VISIONS OF EMPIRE

Visions of Empire

HOW FIVE IMPERIAL REGIMES
SHAPED THE WORLD

KRISHAN KUMAR

PRINCETON UNIVERSITY PRESS

PRINCETON *&* OXFORD

Published by Princeton University Press,
41 William Street, Princeton, New Jersey 08540

In the United Kingdom: Princeton University Press,
6 Oxford Street, Woodstock, Oxfordshire OX20 1TR

press.princeton.edu

Jacket art: Bernhard Strigel (1465–1528), *Portrait of Emperor Maximilian and His Family*, c. 1515, oil on lime, 72.8 × 60.4 cm. (28.7 × 23.8 in.)

Library of Congress Cataloging-in-Publication Data

Names: Kumar, Krishan, 1942– author.
Title: Visions of empire : how five imperial regimes shaped the world / Krishan Kumar.
Description: Princeton : Princeton University Press, 2017. | Includes bibliographical references and index.
Identifiers: LCCN 2016044668 | ISBN 9780691153636 (hardcover : alk. paper)
Subjects: LCSH: Imperialism—Case studies. | World politics. | World history.
Classification: LCC D32 .K86 2017 | DDC 904—dc23
LC record available at https://lccn.loc.gov/2016044668

British Library Cataloging-in-Publication Data is available

This book has been composed in Arno Pro

Printed on acid-free paper. ∞

Printed in the United States of America

10 9 8 7 6 5 4 3 2 1

To my family, empire's children,
in London, Geneva, Charlottesville, Port-of-Spain, Delhi

CONTENTS

ILLUSTRATIONS

Maps

Figures

PREFACE

THE STUDY OF empires is flourishing today as perhaps at no other time since the early twentieth century. Why that should be so is not entirely clear. Following the end of the European empires in the 1960s, there was a marked disinclination in nearly all of the former imperial countries to reflect on the imperial experience. Empire seemed over and done with; there were other pressing concerns, in the case of the Western Europeans the construction of a new European community; a wave of anti-imperial sentiment swept over the Third World, and in courting former colonies it seemed best not to dwell too much on imperial rule. Academics might continue to study and write about empire, but their students on the whole preferred to study other things. I was one of those students who, despite having as my tutor at my Cambridge college, St. John's, the eminent scholar of empire Ronald Robinson, chose not to take any courses on empire. In this I followed the inclination of the general public, which showed little interest in revisiting former imperial triumphs and trials.

The Cold War might indeed have seemed to pit one empire—the American—against another, the Soviet Union, and some certainly sought to portray it as such. But there were other ways of viewing and analyzing that competition—ideological and civilizational—that seemed on the whole more satisfactory. In any case the rise of over fifty new states in the half century following the dissolution of the European empires seemed to point to the nation-state, not empire, as the exemplary form of the future. The fall of the "last empire," the Soviet Union, in 1991, and the establishment of a host of independent successor states on its territory, seemed eloquent confirmation of this.

The renewed interest in empire—detailed in chapter 1—no doubt has many causes, one perhaps being that the European empires are now sufficiently distant in time to be the subject of relatively dispassionate inquiry, if not indeed of nostalgia. But, more important, it may also be an indication that many people are no longer convinced that the nation-state is the best or only form with which to confront the future. Global conflicts—especially those

following the September 11, 2001, attacks on New York and Washington—
seem to demand global solutions, achieved by nations acting in concert.
International terrorism knows no national boundaries, in either its origins
or its effects. Globalization itself—economic, technological, cultural—calls
for cross-national thinking and regulation. Multinational organizations—the
World Bank, the International Monetary Fund, NATO, the European Union,
the United Nations itself—have found fresh demands put upon them, as have
the agencies of "global civil society," many concerned with threats to the environment. Multicultural societies, the result of worldwide flows of migration,
add their own resistance to the idea, or ideal, of the homogeneous nation-state.

Empires are not, of course, seen as the solution, not at least in anything
like their classic form. But empires were after all large-scale, multinational,
multicultural entities. Might they have something to teach us? Might their
study show us something of the mechanisms for the management of difference
and diversity, over large areas? That has been the conviction of a number of
thinkers, most of whom are by no means blind to the faults and iniquities of
empires (though surely no worse than those of nation-states). At the very least
the study of empires forces us to think in the broadest possible terms. Empires
have after all been a part, perhaps the major part, of world history since the
very beginning. They have often lasted for a very long time, their lives to be
measured in centuries, if not millennia. It would be strange if the study of them
were not to offer us some lessons. One of these would be how peoples of many
different kinds, occupying the same political space, come to accommodate to
each other, not necessarily on equal terms. Force is certainly part of the story;
but it cannot be the only part.

This book has no direct pedagogic purpose; but its main concern is certainly to show how empires were ruled, how in particular their ruling peoples
conceived their task in running these vast, rambling, and diverse enterprises
that we call empire. The aim, in other words, is not so much a detailed account
of the mechanics of imperial rule, as rather an examination of the ideas and
ideologies that governed the thinking and at least to some extent the policies
of imperial rulers. How far they were able to carry these out, how far indeed
they intended to, varied from empire to empire, and remains a lively area of
scholarly contention. But ideas of empire were not irrelevant to imperial rule,
not simply a smoke screen that hid other, less idealistic, motives and interests.
Over the course of the empire's history they came to give shape to the imperial mission, to give its rulers a sense of what they were doing in their empires
and why. Without this it is hard to see how the empires could have survived

for so long. Justification and legitimation are as much a part of rule as force and fraud.

After a chapter that considers the idea of empire, and one that examines Rome's pivotal role in it, the bulk of this book discusses the Ottoman, Habsburg, Russian, British, and French empires. The very names suggest a certain progression, not just chronological but also ideological. The first are clearly dynastic empires, in which it is even difficult to say who the ruling people are, at least in the sense of giving them a name. "Turks" and "Austrians" are both highly misleading in the case of the Ottoman and Habsburg empires. "Russians" better suits the tsarist and Soviet empires that were mainly Russian creations, though we should note that the dynastic name of "Romanov" is often attached to the first, and that a national or ethnic designation, as much as a dynastic, is completely lacking in the second. In the British and French cases, the nation is clearly flagged: the empire is British in the first case, made by Britons, though there is the usual confusion as to whether the ruling people are the English or the British. The French Empire is the clearest case of an empire made by a particular nation, an "imperial nation-state," one in which indeed the empire was seen as largely the French writ large.

So there are significant differences in the empires under consideration, one in particular being the extent to which "nationness" is present in the empire. The empires run the gamut from the least degree of nationness, in the Ottoman and Habsburg cases, to the intermediate case of the Russian/Soviet, to the British and French cases where the element of nationality is high, though more so in the French than in the British case. That these differences also map onto the more familiar distinction of land (Ottoman, Habsburg, and Russian) and overseas (British and French) empires is obvious, and points to one possible reason for the relative strength of nationality in the empire (see chapters 1 and 6). But we should remember that both the French and the English/British constructed land empires—the "Hexagon," the United Kingdom—before they built overseas empires. Further, the Habsburgs link land (Austrian) and overseas (Spanish) empires through the two branches of the House of Habsburg—and in the Spanish case, to complicate things even more, the Habsburgs, like the French and British, link both land and overseas empires. The distinction between land and overseas empires is an important one; but we should not exaggerate it. In the cases we are considering, there is often a strong degree of overlap between the two.

Moreover, whatever the differences, there are equally striking similarities in all the empires under consideration. The most important has to do with the extent to which in all of them, however strong the degree of nationness, the ruling people are compelled by the very nature of empire to suppress the expression of their own particular identity as a nation. Not to do so is to put the imperial enterprise at risk. Even though we may discern, within the evolution of empires themselves, a move from "empire to nation," or at least a progressive increase in nationness (which is very different from the conventional understanding of that phrase as meaning the demise and displacement of empire), that is not the same as seeing empires as nations writ large. Even the most "national" of empires, the French, was at pains to stress its universality, the fact that it was open to all, that the French were merely the carriers of the universal message of the Enlightenment and the French Revolution.

As discussed in chapter 1, empires and nation-states may have their similarities, but they are also profoundly dissimilar entities, with sharply differing principles. In the case of empires, one of the most important is to recognize the danger of nationalism, not just of the subject peoples but, perhaps even more, of the ruling people themselves. The moment the ruling people start stressing their own national identity, whether as Turks, Austrians, Russians, English, or French, that is the moment empire begins to decline. The paradox of empire is that it at once creates nations, often where they have never existed before, and at the same time has to act vigorously to suppress them. The national principle denies the imperial principle. The Soviet Union, as shown in chapter 5, is perhaps the best example of this paradox.

A word, finally, about material and method. This book is very evidently a work of synthesis, in the sense that it draws freely on the ideas and findings of a host of scholars, mostly historians but also sociologists and political theorists. But I hope it also attempts something distinctive. It does this by comparing a large and diverse group of empires in order to bring out the common features of ideologies and identities—the identities especially of the ruling peoples, how they got their sense of themselves from their role in empire. In that sense it is very much a view "from the top," not the bottom, of empire. Its subject is the outlook and attitudes of elites and intellectuals, rather than the mass of the subject peoples. My justification of this is that while, particularly in the recent literature, there has been a great concern with the experience of the subjects of empires, there has been much less focus on their rulers, what they thought they were doing in their empires, and how they responded to the empire's needs. If there is not exactly a "logic of empire," there are certainly common problems and challenges, which in the case of the European empires at least drew forth a remarkably similar set of responses.

At the same time, unlike, say, Jane Burbank and Frederick Cooper in their impressive comparative work *Empires in World History*, I find that I can best serve my purposes by treating each empire individually, though of course with comparisons where relevant. This is partly because I want to bring out the chronology of empire, to show each empire's awareness of its predecessors as well as its contemporary rivals (and the awareness of all of the example of Rome). Just as many have discerned a revolutionary tradition stemming from the French Revolution, so one might say that there is a tradition of empire, a notion of imperial succession, in which each empire tries to claim the torch of empire, usually by proclaiming its uniqueness and universality. There is, we might say, a European "repertoire of empire," a common store of ideas, memories, and experiences that each empire draws upon in staking its claim in the world, even as it declares itself not just the latest but also the only true guardian of the imperial tradition.

As for the selection of empires, the Ottoman, Habsburg, Russian, British, and French empires, that is in a sense arbitrary, a reflection of my own tastes and interests as well as of the limits of my knowledge. I would have liked to write about the Portuguese and Dutch empires, among other European empires. It would probably have been even more helpful to include discussion of non-European empires, the Chinese, the Indian, and the Islamic empires, if only to stress differences. There are also of course a host of ancient empires, the study of which seems to be thriving. And what of the Aztecs and the Incas, and other New World empires such as the "American Empire" of today? There are conceptual problems with casting the net so widely, historically and geographically; and one in any case has to draw the line somewhere, even as one regrets the lost opportunities. At least I can say that the empires I have chosen represent by any standard—size, power, impact—the most important of the modern empires, and that all of them would have to be included in any account of the role of empires in the world.

One last point. Have I been too kind to empire? Perhaps. But there are plenty of works lambasting empires, ferociously portraying their dark and often brutal side. I have tried to show them in a different light. I have tried to suggest that they have been ways of dealing with some of the most difficult and challenging problems of modern states, how to manage difference and diversity. That that may not have been their initial goal, that empires arose for a variety of reasons, is not the point. The fact is that in acquiring and governing empires, the ruling peoples found themselves faced with a series of tasks that they had to solve on pain of the quick dissolution of their states. What

I find striking is less the mistakes and occasional brutalities of empire than a remarkable record of success, one that nation-states would be lucky to match.

———

This book, like many of its kind, began life at that unique institution, the Institute for Advanced Study at Princeton, where I was a member in 2004–5. I was particularly fortunate to find myself among a number of other members that year with an interest in empires. Among these were Mark Beissinger, Paolo Desideri, Dan Diner, Marnia Lazreg, and Mary Lewis. Even more fortunate was that Patricia Crone, one of the Institute's faculty, organized on our behalf a seminar on empires that ran throughout the year, and that was able to draw upon not just Institute members but also faculty at neighboring Princeton University. Among these were Linda Colley, Sankar Muthu, and Jennifer Pitts. If one adds to these luminaries the presence at the Institute of Clifford Geertz and Nicola Di Cosmo, with both of whom I had many enjoyable conversations, it is scarcely possible to imagine a better place and time for beginning this study. My thanks to all of them, as well as to the Institute and its always helpful staff. The warmth of my feeling is tinged, though, with sadness at two deaths: that of Clifford Geertz in 2006, and that of Patricia Crone, news of which came just as I was preparing this book for publication. I would so much have liked to place this book in their hands; both were so instrumental in its conception.

Princeton was also the place where I was lucky enough to renew acquaintanceship with Peter Dougherty, of Princeton University Press. It was Peter who encouraged me to prepare a book proposal for the Press. Remarkably when soon after he became director of the Press he continued as my editor, with wise advice that has had considerable effect on the final shape of this book. Later Peter performed an even more valuable service in handing me over to Brigitta van Rheinberg as editor. No one could have had a friendlier, more sympathetic, and more supportive editor than Brigitta. She has brought encouragement and advice during the many years this book has been in the writing, not least during the six years when, as chair of my department, I began to wonder if I would ever finish it. That I have is in no small measure due to her. To Peter for initial encouragement, and to Brigitta for shepherding and sustaining me through the lengthy process of writing—especially in its final stages—I owe an enormous debt of gratitude. Thanks are also due, at the Press, to Lyndsey Claro, Amanda Peery, and, for superb copyediting, Lauren Lepow; to Dimitri Karetnikov, for drawing the maps; and to Melissa Flamson and

Deborah Nicholls, at With Permission, for their invaluable help with maps and illustrations. Thanks too to Dave Luljak for preparing the index.

There are others to thank for intellectual companionship and scholarly support. There are the members of the "empires group"—Julian Go, Peter Perdue, George Steinmetz, Nicholas Wilson—with whom I have shared many stimulating panels at meetings of the American Sociological Association, the Social Science History Association, and other venues. Yale has been another haven for students of empire. The moving spirits there are Julia Adams and Steven Pincus, joint organizers of a number of convivial seminars and conferences on empires where I had the opportunity to learn from a mixed group of historians, sociologists, political scientists, and others. Equally stimulating was the conference "Ancient Writers and Modern Empires" organized by Paolo Desideri at the University of Florence in October 2008, which allowed for some pleasurable conversations with David Lupher and Sabine MacCormack. That discussion on the classics and empire was complemented by an earlier one at the series organized by Arthur Eckstein at the University of Maryland.

Thanks are also due, for their friendship as much as for their invaluable contributions, to David Armitage, Jack Goldstone, John A. Hall, Chris Hann, Siniša Malešević, and Geneviève Zubrzycki. Anthony Pagden kindly invited me to a two-day seminar on empires that he organized at the Folger Institute in Washington, DC: a welcome opportunity to discuss some of the ideas that he has been so influential in diffusing in his many works on empires. I treasure also the discussions I have had with Geoffrey Hosking at the ASEN meetings in London; his work on the Russian and Soviet empires has been fundamental to my understanding of these entities.

Nearer home, my University of Virginia colleague Robert Geraci has also been very generous in sharing with me his great knowledge of the Russian Empire; another colleague, Elizabeth Thompson, set me going on the Ottoman Empire. UVA is also the place where for a number of years I have been running a graduate course on empires; I have learned much from some very lively and enthusiastic students. Also at UVA it would be impossible not to mention, once again, the enormous contribution of the irreplaceable Interlibrary Loan/LEO section of the Alderman Library. I never cease to be astonished by the incredible efficiency of its staff, and their unfailing willingness to help. They have done more perhaps than anyone else to help bring this book to fruition.

Duncan Bell, of Cambridge University, has my thanks for sending me his numerous papers on the political theory of the British Empire, and for his very helpful comments on my own efforts. At Nuffield College, Oxford, Andrew Thompson and John Darwin hosted a very stimulating conference on the impact of the British Empire on British society, a highly contentious subject. I have also profited from their many outstanding works on the British Empire. The work of the late Chris Bayly has also been very influential on me, not just concerning the British Empire but more generally the global context of empire.

I should mention finally the contributions of two people very close to me. Katya Makarova over many years has discussed with me the parallels between the Russian and British experiences of empire, and the predicament of both peoples when faced with loss of empire. Our discussions crystallized some of the central arguments of this book. Kyrill Kunakhovich, a young historian of exceptional promise, is developing ideas about the recent history of Central and Eastern Europe that will illuminate many aspects of a region that has been dominated by empire. To both I owe not just insights into the subject of this book, but the love and support without which its writing would have been an even lonelier and more demanding experience than such endeavors generally are.

Krishan Kumar
Charlottesville, Virginia

VISIONS OF EMPIRE

1

The Idea of Empire

Empires have been, and will be, founded only in the sign of a higher idea. Nations can found only states.

—FRANZ WERFEL (1937: 7)

For to posterity no greater glory can be handed down than to conquer the barbarian, to recall the savage and the pagan to civility, to draw the ignorant within the orbit of reason.

—RICHARD HAKLUYT, LETTER TO SIR WALTER
RALEIGH, 1595 (IN PAGDEN 1995: 64)

The face of the earth is continually changing, by the encrease of small kingdoms into great empires, by the dissolution of great empires into smaller kingdoms, by the planting of colonies, by the migration of tribes. Is there anything discoverable in all these events, but force and violence?

—DAVID HUME ([1748] 1987: 471)

The Rediscovery of Empire

Antipathy to empire is not the same as indifference toward it, or its study. Hobson and Lenin both loathed empire, but thought it a matter of the greatest urgency to study and understand it. Joseph Schumpeter too, convinced as he was that empire was an atavistic throwback to a militaristic past, devoted considerable thought to its anatomy. In the interwar period, as expansionist regimes in Italy, Germany, and Japan sought to build new empires, scholars and intellectuals such as James Burnham and Franz Neumann—not to mention revolutionaries such as Mao Tse-tung—once more felt the need to scrutinize and analyze the springs of the new imperialism.[1]

1

Both politically and intellectually, the period after the Second World War saw a retreat from empire. Politically, the most obvious fact was the dissolution of the great European overseas empires—British, French, Dutch, Belgian, Portuguese—and the rise of new states created out of them. These new states were nation-states, formed in the mold of the modern European nation-state. The important thing therefore seemed to be to understand nationalism, especially "Third World" nationalism. Empire was a thing of the past. The future was a world of nations, seen most spectacularly in the fifty or so new states that joined the United Nations between 1960 and 1980 (Strang 1991: 437).

Marxists, in both West and East, continued to debate imperialism in the 1960s and 1970s, particularly in relation to American foreign policy and the politics of the Cold War. But this was really a discussion about capitalism, and its impact in particular on the Third World of developing nations. Imperialism here was a surrogate for the latest stage of capitalism, in its increasingly global aspect. Hence the common resort to theories of dependency and of "informal empire" (Lichtheim 1974: chaps. 7–9; Mommsen 1982: 113–41).[2] What disappeared—because the entity itself seemed a thing of the past—was interest in the specifics of empires: their principles of operation, their goals, the particular kind of entity they represented. Antipathy to empire was here matched by indifference.

It is this indifference that has been swept away in recent decades. Empire is back, as a steadily growing volume of books, conferences, and mass media treatments testifies.[3] From the viewpoint of scholarly interest, at least in the English-speaking world, one might pick out Michael Doyle's enterprising and ambitious *Empires* (1986) as marking the start of the revival. This was followed almost immediately afterward by Paul Kennedy's much-acclaimed and surprisingly popular *The Rise and Fall of the Great Powers* (1988): a synoptic study of the great European empires of the past, and of the reasons for their rise and demise. The Gibbonesque echo in the title was not lost on most readers, nor the Gibbonesque desire to draw lessons for the contemporary world—and especially for Americans—from the record of past empires. A similar intent lay behind Niall Ferguson's more studiedly popular *Empire* (2004), whose subtitle—*How Britain Made the Modern World*—combatively asserts the link between the British Empire and contemporary globalization ("Anglobalization") that Ferguson was at pains to demonstrate. For the student and scholar, David Abernethy produced an invaluable work of synthesis on the European overseas empires, *The Dynamics of Global Dominance* (2000); Dominic Lieven (2001), focusing especially on Russia, did the same for the land empires in his

Empire: The Russian Empire and Its Rivals (2001). More recently there has been an impressively wide-ranging account of empires as a global phenomenon, Jane Burbank and Frederick Cooper's *Empires in World History* (2010).

Empire, everyone agrees, continues to have the negative, pejorative connotation that it began to acquire in the early twentieth century and that rose to a high point of intensity in the post-1945 period of decolonization.[4] Today no one argues for empire, at least in the sense of formal empire, as many people did in the past. If empire exists today, it is the thing that dare not speak its name. Even talk of "the American Empire" tends to come overwhelmingly from those opposed to current American policies and strategies in the world; it is rare to find anyone advocating American imperialism as such.[5]

But if empire is generally thought to be bad—if, in present circumstances, it is difficult to imagine anyone or any state even attempting it in a formal way—why has it suddenly become popular to study it? Why the outpouring of books and conferences on the subject? What accounts for its fascination today?

There are a number of possible reasons, but one word, "globalization," probably covers a good many of them. Empire, at least as an object of reflection, is back in favor because it retrieves a form that in a practical way engaged with many of the features that preoccupy us today. Do we attempt "multiculturalism," that is, to accommodate a great variety of beliefs and ways of life within existing state structures? Empires were multicultural almost by definition. Are we faced with the challenge of emigration and immigration on a global scale, creating "diasporic" communities of newcomers as large minorities within host populations? Empires were both created by and the cause in turn of vast migrations across the surface of the world. Is the nation-state under stress, perhaps even in crisis, as a result of the transnational movements of finance, industry, people, and ideas? Empires were and are "multinational" and "supranational." They preceded the nation-state and may well succeed it.

Empire, in sum, can be the prism through which to examine many of the pressing problems of the contemporary world—perhaps even the birth pangs of a new world order. Wherever we turn we seem to encounter problems and situations for which there are precedents in the historic empires.[6]

It may be somewhat in jest that some commentators talk of the European Union as a revived "Habsburg Empire," or a revived "Holy Roman Empire"; there may be a degree of nostalgia in speaking approvingly of the *millet* system of the Ottoman Empire as some kind of model for our multicultural societies; the *pax Britannica* as an exemplar of world order may bring a smile to the lips of some hearers. But there is a real sense in which empires achieved many of the things that currently elude us. Stephen Howe, no friend of empire, never-theless suggests that "at least some of the great modern empires—the British, French, Austro-Hungarian, Russian, and even the Ottoman—had virtues that have been too readily forgotten. They provided stability, security, and legal order for their subjects. They constrained, and at their best tried to transcend, the potentially savage ethnic or religious antagonisms among their peoples. And the aristocracies which ruled most of them were often far more liberal, humane, and cosmopolitan than their supposedly ever more democratic suc-cessors" (Howe 2002a: 126–27; cf. Kappeler 2001: 3, 392).[7]

It seems likely that it is this contemporary relevance, arising from some very long-term and deep-seated changes in the political and economic order of the world, that will continue to fuel the revived interest in empires. In that sense it is the most important cause of the revival. But there have also been some more immediate causes. The breakup, in 1991, of what has generally come to be called "the Soviet Empire" was one. It was almost impossible for scholars to resist the urge to compare the Soviet Empire with other empires, past and present, to ask whether there might not be instructive parallels in the course, development, and eventual collapse of similar, far-flung, multiethnic land empires, such as the Habsburg or Ottoman empires. The Soviet Empire increasingly came to be seen within the perspective of Russian imperialism as a whole, to include therefore the previous tsarist phase. Once this was conceded, the way seemed open to comparative inquiry that brought together scholars from a range of disciplines and specializations concerned with empire.[8]

Whether or not talk of "the American Empire" will stimulate so instruc-tive a discussion is a moot point. But there is no doubting the impact of the renewed accounts of America as an empire.[9] This applies as much to the idea of America as itself an empire—as in Alexander Hamilton's belief that the new republic was "an empire in many respects the most interesting in the world" (Lichtheim 1974: 60)—as to the more conventional view that Amer-ica is pursuing, and has long pursued, an imperial policy toward the rest of the world. The current debate about the American Empire is mostly a debate about American intentions in the world today, and about the ideologies that sustain them. But it has had the effect of raising questions about the nature of empires in general, what they are and how they perceive themselves. Nearly every discussion of "the American Empire," whether or not it finds the term satisfactory, begins with an account of what we know about other empires; nearly every conference on empires ends with a session on "the American Empire"—usually followed by a question mark.

It is indeed a widely held view that the new interest in empires springs directly from talk of the American Empire. This seems to take too narrow a view of the matter. There are many other things driving the move. It may be in fact that what has led to the discourse of the American Empire is itself a product of those other, wider, changes. Globalization has impinged on America no less than it has on other societies, even if America has played a central role in bringing it about (so partly disguising the process as simple "Americanization"). What makes America "imperial," or makes it seem so, may simply be the current American responses to a fragmentation and instability in the world order that have in good part been caused by America's own cultural and economic dynamism, and by the victory of American-style capitalism over all its rivals (including Soviet communism). The "American Empire"—which everyone admits does not include the desire to acquire fresh possessions—is what exists when "the lonely superpower" confronts a "new world disorder."[10]

One thing, in any case, is clear from the widespread rediscovery of empire: empire is not just history. It has a contemporary resonance that gives it a strong claim on our attention beyond the purely historical. But it is also contemporary in a further sense. The disappearance of the European empires has, after all, been very recent, in historical terms. The Austrian, German, Russian, and Ottoman empires—the great land empires—collapsed during and after the First World War. The French, Dutch, British, Belgian, and Portuguese overseas empires dissolved more slowly, in the thirty or so years following the Second World War. But in either case we are talking of a period of no more than a hundred years, to be set against many centuries of imperial rule. It is impossible that there should be no "afterlife" of empire, no legacy that continues to haunt the societies of both the colonized and the colonizers (cf. Pagden 1995: 1–2).

This has been a major theme, of course, of many studies of formerly colonized peoples, mostly non-Western but including for some scholars nearer "colonies" such as Ireland and the Balkan countries. Writers such as Frantz Fanon and Edward Said have been the major influences here, followed by various schools of "postcolonial theory" (see, e.g., Ashcroft, Griffiths, and Tiffin 1995; Young 2001). But it is equally important to see that imperial legacies continue to play a significant role in the life of the imperial peoples themselves—the British, French, Russians, Austrians, Turks, and others. This has been clear in a number of ways, most obviously in the post-1945 immigration into European societies of large numbers of people from the former European empires ("the empire strikes back"). But it also shows itself in the impact of empire on the consciousness of the former imperial peoples, their sense of themselves and their place in the world when empire has gone.

This is a subject by itself, to be addressed separately (as I hope to do in a later book).[11] This book touches on it, but its main concern is the outlook and attitudes of the ruling peoples during the period of actual imperial rule, when the empires were at their height. Their formal demise opened a new chapter in the history of empire, one that looked back reflectively but also contemplated future forms of empire. When empires ruled the world, the way they thought about themselves necessarily had a different character. Whatever their doubts and anxieties about their future, their rulers had the immediate, practical task of managing a multiplicity of peoples. How they saw that task, how they conceived their role as an imperial people, what kind of identities that conferred on them: those are the main themes of the chapters that follow.

To concentrate on the rulers rather than the subject peoples of empire is to shift the emphasis away from most recent studies, especially of the "postcolonial" variety. But that does not mean to neglect the impact of empire on the subject peoples. Rather, it is to reconceptualize the relationship, to see it not simply in oppositional terms but as a matter of a shared enterprise that could unite rulers and ruled as much as it divided them. Just as nation-states have divisions—classes, races, religions—but can often act collectively, so too empires aimed at and often achieved a unity that overrode the many differences that were indeed constitutive features.

That brings in ideologies, the way empires sought to portray themselves, often in the form of a universal "mission" that justified their rule and expansion, and in which all peoples of the empire could participate. Often that took religious form—Islam, Orthodoxy, Catholicism; sometimes it was secular, as in the French *mission civilisatrice*. Time played a part in this; generally the later the empire, the more secular the mission. But we should also remember that it was the Romans who pioneered the original "civilizing mission." Some missions are transhistorical.

Nation-states sometimes also have missions; but, premised as they are on the principle of the equality of nations, they are different from the universal missions of empires. That is one way that empires differ from nation-states, despite some important similarities. Another is the extent to which the rulers of empires have to suppress their own national or ethnic identities, in the interests of the more efficient management of their multinational states and the long-term preservation of their rule. That is one of the most distinguishing features of empires, and will get due attention in the succeeding chapters.

All these things follow from focusing on the rule of empire, the ideas and ideals of the ruling peoples. They will concern us in all the main chapters of this book, those dealing with the Roman, Ottoman, Habsburg, Russian/ Soviet, British, and French empires. They provide, as it were, the thematic spine to the chapters. The empires differed from each other in many ways, not least in the way in which they responded to a changing historical environment. Later empires faced different challenges from earlier ones. But all empires had to deal with many of the same problems, those especially of managing difference and diversity across often vast geographical spaces. History and narrative are important, and they find their place in this book. But there are also questions to do with the very form of empire, empire as an entity with some characteristic features. This cuts across history and chronology. This too must be our concern as we analyze the individual empires, in all their particularities.

First we need to turn to the concept of empire. We need to know what it has meant, and whether any of those meanings fit our current usages. How best should we think of empire? What kind of an entity, or entities, is it? What characteristic relations does it establish? How does it differ from other political forms that we are familiar with—most especially, the nation-state?

"Empire without end": Rome and the Imperial Idea

The history of the world is virtually a history of empires (Howe 2002a: 1; Pagden 2003: ix; Ferguson 2005: xii). For much of recorded history, at least, people have lived in empires. But empires have come in many shapes and forms, at many places and in many times. That, according to John Gallagher and Ronald Robinson in a famous article, is why there is so much disagreement among students of empire: they are "writing about different empires," selecting often "eccentric or isolated aspects" and generalizing from them (Gallagher and Robinson 1953: 1; cf. Morrison 2001: 3).

The variety is indeed extraordinary, if we consider the things that are usually called empires. From the time of Sargon of Akkad's conquest of the city-states of Sumeria (third millennium BCE), the Middle East—source of civilization— has been host to a succession of empires—the Akkadian, the Babylonian, the Assyrian, the Persian, the Greco-Roman, the Arab, the Ottoman. In the same area the Egyptian Empire was for more than three thousand years a beacon of civilization and culture—so powerful, so creative, that some have been tempted to see it as the parent of civilization itself. Further east in Asia there were empires in China and India; while to the south were the Aztec and Inca empires of the New World. Later came the European empires—the Holy Roman Empire, the Spanish, Portuguese, Dutch, French, Belgian, and British empires, the Austrian, German, and Russian empires. These empires, taken as a whole, exhibit an enormous range of characteristics, politically, technologically, culturally. What, if anything, unites them? Why call them all "empires"?

It was not so very long ago that scholars still attempted, as had earlier generations, to find common patterns, common principles, linking all empires, ancient and modern, Western and Eastern (e.g., Eisenstadt [1963] 1993; Kautsky [1982] 1997). Nowadays the custom is to be more cautious, to distinguish types and periods of empire and imperialism. Nevertheless, there is a surprising amount of agreement on what constitutes empire at the most general level. What is also convenient is that this understanding derives in the main from our understanding of the Roman Empire. The concept of empire that emerges from considering the Roman case can be fitted, without too much of a stretch, to most of the other political entities that we are in the habit of calling empires—including those, such as the Assyrian or the Persian, that predated Rome. The reason why this is convenient is that the empires that concern us in this book without exception harked back to Rome.

Of course it is not mere chance or good luck that brings about the fit between Rome and empire. To a good extent what, especially in the West, came to be called empire was indebted to the Roman example. To be an empire was to be like Rome. But, once formulated from the Roman case, the same principles are readily found to be at work in many other instances that we have come to think of as empires.

The Roman or Latin word for empire is *imperium*. "Imperium sine fine," "empire without end," with "no bounds in space or time," is what, according to Virgil's celebrated account at the opening of the *Aeneid* (1.278–79), Jupiter promised the Romans, the descendants of the Trojan founders of Rome. But by Virgil's time—the first century of the Principate, the Roman Empire proper—the word had undergone an important shift in meaning. Or, rather, the word had acquired a double meaning, a fact that has been responsible for much of the confusion in later times.

In its main, original, and longest-lasting sense *imperium* referred to the lawfully conferred sovereign power of the magistrate or ruler. "In the language of public law the word denoted the power bestowed by the people on the highest magistrates entrusted with enforcing authority, the consuls, proconsuls, praetors, propraetors, dictators" (Koebner 1961: 5–6; cf. Richardson 1991: 2).[12] Consonant with this sense was the military usage, also common from the beginning, in which *imperium* was bestowed by the people on a supreme military commander.

It is this first meaning of *imperium* that has persisted ever since Roman times, finding an echo in all the European vernacular languages.[13] For English speakers, the best-known example of this is the famous pronouncement in Henry VIII's Act in Restraint of Appeals of 1533, that "this realm of England is an empire" (Elton 1982: 353; see also Ullmann 1979). By this was meant that the king of England acknowledged no superiors in his realm, that his rule was sovereign or absolute, and that there could be no appeal to a higher power, such as the pope. That Tudor England, a kingdom of modest size and moderate power, could make such a claim shows that size and power were not determining criteria. In principle any state—kingdom or republic—could declare itself an empire, as did several of the Italian city-states, such as Milan under the Visconti dukes. It did not have to have extensive territories inhabited by different peoples.

No doubt, "as far as the word referred to the authority of government it seemed more natural to reserve it for some particularly majestic government" (Koebner 1961: 57). The European vernaculars had already begun to use the word "empire" figuratively, to connote majesty and grandeur, whether of the sun or of a great river. But if Shakespeare can refer equally to England, Scotland, and France as all being "an Empery," it is clear that size and grandeur are not for him necessary elements in the understanding of empire; other meanings had to be imported to make these the essential criteria that they became. For early modern thinkers, the key aspect of empire was authority, especially royal authority (though not "despotism").[14] That is why we find so many rulers during the era of European absolutism making this claim for their realms. Empire was no more, and no less, than a synonym for sovereignty—the principal meaning given to it in the writings of Bodin, Hobbes, Grotius, and Spinoza (Koebner 1961: 52).

Returning to the Roman case, it is with such a meaning in mind that we must understand the frequent references to empire in such writers as Cicero. "Cicero's comments on the *imperium populi Romani* never swerved from the intrinsic meaning of 'imperium' to which he paid emphatic tribute in *De Legibus*—the legal power to enforce the law. . . . It was not understood to denote 'the Empire', the political entity of the *orbis* governed by the *imperium populi Romani*" (Koebner 1961: 4–5). This restraint is all the more remarkable given that the Roman Empire, in fact if not in name, was largely a republican accomplishment. As Edward Gibbon correctly put it, "the principal conquests of the Romans were achieved under the republic; and the emperors, for the most part, were satisfied with preserving those dominions which had been acquired by the policy of the senate, the active emulation of the consuls, and the martial enthusiasm of the people" (Gibbon [1776–88] 1995, 1:31; cf. Schumpeter [1919] 1974: 50–51; Finley 1978a: 2).[15] In view of this one might have expected the word *imperium* to be extended to cover the thing, the empire, over which *imperium* was exercised.

In fact this did happen, thereby giving rise to the second main meaning of *imperium* that was handed down to Rome's successors. It was perhaps out of republican sentiment that Cicero, who after all died for the republic, was unwilling to speak of *imperium* as "the empire." But the word apparently was used in this additional sense even in his time. Caesar, for one, fittingly did so use it, even in the period before his actions brought down the republic and inaugurated the empire. Its success as the designation of empire was aided by the fact that the Senate conferred on both Caesar and his successor, Augustus, the title of *imperator*. This was a word that had generally been used in the republic—and for some time after—as "a title of honour, bestowed on a victorious general by the acclamation of the army on the field of battle" (*OED* 1989: *s.v.* "emperor"). In the case of Caesar and Augustus it was meant to refer to the military powers with which the chief of state was invested.

Augustus was at pains to insist that he respected the institutions of the republic, and that the title of *imperator* did not infringe on any of its legal practices. He reaffirmed on several occasions that the *imperium orbis terrarum*— the territorial empire—remained the *imperium populi Romani* (Koebner 1961: 7). However, since not only Caesar and Augustus but every ruler of the empire subsequently (with the exceptions of Tiberius and Claudius) adopted the title of *imperator*, it was inevitable that it would go beyond its purely military meaning to take on all the connotations of political rule. When, in 23 BCE, Augustus's proconsular *imperium* was declared by the Senate to be permanent and to include all of Rome's provinces—a remit that all subsequent emperors claimed—the stage was set for *imperator* and *imperium* to be conjoined. The *imperium populi Romani* now became emphatically the *imperium Romanum*, ruled by a deified *princeps* or *imperator*. It was as such that the Augustan poets Virgil, Horace, and Ovid acclaimed it; other writers, such as Livy and Tacitus, confirmed the link, though with more misgivings (Koebner 1961: 11–16; Lichtheim 1974: 25–26; Woolf 2001: 315).

The passage from *imperium* as authority, the authority of the Roman people, to *imperium* as the province or territory of the emperor, was, as George

Lichtheim notes, "a development of the highest significance, for it coloured the whole subsequent course of Western political history and, more especially, the coinage of Western political terminology" (Lichtheim 1974: 24). Empire never lost its association with absolute rule or sovereignty; but it was fused now with the idea of rule over a vast region occupied by many different peoples—*the* empire, the *imperium orbis terrarum* or *imperium totius orbis*, the territorial empire that included not just Romans and Italians but Greeks, Gauls, Spaniards, British, Egyptians, Africans, Syrians—potentially, and ideally, the whole world.[16]

This is of course the meaning most common today, at least in popular parlance. When we speak of the Russian or the British Empire, we do indeed usually still think of a single ruler, the tsar or the "king-emperor," and there is still the lurking sense that this ruler is absolute. But the British Empire was ruled for most of its history by a parliamentary monarchy, and the French Empire, from 1871, by a parliamentary republic. The earlier meaning of "empire" has been largely superseded by the later one, such that "empire" now means, for most people, a political organization incorporating peoples of many different races and ethnicities—"une état vaste et composé de plusieurs peuples," as it was put by the compiler of a dictionary in early eighteenth-century France.[17] It means more than this, of course, especially in scholarly usage, as we shall see; and the earlier meaning has by no means disappeared.[18] But the fact that empire is thought of as it is today is ultimately due to the shift in meaning that took place as Rome moved from the *imperium populi Romani* to the *imperium Romanum*.

Roman usage had, therefore, by the time of the first century CE linked the two main meanings of "empire": absolute authority or sovereignty, and rule over a complex territorial polity (Richardson 1991: 1, 7; Pagden 1995: 13; Woolf 2001: 313). This duality was continued, if with less assurance, in the "Holy Roman Empire" that, from its founding by Charlemagne in 800 CE, maintained some kind of existence for over a thousand years, until its abolition by Napoleon in 1806. The emperor elected by the German princes was, in theory at least, as sovereign and supreme as the Roman emperors of old; at the same time the empire over which he ruled was made up of a bewildering variety of territories—kingdoms, principalities, bishoprics, independent cities—many of them not German.[19] In the hands of Ottonians and Salians, of Hohenstaufens such as Frederick Barbarossa and Frederick II, and of Habsburgs such as Charles V, the full universalist legacy of Rome could be claimed, and asserted (including the right to govern Italy and to make Rome the seat of the empire); for other Holy

Roman emperors, it was merely an aspiration or a dream, undercut by the reality of rivalry with the papacy and severely limited power over the empire's territories (Folz [1953] 1969: 121–68; Bloch 1967; Heer [1968] 2002: 22–93). But so long as the empire lasted, it perpetuated the notion of empire as a particularly authoritative—if not authoritarian—form of rule over a far-flung territory or territories whose main characteristic was diversity.[20]

There is one further theme deriving from Rome that needs to be mentioned here. That is the theme of the empire's universalism. Here the Romans drew on Greek thought, especially as developed by the Stoics with their idea of a single human community united by the universality of reason—"a single joint community," to use Cicero's later phrase, "of gods and men" (in Pagden 1995: 19). Influenced by the actual conquests of Alexander the Great, Greek philosophers came to see Hellenic civilization as having a universal mission. Greek civilization, the highest level to which mankind had hitherto attained, was in their eyes coterminous with the *oikoumene*, the civilized world; beyond its borders lay barbarism. The purpose of empire was the extension of the global civilizing mission, under Hellenic auspices, begun by Alexander.[21]

It was indeed Greek thinkers such as Polybius who, from the second century BCE on, came to regard the Roman Empire as continuing the mission of Alexander. Roman writers, such as Livy and Virgil, seized on the theme enthusiastically. Rome would bring peace, order, and justice to mankind. Its empire would encompass the *orbis terrarum*, the entire known world, uniting all the peoples of the world in the *pax Romana*. With the Christianization of the empire following Constantine's conversion in the fourth century, Rome's ecumenical mission was given a further spiritual dimension. All medieval emperors, in their various efforts to revive and renew the Roman Empire, emphasized the unity of the *orbis christianus* and the *orbis romanus*: they were two sides of the same universalizing mission, now under God's protection, to realize for the benefit of all mankind the virtues that Romans and Christians had always striven for.[22]

Rome remained, and perhaps still remains, the fount and emblem of empire, certainly in the West. "Rome has consistently provided the inspiration, the imagery, and the vocabulary for all the European empires from early-modern Spain to late-nineteenth-century Britain" (Pagden 2003: 19; cf. Pagden 1995: 11–12). Howe goes further in declaring that "the Romans invented the concept of empire, at least in the forms in which it was to be understood, and constantly referred back to, by later empire builders" (Howe 2002a: 41). And Koebner indicates the depth of the inheritance going back to the earliest times:

The modern concept of empire unfailingly recalls the Roman Empires of the
past: the *Imperium populi Romani* of the Republic, the *Imperium Romanum*
governed by the Emperor Augustus and his successors, the Holy Roman
Empire which was vested in Charlemagne and later on in the kings elected
by German princes. The British empire, the Empire français of the Napo-
leons, the Reich of the Hohenzollern, the Austro-Hungarian Monarchy,
the State of the Tsars have, in whatever mood—whether of glorification,
of misgivings, or even of abhorrence—provoked comparison with one or
other of these predecessors. (Koebner 1961: 18; cf. Richardson 1991: 1)

It was not just the "grandeur that was Rome" that constantly provoked
these comparisons. We need to remember that Rome itself persisted long
after its supposed decline and fall in the West. It persisted even in the West,
in the form of the Holy Roman Empire that was extinguished only in 1806;
and, more unequivocally, it persisted in the East, in the Byzantine Empire
that was the direct continuation of the Eastern Roman Empire established by
Constantine in the fourth century. That empire was overthrown in 1453, by the
Ottomans. But the Ottomans too were dazzled by Rome. They too felt, like
many European emperors, that they had inherited the Roman mantle. They
called their capital Istanbul, the Turkish name for Constantinople, the city
of Constantine.[23] The sultan Mehmed II, conqueror of the Byzantines, had
his portrait painted by the Italian artist Gentile Bellini, and employed Italian
humanists to read him stories from Herodotus and Livy about the glories of
Greece and Rome. "No one doubts," he was assured by the Byzantine scholar
George of Trebizond, "that you are the emperor of the Romans." Noting this
continuity Anthony Pagden has said that "if the Western Roman Empire came
to an end . . . in 1806 . . . the Roman Empire in the East vanished only with the
abolition of the Ottoman Caliphate on March 3, 1924" (Pagden 2003: 176).
    Chapter 2 gives a more detailed account of the Roman legacy of empire—a
legacy that we will have occasion to refer to many times in the course of this
book. First, though, we need to turn to the question of what, deriving from
this particular history, modern scholars have made of the concepts of empire
and imperialism.

Empire, Imperialism, Colonialism

By the eighteenth century, the two central elements of the idea of empire
were firmly established. The older and primary notion of sovereignty was

increasingly overlaid by the newer concept of rule over extensive territories containing many different peoples. Whatever the contribution of the Holy Roman Empire in this respect, there can be no question that it was the dazzling achievements of certain European states in the lands beyond Europe that most definitively set the seal on this development. It was above all the overseas empires of Portugal and Spain, later of Holland, France, and England, that gave the word "empire" its modern connotation. Rome and its empire were constantly invoked in these creations; but Rome had never had anything to match the huge Spanish possessions in the New World, nor the territories of the British Empire, which at its greatest extent occupied a quarter of the world's land surface and included a quarter of the world's population. "Romans are dead out, English are come in," proclaimed Thomas Carlyle in 1840, as he contemplated the "grand tasks" assigned to the English people in "the stream of World-History" (Carlyle [1840] 1971: 202).

But it was not just the Atlantic powers that, from the sixteenth century, were becoming imperial. There were the Habsburgs who, following the building of an overseas empire through the Spanish line, continued through the Austrian line to found another empire, this time a land empire in central and southeastern Europe. There was Russia, which from the sixteenth century to the nineteenth expanded gigantically in an eastward direction, reaching the Pacific by the end of the seventeenth century and mopping up areas in between thereafter. There were the Ottoman Turks, who conquered Constantinople in 1453, so setting the seal on a vast land empire that straddled Asia and Europe, twice bringing them to the gates of Vienna where their advance was finally halted. Even China, which since the Ming dynasty had turned in on itself and seemed uninterested in further expansion, in the eighteenth century under the Qing dynasty engaged in massive expansion to the north and west, giving China a multiethnic and multilingual "imperial" character that it had not previously possessed (Di Cosmo 1998; Perdue 2005). These imposing and long-lasting land empires had their own distinctive patterns and made their own characteristic contribution to thinking about empire.

There are, in other words, many empires ancient and modern, and empires of many varying types, to reflect upon in coming to some sort of definition of what is or makes an empire. One might be, as I am, sympathetic to Max Weber's observation that "definition can be attempted, if at all, only at the conclusion of the study" rather than at its beginning (Weber 1963: 1). No doubt by the end of this book we might have arrived at some different sense of empire from the one with which we began. But it is useful to make an initial stab, helped by a number of authors. What is striking is the general agreement on the main concept of empire, and of such derived terms as imperialism. Moreover, it is clear that, whatever the changes in the intervening centuries, modern definitions derive from empires as they have been known and spoken about for centuries—Rome, of course, being the persisting point of reference.

In a formulation that has found wide acceptance, Michael Doyle has defined empire as "a relationship, formal or informal, in which one state controls the effective political sovereignty of another political society. . . . Imperialism is simply the process or policy of establishing an empire" (Doyle 1986: 45).[24] The key elements here are a one-way flow of power, stemming from the imperial state or "metropole," and a consequent dependence or subordination on the part of the colony or "periphery." What links the metropole to the periphery, besides the asymmetrical relationship of control, is a "transnational society" based in the metropole (Doyle 1986: 81). By this Doyle means the "transnational extension of the domestic society of the metropole" to the periphery, whether this takes the form of the democratic city-state, as with the fifth-century Athenian Empire, the urban legal civilization of Rome in the case of the Roman Empire, or the political institutions of Tudor and Stuart England, as with England's North American empire (Doyle 1986: 129). Imperial states, in other words, export their characteristic institutions to the periphery, thereby building a bridge between the two and creating a common culture that ensures that metropolitan institutions and ideas always have the upper hand.

This conception of empire allows us to distinguish empires simply from large or extensive states lacking both the separation involved in the distinction between metropole and periphery, and the presence of a transnational society and transnational actors bridging the distance between metropole and periphery. Moses Finley has complained that it is only too common to identify empire with any extensive territorial state, whereas what is critical is the exercise of authority "over other states (or communities or peoples)" (Finley 1978a: 1; see also 1978b: 104).[25] We have seen that, deriving from its original meaning of sovereignty, there was indeed a practice of calling large states empires even when there was no obvious connotation of rule over a number of different peoples. We shall also see, later in this chapter, that the line between territorial states—especially nation-states—and empires is by no means as clear-cut as Finley or Doyle would like us to think. Many modern states, such as France or Britain, have an imperial character even when they do not acknowledge it, and before (and after) they have acquired their formal overseas empires. What remains important, however, in these as much as in the better-known and more familiar cases of empire, is that rule is exercised over a plurality of peoples.

It is misleading to suggest, as some scholars do (e.g., Lieven 2001: 25), that the two meanings of empire—simply a large state as opposed to a multiethnic or multinational state—map onto the well-known distinction between land empires and overseas empires. It is true that in the case of land empires, such as the Russian and the Habsburg empires, the fact that territories are contiguous makes it less easy for the casual observer to distinguish between metropole and periphery than in the case of overseas empires, such as the British or the French, where the geographical distances underline the political ones. Nevertheless, land empires no less than overseas empires have fairly recognizable and well-understood metropoles and peripheries. No one could mistake that, say, in the land empire of the Ottomans, where Constantinople stood in a clear metropolitan relationship to its peripheries. The distinction between land and overseas empires is a helpful one, as we shall see, and carries important implications for both imperial and subject peoples. Things become even more interesting in the case of those states, such as Britain, that can be considered both land empires and overseas empires But the distinctions that matter are not those between empires that have metropoles and peripheries and empires that do not. It is a distinguishing mark of all empires that relations of metropole and periphery exist and that they structure much of the political life of those entities.

More problematic is the distinction that some scholars wish to make between "imperialism" and "colonialism." There is some basis for this in the history of the terms. "Empire" is a venerable term, but "imperialism" entered the vocabulary of European nations only in the second half of the nineteenth century, and "colonialism," as a general term, not until the 1950s and 1960s (*OED* 1989: s.v. "imperialism," "colonialism"). Each had its characteristic uses. In the 1880s and 1890s—overcoming an earlier negativity—"imperialism" was generally used with a positive connotation, to mean the advocacy of empire, principally by Western powers. With the publication of J. A. Hobson's *Imperialism* in 1902, followed by the writings of Lenin and others, the word began its career as a term of disparagement, though the positive meaning continued alongside for the first half of the twentieth century (Fieldhouse 1961: 187–88; Koebner and Schmidt 1964: chaps. 4–8; Hobsbawm 1987: 60). In the 1960s, thanks largely to its use by communist and Third World writers and activists, the word "colonialism" began to displace "imperialism" as a term of abuse. Unlike the latter, the former "seems to have been used with almost exclusively hostile intent right from the start" (Howe 2002a: 27).

But, apart from this terminological history, can a more useful distinction be established between colonialism and imperialism? Eric Hobsbawm suggests that, with the imperialism of the capitalist powers of the late nineteenth century, a new type of empire arose, the colonial empire. Imperialism now took on an irreducibly economic character, thereby rendering obsolete all comparisons with earlier precapitalist empires. For Hobsbawm, there is from this time only colonialism—even if the word had to wait to be fully domesticated—rather than old-style imperialism (Hobsbawm 1987: 57–60).

Hobsbawm may believe that latter-day imperialism or colonialism can be reduced to economic causes. But he is perfectly well aware that many people, such as Schumpeter, thought differently, and we are certainly under no obligation to follow the Marxist canon on this. There are in any case too many problems associated with it.[26] It certainly does not help us very much in understanding such twentieth-century phenomena as the Soviet Empire, still less Hitler's Third Reich. It is true that most of the supporters of the European colonial empires expected them to bring in economic dividends, though whether in the event they did remains a hotly contested topic (see, e.g., Offer 1993). But that does not mean that we can ignore military, political, or ideological factors in their creation, or see these simply as the superficial features of a basically economic motivation. To that extent they belong to the same species as other empires of the past, reaching back to Rome and even beyond. There may well be important differences between ancient and modern empires, but the stress on economics does not seem to get to the heart of the matter.

A different way of distinguishing imperialism from colonialism comes in the suggestion that imperialism be restricted to the activities of land empires, leaving colonialism as the proper term to describe the system of overseas empires. Thus the Chinese or the Russians can be said to have had the older form of the more regionally based land empires, while the British and the French engaged in the world-transforming enterprise of overseas colonialism (see, e.g., Adas 1998: 371). But a number of scholars have argued persuasively that, to take the Chinese case as an example, Chinese expansion into "Inner Asia" under the Qing in the late seventeenth and eighteenth centuries had all the basic characteristics of European overseas expansion, and that "Qing rule in Tibet, Mongolia, and Xinjiang did not differ in principle from the European penetration of overseas dependencies" (Di Cosmo 1998: 306; see also Perdue 2005). Moreover, it has long been held that the Russian overland conquest of Central Asia in the nineteenth century had many of the hallmarks of colonial expansion, including the planting of colonists and the establishment of a colonial administration (Carrère d'Encausse 1989; Di Cosmo 1998: 307). Once more, while we may wish to insist on the differences between European and non-Western imperialism, principally on the issue of superior technological and military power (Adas 1998: 382–88), that is a different matter from trying to distinguish between imperialism and colonialism.

One further attempt might be mentioned, even though it might seem to confuse matters even more. Moses Finley (1976) has argued that the term "colonialism" should be applied only in those cases where the metropolitan society deliberately plants settlements of men and women—true colonies or "plantations"—that exist in a relation of dependency on the metropolitan power. By this account, while the Athenians and the Spartans of the fifth century BCE had empires (Finley 1978b), the ancient Greeks generally did not have colonies or colonialism, since the "colonies" set up by the metropolis or "mother-city" were both in intent and in fact self-governing communities of citizens, like the *poleis* from which they derived (see also White 1961).[27] More controversially, Finley argues that while India was part of the British *Empire*, it was not a colony and therefore does not belong to the system of colonialism. Colonialism in the British context can apply only to those settlements where there were considerable numbers of British or European colonists, such as those of North America, Australia, New Zealand, or South Africa. This means that many of those parts of the British Empire, including many territories in Africa, Asia, and the Pacific, where Europeans did not settle in great numbers, cannot be considered colonies. Imperialism and colonialism may overlap, but they have different principles and lead to different relationships between metropole and periphery.[28]

In trying to return to a "technical" and confessedly rather archaic meaning of the term "colony," Finley is aware that the enterprise may appear quixotic (Finley 1976: 170). Indeed it is so. It is as clear to him as to others that colonialism and imperialism have come to be used more or less interchangeably, and no great service is done by attempting to keep them separate. When the attempt is still made, it is done without much conviction (e.g., Howe 2002a: 25–31). Even a concept such as "internal colonialism," which has been put to good use by thinkers such as Michael Hechter ([1975] 1999), turns out not to be very different from what we mean by imperialism, and certainly does not call for the plantation of colonies as suggested in Finley's account (which is why Finley will have none of it). Similarly while "decolonization" is a useful term, for which "empire" and "imperialism" provide no equivalent cognates, its use requires no special theory of colonialism distinct from that of imperialism.

Empire, imperialism, and colonialism make up a family of concepts with varied but overlapping uses. While their histories point to different origins, the passage of time has merged them into a composite about which there is a reasonable degree of consensus. What matters above all from our point of view is the meaning of empire. Rome supplied the basic terms of that meaning. Doyle's definition, quoted above, is a reasonable summation of the tradition of use that derived from that. Empire is rule over a multitude of peoples. Imperialism and colonialism are the attitudes and practices that relate to empire.

Imperialism, in the strict, formal sense, may be a thing of the past. The various institutions of the international community frown on attempts to annex or to incorporate new territories into existing states. Even the most powerful states have come to accept that self-denying ordinance.[29] But there have always been forms of "informal empire," ways of controlling the destinies of other states and societies without formally taking possession of them (Gallagher and Robinson 1953; Wood 2005). The British practiced this on a large scale in the nineteenth and twentieth centuries, the Americans since the Second World War if not earlier; the Russians may be doing so today after the loss of their formal empire of the Soviet Union. "Empires" may have gone, but imperialism may still be with us.

More important, there is a widespread sense that the political institutions that served the world community over the past two centuries or so are no longer capable of doing so in the same way or with the same effect. Whether or not the nation-state and its institutions are in "decline" is a hotly debated question. But virtually no one disputes the changed context of the nation-state, the global forces—economic, political, and military—that play upon it and constrain its actions. There may be some two hundred nation-states in existence. But their ability to determine their own future varies wildly, with perhaps only a handful of states with that capability. That of course was the position of the world in the classic imperial era of the late nineteenth century, when the European empires more or less controlled the world. In that respect there is a certain familiarity about the present time, and a sense that reexamining the history of empires may be more than "mere" history.

There is one further point. We are accustomed to comparing and contrasting empires with nation-states, and to assuming that there has, in the past half century or more, been a passage "from empire to nation" (see further below). Even more, it has been assumed that the national principle, born in the French Revolution, is the "modern" principle, and that empires are in some sense premodern. Their persistence in the nineteenth and twentieth centuries then has to be seen, as Joseph Schumpeter saw it, as some sort of archaic hangover from the past. In which case one must surely say, some hangover! Far from giving way to the nation-state, empires have accompanied and to a good extent over-shadowed nation-states in the past two centuries. Even when empires formally dissolved, in the decades after the Second World War, their place was speedily taken by "superpowers" that were in many ways empires in all but name.

Empires, in short, are not only of the past but also of the present. We need to examine their persisting forms and influence. If empires belong to history, it is to that part of history that has an inescapable afterlife. "The empires of our time were short lived, but they have altered the world forever," says a character in V. S. Naipaul's novel *The Mimic Men* ([1967] 1985: 32); "their passing away is their least significant feature."

Among the features most in need of reexamination is the relation between empires and nations, and the presumed conflict between them. This has always been at the heart of discussions about empires, especially modern empires. How different in fact are they? To what extent have nation-states supplanted empires? What are the similarities, what the differences, between imperial and national identities? If empires are indeed radically different in their principles from nations, what are the implications—in terms of their impact, and of what can be learned from them?

Nation versus Empire

It has long been the conventional wisdom that nations and empires are rivals, sworn enemies. [30] The principle of nationalism is homogeneity, often seen in ethnic terms. Nations strive to embody, or to produce, a common culture. They express a radical egalitarianism: all members of the nation are in prin-ciple equal; all partake of the common national "soul." Nations, moreover, are intensely particularistic. While they do not deny the existence of other nations, and of their right to cultivate their ways, they are generally con-cerned only with their own way, convinced that it is superior to the ways of all other nations. Nationalists are highly inward-looking. They tend to celebrate themselves—"we English," "we Germans," "we French"—simply for their good fortune in being who they are, rather than for any cause or purpose in the world that might justify their existence (Breuilly 2000: 217).

Empires, by contrast, appear to exhibit principles antithetical to those of nations. They are multiethnic or multinational. Far from having or seeking a common culture, they stress the heterogeneity of cultures, especially that between the elite and the local cultures. Empires are hierarchical, opposed in principle to egalitarianism. The lines of solidarity are vertical, between subject and ruler, not, as in nations, horizontal, between equal citizens or fellow members of the same ethnic group. Empires, finally, aspire to universalism, not particularism. As with China or Rome, they see themselves as being at the center of the known world, the source of civilization itself and the carrier of the civilizing process to all the corners of the globe. Far from celebrating merely themselves, they tend to see themselves as the instruments of larger purposes in the world, generally of a moral or religious character. Toward nationalism they are contemptuous, as something petty and self-centered. "I am not *nacional* [*sic*]; that is something for children," declared the count-duke Olivares of imperial Spain, in an expression typical of the imperial mentality (in Elliott 1984: 74).

A powerful statement of what Benedict Anderson in his *Imagined Communities* calls "the inner incompatibility of empire and nation" (Anderson 2006: 93) is to be found in an equally famous study of nationalism, Ernest Gellner's *Nations and Nationalism*. For Gellner empires—seen as essentially premodern in type—belong to what he calls "agro-literate" society, the central fact of which is that "everything in it militates against the definition of political units in terms of cultural boundaries" (Gellner 1983: 11; see also Gellner 1998a: 14–24; Breuilly 2000: 198–99). Power and culture belong to different realms. Crucially, the culture of the elites—often cosmopolitan or international in character—is sharply differentiated from the myriad local cultures of the subordinate strata in the empire. Modern empires, such as the Soviet Empire, perpetuate this division, which is why for Gellner they are inherently unstable in a world in which nationalism is the dominant principle.

For nationalism, argues Gellner, closes what in modernity becomes an increasingly intolerable gap between power and culture, state and nation. It insists that only political units in which rulers and ruled share the same culture are legitimate. Its ideal is one state, one culture—which is to say, its ideal is the "nation-state," since it conceives of the nation essentially in terms of a shared culture. In the eyes of nationalists, for rulers of a political unit to belong to a nation other than that of the majority of the ruled "constitutes a quite outstandingly intolerable breach of political propriety" (Gellner 1983: 1). What, to nationalists, could possibly justify the existence of an entity such as the British Empire, in which a handful of British ruled over millions of Indians, Africans, and others, all of whom contained within themselves the seeds of potential nationhood?

In pitting nation against empire, Anderson and Gellner work within a tradition that stretches back to the eighteenth-century European Enlightenment. Anthony Pagden has drawn attention to the thought in particular of Johann Gottfried Herder, one of the fathers of European nationalism, in "setting up the unalterable opposition of nations and empires." "For Herder, the concept of a people, a *Volk*, and the concept of empire, were simply incompatible. Sooner or later all the world's empires were destined to collapse back into their constituent parts," seen as peoples or nations (Pagden 2003: 131–32; see also Pagden 1994: 172–88; Muthu 2003: 210–58). "Nothing," declared Herder, "appears so directly opposite to the end of government as the unnatural enlargement of states, the wild mixture of various kinds of humans and nations under one sceptre" (in Muthu 2003: 248). This view became a commonplace of nineteenth-century liberal thought as it increasingly allied itself with the national principle. Even those liberals, such as Lord Macaulay and John Stuart Mill, who defended empire accepted that nationality was the "natural" principle, and that empires could be justified only insofar as they were leading "backward" peoples toward independent nationhood (Mehta 1999: 77–114; Pitts 2005: 123–62).

The history of the relations between nations and empires in the past two centuries would seem to bear out the truth of this view of difference and divergence. For what has that history been but one of a revolt against empire in the name of nationality? In the wake of the First World War, the great continental land empires, commonly denounced as the "prison-houses of nations"—the Russian, the German, the Austro-Hungarian, and the Ottoman empires—all came crashing down, to be replaced by independent nation-states that were widely regarded as their legitimate heirs. The victorious Allies' charter of 1918, President Woodrow Wilson's Fourteen Points, loudly proclaimed the triumph of the principle of nationality over that of dynastic empire (Seton-Watson 1964: 19–23; Hobsbawm 1994: 31; Kappeler 2001: 213; Ferguson 2005: 172–73).

Later came the turn of the oceanic or overseas empires of the French, the Dutch, and the British. In a spectacular series of "wars of national liberation" their colonies claimed and enforced their independence on the basis of the nationalist doctrine that had become the norm of the international system. It became common to speak of the movement "from empire to nation" (e.g., Emerson [1960] 1962) to sum up this postwar experience. Moreover, the breakup of these empires too had partly been the result of a cataclysmic war, the Second World War, and, as with the previous war, there was again official endorsement of the nationality principle in the United Nations' Universal Declaration of Human Rights of 1948 ("everyone has the right to a nationality"). Later still, in 1989, the "informal colonies" of the Soviet Empire in Eastern Europe declared their independence, followed swiftly thereafter by similar actions among the various national republics or "internal colonies" of the Soviet Union itself (though, as Gellner rightly noted [1998a: 57], it was not nationalism itself that brought down the Soviet Union).

The collapse of the Soviet Union in 1991 seemed to set the seal on the long-drawn-out encounter between nation and empire. Despite much talk about the new "American Empire," it was clear that formal empire in the classic sense had for the time being at least reached a certain historic terminus (the announcement of the "end of history," and similar claims that liberal democracy had triumphed in the world, were some kind of recognition of this). The opprobrium that had, with increasing force since the Second World War, gathered around the terms "empire" and "imperialism" seemed now to hold sway everywhere. No state called itself an empire anymore; only its enemies did so. If indeed there was or is an American Empire, as Niall Ferguson argued, it was "an empire in denial," an empire that practiced "the imperialism of anti-imperialism," an empire that "dare not speak its name" (Ferguson 2005: xxii, 6, 61–104; cf. Teschke 2006: 137).

Nations as Empires

But there is another way of telling the story of the relation between nation and empire. In this account, nation and empire are not so much opposed as acknowledged to be alternative or complementary expressions of the same phenomenon of power. Empires can be nations writ large; nations empires under another name.

The great historian Sir Lewis Namier once said that "religion is a sixteenth-century word for nationalism" (quoted MacLachlan 1996: 15). This seems to be a typical case of a secular thinker's refusing to accept the sincerity or authenticity of the participants' own protestations. The sixteenth-century conflicts that tore apart most European societies *were* indeed "wars of religion," and any attempt to convert or reduce them to nationalist (or even "protonationalist") conflicts seems, *pace* Anthony Marx (2003), highly anachronistic.[31] But what is insightful in Namier's comment is the recognition that nationalism can take a variety of forms and expressions, and that a concept such as "imperial nationalism" therefore may not be as contradictory as it first sounds.

In the first place it is important to note that, as discussed above, many early modern states—those which later evolved into nation-states—saw themselves as *empires*. David Armitage, among others, has stressed that especially in the sixteenth and seventeenth centuries the term "empire" was often used in its original (Roman) sense of *sovereignty* or *supreme authority*, rather than in its later—and more common modern—meaning of rule over a multiplicity of lands and peoples (Armitage 2000: 29–32; see also Pagden 1995: 12–13). "Rex in regno suo est imperator," the king is emperor in his own kingdom—this common late medieval saying was the basis of many claims to empire among early modern states (Ullmann 1979). Here, then, was an assertion of empire, as sovereignty or self-sufficient authority, very similar to one of the central claims of the nation-state.

There was a further way in which empire and (nation-) state might overlap. Many of the early modern states were what have been called "composite monarchies" or "multiple kingdoms"—states, that is, such as Spain or Britain, where one monarch might rule over several territories, many of them formerly independent kingdoms. Thus the Spanish monarch Charles V—leaving aside what we might think of as Spain's more classically imperial possessions in the New World and elsewhere—ruled over the kingdoms of Castile, Aragon, Milan, Naples, and the Low Countries; Britain, with the accession of James I in 1603, and more firmly with the Act of Union of 1707, was a composite state made up of the kingdoms of England, Scotland, and Ireland and the principality of Wales (Koenigsberger 1987; Elliott 1992; Russell 1995; Armitage 2000: 22–23). Such states, in other words, contained that variety and plurality of peoples and lands that empire connoted, both classically and in modern times. Whether therefore the stress was on sovereignty or multiple rule, state and empire were conjoint terms for much of the early modern period (Koebner 1961: 52; Armitage 2000: 14–23; Pagden 1995: 13–14).

But there is an even more compelling consideration that might lead us to see convergence rather than divergence between (nation-) states and empires. Most nation-states, or what became nation-states, are, like most empires, the result of conquest and colonization. The later ideology of nationalism of course disguises this unpalatable fact, as much as it exhibits amnesia about many other aspects of the violent origins of nations (Marx 2003: 29–32). The rise of nationalist historiography in the nineteenth century drove a wedge between "domestic" and "extraterritorial" history, between the nation-state and empire—both the territorial empires that had preceded it and the extra-European empires that were constructed across the globe in the eighteenth and nineteenth centuries. Nevertheless, as David Armitage says, "the nation-state as it had been precipitated out of a system of aggressively competing nations...functioned as 'the empire *manqué*'"—within Europe itself as much as beyond it (Armitage 2000: 14).

Robert Bartlett (1994) has given the classic account of how European states were formed by a process of "conquest, colonization and cultural change," in the High Middle Ages, from the tenth century to the fourteenth. From their heartlands in the old Carolingian lands—modern France and western Germany—Frankish and Norman knights swept westward, eastward, and southward. Normans conquered England, and went on to take Wales and Ireland. They put enormous pressure on the Scots, forcing them, as a condition of survival, to adapt to Anglo-Norman culture and institutions. In the East, Germans cleared the forests, established new towns, and settled in old ones—such as Prague—in large numbers, opening the way to the eventual incorporation of these lands into Prussia and other German states. Burgundian families established their rule in Portugal and León-Castile and spearheaded the Christian reconquest of Andalucia from the Moors. The Normans conquered Sicily and from this base spread the ways and institutions of Latin Christianity throughout the southern Mediterranean and many parts of the Levant (aided by the crusading movement that established the Crusader Kingdom of Jerusalem). In this massive centrifugal movement, a uniform system of town charters, commercial law, coinage, language (Latin), and educational and ecclesiastical institutions came into being in a huge swath stretching from the Baltic to the eastern Mediterranean. "Europe, the initiator of one of the world's major processes of conquest, colonization and cultural transformation, was also the product of one" (Bartlett 1994: 314).

This dynamic process of conquest and colonization meant that the states and kingdoms that were established in medieval and early modern Europe nearly all had the appearance of empires. England, for instance, once united by the Norman Conquest of 1066, went on in its turn—largely at first under Norman auspices—to "unite" (*sc.* conquer) the peoples of Wales, Ireland, and, eventually, Scotland, into another state, the United Kingdom, and another nation, the British. Observing that "many of the most successful nation states of the present started life as empires," Niall Ferguson asks, "What is the modern United Kingdom of Great Britain and Northern Ireland if not the legatee of an earlier English imperialism?" (Ferguson 2005: xii). Just as Europe itself did, so too England began its great colonizing venture in the world with an initial act of "internal colonization," the construction of an "inner empire" of Great

Britain that became the launching pad for the creation of an "outer empire" of "Greater Britain" overseas (Kumar 2003: 60–88; cf. Cooper 2005: 172).

France too achieved nationhood by a process of conquest launched by the Capetian kings from their base in the Île-de-France (see further chapter 7). They gradually conquered and absorbed the surrounding states: Normandy, Brittany, Burgundy, Languedoc, Provence, and many others of the once-independent principalities that succeeded the Carolingian Empire. As Eugen Weber (1976) showed, it was only in the late nineteenth century that peasants of disparate traditions and many tongues were nationalized, turned into Frenchmen and Frenchwomen. The France of "the Hexagon" has recognizably imperial roots.

Spain shows even more clearly the pattern of unification through conquest—the more so as it remains in several respects still incomplete, with a persistent Basque separatist movement and intermittent calls for independence emanating from Catalonia. From the time of the union of the kingdoms of Aragon and Castile in 1469, Spanish monarchs engaged in a strenuous and only partly successful effort to bring adjacent territories into a single state and to form a Spanish nation. That the process was tortuous, marked by frequent rebellions and civil wars, is made clear in the comment of an eighteenth-century Spanish civil servant, Olavide, that Spain was "a body composed of other smaller bodies separated, and in opposition to one another, which oppress and despise each other and are in a continuous state of civil war. . . . Modern Spain can be considered as a body without energy . . . a monstrous Republic formed of little republics which confront each other" (in Carr 2000: 6).

Spain, France, and England/Britain are the countries most regularly invoked in the literature on nationalism as early, well-formed, nation-states (see, e.g., A. Smith 1991: 55). It is salutary to remember, then, how much of conquest and colonization there was in the formation of these nation-states, and how imperfectly the word "nation," with its suggestion of consensus, community, and homogeneity, sums up the resulting product. "Spain," "France," "Britain," and their respective nations, were the result of the more or less forcible integration of neighboring lands and peoples by dominant groups whose institutions and culture often differed considerably from those of the conquered peoples. This pattern has often been noted for later examples of nation building as well. For example, it was common to say, in the nineteenth century and later, that "Germany" was made by Prussian conquest of the other German states; less commonly, but perhaps equally accurately, it might be said that "Italy" was made by the Piedmontese conquest of the other Italian states (which explains the famous remark of Massimo d'Azeglio in 1868, that "we have made Italy, now we must make Italians"). And it has frequently been pointed out that many of the "new nations" of Africa and Asia are so only in name, that they are artificial creations, the result largely of the wars and political maneuverings of the former imperial powers. What we need to stress is that this pattern is not simply typical of latecomers to nation building but has been the norm since the very earliest examples. Many "nation-states," to put it another way, are empires in miniature; they have been formed as empires have usually been formed. There is in that sense an inescapably imperial dimension to the nation-state.

Empires as Nations: "Imperial Nationalism"

If nations have often been conceived and constructed as empires, might the reverse also be true? If nations can be seen as miniempires, can empires be seen as large nations? Does imperialism converge with nationalism? What are the degrees—and limits—of this convergence?

Anthony Smith has in several places (e.g., 1986, 2004) argued that all nations are constituted by "core" *ethnies*, around which may cohere other ethnic groups in subordinate roles. In the English case, for instance, it is impossible to ignore the contribution over the centuries of Norwegians, Normans, Huguenots, Scots, Welsh, Irish, Jews, Indians, Afro-Caribbeans, and other ethnicities to that mix we call "Englishness." But it is equally clear that, by about the sixteenth century at the latest, there had emerged something like an English nation (which is—*pace* Greenfeld [1992]—quite a different matter from saying that we can find English *nationalism* in this period). The English language, for one thing, had by then come into its own, supremely with the works of Shakespeare, Marlowe, Spenser, and others. Protestantism was beginning to do its work, especially in its nonconformist forms. Parliament and the common law were already beginning to be acknowledged as emblems of the national culture. This was the beginning of something like "racial Anglo-Saxonism," to use Reginald Horsman's (1981) term, though it had little of the biological character ascribed to it in its nineteenth-century guise. It does, though, mean that by this time a distinctive and dominant *ethnie* had emerged in England, setting the terms and conditions within which later groups were invited to find, or to force, a place (for other examples, see Kaufmann 2004). It is this core *ethnie* that lends its peculiar qualities to the nation; it is this group that defines the "national character," difficult as it always is to enumerate its attributes precisely (see, for a good discussion of the English case, Mandler 2006).

Can we not say something similar about empires? Most empires are constructed by a particular people—the Romans, the Spanish, the English/British, the French, the Russians, the Turks, and the like. It is they who name it and oversee its development. Whatever their numbers, it is they who tend to define its character. They are, we may say, the "state-bearing" peoples of the empire. And, just as a particular ethnic group might come to identify itself with the nation it creates, so a particular people or nation might come to identify itself with the empire it founds. Nations and empires, we have seen, tend to think of their purpose or destiny in the world in different terms, the one more inner, the other more outward looking. But it seems fair to say that in both cases we can discern a group or groups that identify with their creation and derive their sense of their collective identity from it.

I have elsewhere (Kumar 2000, 2003: 30–35) argued that we can call the sense of identity of imperial peoples a kind of "imperial" or "missionary nationalism." There is, I agree, a double danger in so doing. In the first place, the ideology of nationalism does not emerge until the late eighteenth century, and it is therefore anachronistic and misleading to speak of nationalism in any form before that time. Since empires for the most part clearly predate the age of nationalism—even if they persist well into it—we obviously need to specify clearly what we might mean by "imperial nationalism." In the second place, for all the suggestive parallels, empires are not nations (and nations are not empires), as we shall see. Hence to speak of imperial nationalism runs the risk of confusing two entities—nations and empires—that for most purposes need to be kept separate.

The reason for nevertheless thinking that "imperial nationalism" might be a useful concept is the gain that comes from seeing two disparate phenomena from a common vantage point. Like nationalists in relation to their nation, imperialists feel that there is something special or unique about their empire. It has a mission or purpose in the world. This may, again as with nationalists, endow imperial peoples with a sense of their own superiority, a feeling of inherent goodness as of a people specially chosen to carry out a task (cf. Smith 2003).[32] Imperialists, like nationalists, are true believers.

What are the causes or missions that have given imperial peoples a sense of their collective identity? For most Europeans, the pattern was set by the Romans with their belief that they were giving nothing less than civilization—Roman laws, Roman institutions, Roman culture—to the world. Hence it was possible for the Romans to identify their empire with the whole known world, the *orbis terrarum*. Later European empires, from the Holy Roman Empire onward, repeated the claim, to an almost wearying degree, though the content might vary depending on the particular place or time. Thus although the Spaniards, like most imperialists, saw themselves in the image of Rome, it was as a Catholic power that they saw their mission, in Europe and in the New World (a role intensified with the Protestant Reformation). The Austrian Habsburgs took up the torch from their Spanish cousins, putting themselves not just at the head of the Counter-Reformation but also—as the Ostmark or Österreich—seeing themselves as the defenders of European civilization on its eastern flank, against the threat of the infidel Turks. The Russians, proclaiming Moscow the "Third Rome" and themselves the legatees of the doomed Byzantines, aspired to continue the struggle for Orthodoxy in the world. A similar resolve, but for a contrary cause, animated the English when as "the Protestant nation" they attempted to lead the Protestant crusade in Europe and the New World, especially against the machinations of the Catholic powers of Spain and France. The French, for their own part, having first hitched their empire to the Catholic cause, after their Great Revolution of 1789 and the turn toward republicanism, increasingly came to identify French imperialism with *la mission civilisatrice* (as, in the later phases of the British Empire, did the British). This too, in its own terms, was the mission of the Russians in their second or Soviet Empire, the spreading of reason and science to the benighted in the form of communism. In this renewed emphasis, begun with the Romans, on the mission to civilize and enlighten, the wheel had come full circle.[33]

Merely to list these causes or missions is to cast doubt on the analogy between nationalism and imperialism. Nationalist causes are not typically like these. For some time in the early nineteenth century, when a form of liberal nationalism flourished under the banner of Giuseppe Mazzini and his followers, nationalism did indeed ally itself with the noble causes of spreading freedom and enlightenment in the world (Alter 1994: 19–23, 39–65; Mazower 2015: 48–54). But the period that followed, the period of "organic nationalism," showed another face of nationalism: one that was vindictive and intolerant toward rivals, one that trumpeted the power and glory of particular nations, one that asked its citizens to die for the nation whatever the cause it chose to embrace. The Nazis' celebration of the Teutonic or Aryan peoples, in and for themselves, indicated the logical end point of this type of nationalism (Alter 1994: 26–38; Hobsbawm 1992: 101–30; Zimmer 2003: 80–106).

Imperialist ideologies are universalistic, not particularistic. That difference has to be borne in mind. Imperial peoples do not, unlike nationalists, celebrate themselves; they celebrate the causes of which they are the agents or carriers. It is from this that they derive their sense of themselves and their place in the world. But the parallel with nationalism is still instructive. In both cases we see the attempt to effect a fusion, a symbiosis almost, between a people and a political entity. Imperial nationalism plays down membership of a "mere nation," with its tendency toward self-congratulation and self-importance; but it does so in order to insist on a higher form of nationalism, one that justifies the nation in terms of its commitment to a cause that goes beyond the nation.

It is somewhat ironic, in view of this, that the greatest apparent convergence between imperialism and nationalism is to be found in the very period—from the 1870s to the First World War—in which nationalism threw off its liberal mantle and presented itself in the guise of naked power seeking. The historian Wolfgang Mommsen speaks of "the deformation of national politics" in this period:

> The idea of the nation state progressively lost those elements which in the first half of the nineteenth century had made it an emancipatory ideology, directed against the arbitrary rule of princes and small aristocratic elites, and an intellectual weapon in the campaign for constitutional government. Instead it came to be associated with the power-status of the established national culture, and the imposition of its values on ethnic or cultural minorities both within and beyond the body politic was now considered essential. (Mommsen 1990: 215; see also Mommsen 1978)

Mommsen sees this deformation as directly connected to the "high imperialism" of the times, when the great powers—in particular Britain, France, Germany—competed for dominance on the world stage through the acquisition of larger and larger territorial empires (Mommsen 1990: 212). This was the view too of another liberal thinker, J. A. Hobson, the great critic of imperialism, who saw imperialism as "a debasement of . . . genuine nationalism, by attempts to overflow its natural banks and absorb the near or distant territory of reluctant and unassimilable peoples" (Hobson [1902, 1938] 1988: 6). For Hobson as for other liberal thinkers, nationality still appeared the natural and desirable principle—a "plain highway to internationalism"—with imperialism a "perversion of its nature and purpose" (Hobson [1902, 1938] 1988: 11).

Such a position has seemed too kind to nationalism, in the view of other thinkers. For them nationalism is inherently imperialistic, just as it was inevitable at this time that imperialism would take the form of nationalist rivalries. Imperialism is then seen not so much as a perversion as a more or less natural extension of a power-seeking nationalism; in its turn, the nation comes to conceive of itself in the image of empire, the traditional emblem of grandeur and the supreme expression of great-power status. "Imperialism and nationalism," says Christopher Bayly, "were part of the same phenomenon. . . . The rise of exclusive nationalisms, grasping and using the powers of the new and more interventionist state, was the critical force propelling both the new imperialism and the hardening of the boundaries between majority and assumed 'ethnic' populations across the world. . . . Imperialism and nationalism reacted on each other to redivide the world and its people" (Bayly 2004: 230, 242–43).

Once again, therefore, the ground between empire and nation, imperialism and nationalism, seems to crumble and disappear. If nations can be seen as empires, empires, especially modern empires, can seem no more than nations writ large. The British Empire, or "Greater Britain" as some termed it, is in this view no more than the expression of British nationalism, the desire to expand the British presence and power in the world (see, e.g., Seeley [1883] 1971); the French Empire, partly in rivalry with Britain, the expression of a wounded French nationalism in the wake of the crushing defeat at the hands of Prussia in 1871 (see Schivelbusch 2004: 103–87). Imperialism appears as hypertrophied nationalism, perhaps; but nationalism nonetheless, expressing its ultimate logic and tendency.

Empire and Nation: Continuing Antagonisms and Tensions

Is this, then, the conclusion? Are Gellner, Anderson, and so many others wrong in drawing such a sharp distinction between the principle of empire and that of the nation? Is imperialism simply nationalism under another name?

Max Weber once observed that while all great powers tend, for reasons of prestige, to be imperialist and "expansive," this was not the case with all nations, some of which sought their principles and sense of national pride from within themselves. "Not all political structures are equally 'expansive'. They do not all strive for an outward expansion of their power, or keep their force in readiness for acquiring political power over other territories and communities by incorporating them or making them dependent. Hence, as structures of power, political organizations vary in the extent to which they are turned outward" (Weber 1978: 2:910). Britain, France, and Germany might feel the need for empire, but not Switzerland or Norway.

This perception might be one way of considering the fact that empire and nation can, at different times, alternate in the striving of states. In the early modern period, the examples of the Spanish and Portuguese empires made it seem that empire was the only way of establishing one's presence in the world. The British, Dutch, and French hurried to imitate the imperial style of those countries, with a considerable measure of success. Later, in the nineteenth century, as the national principle gained in strength, nation-state formation seemed to offer a more fulfilling, as well as for many a more practicable, option. This was especially so in the case of smaller or weaker countries, such as Italy, Poland, Ireland, Norway, and the Slav peoples of the Habsburg Empire. Here empire was the enemy, not the goal.

But nationalism, rather than imperialism, was not just for small or weak countries. The tension between nation and empire could often be seen within the same country, including some of the most powerful, at the same time. Britain in the nineteenth century had its "Little Englanders" who, especially after the loss of the North American colonies, felt that empire was ruinous to British commerce and corrupting in its moral and political effects at home. The way forward was for Britain to renounce imperial entanglements and to exert its influence by the example of its peaceful and prosperous existence as one nation among others (see, e.g., Thornton [1959] 1968: 1–56; Gott 1989).[34] In France, after the loss of Alsace-Lorraine following the Franco-Prussian War of 1871, there was a bitter struggle between the imperialists, keen on matching Britain's imperial power, and the nationalists, who felt that it was essential to France's national honor to recover the lost provinces, and for whom empire was a crippling distraction (Baumgart 1982: 55–68; Schivelbusch 2004: 176–87).

Nationalism and imperialism could therefore, despite their similarities, point in very different directions. A world of nations, accepting the particularities of different peoples, and promoting the cultivation of unique national cultures, was quite different from a world of competing empires, each intent on reforming the world in its own image. J. A. Hobson, the best-known writer on modern imperialism, and one who was fully alive to the connections between nationalism and imperialism, nevertheless felt the need to make it plain at the very outset of his study that the kind of imperialism that was collusive with nationalism was of a very novel and highly untypical kind. It was novel and untypical because it took the form of competing nations, each striving to magnify their empires; whereas the true principle of empire was unitary and universal.

The notion of a number of competing empires is essentially modern. The root idea of empire in the ancient and the medieval world was that of a federation of States, under a hegemony, covering in general terms the entire known recognized world, such as was held by Rome under the so-called *pax Romana*. When Roman citizens, with full civic rights, were found all over the explored world, in Africa and Asia, as well as in Gaul and Britain, Imperialism contained a genuine element of internationalism. With the fall of Rome this conception of a single empire wielding political authority over the civilized world did not disappear. On the contrary, it survived all the fluctuations of the Holy Roman Empire. Even after the definite split between the Eastern and Western sections had taken place at the close of the fourth century, the theory of a single state, divided for administrative purposes, survived. Beneath every cleavage or antagonism, and notwithstanding the severance of many independent kingdoms and provinces, this ideal unity of the empire lived. It formed the conscious avowed ideal of Charlemagne. . . . Rudolf of Habsburg not merely revived the idea, but laboured to realize it through Central Europe, while his descendant Charles V gave a very real meaning to the term by gathering under the unity of his imperial rule the territories of Austria, Germany, Spain, the Netherlands, Sicily and Naples. In later ages this dream of a European Empire animated the policy of Peter the Great, Catherine, and Napoleon. (Hobson [1902, 1938] 1988: 8–9)

There is not much to add to this masterly sketch, merely to say that its accuracy has been confirmed by most later studies of the imperial idea (see, e.g., Folz [1953] 1969; Muldoon 1999; Münkler 2007). Hobson goes on to say that the "internationalism of empire" was continued, with diminishing force, in the "humane cosmopolitanism" of the Enlightenment and the French Revolution, only to "wither before the powerful revival of nationalism" in the nineteenth century. Nationalism properly understood and practiced, he continued to believe, was not in necessary contradiction with internationalism. But linked to an aggressive and competitive imperialism, which transforms "the wholesome stimulative rivalry of varied national types into the cut-throat struggle of competing empires," it threatened "the peace and progress of mankind" (Hobson [1902, 1938] 1988: 10–12).

The revival of interest in empire today, we have noted, has much to do with the revulsion against the excesses of nationalism in the twentieth century, specifically as these were seen to culminate in the fascist regimes of Italy and

Germany, and more recently as the cause of violence in the former Soviet Union and the former Yugoslavia. This has, no doubt, led to a certain amount of nostalgia for empire (including the Soviet Empire), coupled with the feeling that the historic empires have much to teach a world struggling with the problems of globalization and the diminished role of the nation-state, not to mention the management of increasingly "multicultural" societies (themselves to a good extent the product of past empires). Whatever our feelings about this, however, they do underscore the point that in the minds of many people empires and nations, for all the interesting ways in which they overlap, are in the end based on different principles and point to different worlds.

As ideological formations, nations and nationalism may well have occupied center stage in the modern world order, at least in the last two centuries. The American Revolution, the first anticolonial revolution of modern times, may be taken as marking the birth of a strong anti-imperial sentiment in Western thought. It was greeted with enthusiasm by many European intellectuals, not least in France, where it played a significant role in bringing down the old regime in 1789. Enlightenment thinkers such as Diderot and Herder, Adam Smith and Edmund Burke, even Jeremy Bentham, inveighed against empire (Pagden 1995: 156–200; Mehta 1999: 153–89; Muthu 2003; Pitts 2005: 25–122). Empires were widely seen as archaic and outmoded, obsessed with the antiquated virtues of "honor," "grandeur," "greatness," "glory." Their oppression of other peoples readily turned into despotic rule over their own. Though apparently a source of riches, they were ultimately as ruinous to the economies of their countries as they were to its moral health.

But nationalism and anti-imperialism by no means had it all their own way, neither in thought nor, even more, in practice. We are familiar with the late nineteenth-century bout of European (and, for a time, American) imperialism—the "scramble for Africa," the "Great Game" of Anglo-Russian rivalry in Central Asia, the parceling out of the world among the great European powers. What is less well known is how strongly empire, as an idea and a practice, persisted in late eighteenth- and early nineteenth-century Europe, and continued to inform the policies of the major states throughout the nineteenth century. The old idea of a mid-nineteenth-century "hiatus" of anti-imperial liberalism and laissez-faire now looks increasingly illusory, or at best as only a partial truth. The British Empire, for instance, moved seamlessly from the loss of its North American colonies to the acquisition of even more glittering prizes in Asia; France too, having lost its North American empire, began the construction of a new one in Africa as early as 1830, with the conquest of

Algeria—not forgetting, of course, Napoleon's attempt at empire (see further chapters 6 and 7, below).

The persistence of empire in European policy and practice was matched by its persistence in at least one important strand of European thought. This refers not only to racist and right-wing thinkers, such as Thomas Carlyle and Arthur Gobineau, though of course their popularity indicates the appeal of empire in the earlier as much as in the later part of the nineteenth century. Nor should one forget the rehabilitation of the imperial ideal in *les idées napoléoniennes* that, following the death of Napoleon in 1821, proved so seductive to so many French statesmen, not least the founder of the Second Empire, Louis Napoleon (Koebner and Schmidt 1964: 1–26). But more significant is the "turn to empire" in some of the most famous liberal thinkers of the day, such as John Stuart Mill and Alexis de Tocqueville. Mill and Tocqueville, with whatever misgivings, each justified his country's empire in terms of its educative mission of spreading civilization to peoples who had not yet reached the levels achieved by European societies (Mehta 1999: 97–114; Pitts 2005: 123–62, 204–39). In both Britain and France, then, the two leading imperial powers of the nineteenth and twentieth centuries, influential thinkers throughout the nineteenth century lent their intellectual distinction to the imperial idea.

The point that needs stressing, because of our tendency to ignore it, is that empires have been part of the modern world order as much as, and arguably more than, nation-states. An "age of nation-states" did not succeed an "age of empire"; nationalism did not succeed imperialism. Nationalism was certainly the new thing, and nineteenth-century imperialism showed the impress of the new thinking and the new forces. Empires, more than ever before, carried a national label, most obviously in the land empire that Hitler attempted to create in the 1930s and 1940s, as the Third German Reich. The British and the French empires expressed, to an extent, nationalist rivalries, superimposed on the more old-fashioned "great power" rivalries of the eighteenth century. But in no case did they cease to be empires. That meant that they had a principle, and a purpose, different from those of nation-states. Their aims and aspirations were global, not local.

The disappearance of empires—at least in the formal sense—has been relatively recent. The signs of their existence are still all around us, not least in the large populations from the former empires that are now part of the life of most major Western cities. In order to understand our present we need to understand our past. We need to interrogate more closely the principles of empire. We particularly need to turn the spotlight on the ruling peoples themselves, their self-conceptions and justifications of empire. "Force and violence," as David Hume saw, is surely part of the story of empires, but it is not the whole story, and could not have been to have enabled them to last for so long. How did the peoples who made and maintained empire, the "state-bearing" peoples, conceive their role? How did they carry it out? How did it affect their sense of themselves? What are the consequences for them of losing empire?

Since the history of empire is well-nigh coterminous with the whole of recorded history, there is a wealth of examples to draw on. We shall restrict ourselves to some modern examples—the British, the French, the Russian, the Ottoman, and the Habsburg empires. But with empire one is always forced out of any one particular mold, any one historical period. Empires, by virtue of their very principle, are acutely aware not simply of contemporary rivals but also of the great examples of the past. Sometimes this is the relatively recent past, as with the Spanish, Portuguese, and Dutch empires—all of which persisted alongside the newer, more vigorous, empires of Britain and France and indeed continued right up to the twentieth century, if in vastly etiolated form. But for all the Western empires, nothing rivaled Rome, though in their case all roads led not so much to Rome as from Rome. Rome was the inspiration, even as it was a warning in the often-told story of its decline and fall. The modern empires—mostly run by elites educated in the classics—all admired Rome, learned from it, wished to be known as the "New Rome." But they also hoped to go beyond it, to learn from its mistakes and to establish their empires on firmer foundations. All such hopes are of course ultimately illusory, as Thomas Gray recognized—"the paths of glory lead but to the grave." But that is true of all human institutions. Empires are no less subject to this law, but equally no less instructive than any other long-lasting institution.

At any rate, before looking at the more modern examples, we need to glance back at Rome. We have already considered what the Romans meant by empire, as a concept, and how influential this was in the later history of empire. We need now to consider, in brief outline and with the broadest of brushstrokes, what the Roman Empire actually was, how it saw itself and how it was run. For, in however distorted a form, and however misunderstood, these ideas and practices were to have a profound influence on later conceptions of empire, of what an empire was and should be, and how it should conduct itself. No less important, as a dreadful warning, were the causes of its collapse, or what were thought to be its causes, and what that might teach later empires about how to avoid Rome's fate. No empire escaped the shadow of Rome, even as it struggled to break free from what seemed a predestined outcome.

2

The Roman Empire

PARENT OF EMPIRE

Seldom has the government of the world been conducted for so long a term
in an orderly sequence. . . . In its sphere, which those who belonged to it were
not far wrong in regarding as the world, it fostered the peace and prosperity of
the many nations united under its sway longer and more completely than any
other leading power has ever done.

—THEODOR MOMMSEN ([1909] 1974: 1:4–5)

We are all, so far as we inherit the civilization of Europe, still citizens of the
Roman Empire.

—T. S. ELIOT (1957: 130)

We may say that in European cultural tradition any empire must be a Roman
Empire in one sense or another. All the devices to represent the imperial glory
in arts or in literature or even in political thought must, in the last resort, lead
to Rome as their ultimate source.

—MACIEJ JANOWSKI (2004: 79)

The Legacy of Rome

It would be hard to exaggerate the impact and influence of Rome on later
ideas and practices of empire. For one thing—still insufficiently appreciated
even by many educated people—the Roman empire did not "fall" in the fifth
century CE. What fell was the western part of the empire, centered on Rome;
the eastern empire, centered on Constantinople, lived on for another thousand

MAP 2.1. The Roman Empire at its greatest extent, 117 CE

years, as the Byzantine Empire. The Byzantines called themselves Romans, *Rhomaioi*; and so long as the Byzantine Empire lasted, the name and ideals of Rome lived on.[1] When Constantinople finally fell to the Turks in 1453, the Ottoman Empire that succeeded in the region aspired for some time to continue the Roman inheritance, and to see itself in the image of Rome.[2] So we must see the Roman Empire as lasting well into the medieval period, an active player and powerful presence in the whole region stretching from the eastern Mediterranean to the Atlantic.

Even in the West, the idea of the fall of the Roman Empire has to be treated with caution. Many of its practices were continued by its creation, the Catholic Church, insofar as the Church was able to do so in the difficult circumstances of the early medieval centuries. Moreover, the empire was renewed in the West by Charlemagne, founder of the Holy Roman Empire in 800 CE. This too had its vicissitudes; but its survival in some form up to the nineteenth century, when it was abolished by Napoleon in 1806, is a testimony to the enduring appeal of Rome, which the empire self-consciously aimed to revive and continue. And what, allowing for the necessary qualifications, is the European Union but a revived Holy Roman Empire (Zielonka 2006)? All efforts over the centuries to create a unified Europe—if not, indeed, a unified world—have, in some sense or the other, been attempts to resurrect the unity first definitively established by Rome.

The Roman Empire animated the aspirations to "world dominion" of Charles V and Philip II of Spain, and of Louis XIV and the first Napoleon of France. In suppressing the Holy Roman Empire, Napoleon hoped to substitute his own, based on France and Paris; and although he rejected the titles of "Augustus" and "Germanicus" proposed by the Institut de France, there was no question that Roman models inspired him as, in republican form, they had inspired the republic that Napoleon overthrew (Huet 1999). As Marx noted, "the Revolution of 1789 to 1814 draped itself alternately as the Roman republic and the Roman empire" (Marx [1851–52] 1962: 1:247; see also Jenkyns 1992a: 27). It could hardly have been otherwise. "Until not long before [Napoleon's] day there had hardly been a time in Europe when the collective memory had not been stirred by the remembrance of Rome or the medieval Empire as a unified state and when the policies of the leading states had not been shaped by nostalgia for those days, if not by the determination to restore them" (Hinsley 1963: 154).

The British and the French of the nineteenth century also harked back to Rome in the development and rule of their empires (see chaps. 6 and 7). But one might mention here in addition the German Empire created by Prussia in 1871. It was almost inevitable that this empire would be seen as the successor to what after all, since the fifteenth century, had come to be known as "the Holy Roman Empire of the German Nation." Bismarck himself, the architect of the empire, and even the first emperor, the Prussian king Wilhelm I, were themselves personally opposed to such an association but found the tide in its favor irresistible. An unsuccessful attempt was made to get the original imperial crown from Vienna; but in its place a new one was made modeled on that of the Holy Roman emperor Otto the Great, and "the first diet of the Second Reich was opened with the emperor seated on an ancient imperial throne from Goslar, on which Henry IV, Philip of Swabia, Otto IV and Frederick III [all former Holy Roman emperors] had once sat enthroned" (Heer [1968] 2002: 278). The next emperor, Wilhelm II, showed much more enthusiasm for the imperial role, self-consciously cultivating the symbols of the Holy Roman Empire and even of the Roman emperor Constantine (Heer [1968] 2002: 278–79).

It was perhaps even more inevitable that Mussolini's "Roman Empire" and Hitler's Third Reich should see themselves in the image of Rome. "Rome," declared Mussolini, "is our point of departure and reference; it is our symbol, or if you wish, our myth. . . . Much of what was the immortal spirit of Rome, resurges in Fascism." For the Italian people, he claimed, Rome is "eternal and contemporary. For us it is as if Caesar was stabbed just yesterday" (in Nelis 2007: 396, 403). *Romanità*, the quality or character of Romanness, was a dominant theme of much fascist ideology and culture (Visser 1992; Nelis 2007; Arthurs 2012). The very emblem of fascism, the *fasces*—the rods of office—that symbolized the power and authority of the state, was taken from Rome. Fascist intellectuals such as Giovanni Gentile developed the idea of "two Italys," the Italy of Rome and the Italy of the Renaissance. The emphasis on individualism and "culture" in the Renaissance had, they claimed, undermined—not just in Italy but in the West at large—the virility and solidarity of the Roman inheritance, which accordingly needed to be renewed. "Glory" must replace "frivolity"; individualism must give way to the "organic state" of the Roman tradition (Berezin 1997: 57; Visser 1992: 12; Stone 1999: 207).

The architectural schemes drawn up for fascist Rome drew unashamedly and self-consciously on the designs and monuments of imperial Rome. As put by one organizer, "Rome ought to appear marvellous to all people of the world: vast, organized and powerful as it was in the time of the first emperor Augustus" (in Berezin 1997: 125). Murals and mosaics appropriated and reproduced the themes and forms of the Roman Empire. At the vast exhibition of 1937 to commemorate the bimillenium of the birth of the emperor Augustus, monumental statues of Mussolini and Augustus flanked the entrance to the Mostra augustea della romanità. In preparation for the exhibition, and to stress the unity between the Roman past and the fascist present, the Mausoleum of Augustus and the Ara Pacis were excavated and reconstructed for display. As one contemporary reviewer put it, the exhibition was designed to show "the rebirth of *romanità* under Fascism." To underline the point, on the very same day as the Augustan exhibition, the Fascist Party reopened an expanded Mostra della rivoluzione fascista, the exhibition of the fascist revolution. Mussolini inaugurated both within an hour of each other. As the *Corriere della sera* declared, the simultaneous opening of the two exhibitions was meant to show that "*Romanità* and Fascism are manifestations of the same spirit. The two great historical phenomena which led to the creation of the Empire of Augustus and to our Empire represent two moments in the millennial life of a people who have rediscovered their own virtues and reconquered their youth" (Stone 1999: 215–16; Visser 1992: 15–16; Scobie 1990: 10–11, 27–28).

While fascism is usually associated with extreme nationalism, it is often forgotten that it was a species of nationalism with a decidedly imperialist bent. Mussolini's hopes for a new Roman Empire based in the Mediterranean and extending into North Africa and the Balkans followed logically from fascism's idea of its global mission. Maps were prominently displayed showing the successive stages in the conquests of the old Roman Empire, "and Italians enjoyed the implication that history might repeat itself. . . . Fascism was before long said to be imperialist by definition, and Italy to be far more fitted than France or Britain to become a colonial power" (Mack Smith 1977: 32, 84). Much was made of the abundant Roman remains still being found in North Africa, which justified the idea of a recovery and revitalization of a long-neglected imperial legacy (Wyke 1999: 190–91). The establishment of the colonies of Eritrea and Somalia, and the conquest of Libya and Ethiopia, were portrayed as a homecoming ("We were already there . . . We are returning," declared the poet Giovanni Pascoli as Italian troops advanced toward Ain-Zara during the Libyan campaign) . Mussolini's proclamation of Africa Orientale Italiana claimed North Africa as an Italian inheritance, Rome returning to itself as "an empire of civilization and humanity," which it was once more securing for the peoples of North Africa. Millions of Italians were to be settled there, making of North Africa the Quarta Sponda, the "fourth shore," of Italy in the Mediterranean, *mare nostrum* (Taddia 2007; Stone 1999: 209; Nelis 2007: 399–400, 404).

Hitler's Third Reich might not have found such direct inspiration in the Roman Empire—indeed many aspects of Rome's policies and practices were directly antithetical to the racist ideas of the Nazis—but, as with all the empires of the West, the model of Rome was impossible to avoid and the grandeur associated with it difficult to resist. This became especially clear, again, in architecture, where Albert Speer's plans for the redesign of Berlin as the imperial capital strongly echoed classical Rome. Speer boasted that "he and his collaborators had learned how to build in a more Roman manner than the Romans themselves"; and Hitler declared that only Rome was suitable as a model for "a city of the indefinite future that was worthy of a thousand-year-old people with a thousand-year-old historical and cultural heritage." His plans for Berlin were intended to make its architecture more "breathtaking" than Rome's, "our only rival in the world" (Scobie 1990: 6, 35; Koshar 1998: 165).

There were other ways in which Rome functioned as a model for the Nazis. Hitler observed that the reason why Rome had become a world empire was that it was basically a "peasant state"; for him too the maintenance of agrarian ways of life was essential to the health of the nation and the source of its power (Losemann 1999: 222). Though Hitler professed admiration for Spartan society, with its discipline and "racial purity," it was to Rome that he constantly reverted in his thoughts about the Nazi empire—for instance, with reference to Nazi plans for Eastern Europe, in the way that Roman roads showed the importance of good communications in the rule over other peoples. He was fond as well of the comparison of Rome and Carthage, with the British, trade-based, Empire seen as "the modern Carthage" and the Germans as the heirs of the "Nordic Romans." He praised Roman organization of the army and bureaucracy, and the Roman way of both fighting and concluding "peace" ("In every peace treaty the next war is already built in. That is Rome! That is true statesmanship!"). "Even today," he declared to Himmler in 1941, "the Roman empire never had its like. To have succeeded in completely dominating all neighbouring peoples! And no empire has spread so unified a civilization as Rome did." Not just in its rise but as much in its fall Rome carried an important message. It was Christianity, a Jewish religion, whose modern incarnation was Bolshevism, that had undermined the Roman Empire. "Christianity," said Hitler, " was pre-Bolshevism, was the mobilization of the slave masses by the Jews in order to undermine the state" (Losemann 1999: 224–25). Indeed, says Volker Losemann, "in no other historical theme did Hitler express so active an interest . . . as in Roman history. . . . To the very end of his life Hitler clung to the 'Roman example'" (Losemann 1999: 226, 234; Scobie 1990: 20–22).

No one, at least in Europe and even beyond, could escape the spell of Rome. It had created a vast civilization that, in both its cultural and material aspects, extended to the furthest bounds of the Western world, and had repercussions far into the East as well. The city of Rome, with its huge and varied population, was itself said to be in some sense equivalent to the world: "the world," said Ovid, "and the city of Rome occupy the same space." Rome was "the temple of the whole world"; it was the *cosmopolis*, the world-city, and its citizens world-citizens. Goethe's observation, that "the entire history of the world is linked up with this city," is a sentiment expressed by European thinkers again and again (Kennedy 1999: 20; see also Edwards and Woolf 2003; Samman 2007: 70–83).

Rome continued the inheritance of classical Hellenism, preserving and renewing its cultural legacy in literature, philosophy, and the arts—including the art of living (Jenkyns 1992a). The Roman language, Latin, became the language of the educated classes of Europe for over a thousand years; its literature and philosophy, along with that of the Greeks who were its accepted tutors in these domains, were the basis of the educational systems of all the established classes of Europe for even longer. The town-and-country lifestyle of the Roman aristocracy became the model for aristocratic life throughout Europe. Rome built roads and cities whose remains can still be seen throughout Western Europe, and which indeed provided the foundations of much of what is in use today. Above all it furnished the system and much of the content of the laws in use in most of continental Europe; and it contributed forms and concepts of politics that have continued to fertilize thought and practice in all Western societies—even when, as at certain times, there were conscious efforts to reject the Roman models (Feenstra 1992). Freud was not the only famous figure to feel a profound ambivalence about Rome—at once passionately attracted to it and at the same time holding it at a distance, as something with which he could not identify (Schorske 1980: 189–93; 1991). But he like many others would surely have agreed with T. S. Eliot's observation, quoted as an epigraph to this chapter, that "we are all, so far as we inherit the civilization of Europe, still citizens of the Roman Empire" (Eliot 1957: 130; cf. Edwards 1999a: 18).

In the early nineteenth century, as a result partly of the French Revolution and early romanticism, a new enthusiasm for ancient Greece—its literature, philosophy, and politics—did indeed for a while sweep all before it, to some extent displacing the authority of the Roman models that had inspired the "Augustan age" of the eighteenth century. The romantic poets such as Byron and Shelley, Goethe and Schiller, praised Greece as the font of European culture and democracy, and disparaged Rome as materialistic and prosaic. The "glory that was Greece" outshone the "grandeur that was Rome" (Jenkyns 1981; Bernal 1987: 281–336; Vidal-Naquet 1995; Edwards 1999a: 8–13). But the eclipse of Rome was by no means general or complete; and in the later nineteenth century, with the further expansion of the European empires, Rome once more reappeared as the relevant point of comparison, in both its strengths and its weaknesses (Jenkyns 1981: 331–35). Whether or not one believed in empire, whether or not one accepted its claims to be spreading civilization to all parts of the world, Rome was the inescapable example to reflect on.

What was that Rome that everyone aspired to imitate or emulate? What in particular did the Roman Empire mean to its successors? We are not concerned here with the detailed history of the Roman Empire, nor even with the actual workings of its institutions and policies. What matters for our purposes is the image or symbolism of the Roman Empire, what in the broadest terms it was held to have been and to have accomplished. Partly of course this image was the creation of the Romans themselves, especially in the writings of some of the empire's most celebrated poets such as Virgil and Horace. The Romans also supplied the bitterest and most scathing critics of the empire, in the form of such writers as Tacitus and Juvenal. Europe inherited both the celebration and the criticism, and added praise and warnings of its own. We are, in other words, examining the ideology rather than the reality of the Roman Empire; but we should always remember that there is no ideology that does not bear some resemblance to the actual life of the society that it claims to reflect.

The Roman Mission: Alexander, Cosmopolitanism, and Civilizing the World

Chief among the ideas that the Roman Empire bequeathed to European imperialism was that of the mission. Although the Romans cannot be said to have invented it, it was they who popularized it and gave it its most influential formulation. Moreover, for the European empires, especially the early ones, it was particularly important that Rome had expressed the imperial mission not just in secular but also in religious terms. Rome gave the world not simply "civilization"; it also invented and bequeathed Christianity.

To some extent, both the secular and the religious aspects were already fused in the person of Alexander the Great; and it is to Alexander that we owe the earliest, most widespread, and longest-lasting creation of the idea of empire and of its mission. Rome inherited the Alexandrian ideal; but so too did Eastern rulers, from the Persians to the Indians. When Chandragupta, the founder of the third-century BCE Mauryan dynasty in India, was asked how he had conceived his empire, he is said to have replied: "I watched Alexander when I was still a young man." Alexander, he claimed, could have gone on to conquer all of India, because his model of rule was superior to that of all the Indian princes. The Indian cities of Secundra and Secunderabad, named after the "great Secunder," still today testify to the power of the Alexandrian legend in the region.[3]

What, to all his admirers, Alexander seemed to be aiming at was not simply the Hellenization or "Westernization" of the world but something closer to a syncretic world culture and world polity. Alexander linked East and West; his empire, which stretched from the Danube to the Indus, aspired to universality—a central, perhaps the key, imperial ideal (Pagden 2008: 62–68). Through his empire, he would lay to rest the old enmity between East and West, as expressed in the myth of the Rape of Europa—an Asian princess abducted

FIGURE 2.1. Mosaic of Alexander the Great at the Battle of Issus, 333 BCE.
© Everett-Art/Shutterstock.com.

to Western shores—and the story of the Trojan War—a war over a Western woman abducted to Eastern shores.

Everything known—or at least reported or invented—about Alexander pointed to this ideal of universality.[4] He is said, at the famous banquet at Opis (324 BCE) toward the end of his life, to have prayed for "concord and community in empire for Macedonians and Persians" (Bosworth 1993: 161). This followed upon earlier celebrations in which he had married ninety-one of his elite Companions to Persian brides and had himself taken two Persian princesses in marriage—having already married Roxane, daughter of a Bactrian (Afghan) noble.

The first-century CE Latin writer Apuleius claimed that Alexander was "the sole conqueror in the memory of mankind to have founded a universal empire" (in Pagden 2008: 62). This side of Alexander's achievement also formed the centerpiece of the most famous and influential account of Alexander's exploits, that of the first century CE Greek writer Plutarch. Alexander, said Plutarch, deliberately rejected the advice given to him by his tutor Aristotle to treat only Greeks as human and to look upon all "barbarians" as "mere brutes and vegetables." To have done so, says Plutarch, would have "filled his empire with fugitive incendiaries and perfidious tumults."

> But believing himself sent from Heaven as the common moderator and arbiter of all nations, and subduing those by force whom he could not associate by fair offers, he labored thus, that he might bring all regions, far and near, under the same dominion. And then, as in a festival goblet, mixing lives, manners, customs, wedlock, all together, he ordained that every one should take the whole habitable world for his country, of which his camp should be the chief metropolis and garrison. (Plutarch 1871: 481)

The great Hellenistic scholar Sir William Tarn believed that Alexander pursued a consistent policy of fusion of Greeks and barbarians. Alexander, says Tarn, had a cosmopolitan vision with three facets.

> The first is that God is the common father of mankind, which may be called the brotherhood of man. The second is Alexander's dream of the various races of mankind, so far as known to him, becoming of one mind together and living in unity and concord, which may be called the unity of mankind. And the third . . . is that the various peoples of his Empire might be partners in the realm rather than subjects. (Tarn 1948: 1:400)[5]

Alexander's death at the early age of thirty-two meant that he did not live long enough to carry out that vision—if indeed that is what he had—in anything but the sketchiest ways. But it is generally agreed by historians of political thought that the cosmopolitanism of the Cynics and Stoics, whose schools appeared in the wake of Alexander's empire, was a direct response to that empire, and what it had shown of the possibilities of a universal human community and of the "world citizen" (Sabine 1960: 117–53; Burn 1962: 187–88). For H. G. Wells in his *Outline of History*, searching for the origins of his own conception of the "world-state," the career of Alexander was indeed "the first revelation to the human imagination of the oneness of human affairs," breaking with all that had gone before it. After him "the conception of a world law and organization was a practicable and assimilable idea for the minds of men" (Wells 1937: 372–73).

The earliest surviving accounts of Alexander are by Romans, or at least Roman citizens: Diodorus Siculus, Arrian, Plutarch, Curtius (Gergel 2004). All but Curtius wrote in Greek, and all wrote nearly four hundred years after the events they describe; no contemporary accounts survive. So the Alexander story is mostly myth, one largely created by Greek scholars in the early Roman Empire (though those scholars did have access to primary sources since lost). But it was a myth with astonishingly long-lasting and widespread power, inspiring kings and emperors East and West over two millennia (Lane Fox 1986: 26; Bosworth 1993: 180–81; Pagden 2008: 66; Baynham 2009). Particularly important, from our point of view, was its influence among Roman leaders, in the empire that was their creation. From Pompey and Caesar—who was moved to tears because "Alexander had died at the age of thirty-two, king of so many peoples, and he himself had not yet achieved any brilliant success"—to Trajan and Caracalla—"who carried Alexander-imitation to absurd lengths" (Bosworth 1993: 260)—the Roman rulers were dazzled by Alexander's vision and sought to realize it in a more lasting way (Brunt 1978: 178–79, 1990c: 449; Spencer 2009). Moreover, they were the more inspired to do so by inheriting the idea of divine kingship from Alexander and his Hellenistic successors. Alexander believed himself, and was believed to be, the son of Zeus. Caesar, after his assassination, was proclaimed a god, as were all the pagan Roman emperors thereafter. Only a god could rule the universe and unify mankind— the aspiration of both Alexander and the Roman emperors (Tarn 1948, 1:145– 48; Bosworth 1993: 278–90).

We can consider the nature of the Roman civilizing mission, in its broadest terms, through the "orations" of two rhetoricians, Aelius Aristides and Claudian (Claudius Claudianus). Both wrote in a rhetorical tradition of offering encomia and eulogies to cities and rulers, in the process stating what their aspirations and achievements were. The reason for singling out these two contributions is that they became among the best-known, among later generations, for what Rome stood for, and what later empires had therefore to live up to. Particularly in the nineteenth century, in Britain and France and elsewhere, Aristides and Claudian were frequently quoted by statesmen and publicists in support of their views of empire.[6]

Somewhere around 143 CE, the Greek rhetorician Aelius Aristides delivered his oration "To Rome" at the imperial court in Rome.[7] James Oliver calls it "the greatest literary expression of what the Golden Age could mean to the world of Hadrian and the Antonines" (Oliver 1953: 887). This was indeed the great period of Antonine Rome—the emperor Antoninus Pius himself may have been in the audience for Aristides's oration, and Aristides later met an admiring Marcus Aurelius. It was also famously praised by Gibbon as the golden age of the Roman Empire, if not of the whole world. Aristides himself had no doubt. For him Rome is the center of world civilization, the place to which all things and people come, and from which flow, to all the corners of the globe, all civilizing influences, material, moral, cultural, and political.

There is first of all Rome's size and greatness, the largest empire the world has known since Alexander. And indeed it is greater than Alexander's, because more durable and longer-lasting. Alexander, "who acquired the great empire—so it looked until yours arose—by overrunning the earth, to tell the truth, more closely resembled one who acquired a kingdom than one who showed himself a king." He left many memorials, notably Alexandria, "the greatest city after yours," but died too soon to lay down a lasting legacy of just and firm rule (Oliver 1953: 898). Not only did Rome take up this task, but in the process expanded to all the boundaries of the known world, to such an extent "that one cannot even measure the area within them." "Your possession is equal to what the sun can pass, and the sun passes over your land . . . nor do you reign within fixed boundaries, nor does another dictate to what point your control reaches; but the sea like a girdle lies extended, at once in the middle of the civilized world and of your hegemony" (Oliver 1953: 896).

Then there is Rome's wealth and prosperity, the result of its being at the crossroads of the world's trade and commerce.

> Whatever the seasons make grow and whatever countries and rivers and lakes and arts of Hellenes and non-Hellenes produce are brought from every land and sea, so that if one would look at all these things, he must needs behold them either by visiting the entire civilized world or by coming to this city. For whatever is grown and made among each people cannot fail to be here at all times and in abundance. And here the merchant vessels come carrying these many products from all regions in every season and even at every equinox, so that the city appears a kind of common emporium of the world. . . . Just as Hesiod said about the ends of the Ocean, that there is a common channel where all waters have one source and destination, so there is a common channel to Rome and all meet here, trade, shipping, agriculture, metallurgy, all the arts and crafts that are or ever have been, all the things that are engendered or grow from the earth. And whatever one does not see here neither did nor does exist. (Oliver 1953: 896–97)

What Aristides wishes to stress and to praise, however, is not just the power and wealth of Rome but above all Rome's moral and political gifts to the world: the inestimable boons of order, tranquillity, concord, justice, and—properly understood—equality. "Vast and comprehensive as is the size of it, your empire is much greater for its perfection than for the area which its boundaries encircle. . . . You who hold so vast an empire and rule it with such a firm hand and with so much unlimited power have very decidedly won a great success, which is completely your own. For of all who have ever gained empire you alone rule over men who are free" (Oliver 1953: 898–99). Aristides is aware that this statement needs careful explanation; Rome is after all an empire, with a distinct order of ranks and with an emperor who is not simply autocratic but also a god. But what he wishes to show is how, in comparison with all other empires and even with the "Free Republics" of the old Greek city-states, Rome has established a system of rule in which justice is done to all, in which subordinate officials are controlled, corruption punished, and the law gives protection to all of whatever rank and in whatever part of the empire. Thus "there is an abundant and beautiful equality of the humble with the great and of the obscure with the illustrious, and above all, of the poor man with the rich and of the commoner with the noble, and the word of Hesiod comes to pass, 'For he easily exalts, and the exalted he easily checks,' namely this judge and princeps as the justice of the claim may lead, like a breeze in the sails of a ship, favoring and accompanying, not the rich man more, the poor man less, but benefiting equally whomsoever it meets" (Oliver 1953: 899).

It is in the context of praising Rome's justice and its equal treatment of its subjects that Aristides comes to the thing that, he says, "very decidedly deserves as much attention and admiration as all the rest together."

> I mean your magnificent citizenship with its grand conception, because there is nothing like it in the record of all mankind. Dividing into two groups all those in your empire—and with this word I have indicated the entire civilized world—you have everywhere appointed to your citizenship, or even to kinship with you, the better part of the world's talent, courage and leadership, while the rest you recognized as a league under your hegemony. Neither sea nor intervening continent are bars to citizenship, nor are Asia and Europe divided in their treatment here. In your empire all paths are open to all. No one worthy of rule or trust remains an alien, but a civil community of the World has been established as a Free Republic under one, the best, ruler and teacher of order; and all come together as into a common civic center, in order to receive each man his due. (Oliver 1953: 901)

It is indeed the cosmopolitanism of the Roman Empire, its drawing in of so many diverse lands and peoples, and its opening itself to the whole world by incorporating all within its own system of enlightened rule, that is the repeated subject of Aristides's admiration. Neither race nor ethnicity, neither nationality nor religion, is a barrier to membership and to advancement within the empire. Here Rome has gone beyond the policies and practices of the Hellenic states—including Alexander's and its successors—who so prided themselves on the rights of citizenship, and who were nevertheless so jealously possessive of it. Rome's greatness consists in its generosity, its extension of citizenship such that "you made your citizenship an object of wonder."

> You sought its expansion as a worthy aim, and you have caused the word Roman to be the label, not of membership in the city, but of some common nationality, and this not just one among all, but one balancing all the rest. For the categories into which you now divide the world are not Hellenes and Barbarians, and it is not absurd, the distinction which you made, because you have shown them a citizenry more numerous, so to speak, than the entire Hellenic race. The division which you substituted is one into Romans and non-Romans. To such a degree have you expanded the name of your city. Since these are the lines along which the distinction has been made, many in every city are fellow-citizens of yours no less than of their own kinsmen, though some of them have not yet seen this city. There is no need of garrisons to hold their citadels, but the men of greatest standing and influence in every city guard their own fatherlands for you. (Oliver 1953: 902)

Aristides is aware of how enormous a step this is, and how far it distances Rome from all previous conceptions of citizenship. It is here that Rome's civilizing effect is at its most fundamental, for what Rome has done is nothing less than to have turned nature into culture, to have transformed mere "bodies" of men—defined for the most part by "biological" divisions of race and ethnicity—into communities of citizens with equal rights and responsibilities. Previously,

> all those of the past who ruled over a very large part of the world ruled, as it were, naked bodies by themselves, mere persons composing the ethnic groups or nations. . . . Hence the inferiority of those who lived in former times appears, because the past is so much surpassed, not only in the element at the head of the empire, but also in cases where identical groups have been ruled by others and by you. Those whom the others ruled did not as individuals have the equality of civil rights and privileges, but against the primitive organization of an ethnic group in that time one can set the municipal organization of the same group's city of today. It might very well be said that while the others have been kings, as it were, of open country and strongholds, you alone are rulers of civilized communities. (Oliver 1953: 905)

Citizenship, a complex story, is one of the central legacies of Rome to the European empires. We will consider it in more detail below. But let us hurry on to Aristides's grand peroration, a paean to Rome's greatness and benevolence, Rome as the fulfillment of the promise of Hellenic civilization, Rome as the Demiurge of a universal order of peace and civility.

One can say that the civilized world, which had been sick from the beginning, as it were, has been brought by the right knowledge to a state of health. . . . Cities gleam with radiance and charm, and the whole earth has been beautified like a garden. . . . It is you who have best proved the general assertion, that Earth is mother of all and common fatherland. Now indeed it is possible for Hellene and non-Hellene, with or without his property, to travel wherever he will, just as if passing from fatherland to fatherland. Neither Cilician Gates nor narrow sandy approaches to Egypt through Arab country, nor inaccessible mountains, nor immense stretches of river, nor inhospitable tribes of barbarians cause terror, but for security it suffices to be a Roman citizen, or rather to be one of those united under your hegemony. Homer said "Earth common of all," and you have made it come true. You have measured and recorded the land of the entire civilized world; you have spanned the rivers with all kinds of bridges and hewn highways through the mountains and filled the barren stretches with posting stations; you have accustomed all areas to a settled and orderly way of life. . . . Though the citizens of Athens began the civilized life of today, this life in turn has been firmly established by you, who came later but who, men say, are better. . . . Before the rule of Zeus, as the poets say, the universe was full of strife, confusion and disorder, but when Zeus came to the rule he settled everything. . . . Thus one who reflects about the world before your time and about the conditions of affairs in your period would come to the opinion that before your empire there had been confusion everywhere and things were taking a random course, but when you assumed the presidency, confusion and strife ceased, and universal order entered as a brilliant light over the private and public affairs of man, laws appeared and altars of gods received man's confidence. (Oliver 1953: 906)

Aristides's Roman oration was famous in its own day and for centuries afterward. Its figures and tropes found their way into a hundred accounts of empire, by those especially seeking to justify its existence. But it could equally influence the accounts of those who tried to indicate the appeal of Rome by pointing to its greatest and most successful period, before the long slide into decline and downfall. One of the most famous and influential of such accounts is to be found in the first three chapters of book 1 of Gibbon's *Decline and Fall of the Roman Empire*—the chapters where he describes Rome in the age of the Antonines, the very period in which Aristides delivered his oration and whose world he evokes. These chapters breathe the spirit of Aristides's oration, from the very opening lines of chapter 1:

> In the second century of the Christian Æra, the empire of Rome comprehended the fairest parts of the earth, and the most civilized portion of mankind. The frontiers of that extensive monarchy were guarded by ancient renown and disciplined valour. The gentle, but powerful influence of laws and manners had gradually cemented the union of the provinces. Their peaceful inhabitants enjoyed and abused the advantages of wealth and luxury. The image of a free constitution was preserved with decent reverence. (Gibbon [1776–88] 1995: 1:31)

The opening of chapter 2 again evokes Aristides, who indeed is directly referred to twice in this chapter. Here also we find that series of comparisons with other rulers and empires that Aristides, reflecting the rhetorical tradition, is so fond of:

> It is not alone by the rapidity, or extent of conquest, that we should estimate the greatness of Rome. The sovereign of the Russian deserts commands a larger portion of the globe. In the seventh summer after his passage of the Hellespont, Alexander erected the Macedonian trophies on the banks of the Hyphasis ["midway between Lahore and Delhi"]. Within less than a century, the irresistible Zingis [Genghis], and the Mogul princes of his race, spread their cruel devastations and transient empire, from the sea of China, to the confines of Egypt and Germany. But the firm edifice of Roman power was raised and preserved by the wisdom of ages. The obedient provinces of Trajan and the Antonines were united by laws, and adorned by arts. They might occasionally suffer from the partial abuse of delegated authority; but the general principle of government was wise, simple, and beneficent. They enjoyed the religion of their ancestors, whilst in civil honours and advantages they were exalted, by just degrees, to an equality with their conquerors. (Gibbon [1776–88] 1995: 1:56)

Summing up this era of felicity, Gibbon includes a composite quotation that explicitly draws on similar passages in Aristides, as well as Pliny and Tertullian:

Notwithstanding the propensity of mankind to exalt the past, and to depreciate the present, the tranquil and prosperous state of the empire was warmly felt, and honestly confessed, by the provincials as well as Romans. "They acknowledge that the true principles of social life, laws, agriculture, and science, which had been first invented by the wisdom of Athens, were now firmly established by the power of Rome, under whose auspicious influence, the fiercest barbarians were united by an equal government and common language. They affirm that, with the improvement of arts, the human species was visibly multiplied. They celebrate the increasing splendour of the cities, the beautiful face of the country, cultivated and adorned like an immense garden; and the long festival of peace, which was enjoyed by so many nations, forgetful of their ancient animosities, and delivered from the apprehension of future danger." Whatever suspicions may be suggested by the air of rhetoric and declamation, which seems to prevail in these passages, the substance of them is perfectly agreeable to historic truth. . . . If a man were called to fix the period in the history of the world during which the condition of the human race was most happy and prosperous, he would without hesitation, name that which elapsed from the death of Domitian to the accession of Commodus. The vast extent of Roman power was governed by absolute power, under the guidance of virtue and wisdom. The armies were restrained by the firm but gentle hand of four successive emperors, whose characters and authority commanded involuntary respect. The forms of the civil administration were carefully preserved by Nerva, Trajan, Hadrian, and the Antonines, who delighted in the image of liberty, and were pleased with considering themselves as the accountable ministers of the laws. (Gibbon [1776–88] 1995: 1:82, 103)

Commenting on the similarities of Aristides's and Gibbon's accounts of the Roman Empire in the second century—"the images of modernity and those of antiquity, fashioned through Aristides' lens, shade into one another to the point of becoming intermingled"—Aldo Schiavone observes, "But Gibbon had knowledge of something that Aristides could not have foreseen: the violent end that this world was to meet" (Schiavone 2000: 16–17). The decline and fall of Rome—at least in the West—was to become another of the great legacies of Rome to later empires. Here, however, the obsessive question was not imitation or emulation but its opposite: how *not* to be like Rome. How to avoid the fate of Rome, and was it possible to do so? How could any empire, which almost by definition saw itself as universal and eternal, stop that decline and decomposition which had afflicted Rome, the exemplary empire? If Rome had fallen, could any empire do differently? Was "decline and fall" inscribed on the banners of all empires? This became the theme of nearly all philosophical and literary reflections on empire, from Gibbon's *Decline and Fall* to Rudyard Kipling's "Recessional" (1897), by way of a whole literature and iconography of the "ruins of empires."[8] Charles Maier speaks of "the melancholy of empire, the intimations of mortality that tinge all its triumphs.... The end of empire is always present.... Ultimately the lights will go dim on the imperial stage and the curtain will descend.... Empires are epics of entropy" (Maier 2006: 76–77, 286). Here was food for thought, on an epic scale; and here too Rome supplied the materials in abundance, not least because of the scintillating reflections of its own writers, such as Tacitus and Juvenal (Shumate 2006).

But before the catastrophe of Rome's fall there were those who still saw in Rome the shining beacon to the world, the empire that outshone all others and would outlive them all. As with Aristides (from Mysia, in Asia Minor), it was another provincial, Claudius Claudianus (Claudian), from Egypt, who once more gave utterance to Rome's glorious achievements, again in the form of a rhetorical panegyric.[9] In Claudian's case it was delivered in Latin, even though as with Aristides Greek was his first language; and it was delivered not to the city of Rome but to one of Rome's great generals, Flavius Stilicho, son of a Vandal. Stilicho had been employed by the emperor Theodosius against Alaric the Visigoth, and had indeed married Theodosius's niece and adopted daughter Serena, while his own daughter Maria married the young emperor Honorius—thus making Stilicho, as Claudian never tires of calling him, "father-in-law and son-in-law of an emperor." Stilicho defeated Alaric at the Battle of Pollentia in 402 CE; two years later Claudian died, therefore missing the murder of Stilicho by a jealous Honorius in 408, and the sack of Rome by a resurgent Alaric in 410. He lived, however, to deliver two orations in praise of Stilicho, "On Stilicho's Consulship" (400), and "The Gothic War" (402), the latter celebrating Stilicho's victory at Pollentia. It is the former that achieved lasting fame for its eulogy of Rome.

Vandal and Visigoth, rebel against rebel: the one in the service of the empire, the other one of the architects of its destruction. We are very much in the late Roman Empire, the period of the early fifth century, on the eve of Rome's downfall. Perhaps this is why Claudian, whom his editor and translator Maurice Platnauer calls "the last poet of classical Rome" (Claudian [c. 370–404 CE] 1922: 1:vii), is so passionate, so fulsome, in his praise of Rome, going it seems even beyond the conventions of the traditional panegyric. Just as a species on the verge of extinction displays its most glorious plumage, so Claudian's panegyrics to Stilicho pull out all the rhetorical stops in their celebration of Rome.[10]

Since Claudian's orations were formally delivered to a person, Stilicho, and not directly to the city of Rome or its empire, they naturally spend much of their time praising the particular deeds of a particular person—albeit with specific reference to their importance for Rome, as for instance in Stilicho's defeat in 397 of Gildo's rebellion in Africa, which had threatened Rome's grain supply; or his defeat of Alaric at Pollentia, "which dispersed the darkness that enshrouded our empire and restored its glory" (Claudian [c. 370–404 CE] 1922, 1:385, 2:129). In general Stilicho is seen as the embodiment and regenerator of all the old Roman virtues, as when he turns to the Senate for permission to wage war in Africa (1:389).

But at certain points, especially in "On Stilicho's Consulship," Claudian has occasion to reflect on Rome more directly, as he waxes eloquent on the regeneration of Rome represented by Stilicho.

> Stilicho gives scope for the virtues of a bygone age and rouses a people, forgetful of their former glory, to resume their accustomed sovereignty, to make themselves feared, to tread powerful magistrates beneath their heel, to mete out to crime its due reward, to show mercy towards the erring, favour to the innocent, punishment to the guilty, and to exercise once more their native virtue of clemency. . . . Thanks to him dishonour is banished and our age blossoms with Rome's ancient virtues; thanks to him power, long degraded and all but transferred [i.e., to Constantinople], no longer, forgetful of itself, is exiled in lands of servitude but, returned to its rightful home, restores to Italy its victorious destiny, enjoys the promised auspices of its foundation and gives back its scattered limbs to the head of the empire. (Claudian [c. 370–404 CE] 1922: 2:51)

Shortly after this passage occurs another in which Stilicho is hailed as the protector of the city, and thus the guardian of all the greatness that Rome represents. It is here that Claudian rises to heights of acclamation, offering a transcendent vision of Rome and of its mission in the world.

> Consul, all but peer of the gods, protector of a city greater than any that upon earth the air encompasseth, whose amplitude no eye can measure, whose beauty no imagination can picture, whose praise no voice can sound, who raises a golden head amid the neighbouring stars and with her seven

hills imitates the seven regions of heaven, mother of arms and of law, who extends her sway o'er all the earth and was the earliest cradle of justice, this is the city which, sprung from humble beginnings, has stretched to either pole, and from one small place extended its power so as to be co-terminous with the sun's light. Open to the blows of fate while at one and the same time she fought a thousand battles, conquered Spain, laid siege to the cities of Sicily, subdued Gaul by land and Carthage by sea, never did she yield to her losses nor show fear at any blow, but rose to greater heights of courage after the disasters of Cannae and Trebia, and, while the enemy's fire threatened her, and her foe smote upon her walls, sent an army against the furthest Iberians. Nor did Ocean bar her way; launching upon the deep, she sought in another world for Britons to be vanquished. 'Tis she alone who has received the conquered into her bosom and like a mother, not an empress, protected the human race with a common name, summoning those whom she has defeated to share her citizenship and drawing together distant races with bonds of affection. To her rule of peace we owe it that the world is our home, that we can live where we please, and that to visit Thule and explore its once dreaded wilds is but a sport; thanks to her all and sundry may drink the water of the Rhone and quaff Orentes' stream, thanks to her we are all one people. Nor will there ever be a limit to the empire of Rome, for luxury and its attendant vices, and pride with sequent hate have brought to ruin all kingdoms else. (Claudian [c. 370–404 CE] 1922: 2:53–55)

How devastating, then, for this mighty empire, destined to last for all time, to suffer the sack of the eternal city, Rome, in 410, only a decade after this paean was penned. No matter that the "sack of Rome" was, in truth, relatively minor in its actual material effect, by no means in itself signaling the end of empire.[11] The fact is that it was the first time that Rome had fallen since its capture by the Gauls in 390 BCE; and that it was followed, not so long afterward, by the deposition in 476 of the last Roman emperor in the West, Romulus Augustulus. In retrospect therefore it came to be seen as the first major blow in the chain of blows that brought Rome to its knees. Certainly at the time it caused consternation among educated people throughout the empire. From Jerusalem St. Jerome lamented that "when the brightest light in the world was extinguished, when the very head of the Roman empire was severed, the entire world perished in a single city" (Kelly 1975: 304). In North Africa St. Augustine pondered the meaning of the event, and in particular the charge that it was Christianity that had been responsible for Rome's suffering, a punishment meted out by the empire's old gods for being forsaken in favor of the new God of the Christians. In the *City of God* (413–26) Augustine eloquently refuted this claim, at the same time pouring scorn on all earthly cities and their empires, by comparison with the "Heavenly City" of God, where alone salvation and eternal life are to be found (Coyle 1987).

We will return to the question of Rome and Christianity later in this chapter. For the moment what needs to be noted are Claudian's claims for Rome, and the fact that Claudian's eulogy achieved great fame in later years, long after Rome was gone (Cameron 1970: 419–51). As late as the nineteenth century Claudian was being quoted approvingly, as a statement of what the aims of empire should be, by British imperialists such as Lord Cromer and Sir George Bowen, proconsuls in Egypt and India, respectively; his eulogy was even quoted about the same time by an American scholar, R. Y. Terrell, intent on urging America's own imperial claims, as "a splendid expression of what ought now to be the ambition and aspiration of at least one great empire and one great republic" (Vance 1997: 233–34). For later imperialists, Claudian had delineated in the most striking possible way what Rome had stood for, and what ought to be the aspirations of all empires that sought to measure themselves by Rome's greatness.

Rome's greatness lay, in Virgil's famous formulation, not in size or power itself but in the uses to which that power was put. Rome was indeed granted *imperium* over all other peoples, but its allotted task, what marked it out from the rule of others, was "to impose peace and morality, to spare your subjects and to conquer the proud" ("pacisque imponere morem // parcere subiectis et debellare superbos," *Aeneid* 6.851–53). At the heart of the Roman civilizing mission was the carrying to the world of the very thing itself, "civilization," the usual English translation of what the Romans generally referred to as *humanitas*. "Civilization" was an ideal of the humane, enlightened, and cultivated man (cf. German *Bildung*). Roman authors such as Cicero readily admitted the Greek origins of this vision, in such concepts as *philanthropia* and *paideia*. But it was they, they insisted, the Romans, who had brought it to perfection. More important, it was the Romans who were promoting and diffusing it throughout the world. It was the Roman Empire that was the carrier of the civilizing mission. Rome, said Pliny the Elder in his *Natural History*, is called "the nurse and parent of all other lands, elected by the gods' will in order to make heaven itself brighter, to bring scattered peoples into unity, to make manners gentle, to draw together by community of language the jarring and uncouth tongues of nearly countless nations, to give civilization to mankind [*humanitatem homini*], and put simply to become throughout all the lands the single father-land of humanity" (in Champion 2004: 259–60; see also Nutton 1978; Woolf 1994: 119, 1998: 54–60; Edwards and Woolf 2003; Woolf 2012: 226–29).

The civilizing mission legitimated Roman power and its worldwide expansion.[12] In the writings of Caesar, Strabo, Pliny, and others, says Greg Woolf, "Roman rule is presented as providing the conditions for human beings to realize their potential fully, by becoming civilized, and so truly human. . . . Roman expansion could thus be understood as the means by which the potential of the world and the entire human race might be fulfilled. Earlier justifications of imperialism had been based on the idea that each war was individually righteous, a *bellum iustum*, but the notion of Rome as the propagator of *humanitas* provided a sanction for the entire process of world conquest" (Woolf 1998: 57).

It was crucial that the Roman concept of civilization was divorced from ethnicity or nationality. Here Romans parted company with Greeks, whose culture and accomplishments they in so many other ways venerated. For the Greeks, some kind of common descent, real or fictive, was necessary for individuals or groups to be counted among the Hellenes, and so part of the civilized world (as opposed to "barbarians"). For the Romans, civilization—Romanization—was in principle open to anyone, foreign barbarians as well as the neighboring Italians. Rome itself had been a "hybridized" city, made up of a mixture of tribal and racial groups, not one ethnically based. In their foundation myths and speculative accounts of their history, the Roman people "did not define Romans as a descent group like the Greeks or a chosen people like the Jews but as a community that had grown by recruiting others to its values, loyalties, customs and cults" (Woolf 1994: 120, 1998: 74; cf. Walbank 1972: 149–50; Sherwin-White 1973: 8; Miles 1990: 633–38; Dench 2005).[13]

Moreover, not only could civilization be acquired by anyone; it could also be acquired by degrees. The "civilizing process" was exactly that—a gradual and progressive increase in the traits and qualities associated with *humanitas*. What crowned and confirmed the acquisition of civilization was the grant of citizenship. That too could be acquired by degrees. A group like the Latins, near neighbors of the Romans and sharing with them a language and some cults, could be considered as having progressed some way along the path to civilization, and accordingly granted some kind of citizenship rights—the "Latin right," the *ius Latii*, as it was called. Only when they were thought fully assimilated to Roman ways were they granted full citizenship rights (Sherwin-White 1973: 32–37, 96–116; Woolf 1998: 65–67, 2012: 219–20). Here was the model for the incorporation of other foreigners and even the most distant barbarians, in the wilds of northern Gaul and Britain. "The *ius Latii* . . . became one of the favourite weapons in the store of Rome for the gradual elevation of provincial communities to a parity with herself" (Sherwin-White 1973: 114; see also 414–15; but see also the demur of Brunt 1990b: 268). It was a precedent not forgotten in the later European empires, as they opened their citizenship to their subjects, not immediately and not unconditionally, but on the basis of the achievement of a certain level of "civilization."

Rome: Citizenship, Race, Nationality

Among the parts of Claudian's oration that were most frequently quoted were those that dealt with Rome's attitudes toward its subjects. Rome was praised by Claudian for "summoning those she has defeated to share her citizenship and drawing together distant races with bonds of affection." It was an aspect of Rome's rule that drew the attention of a host of commentators over the centuries. Shortly after Claudian, the poet Rutilius, a native of Toulouse, wrote an epic poem on his return to Gaul, *De reditu suo* (417), which again pointed to this feature as a central aspect of Rome's civilizing mission in the world.

> Thou has made of alien realms one fatherland;
> The lawless found their gain beneath thy sway;
> Sharing thy laws with them thou hast subdued,
> Thou hast made a city of the once wide world.

(IN HEATHER 2006: 234)

In the Renaissance, Rome was often seen as having distinguished itself in the ancient world by its enlightened attitude toward non-Romans. In his *Discourses on the First Ten Books of Titus Livius* (1531), Machiavelli observed that the Greek states, such as Athens and Sparta, had stagnated and finally been extinguished because of their hostility to "strangers" and foreigners; Rome by contrast had "ruined her neighbours" and grown more powerful because it had kept the road "open and safe for foreigners who propose to come and dwell there," and had granted them "easy access to her honours," including the prize of Roman citizenship (Machiavelli [1531] 1970: 281–82).[14]

Francis Bacon, like Machiavelli, pointed to Rome's policies of citizenship as the key to the rise and maintenance of its power. "All States that are liberal of naturalization towards strangers are fit for empire. . . . Never any State was, in this point, so open to receive strangers into their Body as were the Romans;

therefore it sorted with them accordingly, for they grew to the greatest monarchy." Add to this, says Bacon, "their custom of plantation of colonies, whereby the Roman plant was removed into the soil of other nations; and, putting both constitutions together, you will say, that it was not the Romans that spread upon the world, but it was the world that spread upon the Romans—and that was the sure way of greatness" (Bacon [1625] 1906: 120–21). Other nations closed in on themselves, jealously guarding their culture and their citizenship; Rome, like Alexander according to the tradition, opened its doors to the world outside, taking in peoples, customs, and religions from all over, while at the same time infusing its own politics and culture into that world.

"Romanization" is the term generally used to describe the process whereby the laws, language, urban forms, and administrative structures of Rome spread to every corner of the empire.[15] This did not necessarily mean the elimination of local differences of culture or ethnicity, especially at popular levels of society. Romans were generally tolerant toward local cultures, allowing the persistence of local cults and language.[16] But there was in the main a remarkably uniform process in which the material and political culture of Rome stamped itself on the consciousness and practices of the elites in every region of the empire. Provincial cities showed the same pattern of temples, theaters, town palaces, suburban villas, roads, baths, forums, stadiums, and public statues and monuments as were to be found in Rome itself and throughout Italy. At first in the town councils, then later, as the localities lost their power, in the imperial bureaucracy and army, a provincial and thoroughly Romanized landed aristocracy ruled through a system of indirect rule that was later to appear highly attractive to the British in their own far-flung empire. Latin was the language of the provincial upper classes—at least in the West—and of anyone aspiring to join them, throughout the history of the empire.[17] Aristides and Claudian, as we have seen, were both provincials, and to them we can add one such as Merobaudes, born in southern Spain of a Romanized general of Frankish origins (cf. Stilicho), who went on to become a famous Latin poet and orator (and soldier), and ended up at the imperial court in Ravenna (Heather 2006: 283–84).

Citizenship—the right to say "civis Romanus sum"—was the prized object of most of Rome's subjects. What is more, it was a prize that Rome dangled in front of its subjects as an attainable object, a just reward for loyalty to Rome and respect for its laws and institutions. It was precisely in this respect that Rome distinguished itself from its Greek (though not Macedonian) predecessors. In arguing the case for the admission of leading Gauls from northern and central Gaul—Gallia Comata, "long-haired Gaul," as opposed to the Roman-ized area of Narbonese Gaul in the south—to the Roman Senate, the emperor Claudius made exactly the point that was to be made by Machiavelli and Bacon centuries later. "What proved fatal to Sparta and Athens, for all their military strength, was their segregation of conquered subjects as aliens. Our founder Romulus, on the other hand, had the wisdom—more than once—to transform whole enemy peoples into Roman citizens within the course of a single day." This, claimed Claudius with a wealth of examples, was the Roman way, going back to the very beginnings of Rome's rise to greatness, and indeed the source of that greatness. The founder of his own family had been a Sabine, Clausus, "who was simultaneously made a Roman citizen and a patrician"; thus was Claudius encouraged "to adopt the same national policy, by bringing excellence to Rome from whatever source." He pointed to the fact that since the end of the Gallic Wars, "peace and loyalty have reigned unbroken. Now that they have assimilated our customs and culture and married into our fami-lies, let them bring in their gold and wealth rather than keep it to themselves." The Senate, says Tacitus, approved the emperor's speech, thereby conceding that not merely Roman citizenship but the right to the highest offices should be open to former barbarians who became Rome's loyal subjects and learned Rome's ways (Tacitus 1996: 242–44 [*Annals* 11.22–24]; see also Sherwin-White 1973: 237–41; Griffin 1990; Woolf 1998: 64–65; Dench 2005: 117–18).

The extension of Roman citizenship was a slow but steady process, starting first with Rome's Latin neighbors, then, after the Social War (91–89 BCE), adding its Italian allies (89 BCE), and a little later the Romanized Celts of Cisalpine Gaul (49 BCE). This completed the unification of the whole of Italy under Rome. Under the empire citizenship was gradually conferred on peoples of the non-Italian provinces. The process culminated in the famous decree of 212 CE in which the emperor Caracalla extended Roman citizenship to virtually all free subjects of the empire. In practical terms, it has been said, this did little more than tidy up and complete what had been a steady develop-ment for a century or more. But no one has denied the enormous symbolism of the edict. It proclaimed in unmistakable tones the unity and grandeur of the empire, the *maiestas populi Romani*, "the greatness of the Roman people."[18] By making them all citizens, it elevated all subjects to an equality in the *orbis Romanus*, the Roman world, increasingly identified with the whole civilized world, the *orbis terrarum*. "Henceforth a man was a Roman citizen simply because he was a free inhabitant of the civilized world" (Sherwin-White 1973: 287). Beyond were the "barbarians," now more clearly seen as those outside

FIGURE 2.2. The Claudian Tables, showing the speech to the Roman Senate of the emperor Claudius as he argued for the admission of leading Gauls to the Senate. Photograph by Rama, licensed under Wikimedia Attribution-ShareAlike 2.0 France (CC BY-SA 2.0 FR) https://creativecommons.org/licenses/by-sa/2.0/fr/deed.en.

the empire without the benefits of civilization. It was no longer possible, as it had been previously, to be one of several groups of "internal barbarians" enjoying varying citizenship statuses (Burns 2009: 35; Sherwin-White 1973: 445–46, 451–60). "Romans" and "barbarians," the civilized and the uncivilized, increasingly at war, now divided the world.

The result of a steady progression it may have been; but for some the Edict of Caracalla nevertheless marks a certain "threshold" in Rome's evolution. It symbolized the point at which the empire passed beyond any control by the Roman people of its destinies, becoming instead the creature entirely of the emperor and his servants, the army and bureaucracy. For Richard Koebner, "universal citizenship was in fact incompatible with *Imperium populi Romani.*" What Caracalla's edict amounted to was a claim to "administrative omnipotence," revealed by the use of the phrase *orbis Romanus,* "the Roman world," in the edict rather than the more usual *imperium populi Romani,* "the empire of the Roman people" ("In orbi Romano qui sunt, cives Romani effecti sunt"; "those within the Roman world have become Roman citizens"). The

FIGURE 2.3. Bust of the emperor Caracalla, who in 212 CE issued a decree making
all free subjects of the empire Roman citizens. Shakko/Wikipedia licensed under
Attribution 3.0 Unported (CC BY 3.0) http://creativecommons.org/licenses/by/3.0.

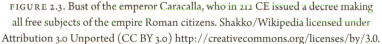

stage was set, according to Koebner, for the Christian concept of the Roman
Empire, the "Emperor's Empire," which attached the empire entirely to the
person of the emperor. Hence it was that the empire could find its seat now in
Constantinople, now in Milan, now in Ravenna, and later in the Holy Roman
Empire, even in distant parts of Gaul and Germany: wherever in fact the
emperor chose to reside, there was "Rome" (Koebner 1961: 15–17; cf. Miles
1990: 649; Brown 2003: 101).

Michael Doyle, writing of a "Caracallan threshold," expresses a similar sense
of change though from a somewhat different perspective. He too sees a decline
in freedom and participation. But, more far-reachingly, he questions also how
far, after Caracalla, Rome could be called an empire in the strict sense of the
"interaction between two political entities," one of which controls the other.
"Under Caracalla, Rome became a political community in which citizens

possessed attenuated but equal rights. Was Rome still an empire in the sense of one people controlling another? Rome had in fact reached an imperial apotheosis: the political distinction between peoples was removed" (Doyle 1986: 97; see also 12, 45). Doyle here follows closely Moses Finley's conception of empire, which rejects any definition in terms of a large territorial state and restricts it to rule by one people or state over other peoples or states. Hence Finley can state firmly that "when the emperor Caracalla extended Roman citizenship to virtually all the free inhabitants of his realm . . . that not too significant administrative measure symbolized that what we call the Roman empire had ceased to be an empire" (Finley 1978a: 2; cf. Crone 2006: 109).

What Doyle and Finley seem to be suggesting is that, with the equalization of citizenship, Rome in effect became something like a large nation-state, rather than an empire, since equal citizenship has always been held to be one of the cardinal principles of the nation-state. If so, the invention of the nation-state has to be added to the many other things that can be attributed to the Roman Empire, since no other state in the ancient world ever approached Rome in its attitude toward citizenship (Brunt 1978: 185; Dench 2005: 131).

Empires and nation-states, as we saw in chapter 1, can indeed often look alike, in practice at least, if not in principle. What description we choose in any particular case seems to depend to a good extent on what we are interested in. But, in whatever other directions Caracalla's edict may be said to point, it is hard to see it as pointing to the end of empire. For Cicero, Aristides, Pliny, Strabo, Claudian, Rutilius, and a host of other commentators, Roman and provincial, the extension of citizenship to all of Rome's subjects was of the essence of Rome's empire, expressing its highest and most characteristic principle. It was the thing that made it distinctive in the world, setting it off from all other states and empires, past and present. It was just this that was seized upon by the great nineteenth-century historian and jurist James Bryce, comparing the Roman and British empires, and noting the British aspiration to imitate Rome in this respect. "Nothing," he said, "contributed more powerfully to the unity and the strength of the Roman dominion than this sense of an imperial nationality. . . . In the third century A. D. a Gaul, a Spaniard, a Pannonian, a Bithynian, a Syrian called himself a Roman, and for all practical purposes was a Roman. The interests of the Empire were his interests, its glory his glory, almost as much as if he had been born in the shadow of the Capitol. There was, therefore, no reason why his loyalty should not be trusted, no reason why he should not be chosen to lead in war, or govern in peace, men of Italian birth" (Bryce [1901] 1914: 40–41).

The political scientist C. P. Lucas, Bryce's contemporary, remarked that "in truth the Romans were the one people in the history of the world who gradually and surely expanded a town into a worldwide community" (Lucas 1912: 95). Here too is the difference between the Roman Empire, even after Caracalla, and the nation-state. What nation-state encompasses the globe? Which aspires to? Nation-states, however self-regarding, accept a world of other nation-states. Empires, however much they are forced in practice to deal with other states and empires, do not. Ultimately there can be only one empire, the universal empire, the carrier of the universal civilizing mission (see chapter 1). No other empire has ever expressed that belief with greater conviction than the Roman. As Theodor Mommsen put it, it was "a familiar concept to the Romans that they were not only the first power on earth, they were also in a sense, the only one" (in Pagden 1995: 23). Rome was the world, the *urbs* the *orbis*, the Roman emperor, as the second-century *Lex Rhodia* put it, *dominus totius orbis*, "lord of all the world." When the pope at Easter delivers his message "urbi et orbi," "to the city and the world," he is, as the head of the Roman Catholic (i.e., universal) Church, precisely expressing that idea of unity and identity claimed by the Roman Empire whose successor the Catholic Church claims to be.

Rome's cosmopolitanism involved a plurality and diversity of peoples that square uneasily with the homogenizing tendencies of the nation-state, however much it struggles with the problem of ethnic minorities and "multiculturalism." For the other side of the coin of universal citizenship was indifference to race, ethnicity, and nationality. With remarkably few exceptions nearly all students of the Roman Empire agree on that.[19] Romans could express contempt for "barbarians," both beyond and within the empire, but the overwhelming consensus was that there was no insuperable "racial," biological, barrier to their eventual absorption (only a stubborn unwillingness, as with the Jews, to accept Roman ways). Barbarians could be civilized, trousered (and "long-haired") Gauls become togaed Gauls. They could be made to cultivate the grape and the olive, to give up porridge for bread, to drink wine instead of beer, to live in cities, to take baths. In a word, they could be Romanized. It was an attractive prospect, and most barbarians, especially the upper classes among them, rushed to embrace it. As Strabo said of the Turdetani of Spain, "they have adopted the Roman style altogether, no longer remembering their own language, and become a people of the toga" (in Sherwin-White 1967: 3).

Compared to modern empires, Rome's singularity as a political entity, as many commentators observed, was the move from city-state to empire without any sense of nationality. The myths of Rome's origin all stress its heterogeneity as a foundational principle. "Many nations," says Ronald Syme, "are prone to embellish and exalt their birth and origins but the legend of the foundation of Rome is anything but flattering—bastards and brigands" (Syme 1958: 17; see also Ando 2000: 52). Rome's founder Romulus, according to Livy, made the city an "asylum for fugitives. A motley mob from the neighbouring peoples flocked to the spot, with no distinction made as to whether they were free or slave, and all eager for a new start in life. These men were the beginning of the real strength of the city" (Livy [c. 25 BCE] 1998: 13 [1.8]).[20] Sallust also notes the mixed ethnic origins of Rome, and comments, "When once they had come to live together in a walled town, despite different origins, languages, and habits of life, they coalesced with amazing ease, and before long what had been a heterogeneous mob of migrants was welded into a united people" (in Champion 2004: 209).

But this was not a people as a nation in any modern sense, certainly not in an ethnic sense. The "mongrel" character of the Roman people continues with the story of the capture of the Sabine women by the Romans. Faced with the threat of war between the two peoples because of the crime, the Sabine women successfully plead for peace and reconciliation between the contending parties. The result was the fusion of the Sabine people in the Roman state. As Livy puts it, Roman and Sabine leaders "not only made peace, but united the two peoples in a single community" (Livy [c. 25 BCE] 1998: 18 [1.13]; see also Edwards and Woolf 2003: 9–10; Dench 2005: 11–26). Claudius, we may remember, boasted of his Sabine ancestry; and Cicero thought that the act of statesmanship that bound the Sabines to Rome—so establishing the principle that "this state should be increased even by the admission of enemies to the citizenship"—was the beginning of its rise to greatness (in Champion 2004: 209).

As Rome expanded and incorporated more and more regions, progressively granting their peoples citizenship, non-Romans and non-Italians came to feature prominently at all levels of the imperial administration. Later commentators, with an eye on modern empires, have all remarked on the extraordinary extent to which the Romans in effect gave over their empire to others. What mattered was the preservation of the imperial ideal—as elaborated of course by Rome, which continued to name the empire. But "Rome" became a remarkably open and flexible signifier. After the second century CE even the city of Rome itself ceased to be the effective seat of the empire: "Rome" was where the emperor was, mostly in the frontier regions. As Bryce put it, "the City of Rome became the Empire, and the Empire became Rome. . . . In the end, Rome ceases to have any history of her own, except an architectural history, so completely is she merged in her Empire" ([1901] 1914: 40, 71; see also Cromer 1910: 37–38). Not only do non-Italian provincials, from Gaul, Spain, Africa, the Balkan provinces of Dalmatia and Pannonia, the eastern provinces of Syria and Asia, swell the equestrian ranks and hold major offices in the army and bureaucracy. At the very top too, among the emperors, it becomes common to find non-Italians, such as Septimus Severus the African; Spaniards such as Trajan, Hadrian, and Theodosius; Diocletian and Constantine from Dalmatia; the Syrians Heliogabalus and Alexander. As P. A. Brunt puts it, "under Rome such men as Nehru and Nkrumah would have been eligible for the highest imperial offices. In the third century most senators were not Italians. From Trajan onwards most emperors came from the provinces and the eternal city celebrated its millennium in A.D. 247 under the rule of an Arab sheikh" (Brunt 1965: 274).[21]

For those concerned to compare Rome with later empires, the cosmopolitanism of the Roman Empire, its reversal of the traditional xenophobia of the ancient world, was among its most striking features. But there remained this question: Could modern empires, with their large admixtures of non-European peoples, attain the degree of assimilation that Rome seems to have aimed at and, to an extent, attained through the policies and processes of Romanization? This problem preoccupied most commentators on empire in the later period. The French, with their assimilationist policies, came nearest to the Roman model, in aspiration at least if not always in practice. The British always remained ambivalent on the issue, unsure how far Indians and Africans really could become British (and, even more, English). For the land empires of the Romanovs, the Habsburgs, and the Ottomans, with their more adjacent populations, the Roman model of assimilation would have seemed the most obvious one. Yet for differing reasons they mostly preferred to follow another aspect of the Roman experience: to establish a common membership and common loyalty to the empire but to allow the different peoples within it a good deal of latitude in the maintenance of their own religions, languages, and customs. The Roman legacy in this respect was indeed complex, allowing both for the pursuit of a common imperial culture and for a degree of pluralism and diversity that was less demanding of uniformity.

We shall see later how these questions affected developments in these empires. But we must turn now to one last aspect of the Roman legacy, in some respects the most momentous: the invention and diffusion of the new religion of Christianity.

Rome: The Universal Religion

In his monumental *A Study of History*, Arnold Toynbee traces a pattern common to all civilizations whereby after a period of creative efflorescence the creative energies die away, to be consolidated in a "universal state" and a "universal religion." Thus, in what was for him the exemplary case, Hellenistic civilization gave rise to the universal state of the Roman Empire and the universal religion of Christianity. The universal state, the Roman Empire, could fall because the universal religion, institutionalized in the Church, incorporated the Hellenistic culture, which, chrysalis-like, it could pass on to the nascent Western civilization (Toynbee 1962–63: 1:52–58; see also vols. 7a and 7b).

Whatever one thinks of Toynbee's philosophy of history, there is no doubting the link between Rome and Christianity, and the fact that of all the legacies of Rome that of Christianity has to be reckoned the most important and longest-lasting. That should seem obvious, in the rise and persistence over two millennia of what is after all called the Roman Catholic Church. The fact that it is not so obvious, and to many people still a matter of dispute if not denial, has to do with the long-standing charge, first voiced by pagan thinkers of the fourth and fifth centuries, that Christianity, far from consolidating and continuing the Roman tradition, in fact undermined it, leaving Rome defenseless before the hordes of barbarians that eventually overwhelmed it. Despite the evidence to the contrary, despite the fact that many of those barbarians, such as the Visigoths who sacked Rome in 410, were Christians, and despite the persistence of the thoroughly Christianized Byzantine Empire in the East for another thousand years, there remains a lurking sense that Christianity and Rome are somehow opposed. Rome is seen as pagan in spirit, militaristic and overbearing, its institutions shot through with such practices as emperor worship, its pleasures the cruel and sensual ones of gladiatorial combats and gluttonous feasting. Christianity brought a philosophy of peace and reconciliation, and a taming of the militaristic ethos of the empire. It preached meekness and forgiveness, austerity and asceticism. It aspired to carry its message to foreign lands where Rome had no presence and no hope of establishing one. How could these two entities be thought compatible, let alone complementary?[22]

It is important first to see that in one of the most influential statements of what appears to be such a view—Edward Gibbon's in *Decline and Fall*—that is not precisely what is meant. True, at one point in his great narrative Gibbon says that "as the happiness of *future* life is the great object of religion, we may hear without surprise or scandal, that the introduction, or at least the abuse, of

Christianity, had some influence on the decline and fall of the Roman empire." He goes on to say, in a famous passage, that "the active virtues of society were discouraged," "the flames of religious discord" kindled, "the attention of the emperors was diverted from camps to synods," and "the Roman world was oppressed by a new species of tyranny" (Gibbon [1776–88] 1995: 2:510–11).

But not only, as always and especially with Gibbon, must one pay attention to the tone and careful wording of his account, but even more should one note that Gibbon immediately qualifies and to an extent refutes the charge. Christianity, he goes on to say, was actually a force for unity as much as division, binding the empire at a time when it was threatened with dissolution by many other forces. "The bishops, from eighteen hundred pulpits, inculcated the duty of passive obedience to a lawful and orthodox sovereign; their frequent assemblies, and perpetual correspondence, maintained the communion of distant churches; and the benevolent temper of the gospel was strengthened, though confined, by the spiritual alliance of the Catholics." Moreover, Christianity can be held to have softened the impact of the barbarian invasions, since so many of the barbarians were themselves converts to Christianity. "The pure and genuine influence of Christianity may be traced to its beneficial, though imperfect, effects on the Barbarian proselytes of the North. If the decline of the Roman empire was hastened by the conversion of Constantine, his victorious religion broke the violence of the fall, and mollified the ferocious temper of the conquerors" (Gibbon [1776–88] 1995: 2:511; see also 3:1068–70).[23]

Gibbon's caution against putting the blame on Christianity sets him at variance with some of the commoner varieties of Enlightenment thought, which saw Christianity, and religion in general, as an offense against reason, and so in good measure responsible for weakening Rome's morale and resilience. But here the Enlightenment was reacting against a much longer tradition of Christian apology, in which far from undermining the Roman Empire Christianity could in some sense be seen as its fulfillment. The basic form of the argument, formulated in the early Christian centuries, was that Rome was the providential vehicle for the origin and rise of Christianity, culminating in Christianity's triumph within the empire itself and so presumptively throughout the world as a whole. Rome and Christianity were not opposed; they were destined for each other. Christianity continued, complemented, and completed the civilizing mission begun by Rome; but on a higher, spiritual plane. Thus the fall of the material structures of the Roman Empire, the decline of its political and even its economic institutions, were not necessarily the end of Rome; for its inheritance was now carried by a greater power, the Catholic Church. The

Church was the continuation of the Roman Empire by other means, and in another form. As the great medieval historian Henri Pirenne put it, the Church was "the most striking example of the continuity of Romanism." "Had not the Fathers told it that the Roman Empire existed in accordance with the will of God, and that it was indispensable to Christianity? Had it not modelled its organization upon that of the Empire? Did it not speak the language of the Empire? Had it not preserved the law and culture of the Empire? And were not all its dignitaries recruited from the ancient senatorial families?" (Pirenne 1939: 45, 124).

Among the first proponents of this influential and long-lasting view was the third-century theologian Origen of Alexandria, generally regarded as the first great scholar among the Greek Fathers of the Church. Quoting Matthew 28:19, "Go therefore and make disciples of all nations," Origen comments: "It is clear that Jesus is born in the reign of Augustus who had, so to speak, united into one kingdom most of the peoples of the earth. The existence of many king-doms would have been an obstacle to the spread of Jesus's teachings all over the world" (in Isaac 2006: 491). In the early Christian view, only a simpleton or an ignoramus could suppose it an accident that Jesus was born at the same time as the establishment of the *pax Augusta*, or think that the destruction of Jerusalem by the emperor Titus in 70 CE could be for any other purpose than the chastisement of the Jews for the murder of Christ.[24]

It was Augustine, in book 5 of the *City of God*, who gave the canonical expression of this view of the relation between the Roman Empire and Christianity. Augustine explicitly drew on the Roman imperial tradition, as expressed by Virgil, that the gods had given Rome dominion over all other nations because it had a sacred mission to carry out, that of bringing law and peace to the world ([413–27 CE] 1984: 198–99; see also Heather 2006: 125; Ando 2000: 48, 63–64, 346–51). For Augustine this was all part of God's plan for humanity. He chose the Romans as the vehicle of his purpose because they had clearly displayed their virtues to the world. "The kingdoms of the East had enjoyed renown for a long time, when God decided that a Western empire should arise, later in time, but more renowned for the extent and gran-deur of its dominion. And, to suppress the grievous evils of many nations, he entrusted this dominion to those men, in preference to all others, who served their country for the sake of honour, praise and glory, who looked to find that glory in their country's safety above their own and who suppressed greed for money and many other faults in favour of that one fault of theirs, the love of praise" (Augustine [413–27 CE] 1984: 201–2).

Imperfect and worldly as these virtues were, they schooled the world for the reception of the virtues of Christianity and prepared it for entry into the "Eternal and Heavenly Country":

> The Roman Empire was not extended and did not attain to glory in men's eyes simply for this, that men of this stamp should be accorded this kind of reward. It had this further purpose, that the citizens of the Eternal City, in the days of their pilgrimage, should fix their eyes steadily and soberly on those examples and observe what love they should have towards the City on high, in view of life eternal, if the earthly city had received such devotion from her citizens, in their hope of glory in the sight of men. (Augustine [413–27 CE] 1984: 205)

The thought is expressed repeatedly in Augustine: if the Romans could do so much, cultivate such virtues, for the sake of the earthly city, how much more should we strive to acquire those virtues necessary for achieving the greater glory of the heavenly city. "If we do not display, in the service of the most glorious City of God, the qualities of which the Romans, after their fashion, gave us something of a model, in their pursuit of the glory of their earthly city, then we ought to feel the prick of shame" (Augustine [413–27 CE] 1984: 211). We must learn from their example. The Romans prepared the way, providentially providing the place for Christ's birth and mission, punishing the Jews who put him to death, establishing through their empire the space within which, carried by evangelists such as Paul, Christianity's message could spread throughout the world. Eventually—again providentially—Rome itself threw up emperors such as Constantine and Theodosius who saw the light and made Christianity the religion of the empire. Nothing could more clearly show the deep affinity between the Roman Empire and Christianity. The heavenly city merely completes and perfects what has been achieved in the earthly city of the Romans.

In later years, thanks to Augustine and a host of other Christian Fathers, this claim for Rome as the cradle of Christianity had great appeal, and served to offset the less endearing image of the Roman Empire as the seat of a cruel and heartless despotism. The idea was particularly congenial to several nineteenth-century thinkers, such as John Henry Newman, who famously converted to Catholicism and became an ardent defender of the Catholic Church. But it appealed also to Thomas Babington Macaulay, usually portrayed as a doughty Protestant hostile to the pretensions of the Roman Catholic Church. It was Macaulay who opened his great paean to the Catholic

Church, his essay on Ranke's *History of the Popes*, with the statement "The history of [the Roman Catholic] Church joins together the two great ages of human civilization. No other institution is left standing which carries the mind back to the times when the smoke of sacrifice rose from the Pantheon, and when camelopards and tigers bounded in the Flavian amphitheatre" (Macaulay [1840] 1907: 38). For Macaulay the Catholic Church established a continuity with Roman times, and the Roman spirit, like no other; and he saw no end to its power and influence in the world.[25] Christianity had prolonged the Roman inheritance: "the idea of Christendom itself," Richard Jenkyns says, as "a Roman-ness transcending geographical boundaries, . . . is in part a legacy of Rome" (Jenkyns 1992a: 9).

Frank Turner observes that "for the Victorians the shared presence of the Christian faith constituted the single most important connection between their lives and those of the Romans under the empire. . . . The rise of Christianity within the Roman empire for the Victorians and even many Edwardians more than compensated for the disappearance of the empire itself. Indeed for many Victorian writers the empire had simply served as a providential vehicle for the emergence of the faith" (Turner 1999: 173–74; see also Vance 1997: 236, 1999: 121). While this might be true for some thinkers, it was by no means the general perception. The decline and fall of the Roman Empire was a theme of perennial interest to Western thinkers, and continued to preoccupy scholars and statesmen in the heyday of European imperialism, in the nineteenth century and beyond. If they thought of Christianity in this context, it was often as the antithesis to, and antagonist of, Rome—perhaps even as the solvent that dissolved the fabric of empire. The fall of Rome, in this view, marked the beginning of a new era—the "Christian Middle Ages"—and the end of antiquity. For secular humanists, in the Renaissance and beyond, this could be something to be mourned, as the loss of a valued way of thinking and living.

But there were continuities too, of particular interest to those who thought about empire. The fact that Rome had incubated Christianity and then been its principal carrier was immensely important to those early modern empires, such as those of Portugal and Spain, which saw their mission in Christianizing terms, in the New World and the East. The same was true of the land empires of the Romanovs and the Habsburgs, the one the standard-bearer of Orthodoxy and the Byzantine tradition—"Moscow the Third Rome"—and the other of Roman Catholicism, as the leader of the Counter-Reformation and defender of the faith in the borderlands of the empire in the East (Österreich).

For later Western empires—those of the Dutch, the French, the British, and others—while Christianity remained important, especially in the face of the Islamic empire of the Ottomans, other aspects of the Roman legacy loomed larger. The "civilizing mission" to some extent changed its character, no longer being primarily about spreading the faith but more concerned with the legal, political, and cultural order created by empire. Here again Rome had a rich storehouse of ideas and experience from which others could draw, in its policies of citizenship and its attitudes toward the customs and beliefs of the many peoples that inhabited the empire. Could Caracalla's example be followed, with its grant of citizenship to all subjects of the empire? What was the precise intent and effect of Romanization: to create a common imperial culture or simply to buy off the elites of the conquered nations? And how meaningful was Rome's global pretensions to universality, to be an *imperium totius orbis*? Can empires aim at universality, in a world of other empires and other states? All these questions pressed upon the European empires; and for answers, or at least material for reflection, they turned almost instinctively to Rome.

In his essay, "On Vehicles" (1580), which contains one of his most famous diatribes against the Spanish conquest of the New World, Michel de Montaigne laments the lost opportunity of gaining the trust and consent of the native Indian population, and expostulates: "Why did not so noble a conquest fall to Alexander, or to the ancient Greeks and Romans! Why did not this vast change and transformation of so many empires and peoples fall to the lot of men who would have gently refined and cleared away all that was barbarous, and stimulated and strengthened the good seeds that nature had sown there, not only applying to the cultivation of the land and the adornment of the cities the arts of this hemisphere, in so far as they were necessary, but also blending the Greek and Roman virtues with those native to the country?" (Montaigne [1580] 1958: 278–79). It is a vivid example of what Rome—as the inheritor and transmitter of Hellenistic civilization—meant to many educated Europeans of the modern era. It is also a reminder that, to many of them, the problem with modern empires was precisely their departure from the Roman model. In one way or another, modern imperialism evolved in dialogue with Rome.

3

The Ottoman Empire

Some historians have written about the Ottoman Empire as if it were a nation-state, with the Turks in control and administering minorities. This approach is flawed. The system encompassed multiple groups, all accepted as "different." Difference was not horizontally eradicated but vertically integrated into the political system.

—ARON RODRIGUE (1995: 84)

The makers of the Ottoman slave-household forged an instrument which enabled a tiny band of Nomads, who had been ejected from their native Steppe and cast away in an alien environment, not merely to survive and hold their own in this strange world, but to impose peace and order upon a great Christian society [Orthodoxy] which had gone into disintegration, and to threaten the life of a yet greater Christian society which has since cast its shadow over the whole of the rest of Mankind.

—ARNOLD TOYNBEE (1962–63: 3:49)

The attempt to frame late Ottoman history in a narrative of imperial collapse to the relentless drumbeat of the march of progress—usually associated with Westernization, nationalism, and secularization—prevents a clear understanding of the developments in question.

—M. SUKRU HANIOGLU (2008: 1–2)

Alien Empire

The Ottoman Empire can be made to sound very alien to Western ears. Unlike the Western empires, it was a non-Christian empire, the center and carrier of Islam, protector of the Holy Places. It inherited the mantle of the Caliphate from the Arabs, and something of the mission to spread Islam around

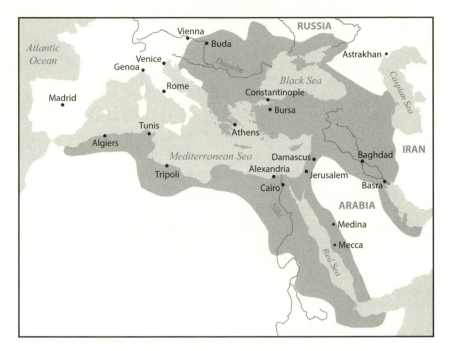

MAP 3.1. The Ottoman Empire at its greatest extent, 1683

the world. For the West the conflicts with the Ottomans could be seen as a continuation of the medieval Crusades against the Arab lands. In the early modern centuries especially, when religion was a central preoccupation of the European empires, the religious divide with the Ottomans could seem the most profound marker of difference. The Ottoman invasions of Europe in the fifteenth and sixteenth centuries produced consternation throughout the continent, especially in Central Europe, in Germany and the Habsburg lands (Elliott 1993: 155). Catholics and Protestants alike expressed profound anxieties about the apparently unstoppable advance of Islam. Twice—in 1529 and 1683—the Ottomans besieged Vienna, the capital of the Habsburg Empire and principal bulwark of Christendom against the Ottomans. The Ottomans, with their strange ways and alien religion, threatened to overrun Europe just as had the Arabs centuries earlier.

The Habsburgs represented the Catholic Counter-Reformation; but Protestants were almost equally aroused. Martin Luther indeed thundered that "the Turk is the rod of the wrath of the Lord our God," a just chastisement of Christians for their failings, and for allowing the corruption of their Church. But, on the grounds of a "just war," he urged his followers to support the

Habsburgs in their conflict with the Ottomans. For, "just as the pope is the Antichrist, so the Turk is the very devil incarnate. The prayer of Christendom against both is that they shall go down to hell." Increasingly pope and Turk are conflated by Luther: "The person of the Antichrist is the pope, his flesh is the Turk" (in Smith 2007: 354; see also Elliott 1993: 157–58).

For Renaissance thinkers and beyond, "Turks"—the common but mistaken European term for the Ottomans—were the new barbarians, the counterpart of the old foes of Greece and Rome, the modern equivalent of the cruel and savage *barbari* that had overwhelmed the Roman Empire. They were, in the words of the English writer Richard Knolles, "the present terrour of the world" (Woodhead 1987: 22; see also Mantran 1980: 231–33; Yapp 1992: 148; Cirakman 2001: 53). A whole series of impressions and perceptions of the Ottomans underwrote this judgment. There were the peculiar institutions and practices, as bizarre in Western eyes as the Ottomans' religion: the practice of mass fratricide, with the new sultan killing off all his brothers on acceding to the throne, to preempt rival claims and bloody succession struggles; together with the practice of confining the young princes, sons of the sultan, to "cages" within the harem of the Topkapi Palace. There was the harem itself, the women's quarters, where the *valide sultan*, the queen mother, lorded it over the sultan's wives and concubines, and black African eunuchs oversaw their daily life. There was the striking institution of the *devshirme*, the "levy" of Christian youth for service in the palace and in the military corps of the Janissaries, as slaves of the sultan. Add to this bearded and turbaned muftis, whirling dervishes, the murderous violence that often broke out in and around the Topkapi Palace as the Janissaries launched one of their frequent bouts of insurrection, and it is not difficult to see why the Ottoman Empire provided the prime site of that "Orientalism" that Edward Said so influentially delineated as inscribed in the Western imagination. "Until the end of the seventeenth century the 'Ottoman peril' lurked alongside Europe to represent for the whole of Christian civilization a constant danger." It was the latest expression of the "lasting trauma" of Islam, which for Europeans came to symbolize "terror, devastation, the demonic, hordes of hated barbarians" (Said 1979: 59; cf. Yapp 1992: 135). The Ottoman Empire was for centuries the classic "other" of Western civilization, at once outlandish and menacing, fascinating and seductive, threatening to overwhelm it with its alien ways.

Paradoxically, as the Islamic threat receded in the nineteenth century and the Ottoman Empire became "the sick man of Europe," European perceptions of the difference between their civilization and that of the Ottomans reached a new and heightened intensity. For the great British thinker Cardinal Newman, the Ottomans represented the principle of nullity, a barbarian civilization lacking any internal life and entirely dependent on others—"Franks," Armenians, Greeks, Jews—for their existence. They are, asserted Newman, "in the way of the progress of the nineteenth century. . . . There they lie, unable to abandon their traditionary principles, without simply ceasing to be a state; unable to retain them, and retain the sympathy of Christendom;—Mahometans, despots, slave merchants, polygamists, holding agriculture in contempt, Europe in abomination, their own wretched selves in admiration, cut off from the family of nations, existing by ignorance and fanaticism" (Newman [1853] 1894: 220, 222–23).

Newman's uncompromisingly hostile view of the Ottomans was more than matched by that of the British prime minister William Gladstone, whose immensely popular tract on the "Bulgarian Horrors" of 1876 contained a searing indictment of "the Turkish race" and its character.

> It is not a question of Mahometanism simply, but of Mahometanism compounded with the peculiar character of a race. They are not the mild Mahometans of India, nor the chivalrous Saladins of Syria, nor the cultured Moors of Spain. They were, upon the whole, from the black day when they first entered Europe, the one great anti-human specimen of humanity. Wherever they went, a broad line of blood marked the track behind them, and, as far as their dominion reached, civilization disappeared from view. They represented everywhere government by force, as opposed to government by law. For the guide of this life they had a relentless fatalism: for its reward hereafter, a sensual paradise. (Gladstone 1876: 9)

The cruel, sensual and despotic Turk became a standard stereotype in the West. But, from the earliest days of the Ottoman presence in Europe, there was an alternative view, though never one that matched the negative one in power and popularity. For some Western thinkers the very differences with the West could be the source of critical and satirical reflection on Western beliefs and practices. Some, such as Richard Knolles, commented on the advantages of a lack of an aristocracy of birth, arguing that the *devshirme* system allowed for the selection of a ruling class based solely on merit and service to the state (Woodhead 1987: 23). The sixteenth-century French thinker Jean Bodin contrasted the fanaticism of religious authorities in Europe with the much more tolerant policies of the Ottomans:

The great emperour of the Turkes doth with as great devotion as any prince in the world honour and observe the religion received from his auncestours, and yet detesteth hee not the straunge religion of others; but to the contrarie permitteth every man to live according to his conscience: yea and that more is, neere unto his pallace at Pera, suffereth foure divers religions, viz. That of the Jewes, that of the Christians, that of the Grecians, and that of the Mohametanes: and besides that, sendeth almes to the Calogers or religious Monkes, dwelling upon mountaine Athos (being Christians) to pray for him. (Bodin [1586] 1962: 537; see also Hentsch 1992: 68–75)

A similar point was made by John Locke, in his *Essay on Toleration* (1689), when he imagined two Christian churches in Constantinople attempting to "savage" each other, while "the Turks meanwhile say nothing and laugh up their sleeves at the cruelty of Christians beating and killing each other" (Locke [1689] 2010: 14). Bodin's compatriot Voltaire, writing two centuries later, was even more vehement in contrasting Ottoman practice with that of Europeans:

The Sultan governs in peace twenty million people of different religions; two hundred thousand Greeks live in security at Constantinople; the *muphti* himself nominates and presents to the emperor the Greek patriarch, and they also admit a Latin patriarch. The Sultan nominates Latin bishops for some of the Greek islands, using the following formula: "I command him to go and reside as bishop in the island of Chios, according to their ancient usage and their vain ceremonies." The empire is full of Jacobites, Nestorians, and Monothelites; it contains Copts, Christians of St. John, Jews, and Hindoos. The annals of Turkey do not record any revolt instigated by any of these religions. (Voltaire [1763] 1912: 23; see also Hentsch 1992: 104–7)

The generally tolerant nature of the Ottoman state, institutionalized in the *millet* system, was always one of the principal aspects singled out by those who defended it against the opprobrium heaped upon it by its detractors. But that too might also perversely highlight its difference from the West, at least in the earlier centuries when religious orthodoxy was regarded by most European states as one of the chief objects of public policy. It was telling that the other instances of toleration that Voltaire contrasted with European intolerance were India, Persia, Tartary, China, and Japan (until the arrival of the intolerant Jesuits): all societies markedly different in outlook and practices from European ones. Thus the very thing that might commend the Ottomans to Europeans served rather to show up their exoticism.

A European Empire

It is indeed possible to stress the non-European—Turkic, Arabic, Persian—aspects of the Ottoman Empire. Yet properly considered it has at least as much claim to be thought European as, say, the Russian Empire.[1] This comes out clearly in its origins, the manner of its development, its geographical spread, and its impact on Europe.

Origins do not determine destinations; there is plenty of room for deviations and novelties on the way. But they are a good guide to general orientations and directions. The great Ottoman scholar Paul Wittek indeed claims that "the well-known saying, that every state owes its existence to the same causes that created it, holds good to the full extent for the Ottoman state"—right to the very end of its life, according to Wittek (Wittek 1938: 5). This may be too strong a statement; but undoubtedly how the Ottoman Empire came into being and how it was formed tell us much about its basic character and outlook.

Because of the almost total absence of records for the crucial thirteenth and fourteenth centuries, the origins of the Ottoman Empire are shrouded in myths and scholarly controversy. Were the Ottomans, as the American historian Herbert Gibbons argued, a relatively small tribal group that assimilated Byzantine traditions and made extensive use of Christians, or ex-Christians, as administrators and military commanders? Were they rather, as the Turkish scholar M. Fuad Köprülü insisted against Gibbons, impeccably Turkish, bringing with them the Turkic traditions of Central Asia, and at least in the early stages wholly reliant on Turks for running the empire? Or were they, as the French scholar Paul Wittek in turn urged, not tribal at all but a *gazi* warrior band from the marches, committed to spreading the faith of Islam in a ceaseless and all-out battle with the infidel?[2]

Let us begin with what seem some generally agreed-upon facts, or at least perceptions.[3] Sometime in the early thirteenth century, the ancestors of Osman, the founder of the Ottoman (Osmanli) dynasty, arrived in Anatolia. They were part of the second wave of the great Turkic migrations, those that took place in the wake of the conquests of Genghis Khan in Central Asia, home of the Turkic or Turcoman tribes. In Anatolia they encountered Turkic groups from the first wave of Turkic migrations that began in the eleventh century. Most evident among such presences were the Seljuk Turks, whose empire at one time extended over much of Asia Minor. In 1071, at the Battle of Manzikert, the Seljuks defeated the Byzantines and established their rule in

Anatolia, with bases at Iznik (Nicaea) and later Konya (Iconium), in central Anatolia. With varying degrees of effectiveness they made vassals of most of the other Anatolian Turkic emirates or principalities. The Seljuks called themselves the Seljuks of Rum, that is, of the lands of the (eastern) Roman Empire, thereby distinguishing themselves from the Seljuks of the Great Seljuk Empire of Iran and Iraq. Here was established the idea that whoever ruled in "Rum" was in effect the successor to the Roman Empire.

Seljuk rule was rudely and peremptorily ended by the Mongol invasion of Anatolia in the thirteenth century. The Seljuks were decisively defeated by the Mongols at the Battle of Kösedag in 1243; their successors in Anatolia were the Mongol Ilkhanids. Avoiding or evading Ilkhanid control, some of the Turkic groups pushed northward and westward, to the borderlands of the Byzantine Empire (Köprülü [1935] 1992: 32–42; Inalcik 1981–82: 72–75; Darling 2000: 156). Among these were the followers of Osman, who established themselves in the border region of Bithynia. By the end of the thirteenth century the Ottoman emirate was in effective control of Bithynia. In 1301, the Ottomans defeated the Byzantines at the Battle of Bapheus: the first encounter between the two powers, and harbinger of many more to come in the next century and a half.

It is at this point, with the Ottomans the dominant group in Bithynia at the beginning of the fourteenth century, that controversy rages over who exactly the Ottomans were and what they might have represented. It was during the course of the fourteenth century that the Ottomans built up their power, in Anatolia and the Balkans. But with what purpose, and under what ideology? The dominant interpretation for many decades has been what has come to be called the *gazi* thesis, as expounded most influentially by Paul Wittek. The Ottomans, says Wittek, were "a community of *Ghazis*, of champions of the Mohammedan religion; a community of Moslem march-warriors, devoted to the struggle with the infidels in their neighbourhood" (Wittek 1938: 14). For Wittek the conquest of Constantinople in 1453 was not simply the climactic but also the defining act of the Ottoman mission. Even though the later acquisition of the Arab lands, including the holy cities of Mecca and Medina, made the Ottomans the greatest Muslim power of modern times, the heart of the empire was always the possessions in Anatolia and the Balkans won from the Byzantines. When the Ottomans conquered Constantinople, "the natural centre of this area," they "obtained a capital which for more than a thousand years past had been the seat of imperial traditions." Constantinople was the center of this essential "inner" empire, the empire that the Ottomans themselves called "the Sultanate of Rhum," to emphasize its character as successor to the "Rhomaean," that is, Byzantine, state. This "older Ottoman Empire," says Wittek, "was never completely absorbed in the later and larger Moslem one; it distinctly retained its position as the vital nucleus of the whole and imposed upon the latter the continuation of its peculiar political tradition" (Wittek 1938: 2).

For Wittek, this tradition grew out of the *gazi* ethos, and hence meant that for the Ottomans, even before they became caliphs and formal guardians of the Islamic faith, "the struggle against their Christian neighbours" marked both their origins and the continuing principle of their history right down to the end. Following the conquest of Constantinople the Ottomans carried out a ceaseless struggle against the Christian powers of Europe, capturing most of Hungary and twice besieging Vienna. Not until the Peace of Karlowitz in 1699 did the slow rollback and decomposition of Ottoman power begin. For Wittek it is significant that it was setbacks in Europe, and not in its Arab lands— the larger part of its possessions, most of which remained securely within the empire—that most severely weakened the Ottoman state. "The wounds which the empire received in Europe were closely followed by its decline and ruin." Nevertheless, the decline was slow and fitful; not until the end of the nine-teenth century did it accelerate, the end coming in the early twentieth century. "It is very characteristic that the accomplishment of the final breakdown was closely preceded by the loss of nearly all the European possessions consequent upon defeat in the Balkan War [1912–13]. This defeat obliged the Ottomans to resign definitely and for ever any ambition of ruling over Christian countries, and this meant not less than the renunciation of their dominant idea, of the *raison d'être* of their state" (Wittek 1938: 2–3).

We shall come back to Wittek's *gazi* hypothesis, the specific claim for the nature of the original warrior band that founded the Ottoman Empire. What we have to see first is that Wittek's stress on the European element in the Otto-man Empire—his argument about its "Rhomaean" core—is to a good degree separable from any speculation as to the religious motivation of the original Ottomans. For whatever the nature of the original band, it seems clear that conquest of the European lands across the Sea of Marmara, and aspirations to take control of Constantinople, were and remained animating principles of the empire from the very start. Moreover, the more their contact with the West, and the greater the realization that they were slipping behind in science, technology, and forms of modern government, the more pronounced became this "European" element in Ottoman consciousness. The Ottoman Empire was indeed an Islamic empire; but it was also a European empire. The two of course are not in conflict, despite popular—and to some extent scholarly—perceptions. Islam has been part of Europe ever since the Arab conquests in (formerly Roman) North Africa and Spain in the eighth century. Ottoman rule, in the Mediterranean and the Balkans, simply continued this trend. But, because of the conflicts between Islam and Christianity, and because for many Europe has been identified with Christendom, it is important to stress that even without its Islamic character the Ottoman Empire can be seen as part of the family of European empires.

It is generally agreed that what distinguished the Ottomans from the other Turkic emirates in Anatolia—including the Seljuks—was their interest in the European territories across the Straits of the Dardanelles. Their occupation of Bithynia, in the northwest corner of the Anatolian peninsula, put them in a favorable position for raiding and plundering the Byzantine towns and villages on their borders, and for attempting to penetrate the heartlands of the crumbling Byzantine Empire. From 1204 to 1261 Latin forces, in the midst of the Fourth Crusade, had occupied Constantinople, forcing the Byzantine court to retreat to Nicaea, and severely undermining Byzantine power and authority in the region. The Ottomans made full use of the opportunities offered, even when the Byzantines recovered Constantinople late in the thirteenth century. In 1326 Osman's son Orhan captured the important Byzantine city of Bursa, which he made his capital. But it was the Ottoman occupation of Thrace, on the southeastern tip of the Balkans, that marked the decisive passage of the Ottomans from Asia to Europe, and the making of them as a European power.

The move was significantly accomplished by a typical mix of Ottoman alliances and entanglements with a variety of Christian powers—again, a pattern that was to characterize Ottoman rule right to the end of its existence (including the bizarre alliance with the Habsburg Empire, its long-standing and most uncompromising antagonist for most of its history, during the First World War). Between 1351 and 1355 Genoa and Venice were engaged in a war over control of the lucrative Black Sea trade. Orhan opted to side with Genoa, and it was the Genoese, as reward for Ottoman support against Venetian attacks on the Genoese trading colony at Galata, who supplied the boats that ferried the Ottomans across the Dardanelles Straits in 1352. But Orhan had also been negotiating with Byzantium, which from 1341 had been plunged in civil war following the death of Emperor Andronicus III. Orhan allied with Andronicus's successor John VI Cantacuzenus, and in an elaborate ceremony in 1346 married his daughter Theodora. In 1352 John Cantacuzenus invited a "Turkish" (probably Karesi) contingent to garrison the Byzantine fort of Tzympe on the Gallipoli (Gelibolu) peninsula, on the northern, European, side of the Dardanelles. These Turkish warriors declared allegiance to the Ottomans, in the person of Orhan's son Suleyman Pasha, who crossed the Dardanelles with his troops—in Genoese boats—and occupied Gallipoli. Thus did Thrace pass over to the Ottomans, helped by an earthquake in 1354 that destroyed the walls of the Gallipoli fortress and those of other towns in the peninsula. By the time of Orhan's death in 1362 the Ottomans had expanded beyond Thrace into the adjoining regions of the Balkans. Edirne (Adrianople), captured in 1361, became the new capital of the region now known as Rumeli, or Rumelia.

The Ottomans had now established their bridgehead in Europe, and in the second half of the fourteenth century went on to take most of the remaining kingdoms and principalities in the Balkans. In 1389 they defeated the Serbs at the Battle of Kosovo Polje (the "Field of Blackbirds"), effectively ending Serbian independence. In 1393 the Bulgarian lands were annexed; in 1395 Wallachia fell to the Ottomans. In 1394–1402 the Ottomans laid siege to Constantinople itself, but the city held out—aided by the Mongol threat.

For now another Mongol incursion into Anatolia—that of Timur or Tamerlane—seriously disrupted the pattern of Ottoman expansion. In 1402 at the Battle of Ankara the Ottomans were routed by Timur, thereby allowing the Anatolian emirates to regain their independence. Slowly the Ottomans regrouped, and by 1425 had retaken most of the Anatolian principalities. They continued their operations in the Balkans, taking Thessalonica in 1430, and defeating the Hungarians at Varna in 1444, thus ending Hungarian ambitions in the Balkans. Finally in 1453 came the great prize, the taking of Constantinople. From here, the new imperial capital, flanked on either side by the imperial cities of Bursa (Anatolia) and Edirne (Rumelia), the Ottomans carried out the conquest of the remaining Balkan powers, incorporating the Peloponnese in 1460, annexing Bosnia and Herzegovina in 1463, and subduing Albania in 1464–79.

Two points need to be brought out in this brief account of the early years of the Ottomans. First, it is clear that the conquest of Constantinople was the culminating act of a European strategy, grounded in the Balkans. The Ottomans did not, like some Asiatic conqueror, burst out of the East, to descend upon Western civilization with their alien culture and religion. Rather, from their earliest days, even before they had fully secured Anatolia, they slowly and carefully built up their power in the Balkans, creating their capital at Edirne and lavishing attention upon it. Deflected by Timur's invasion of 1402, they patiently returned to their task after his departure, continuing their design of

FIGURE 3.1. Sultan Mehmed II ("the Conqueror"), who in 1453 conquered
Constantinople and put an end to the Byzantine Empire. Portrait attributed
to Gentile Bellini. © National Gallery, London/Art Resource, NY.

gaining mastery over the whole of the Balkans as the best means of overcoming the Byzantine Empire. It was from the west, from Edirne, not from the
other Ottoman capital of Bursa on the eastern side of the Bosphorus, that
Mehmed II "the Conqueror" marched on Constantinople. Heath Lowry has
rightly said that in understanding early Ottoman traditions and institutions

we must focus on the Balkans, not, as is traditionally done, on Anatolia. "For, while originating in the latter, the Ottoman state came of age in the Balkans and only really began to turn its attention fully . . . to eastern Anatolia and the heartlands of the Islamic world in the sixteenth century. From the early 1350s forward, the primary Ottoman focus was Balkan oriented and it is in that steady westward movement that we must begin searching for the institutional origins underpinning Ottoman success . . . [T]he Ottoman polity in its formative centuries was nurtured and grew in the late-Roman, Byzantine Christian milieu of the Balkans" (Lowry 2003: 96).

The second thing to stress is that the idea of a permanent, unremitting war between Ottoman Muslims and European Christians is a myth, convenient both for certain Ottoman propagandists and even more for Europeans. From the very start the Ottomans were entirely prepared to enter into alliances, and indeed marriages, with Christian powers. We have seen this in the case of the opportunity given to the Ottomans to make their first entry in the Balkans in the mid-fourteenth century. Even in the case of the conquest of Constantinople in 1453, alliances with Christian rulers— Władysław of Hungary-Poland, George Brankovic of Serbia (whose daughter Mara had married Murad II), John Hunyadi, regent of Hungary, as well as the Venetians—were critical to the Ottomans in securing their flank in the Balkans (Imber 2002: 28; Finkel 2007: 48). Moreover, among the Byzantine defenders of Constantinople was Orhan, pretender to the Ottoman throne (executed after the conquest); while there is evidence that within Constantinople itself there were Orthodox elements, alarmed by the recent union of the Orthodox and Catholic Churches, and mindful of the brutal rule of the Latins in Constantinople in the thirteenth century, which were more prepared to accept Ottoman rule than be yoked with the Catholics (Inalcik [1973] 2000: 23; Finkel 2007: 50).[4] Such was the complexity of crisscrossing Muslim-Christian alliances in this momentous event.

This pattern of realpolitik continued to the end of Ottoman rule. Even before the acceptance of the Ottomans in the European state system in the eighteenth century (which, however, was not formalized until the Treaty of Paris in 1856), Ottomans had actively engaged in intra-European rivalries and conflicts, showing a willingness to establish cordial relationships with European powers. In the sixteenth century they allied with France against the Habsburgs, and—despite Luther's fulminations against them—they supported the German Protestant princes against the Counter-Reformation, arguing that Muslims and Protestants had much in common in their antipathy both to idols and to the pope (an argument that also endeared them to the English queen Elizabeth). In the eighteenth and nineteenth centuries, fear of Russia drew them to the British and French, while in the later nineteenth and early twentieth centuries Germany seemed the better partner. At no point does one see a massive fault line separating a militant Islamic power from a bloc of Christian ones. The Ottomans inserted themselves fully into the European game, as one of its most active and powerful players. "Throughout nearly all of its 600-year history," says Donald Quataert, "the Ottoman state was as much a part of the European political order as were its French or Habsburg rivals" (2000: 2; see also Elliott 1993: 154, 162; Goffman 2002: 103, 110–11; Goffman and Stroop 2004: 135–41).

Muslims and Christians

If we now return to Paul Wittek's *gazi* thesis, and the criticisms that have been made of it, we can see further how mistaken it is to view the Ottoman Empire as an "Eastern," Islamic, state, implacably opposed to everything Western and Christian. As is usual with such historiographical controversies, participants tend to exaggerate the differences, and a careful reading of Wittek shows a subtlety and a nuance that are lost in the summaries of his position. Nevertheless, insofar as Wittek stressed the overwhelmingly religious—Islamic—character of the early Ottomans, later work has rightly suggested that he and other Ottomanists of his generation, such as Köprülü and even Köprülü's disciple Halil Inalcik, have allowed themselves to be unduly influenced by the Ottoman chroniclers of the late fifteenth and sixteenth centuries, who were concerned to stress the traditionally Islamic character of the Ottoman Empire.

Some, such as Cemal Kafadar, have stressed the "fluidity of identities" in the Ottoman community in Bithynia and the surrounding region, allowing for much intermingling between Muslims and Christians, and leading to the formation of a syncretic culture, as in medieval Iberia. Ottoman success, he says, lay in harnessing the "mobility and fluidity" of Anatolian frontier society, and subduing it to their own "stability-seeking, centralizing vision" (1995: 140–41; see also Lindner 1983: 1–50).

Heath Lowry has gone even further in his characterization of the early world of the Ottomans. Bithynia in the fourteenth century was "a multireligious, polygot, multiethnic society." The evidence suggests that "Osman and Orhan were far more interested in accommodation with their Bithynian Christian neighbors than in converting them to Islam." Conversion to Islam was not necessary for acceptance into the Ottoman ruling elite in the fourteenth and early fifteenth centuries. However, conversion appeared attractive for a number of reasons to a number of people. "Whether facilitated by a state policy of kindness and good treatment (for the peasants), or a desire to share in the spoils of conquest and *Realpolitik* concerns (for the local Byzantine nobility), ever increasing numbers of Bithynian (and later Balkan) Christians, inspired primarily by the promise of shared booty, opted to join the Ottoman banner. The manumission of slaves, gradual assimilation and intermarriage were all to become means whereby the Ottoman manpower base was provided with a steady flow of religious and cultural converts" (Lowry 2003: 132). All this requires a decisive rejection of Wittek's *gazi* (Holy War) thesis. The goal of the Ottomans was not conversion to Islam but "booty, plunder, and slaves. . . . The . . . Ottoman juggernaut rolled through Bithynia and into the Balkans, fueled not by the zeal of a religious brotherhood, but by the greed and ambition of a predatory confederacy" (Lowry 2003: 43, 46, 54; see also Darling 2000: 137).

Drawing upon the work of Kafadar and Lowry, Karen Barkey has skillfully employed network analysis to show the formation of the early Ottoman state, and the reason why the Ottomans won out against their rivals in Anatolia. She describes "a frontier where boundaries were acknowledged but continually evaded. Osman, Mihal, and Evrenos [founders of the Ottoman state] in many ways succeeded in crossing boundaries, bringing different communities together, and enlisting them in a common project. . . . The foundation of Ottoman power then was the result of brokerage across boundaries, especially religious ones. The irony of this construction should not be missed because it is clear that as the West consolidated Latin Christendom, opposing and oppressing Orthodox Christianity at every turn, Muslims and Greek Orthodox Christians were laying the foundations of a hybrid state" (Barkey 2008: 54–55; see also Lowry 2003: 56–57, 136; Goffman and Stroop 2004: 137).

Lowry speaks of "the spirit of latitudinarianism" in early Ottoman rule, allowing for easy conversion and assimilation, and enabling both Christians and ex-Christians to ascend the administrative and military hierarchies. The Ottomans practiced a policy of "accommodation" (*istimalet*) and "allurement" toward the indigenous Christians, returning lands to the peasants displaced by the conquests, confirming them in their rights, and lightening the tax burden, so that in many respects peasants were better off under Ottoman rule than Byzantine. Christian landowners too, who accepted Ottoman rule, had their landholding rights confirmed, and their position as seigneurs converted to the comparable status of Ottoman timariots, holders of land, *timars*, from which they gained an income.

Lowry shows that not just Christian peasants but large numbers of the Byzantine-Balkan aristocracy were recruited into the Ottoman ruling elite. It has commonly been thought that the rise of Christians or former Christians can largely be attributed to the *devshirme* system instituted in the late fourteenth century by the sultans Murad I and Bayezid I. It was Murad who, continuing an older practice of using prisoners of war as fighters, formed the first infantry corps of the Janissaries (*yeneceri* in Turkish, meaning "new forces") from Christian captives. Bayezid institutionalized this as the *devshirme*, the periodic levy of Christian youth from Balkan villages and later elsewhere.[5] The youths thus chosen were obliged to convert to Islam, and were then brought to the Palace Schools to be trained as soldiers and administrators.

It has long been known that many of the most senior administrators in the early centuries of Ottoman rule rose through the *devshirme* system. Of 34 grand viziers—the highest office in the Ottoman state, making them deputies of the sultan—all but 4 between 1453 and 1600 were *devshirme* conscripts. Indeed, over the course of the empire's history as a whole, of the 215 grand viziers more than two-thirds were of Christian origin. But these ex-Christian members of the Ottoman elite were not necessarily of peasant background, as is generally assumed about *devshirme* recruits; many of them came from the Byzantine-Balkan aristocracy—the very group that might have been thought most recalcitrant to Ottoman rule (Lowry 2003: 117, 119; Inalcik 1954: 114–17; Kunt 1982; Toynbee 1962–63, 3:40).

The "hybrid state" constructed by the Ottomans—a hybrid of high Islamic culture and administration and Byzantine Christian culture and administration—together with the partial rapprochement between Muslims and Christian that it represented, was not without its dangers. Scholars have noted the relatively large number of "heretical" preachers in the Ottoman lands who, in the fourteenth and early fifteenth centuries, proclaimed Jesus and Muhammad of equal worth and standing, and looked toward a syncretism of Islam and Christianity. Such scholars have often been puzzled by the massive Sheikh (Seyh) Bedreddin Revolt, which broke out in Rumelia and Anatolia in 1416, and which until it was brutally crushed threatened to undermine an Ottoman state already weakened by Timur's invasion. Since Bedreddin—and especially his disciple Borkluce Mustafa—preached a reconciliation of Islam and Christianity similar to that urged by these other preachers, Lowry plausibly suggests that "in a state formed by Muslims and Christians, in which the role of popular religion had, from its inception, brought Muslims and Christians together, this movement was nothing more than an attempt actually to unite the two faiths as one," in a projected "Islamo-Christian syncretism" (Lowry 2003: 138; cf. Inalcik [1973] 2000: 188–90; Kunt 1982: 57–58; Goffman 2002: 39; Barkey 2008: 65). Despite their attitude of accommodation, and their dependence on Christian recruits for the army and civil administration, this was one step too far for the Ottomans, who never wavered from proclaiming their Islamic faith. But the savagery of the suppression of Bedreddin's revolt suggests how serious the movement was, and how powerful the tendency that it represented in Ottoman society toward an "Islamo-Christian syncretism."

Ottomans and Romans

When the Ottomans captured Constantinople they called it "Istanbul." This was not, as used to be thought, a corruption of Constantinople, but a name derived from the classical Greek *eis tin polin* ("to the city"), often shortened in colloquial Greek to *stin poli*, meaning both "to the city" and "in the city," that is, of Constantinople (Georgacas 1947: 367). But not only was the new name a continuation of Byzantine Greek practice; the old name of Constantinople, rendered in Turkish as Kostantiniyye, continued to be used for centuries alongside the newer coinage. It was in fact only in 1930, in the new Turkish Republic, that Istanbul was adopted as the official name of the city (Finkel 2007: 57).

Here we have, in a particularly telling form, another indication of the element of continuity in the Ottoman conquest of the Byzantine Empire. Other names tell the same story, the names often used by Ottoman rulers from the time of Mehmed II: *Kaysar* (Caesar), *Basileus* (king—the primary title of the Byzantine emperors), *Padisah-i Kostantiniyye* (emperors of Constantinople), *Padisah-i Rum* (emperors of the Romans) (Lowry 2003: 119; Goffman and Stroop 2004: 132). These titles clearly show that in one aspect at least the Ottomans, as the conquerors of the Eastern Roman Empire, wished to consider themselves as the heirs of Rome. Nor did they stop with Constantinople. Mehmed II's campaign against Otranto was intended as a first step in the conquest of Rome itself, a plan aborted by his death. Suleyman also contemplated, during his campaign in Corfu in 1537, invading Italy and capturing Rome; his support for the Protestants in Europe was in pursuit of this end, designed as it was to destroy the unity of Christendom symbolized by the pope and Holy Roman emperor. As late as the seventeenth and eighteenth centuries the Ottoman sultans were still styling themselves "Caesar" or "Caesar of Caesars"—at the same time denying that title to the other most obvious claimants, the Holy

Roman emperors (Inalcik 1993: 68; Göçek 1993: 93, 96; Imber 2002: 125; Goffman 2002: 107–9; Şahin 2015).

The Venetian traveler Giacomo de' Languschi, who met Mehmed II shortly after the conquest of Constantinople, reported him as saying that "the world empire must be one, with one faith and one sovereignty. To establish this unity, there is no place more fitting than Constantinople." The Greek scholars and Italian humanists at his court instructed him in Roman history. The Greek scholar George Trapezuntios wrote that "no one can doubt that he is emperor of the Romans. He who holds the seat of empire in his hand is emperor of right; and Constantinople is the centre of the Roman Empire" (in Inalcik [1973] 2000: 56–57; see also 26, 29–30, 181). Others wrote of Mehmed's fascination with Greek and Roman history, his visit to Troy to see the graves of the Greek heroes Ajax and Achilles, the copying of the *Iliad* for his library, and his identification with Alexander the Great and Julius Caesar. Even in death Mehmed continued to insist on the succession. Eschewing the old imperial capital of Bursa, where earlier sultans had been buried, he chose to be buried in the new capital of Constantinople. Moreover, the ceremonial at his funeral has been shown to have been modeled on that of Constantine the Great, founder of Constantinople (Finkel 2007: 80, 82; Göçek 1993: 97–98).

The capture of Constantinople had obvious logistic and strategic point, giving the Ottomans control of the Bosphorus and establishing a critical link between their domains in Rumelia and Anatolia. But as all commentators have pointed out, there was a high symbolic value placed on it as well. Constantinople had long occupied a special place in both sacred and secular Islamic thought (Goffman 2002: 13). Legend held that the Prophet Muhammad himself had prophesied that "one day Constantinople will certainly be conquered. A good emir and a good army will be able to accomplish this." Late fifteenth-century Ottoman tradition linked the city with the grave of one of the Companions of the Prophet, Abu Ayyub, who had fallen during the first Muslim siege of Constantinople in 668 CE. After the Ottoman conquest of Constantinople, Abu Ayyub's tomb was "discovered" as being at Eyüp, just outside the city. Eyüp became a major site of Muslim pilgrimage, and a visit to it an essential element in the ceremony of accession of a new sultan. Thus was the city linked with the Prophet, and its capture placed within Muslim apocalyptic tradition. Constantinople was indeed the "Red Apple," as the Ottomans expressed it: their highest aspiration and the ultimate prize (Imber 2002: 116–18; Finkel 2007: 48, 54, 153). By conquering Constantinople the Ottomans showed themselves to be the direct heirs of Rome and Byzantium, together with the claims to world empire and universality that that implied. Here was a *translatio imperii* every bit as direct as that from the Roman to the Holy Roman Empire.

Even after the conquest of Egypt and Syria in 1516–17 by Selim I, and so the acquisition of the Muslim heartlands with their very different traditions, Ottoman sultans continued to see themselves in something of the same universal terms marked out by the Romans. Selim I called himself the "world conqueror," and his son Suleyman I ("the Magnificent"), with his further conquests—Hungary among them—continued in the same vein. In an inscription of 1538 affixed to the fortress of Bender on the Dniester, Suleyman proclaimed himself "God's slave and sultan of this world." In his person he linked Muslim and Christian lands and peoples, making of them, like Alexander, one *ecumene*, one great world community.

> I am Suleyman, in whose name the *hutbe* [public sermon] is read in Mecca and Medina. In Baghdad I am the shah, in Byzantine realms the Caesar, and in Egypt the sultan; who sends his fleets to the seas of Europe, the Maghrib and India. I am the sultan who took the crown and throne of Hungary and granted them to a humble slave. The voivoda Petru raised his head in revolt, but my horse's hoofs ground him into the dust, and I conquered the land of Moldavia. (in Inalcik [1973] 2000: 41; see also Inalcik 1993: 67–68; Şahin 2015)

Of the number of ways in which the Ottomans can be seen as the successors of the Romans, that relating to Christianity is especially striking. In a typically paradoxical but revealing way, Arnold Toynbee suggests that, appearances to the contrary notwithstanding, the Ottoman Empire at least in its early stages can be seen not as a rebuff and a reverse but as a direct continuation of the Roman mission of incubating, protecting, and promoting the Christian religion. In both West and East Christianity faced grave threats in the medieval centuries that it was able to overcome only with the aid of new empires. Western, Latin, Christianity experienced its "time of troubles" with the barbarian invasions and the fall of the Roman Empire in the West, from which it was rescued by the Holy Roman Empire. The Ottoman Empire did the same for Greek Orthodox Christianity, as embodied in the Byzantine or Eastern Roman Empire. The Byzantine Empire experienced its "time of troubles" from the eleventh century onward, with its defeat by the Seljuks in 1071, and, most calamitously, with the capture and sack of Constantinople by Latin troops in 1204 and the subsequent establishment of a Latin Kingdom there. It was from this weakness and degradation that the Ottomans rescued Greek Orthodoxy. "The historical function of the Ottoman empire-builders," says Toynbee, "was to bring the Orthodox Christian Society's 'Time of Troubles' to a close by uniting the whole of the main body of Orthodox Christendom politically into one universal state under an alien Pax Ottomanica" (Toynbee 1962–63, 1:370; see also 3:26–27; and cf. Shaw 1976: 59).

"Alien," as we have seen, may be too strong a word, and Toynbee indeed reads that backward from later Ottoman history, rather than in terms of what the early Ottoman rulers intended, which was—as Toynbee himself expresses it—fundamentally a reconstitution of the now-decrepit Byzantine Empire. Like many other scholars, Toynbee believes that with the rise of Safavid Iran and the challenge of Shiite Islam in the East, the Ottoman Empire was forced to adapt itself to a new environment, and to change its character. We shall see later what that argument involves, and how far it holds up. But what is illuminating about Toynbee's approach is that he sees the Ottoman Empire in its formative years as being as much a regenerator of the Byzantine Empire as its executioner. For large parts of the Orthodox Christian world it brought peace and a measure of security that had been lacking for centuries. The Orthodox Church and clergy were confirmed in their authority and given an established place within the Ottoman administration.[6] The Orthodox community was allowed to practice its religion under the supervision of its own religious officers. The Latin powers were kept at bay by Ottoman supremacy in the Balkans and by its control of large parts of the Mediterranean.

The Orthodox Church indeed developed at the highest level of the hierarchy the doctrine that the establishment of the Ottoman Empire was part of the divine dispensation, created to defend the integrity of Orthodox Christianity. This view stressed the continuity of empire, the Byzantines giving way to the Ottomans, to whom had now, as with Rome of old, fallen the task of protecting and promoting the true faith. The sultan was seen as "the direct inheritor of the last Christian *Basileus* of the Romans, and so of Constantine himself" (Nicol 1967: 334). As late as the eighteenth century the doctrine was still being enunciated by the Orthodox hierarchy, as in the *Paternal Exhortation* of the patriarch of Jerusalem in 1798: "Behold how our merciful and omniscient Lord has managed to preserve the integrity of our holy Orthodox faith and to save (us) all; he brought forth out of nothing the powerful Empire of the Ottomans, which he set up in the place of the Empire of the Romaioi, which had begun in some ways to deviate from the path of the Orthodox faith; and he raised this Empire of the Ottomans above every other in order to prove beyond doubt that it came into being by the will of God" (in Nicol 1967: 334; cf. Clogg 1982: 191). Orthodoxy and the Ottomans were reconciled; the latter were not the barbaric foes of the Christian religion but its custodian. It is telling that until the nineteenth century the gravest internal threats to the Ottoman state came not from its Christian communities but from movements of radicals and rebels among its Muslim subjects.[7]

Ottomans and Turks

The Ottomans were not "Turks," and the Ottoman Empire was not the "Turkish Empire." This much is agreed upon by practically every qualified commentator. There are differences of view as to how far Turks constituted the core of the empire, and how much Turkish language and culture may have been the dominating influences within it. But even here it is clear that whatever we may mean by "Turkish" in the context of the Ottoman Empire has a very different significance from its meaning in the new Turkish state created by Mustafa Kemal Atatürk.

The situation is complicated by the fact that Westerners from very earliest times—since the first arrival of the Turks in Anatolia in the eleventh century, in fact—were accustomed to calling the Ottomans Turks, and to referring to their empire as a Turkish empire (Lewis 1968: 1). In addition Turkish nationalists, from the late nineteenth century onward, were only too keen to stress the essentially Turkish character of the empire and to portray other groups as alien minorities that were a persistent threat to its Turkishness. This was so even though, after the declaration of the Turkish Republic in 1923, Mustafa Kemal wished to obliterate the Ottoman inheritance as far as possible and sought to emphasize the novelty and modernity of the new, Western-style, republic. Turkish scholars who studied the Ottoman period, such as Fuad Köprülü, nevertheless took pride in the fact that the great Ottoman Empire had been as they saw it an essentially Turkish creation, an expression of Turkish genius for civilization and evidence of Turkish skill in state building. "The Ottoman state," averred Köprülü ([1935] 1992: 87), "was founded exclusively by Turks in the fourteenth century"—a view that Colin Imber calls "nonsense" (2002: xiv).

The Ottoman dynasty did indeed claim descent from the Turkic Oguz clan, and in the early years of rivalry with the other principalities in Anatolia of Central Asian origins it made a point of stressing its Turkic roots. But with the extirpation of those rival principalities, and above all with the capture of Constantinople and the claim to the Roman-Byzantine inheritance, references to the Turkic identity of the empire rapidly dropped off. By the sixteenth century "Turk" was more a term of abuse than one of approbation. "In the Imperial society of the Ottomans," says Bernard Lewis, "the ethnic term Turk was little used, and then chiefly in a rather derogatory sense, to designate the Turcoman nomads or, later, the ignorant and uncouth Turkish-speaking peasants of the Anatolian villages. To apply it to an Ottoman gentleman of Constantinople would have been an insult" (Lewis 1968: 1–2; see also 332–33).[8]

To be a "Turk" or "Turkish" was, to the educated inhabitants of the empire, to be "ignorant," "witless," "senseless," "stupid," or "dishonest." Turks were called "country bumpkins" and "mischief-makers"; they could also be deviants and heretics, such as those who rallied to the Safavid Shah Ismail in the sixteenth century, or those who rebelled against the central government in the seventeenth century (Imber 2002: 3; Finkel 2007: 548). In the face of this history of disparagement and ridicule it is not surprising that the Turkish nationalist Ziya Gökalp should exclaim that "the poor Turks inherited from the Ottoman Empire nothing but a broken sword and an old-fashioned plow" (quoted Armstrong 1976 : 397). This is by no means the only case, as we shall see, when the ostensible "imperial people"—in this case the Turks—feel that they got a raw deal out of "their" empire.

Not only were Ottomans not Turks; "Turk" and "Turkish" were themselves vague and shifting designations. There was no sense of nationhood among the backwoods peasants of Anatolia who were usually referred to as Turks. Their affiliations were to their village or clan, or to the wider community of Islam. They made up a majority of the population of Anatolia, but about one-third of that population was non-Muslim, and of the Muslims not all were ethnic Turks. Moreover, there were many ethnic Turks in other parts of the empire, especially in the Balkan provinces (Kafadar 1995: 4; Lieven 2001: 133). Even ethnicity seems too strong and specific a term to define the Turks: "'Turk,'" says Amira Bennison, "was a socio-linguistic not ethnic distinction which included members from the Balkans, Anatolia, the Arab lands and renegades from European societies" (Bennison 2002: 90).

When Turkish nationalists later tried to make the case for the "imagined community" of the Turkish nation, they were—as with many other nineteenth-century nationalists elsewhere—faced with formidable obstacles of history, geography, and culture. In effect they were forcing upon the region a designation as Turkey, and upon the people an identity as Turkish, that reflected European usage—*Turkiye*, the Turkish term, was clearly of European origin—but which ran counter to the understandings of most peoples in the empire.[9] "The introduction and propagation of this idea in Turkey," says Bernard Lewis, "and its eventual acceptance by the Turkish people as expressing the nature of their corporate identity and statehood, has been one of the major revolutions of modern times, involving a radical and violent break with the social, cultural, and political traditions of the past" (Lewis 1968: 1).

If the Turks were not a clearly delineated national or ethnic group, still less, of course, were the "Ottomans." The Ottomans or Osmanli were, originally and in a sense always, simply "those who follow Osman," the founder of the dynasty. They came to constitute the ruling class of the Ottoman Empire, but they always remained the sultan's creations and his servants. "No Ottoman people ever existed," says Fuad Köprülü; "according to the old annalists, the word 'Ottoman', which was not an ethnic but simply a political term, always had the meaning of 'a dominant or administrative class which was in the service of the state and earned its living from the state budget'" ([1935] 1992: 5; cf. Goffman 2002: 65; Finkel 2007: 74). Drawn from all over the empire, largely composed in the earlier centuries of ex-Christians recruited through the youth levy (the *devshirme*), the Ottomans were "a cosmopolitan ruling class distinguished by the imprint of Ottoman court culture" (Findley 2005: 230; see also Goffman and Stroop 2004: 141). They included—"like all imperial ruling classes"—"individuals from an astonishing array of different backgrounds—Albanian, French, Venetian, Arab, Jewish and Circassian" (Mazower 2005: 281; cf. Goffman 2002: 51). Even the language of the Ottomans—Ottoman Turkish—was not the Turkish-Persian synthesis of most Central Asian Turks but an amalgam of Turkish, Arabic, and Persian, embellished with Greek, Slavic, and Italian additions—a truly cosmopolitan creation, and one largely inaccessible to the mass of Turkish peasants (Findley 2005: 156; Hanioglu 2008: 34–35). It was by engaging in and identifying with Ottoman culture that one showed oneself a member of the Ottoman elite; hence any educated and cultivated denizen of the empire would think of and call himself an Osmanli. "Only when the last European provinces were almost lost, and the loss of the Arab provinces was well within sight, did political leaders in Istanbul begin to think and to speak of themselves as Turks" (Seton-Watson 1964: 10).

"The Ottoman ruling class eventually emerged as a combination of Muslims (some by conversion) who spoke Turkish (though not necessarily as a native tongue) affiliated (some voluntarily and some involuntarily) with the dynastic state under the rule of the House of Osman" (Kafadar 1995: 4). The Ottoman Empire, perhaps more than any other of the European empires, was a dynastic, multinational, empire, ruling over a variety of peoples. As Colin Imber puts it, "the Ottoman Empire was not ... exclusively Islamic; nor was it exclusively Turkish. Rather, it was a dynastic Empire in which the only loyalty demanded of all its multifarious inhabitants was allegiance to the sultan. ... It was in the end the person of the sultan and not religious, ethnic or other identities that held the Empire together" (Imber 2002: 3; cf. Rodrigue 1995: 84; Bayly 2004: 220). Ottoman theory stressed that all subjects and lands within the realm belonged to the sultan, and that all rights stemmed from his will. Unlike the European nobility, the Ottoman ruling class enjoyed no hereditary rights. It was a purely functional ruling class, defined not by ethnicity, language, or religion, but by its role in the running of the state (Sugar [1977] 1993: 273). When the Ottomans acquired a territory, they abolished, at least in principle, all local and inherited rights and privileges (though, as we have seen, in the early years they were careful to respect these rights in the case of their Balkan subjects). At the death of the reigning sultan all commissions and rights became invalid and had to be reconfirmed by his successor. Louis XIV famously claimed that "l'état, c'est moi"; but given the strength and customary rights of the French aristocracy, this was a pale reflection of the power of the Ottoman sultan. For the Ottomans, as Halil Inalcik says, "there was real meaning in the common expression, 'the Sultan was the state itself'" (Inalcik 1954: 113).

The dynastic principle undergirded the social structure of the empire. There was only one basic division running throughout Ottoman society: that between the ruling class, the *'askeri*, who were exempted from paying taxes, and the ruled, the *re 'aya*, the subject and tax-paying class—peasants, craftsmen, traders, whether Muslim or non-Muslim. As befitted a conquest society, *'askeri* referred originally to the military leaders, but it came to include all public servants— palace officials, provincial administrators, religious officials, *medrese* teachers and scholars—and the members of their households. "Ottomans" were in effect the whole educated and cultured stratum of society. This was not a hereditary aristocracy on the European model but a service class created by the sultan and always dependent on his will. The class structure of the empire therefore flowed directly from the political principle of sultanic rule. This can be called "oriental despotism," if we wish, so long as we remember that no Middle Eastern ruler ever thought that his absolute power dispensed him from the primary obligation to rule according to the principle of justice, *'adâlet*—a charge that related especially to the subject class, his "flock," the *re 'aya*.[10]

"Turks" and "Ottomans" therefore represented entirely different facets of imperial society. Turks, if we choose to designate them as an ethnic group, were only one element among many, and certainly not the *Staatsvolk*, the "state-bearing" people. The people who ran the empire, the people who named it, were not an ethnic group, not a "people" in the modern sense, but an educated elite closer to the mandarins of China than to a Western ruling class. Like all imperial ruling classes, the Ottomans had a mission, primarily to protect all Muslims and to advance the cause of Islam in the world. But, less than in any of the other empires was this mission identified with a particular people and their peculiar culture. Unlike, say, the English in their empire, or the Russians in theirs, the Ottomans did not have a culture and a tradition that could be derived from the history of a particular ethnic group (complex as that was even in those clearer cases). The Ottomans were a class that was made exclusively by empire, and that evolved along with it, changing as it changed. Starting as the followers of Osman—and already in the earliest stages, as we have seen, including non-Turks and non-Muslims—it developed, as the empire developed, into a wide-ranging cosmopolitan formation that included individuals from a host of ethnicities and nationalities: Turkic, Arabic, Persian, Jewish, Armenian, European. That ethnic mix, as we shall see, has also largely been true of most imperial ruling classes, noticeably the Habsburg, which probably comes closest to the Ottomans of all the European empires in this regard. But the Ottomans, as it were, excelled all of these in its nonspecificity, its fundamental lack of an ethnic core. When therefore in the nineteenth century Turkish nationalists claimed the Ottoman mantle, and attempted to assert themselves as the natural successors to the Ottomans, they were running right against the grain of Ottoman tradition. Turkish nationalism was an explosive force, whose outcome could only be the dissolution of the empire itself— though it might need other elements to aid it in this.

Muslims and Non-Muslims

The Ottoman Empire, like the empires of the Safavids and the Mughals, was a Muslim empire.[11] Islam was throughout its history a key part of its identity. But the extent to which it stressed its Muslim character varied, depending on circumstances. Moreover, like the Mughals with their Hindu, Jain, Buddhist, and Christian subjects, it was always aware that a large number of its subjects were not Muslim. This fact was mirrored centrally in its institutions and its practices.

Michael Walzer has argued that multinational empires are forced by their very nature to pursue policies of toleration, which they then enforce on the population. "Groups have no choice but to co-exist with one another, for their interactions are governed by imperial bureaucrats in accordance with an imperial code" (Walzer 1997: 14). Toleration implies both sufferance and acceptance, an awareness both of difference—often seen as repugnant—and of the need nevertheless to allow the differences. Sometimes that acceptance can be in a spirit of celebration, as seeing in the differences a source of strength and vitality. Both these attitudes can be found for most of Ottoman history, until late in the nineteenth century the calls for unity and homogeneity began to drown out the voices on behalf of diversity.

In a powerful passage that opens their highly regarded edited volumes on the plural nature of Ottoman society, Benjamin Braude and Bernard Lewis write:

> For nearly half a millennium the Ottomans ruled an empire as diverse as any in history. Remarkably, this polyethnic and multireligious society worked. Muslims, Christians, and Jews worshipped and studied side by side, enriching their distinct cultures. The legal traditions and practices of each community . . . were respected and enforced through the empire. Scores of languages and literatures employing a bewildering variety of scripts flourished. Opportunities for advancement and prosperity were open in varying degrees to all the empire's subjects. During their heyday the Ottomans created a society which allowed a great deal of communal autonomy while maintaining a fiscally sound and militarily strong central government. (Braude and Lewis 1982b: 1)

Braude and Lewis are at pains to stress that, just as they are concerned to oppose the stereotype of Islam and Muslims as "bigoted, intolerant and oppressive," so they are equally opposed to the myth of "an interfaith, interracial utopia in which Muslims, Christians, and Jews worked together in equality and harmony in a golden age of free intellectual endeavor." Ottoman society, they insist, was a plural society in the strict meaning of that term: that is—quoting J. S. Furnivall's well-known account—the various peoples form "'a medley, for they mix, but do not combine. Each group holds by its own religion, its own culture and language, its own ideas and ways. As individuals they meet, but only in the market place, in buying and selling. There is a plural society, with different sections of the community, living side by side, but separately within the same political unit. Even in the economic sphere there is a division of labor along racial lines.'"[12]

Like all Muslim states the Ottomans discriminated against non-Muslims—such was the requirement of Islamic Holy Law, the *Sharia*—but did not, on the whole, persecute them. Again, this followed the injunction in the Quran that people should not be forced to change their religion. The route to preferment in the Ottoman Empire was conversion to Islam, and this was made relatively easy, whether through the *devshirme* system or in other ways. But the Ottomans did not go in for forced conversion or even much for peaceful proselytization. Non-Muslims were sometimes humiliated; there were various formal restrictions on such things as dress, the type of beasts they might ride—saddled horses were forbidden—and the size and number of places of worship. As in all Muslim societies, nonbelievers were taxed at a higher rate than Muslims. There were sporadic efforts to enforce these rules, but with the exception of the fiscal penalty they seem to have been rarely applied with much severity (Braude and Lewis 1982b: 5–6; Bosworth 1982: 46–48; Finkel 2007: 213; Barkey 2008: 121, 151). For much of the history of the Ottoman Empire, at least down to the latter part of the nineteenth century, Muslims and non-Muslims do indeed seem to have coexisted pluralistically, side by side. We do not have to exaggerate or idealize this in recognizing the real achievement of the Ottoman Empire in this respect, by comparison with the practices of most nation-states and even of other contemporary empires.[13]

Christians and Jews in the Ottoman Empire, as in other Muslim empires, were undoubtedly second-class citizens, consistent with their status as *dhimmis* (Turkish *zimmis*), protected "people of the Book" (*ahl al-kitab*) whose chief failing was that they refused to accept the true faith of Islam (Bosworth 1982: 41; Sugar [1977] 1993: 5; Karpat 1982: 149; Shaw 1991: 10). They were required to pay a special poll tax (*jizya/cizye*) and to perform certain services for Muslims, such as giving Muslim travelers hospitality. But in return for this, their lives and property were protected, and they were free to work and worship as they liked, under the supervision of their own religious leaders. Here we come to the famous *millet* system, perhaps the best-known and most acclaimed of the Ottoman institutions, and commonly viewed as the cornerstone of its policies of toleration.

It has been shown that there are many myths—both in the West and, through Western influence, in contemporary Ottoman historiography—concerning the *millet*. A *millet* was simply "a religiously defined people," and in fact before the nineteenth century the term was more often used to describe the community of Muslims than—as it has generally come to be used—the various communities of non-Muslims, Greeks, Armenians, and Jews (Braude 1982; cf. Lewis 1968: 335). Moreover, there was never a fully developed, unchanging, *millet* "system" but rather "a set of arrangements, largely local, with considerable variation over time and place" (Braude 1982: 74; cf. Goffman 1994: 153–54). Accepting these scholarly qualifications, there seems neverthe-less general agreement that the Ottomans did follow older Muslim practices in allowing each major non-Muslim religious community a remarkable degree of autonomy and control over its internal affairs, under the direction of leaders chosen according to their own rules. In the cases of the Greek Orthodox and the Armenian Christians this meant the authority of their respective Patriarch-ates in Istanbul; in the case of the Jews the leadership of locally chosen rab-bis.[14] *Millets*, it needs to be noted, were strictly religious, not ethnic, divisions; the "Greek" *millet, millet-i Rum*, for instance, included many different ethnic groups—not just Greeks, but Bulgarians, Serbians, Albanians, Romanians, even Arabs of the Orthodox faith (Clogg 1982: 185; Karpat 1982: 146). Eventu-ally that ethnic diversity, and the attempts by some *millet* leaders to impose an ethnic character on the *millet*—such as Greek attempts in the eighteenth century to "Hellenize" the Greek *millet*—were to lead to the breakup of the system (Karpat 1982; Sugar [1977] 1993: 252–54). But more or less until the end of the empire the *millet* system remained the principal and on the whole remarkably successful way of acknowledging and managing the enormous ethnic and cultural diversity of the Ottoman Empire.

But it would be wrong to imagine that the place of non-Muslims in the empire was simply to pursue their own lives within the confines of the *millet*. The institution of the *millet* was indeed indispensable for affording protec-tion, and for enabling common negotiations with the Ottoman authorities on a host of matters, from taxation policies to the resolution of disputes with local officials. But *millets* were not self-contained, hermetically sealed enti-ties. There was considerable intercommunal cooperation, especially in com-mercial undertakings, in which rivalries might as readily cut across *millets* as between them (Goffman 1994: 146–50). Greeks, Armenians, and Jews also played important roles in the wider life of the empire, sometimes achieving such prominence as to make them subject to the envy and hostility of their Muslim fellow subjects. In trade and finance, and in certain crafts, the non-Muslim minorities brought important and much-needed skills and expertise. Their value was enhanced by their contact and familiarity with foreigners, especially Europeans, with whom they interacted as brokers and transla-tors on behalf of the Ottomans (Armstrong 1976: 400; Goffman 2002: 16–18, 85–91). The Istanbul districts of Galata and Pera, on the northern side of the Golden Horn, were dominated by non-Muslims, especially Greeks; the fact that many foreign traders and consuls—Venetian, Genoese, French, English,

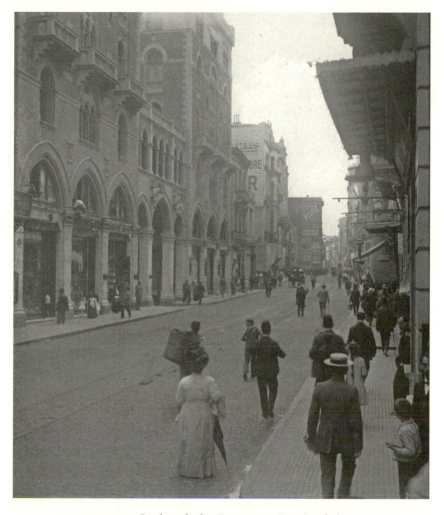

FIGURE 3.2. Greeks and other Europeans in Pera, Istanbul, 1912.
Pera was the Ottomans' "window on the West." Library of Congress.

Dutch—also had their residences here accentuated its "European" character and its role as an Ottoman window on the world (Mantran 1982: 129; Goffman 2002: 172–73, 185).

Jews were especially welcomed in the empire. They came in large numbers following their expulsion from the Iberian peninsula at the end of the fifteenth century; but they also came from Italy and Central Europe.[15] Jews flourished in such cities as Bursa and Edirne, which they helped to turn into imperial capitals; after the conquest of Constantinople they were brought in large numbers to the city to help in its repopulation and rebuilding (Olson 1979: 76; Shaw 1991: 26–29). In Salonica, another major Jewish center, they became principal suppliers to the Ottomans of woolen goods for the army, as well as wheat, salt, silver, and other commodities. Notably Jews were bankers and money changers, and were also heavily involved with the collection of customs dues—all activities that involved close relations with foreign merchants and ship captains. A famous figure of this kind was the wealthy and influential Don Joseph Nasi, banker, adviser, and tax farmer, who was elevated by Selim II to be duke of Naxos and the Cyclades (Shaw 1991: 88–89).[16] The Jews became the intermediaries par excellence between the Ottomans and the outside world. Even during times of war, as for instance that between the Venetians and the Ottomans in 1645–69, Jews were able to use their foreign contacts to allow trade to continue between the warring countries (Mantran 1982: 133; Goffman 1994: 147, 2002: 179–82; Mazower 2005: 52–55).

Jews, like other non-Muslims, had their difficulties and disabilities in the Ottoman Empire. But later Jewish memories of the Ottoman period as a "golden age" were not entirely fanciful. Stanford Shaw claims that, with between 100,000 and 250,000 people, "the Ottoman Jewish community [was] not only the largest but also the most prosperous in the world" in the sixteenth and seventeenth centuries; and, though Jewish fortunes suffered some decline in the eighteenth century, there was a strong revival in the nineteenth and twentieth centuries (Shaw 1991: 36, 147ff.; see also Olson 1979: 77–78). Certainly to the end Jews remained the most loyal of the Ottomans' non-Muslim subjects (Sugar [1977] 1993: 48; Dumont 1982: 221–22; Mazower 2005: 10; Gilbert 2010). In the light of the fate of the Jews in Europe in the twentieth century it is not difficult to understand why the memory of a golden age should only become more vivid and nostalgic with the passing of time.

Greeks, as former rulers of Byzantium and possessed of valued skills and experience, occupied the highest place among non-Muslims in the Ottoman Empire. Their patriarch was given special privileges by the sultans and confirmed in his position as the supreme authority in both civil and ecclesiastical matters over all Orthodox Christians, Greek and non-Greek, in the empire—giving the Orthodox Church greater authority than it had enjoyed under the Byzantines (Sugar [1977] 1993: 45–47; Clogg 1982: 186–87; Kitsikis 1994: 69). We should remember, too, that before the conquest of the Arab lands in the sixteenth century, the Orthodox Christian population—dominated and ruled by Greeks—was the majority population in the empire, outnumbering Muslims. Thus during one of the most important periods in the growth and

FIGURE 3.3. Jews in Salonica, early twentieth century. Jews were among the most loyal subjects of the Ottoman Empire. NGS Image Collection/The Art Archive at Art Resource, NY.

development of the empire, the Ottoman Empire could, without too much exaggeration, be called "Greek" as much as "Turkish" (Kitsikis 1994).

Economically Greeks probably fared the best of all groups in the empire. They dominated navigation, as shipowners and ship suppliers. Being dispersed throughout the empire, they were also able to play an important role in internal trade, linking distant provinces and acting as agents for foreign merchants in the provinces. They were also well represented in banking, railways, and manufacturing. But just as important were their administrative and diplomatic skills. Greeks were appointed as ambassadors and diplomats, and were well placed in other spheres of the Ottoman administration concerned with foreign affairs (Mantran 1982: 130; Clogg 1982: 196).

In the eighteenth century, following the Ottoman repulse at the second siege of Vienna in 1683, Greek influence in the empire actually increased. The Ottomans now found themselves engaged in a more or less continuous round of diplomacy and treaty negotiations with Western powers. They were more than ever conscious of the need to conciliate their Christian subjects, especially following the Treaty of Küçük Kaynarca (1774), which Russia controversially interpreted as giving it the right to intervene on behalf of all Orthodox Christians in the Ottoman Empire (Finkel 2007: 378). There was hence an intensified requirement for intermediaries with international connections and administrative expertise, and Greeks were on hand to supply both in rich measure.

Especially important in this regard were the Phanariot Greeks, Greeks from the Phanar quarter of Istanbul (so-called because of the Phanar, "lighthouse," in the northwest corner of the city). This community, within which the Greek Patriarchate was situated, and among whom many of the wealthiest merchants were based, had quickly established itself as the religious and commercial heart of the Greek population in the wake of the Ottoman conquests. In the new international climate of the eighteenth century, the accomplishments acquired in these spheres made the Phanariots invaluable to the Ottomans in their dealings with the West and in the administration of some of their strategically sensitive Christian communities. From the late seventeenth century to the early nineteenth, Phanariot Greeks monopolized the two new positions of dragoman of the Sublime Porte and dragoman of the fleet. The modest meaning of dragoman ("interpreter") disguised the fact that these were in fact two of the most important positions in the Ottoman administration, being equivalent in effect to secretary of state for foreign affairs and secretary of state for the navy. In addition from 1711, again up to the early nineteenth century, Phanariots replaced local Romanian princes as *hospodars*—governors—of the autonomous Danubian principalities of Wallachia and Moldavia. Thus was acknowledged the new political and strategic importance of these regions as marches of the Ottoman Empire over against both the Habsburgs and the Romanovs (Toynbee 1962–63, 2:223–25; Lewis 1968: 62, 87; Sugar [1977] 1993: 128).

So important do the Phanariots become in the eighteenth-century empire that many have seen this as an incipient Greek *reconquista* of their old territory, or at least a bid to achieve parity with the dominant Muslims. It is known that, after the crushing defeat of the Ottomans by the Russians in the Russo-Turkish War of 1768–74, Catherine the Great played with the idea of reestablishing the Byzantine Empire under Phanariot management (though perhaps with a Romanov on the throne). When in 1821, from his base in southern Russia, the Phanariot prince Alexander Ypsilantis crossed the Prut and invaded Moldavia—an event usually seen as the opening act of the "Greek War of Independence"—he too seems to have aspired to re-create the Byzantine Empire under Greek rule, rather than to establish a separate Greek state (Toynbee 1962–63, 2:225, 7a:30; Armstrong 1976: 401; Finkel 2007: 430; Findley 2010: 26).

The Phanariots hoped for peaceful penetration of the Ottoman Empire, a reconquest by stealth, not violence. Ypsilantis's escapade, and even more the achievement of Greek independence in 1830, at a stroke dashed these hopes. From being among the most favored, Greeks were suddenly the most distrusted group in the empire, suspected of plotting its dismemberment. Despite his vigorous denunciation of both Ypsilantis and the rising in the Peloponnese, the Greek patriarch Gregory V was unceremoniously hanged in 1821 at the gate of the Patriarchate in Istanbul. At the same time two successive Greek grand dragomans were executed, and the post passed out of Greek hands forever (Lewis 1968: 87; Clogg 1982: 192–93; Finkel 2007: 429–30).

Nevertheless, this sharp reversal of fortune was not the end of the story of Greek success in the Ottoman Empire. The creation of an independent Greek state did not by any means square with the aspirations and desires of all Greeks, least of all the Greek Orthodox Patriarchate and the Phanariot elites. The new state was too poor and undeveloped to compete with the economic opportunities offered by the Ottoman Empire. Greeks from the new state poured into the empire in increasing numbers shortly after independence and throughout the second half of the nineteenth century. Greeks within the empire, moreover, outperformed Turks demographically. By the 1860s the town of Izmir in western Anatolia had a majority Greek population, replacing the Muslim majority of the previous generation. The same was true of several other towns in the region. In the 1890s a quarter of the population of Istanbul was Greek. Greeks prospered, as in the past, in commerce, manufacturing, banking, shipping, and the professions. They even continued to be employed by the Ottoman state in the conduct of foreign affairs. Nearly 30 percent of all Foreign Ministry officials in the later nineteenth century were Greek—a proportion far outstripping their numbers in the total Ottoman population—and a Greek, Alexander Karatheodori Efendi, became deputy foreign minister (Quataert 2000: 81). Once more, as in the eighteenth century, one began to hear talk among Greeks both in the empire and beyond of the steady but sure "Hellenization" of the Ottoman Empire. "By the second half of the nineteenth century," writes Richard Clogg, "the Greeks had largely regained the economic, and to a somewhat lesser degree, the political influence in the affairs of the Ottoman Empire which they had enjoyed prior to 1821" (Clogg 1982: 196; see also Zürcher 1997: 50; Lieven 2001: 153).

As with the Armenians, the Greeks in the empire were to be the casualties of the growth of Turkish—and Greek—nationalism, and the machinations of all parties during the First World War.[17] But, as Clogg says, "what is most surprising is that the *Millet-i-Rum* should have survived for so long after the creation of an independent Greek state" (Clogg 1982: 200). It is a testimony to the key role of the Greeks in the Ottoman Empire throughout its history, and to the fact that Greeks at all levels found a place for themselves in the empire even after the existence of a separate Greek state. When, in the Greek-Turkish population exchange of 1923, over a million Greeks were expelled from the new state of Turkey—and half a million Turks were forced out of Greece—it ended over five hundred years of a remarkable experiment in cohabitation (Zürcher 1997: 171; Clark 2006).

Some general remarks, finally, on the two institutions most commonly associated with Ottoman treatment of the empire's non-Muslim subjects: the *devshirme* and the *millet* system. The *devshirme* flourished for over two hundred years, from the late fourteenth to the mid-seventeenth century, its abolition being traditionally attributed to Ahmed II (1691–95). Scholars estimate that something of the order of 200,000 Christian youth, mostly Slavs from the Balkans, were taken during the peak period of the levy, in the fifteenth and sixteenth centuries (Sugar [1977] 1993: 56; Itzkowitz 1980: 49–54; Braude and Lewis 1982b: 11–12; Imber 2002: 137).

For many Europeans, the *devshirme* was the epitome of Ottoman outlandishness and barbarism, and many piteous stories circulated of Christian boys being ripped from the arms of their weeping mothers (Yapp 1992: 137). The degree of personal hardship and suffering has been much debated. But most scholars accept that many Christian families were glad to have their sons "lifted out of provincial, impoverished, and oppressed surroundings into the ruling class of arguably the most powerful and refined polity in the world" (Goffman 2002: 68).[18] We also have the telling example of the Bosnian Muslims, who, as Muslims, were exempted from the *devshirme*, but as a group that had early converted to Islam were able successfully to request as a reward from the sultan that they should be subject to the *devshirme*—clearly for them a prize rather than a punishment (Imber 2002: 136–37). Moreover, in several cases, high-ranking Ottoman officials of Christian birth maintained connections with their families and regions of origin and were able to help them in various ways. One of the best-known examples of this is the story of the two Serbian brothers, one of whom, Mehmed Sokullu, rose through the *devshirme* to become grand vizier, the other—Makarius—who with his brother's help

FIGURE 3.4. *Devshirme* for Sultan Suleyman. The *devshirme* was the levy
of Christian boys, mostly from the Balkans, for eventual service in the
Ottoman bureaucracy and military. From Ali Amir Beg, *Suleymanname*
(1558). Topkapi Palace Museum, Istanbul, Turkey/Bridgeman Images.

became head of the Serbian Orthodox Church. The two brothers continued to correspond in Serbian. In such a way, through a system of personal ties and favors, the *devshirme* may have helped to bind Christian provinces to the Islamic Ottoman state (Sugar [1977] 1993: 58; Goffman 2002: 68; Barkey 2008: 124).

So far as the *millet* system is concerned, the important thing is not to conceive it in terms of "majority-minority" relations, nor to think of it as expressing modern ideas of pluralism and "multiculturalism" (Rodrigue 1995). Both of these concepts echo post-Enlightenment Western political thought, and ultimately all of them depend upon certain assumptions of sameness and universality, usually linked to some idea of natural or human rights.

The Ottomans did not accept or aspire to sameness, nor did they embrace any idea of natural rights. They postulated and respected difference and had no desire to bring about homogeneity. Hence, though they were undoubtedly convinced of the truth and superiority of Islam, there was little attempt to impose it on non-Muslims. The *millet* system in that sense breached the principle of universality even in relation to the dominant religion of Islam, since it accepted the persistence of the differences embodied in the separate *millets*. But nor, at the same time, did the Ottomans embrace equality in the modern sense. "Islam was ultimately the hegemonic system.... Therefore, we can perhaps say that difference was recognized but not on the basis of equality. This was very much a hierarchical difference. This was not an issue of pluralism, rather it was about plurality. In other words, difference was one of the organizing principles of society and sustained a certain inequality. But it was not linked to the universalizing project of homogenizing differences and hence engendering intolerance" (Rodrigue 1995: 90).

It followed that nationalism of any group, including their own, was anathema to the Ottomans, since nationalism's fundamental drive is to eradicate difference and bring about uniformity among all those considered to belong to the same nation. This too breached the principle of the *millet* system, which was not based on ethnicity or nationality but strictly on religion. It would thus be a fundamental error to see the *millets* as the "building blocks" for the later development of nationalism within the empire. The rise of nationalism heralded the death of the *millet* system as much as it did the death of the empire that had established and sustained it. This is particularly clear in the case of the "Greek" *millet*, which came under increasing strain with the rise of the nationalism of Serbs, Bulgarians, Romanians, and other Orthodox members of the *millet*. *Millets* expressed in the most direct way the Ottoman Empire's fundamental commitment to heterogeneity, as a principle both of imperial rule and of the Ottoman's understanding of the religion of Islam.

With the decline of the *devshirme* in the seventeenth century, and the weakening of the *millet* system in the nineteenth century, we have what many observers at the time and since have seen as the signs of Ottoman decline and imminent dissolution. We need to turn therefore to the later development of the empire, beyond its "classical" period, and ask what that might mean for questions of its identity and purpose. Did the Ottoman Empire fundamentally change direction? Was that the harbinger of its eventual downfall? Was the death of empire self-inflicted or the result of external forces over which the Ottomans had little control?

Decline or Change? The Transformation of the Empire

The reassessment of the "classical" period—from the fourteenth to the seventeenth century—of the Ottoman Empire has not so far, in any commanding synthesis, extended to the later history of the empire, down to its dissolution after the First World War. For the earlier period we have the wide-ranging works of Cemal Kafadar, Heath Lowry, Colin Imber, Daniel Goffman, Suraiya Faroqhi, and several others, building on the work of Halil Inalcik and other earlier Ottoman scholars. These have refined the earlier assumptions of the *gazi* character of the early Ottoman state, stressing instead its composite and hybrid character, its openness to the culture and institutions of the lands it conquered, its willingness to allow its non-Muslim subjects to pursue their own ways, its eagerness to employ them fully in its economic, commercial, and diplomatic life, and its active engagement with the European powers it encountered, as rivals and allies. The Ottoman Empire in this perspective belongs fully to the early modern world of Europe, whatever its other face to the East.

For the later period there are an increasing number of excellent contributions that challenge received assumptions, and we shall be drawing upon them in the following discussion. What we do not have, however, is a body of synthetic work, comparable to that for the classical period, which shows the basic form and character of the empire in its last three centuries. On the contrary, a good deal of even very recent writing continues to insist that, however much we need to change the picture for the earlier time, for the later period the older accounts remain essentially accurate.

The central burden of these accounts is that, sometime in the seventeenth century, perhaps even earlier, the Ottoman Empire experienced a fundamental reorientation of direction, one which led it along a quite different path from that which it had earlier been following. More consequentially, that change of direction is held by many—by no means all—to have contained the seeds of Ottoman decline, so much so that the later history of the empire is mainly seen as an increasingly desperate effort to hold together the empire and to prevent it from being overwhelmed by its more powerful rivals. In this perspective what we see in the last three centuries of the empire is a relentless, slow-motion decline, punctuated by spirited but in the end unavailing efforts to reform the empire and stem the decline.

There are a number of strands in this account. The first, and in many ways the most important, is what is seen as the profound and long-lasting impact of the defeat of the Mamluks by Selim I in 1516–17, and the consequent acquisition of the Arab lands of Egypt, Syria, and the Hijaz. In 1534, under Suleyman I, also came the conquest of Iraq. At virtually a stroke, the Ottoman Empire now included the vibrant Muslim cities of Cairo, Damascus, and Baghdad, together with the holy cities of Mecca and Medina. From ruling an empire in which Muslims were a minority the Ottomans had now come to rule an empire in which Muslims were a clear majority. They were heirs to the great Islamic cultures and traditions of the Umayyads, Abbasids, and Fatimids. Scholars, bureaucrats, and traders from the Arab lands made their way to Istanbul and the other great Ottoman cities, such as Bursa and Edirne. The Ottomans were now the guardians of the Holy Places and protectors of the pilgrim routes to Mecca and Medina. From the time of Suleyman I (1520–66) onward, Ottoman sultans also claimed the title of caliph, making them the spiritual heads of the entire Islamic world (Inalcik 1993: 67–69; Imber 2002: 126).

Not surprisingly, many scholars see in these developments a far-reaching "Islamization" of the empire, in many respects reversing an earlier tendency toward eclecticism and syncretism. Heath Lowry, who has made one of the most powerful cases against the *gazi* thesis of an originally Islamic Ottoman state, feels that with the Arab conquests a new direction set in.

> What eventually was to emerge as a classical Islamic dynasty, did so less as a result of developments during its formative period than due to the impact of its having annexed the traditional Arab heartlands of the Islamic world at the end of the second decade of the sixteenth century. Thereafter, we see the implantation of a centuries' old Islamic bureaucratic tradition to a body which had theretofore been a vibrant, syncretic, multiethnic, multicultural entity. In this sense, the question of who conquered whom is debatable. (Lowry 2003: 96)[19]

FIGURE 3.5. Suleyman the Magnificent, who continued the work of his father Selim I in extending Ottoman rule over Egypt, Syria, and the holy cities of Mecca and Medina. He also conquered Hungary. Portrait, Italian School, (sixteenth century), Kunsthistorisches Museum, Vienna, Austria/Bridgeman Images.

The turn toward Islam, it is further held, was powerfully reinforced by the resurgence of Iran under the new Safavid dynasty that arose in the early fifteenth century. The Ottoman Empire now had on its eastern flank a rival Islamic power, one indeed that proved an insuperable obstacle to the empire's further eastward expansion. More significantly, Safavid Iran was Shiite, opposed to the Sunnism of the Ottomans. Here was a competing version of Islam that was attractive to many of the Ottoman sultan's subjects, particularly the nomadic Turcoman tribes of eastern Anatolia. They now had a powerful patron on the eastern border of the empire. Numerous Shiite revolts with Iranian support, such as that of the Kizilbas ("red-heads"), repeatedly shook the empire in the fifteenth and sixteenth centuries.[20] It is indeed generally considered that, at least until the fall of the Safavid dynasty in 1722, Shiite Iran constituted a graver threat to the Ottoman Empire than did the Christian powers of the West.

The natural response of the empire in the face of this threat, it is argued, was to reemphasize its Islamic credentials. It had to stress its role as the protector of the true, Sunni, Islam against the heresy of the Shiites. It could not afford to be charged with laxity or indifference to its religious identity. It had to proclaim its Muslim character in the clearest possible way, avoiding any taint of heresy or backsliding. One consequence was a greater rigidity and narrowness in its interpretation and application of Islamic doctrines, together with a stricter delimitation of the line separating Muslims from non-Muslims.[21]

No one can deny the importance of Islam in the identity of the Ottoman Empire. For some, such as Bernard Lewis, this fact marked the empire from the very beginning. "From its foundation until its fall," he says, "the Ottoman Empire was a state dedicated to the advancement or defence of the power and faith of Islam." The conquest of the Arab lands only confirmed what had always been the case: "For the Ottoman Turk, his Empire, containing all the heartlands of early Islam, was Islam itself" (Lewis 1968: 13; see also Lewis [1982] 2001: 171–73; Imber 1995: 139; Findley 2010: 64).

We have seen that this is an overstatement for the early centuries of the empire. The question is whether things changed, whether the acquisition of the traditional lands of Islam in the sixteenth century fundamentally redirected Ottoman society. What we have to see is that, while there was a new emphasis on the sultan's role as caliph and guardian of the true faith, this was a fitful enterprise, qualified as always by a pragmatic awareness of the needs of empire. What was asserted in theory, as an official doctrine, was not always followed in practice. Moreover, even official doctrine could be bent. If it suited the state to assert its strict Islamic identity, as for instance in competition with Shiite Iran or to counter the claims of various heresies, it did so. If, however, this had the effect of antagonizing its non-Muslim subjects, it might mute or even ignore its Islamic character, as it did especially during the reform movement of the nineteenth century.

There was a further reason for the empire's rulers to be circumspect in their assertion of an Islamic identity. During the eighteenth and nineteenth centuries the Ottoman Empire began to open up, to an increasing extent, to the West. The traffic in people and ideas between the Ottoman Empire and the rest of Europe grew steadily. Ottoman diplomats and travelers began to report back on the new ideas and practices of Western European societies. Western travelers and scholars likewise wrote descriptions of the Ottoman Empire, to some extent offsetting the unfavorable image of the earlier centuries. More and more Westerners, as traders, diplomats, or simply curious and enterprising visitors, such as the intrepid Lady Mary Wortley Montagu, were to be found in the Ottoman cities of Istanbul, Izmir, and Aleppo.[22]

Most significantly, Ottoman statesmen began to be acutely conscious that, in economic and technological developments, as well as in certain aspects of military and civilian administration, the empire was lagging dangerously behind the West. If the empire were to survive, ran the emerging consensus, major structural reforms would be necessary. "Modernization" became the aim if not the preferred term of the Ottoman government. Correspondingly the vocabulary of "the sick man of Europe" and "the Eastern Question"— what to do about a possibly disintegrating Ottoman Empire—began to enter the lexicon of Western European statesmen, and to influence their policies. Having previously inspired anxiety as a dangerous and dynamic power, the Ottoman Empire became increasingly seen in terms of what Montesquieu characterized as "oriental despotism"—a social order at once static and servile, backward and corrupt, lacking all progressive features (Cirakman 2001; see also Hentsch 1992: 107–13; Faroqhi 2006: 61; Pitts 2016).

This was not the time to insist on the religious, Islamic, character of the empire.[23] Secularizing currents affected the Ottoman elites as much as the elites of Western Europe. Learned, elegant, and cosmopolitan Ottoman diplomats and travelers graced the salons and drawing rooms of the European upper classes. Products in many cases of the elite Galatasaray Lycée, where instruction was mostly in French, they often then passed through the Translation Bureau, set up in 1821 to replace the Greek-dominated office of dragoman, and once more providing a training ground in European languages and culture (Quataert 2000: 80; Lewis 1968: 118, 122).[24] For many of these elites religion was more a matter for the country people—"the Turks" and Balkan peasants—than for educated and sophisticated Ottoman gentlemen. In the central government, professional bureaucrats challenged the power of the religious elites, the *ulema*, leading the latter to increasingly desperate and disorderly alliances with the Janissaries. Only with the loss of so many European provinces in the later nineteenth century did the empire—or at least its reigning sultan—consider it politic once more to stress its Muslim identity; and it is telling that this move stirred up bitter controversy among its subjects (not least its Muslim ones), and certainly did little to resolve the empire's problems. But in general, in the conflict "Mecca versus Europe," Mecca was not always or even predominantly triumphant.[25]

It is important also to see that right from the start the Ottoman Empire recognized the need to qualify the purely Islamic nature of the state and society. It did so by institutionalizing a code and practice of sultanic or secular law—*kanun*—that paralleled and often overrode holy law, the *Sharia*. It was largely through *kanun* in fact that the Ottoman state governed and administered its realms, so much so that Halil Inalcik considers it "the cornerstone of the autocratic and centralizing Ottoman regime" (Inalcik [1973] 2000: 73). Metin Kunt notes that by the early fifteenth century, with the establishment of the sultanate as the key institution of society, "the laws of the sultan, *kanun*, made no reference to *seriat (Sharia)*; they were completely outside its sphere; in certain respects, as in parts of the criminal code, *kanun* unhesitatingly replaced *seri* injunctions" (Kunt 1982: 58; see also Imber 2002: 244–51). The decrees of the sultan, codified as *kanunname*, expressed the specifically "Inner Asian" and distinctively Ottoman aspect of the empire. They derived from *kanun ve adet-i osmani*, "Ottoman laws and traditions," or "Ottoman customary laws" (Kafadar 1993: 38; Göçek 1993: 104; Howard 1988: 58; Inalcik [1973] 2000: 70–72). As such they gave the empire a unique flexibility in adapting to the changing conditions and challenges it faced over the course of its long evolution. They were a recognition that *Sharia* law, developed largely in response to the conditions existing in eighth-century Arabia, might not be fully suitable for a multifaith, multicultural empire that sought to rival the great empires of the past and present. One of Suleyman's great achievements indeed was seen as his successful fusion of religious, *Sharia*, law and sultanic, *kanun*, law (Göçek 1993: 103).

An impressive list of representatively and distinctively Ottoman institutions derived their authority from *kanun*. These included the *kul* (slave) system of state officials, based in part on the *devshirme*, itself a deviation from and indeed infringement of *Sharia* law. *Kanun* also regulated the relations between the ruling *askeri* and the subject *re 'aya* classes: a distinction that was strictly functional, between those who performed services for the state and therefore received remuneration as opposed to those who paid taxes. It therefore paid no attention to religious differences; the *re 'aya* included Muslims as well as non-Muslims, and in the early period so did the *askeri*. This set it apart from the *Sharia*, with its strict separation of Muslim and non-Muslim as the principal and in a sense the only dividing line in society.

Similarly outside the *Sharia*, or in serious qualification of it, were two other key Ottoman institutions. One was the *wakf*, a grant of land or other source of revenue that was established in perpetuity for pious or charitable purposes. This was a traditional Islamic practice, but, through the institution of *temlik* or the royal grant of property rights, the Ottomans had used it for a wide variety of secular public purposes, including the construction of markets, the building of bridges, and the establishment of caravanserai for travelers (Inalcik [1973] 2000: 141–50). The other institution was the *timar* system, whereby the Ottoman state bestowed on certain state servants the right to collect, for their support, tax revenues from the subjects living on the land of a certain area. The Ottoman cavalrymen, the *sipahi*, were the preeminent *timar*-holders, and their strength and well-being were often seen as an index of the strength and health of the empire as a whole (Inalcik [1973] 2000: 111–16; Imber 2002: 194–206).

Both the *wakf* and *timar* systems, like the *kul* and *devshirme* systems, depended almost entirely on *kanun* (Howard 1988: 59; Inalcik [1973] 2000: 73; Imber 2002: 244–46). By the sixteenth and early seventeenth centuries what has been called "*kanun* consciousness" had become so extensive that it vied with *Sharia* as the dominant source of law and regulation. Thus the chancellor (*nisanci*) who sat on the Imperial Council and who was the Ottoman official most involved in the daily interpretation of *kanun*, could be called in the contemporary literature the "*mufti* of *kanun*," on a parallel with the chief mufti, the *seyhulislam*, the head of the body of religious scholars, the *ulema*. "The concept of *kanum* in Ottoman society had achieved such prominence that it could be compared to the holy law, and its chief interpreter to the supreme religious authority in the empire" (Howard 1988: 59). It is perhaps significant that to Turks today as in the past the great sultan Suleyman I is more known as Kanuni, "the Lawgiver," than, as generally in the West, "the Magnificent."

The importance of *kanun*, and its role in mitigating the purely Islamic character of the Ottoman regime, provides a convenient bridge to the theme of "decline" that became so prominent a feature in Ottoman thought and subsequent Western commentary on the empire. For a central claim of the decline literature that began in the late sixteenth century and continued throughout the seventeenth was that the sultans and their advisers were rashly disregarding *kanun* and as result causing the corruption and decline of hitherto central Ottoman institutions. Thus insofar as there was a tendency toward

Islamization as a result of the Arab conquests and other causes, this was seen as bringing about a potentially fatal weakening of the Ottoman state.

Bernard Lewis has noted that "the debate on the decline of the Ottoman Empire began when the Empire was at its zenith—and it began among the Ottoman Turks themselves" (Lewis 1962: 73–74; cf. Itzkowitz 1980: 37; Howard 1988: 53). More or less immediately in the wake of the glories and achievements of Selim I (1512–20) and especially Suleyman I (1520–66), a group of officials and scholars— Lütfi Pasha, Taliki-zade, Kochu Bey, Kâtib Çelebi, Mustafa Ali being among the most influential—began a series of reflections pointing to growing sources of corruption and weakness in the empire, and offering, with varying degrees of hope, their advice to the sultan on how to remedy them.[26] In these accounts the reign of Suleyman the Magnificent was generally singled out as a golden age, marking the pinnacle of Ottoman achievement.[27] From this several writers concluded, in the melancholy vein that often characterizes the literary genre of "decline" found in most empires, that the only way ahead was down, that the Ottoman Empire was doomed to dissolution. But others were convinced that by a determined effort the empire could avert the disaster and return to the healthy ways of the past.

In their accounts, the reformers portrayed an established normative order underwritten by *kanun* (Howard 1988: 62; Kafadar 1993: 42; Woodhead 1995: 187). Successive sultans—the "first ten good sultans"—from the early Ottomans through Mehmed II the Conqueror and culminating in Suleyman the Lawgiver, had built up an institutional system that had proved itself magnificently in its conquests and the growing prosperity of the empire. This classic system was identified with *kanun-i kadim*, "ancient tradition" or "customary law," which should serve as the standard by which present practices were to be measured (Howard 1988: 64). It was this order that was in the process of decay.

The litany of complaints in these early accounts became standard tropes in their successors, not least in those of Western commentators and scholars who drew almost slavishly on these native Ottoman writers. They included the decline of the *devshirme*, as native-born Muslims swelled the ranks of the Janissaries and occupied other positions—including the chief viziership—previously occupied by Christian-born slaves. For many this introduced favoritism and promotion by family connection rather than merit. Similarly corrupting influences were held to attend change in the *timar* system. No longer was it largely the preserve of, and for the support of, the *sipahi*, who had constituted a provincially based army of sturdy warriors and their sons. Now it had been invaded, from above, by government officials and palace favorites and, from below, by the common peasantry. Hence the military weakness and military disasters of the post-Suleymanic period. If the *kanun* that had established the original system—codified in numerous *kanunname* dealing with *timars*—were adhered to, the *timar*-based army would once more flourish and the empire regain its military strength.

Then there were, according to the critics, other significant departures from classic Ottoman practice. The custom of fratricide, whereby disabling succession struggles were avoided by the killing of the brothers of the sultan on his accession to power, gave way in the late sixteenth century to the principle of seniority, the throne going to the eldest male of the House of Osman. The fact that Suleyman I was followed by a succession of weak and inept sultans over the next century, and that fear of their surviving brothers led many sultans to act in a capricious and often savage manner, made many feel that the change had been for the worse (Imber 2002: 108–15; Finkel 2007: 196–97). One consequence was a loss of sultanic authority, as the sultan secluded himself behind the walls of the palace and power was exercised increasingly by palace factions. Since, also, princes were no longer sent out as governors of the provinces but were confined in "cages" (*kafes*) within the harem of the Topkapi Palace, there was plenty of opportunity for intrigue by designing mothers and their supporters in the palace. Sultans, moreover, no longer as in the past married the daughters of foreign potentates but, following Suleyman's precedent with Hurrem, their favorite concubine, thus also providing rich material for palace intrigue and jockeying for position among the sultan's wives as they promoted the interests of their sons. There was a chorus of complaints of the "pernicious" influence of the harem, presided over by the *valide sultan* and the black eunuch.[28] The sense of an enfeebled and "feminized" sultanate was enhanced by the fact that, from the time of Selim II (1566–74), with rare exceptions sultans no longer led their troops into battle (Woodhead 1987: 26; Imber 2002: 119, 143).

There were important fiscal and administrative changes that were also, at the time and since, seen as disabling developments. Chief among these was the growth of the system of tax farming by which the state now sought to obtain the increased revenue needed for several purposes, including the expansion of its military forces. New forms of fighting required an enhanced infantry at the expense of cavalry. To pay for the larger number of Janissaries and other forms of infantry, *timars* were converted into tax farms: a particularly disturbing development for the reformers (Imber 2002: 210–13, 284–85; Itzkowitz 1980: 90–91; Shaw 1976: 173–4). The widespread use of tax farming also, it has been held, led to a serious decline in the power of the central government and a corresponding increase in the power of the provinces and of local leaders. Life-term tax farming enriched a new breed of *ayans*, or provincial notables. What has been called the "Age of Ayans"—a development particularly related to the eighteenth century—has been widely taken to mark a profound crisis of Ottoman government, shown by such events as the unprecedented pact (the Sened-i Ittifak) of 1808 between the *ayans* and the central government, following a major revolt of the *ayans*.[29]

The signs of internal decline were matched, in an even clearer fashion, by what seemed the spectacular decline in the power and prestige of the Ottoman Empire in the international sphere (Lewis 1968: 36–38). Following the triumphs of Selim and Suleyman in the earlier part of the sixteenth century came the defeat at the great naval Battle of Lepanto (1571)—hailed by Western powers as the decisive reversal of Ottoman power, and celebrated throughout Christian Europe. A period of consolidation and stability, under the direction of the Köprülü vizierate, in the middle and latter part of the seventeenth century, was followed, in rapid succession, by the failure of the second siege of Vienna (1683), and losses during the war with the Holy League (1683–99). This culminated in the crippling Treaty of Karlowitz (1699), in which the Ottomans were forced to cede Hungary and Transylvania to the Habsburgs.

In the eighteenth century Russia replaced the Habsburgs as the chief antagonist of the Ottomans. Here too there were serious losses to record, principally the Khanate of Crimea, whose independence—the preliminary to its incorporation in the Russian Empire in 1783—was acknowledged in the Treaty of Küçük Kaynarca (1774), which heaped further humiliation on the Ottomans by making the Porte accept a vaguely defined Russian "right of protection" of the Ottomans' Christian subjects. The familiar story of Ottoman decline can be taken one step further with the mention of Napoleon's conquest of Egypt in 1798 and, under the influence of French revolutionary ideas, the subsequent rise of the rebellious Mehmed Ali Pasha in that province.

This is not the place to interrogate in any detailed way this account of a long-drawn-out decline, seen as forming what is in effect a massive, melancholy coda to the triumphant period of the first three centuries of Ottoman power and prosperity. But a number of things can be said about it. In the first place, all empires experience a "time of troubles," sometimes several. For the Roman Empire it was the third century CE, for the Spanish and Russian—like the Ottoman—the seventeenth century, for the Habsburgs the eighteenth. This did not stop, in most cases, reform, reinvention, and recovery. It would be surprising if the Ottoman Empire were such an exception to this general pattern. The fact that it "survived"—the very word is of course questionable—for a further three centuries, extending into the twentieth century, should itself make us suspicious of this narrative of decline.

Second, it is important to note that the decline story, still such a prominent feature of Ottoman historiography, was taken over almost unchanged from the post-Suleymanic reform literature of the sixteenth and seventeenth centuries.[30] That literature remains of course significant in itself, telling us much about Ottoman consciousness of the time. But we need to remember the specifically literary quality of the writing, the reliance on traditional tropes, the rhetorical devices employed in partisan or apologistic mode. It is highly unlikely to have provided a full or objective picture of what was going on at the time. The fact that so many current accounts continue to repeat the received story, in very much the same terms, should again warn us against taking too literally what was claimed by contemporary authors.[31]

Finally, and most important, we should recognize that much recent research has radically reshaped our understanding of the last three centuries of Ottoman rule. Ignoring or questioning the narrative of decline, it has focused on the way that the Ottoman state and Ottoman society attempted to respond to the challenges posed by a changed internal and external environment. The story is still one of only partial success; but that can be said about practically any major changes or reforms introduced or experienced by states over the course of their histories. What is more remarkable in the Ottoman case are the sustained efforts at change, and the considerable measure of success these achieved. If finally the Ottoman Empire succumbed to the pressures of war and revolution, it did so alongside many others, and with no less evidence of vitality than in those cases. The "bonfire of empires" after the First World War had many causes. There was no single-line chain of deficiencies making the downfall of any of them inevitable.

The work of revisionist scholars has produced a much more qualified picture of Ottoman "decline," suggesting reorganization and reform as much as the signs of weakness and failure. Though the *devshirme* system did end, there is no evidence that this brought about a "Moslem revolt" against prior non-Muslim dominance of state offices. Non-Muslims—including a good many grand viziers—continued to be found among the highest ranks of Ottoman government throughout the eighteenth century and beyond (just as Muslims are to be found in such positions in the time of Suleyman and earlier). In general, as Norman Itzkowitz has argued, in the eighteenth century religion ceased to be a decisive factor in the appointments of grand viziers, provincial governorship, and top-level military positions. More important were "career lines" determined by proficiency and performance in the bureaucracy, the military, and the religious hierarchy, together with emerging family traditions in all these spheres (Itzkowitz 1962: 85, 91, 1977). If decline is to be attributed, as it often is, to the "Islamization" of the empire, close attention to the ruling structures of government show little evidence of this Islamization but rather a growth of secularism and professionalism (Faroqhi 1994: 552–61; see also Quataert 2000: 98–100).

The view that the rise of the provincial notables, the *ayans*, brought about a weakening and fragmentation of government has also been seriously questioned in recent years. Rather, what seems to have taken place is a realignment of elites, with new men now competing for power in the palace but with no fundamental loss of control at the center. Tax farming and the growth of a more commercialized economy certainly produced "new Ottomans," but as with the older families their sights were on the centralized institutions of power, in the military and bureaucracy, not in strengthening provincial power against the center. Moreover, older elites bid just as vigorously for the tax farms as did newer men, and their connections at court meant that they often won the day. In addition they controlled the auctions that allotted the tax farms, thus maintaining a good deal of patronage over local notables. "Privatization" and "decentralization," it is clear, were not opposite poles to centralization but can in fact be seen as relatively successful measures to modernize the government: an "alternative modernization" to the centralizing policies that characterized most of the absolutist states in the West.[32]

Failure and humiliation in the international sphere no longer appear quite so obvious either. The naval defeat at Lepanto (1571) had long-term strategic consequences—it ended the era of galley-based conflict in the Mediterranean—and it certainly put heart in the Christian nations, after so many Ottoman triumphs. But for the Ottomans it represented a minor setback. Naval strength, with better and stronger ships, was restored within a few years. More important, the defeat has to be set in the context of significant gains. In 1565 Malta was besieged; in 1566 the Ottomans took Chios and in 1571, the very same year as Lepanto, Cyprus from the Venetians: two key islands that had long been bitterly contested. Tripoli was taken in 1551, Tunis in 1569 and again in 1574, thus ensuring Ottoman supremacy along the whole coast of North Africa and ending Spanish ambitions there forever. In 1578 the Ottomans crushed the Portuguese at Alcazar, one consequence of which was the Spanish absorption of Portugal in 1580 and the weakening of Portuguese power in the Indian Ocean, where it had challenged Ottoman trade with the East. In 1580 Spain signed a formal peace with the Ottomans. A fundamental realignment of geopolitical power was taking place, with the Venetians pushed out of the eastern Mediterranean and the Iberian states contained within Europe, leaving the Ottomans with undisputed mastery over North Africa and the Levant.[33]

In 1669 Crete fell to the Ottomans, thus completing—with the exception of Malta—a more or less clean sweep of all the strategically important islands in the Mediterranean. In 1669 much of Ukraine once more became part of the Ottoman Empire, and—under the personal leadership of Sultan Mehmed IV—Ottoman forces struck deep into Poland-Lithuania, creating in 1672 the Ottoman province of Kamenets in Polish Podolia and threatening to make the Polish king an Ottoman vassal (Finkel 2007: 273–75). Any idea that the Ottomans had given up on expansion in Europe, after Lepanto, was clearly premature, as the almost-successful siege of Vienna in 1683 demonstrated even further (Faroqhi 2006: 57, 73).

Even the period following the Treaty of Karlowitz (1699), when Hungary was ceded to the Habsburgs, is not one of unalloyed disaster. Russia—making its first serious move, under Peter the Great, against the Ottomans—was heavily defeated in the Crimea in 1711. The great fortress of Belgrade, lost to the Habsburgs in 1688, was recovered in 1739 and again in 1789–90; other earlier losses to the Habsburgs (Bulgaria, Serbia, Transylvania) and to Russia (Azov and other Black Sea fortresses) were reversed by the end of the eighteenth century. The Greek province of Morea was regained from the Venetians in 1714–18 and retained for more than a century (Quataert 2000: 41). Ottoman control of the North African provinces—the Maghreb—remained firm throughout the eighteenth century (Hess 1977). We should remember in fact that, after the losses conceded in the Treaty of Küçük Kaynarca, there were no further significant losses for a century—hardly what one would expect of "the sick man of Europe" (Lewis 1968: 37).

Probably even more consequential for the Ottomans was the fall of the Safavid dynasty in Iran in 1722, leaving the way open for both Ottomans and Russians to gain territory at Iran's expense and giving the Ottomans a much-needed respite on their eastern flank. There is thus a certain degree of unwarranted hindsight in describing the Treaty of Karlowitz as a turning point or a watershed in Ottoman fortunes. What one sees rather in the eighteenth century is increasing Ottoman integration into the European state system, with a pattern of alliances, reverses, and successes similar to that of other states of the time (Naff 1977b; Faroqhi 2006: 73).

Renewed war with Russia (1768–74) did indeed lead to the humiliating Treaty of Küçük Kaynarca and the loss of the Crimea. It also revealed glaring weaknesses in Ottoman administration and military technology, as did Napoleon's invasion of Egypt in 1798. But again what needs to be noted alongside these undoubted reversals is Ottoman awareness of the deficiencies, and the sustained effort that was launched to remedy them. The nineteenth century was to see an even more strenuous pursuit of reform, extending to the very end of the century. If these endeavors ultimately failed to save the empire, the same can be said about parallel efforts in the Russian and Habsburg empires at about the same time. Yet there is no tradition, in those cases as compared with the Ottoman, of talking about a three-hundred-year period of "decline," as if the Ottoman Empire were doomed from the late sixteenth century onward. Why should that be so? We have to see that very different standards are being applied to what are in many ways very similar cases.[34]

Ottomans to Turks

At the Treaty of Küçük Kaynarca of 1774, when the Ottomans had been forced to concede to Russia certain vaguely defined rights of intervention on behalf of the Porte's Orthodox Christian subjects, the sultan countered with a claim of his own: that, as the "supreme Mohammedan Caliph," he had rights of regulation over the Muslim subjects of the newly independent (and soon to be Russian) Crimea. This claim, says Bernard Lewis, was "new and unprecedented."

> Since the extinction of the classical Islamic Caliphate in medieval times, there had been no single, universally recognized titular head of the whole Islamic community, and each monarch had become, in effect, a Caliph in his own realms. . . . The assertion of religious authority beyond the frontier was a radical departure—an attempt, for the first time since the fall of the Abbasids, to establish a universal Islamic leadership, and to claim it for the house of Osman. (Lewis 1968: 324; cf. Findley 2010: 25–26)

If this was indeed so, there was a certain irony in this claim—in any case, of dubious and "murky" character (Deringil 1999: 46–47, 174–75; Hanioglu 2008: 130, 142). It took place as the Ottoman Empire was facing the most serious challenges to its existence—not least from Russia—since its foundation in the fourteenth century. Everywhere indeed—in North Africa, India, Southeast and Central Asia, the Caucasus—Islam was on the defensive, pushed back by European colonial powers. The Ottoman claim to universal authority over all Muslims might seem a classic instance of Arnold Toynbee's idea that, in their period of decline, all civilizations throw up a "universal state" claiming worldwide authority.

There would in fact be a double irony in this claim of Islamic leadership: because it took place, as we have seen, precisely at the time that secularization was making inroads into the culture of the Ottoman elites. This secularization continued apace in the nineteenth century. The vigorous spate of reforms attempted by practically every sultan from the beginning of the century to its end left in its wake a shoal of schools, universities, medical and military colleges, and new courts and legal codifications that were heavily imprinted with the secular and scientific culture of the West. Educated Ottomans traveled all over Europe, and brought back many of the social and political ideas being developed by European intellectuals in Paris, London, Vienna, and Berlin. The printing press, finally admitted into the Ottoman Empire from the early eighteenth century onward, was the powerful carrier of these ideas in the newspapers and journals that flourished in the nineteenth century.

This is not meant to suggest that the proud assertion of the empire's Islamic credentials was an empty gesture. Secularization and the survival—indeed renewal—of religion are, as we now know very well, not contradictory but complementary phenomena. So it was with Christianity in the West, where the undoubted progress of secularization in the nineteenth century was accompanied by a massive upswing, in Europe and North America, of evangelical Christianity—one of the greatest movements of renewal in the history of Christianity. In the Ottoman Empire too, as elsewhere in the Islamic world, secularizing currents had to contend with repeated bursts of Islamic vigor, not just among the rural peasantry but at the very top of society (cf. Findley 2010: esp. 18–22). At various times, right up to the end of the empire in the early twentieth century, the ruling establishment sought to reinvigorate the society and polity of the empire with infusions of religion. That this ultimately failed to save the empire can no more be attributed to Islam than can the equal failure of more secular reforms be blamed on secularism. Both had to contend with a world that, in the maelstrom of the First World War and the increasing power of nationalism, was no longer so hospitable to empire.

Two main developments in the nineteenth century affected the character and outlook of the Ottoman Empire. The first was the loss, especially in the latter part of the century, of most of the Christian provinces of the empire. It was this that lent plausibility to the arguments of those who insisted that it was only through stressing the Islamic character of the empire that it would have any hope of survival. Right to the bitter end, in the controversies over the abolition of the *Sharia* and the Caliphate in the early years of the Turkish Republic, this view continued to have powerful adherents.

The second development, associated especially with the Tanzimat reforms of the midcentury, was the attempt to equalize the legal and political condition of all Ottoman subjects, Muslim and non-Muslim alike. This had a profoundly unsettling effect on the population, reversing as it did a centuries-old tradition of maintaining and institutionalizing difference. Here the effects of the French Revolution, and the worldwide impact of its ideas, showed itself in the clearest possible way. The espousal, by reforming sultans and their advisers, of French and generally Western ideas of equality and uniformity was a revolutionary development within Ottoman society, threatening to disrupt many of its central principles and practices.

These two developments cut across the three main strategies that were promoted by Ottoman statesman and intellectuals in the course of the century. The first, linked especially to the reforms of the Tanzimat era, was the policy of "Ottomanism": the effort to provide a common basis of citizenship for all the sultan's subjects, thus ending discriminations between Muslims and non-Muslims. The second was to revert to a definition of the empire as primarily Islamic, and to seek to give new strength to Islamic law and Islamic institutions as a way of revivifying the empire. The final strategy—which did not emerge until the last third of the century at the earliest—was to insist on the Turks as a nation, and to reject the idea of a multinational empire in favor of the formation of a Turkish national state. In the end it was this third option that won out; though, as in a palimpsest, the other two tendencies continued to exercise some power even after the founding of the Turkish Republic in 1923, and, especially in the case of Islam, in later years began to show that their force was by no means spent.

Finally—a Muslim Empire?

Before 1850, despite the acquisition of the Arab territories in the previous centuries, approximately 50 percent of all Ottoman subjects—Muslim and non-Muslim—still lived in the Balkans. By 1906, the European provinces of the empire contributed only 20 percent of the population (Quataert 2000: 54). Put another way, the balance between the Muslim and non-Muslim subjects of the empire shifted decisively in favor of the former. As late as 1874, non-Muslims made up over 50 percent of the population; by 1881–93, following the Russo-Turkish War and Ottoman losses, nearly three-quarters of the Otto-man population were Muslims, and fewer than a quarter Christians (Qua-taert 1994: 782; Findley 2010: 115). This was the hard demographic basis of the view, urged by many in the second half of the nineteenth century, that the best way to revive the empire was vigorously to reassert and reestablish its Islamic character.

We may remember here Paul Wittek's assertion that it was Rumelia, not Anatolia or the Arab lands, that constituted the "vital nucleus" of the Ottoman Empire right to its end, and that the loss of this core "inner empire," its animat-ing principle, was the signal of its imminent demise. Carter Findley, too, more recently has argued that "as late as the Balkan Wars of 1912–13, the real home-land of many Turks, especially those in leadership positions, was not Anatolia but Rumelia, the Ottoman Balkans. For many of them, the sudden necessity to rethink Anatolia as their homeland was a wrenching, unwelcome change" (Findley 2010: 4; cf. Hanioglu 2011: 199). The movement from "Ottomans" to "Turks" is accordingly, for many commentators, the direct consequence of the more or less wholesale loss of the European provinces in the nineteenth and early twentieth centuries.

Late Ottoman history, in one of its aspects, can readily be portrayed as one of a steady succession of reversals starting with the loss of the Crimea as recognized in the Treaty of Küçük Kaynarca (1774), and culminating in the final loss of most of the European provinces in the Balkan Wars of 1912–13. In between would come such landmarks as Napoleon's conquest of Egypt in 1798, a short-lived occupation that nevertheless left a lasting impact not just on Egypt but on the empire as a whole. With it came the rise of Mehmed Ali (governed 1805–48) and a modernizing drive in Egypt that dramatically chal-lenged the Ottoman state to equal it, on pain of even greater failure.

This episode was speedily followed by the Serbian uprising in 1804—like the Greek and most other nationalist movements in the Balkans, inspired more by outsiders than by Ottoman subjects—leading eventually to Serbian autonomy in 1838 (Hanioglu 2008: 51–53). Greece got its independence in 1830—largely as a result of outside intervention, again setting a pattern for future settlements. In 1830 also the French occupied Algiers, and although it would take several decades of bloody conflicts for them to make Algeria the foundation stone of their "second empire," they had laid down an unmistak-able, and unshakable, marker.

There was then a breathing space—and indeed a major victory, in the Crimean War (1853–56), against the Russians, the empire's principal antagonist. There was also formal admission, in the Treaty of Paris (1856), to the "European club" of major powers, together with "an unprecedented guarantee of the territorial integrity of the Ottoman state" (Hanioglu 2008: 82). But in the Crimean War Ottoman dependence on Britain and France had been made manifest; and the guarantee of territorial integrity turned out to be unenforceable. Great power interests again determined the fate of the empire in renewed conflict with Russia in 1877–78. Russia this time firmly got the upper hand in the military engagement—the war was "a disaster for the Ottomans"—and imposed a crushing settlement on the Ottomans at the Treaty of San Stefano (1878). But the great powers once more intervened, unwilling to allow Russia such an extension of power in the Balkans. The losses were nevertheless enormous. By the terms of the treaty agreed at the Berlin Congress (June–July 1878), Serbia, Montenegro, and Romania (formed mainly from the old Ottoman principalities of Moldavia and Wallachia) gained their independence; Bulgaria—though denied the extent of territory agreed at San Stefano—achieved autonomy; Russia acquired southern Bessarabia and the Ottoman territories of Kars, Batum, and Ardahan on the Black Sea; Austria-Hungary won the right to occupy and partly to administer Bosnia-Herzogovina; Britain won similar rights over Cyprus.

Such losses amounted, in the view of several scholars, to a massive transformation in the character of the empire. "The war of 1877–8 and the Treaty of Berlin that ended it," says Caroline Finkel, "hastened the culmination of a process begun with the defeats suffered by the Ottomans at the hands of the Habsburgs in the last years of the seventeenth century: the empire lost more than a third of its territory, and much of its non-Muslim population" (Finkel 2007: 486; see also Zürcher 1997: 85; Hanioglu 2008: 121–23). More was to follow. In 1912 the Italians effectively took—leaving a shadowy Ottoman suzerainty—the Ottoman province of Tripoli, the last of the African territories still ruled from Istanbul. The concession was in part forced on the Ottomans by the outbreak, in the same year, of war with the Balkan states of Serbia, Bulgaria, Montenegro, and Greece. Once more the Ottomans suffered military humiliation; once more the great powers intervened to enforce a peace. But now the Ottomans lacked the great protective hand of Britain, which since the 1880s, and under the powerful lead of William Gladstone and the Liberals, had turned decisively against the Ottomans. At the Treaty of London (1913), the Ottomans were forced to make substantial territorial concessions to Greece (which acquired Crete), Serbia, Montenegro, and Bulgaria. Albania achieved independence. The Dodecanese Islands came under Italian occupation. The

Ottoman presence in Europe was at an end. An "empire of three continents" was reduced to "an Asiatic state." "For centuries, the empire had rested on two central pillars, Rumelia and Anatolia, between which nested the imperial capital. Suddenly, the Arab periphery became the only significant extension of the empire outside its new Anatolian heartland" (Hanioglu 2008: 173). Why not, therefore, as some Ottoman thinkers urged in the wake of the Balkan Wars, transfer the capital to some major town in central Anatolia—Konya or Ankara—or even northern Syria: Damascus? (Finkel 2007: 524–25; Hanioglu 2011: 200–201). The movement from "Ottomans" to "Turks" appeared to have taken on the character of a rout.

How easy it is to read into this narrative the story of a slow but steady and relentless decline, leading to a more or less inevitable dissolution and death. That has been the burden of innumerable accounts, old and new. But we should by now surely be wary of such perceptions. The French, after all, in the eighteenth century lost territories—in North America and India—greater by far than those lost by the Ottomans in the nineteenth. But that did not stop them from rebuilding their empire, so that by the early twentieth century they had an empire second in the world only to that of the British. The Russians too lost one empire and—under the guise of the Soviet Union—acquired another. The "decline of empire," as a trope, is appealing to the romantic and poetic temperament. But it should not be allowed to color a more sober assessment of an empire's character and prospects. Shortly after its reduction to its Asiatic parts, the Ottoman Empire did indeed collapse. But so too, at about the same time, did several other empires, for a variety of reasons including the common experience of the First World War. It is as dangerous, in the case of the Ottoman Empire, to read into its history the element of inevitability as it would be in theirs.

What the loss of much of its non-Muslim population meant, though, was clearly the need for a rethinking of the forms of rule and legitimacy in the empire. This, emphatically, did not mean giving up on empire. That thought does not seem to have crossed the minds of any significant section of the educated population until well into the First World War. Nationalism, as espoused by its former Balkan subjects and increasingly powerful throughout Europe, undoubtedly had some influence on the thinking of late Ottoman statesmen and thinkers. But that did not, until a much later date than is generally realized, lead in the direction of an ethnically based, Turkish national state. For one thing, there were still substantial numbers of Greeks, Jews, and Armenians in the empire who flourished in its expanding commerce and economy, and who remained loyal subjects of the sultan or looked to him for protection. There were also the sultan's Arab subjects, who while they agitated for various degrees of autonomy, in only the rarest of cases were interested in the breakup of the empire ("Arab nationalism" was more a creation of foreign sympathizers, such as "Lawrence of Arabia," than it was of native Arabs). What, in the relative absence of non-Muslims, was a tempting candidate for holding the empire together was Islam. This card, as we shall see, was duly played, though not as straightforwardly as usually portrayed. But Islam is not nationalist—quite the contrary. If Islam was to be the salvation of the empire, this suggested policies that might be Pan-Islamic but could in no way focus on the nation-state.

The movement from the Ottoman Empire to a Turkish national state was not foreordained. The route was far more twisted and tortuous than one might imagine from the accounts written by later Turkish nationalists or their supporters. Without the astonishing energy and capability of Mustafa Kemal, indeed, it is quite possible that the Ottoman Empire might have suffered the fate of Poland in the eighteenth century: dismemberment and division among the victorious powers parceling out the post-1918 world.

Tanzimat, Ottomanism, Turkism

The sustained attempt at reform of the empire that occupied Ottoman statesmen for much of the nineteenth century is usually associated with the era of the Tanzimat (1839–76). *Tanzimat* means "Reforms" or "Reorganization." Launched in the final years of the reign of Mahmud II (1808–39), and continued by his successors Abdulmecid I (1839–61) and Abdulaziz I (1861–76), the principal measures of the reforms are by convention listed as the Gülhane Decree (Gülhane Hatt-i Serifi, the "Noble Edict of the Rose Garden") of 1839, and the Reform Edict (Islahat Fermani) of 1856, which explicitly built on the earlier measure. The Imperial Constitution of 1876, the first constitution in Ottoman history, can also be seen as a continuation of the Tanzimat, together with a number of other measures—such as the new penal code of 1840 and the commercial code of 1850—that promoted the Tanzimat's goals of centralization, equalization, and modernization.[35]

But practically everyone agrees that the formal era of the Tanzimat was merely a culmination of a reform movement that had started much earlier, following the defeats of the late seventeenth century and the growing threats posed by great power pressures. The reign of Ahmed III (1703–30)—the "Tulip era"—had shown a marked opening up to the influence of Western

FIGURE 3.6. Sultan Abdulmecid, in whose reign the Tanzimat
reforms were implemented. © HIP/Art Resource, NY.

mores and ideas. Ottoman embassies were for the first time established in the
major European capitals, allowing for extensive reports on European societies
to reach Ottoman statesmen. A critical development was that, after centuries of prohibition, printing was—in 1727—finally allowed to Muslims in the
empire, a revolutionary departure in Ottoman society that spearheaded the

rise of a thriving press and more generally a vibrant literary culture, though mostly in the nineteenth century (Lewis 1968: 50–52, 187–94; Hanioglu 2008: 94–96). Spurred on by Napoleon's conquest of Egypt (1798) and Mehmed Ali's subsequent modernizing drive there, Selim III (1789–1807) announced a "New Order" (Nizam–i Cedid), especially in the military, and attempted to curb the power of the provincial *ayans*. He was finally stopped by a bloody revolt of the Janissaries in 1807 and his own murder, but the message was clear. As Thomas Naff sums up the effects of the changes, "during the eighteenth century, the bonds of tradition were permanently loosened, the old institutions were shaken to their foundations, and the idea of reform itself acquired an inexorable momentum within Ottoman circles" (1977a: 14; see also Lewis 1968: 40–73; Zürcher 1997: 23–31; Findley 2010: 24–34).

Mahmud II (1808–39) took up where his cousin Selim III had left off. Gradually building up his power base in the palace, and reestablishing central control over the *ayans*, he embarked on "a great programme of reforms; in them he laid down the main lines along which later Turkish reformers, in the nineteenth and to some extent even in the twentieth century, were to follow" (Lewis 1968: 80; cf. Zürcher 1997: 41). He suppressed the Janissaries in 1826—an act known in Ottoman history as the "Beneficent Event" (Vaka-i Hayriye)—and refounded the "New Order" army created by Selim III. He had the military adopt the fez, instead of the turban or other traditional headgear, and then had this enjoined on all government civilian employees as well—a symbolic move of great importance (Lewis 1968: 101–3; Quataert 2000: 65). He brought the great holdings of the religious foundations, the *wakfs*, under government control, and centralized the *ulema* under the *seyhulislam*, the chief mufti, thus depriving it of its independence and subjecting it to the direct influence of the state. He conducted the first-ever census of the empire. It was also Mahmud II who established the "Translation Office" (Tercume Odasi) (1833), where young bureaucrats were taught to read, write, and speak French, and which became the great training ground and launching pad for many of the leading Ottoman statesmen of the nineteenth century. Indeed it was under Mahmud too that the first of the formal Tanzimat decrees, the Gülhane Decree, was drafted, though he died weeks before its official declaration. The main feature that distinguished Mahmud II's efforts from those of his successors to 1876 was that under him the impetus for reform came from the sultan himself, from the palace, whereas under Abdulmecid I and Abdulaziz I the bureaucrats of the Sublime Porte—principally Grand Viziers Mustafa Reshid Pasha, Fuad Pasha, and Ali Pasha—took the leading role, and the palace, though compliant, was sidelined.[36]

It is indeed the very fact that the Tanzimat was, in effect, so long in preparation that it was able to achieve such a remarkable degree of success (contrary to earlier dismissals). By itself the period normally allotted to the Tanzimat— 1839–76—would be too short to have brought this about. It was because it was so long in gestation that the wave of reforms that followed the Gülhane Decree had such an impact. As to their significance, "modernization" and "Westernization" still to a good extent sum up the content and direction of the reforms, so long as we recognize—as most scholars now do—that these can be accomplished in their own distinctive way and are not necessarily slavish imitation of Western forms. The slogan, *alafranga* (*alla franca*, Frankish or European style) which summed up the aim of many of the reformers, was countered by *alaturka* (*alla turca*, Turkish style) (Hanioglu 2008: 100; Findley 2010: 177). But these were not necessarily in direct conflict, and Ottoman and Turkish history have indeed shown their continual interweaving.

Be that as it may, the Tanzimat reforms had a lasting impact, creating many of the institutions inherited by the Turkish Republic (cf. Zürcher 2010: 61; Reinkowski 2011: 457). By the late nineteenth century the empire had rationalized its bureaucracy and established a reasonable degree of centralized control over the provinces. It had created a regular system of boards and ministries in the central government, on the European model. It had reformed the system of taxation, abolishing tax farming and removing the traditional distinction between tax-paying and non-tax-paying groups (including abolishing the poll tax, the *ciziye*, on non-Muslims). It had introduced conscription, and imposed the obligation for military service on non-Muslims as well as Muslims, though until the Balkan Wars non-Muslims could buy their way out of this (as most did). New schools and academies, such as the Galatasaray Lycée, the army medical school, and the military academy, were beginning to produce a new educated and Westernized elite among Muslims. European capitals, Paris especially, began to feature more and more in their experience. The Constitution of 1876, though suspended—not abolished—after only two years, was a landmark reform, becoming a rallying point for reformers of all kinds in subsequent years. In all this, due obeisance was paid to Islam and the *Sharia*, as was traditional in all reforms. But it cannot have escaped anyone's attention that it was mainly through secular, *kanun*, decrees that the bulk of the reforms were carried out—for instance the new penal code of 1840 that asserted the equality of all subjects before the law was called *ceza kanunnamesi*. In practice the scope of the *Sharia* was limited henceforth almost entirely to family law (Zürcher 1997: 64; Findley 2010: 24, 94).

Not surprisingly the Tanzimat called up vigorous resistance from traditional elements in Ottoman society—the *ulema*, the *medreses*, the provincial notables. What is more noteworthy is that it also provoked alarm and resistance among Christians, especially Christian landowners in the Balkans who saw their local privileges coming under threat (Inalcik 1973). This indicates the extent to which non-Muslims as much as Muslims had found an established place for themselves in the empire—in the nineteenth century as well as earlier—and were prepared to fight to maintain it, opting for separation only when their position became or seemed untenable. Both traditional Muslims and Christians were reacting to what was the unprecedented and indeed (French) revolutionary principle of the Tanzimat—the formal equalization of all Ottoman subjects, Muslim and non-Muslim, before the law and in the eyes of the state. This struck at the heart of the principle of difference that had marked the old empire, based as it was on traditional Islamic doctrines. It aimed to transform the Ottoman state and society as much, and in the same way, as according to Alexis de Tocqueville the principle of equality transformed French society of the ancien régime.

But equality could save the empire as much as threaten it. This became the conviction of the Young Ottomans (Yeni Osmanlilar), an opposition group that flourished in the 1860s and 1870s. This, it has been held, was the first modern-style opposition movement among Ottoman intellectuals, and in many ways, especially in its use of literary and poetic forms, the exemplary one (Mardin 1962: 4; Findley 2010: 104). The Young Ottomans were not against the reforming intent of the government; on the contrary they were for it. They held, though, that it had not gone nearly far enough, and that above all a constitution and a parliament were needed to complete and further the Tanzimat. What was required in their view was the creation of a sense of common citizenship among all the inhabitants of the empire, and a common commitment to the "fatherland" (*vatan*). In their writings—especially that of their leading light, Namık Kemal—they infused old terms—*vatan, millet, hürriyet*—with new meanings, just as the French in the course of their Revolution infused new meanings in the old terms *pays* and *nation*. *Vatan*, an Arabic word signifying birthplace, became the equivalent of "fatherland" or the French *patrie*. *Millet*, the old word for community, took on the modern meaning of nation (as *nation* for the French). *Hürriyet* —which traditionally meant simply being a free man rather than a slave—now came to mean liberty—*liberté*—in the full (French Revolutionary) political sense (Deringil 1993; Zürcher 1997: 72; Findley 2010: 123–32).

Understanding the Young Ottomans has been complicated by the fact that, though reformers influenced especially by French ideas, they also put stress on the Islamic heritage of the empire, and accused the government of a too-hasty Westernization and indifference to Islamic values. It has been said that the sense of identity of the Young Ottomans "oscillated between Ottoman cosmo-politanism, Islamic solidarity, and Turkish self-consciousness"—a pattern that was to persist for many generations of intellectuals (Findley 2010: 106). But undoubtedly their most important impact, in the political sphere, was in their efforts to get the Ottoman Empire to adopt a parliamentary constitution. This began with the formation in 1865 of the Patriotic Alliance (Ittifak-i Hamiyet), a secret society whose declared aim was to change "absolute into constitutional rule" (Mardin 1962: 13). It culminated in the promulgation, by the new sultan Abdulhamid II, of the 1876 Constitution, in the drafting of which Young Ottomans such as Namık Kemal were heavily represented. Inasmuch as the Young Ottomans criticized the Tanzimat statesmen Ali and Fuad Pasha for their subservience to Europe—intellectually and politically—they also criticized them for their bureaucratic despotism, which they saw as removing the traditional checks on authority exercised by such independent institutions as the *ulema* and even the Janissaries (shades, once more, of Tocqueville's criticism of the leveling impact of the French Revolution). The establishment of a representative, constitutional, and parliamentary system would, they were convinced, instill a new sense of citizenship and loyalty toward the empire on the part of all its inhabitants, Muslim and non-Muslim alike. It would also, they argued, enable a return to some fundamental principles of Islamic law, flouted by the bureaucratic reformers, including a recognition of the contractual nature of the bond between ruler and people (as shown for instance in the traditional oath of allegiance, the *baya*, given by leaders of the Islamic community to a new sultan). Alongside "Love of One's Country is Part of the Faith," a quotation from the Koran used as a plea for consultative government—"And Consult with Them in the Matter"—also featured prominently in the Young Ottoman journal *Hürriyet* (Lewis 1968: 155).[37]

Abdulhamid II (1876–1909) suspended the Constitution in 1878, and prorogued the parliament (it was not to meet again for thirty years). An indefatigable worker, he also reasserted the authority of the palace over the Porte; during his reign he changed his grand vizier over twenty-five times, and took personal control of many of the ministries (Fortna 2008: 50). Since he also put a renewed stress on Islam, it was once common to portray the "Hamidian era" as one of autocratic and reactionary rule, a throwback to the past and a last-ditch attempt to shore up an empire manifesting clear signs of dissolution. European contemporaries in particular, appalled by such events as the Armenian Massacres of 1896—which brought out an aging Gladstone from retirement once more to thunder against the "abominations of Turkish rule"—were responsible for spreading the view that Abdulhamid's reign marked "an atavistic return to fanaticism" (Zürcher 1997: 83).

No serious scholar now holds that view.[38] What is now clear are the marked continuities with the preceding period. Despite his suspension of the Constitution, Abdulhamid in many ways shared the outlook of the Young Ottomans. He held strong Islamist beliefs, and he distrusted what he saw as the overly Western orientation of the Tanzimat statesmen.[39] With the loss of many of the empire's Christian subjects following the war with Russia in 1877–78, Abdulhamid saw the need to employ Islam as a unifying force for the empire's now predominantly Muslim population. He paid particular attention to the Arab lands, hitherto relatively neglected by Ottoman administrations. Although Arab nationalism was a negligible force at this time, there were powerful Arab leaders with a strong sense of independence. Abdulhamid moved to counter this with an assertion of the Ottoman sultan's historic role as the caliph, spiritual head of all Muslims in the world. He was fond of quoting the *hadith* (saying) of Muhammad "Other prophets before me were sent only to their peoples; I have been sent to all humanity" (Samman 2007: 136). The Hijaz, home of the Holy Cities of Mecca and Medina, was a focus of particular concern, especially in view of the ambitions of the Hashemite sherifs of Mecca. Abdulhamid stressed his position as protector of the Holy Places and commander of the faithful. The building of the Hijaz railway, one of the high points of his reign, was designed to make it easier for Muslims from all over the empire—and beyond—to make the obligatory pilgrimage to Mecca. It symbolized the sultan's concern for the welfare of all Muslims.[40]

But it would be wrong to see the renewed stress on Islam as an attempt to put back the clock, to return to some mythical golden age of an Islamic empire. Throughout their history the Ottomans had shown a thoroughly pragmatic attitude toward the Muslim religion, privileging it while at the same time qualifying its influence in the interests of the management of a multinational and multifaith empire. With the loss of the Christian provinces, and unrest in the Arab ones, it made perfectly good sense to turn to Islam as a rallying and mobilizing force. But this was Islam in the context of continuing modernization. Selim Deringil has written of "the Ottomanization of the Seriat" under Abdulhamid, a standardization and regularization of Islamic practice that was designed

to make it an effective ruling tool for the whole empire, overriding local customs and interpretations (Deringil 1999: 50–52). He also speaks of "Islam and
Enlightenment" as both being preoccupations of the scholar-bureaucrats of
Abdulhamid's time. Secular reforms proceeded within "the 'cocoon' of a religious vocabulary." The Tanzimat reforms had produced a society "where the
religious could express itself in secular terms, just as the secular could use religious motifs" (Deringil 1999: 14, 19, 168, 176). Islam in the service of empire
meant of necessity constantly "updating" it. In the present era that meant rationalizing and popularizing it in such a way as to make it compatible with the
ends of modernization that seemed the overriding condition of the empire's
survival. Deringil quotes Ahmet Yaşar Ocak's view as "summing up the matter
in a nutshell": "The Islamism of the Hamidian period . . . was entirely a reaction
against classical Ottoman Islam. As such, essentially it was a *modernist* movement. Despite all its anti-Western posturing, because it favoured of modernization, it must be considered together with the other modernist movements in
Turkish history" (in Deringil 1999: 66–67). Bernard Lewis concurs: "It would
not be an exaggeration to say that it was in . . . the reign of Abdulhamid that the
whole movement of the *Tanzimat*—of legal, administrative, and educational
reform—reached its fruition and its climax" (Lewis 1968: 178–79).[41]

Educational reform, at both secondary and higher levels, was one of the
keynotes of Abdulhamid's policy (Lewis 1968: 181–83; Deringil 1999: 93–111,
130–33; Fortna 2008: 51). But his success can perhaps best be judged by the
performance of the Ottoman military. After the humiliations of the 1870s,
serious attention was once more paid to military reform. The Ottomans here
turned toward Germany, which had incontrovertibly demonstrated its military prowess in the Franco-Prussian War of 1871. The German officer Field
Marshal Colmar von der Goltz from 1883 to 1895 played a leading role in the
reorganization of the Ottoman army. The fruits of the reform were quickly
shown when in 1897 the Ottoman army routed the Greeks, who had intervened to support an insurrection in Crete. The startling defeat of Russia by
Japan in 1904–5—the first major defeat of a European power by an Asiatic
state—provided additional lessons, closely studied by Goltz through the Ottoman military observers who had accompanied the Japanese forces. After the
Young Turk Revolution of 1908, Goltz was once more called upon to assist in
military reform. So great was his success that by 1918 every major European
combatant had adopted the Ottoman model. "The reorganization brought the
Ottoman army in line with contemporary armies in operational doctrine and
ahead of the Europeans in organization. . . . The reason for Ottoman defeat

in the Balkan Wars of 1912–1913 has to be sought elsewhere than in military backwardness" (Findley 2010: 199–200). Nevertheless, that defeat revealed serious weaknesses, to remedy which the Committee of Union and Progress once more turned toward Germany, in the person of General Otto Liman von Sanders. Building upon Goltz, Sanders was able to achieve remarkable results. In the First World War the performance of the Ottoman army surprised many European observers, notably in the great defense of Gallipoli of 1915–16 (where the young officer Mustafa Kemal won his spurs). The Ottoman army surprised them even more during the "Turkish War of Independence" of 1920–23 when, under Mustafa Kemal's inspired command, it fought off the combined forces of Greece, Britain, and France—and held off the Armenians and Russians—to save Anatolia and establish the new Turkish Republic (Zürcher 1997: 138–70; Findley 2010: 245; Hanioglu 2011: 33–43).

So the last breath of empire was in giving life to the new Turkish nation-state. But this was not the intended result of the Young Turk Revolution of 1908, despite the mythology so carefully built up and propagated by the new state. Following the declaration of a republic in 1923, the new state under Atatürk portrayed the Young Turks as Turkish nationalists who had prepared the way for the new regime. Nothing could be further from the truth. The Committee of Union and Progress (CUP) that supervised, with short breaks, the politics of the whole period from 1908 to 1918 (the "Second Constitutional Period") underwent a number of changes of direction during these tumultuous years. But, like the Young Ottomans before them, they came to save the empire, not put an end to it in the interests of Turkish nationalism.

All the key events and personalities show this. Among the four medical students whose meeting in May 1889—on the centenary of the French Revolution—at the Military Medical College in Istanbul is traditionally seen as the founding moment of the Young Turk movement, not one was an ethnic Turk. Ibrahim Temo was an Albanian, Memed Reshid a Circassian, Abdullah Cevdet and Ishak Sukuti were Kurds (Lewis 1968: 197; Zürcher 2010: 99). Their heroes, as with many of the Young Turks, were the Ottomanist thinkers Namık Kemal (from whom Mustafa Kemal took his second name) and Ziya Pasha, whose writings were banned under Abdulhamid (Lewis 1968: 195–97; Hanioglu 2011: 23). What united them—what led them to adopt the name Ottoman Unity Society (Ittihad-i Osmanli Cemiyeti)—was a concern with the separatism, supported by European powers, among non-Muslims in their various communities (Hanioglu 2008: 145; Findley 2010: 161). The group of exiled Ottoman liberals in Paris with which they established contact—by means of the French post office in Galata—was led by a Lebanese (Christian) Maronite and former member of the Ottoman parliament, Khalil Ghanim. It was Ghanim who had founded the journal, in Paris, *La Jeune Turquie*—"no doubt a conscious evocation of the memory of the Young Ottoman exiles of the 1860s" (Lewis 1968: 197). In Paris the group called themselves Jeunes Turcs; and though "Young Turks" (*Jön Türk*) was no doubt a more literal translation than "Young Ottomans," which also derived from the same French term, the conflation of terms was a further symptom of the obstinate refusal to distinguish between Ottomans and Turks.

The Young Ottoman connection continued with the dominating influence in the early years of the Ottomanist intellectual Ahmet Riza, one of the founders of the Paris-based Committee of Union and Progress (Ittihat ve Terakki Cemiyeti)—a title that was an adaptation of the Comtean slogan "Order and Progress." Comte's—and his disciple Durkheim's—influence was pervasive among the Young Turks. It was under this influence that the young radicals of the Istanbul group decided to change their name from the Ottoman Unity Society to that of the Paris group, the Committee of Union and Progress. It was Ahmet Riza also who began to publish a biweekly journal, the *Mesveret* (Consultation), whose very name evoked the Young Ottomans' use of the Koran to argue for consultative government. At the same time the journal bore the Comtean subtitle *Order and Progress* (Lewis 1968: 198; Zürcher 1997: 91; Fortna 2008: 59). Add to this that the one unifying call among the Young Turks was for the restoration of the Constitution of 1876 and the recalling of parliament, and the connection and continuity with the Young Ottomans of the 1860s and 1870s become impossible to ignore (which does not mean that it has not in fact frequently been ignored).

The young army officers from Salonica and Monastir—among them Enver Pasha and Cemal Pasha—who gave military muscle to the Young Turks were equally committed to the salvation of the empire, not its dissolution. Their anxieties were focused on the separatist movement in their province of Macedonia, and the feeling that Abdulhamid's government was too weak to deal with it and the other threats to the empire's unity. It was indeed the revolt in Macedonia that sparked the Young Turk Revolution in 1908—a year that also saw the Austrian annexation of Bosnia-Herzegovina, the Bulgarian annexation of East Rumelia and declaration of Bulgarian independence, and the absorption of Crete by Greece. "Macedonia's independence," declared the CUP leaders, "would mean the loss of half of the Ottoman Empire and, therefore, its complete annihilation. . . . Without Macedonia in between, Albania would naturally be lost. Since our border would have to retreat to the gates of Istanbul, the capital would not remain in Istanbul. The removal of our capital from Europe to Asia would exclude us from the European powers and turn us into a second or third class Asiatic state. If, Heaven forfend, we lose Rumelia, then . . . Ottoman sovereignty will be reduced to the level of Iranian power" (in Hanioglu 2011: 200; see also Zürcher 2010: 31).

Rarely can a declaration have been so prophetic; but the Young Turks did everything to try to stave off its realization. Since most of them came from the Balkan provinces, they were in a very real sense fighting for what they regarded as their homeland (Zürcher 2010: 95–109, 118–19). It was their conviction that only the recall of parliament could provide the representative strength necessary to save the empire in a time of crisis. Following the restoration of the Constitution in 1908, elections for a new parliament were immediately held. Abdulhamid clung on for a time but a countercoup in 1909, supposedly engineered by him, led to his deposition and exile (Finkel 2007: 516–17; Aksin 2007: 57–64; Zürcher 2010: 73–83).

If one considers the ideological alternatives widely debated among the Young Turks in the first two decades of the century, it quickly becomes obvious how far a Turkish nation-state was from their thoughts.[42] In 1904 the Tatar writer Yusuf Akçura, whose family had emigrated to Istanbul, published a long and much-discussed article in the Young Turk émigré paper *Türk*, entitled "Three Types of Policy" (Lewis 1968: 326; Zürcher 1997: 134). In it he compared the relative merits of Ottomanism, Islamism, and Turkism. He was skeptical of the Ottomanist goal, feeling that the elements of the empire were too diverse to make it a reality. He also felt that Pan-Islamism, the aim at various times of Abdulhamid and his advisers, was an impossibility in the face of the opposition of the Western colonial powers. He advocated therefore Turkism. But by that he did not mean Turkish nationalism, as that came to be understood after 1923. For Akçura Turkism was Pan-Turkism, or "Pan-Turanianism," the union of *all* the Turkic peoples, those of the Caucasus and Central Asia as much as those of Anatolia. Far from privileging the Turks of Anatolia, as Turkish nationalism was to do, Pan-Turkism reached out to all the elements of an alleged common Turkish civilization, within the empire as well as outside it. It was in pursuit of this dream that Enver Pasha, for long the leading figure among the Young Turks, gave his life fighting the Soviet army in Central Asia in 1922 (Lewis 1968: 351; Zürcher 1997: 124).

Even the most ardent nationalist thinker among the Young Turks, the sociologist Ziya Gökalp—who had a profound influence on Mustafa Kemal—did not advocate a purely ethnic Turkish nationalism. Gökalp, a follower of the French sociologist Emile Durkheim but also a student of the German sociologist Ferdinand Tönnies, made a key distinction between "culture" and civilization," similar in many ways to Tönnies's distinction between *Gemeinschaft* and *Gesellschaft*. The one was national, the other international; all societies partook of both. What Gökalp called "Turkism"—the language and popular culture of the ordinary people, as opposed to the "alien" Ottoman language and culture—expressed the national culture of the Turks; but Turks also drew on the international civilization of Islam, just as European nations drew upon the international civilization of Christianity. "Our national ideal will be Turkishness; our international ideal will be Islam"" (Gökalp 1959: 103). Unlike Mustafa Kemal, Gökalp never renounced Islam as an essential part of Turkishness. But he did argue that for Islam to play its part in the national culture, it would have to divest itself of its outward, "churchly" (*ümmet*) aspects, taking on more the character of a private religion—as Protestantism, severed from the state, had become the privatized religion of many northern European nations. That would leave the way clear for Turkey to participate increasingly in the new international civilization of science and industry, the civilization that in the West had increasingly displaced Christianity in the public life of society. Hence the threefold aspects of modern Turkish nationality—Turkism, Islam, and Western modernity—would be harmonized (Gökalp 1959: 71–76).[43]

The late arrival of Turkish nationalism is attested to by Gökalp himself. "Until the revolution in Anatolia [1920–23], the name of our state, our nation, and even our language, was 'Ottoman'. No one could dare use the word 'Turkish' for them. Nobody could claim to be a Turk" (Gökalp 1959: 305). Allowing for the rhetorical exaggeration in this claim, it makes a fundamental point. Throughout the whole "Second Constitutional Period" (1908–18), it was the struggle for the Ottoman Empire, not for a national Turkish state, that dominated thought and policy. It is true that in the wake of "the Balkan catastrophe"—the Balkan Wars of 1912–13 as seen by Turks—and the reduction of the empire to the condition of an "Asiatic state," some members of the CUP—Mustafa Kemal among them—began to envisage a new Turkish state centered on Anatolia; and indeed in 1913, for the first time in its entire history, the Ottoman Empire had a Turkish majority (Zürcher 2010: 120; Hanioglu 2011: 37–38). But this remained a distinctly minority view, not shared by most of the leaders of the CUP. Only the further catastrophe of defeat in the First World War, and the threat of the total breakup not just of the Ottoman Empire but of any viable successor state, brought Turkish nationalism to the forefront as the only possible solution to the crisis. It is a measure, though, of the obstacles it faced that even the "National Pact" (Misak-i Milli) adopted by the last Ottoman parliament in January 1920 referred to territories "inhabited by an Ottoman-Muslim majority," not a "Turkish" majority. It was fully in keeping with this view that the National Pact still contemplated recovering the Arab provinces, demanding plebiscites there and also in western Thrace and the Black Sea provinces of Kars, Ardahan, and Batum (lost to Russia in 1878) (Kayali 2008: 127; Zürcher 2010: 137–38, 148, 228). Even at this late date therefore there were many who were reluctant to consign the empire to history (cf. Aksin 2007: 146).

So long as Islam—in the formulation "Ottoman-Muslim"—featured in the aims and demands of the CUP and its successors, it was impossible for Turkish nationalism in the strict sense to establish itself. In 1914 the Ottoman government formally announced the war effort as a *jihad*, and throughout the war Ottoman propaganda appealed to Muslims the world over, asserting the claims to allegiance of the Ottoman sultan-caliph (a claim that particularly worried the British with their millions of Indian Muslim subjects). In the numerous "Defence of National Rights" organizations that sprang up all over the empire in the years 1918–20, Gökalp's formula—"Turkish culture and Islamic civilization"—appeared widely in various guises; and even in the "War of Independence" (1920–23) Mustafa Kemal and others used Islam as a means of mobilizing the peasantry of Anatolia.

We can, if we wish, speak of "religious nationalism" (Zürcher 2010: 278) in this as in certain other cases (e.g., the use of Catholicism in Polish nationalism) as long as we remember the possible contradiction. Islam always carried a transnational, indeed universal, message; and even if for practical purposes it might sometimes be restricted to the Muslim subjects of the Ottoman Empire, it would at the very least have had to include not just Turks but other such Muslim groups as the Kurds ("Turks and Kurds," as a common community, is indeed a formulation that we encounter frequently in the proclamations of the resistance movement).[44]

It was indeed in the War of Independence—but not before, and not without controversy—that something that can properly be called Turkish nationalism first found utterance. In April 1920 the "Grand National Assembly of Turkey" (Türkiye Büyük Millet Meclisi) was formed in Ankara. This was the first time that the term "Turkey," long in use by Europeans but until recently rarely by Ottomans—was given formal status; it was also the first time that the Ottoman dynasty, and the Ottoman state, were formally repudiated (Kayali

2008: 129; Zürcher 2010: 143). It was a historic moment, and a historic turn-ing point. It announced the arrival of a new state, a national state supposedly founded on the "historic culture" of the Anatolian Turks, one that had roots stretching back to a distant past well before the importation of the "alien" reli-gion of Islam.

From then on Mustafa Kemal moved steadily against Islam, aiming to eradi-cate it as far as possible from the secular, scientific, thoroughly Westernized republican state that he set about creating in the second half of the 1920s and the 1930s. Islam was declared an "Arab religion." Not just "Ottoman Muslims" but Gökalp's Turkish-Muslim synthesis were rejected; the conjunction "Turks and Kurds" disappeared from formal pronouncements, and Kurdish rebel-lions, notably that of 1925, were put down with great ferocity. The Caliphate was abolished in 1924, amid bitter controversy within the new state and to the consternation of millions of Muslims outside Turkey. The religious schools, the *medreses*, were closed down, as were the dervish lodges (*tekkes*). Even the Quran was "Turkified," given a Turkish translation and a Turkish commentary on the text. Mustafa Kemal knew he had to tread warily in this area, given the strength of religious belief among the bulk of the mainly rural population. In the Constitution of 1924, it was stated that Islam would remain the state religion; only in 1928 did he feel confident enough to abolish this provision. Mustafa Kemal seems to have felt—here echoing Gökalp to some extent—that something akin to the Protestant Reformation could be brought about in Turkey, thereby not merely rendering religion a private affair but prepar-ing the way for the wholesale secularization that he thought had occurred in Protestant countries (Hanioglu 2011: 131–59; see also Deringil 1993: 176–81).

Rejecting Islam, and Ottomanism, was one thing; defining Turkish nation-alism was another, one that proved far more difficult in the succeeding years. In the early 1920s, as Turks struggled to ward off Greek, British, and French claims, and the support of the Soviet Union became imperative, Turkish nationalism expressed itself in stridently anti-imperialist, anti-Western terms. Mustafa Kemal even flirted with the new Bolshevik leaders of the Soviet Union, and professed to espouse a form of "Muslim communism" (Hanio-glu 2011: 86–109). The episode was short-lived but revealing. It showed the originally protean nature of Turkish nationalism, and the difficulty it had in establishing clear credentials. In attempting to define Turkishness, Mustafa Kemal (Atatürk, "Father-Turk," after 1934) and his supporters called upon a formidable but bewilderingly diverse array of historical, anthropological, and religious ideas, replete with notions such as the Turks being the creators of human civilization, and Turkish as the original source of all civilized languages. Much of this intellectual baggage was discarded after Atatürk's death in 1938, indicating its unpersuasiveness and the fact that it had not penetrated very deeply into the general population. But the very ingenuity and thoroughness of the search, into which Atatürk personally and energetically threw himself, showed how desperate the founders of the new republic were to promote a new sense of national identity, and how anxious to provide a respectable scholarly base for it.

Turkish nationalism faced an even greater problem in having to square itself with Atatürk's unswerving commitment to Westernization on the European model. Here he identified himself with the extreme Westernizers of the late Ottoman period. "There is no second civilization; civilization means European civilization," declared the Young Turk writer Abdullah Cevdet in 1911 (Lewis 1968: 236, 267). Atatürk did not just believe that, he even attempted to show that Turkish culture was the source of European civilization; in Westernizing, the Turks were only returning to the original path from which they had been diverted by the foreign influence of Islam (Hanioglu 2011: 201–4; Lewis 1968: 358–60). But this claim sat rather uneasily with the equal emphasis on the Central Asian roots of Turkish culture, as did the need to insist—against all Ottoman tradition, including that of the Young Turks themselves—that Anatolia, not Rumelia, had constituted the heartland of the Turks for the past five centuries, and indeed longer still, ever since the Turks had migrated from Central Asia to Anatolia in Neolithic times (Hanioglu 2011: 165–66). The attempt to show the Turkic character of the ancient Anatolian civilization of the Hittites added to the discrepant mix. Atatürk's attempt at a thoroughgoing Europeanization of Turkish culture and society—the adoption of a Latin script in place of the Arabo-Persian one, the replacement of the Muslim calendar by its Gregorian Christian counterpart, the promotion of European dress and manners and Western forms of literature and the arts—all added to the Janus-faced quality of Turkish nationalism: looking westward while at the same time insisting on its distinctively Eastern and Asiatic origins.

As with all nationalist ideologies, their inconsistencies are no bar to their fervent acceptance by a population—quite the opposite seems to be the case. For Turkish nationalism, in its Kemalist variety, the problem seems to have been more its insufficient penetration into the main body of society, beyond a relatively thin stratum of educated urbanites. It was a nationalism of intellectuals, bureaucrats, and military officers rather than of ordinary people whether in the towns or, especially, the countryside. The resulting imbalance, the deep fissures that ran throughout Turkish society, were sharply shown by the repeated interventions of the military in politics after 1950, once multi-party politics was allowed. At a rate of almost once a decade—in 1960, 1971, 1980, and 1997—the military, as the self-styled guardians of the Kemalist heritage, sought to safeguard the secular, unitary state that for them represented the modern Turkish nation. Religion was one kind of threat; the demand for autonomy or even independence by the large Kurdish minority was another. The resurgence of both in recent decades, especially during the rule of the Justice and Development Party of Recep Tayyip Erdoğan has shown how incompletely Attatürk was able to realize his vision.[45]

Coda

The breakdown of empires is one thing; what emerges from the wreckage is another. The causes of the one are not necessarily the causes of the other. In the conflagration of the First World War, the dynastic land empires of the Ottomans, the Habsburgs, the Hohenzollerns, and the Romanovs all collapsed. Their successors were formed as the result of various elements: the interests and ideals—often conflicting—of the victorious Allies; the social and ideological forces contending within the defeated empires; the ingenuity and ability of popular leaders. Luck and contingency as usual played their important roles. Ideas, especially the idea of self-determination as powerfully formulated by Woodrow Wilson in his Fourteen Points, were also a part, but only a part, of the story. The resulting creations could all have been different had the elements fused in different ways.

Out of the Habsburg Empire came little Austria, soon to be absorbed by another empire, the Third Reich of its more powerful German neighbor. From the Hohenzollern realms came the Weimar Republic, which lasted a brief decade or so before also giving way to the same German empire (itself of relatively brief duration). The Bolsheviks ensured that, alone of all the defeated empires, the Romanov Russian Empire would give rise to another empire, the Soviet Union.

There was nothing logical or inevitable about the emergence of the Republic of Turkey from the Ottoman Empire. The very name "Turkey," as we have seen, was first used only in the 1920s. The crushing terms agreed by the Allies at the Treaty of Sèvres (1920) called for Turkey to be reduced to no more than a rump consisting of Istanbul and parts of central Anatolia—probably under British supervision, in a manner comparable to rule over the other British mandates granted by the League of Nations. Only the determined resistance led by Mustafa Kemal made possible the creation of a more viable state. That it took the form that it did—of a secular nationalist state formed in the image of Western modernity—was itself the result of a highly improbable constellation of forces, of which the attempt to suppress Islam appears in retrospect as the one least likely to have succeeded.

The comprehensive rejection of the Ottoman Empire, and of the Ottoman past, was another striking feature of the new state, one that like Islam was likely to return to haunt it. Of all the empires considered in this book, the Ottoman was the most "imperial," in the sense of conforming most closely to the principles of empire. It practiced, more thoroughly than any other empire, the principles of difference and diversity, while seeking to maintain an overarching identity as a universal civilization. Race, ethnicity, and nationality were anathema to it. Religion was important—indeed part of its missionary goal—but not to the extent of undermining its commitment to the communities that did not share its religious beliefs. To call this toleration is, as we have seen, misleading, since that presupposes an acceptance that was alien to the Ottoman way of thinking. But what the Ottomans showed was a pragmatism and a realism that go a long way toward explaining the six-hundred-year survival of the empire. Only when the constellation of international forces changed decisively against it was its survival threatened. Whether or not it had to disappear—whether it did not in the end belong to the modern world—will always remain a moot point, as in the case of many other empires. What can at least be said is that, at its best, the Ottoman Empire offered to the world a remarkable model of how different communities can coexist under the shelter of a supranational power. The replacement of the Ottoman Empire by the Turkish state can in that sense be seen as a loss—though not one that can be blamed upon the Turks alone.

4

The Habsburg Empire

In other countries dynasties are episodes in the history of the people; in the Habsburg Empire peoples are a complication in the history of the dynasty.

—A.J.P. TAYLOR ([1948] 1990: 12)

Habsburg history is in both the particular and the general sense not national but European history. From its earliest origins the family was entrusted with the task of resolving the tensions between the west and the east, north and south.

—ADAM WANDRUSZKA (1964: 183)

Your Majesty can now eliminate the Austrian monarchy or re-establish it. But this conglomeration of states must stay together. It is absolutely indispensable for the future well-being of the civilized world.

—COUNT TALLEYRAND TO NAPOLEON BONAPARTE, AFTER AUSTRIA'S DEFEAT AT AUSTERLITZ, 1805 (INGRAO 1994: 237)

The Habsburg Empire in Retrospect

Of all the empires discussed in this book, the Habsburg Empire is the most tortuous, treacherous, and protean. There are even, as we shall see, difficulties and disputes about what exactly to call it, how to name it. But at the same time it is also—if such a thing is permitted of empires—the most *lovable*. All empires inspire a certain degree of nostalgia after their demise. In the case of the Habsburgs, this can border on the clinical. Partly this has to do with the sad fate of Austria in the decades after the fall of the empire, as it got swallowed up in the greater German Reich of the Nazis and suffered something of the consequences of their infamy and downfall. More probably it is owing to the glow cast over the empire by its twilight years, in the late nineteenth and early twentieth centuries.

For it was in the great cities of the empire—Vienna, Prague, Budapest—that at this time much of the intellectual and artistic equipment of the twentieth-century world was fashioned. The great names say it almost all: in philosophy, Ernst Mach, Ludwig Wittgenstein, Karl Popper, Moritz Schlick, and the members of the Vienna Circle; in psychoanalysis, Josef Breuer, Sigmund Freud, Alfred Adler, and Wilhelm Reich; in anthropology and sociology, Bronisław Malinowski, Paul Lazarsfeld, and Marie Jahoda; in economics, Joseph Schumpeter, Ludwig von Mises, Friedrich von Hayek, and the "Austrian school" of economics; in architecture, Otto Wagner and Adolf Loos; in literature, Karl Kraus, Arthur Schnitzler, Hugo von Hofmannsthal, Stefan Zweig, Joseph Roth, Robert Musil, Franz Kafka; in music, Anton Bruckner, Gustav Mahler, Hugo Wolf, and the "Second Viennese School" of Arnold Schönberg, Alban Berg, and Anton von Webern; in painting Gustav Klimt, Egon Schiele, and Oskar Kokoschka. Look into virtually any field of thought and the arts of our own time, and there one will almost certainly find the pioneers among that astonishingly creative generation that lived in the last years of the Habsburg Empire. The contrast between that era and the provincial status of Austria after the end of empire only serves to deepen the nostalgia for that lost "Golden Autumn."[1]

There will be those who will immediately remind us of the other, darker, side of these years: that Adolf Hitler, Austrian-born, found much material for his thought in the rampant anti-Semitism of the cities, and learned much of his brutal politics from the racist Viennese politician Georg von Schönerer and his German Nationalism movement; that, reacting to all this, the Viennese journalist Theodor Herzl felt himself forced to choose the Zionist path. The twilight of the Habsburg Empire was not all sweetness and light, not even when allowed to be bathed in melancholy. But it was precisely in the clash and conflict of peoples and ideas, and in the very violence of the encounter, that the creativity flourished. The end of empires is never an easy time; the rash of suicides in Austria at this time is some testimony to the strain. But, rather as evolution shows in the case of the end of species, it is in the prelude to extinction that a culture sometimes throws up its most dazzling and flamboyant exhibits. Whether the Habsburg Empire was in fact destined for extinction, at least at the time when it occurred, is of course a much-debated issue. But there is no denying a certain sense of urgency, a feeling of apprehension and even desperation, in the atmosphere of the late nineteenth-century empire. This was the general mood of the fin de siècle throughout Western Europe, but it seems to have achieved a particular crystallization in Austria, especially in the city of Vienna. "People have to be prepared for the world war looming ahead," wrote the countess Marie Ebner-Eschenbach in 1899. "In order to gobble each other up, they must now sharpen their teeth" (in Spiel 1987: 97).

We will return to the late Habsburg Empire. First, though, we must consider the principle features of the empire, as it evolved especially from the sixteenth century. Here we immediately encounter one of the most distinctive aspects of the dynasty, its far-flung, Europe-wide, character. At one time Habsburgs ruled a bewilderingly disparate group of territories that stretched from the Atlantic to the Carpathians and beyond, and from the North Sea to the Mediterranean and the Adriatic. There was Habsburg rule in Spain, Italy, Burgundy, and the Netherlands; Austria, Bohemia, Hungary, Croatia, and parts of Germany. For a time Portugal was annexed to Spain. As more or less hereditary Holy Roman emperors the Habsburgs had a diffuse but nonetheless real influence over many German, and some non-German, states. The Habsburgs shared in the partition of Poland; later they acquired more territories in the Balkans from a weakened Ottoman Empire. This leaves out the vast swath of New World lands, and possessions in Africa and Asia, conquered by Habsburgs in the sixteenth century. No other European dynasty ever combined on such a scale continental and overseas holdings.

Of course this can give a misleading impression of unity. Though Habsburgs might rule in all these lands, they did not rule as a single unified entity. Most significant was the distinction between the Spanish and the Austrian Habsburgs, a distinction that lost its meaning only with the death of the last Spanish Habsburg in 1700. We shall in this chapter be dealing mainly with the Austrian Habsburgs; but it is right that we should start with the senior branch, the Spanish Habsburgs, rulers of one of the greatest empires the world has ever known.

Habsburg Spain and the Spanish Empire

"This monarchy of Spain," wrote the visionary and widely read Calabrian friar Tommaso Campanella in 1607, "which embraces all nations and encircles the world, is that of the Messiah, and thus shows itself to be the heir of the universe" (in Pagden 1990: 50). Campanella, author of the famous utopia *City of the Sun* (c. 1602), expressed an apocalyptic and millenarian view of the role

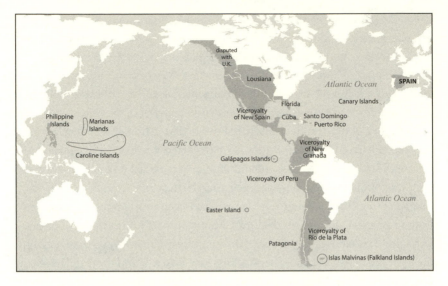

MAP 4.1. The Spanish Empire at its greatest extent, 1790

of Spain that was, as Anthony Pagden has shown, quite widespread in the sixteenth- and seventeenth-century Spanish Empire, and even beyond. To Campanella's contemporary the Piedmontese scholar Giovanni Botero, the Spanish Empire "surpasses every empire that has ever been." It is the only one to encompass such a vast area and to embrace "such a great variety of peoples, divided by language, customs, religion, and by every other quality" (in Pagden 1990: 55). Such views were not restricted to Spanish subjects like Campanella and Botero. The French nobleman Pierre de Bourdeille, lord of Brantôme, who had served with the Spanish army, in 1600 wrote admiringly of the Spaniards:

> They have conquered the Indies, East and West, a whole New World. They have beaten us and chased us out of Naples and Milan. They have passed to Flanders and to France itself, taken our towns and beaten us in battle. They have beaten the Germans, which no Roman emperor could do since Julius Caesar. They have crossed the seas and taken Africa. Through little groups of men in citadels, rocks, and castles, they have given laws to the rulers of Italy and the estates of Flanders. (in Kamen 2003: 487)

Henry Kamen (2003), in his comprehensive account of the Spanish Empire, is at pains to emphasize that Spain did not accomplish this staggering feat entirely on its own. Far from it: it depended throughout on contributions, of men, money, material resources, and technical knowledge, from Italians,

Flemings, Germans, Portuguese, even French and English. Madrid might, at least from the time of Philip II, be the head of the empire, Castilians the "state-bearing people," and Castilian the language of empire. It is this that allows us to speak at all of "the Spanish Empire," allowing, as is common, Castile to stand for Spain. But, like most empires, the Spanish Empire was multinational not just in the composition of its far-flung population but in its ruling elites and many of its key figures. It depended critically on such leaders as Allesandro Farnese, prince of Parma, a brilliant commander who became governor of the Netherlands; the Genoese Ambrogio, marquis of Spinola, a banker who went on to become one of Spain's most successful generals in the war against the Dutch; Antoine Perrenot de Granvelle, later cardinal, from the Franche-Comté, a trusted adviser to a succession of Habsburg rulers and later viceroy of Naples. We are reminded that, though sailing under the Spanish flag, Christopher Columbus was Genoese, and Ferdinand Magellan Portuguese. Even Charles V, the great architect of Spain's empire, was more Flemish than Spanish, and learned Castilian as his second language (his first was always French). "The truth was," says Kamen, "that Spain was a poor country that made the leap into empire because it was aided at every turn by the capital and expertise and manpower of other associated people" (Kamen 2003: 489; see also 2005: 244–47; Braudel 1975, 1:208–14).

But the very term "Spanish Empire" is disputed, in respect of both its elements. For what was "Spain" at this time? Was it any more than the "geographical expression" that was Italy in Metternich's eyes in the nineteenth century? The fight against the Moors had certainly rallied many Spaniards to the cause, and brought about a certain sense of unity. From the time of the victory at Granada, in 1492, soldiers of all nations fighting for the Spanish crown were exhorted to go into battle under the battle cry, "Santiago, España!" (Kamen 2003: 332). Even though the medieval concept of Hispania related to Spain mainly as a geographical entity, a certain sense of commonality, as against foreigners such as the French or English, had begun to appear among the inhabitants of the Iberian peninsula as contact with the outer world developed. This was heightened by the work of humanists who looked back to the old Roman Hispania, when Spain was not many provinces but merely two, Hispania Citerior and Ulterior. One could therefore hope to reunite Spain on that historical basis (Elliott 1970: 19).

In addition, there was the undoubted prominence of Castile, and its growth as a synecdoche for the whole of Spain. With the acquisition of Granada, the Crown of Castile in the fifteenth and sixteenth centuries occupied about two-thirds of the Iberian peninsula, and accounted for more than three-quarters of its population (the Crown of Aragon and the kingdoms of Navarre and Portugal shared the rest). Aragon, centered on Catalonia and the great commercial port of Barcelona, had flourished in the fourteenth century. But in the fifteenth century it went into steep decline with the eclipse of Catalonia, battered especially by the ravages of the Black Death, which afflicted Catalonia far more than other parts of Spain. Making use of Genoese financiers and traders, Castile in these years by contrast greatly expanded its wool trade, and through building up Seville in the south and the Cantabrian ports in the north strengthened its maritime links with the northern nations (Braudel 1975, 1:343–44, 500–508).

In the marriage of Isabella of Castile and Ferdinand of Aragon in 1469, and the Union of the Two Crowns in 1479, it was evident by this time that Castile would be the senior partner. In the works of the Castilian chroniclers and historians of the sixteenth century, which tended to provide the master narrative then and since, Castile and Castilians were presented as the makers of Spain and of the Spanish Empire (Kamen 2003: 333–35). Just as happened later with "England" and "Britain," the elision and equation of "Castile" and "Spain" became natural, at least to the numerically preponderant Castilians as well as many outsiders. Castilians took the lead in the exploration and exploitation of the New World. Their language, achieving predominance in Spain itself, was clearly marked out to be the master language of empire. In 1492 the humanist Elio Antonio de Nebrija published a Castilian grammar—the first of its kind in Europe. When asked by Isabella what it was for, the reply given by the bishop of Avila was "Your Majesty, language is the perfect instrument of empire." This was to prove prophetic. In both Spain and the wider empire, Castilian language and literature established themselves as the dominant culture, the culture of an empire spearheaded and directed by Castilians. "Ferdinand and Isabella, in giving Castile a new sense of purpose and direction, had released the springs of action. It was Castile, rather than Spain, which burst into life in the late fifteenth century. . . . Already, to the Castilians, Castile was Spain" (Elliott 1970: 128–29; cf. Braudel 1975, 1:163; Lynch 1991: 3–4, 25–26).

But for many especially within Spain, the assumption of superiority by Castile, and the equation of Castile and Spain, were hotly contested. Local and regional sentiment was profound, then as now. Catalans, Aragonese, Valencians, Navarrese, Basques, and Andalusians took pride in their regional identities and carried them into the New World settlements (Kamen 2003: 348–49). Despite some centralizing moves by Isabella and Ferdinand, the kingdoms of Castile and Aragon continued to have separate political systems, and to operate according to their own traditional ways. Economically too the peninsula remained divided, each part pursuing its traditional activities and jealously guarding its privileges. "Economically as much as politically," says Elliott, "*Spain* existed only in embryo" (1970: 125; cf. Lynch 1991: 5–9). Only in the persons of "the Catholic kings" did it exhibit any unity. If this was indeed a "Spanish Empire," it was an empire of many Spains.

If the Spanishness of the empire can be questioned, so too, according to some, can its very status as an empire. "There never was, of course," claims Anthony Pagden, "a 'Spanish Empire'":

> Although contemporaries sometimes referred to the territories over which first the Habsburgs and then the Bourbons ruled as an empire, and although in many respects the administration of those territories was an imperial one, they were always, in theory and generally in legal practice, a confederation of principalities held together in the person a single king. Naples remained a kingdom ruled by a viceroy, the king's *alter ego*, and Milan never ceased to be a duchy with the current Spanish sovereign as its duke. The Americas, as the *criollos*, the American-born Spaniards, were later forcibly to remind their king, were never colonies but kingdoms, and—in this they were unique—an integral part of the crown of Castile. (Pagden 1990: 3)[2]

It is true that the Spanish Empire was rarely if ever so-called—not even in relation to its overseas possessions. The usual term was *monarquia española*, "the Spanish Monarchy" (Muldoon 1999: 114–27; Elliott 1989b: 7; Pagden 1995: 15–16). It was as king of Castile, Aragon, and the other territories held by the Spanish crown that Charles V ruled his vast inheritance. If he was an emperor—which he was—it was as Holy Roman emperor, an office to which he was elected in 1519. This gave him rights and responsibilities in Germany, to which he was also bound by his relationship to his brother Ferdinand, ruler of the Austrian lands. Since it was Ferdinand, not Charles's son Philip, who succeeded Charles as Holy Roman emperor, the tendency was reinforced of speaking of "the Spanish Monarchy" and thinking of the Habsburg Empire largely in terms of the Austrian branch.

But this should be seen as a matter of mere words. If Charles V did not have an empire, it is difficult to think to what entity the word should apply. The Spanish humanist Antonio de Nebrija observed that "though the title of Empire is in Germany, the reality of power is held by the Spanish monarchs who, masters of a large part of Italy and the Mediterranean, carry the war to Africa and send all their ships, following the course of the stars, to the isles of the Indies and the New World" (in Kamen 2003: 9). It was indeed the combination of German empire and Spanish monarchy that conferred such power on the Habsburgs, making of their lands a world empire. The astute dynastic alliances forged by Ferdinand and Isabella, linking their family with the Habsburgs through a double marriage between the two royal houses, had unexpectedly brought the succession to their grandson, Charles of Ghent, on the early deaths of other possible, and from the point of view of the Catholic kings, more desirable heirs. The joint Spanish and Habsburg inheritance delivered to Charles—as Charles I of Spain and Charles V, Holy Roman emperor of the German people—the greatest realm in all Europe. As king of Aragon (which included the territories of Catalonia and Valencia), at his accession in 1517 Charles also ruled over Naples, Sicily, and Sardinia; in 1535 he added the Duchy of Milan to his titles, thereby consolidating Spanish predominance in the Italian peninsula, which was to last for more than two centuries (after which it was handed over to the Austrian Habsburgs). From his paternal grandmother, Mary of Burgundy, and via his father, Philip the Fair of Burgundy, Charles inherited the Franche-Comté and the Netherlands. Through his paternal grandfather, Maximilian of Austria, as the eldest son he was the senior ruler in the Habsburg's Austrian territories—which during his reign came to include the crown lands of Bohemia, Croatia, and Hungary. As Holy Roman emperor he could call upon the imperial German states and cities for aid and assistance in all his campaigns. And as king of Castile he was the ruler not simply of the largest, richest, and most populous part of Spain but of the vast Castilian possessions in the Americas, Africa, and Asia. Truly was Charles, as was said of his great predecessor, Frederick II, as Holy Roman emperor, *stupor mundi*—the "wonder of the world."

His son Philip II inherited these immense possessions and even increased them. He might not be Holy Roman emperor—that title passed to his uncle Ferdinand of Austria. But Philip at his accession was married to Mary Tudor, and had hopes that England and Ireland might be added to his realms (her death in 1558, without an heir, cut short these hopes, though he had designs also on her half sister Elizabeth, and later hoped to marry his son Carlos to Mary Stuart). In 1580 he added, by an enforced family claim, the throne of Portugal to his domains, thereby at a stroke inheriting all of the many overseas Portuguese colonies in South America, Africa, and Asia. His might be more of a Spain-based, Atlantic empire, unlike the Flemish-based, Central European empire of his father. But it was without question the greatest empire in the

FIGURE 4.1. Juan Pantoja de la Cruz, *Emperor Charles V with a Baton*
(copy of a portrait by Titian). © Museo Nacional del Prado/Art Resource, NY.

world at that time. Philip himself seems to have thought that, despite not possessing the imperial title, he, rather than the emperor Ferdinand, had inherited the imperial mission of his father Charles and, through him, that of Charlemagne. With him there had been a *translatio imperii ad Hispanos*. Through the *monarquia del mundo* (the world monarchy) that was Spain, he would continue the universalizing mission of the Roman and medieval empires (Muldoon 1999: 120). It was to Philip's monarchy, as "the heir of the universe," that Campanella attached his messianic hopes. The English Elizabethan chronicler William Camden did not hesitate to call Philip's realms an empire, declaring that it "extended so farre and wide, above all emperors before him, that he might truly say, *Sol mihi simper lucet*, the sunne always shineth upon me" (in Kamen 2003: 93).

Moreover, we should not take too seriously the other objections to speaking of the Spanish Empire—that the empire was not, strictly speaking, Spanish, and that it was created by many nationalities both within and outside its borders. Both of these features have been true of most empires. The Spanish Empire was normal in having a "state-bearing" people, the Castilians, who stood in for the other peoples of the Spanish peninsula, much as the English stood in for the other peoples of the United Kingdom. It was also normal in being strongly multinational, at all levels of society. We are accustomed to speaking of the multinational character of the Habsburgs' Austrian Empire, without pausing to think of how equally that applies to the branch of empire ruled by their Spanish brethren.

If empire it was, of what kind was the Spanish Empire? To the humanists who accompanied Charles on his journey south to take up his inheritance in Spain, Charles represented the renewal of the Roman Empire as continued by the medieval Holy Roman Empire of Charlemagne and his successors (Yates 1975: 20–28; Braudel 1975: 2:674–75; Pagden 1995: 40–46; Headley 1998). Charles's tutor and lifelong adviser, the Piedmontese Mercurino Arborio di Gattinara, was a student of Dante's *De Monarchia* and saw in Charles the universal monarch, the *Dominus Mundi*, Lord of the World, that Dante had regarded as necessary for the peace and happiness of the world. Gattinara's hopes chimed with the mood of apocalyptic expectation powerfully present at this time. Ariosto's *Orlando furioso* of 1516 prophesied the rule of a new Charlemagne in the person of Charles, who like the best Roman emperors of old would bring back the reign of Justice. Ariosto adds that with the conquest of the New World, unknown to the Romans, Charles will surpass Rome: that was the meaning of Charles's famous device of the two columns of Hercules with its motto, *Plus Oultre*—"still further"—that came to be known throughout Europe (Yates 1975: 22–23; Elliott 1989b: 8).

If Charles represented a renewal not just of the classical Roman Empire but of the Christianized Holy Roman Empire, then his mission was marked out for him. He had to defend Christianity against its enemies and to carry it into infidel lands. "In defence of Christendom," he declared to the Diet of Worms in 1521, "I have decided to pledge my kingdoms, dominions and friends, my own body and blood, my soul and my life" (in Lynch 1991: 96). He might even, as urged by the Erasmians at the Spanish court, reform the Church, rooting out the abuses that were attracting the attention of others such as Luther (the sack of Rome by imperial troops in 1527, though condemned by Charles himself, was seen by some of his supporters as a providential warning to the papacy that it needed to mend its ways) (Yates 1975: 25).

The reforms were not carried out—not, at least, to the satisfaction of the Lutherans—and Charles and his Habsburg successors found themselves put at the head of the Counter-Reformation, the century-long struggle against the Protestant heresy that achieved some sort of weary resolution at the Peace of Westphalia in 1648. At the same time there was the growing "Turkish threat," the onslaught of the Ottomans that resulted in the first siege of Vienna, in 1529–30, the loss of most of Hungary, and the Ottoman challenge to Spain in the western Mediterranean. Austrian and Spanish Habsburgs found themselves menaced on both fronts, in Central Europe and the west. They united against the common enemy and, as Holy Roman emperors, assumed the role of defender of the faith against the infidel. Here, then, was a Habsburg mission—the defense of Christian Europe against its enemies both within and without—that could and did become a rallying cry for Habsburgs down the centuries, from the sixteenth to the nineteenth.

It was, though, Charles V himself who first and most spectacularly provided the inspiration for the theorists of empire. It was because his career and ambitions most readily brought to mind the greatest empire of classical antiquity, that of Rome. Italy was, at least in the eyes of his humanist advisers such as Gattinara, the key to Charles's empire, and it was in Italy that he most energetically pursued the imperial goal (Headley 1998: 59–65). His Aragonese inheritance had already given him Naples, Sardinia, and Sicily. Following the defeat of the French at the decisive Battle of Pavia (1525), he was able to enforce his title to the Duchy of Milan and go on to establish unquestioned Spanish dominance of the peninsula. The parallel with Rome inevitably and as it were naturally suggested itself As Anthony Pagden puts it:

Spain . . . became part of a wider Italian project for the creation of a European *imperium* which would provide a defence against the Turks without and the menace of the religious conflict offered by the presence of Calvinism within. In this there could be little doubt that the new Carolingian empire provided the same goods as the old Roman one had: protection and the security of the *civitas*, now understood not as civil society under threat from the barbarians but as Christianity under threat from unbelievers and heretics. The continuity between the ancient and the modern *imperia* was guaranteed as much by the translation of power from Augustus to Constantine the Great and from Constantine to Charles V, the *alter Karolus*, via Charlemagne, as it was by the objectives which all these monarchs had pursued. As the imperial historian Pedro de Mexia (1500–52) observed, the history of Rome was the history of an empire which in "longevity, size and power" was the greatest of all empires because it had begun "a little less than 2300 years ago and is still alive today." (Pagden 1995: 41–42; cf. Elliott 1989b: 8–9)

The principles of the classical and Christian empires could be merged in a stupendous effort that led not just to the unification of Spain and the conquest of the Muslim state of Al-Andalus—the process usually though somewhat misleadingly known as the Reconquista—but also to Spain's outpouring overseas and the construction of an entirely new empire in the New World. It could scarcely escape anyone's attention that 1492, which saw the final victory over the Moors at Granada, was also the year that Columbus set sail for the Indies. The conquest and colonization of the New World seem only too clearly an extension of the imperial drive within the peninsula itself. As Ronald Syme put it, "the enterprises across the ocean are a direct continuation both of the Reconquest and of the campaign against the infidel in North Africa." Moreover, this was "not only a religious crusade. The Spaniards, ever conscious of imperial Rome (and haunted perhaps by the fame of their Trajan), were impelled by a deep sense of mission to conquer and also to govern" (Syme 1958: 27; cf. Parry [1966] 1990: 37; Fradera 2007: 45; Kamen 2003: 16–17; Elliott 2006: 20).

But that mission, in a religious age and under the aegis of the Holy Roman emperors, was bound to be overwhelmingly colored with a religious hue. "Christendom," argues Michael Doyle (1986: 110), "is . . . the proper perspective from which to view the religious drive behind the Spanish justification for empire. Colonization, in effect, was an entrepreneurial venture of Christendom." It is necessary to be reminded of this in view of the tendency, common in a secular age, to take a largely materialist view of the Spanish as of most modern empires. Was it not Hernán Cortés himself, conqueror of Mexico, who asserted, "I came here to get rich, not to till the soil like a peasant"—nor, presumably, to convert the heathen? Gold and silver, it is said, constituted the main motive of empire and the "sheet anchor of Spain's power" (Kamen 2003: 493). When, in the seventeenth century, Spain went into decline—or so it seemed to many, then and since—it was common to blame the excessive dependence on American bullion, and the corrupting effects of that dependence. The Flemish scholar Justus Lipsius wrote to a Spanish friend in 1603, "Conquered by you, the New World has conquered you in turn, and has weakened and exhausted your ancient vigour" (in Elliott 1989b: 25).

The sources of Spain's weaknesses in the seventeenth century, after the glories of the sixteenth under Charles V and Philip II, have been much debated.[3]

The dwindling supply of New World silver, and consequent inability to keep up the expenses of great power status, have always been seen as one of the main causes. But a concentration on such factors blinds us to the powerful ideological drive that underlay the imperial enterprise alike in Spain and the New World. The monumental achievements of the Spanish kings, conquistadors, and clergy are inconceivable without it. Greed and riches have always been strong motives for empire, but no empire would be sustained for very long by those motives alone. The Spanish Empire lasted from the sixteenth to the nineteenth century, and missionary zeal, as with the Roman Empire, is a central part of the explanation of its longevity. The Castilians, as the driving force of that empire, had developed, as J. H. Elliott puts it, "a powerful strain of messianic nationalism. The achievement of world-wide empire and an extraordinary run of victories had helped convince Castilians that they were the chosen people of the Lord, especially selected to further His grand design—a design naturally cast in cosmic terms as the conversion of the infidel, the extirpation of heresy, and the eventual establishment of the kingdom of Christ on earth" (Elliott 1989d: 246; see also Elliott 2006: 67). For Thomas Babington Macaulay indeed, writing in the mid-nineteenth century, the whole of modern Spanish history should be seen in the perspective of the Christianizing mission.

> The Crusades had been merely an episode in the history of other nations. The existence of Spain had been one long Crusade. After fighting Mussulmans in the Old World, she began to fight heathens in the New. It was under the authority of a Papal bull that her children steered into unknown seas. It was under the standard of the cross that they marched fearlessly into the heart of great kingdoms. It was with the cry of 'St James for Spain', that they charged armies which outnumbered them a hundredfold. . . . In the year in which the Saxons, maddened by the exactions of Rome, broke loose from her yoke, the Spaniards, under the authority of Rome, made themselves masters of the empire and of the treasures of Montezuma. Thus Catholicism which, in the public mind of Northern Europe, was associated with spoliation and oppression, was in the public mind of Spain associated with liberty, victory, dominion, wealth, and glory. (Macaulay [1840] 1907: 50)

Thus was the empire in the New World fitted into a missionary conception already elaborated for that in the Old. Shortly after Charles was elected Holy Roman emperor, Hernán Cortés wrote to him from Mexico: "The things of this land are so many and of such a kind that one might call oneself emperor of this kingdom with no less glory than that of Germany, which, by the Grace of God, Your Majesty already possesses." Anthony Pagden comments on this: "'New Spain' was to be no mere province, much less a colony. It was to be a kingdom within the world empire of Charles V. . . . New Spain was to be a Germany overseas, with the emperor as its sovereign lord and Hernán Cortés as its governor and de facto ruler. The whole history of the conquest of Mexico was conceived as a *translatio imperii* from the old world to the new" (Pagden 1987: 52; cf. Muldoon 1999: 88; Elliott 2006: 5).

Despite the fact that the American possessions had been incorporated into the crown of Castile as early as 1523, the *criollo* elites of Mexico and Peru insisted that their lands were "kingdoms" in very much the same sense as Aragon, the Netherlands, and Naples were kingdoms within a "Greater Spain," *magnae hispaniae*, ruled by a single sovereign. As such they had the same rights as had been granted by the Spanish sovereigns to their European counterparts. They should, that is, be treated as self-governing entities with their own customs and traditions, owing allegiance only to the sovereign. As kingdoms, not colonies—a word never used of the American possessions—they saw themselves as part of the empire of Greater Spain with a mission to colonize, civilize, and Christianize the heathens they encountered in the New World (Pagden 1987: 63–64, 1995: 137–40; MacLachlan 1991: 17, 25; Elliott 2006: 66–69, 121–22, 238).

The *criollos* were not above making use of a mythologized Indian past as a way of authenticating their title to rule in the Indies. The Aztec and Inca empires could be seen as the equivalent of Greece and Rome, and the *conquistadores* as the heroic successors to those ancient empires, just as the European empires saw themselves as successors to Rome.[4] But this sat uneasily with the increasing emphasis on purity of blood, *limpieza de sangre*, that became such a distinctive feature of the Spanish Empire both at home and overseas.[5] A taint of Indian blood was not something that the status-conscious *criollo* aristocracy wished to admit to, at least after an earlier period in which marriages with the Inca and Mexica nobility were relatively common. Nor did calling upon an Indian past help the case for being regarded as Spaniards, with all the rights and privileges of Spaniards. This became increasingly important in the eighteenth century, under the Bourbon kings, with the arrival of large numbers of peninsular Spanish as merchants and officials who looked upon the *criollos* as provincial boors, corrupted by their life in the New World.

Eventually the competition between *criollos* and *peninsulares*, and a growing sense of a distinctive American identity among the former, brought about rebellion and independence for the *criollo* nations (Elliott 2006: 234–42, 319–24). What is more remarkable, however, is the success of the Spanish crown over a very long period in preventing just such a break, and in maintaining a sense of common purpose between their European and their New World subjects. "Greater Spain," the Spanish Empire in Europe and America, held together its constituent parts even longer than did "Greater Britain" some centuries later. As John Elliott writes, "apart from the struggle between the crown and the followers of Pizarro in the aftermath of the conquest of Peru and the abortive conspiracy by Martin Cortés in Mexico in 1566, there was no major challenge to the crown from the settler community in the New World in the nearly three hundred years of Spanish rule before it was overthrown by the independence movements of the early nineteenth century." Considering the difficulties posed by time and space in the early modern world, as compared to those facing later empires, this is indeed, as Elliott says, "an extraordinary achievement," and a testimony to the strength of the connection throughout the vast empire of the Spanish Habsburgs (Elliott 1989b: 14; cf. Pagden 1987: 54–56; Parry [1966] 1990: 274).

The relation between *criollos* and *peninsulares*, and between both and the Indians, revealed something of the fault lines apparent in all overseas empires. There is the metropole, striving to maintain central control over its dependencies and sending out its agents to oversee and enforce its policies. There are the settler communities, whose goal is to achieve as much freedom and independence of the mother country as possible without breaking the family ties or losing their metropolitan identities. There are the indigenous populations, alternately protected and abandoned by the metropolitan authorities. In this as in many other respects the Spanish Empire was exemplary. There as elsewhere assertions of settler autonomy were met with reimposed central controls. Settler attempts to exploit the natives were countered with vigorous measures of protection. Eventually a relatively long period of metropolitan control ended with the rejection of metropolitan rule. The successors were either *criollos*, as in both British North America and Spanish South America, or, where European settlements were thin, native peoples, as in British Africa and Asia and in the French, Belgian, and Dutch empires.

In the case of the Spanish Empire, native succession was out of the question owing to the wholesale decline and depopulation of Indian society. The Indians following the Spanish conquest experienced a "demographic catastrophe" of colossal proportions, caused largely by the importation of European diseases (Parry [1966] 1990: 213–28; Crosby 1972: 35–63). All the more poignant therefore was the extraordinary and impassioned debate over Indian rights and metropolitan responsibilities that absorbed some of the best minds of sixteenth-century Spain. The questions were ones that were to exercise all subsequent European colonizers, intent on saving souls as much as on promoting European influence overseas. "Did the duty of conversion involve the right of conquest?—the deposition of native rulers, if indeed the Indians had legitimate rulers? the seizure of their lands? the assertion of Spanish sovereignty over their former subjects? And if the Indians should be reduced, by a just conquest, to the position of vassals of the Spanish crown, what legal and political rights remained to them? Should they be 'converted' by force? Might they be enslaved, or robbed of their property? Were they subject to Spanish courts of law, civil and ecclesiastical? Above all, what justification could be found for those all-important institutions, the *encomienda* and the *repartimiento*?" (Parry 1940: 5; see also Parry [1966] 1990: 139). It is a measure of how seriously the Spanish crown took its responsibilities as a Christian power that it actively encouraged discussion of these questions. In the contributions of the jurist Francisco de Vitoria, in the great debate in Valladolid in 1550 between Fray Bartolomé de Las Casas and Juan Ginés de Sepúlveda, the issues were debated with a subtlety and sophistication unparalleled elsewhere.[6] Nor were they without consequence, mere scholastic exercises. The influence of Las Casas in particular, with his denunciation of the atrocities committed by the settlers and his defense of Indian rights, can be clearly seen in such acts as the New Laws of the Indies of 1542 and the Ordinances of 1573, all aimed at restraining the settlers and affirming Indian rights.

In the debates over Indian rights and capacities, Rome was frequently invoked by all parties (Lupher 2006; MacCormack 2009). It was inevitable that this should be so. Roman law, and Roman history, were central points of reference for all the classically trained Spanish humanists. Romans were, as the anthropologist Claude Lévi-Strauss might have put it, "good to think with." More to the point, the Spanish Empire saw itself as being in direct succession from the Roman Empire, via Charlemagne and the Holy Roman Empire, whose title the Habsburgs had made more or less a family possession. But, being later and more thoroughly Christianized, Spaniards had the ability, and the obligation, to go further than the recently pagan Romans—as Cortés proudly pointed out on more than one occasion (Díaz 1963: 131, 158–59). Moreover, they had conquered parts of the world unknown to the Romans, and had encountered new and different challenges. Their empire must act, in significant respects, differently from the Roman, even as it inherited the basically civilizing mission from its great predecessor.

David Lupher, in his searching exploration of the use of Rome in learned Spanish debates on empire in the sixteenth century, has emphasized that "again and again, Spaniards' application of the Greco-Roman patterns and perspectives to the New World inspired a revaluation of the classical interpretive framework itself. . . . When the 'other' is interpreted and 'domesticated' by an appeal to the familiar, there is always the risk that the current will be reversed and that the familiar will be 'defamiliarized' by the conceptually unruly 'other'" (2006: 321). Such was frequently the fate of comparisons of the Roman and the Spanish empires. This made the classical Roman experience not irrelevant—on the contrary—but it served to bring out the differences between Spain in the New World and the Romans in the Old.

In this respect indeed Spain blazed a new path. What is important about the Spanish Empire, in the history and comparative study of empires, is that Spain was in many ways the first of the modern empires (Elliott 2006: 405–10; Fradera 2007: 67). In its combination of a land and a worldwide overseas empire it added a dimension lacking in all the ancient empires, Alexander's and Rome's included. In its wrestling with the problems of governance of so huge and variegated an entity, in the sophisticated thinking about empire that took place in the first century of imperial rule, the Spanish Empire laid down, as it were, the template of empire, the ground rules for the analysis of modern empires and of the challenges facing them. As the overseers of a land empire, the Ottomans were offering to thoughtful observers at about the same time lessons in the management of diversity. But the non-Muslim peoples they mainly dealt with were "people of the Book," Jews and Christians, who were in many ways kin to them. In the New World, the Spanish had to deal with peoples and customs that were completely outside the experience and even the comprehension of Europeans. This was uncharted territory. The Spaniards were the first to attempt to map out this territory, to set the terms of the discussion and debate that were to occupy European empires for centuries after. If "civility and Christianity" were the declared goals of European conquest, it was the Spaniards who first wrestled with the problems of how this was to be accomplished, and the inevitable contradictions that would arise when these aims conflicted with other, more mundane and material ones.

Spanish and Austrian Habsburgs

On October 25, 1555, in the great City Hall in Brussels, before an audience of dignitaries from nearly all his European realms, Charles V announced his abdication. In his farewell speech he spoke of his travels throughout his lands:

I have been nine times in Germany, six times in Spain, and seven to Italy; I
have come here to Flanders ten times, and have been four times to France in
war and peace, twice to England, and twice to Africa . . . without mention-
ing other lesser journeys. I have made eight voyages to the Mediterranean
and three in the seas of Spain, and soon I shall make the fourth voyage when
I return there to be buried. (in Kamen 2003: 92)

It is a revealing account, telling us much about Charles's priorities and
interests. His Spanish—especially Castilian—subjects frequently complained
about his long absences, as well as his choice at least initially of Netherland-
ers, Burgundians, and Italians, in preference to Spaniards, as his officials and
advisers. Early in his reign Charles had to deal with the revolt of the Castilian
comuneros against what was seen, among other grievances, as excessive foreign
influence and the sacrifice of Castilian interests to those of Charles's other
realms (Lynch 1991: 51–59).

In the end Charles won over his Spanish subjects, and pointedly chose
Spain as the place to end his days. But nevertheless, just as his Spanish subjects
often showed indifference to his Flemish and German affairs, he too often
seemed not to care for Spain as much as for his other lands and their concerns.
As well as being king of Aragon and Castile, he was a Habsburg and Holy
Roman emperor. The fate of the Netherlands and of Germany mattered deeply
to him. That is why his travels took him there more than anywhere else. Next
in importance was Italy, for all Holy Roman emperors since Charlemagne the
symbolic heart of their empire. Not to have an Italian presence, and a commanding influence in Italy, was not to be a Roman emperor, however successful elsewhere. As for the New World, Charles was grateful for the wealth it
brought him—though to a far greater degree to his son Philip II—in support
of his European ventures. But it was not as emperor of the Indies that he primarily saw himself; it was as ruler of a European empire, with Europe-wide
interests and responsibilities. In that sense, as has frequently been observed,
Charles continued in the medieval tradition of the Holy Roman Empire rather
than, as with his son Philip, inaugurating the age of the overseas empires (e.g.,
Chudoba 1952: 14).

It was this tradition too that preoccupied the Austrian Habsburgs who
regained the Holy Roman Empire after Charles's abdication and death. It is
not true to say that the Austrians never interested themselves in an overseas
empire—several attempts were made, though they were all abortive (Kann
1980: 92). But they never acquired one. Their empire remained resolutely,

indeed quintessentially, European. Along with the Ottoman and the Russian empires, from the sixteenth to the twentieth centuries they became one of the leading representatives of the European land empire, sharing much in outlook and preoccupations, and sharing too the same ultimate fate, defeat and collapse after the First World War.

It is important to stress the overlap and continuities between the Spanish and the Austrian Habsburgs, owing to the tendency to treat them separately and differently: the usual result of the regional and specialist concerns of professional historians, together with a conventional periodization that tends to regard the Spanish Empire as mainly "early modern"—a sixteenth- and seventeenth-century development—and the Austrian Empire as mainly an eighteenth- and nineteenth-century affair. But Spanish and Austrian Habsburg concerns were intertwined from the start, and continued throughout the reign of Charles V and his successors. The Habsburgs were a family, a house, with common interests in power—*Hausmacht*—and survival, which they rarely forgot (Wandruszka 1964). The famous marriage alliances—*tu, felix Austria, nube*—that brought the Habsburgs such fabulous possessions and entangled them in virtually every corner of Europe, were a fitting symbol of a family inheritance.

The connection between the Spanish and the Austrian Habsburgs, and their respective possessions, was not just familial but also directly physical and geographical. Their realms were not as physically separate as is usually thought. This was one reason why Italy was so important to the Spanish Habsburgs. Through Spain's rule in northern Italy, the Spanish Habsburgs had a direct connection to the Austrian Habsburgs through the famous mountain route—the Valtelline—that linked Milan with the Tyrol and Habsburg Austria. Troops passing up and down this route had safe passage in Habsburg lands throughout. When Spain was at war with France over the Mantuan Succession (1627–31), it was through the Valtelline that in 1629 units of Count Wallenstein's army were able to come from Germany to the aid of the Spanish crown. Again it was through the Valtelline that in 1634 Spanish troops under the command of the infante Ferdinand linked up with the imperial forces of his cousin Ferdinand II, king of Hungary and later Holy Roman emperor. The "two Ferdinands" then inflicted a crushing defeat on the Swedes and the German Protestant princes at the Battle of Nördlingen (Kamen 2003: 382–86; Chudoba 1952: 242).

Even after the Holy Roman Empire passed to the Austrian Habsburgs, Spain continued to be heavily involved in German affairs. This was partly because of the weakness and vulnerability of Austria in the sixteenth century and the first half of the seventeenth. Charles's brother Ferdinand, ruler of the Habsburgs' Austrian lands, might as Ferdinand I inherit in 1526 the crowns of Hungary, Croatia, and Bohemia—a powerful legacy for the future. But the reason for this inheritance—the result ultimately of the astute marriage policy of his grandfather Maximilian I—was the death without heir of the Hungarian king, Louis II, in the Battle of Mohács (1526), in which the Ottomans routed the Hungarians and took control of the greater part of Hungary. In 1529 the Ottomans not only occupied Buda but also laid siege to Vienna—a threat far more dangerous than the later and more celebrated siege of 1683, when Ottoman power was on the defensive rather than, as with Suleiman II in 1529, sweeping all before it. Suleiman withdrew from the siege not because he was defeated but because he calculated that his losses—many of them due to plague—militated against the further effort required. Hungary was what mattered, and it remained under Ottoman rule for the next 150 years. The Austrian Habsburgs had to wait a long time to come into the inheritance of what became one of the two pillars of the empire.

Despite Ferdinand's succession—at Charles V's instigation—as Holy Roman emperor in 1556, the Austrian Habsburgs remained very much the junior partner in the dynasty (Wandruszka 1964: 102–23). Ferdinand himself never forgot his early education in Spain, and continued to look to it for guidance. For much of the later sixteenth century and the first half of the seventeenth, Habsburg Austria was caught up in the struggles of the Counter-Reformation. Here again Spain and the Spanish Habsburgs, in the reigns of Philip II and his successors, took the lead (Lynch 1991: 342–85; Kamen 1991: 177–90). Charles V had regarded the threat of Lutheranism as the most serious to the integrity of his European empire, but it was only after his death that the conflict came to dominate Europe.

It was from Spain that the Inquisition, with its headquarters in Seville, exercised its powerful influence. It was in Spain that the Jesuits, founded in 1534 by the Spanish soldier and scholar Iñigo López de Recalde (Ignatius de Loyola), began their vigorous campaign against the doctrines of the Reformers, and sent out their missionaries to all lands, including those of Austria. Philip II, in a distinctly coordinated family strategy, made sure to engage his uncle, the emperor Ferdinand, in all his moves against reformers and rebels in his realms, especially those in the Netherlands, and there was a constant exchange of ambassadors and advisers between Madrid and Prague. Ferdinand's successor, his son the emperor Maximilian II, thought by Philip to be too lax toward the Protestants in his realms, was also the recipient of numerous envoys from his cousin—who was also his brother-in-law—pressing stronger measures against the reformers (Chudoba 1952: 132–33, 147–52, 179–82).

Spanish statesmen were clear that the fate of Spain was linked to that of Austria in the Thirty Years' War (1618–48) in Germany, the climactic episode of the Counter-Reformation. "The answer to everything must come from Germany," declared the count-duke of Olivares, convinced that only by shoring up the Austrian Habsburgs in Germany could Spain sustain its rule in northern Europe, by keeping open the crucial route between northern Italy and Flanders (Kamen 2003: 385). The crushing defeat of the Protestant Bohemian nobility at the Battle of the White Mountain (1620) was achieved with Spanish money, Spanish coordination of imperial strategy, and large numbers—over three-quarters of the imperial forces—of Italians, French, and Flemings from Spain's territories in Italy and the Netherlands (Chudoba 1952: 239–48; Ingrao 1994: 32–33). Spanish troops were involved in the victory over the Protestant forces at Nördlingen in 1634. This decisive battle of the Thirty Years' War was in many ways a reprise of an earlier Habsburg victory, that of Charles V against the Lutheran princes of the Schmalkaldic League at Mühlberg in 1547. Here too Germans, assembled by his brother Ferdinand, combined with Spaniards, Italians, and Flemings in an all-Habsburg effort to achieve a famous victory over the Protestant Reformers. Again, in the defeat of the Ottomans at the great naval Battle of Lepanto (1572), generally accounted a Spanish triumph, five thousand German troops from the empire fought alongside Spaniards and Italians, and the entire fleet was commanded by Philip II's half brother, Don John of Austria. Throughout the sixteenth and seventeenth centuries there was to be close cooperation in military as much as ideological matters between the Spanish and Austrian rulers, and a recognition of their mutual dependence (Kamen 2003: 68, 71, 80, 184).

Charles in fact had always thought of the Habsburg inheritance as a joint one, with a common interest and purpose. There was a rough division of labor, with the Spanish arm active in the north and west and the Austrian arm in the south and east. But both sides could expect to draw on a common store of men and money. Thus it was that Spanish troops played an important role in the defense of Vienna against the Ottomans in 1529, just as they were to do again in 1683 (Lynch 1991: 117). Moreover, the impression of a disconnected and dispersed empire—with disparate Spanish, Flemish, Italian, and Austrian parts—is misleading. Charles constructed an elaborate network of postal communication linking all the major cities of empire—those in Spain to Brussels,

Vienna, Milan, and Naples. The system was organized and run by an enterprising family, the Tassis, originally from northern Italy but establishing branches in the Netherlands and Germany, and becoming distinguished members of the Castilian aristocracy (Kamen 2003: 54–55). Such cosmopolitanism and internationalism was typical of Charles's empire, as it was to be of Ferdinand's. It was to be found in the army, the bureaucracy, and the diplomatic corps that served the empire. It was to be seen in the operations of the great German banking family, the Fuggers, who not only supplied the funds that had helped Charles secure the imperial crown in 1519 but at various times came to the financial aid of his brother Ferdinand in his dealings with recalcitrant German princes in his territories (Chudoba 1952: 73; Lynch 1991: 52).

It was not in fact until the heirless death of the last Spanish Habsburg king, Charles II, in 1700, that the Austrian Habsburgs fully came into their own. Before that their own weakness, set against the power and influence of Spain, of necessity made them the subordinate branch of the family, dependent on their Spanish relatives for guidance and support. In the sixteenth and early part of the seventeenth centuries, Protestantism made huge inroads in the Habsburg lands, in Hungary, Bohemia, and Austria itself, reaching into the highest levels of the court and aristocracy. The Austrian Habsburgs, as Holy Roman emperors committed to the Catholic cause in partnership with their Spanish brethren, came close to losing the battle against the Reformers (Evans 1991: 3–40; Ingrao 1994: 28–29). In the Thirty Years' War, sparked by the defenestration of the imperial ambassadors in Prague in 1618, they struggled to make way against the Protestant princes, leading to a peace of exhaustion in the Treaty of Westphalia (1648). The Augsburg formula, *cuius regio, eius religio*, was confirmed, and the Habsburgs were forced to recognize the practical independence of the German Protestants. In 1683 the Ottomans were once more at the gates of Vienna, showing that the Ottoman threat had by no means diminished. Despite Spain's own increasing weakness in the seventeenth century, the balance still favored the western over the eastern Habsburgs. But change was in the air. The feebleness of the last Spanish Habsburg, Charles II, in retrospect could be seen as the harbinger of a remarkable shift in the balance of power in Europe, and in the world.

The Rise of the Austrian Habsburgs

The end of the Habsburg line in Spain in 1700 did not by itself of course ensure the rise of the Austrian Habsburgs. The Thirty Years' War had been a brutal and an exhausting trial of strength, and the Austrian Habsburgs, as Holy Roman

MAP 4.2. The Austrian dominions after 1815

emperors, emerged weakened by the experience, their influence in Germany especially diminished (Kann 1980: 46–47; Ingrao 1994: 48). But, as R.J.W. Evans (1991) has convincingly shown, it was during these years, and especially in the second half of the seventeenth century, that the Austrian Habsburgs gradually recovered and consolidated their power in their realms. Apart from a few pockets, especially in Hungary, they virtually eradicated Protestantism in a triumphant vindication of Catholicism and the principles of the Counter-Reformation. They constructed a powerful, Catholic-based, baroque civilization that extended throughout the Habsburg lands. They at last began to push back the Ottomans, lifting the second siege of Vienna of 1683 and retaking Buda in 1686. At the Peace of Karlowitz (1699) the Habsburgs regained much of Hungary, which had been under Ottoman rule since the Battle of Mohács in 1526. It was a decisive turning point. "Never again could the Ottoman power single-handed threaten the existence of Habsburg power" (Kann 1980: 67; cf. Bérenger 1994: 335–36; Ingrao 1994: 83).

In the War of the Spanish Succession (1701–14) the Austrian Habsburgs failed to secure the Spanish throne for their candidate, but in some sense this seemed also to clear the way for the Habsburgs to concentrate their energies and to make themselves the commanding power in Central Europe. That indeed might make their reach and ambitions sound almost too limited. In return for renouncing their claim to Spain, the Austrians received the Spanish Netherlands and nearly all the Spanish holdings in Italy (Milan, Mantua, Naples, Sicily, Sardinia).[7] Here was at least a partial *translatio imperii*, as Austria took on the Spanish Habsburgs' rule and responsibilities in these widely dispersed European regions. Indeed throughout the succession crisis and subsequent war the Habsburg emperors—Leopold I, Joseph I, and Charles VI—showed their determination to reunite the Habsburg realms and re-create the empire of Charles V. Their failure to achieve this, in the face especially of British opposition, seems only to have strengthened their resolve to buttress their Central European position by establishing themselves firmly in Italy. Italy, until its loss in the later nineteenth century, became a permanent feature of the Habsburg landscape, and a symbolic claim, as of old, to universality. Where Charles V had been, so his successor, the Holy Roman emperor Charles VI, hoped to go. This aspiration extended even to the dream of a colonial empire, which the acquisition of the Spanish Netherlands, and an Atlantic outpost, seemed for the first time to make possible for the landlocked Austrians (Kann 1980: 91–93).

Further gains came following renewed war with the Ottomans, in which the Habsburg hero Prince Eugene of Savoy achieved some of his most famous victories, such as that at Petrovardin in 1716, culminating in the capture of Belgrade in 1717. By the Treaty of Passarowitz (1718) the Ottomans recognized Habsburg rule over Belgrade, the Banat, and the greater part of Serbia, so completing the Habsburg reconquest of Hungary that had begun in 1686. With this, taken with the gains made at Utrecht and Rastatt, Habsburg power reached its greatest extent, the springboard for its enormous influence in Europe in the eighteenth and nineteenth centuries. "Never before had the Viennese Habsburgs ruled over so vast a territory. It was now a great continental power extending from the North Sea to the Carpathians, from Bohemia to the Straits of Messina. It exercised its hegemony over Italy and remained the preponderant power in Germany. Ferdinand would have found it hard to imagine such a revenge in October 1648, at the end of the Thirty Years War" (Bérenger 1997: 24; cf. Kann 1980: 68).

It has indeed seemed possible to speak of the creation at this time of a "second Habsburg empire," nearly as extensive as Charles V's European empire and in territory second only to the Russian Empire of the time (Ingrao 1994: 121). And it was during the second half of the seventeenth century and the first half of the eighteenth that the Habsburgs constructed the social and political system that was the fundamental basis of their existence until the end of empire. It was during these years, especially under the Habsburg rulers and Holy Roman emperors Leopold I (r. 1657–1705), Joseph I (r. 1705–11), and Charles VI (r. 1711–40), that crown, church, and nobility were forged into a powerful, empire-wide, ruling alliance that resisted all challenges to their dominance for over two hundred years. A common set of interests and a common culture, founded on Catholicism and an allegiance to the dynastic principle, bound them together and, in the last resort, overcame the many differences among Czechs, Hungarians, Austrians, Germans, and others, at least at the level of the elites.

Vienna, emerging in these years as the imperial capital and the font of all privileges and honors, drew the nobility from all parts of the empire to set up their residences there and to cultivate a common style of life, centered on the court. The emperors, nobility, and clergy embarked on a massive program of construction, of palaces, churches, and monasteries. By 1730 some 230 aristocratic residences had sprung up in and around Vienna, many of them designed and built by the great baroque architects Johann Bernard Fischer von Erlach and Johann Lukas von Hildebrandt. It was Hildebrandt who built the sumptuous Belvedere Palace for the great military leader Prince Eugene of Savoy; Erlach who designed the Habsburgs' grandiose summer residence of Schönbrunn, aimed at rivaling Versailles. It was Erlach too who began— his son Johann Michael completed—the immense baroque church in Vienna's Karlsplatz, the Karlskirche, with its two giant flanking pillars modeled on Trajan's Column—or perhaps, as with Charles V's emblem, the Pillars of Hercules. The Karlskirche was dedicated to the sixteenth-century saint Carlo Borromeo, but it was probably no accident that it could also be held to glorify his namesake the emperor Charles (Karl) VI, its founder, and the empire he ruled—the imperial references on the columns, going back to classical Rome, were unmistakable. Along the Danube, just outside Vienna, Charles VI also planned a grand imperial palace along the lines of Philip II's Escorial near Madrid—no doubt, once more, to emphasize the *translatio imperii* from the Spanish to the Austrian Habsburgs, now that Spain was ruled by Bourbons. Only one wing of the palace was ever built, but in compensation Charles renovated the adjoining monastery of Klosterneuberg, to make it the grandest and richest in the land. Almost equally imposing were the other monasteries of the time built or reconstructed along the Danube, such as Stift Göttweig, St. Florian, and the towering, fortress-like, Melk.

All scholars have emphasized the extraordinary importance of the arts in creating the common culture that gave the Habsburg lands so distinctive and recognizable a character, one still discernible today in the various successor states of Central and East-Central Europe. Its hallmark was the exuberant Austrian baroque, the *Kaiserstil* or imperial style, adapted from the more restrained Italian baroque to trumpet the triumph of the Counter-Reformation in church and state.[8] It is common to speak of the baroque as an art of elaborate façade, a fantastic and intricate style that strains to produce its effects and seeks to conceal the cracks and strains that eventually show through (e.g., Taylor [1948] 1990: 14; Evans 1991: 443). No doubt there were persisting fault lines in the glittering social order laboriously and quite self-consciously constructed in the years after the Peace of Westphalia. The relations between the center and the regions, among Vienna, Pressburg, and Prague, remained uncertain and unstable, despite the unifying force of an integrated aristocracy. Pockets of Protestantism, in Hungary and Silesia especially, but also in Bohemia, remained to provide the ground of protest, subterranean as much of that had to be. The empire's ambitions frequently outran its reach and its resources, as in its abortive overseas ventures (under British pressure, Charles VI's Ostende Trade Company was wound up in 1731).[9] It remained perilously dependent on the balance of power in Europe, and on its diplomatic skills in preserving Austria's interests.

But the same could be said about practically every other ancien régime in eighteenth-century Europe. In the French case, failure to resolve its problems led to the French Revolution, and several other states also came unstuck in the general crisis of legitimacy that swept over most of Europe in the later eighteenth century. What has to be stressed is the relative success of the Habsburgs in riding the storm, the fact that they emerged from the turmoil with the social order of the ancien régime more or less intact. It is a testimony to the strength of the ruling coalition of crown, church, and nobility forged in the earlier part of the century.

Austria[10] certainly had its reverses in the eighteenth century. Following the War of the Polish Succession (1733–38), the imperial fief of Lorraine was lost to France, and Naples and Sicily went to the Spanish Bourbons; but in compensation the Habsburgs received further territories in central Italy (Parma, Piacenza, and Tuscany) and thereby consolidated their Italian possessions into a more homogeneous and readily defensible whole. Soon after, following another war with the Ottomans, some of the gains in the Balkans—including Belgrade—made at Passarowitz were lost at the Peace of Belgrade (1739); but at the same time a powerful military frontier zone (*Militärgrenze*), peopled by Serbian refugees, was constructed against the Ottomans in the Croatian enclave of Slavonia, and proved one of the Habsburgs' most important redoubts.

More consequential was the loss, in the War of the Austrian Succession (1740–48), of the prosperous province of Silesia to the rising power of Prussia, under its king Frederick II ("the Great"). Once more, though, there were compensations. The great powers accepted the "Pragmatic Sanction" of 1713, which meant that not only was Charles VI's daughter, Maria Theresa, allowed to inherit the Austrian throne but, more important, the powers acknowledged the unity of all the Habsburg lands and the Habsburgs' right to rule over them. In the light of the powerful local institutions and traditions of autonomy in the varied Habsburg domains, this has to be accounted a major accomplishment, one with lasting effects right up to the dissolution of the empire in 1918 (Kann [1950] 1970, 1:9–12, 1980: 58–60; Ingrao 1994: 129–30; Judson 2016: 22–23). Also important was the recognition of Maria Theresa's husband, Francis of Lorraine, as Holy Roman emperor, thereby ensuring that the empire remained a Habsburg—now more correctly a Habsburg-Lorraine—preserve.

With what seems uncanny good fortune, every Habsburg reversal was accompanied by some sort of positive gain. To some observers the Habsburg Empire, having got off to a flying start in the early years of the eighteenth century, was on the shoals by the midcentury. But others, including the Prussian monarch Frederick II, knew otherwise. By midcentury the empire had made itself indispensable to the international system, in particular as a hedge against the constant threat of French power. The idea of "the Austrian necessity," the centrality of the Habsburg lands to the stability of the European order, was established in these years, to become an item of conventional wisdom in the diplomacy of the succeeding century (Ingrao 1994: 237; Taylor [1948] 1990: 38, 137; Sked 2001: 107–8). In the second half of the eighteenth century the empire even managed to reform itself, making enormous strides in rationalizing and modernizing its somewhat ramshackle administration. It is sometimes said that Austria made very little contribution to the European Enlightenment, that the great intellectual movement somehow slipped Austria by. One explanation is that the very strength and success of the culture of the ruling elite, stretching across the whole empire, made critical Enlightenment thought less appealing and less necessary. As Charles Ingrao puts it: "While the obvious shortcomings of Bourbon and Stuart regimes inspired French and British philosophers to seek different values represented by the Enlightenment, the monarchy's

FIGURE 4.2. The empress Maria Theresa. Portrait (1759) by Martin van
Meytens the Younger. © Scala/White Images/Art Resource, NY.

coalition of church, aristocracy, and crown was able to legitimize a system
that had reestablished Catholicism, expelled the Turks from Hungary, and
restructured and revived the *Erblande*'s economy. Rather than resort to skepticism and introspection, the ruling elites spread their own values through their
patronage of the various media of the baroque" (Ingrao 1994: 102).

There is some truth in this. But more to the point, it is not so much that the
Enlightenment passed the Habsburgs by as that they annexed it. "Enlightenment from above" was what the Habsburg lands received, through the thinking and policies of the "Enlightened despots" Maria Theresa and Joseph II.

They thoroughly overhauled the financial, civil, and military administration, well served by statesmen and advisers such as Friedrich Wilhelm Haugwitz, Wenzel Anton Kaunitz, Joseph Sonnenfels, Ignaz Born, and Gottfried van Swieten (Wangermann 1973: 60–105, 158–59; Okey 2002: 25–39; Judson 2016: 28–36). With the dissolution of the Society of Jesus by Pope Clement XIV in 1773, Maria Theresa seized the opportunity to embark on a wide-ranging program of public education, surpassing Prussia in both the availability and the quality of its schools (Ingrao 1994: 188–91). Joseph added to this with measures promoting freedom of expression and extending toleration to Jews, Protestants, and Orthodox subjects. He established firm state control over the Church, seizing many monasteries and reforming clerical education. He abolished serfdom and unpaid labor service (*robota*) throughout the Habsburg lands. Though, owing to the resistance they had stirred up among conservative elements, some of these bold measures were rescinded or moderated after Joseph's death in 1790, his short-lived but astute successor Leopold II (r. 1790–92) managed to preserve most of his legacy, together with Joseph's reputation as an Enlightened reformer, if not the "royal revolutionary" of nineteenth-century liberal imagining (Wangermann 1973: 175–76; Okey 2002: 40–67; Judson 2016: 51–85).[11]

At the same time—*tu, felix Austria, nube*—strategically placed marriages of Maria Theresa's many children—she and Francis Stephen had sixteen—gave the Habsburgs influence in Spanish, French, and many Italian courts, most notably with the marriage of her daughter Marie Antoinette to the French dauphin and future king Louis XVI of France. Most of these states were indeed ruled by Bourbons, and a solid alliance with the Bourbons, ending more than a century of wars with them, was one of the foundations of Austrian security in the second half of the eighteenth century. More solid gains came with the First Partition of Poland (1772), in which Austria received the lion's share with Galicia; Austria also acquired Bukovina—a strategically useful corridor linking Hungary with the new territory of Galicia—from the Ottomans when they were forced to sue for peace with Russia at Küçük Kaynarca (1774).

Culturally too the empire flourished, crowning its accomplishments in painting, architecture, and the plastic arts with an astonishing musical efflorescence. The Habsburg crown and nobility, together with an increasingly wealthy bourgeoisie, opened its doors to and lavished its patronage on some of the greatest composers of all time: Gluck, Haydn, Mozart, Beethoven, Schubert (even Bach was attracted to the Habsburg court, but was turned down by Maria Theresa on the grounds of his Protestantism). For Franz

Werfel, music was the universal language of the empire, and Mozart "the idea of Austria, made vocal" (1937: 39). Wherever they were born—many from neighboring Germany—musicians flocked to Vienna, or to the country estates of the aristocracy, such as the Esterhazy estates at Fertöd and Eisenstadt in Hungary where Haydn composed and performed many of his works. Prague too became a great musical center, nourishing a thriving school of Czech composers as well as being the scene of some of Mozart's greatest triumphs. To the whole world, for more than a century afterward, Austria became synonymous with music, not least in the Indian summer of the empire's existence in the late nineteenth and early twentieth centuries.

On the eve of the French Revolution, the Habsburg Empire was in as strong and healthy a condition as it had ever been or was ever to be again. It had broadly established the institutions and outlook—"a curious mix of authoritarianism and benevolence"—with which to confront the coming century (Okey 2002: 33). It had laid the foundations of an industrial economy, especially in Bohemia and Lower Austria, which was to develop strongly in the nineteenth century (Wangermann 1973: 107–11). It remained a multinational, dynastic empire, with strong and diverse local traditions. But it had developed, thanks largely to the reforms of Maria Theresa and Joseph II, something approaching a common identity and widespread acceptance of its rule. Charles Ingrao's assessment is not wide off the mark: "By the second half of the eighteenth century it not only had the continent's most innovative government and largest army, but was also a leader in public education and the world of music. It subsequently played a leading role in turning back the French Revolution and crafting an international system that remained in place until 1914. When it finally collapsed four years later, it had already outlasted every other major monarchy in both longevity and dynastic continuity" (Ingrao 1994: xi–xii; see also 212–19; cf. Judson 2016: 97–102).

What Was the Habsburg Empire?

In *The Man without Qualities* (1930–32), Robert Musil's sparkling novel of the late Austro-Hungarian Empire, he writes of the contradictory nature of "Kakania," his somewhat scatological name for an empire for which, however, he shows great affection:

> For instance, it was *kaiserlich-königlich* (Imperial-Royal) and it was *kaiserlich und königlich* (Imperial and Royal); one of the two abbreviations,

k.k. or *k.&k.*, applied to every thing and person, but esoteric lore was nevertheless required in order to be sure of distinguishing which institutions and persons were to be referred to as *k.k.* and which as *k.&k.* On paper it called itself the Austro-Hungarian Monarchy; in speaking, however, one referred to it as Austria, that is to say, it was known by a name that it had, as a State, solemnly renounced by oath, while preserving it in all matters of sentiment, as a sign that feelings are just as important as constitutional law and that regulations are not the really serious thing in life. By its constitution it was liberal, but its system of government was clerical. The system of government was clerical, but the general attitude to life was liberal. Before the law all citizens were equal, but not everyone, of course, was a citizen. There was a parliament, which made such vigorous use of its liberty that it was usually kept shut; but there was also an emergency powers act by means of which it was possible to manage without Parliament, and every time when everyone was just beginning to rejoice in absolutism, the Crown decreed that there must now again be a return to parliamentary government. Many such things happened in this State, and among them were those national struggles that justifiably aroused Europe's curiosity and are today completely misrepresented. They were so violent that they several times a year caused the machinery of State to jam and come to a dead stop. But between whiles, in the breathing-spaces between government and government, everyone got on excellently with everyone else and behaved as if nothing had ever been the matter. Nor had anything real ever been the matter. (Musil [1930–32] 1979, 1:32–33)[12]

This masterly sketch touches on almost every aspect of the nineteenth-century Habsburg Empire, with an irony that seems entirely appropriate to the mixture of exasperation and affection with which virtually everyone, native and foreigner alike, regarded it. It points first to the difficulties simply of naming the empire, a puzzle that has perplexed everyone: should it be the Habsburg Monarchy, the Habsburg Empire, the Austrian Empire (after 1804), the Austro-Hungarian Empire or Austria-Hungary (after 1867)? Should indeed "Austria" stand for all of these, as was common? Then there are the alternations of constitutionalism and absolutism or authoritarianism that marked the history of the empire for much of the century, and the punctuations brought about by revolutions and nationalist uprisings, such as those of 1848. Against expectations, the Habsburg Empire got through all of these, to collapse finally in the conflagration of the First World War. What is also remarkable, and perhaps the most important thing to note, is how unwilling anyone was to destroy it, how necessary it appeared even to those who found it oppressive and wished for radical changes. The "Austrian necessity" was not simply, as it is normally presented, a feature of the nineteenth-century international scene; it applied also to practically all of the major actors on the domestic stage of the empire. "Everyone got on with everyone," not necessarily easily or comfortably but with a profound sense that each needed the other.

R.J.W. Evans described the late seventeenth-century Habsburg Empire as "a complex and subtly-balanced organism, not a 'state' but a mildly centripetal agglutination of bewilderingly heterogeneous elements" (Evans 1991: 447). By the nineteenth century there had been some significant changes in the direction of uniformity, thanks largely to the centralizing policies of Maria Theresa and Joseph II. In particular the powers of the historic diets of Bohemia and Hungary had been drastically reduced. But the empire remained a highly varied multinational entity, at once its strength but also the source of many of its problems.

By general agreement, the Habsburg lands are usually divided into three main parts.[13] The first part consists of Austria proper, Austria narrowly defined. "Austria" here means the Erblande, the hereditary lands directly ruled by the Habsburgs and excluding Bohemia and Hungary. The Habsburgs took their name from the *Habichtsburg*, the "Castle of the Hawk," their ancestral eleventh-century home in the present Swiss canton of Aargau in northern Switzerland. Recognized as dukes by the Holy Roman emperor early in the twelfth century, they steadily expanded their domains, acquiring lands in Alsace and Breisgau on both sides of the Upper Rhine, and in the southern Swiss valleys. In 1273 Rudolf of Habsburg was elected Holy Roman emperor, the first of a long line of Habsburg emperors. Defeating his rival Ottokar Przemsyl, king of Bohemia, at the Battle of Marchfeld in 1278, Rudolf successfully established his claim to the Duchy of Austria, vacant since the death of the last duke of the House of Babenberg in 1246. With this the Habsburgs shifted the center of their power to Austria—Österreich—which originated as the Ostmark, the "Eastern March," of Charlemagne's empire.

The Babenberg legacy, and its close association with the Hohenstaufen emperors, was claimed as the Habsburgs' own, and the Babenbergs merged with the Habsburgs in the family tradition, as "quasi-Habsburgs" (Wheatcroft 1996: 48). The name "Austria" came to embrace the other Central European territories acquired by the Habsburgs under Rudolf and his successors—Styria, Carinthia, Carniola, Istria, and the Tyrol, collectively known as "Inner Austria." Also included in Austria was a conglomeration of territories, known as the Vörlande or "Further Austria," in the Swabian part of the Holy Roman Empire. In 1500 the emperor Maximilian I added Gorizia to the hereditary lands, thus gaining easier access to the port of Trieste and the Adriatic Sea. Together all these possessions made up the Erblande, the core territories of the House of Habsburg.

The second part of the Habsburg lands consisted of the "Lands of the Crown of St. Wenceslas" (i.e., Bohemia and its dependencies, such as Moravia and Silesia). In the tenth century Bohemia became a fief of the Holy Roman Empire, and remained so until the empire's dissolution in 1806. In 1156 the emperor Frederick Barbarossa granted it a royal crown—the only one of the empire's fiefs to be so distinguished—and when the empire became an elective monarchy, Bohemia became one of the seven imperial electors. Briefly—with Hungary—under Habsburg rule in the fifteenth century, it became a permanent part of the Habsburg Empire in 1526 as part of the inheritance of Ferdinand, brother of Charles V. The strong development of Protestantism among the Bohemian nobility brought their fief into sharp conflict with its Habsburg rulers. At the Battle of the White Mountain (1620) the native Bohemian nobility was crushed, and subsequently almost wholly displaced by landholders from other parts of the empire (thus ensuring a high degree of loyalty to the dynasty, lasting well into the nineteenth century, on the part of the newly created aristocracy). Protestantism too was almost completely eradicated. It took almost a century for popular Bohemian sentiment to accede to Habsburg rule, but by the eighteenth century Bohemia had become so firmly integrated into the Habsburg structure as to be often included in the designation of the Erblande, the hereditary lands. In the nineteenth century it became the powerhouse of the empire's considerable industrial development.

Hungary—the "Lands of the Crown of St. Stephen"—made up the third main portion of the Habsburg patrimony. Included with Bohemia in the joint inheritance of 1526–27, it had already been largely lost to the Ottomans after their great victory at Mohács (1525). Only in 1699 was it recovered, though the recovery was not complete until 1718. Hungary was a vast territory, including much of what today forms Romania, Croatia, and Slovakia, as well as modern Hungary. From the eighteenth century it made up nearly a half (45 percent) of the Habsburg lands. It also had the highest degree of autonomy of any of them, which it clung to tenaciously. Eventually this led to a formal sharing of power, in the Austro-Hungarian Compromise (Ausgleich) of 1867. Henceforth, to the end of its existence, the empire was known as the Austro-Hungarian Empire or Austria-Hungary.

Apart from these three main divisions of the Habsburg Empire, certain other territories also played an important part in its life for shorter or longer periods. From the Spanish Habsburgs the Austrians took over significant sections of Italy. By the middle of the eighteenth century these included Lombardy and several of the central Italian states. After the Napoleonic Wars they also gained Venetia, in exchange for the Austrian Netherlands, which they had held from 1714 to 1797. At the First Partition of Poland (1772) they acquired the prosperous province of Galicia, some compensation for the loss of Silesia to Prussia in 1742. These changes meant that, after the Congress of Vienna (1815), the Habsburgs for the first time in their history had a more or less territorially compact empire: an empire firmly based in Central and East-Central Europe, with a strategically important extension in Italy. It was this entity, the "Danubian Monarchy," that most firmly established itself in the imagination of Europeans in the nineteenth century; it is this that is most fondly conjured up today in retrospective reveries of the Habsburgs.

That Danubian image was paradoxically made all the more possible by the loss of one of the most important roles that the Habsburgs had played in their six-hundred-year history: that of Holy Roman emperor. Rudolf of Habsburg, elected in 1273, was the first Habsburg Holy Roman emperor. There was then a break until the election of Albrecht II (r. 1438–39), a short-lived reign which nevertheless established a pattern of Habsburg monopoly of the Holy Roman Empire that was not broken, with a minor exception in the eighteenth century, until the extinction of the empire in 1806.

In the earlier centuries, the usual formula for selecting the Holy Roman emperor was first election by the imperial electors, as "king of the Romans," with a coronation in the imperial city of Aachen; this was then followed in due course by a coronation as Holy Roman emperor, blessed by the pope, in Rome. Frederick III (r. 1440–93) was the last emperor to be crowned in Rome; his son and successor Maximilian I (r. 1493–1519), chosen during his father's lifetime as king of the Romans, but prevented by his enemies from going to Rome, had himself in 1508 declared "emperor elect" and crowned himself, without the assistance of the pope, as Holy Roman emperor. He also made a significant modification to the title of the empire: it was henceforth to be called "the Holy Roman Empire of the German Nation" (sacrum imperium Romanum nationis Teutonicae) (Mamatey 1995: 6). This was to be consequential not just for later German nationalism, viewing the empire as an earlier incarnation of German unity; it was also important as signaling Habsburg claims to leadership in Germany. Even when the empire was abolished under French pressure in 1806—there could be only one emperor, and Napoleon had declared himself that—the Habsburgs were able to keep alive their hopes in Germany when Austria was given the presidency of the "German Confederation" formed with a membership of thirty-nine states in 1815.

At the same time, anticipating the dissolution of the Holy Roman Empire, the Habsburg Holy Roman emperor Francis II in 1804 declared himself Emperor Francis I of the newly designated "Austrian Empire": the first formal statement of a purely Austrian or Habsburg Empire, divorced from "the Holy Roman Empire of the German People." This made it easier for the Habsburgs to emphasize their Central European, Danubian, identity. Austria did not give up its claim to be the leading German power until it was forced to do so by Prussia, in the wars of the 1860s; but the dissolution of the Holy Roman Empire undoubtedly broke a historic association with the German states, one cherished by Habsburg monarchs going back to Maximilian I and Charles V (Whaley 1994, 2012). The question of the "Germanness" of the Habsburg Empire indeed became one of the central questions of the nineteenth-century empire.

Nationality and Identity in the Nineteenth Century

If the territories of the Habsburg Empire were heterogeneous, the nationalities were even more so. Moreover, nationality did not necessarily overlap territory, making statements about nationalism and national identity in the Habsburg lands even more treacherous than elsewhere.

Numerically Germans were the largest single group in the Habsburg Empire.[14] In 1910 they made up 23 percent—12 million out of a total population of 51 million. Even in the "Austrian" half of the Dual Monarchy Germans made up only 35 percent, the majority—nearly 59 percent—being Slavs: Czechs, Poles, "Little Russians" (Ruthenes/ Ukrainians), Slovenes, Serbs, and Croats (the remainder were made up of Italians and Romanians).[15]

But who or what were the "Germans"? It is true that the German language and German culture became dominant at the imperial court and eventually the local administration (Kann [1950] 1970, 1:361–62, 1991b: 53–55; John 1999: 30). It was the language of the imperial bureaucracy and the officer corps in the army. The towns too, throughout the empire—Prague, Pressburg (Bratislava), Brno, Budapest, and Zagreb as much as Vienna, Linz, Innsbruck, or the other Austrian towns—were German in character. The traders and educated professionals spoke German, as did the nobility. The language of instruction at the universities was German, and scholars and poets wrote in German. It was possible to argue that German was the empire's "language of state," and German its universal high culture. Only in Polish Galicia and the Habsburgs' Italian lands—once the Low Countries had gone—did a native nobility and bourgeoisie retain the local language and culture. Elsewhere, as Austrian German nationalists were later to claim, the Habsburg Empire—the Austrian Empire—could be thought a German Empire, a fit successor to the "Holy Roman Empire of the German Nation," and the natural leader of a united "Greater Germany."

But the "German" of Austrian Germans was almost entirely a matter of culture, not of race or even of ethnicity. You became German by adopting the German language and German culture, whatever your origins. Many self-defined "Germans" in the nineteenth century had Czech, Slovenian, Croatian, Serbian, or Romanian roots (Taylor [1948] 1990: 27, 285; Déak 1990: 14). At home, especially in the villages and smaller towns, they might even still speak their native language, as with the Slovenian spoken by the older generation of the von Trotta family in Joseph Roth's novel *The Radetzky March* (1932). To be "German" was essentially a matter of class and culture. It was to proclaim one-self urban, a member of the predominantly German culture of the towns, not a "peasant" from the countryside, but a bureaucrat, a trader, a schoolteacher, a lawyer, a doctor, or any other member of the educated classes. It meant to be cultured and learned. Even music, the most international language of the empire, took on, with Gluck, Mozart, Beethoven, Schubert, and Weber, an increasingly German hue, until the nationalist movements of the second half of the nineteenth century provoked a reaction in the music of such composers as Dvořák and Smetana.

Crucially, what being German meant was not the German of German nationalism, whether in the Habsburg Empire or beyond it. Germans in Austria thought of themselves as Austrians, or perhaps as "Austrian Germans," not as Germans pure and simple. Their loyalty was to the empire and above all to its head, the Habsburg emperor and the Habsburg dynasty (Kann [1950] 1970, 1:51–53; Taylor [1948] 1990: 25). Their nationalism, if they had one, was what we have earlier (chapter 1) called "imperial nationalism," the national-ism of a "state-bearing group" that identified itself with the imperial cause or mission ("state patriotism" would be another possible designation). But this was not nationalism in the conventional, nineteenth-century, sense, the nationalism of a group defining itself by race or ethnicity. Such a nationalism, as all recognized, especially most Germans, would destroy the evidently multinational empire. Other nations in the empire—the Hungarians, the Czechs, the Poles, even the Croats, Slovenes, and Ruthenes—might espouse nationalist ideas and identities, so long as this tendency did not threaten the basic integrity of the empire. For them it might offer some sort of cover, or consolation, for their more dependent roles in the empire. But for the Germans, it was acknowledged, this was a dangerous path to take. For much of the nineteenth century Germans were the least nationalistic of all the groups within the empire. Most Austrian Germans rejected the aspirations of German nationalists to break up the empire and unite all Germans in a pan-German nation-state (the *Grossdeutsch* program). Only in the very last years, in reaction to the increasingly loud claims of Czechs and other non-German nationalities, and mainly after the breakup of the empire in 1919, did German Austrians develop a specifically German nationalism that was to lead, eventually, to a willing absorption into Hitler's Third German Reich in the *Anschluss* of 1938.

For similar reasons, many Hungarians rejected the siren call of nationalism, and worked to achieve their ends within the confines of empire. Hungarians, at 19 percent or 10 million, represented the second-largest single group in the empire in 1910. Together therefore Germans and Hungarians made up just under half—42 percent—of the total population of the empire at that time. That had been one of the justifications of dividing rule in the empire between Austria and Hungary in the "Compromise" of 1867. The other, perhaps more realistic, cause was the persisting strength of local Hungarian institutions and traditions of autonomy. Unlike Bohemia and Croatia, the "Crownlands of St. Stephen" were never thought of as part of the Erblande, the Austrian hereditary lands.

But much as they might insist on their "liberty" and independence, much as they might stress their historic rights and privileges, the Hungarian nobility, which until the late nineteenth century dominated all local institutions, had every reason to throw in their lot with the Habsburgs and remain loyal servants of the imperial state. For one thing, despite their claim to be the custodians of a "thousand-year-old Hungry," many of the nobility were relatively new creations, the result of lands and titles allocated after the recovery of Hungary from the Ottomans in the late seventeenth and early eighteenth centuries. The more than a century-and-a-half rule by the Ottomans, from the 1520s to the 1680s, marked a deep divide in Hungarian history. Though not an almost entirely new aristocracy on the Bohemian model, the Hungarian nobility were sufficiently reconstructed by the Habsburgs to be integrated, at least at the upper levels, into the structure of Habsburg rule and culture. Most of the leading magnates, such as the Esterhazys, the Palffys, and the Batthyánys, had their large town palaces in Vienna, and entered fully into the life of the capital (becoming among other things, some of them, patrons of Beethoven as well as Haydn). Like the Bohemian aristocracy they knew that they owed their power and privileges to the Habsburgs. The lesser nobility might flirt with Hungarian nationalism, but they too recognized that Habsburg rule was better for them than bourgeois or peasant nationalism. The Ausgleich or Compromise of 1867 was satisfactory to most of the Hungarian nobility, and ensured their loyalty right to the end of the empire (Evans 2006: 175–92).

There was an even more compelling reason why the Magyar nobility should be content with Habsburg rule: it was necessary for their control of the many other ethnic groups that existed in "Hungary"—that is, what, after the 1867 Compromise, became known as the "Hungarian half" of the empire (Kann [1950] 1970, 1:109–11; Sked 2001: 212–23). The "Lands of the Crown of St. Stephen"—"Greater Hungary"—included Croatia and Transylvania as well as Hungary proper, "lesser Hungary." In 1848 and again more firmly in 1867 Transylvania lost its identity and was absorbed into a unitary Hungary. What later became "Slovakia" had since the eleventh century also been part of Hungary ("Upper Hungary").

In this Hungary, including Transylvania but excluding Croatia, the nearly 10 million Magyars recorded in the 1910 census made up a bare majority (54 percent). In addition, there were nearly 3 million Romanians (16 percent), nearly 2 million Slovaks (10.7 percent), nearly 2 million Germans (10.4 percent), half a million each of "Little Russians" (Ruthenes or Ukrainians) and Serbs (2.5 percent each), and 195,000 Croats (1.1 percent).

Even this conceals the extent of the non-Magyar population. Jews (5 percent), for instance, were counted as Magyars in the 1910 census; if they are deducted, the Magyars become a minority (49 percent) even in "lesser Hungary." They are even more of a minority—43 percent—in "Greater Hungary," if we add the Serbs and Croats of Croatia, often excluded in population statistics when the Magyars wished to show that they were a majority. Moreover, the Magyar population had experienced a suspicious inflation by 1910. In the eighteenth century they had made up less than a quarter of the population, and even in 1880 they were a minority, at 46 percent. A deliberate policy of "Magyarization" following the Compromise of 1867 had produced many more "Magyars" than previously, as revealed by the censuses of the various successor states after the collapse of the empire in 1919. Just as with "Germans" in

FIGURE 4.3. Croatian National Theatre, Zagreb. A common neo-baroque style
covered all the Habsburgs' lands. © DeymosHR/Shutterstock.com.

other parts of the empire, in Hungary it paid to be "Magyar," until the rise of
nationalism among non-Magyar groups discouraged this identification.

Germans and Hungarians might make up 42 percent of the empire; but if
the Slavs and Romanians, as "subject peoples," are taken together, they actually made up a majority of the empire, at 51 percent (45 percent or 23.5 million
Slavs, 6 percent or 3 million Romanians). Only if the Polish group of Slavs, at
5 million or 10 percent, are deducted and added to the Germans and Hungarians as the historic "master nations" of the empire—a conventional enough
practice in the nineteenth century—do the Slavs and Romanians become a
minority. However, whether as a majority or a minority there was no unity
among these groups. Romanians were not Slavs, of course, and held to a proud
if somewhat historically dubious consciousness of themselves as "Romans,"
descendants of the Dacians of the short-lived trans-Danubian province of the
Roman Empire (hence the change of name from the earlier "Rumania," remi-
niscent of the Turkish period, to "Romania" in the twentieth century). Among
the Slavs themselves there were faint stirrings of Pan-Slavism, stronger as the
nineteenth century progressed. But this was incapable of preventing the even
stronger sense of difference among Poles, Czechs, Slovaks, Slovenes, Serbs,
Croats, Ruthenes/Ukrainians.

But it would be mistaken to think of the Slavs as somehow weakened by their disunity, and Germans, Hungarians, and Poles as strengthened by some greater national consciousness. This would be seriously to misunderstand the role of nationalism in the Habsburg Empire. Nationalism was to become a problem, and the empire struggled with it to the end. But it was not nationalism that brought down the empire. We shall consider the national question in greater detail later, but here it is important to stress that in detailing the *nationalities* in the Habsburg Empire, we are not engaged in documenting the *nationalisms* in the empire. The various ethnic groups composing the empire were conscious of their differences and strove to improve their positions relative to others; but rarely did these differences by themselves, or the consciousness of them, threaten the existence of the empire (Cohen 2007: 242–43).

This is because, to an extent greater than perhaps with any other empire except the Ottoman, the imperial idea was tied strictly to the dynastic idea, and as such was firmly opposed to the national idea and also allowed for a strong personal loyalty to the person of the emperor—shown most clearly in the long reign of the emperor Franz Joseph (r. 1848–1916) (Wandruszka 1964: 2–13; Kann 1991b: 65; Urbanitsch 2004; Unowsky 2011: 238). The Habsburgs, like the Ottomans, ruled without a break for over six hundred years. Throughout their existence the Habsburgs clung tenaciously to the idea of *Hausmacht*, the power of the House of Habsburg. The Habsburgs, like the Ottomans, were in other words a dynasty, not just a family but a *ruling* family (from Greek *dunasteia*, power or domination). It was their duty to defend and extend their territories, for the greater power and glory of the dynasty.

"Empire"—whether the Holy Roman Empire or the Austrian Empire—and "Habsburg" became virtually synonymous. The House of Habsburg was the unifying symbol of the disparate elements of the empire and the principal link connecting them. It was crucially important, for the strength and stability of the *Hausmacht* principle, that the dynasty did not become identified with any of its subject peoples, including and especially its German subjects, who sometimes saw the empire as "theirs." The archduke Albert, cousin to the emperor Franz Joseph and one of the most passionate advocates of the dynastic idea as the linchpin of the empire, once said: "In a polyglot Empire inhabited by so many races and peoples, the dynasty must not allow itself to be assigned exclusively to one of these. Just as a good mother, it must show equal love for all its children and remain foreign to none. In this lies the justification for its existence" (in Sked 2001: 270).

From the very beginning the Habsburgs created elaborate genealogical histories linking their family with ancient Trojans (Aeneas) and Roman emperors (Julius Caesar) as well as sundry early Christian saints and early German emperors, including Charlemagne himself. The Habsburgs presented themselves as Roman, Christian, German—exactly the lineage necessary to lead not just Germany but the whole of Europe (Wandruszka 1964: 15–23; Wheatcroft 1996: 41–50). And why stop at Europe? The emperor Frederick III (r. 1440–93) adopted the grand motto A. E. I. O. U.—"*Austria Est Imperare Orbi Universo*" ("Austria will rule over the entire globe") (Wheatcroft 1996: 81).[16] As the Habsburgs took on the task of defending Western Christendom against the infidel—the Ottomans—and against the enemy within—Protestantism— they increasingly identified themselves with civilization itself, and their role as that of its God-appointed guardians (Werfel 1937: 14; Wessel 2011: 344). For many of their subjects that gave the Habsburgs near-divine status (Johnston 1986: 183).

The Habsburgs were masters at elaborating the trappings of rule—in architecture, in painting, in music, in the rituals and ceremonies of coronation, in imperial tours, in the titles and honors flowing from the emperor (Bucur and Wingfield 2001; Cole and Unowsky 2007; Judson 2016: 233–44). As the champions of Catholicism, and exponents of the *pietas austriaca*, they paid particular attention to religious ceremonies, such as the foot-washing ceremony on Maundy Thursday and the annual Corpus Christi procession in Vienna, whose pageantry drew thousands not just from the empire but from all over Europe (Unowsky 2001: 23–26; Wessel 2011: 346–47). Important too was Habsburg patronage of the great pilgrimage sites, especially that of the most venerated, Mariazell, visited by pilgrims from all over the empire (Frank 2009). Austrian Catholicism was always best in its showy and liturgical aspects, as gloriously expressed in the exuberant baroque of its churches and abbeys (Francis 1985: 31–35). In the second half of the nineteenth century the Church experienced vigorous growth—though now expressed more in neo-Gothic than baroque architectural styles—and despite some conflicts with the state over such matters as civil marriages remained a stalwart bulwark of Habsburg rule, one of the three pillars of the empire along with the army and the bureaucracy (Judson 2016: 281–88).[17]

Imperial tours established a personal and as it were physical contact between the emperor and his peoples in his far-flung and culturally diverse lands. Joseph II's popularity as "Emperor-Liberator" was rekindled in Franz Joseph's tours to Galicia in 1851, 1880, and 1894, where the emperor made a point of attending both Roman Catholic and Greek Catholic masses (the bulk of the peasants in eastern Galicia were Uniate Ruthenians). He also visited the Jewish synagogues in Lemberg, where the rabbis raised Torahs in expressions of loyalty. Even the Polish nobles, smarting since the failure of their risings in 1846 and 1848, were won round by the devolution measures of 1867 and in 1880 greeted the emperor warmly. Similar tours by Franz Joseph to Bukovina, Hungary, Bohemia, Moravia, Lombardy, Venice, Trieste, and the Tyrol—more than any of his predecessors since Joseph II—worked to mobilize popular feeling on behalf of the dynasty and its empire, and to stress common patterns of rule and ritual (Unowsky 2001: 27–34, 2005: 33–76; Judson 2016: 233–35).

Similarly Franz Joseph's two imperial jubilees–the Golden Jubilee of 1898 and the Diamond Jubilee of 1908—were celebrated with due pomp and ceremony, and were occasions for the display of a genuinely popular imperial patriotism. The theme of the multiplicity of nationalities, and of the emperor as the symbol and representative of all, was prominent on both occasions (Beller 2001; Unowsky 2005: 77–112).[18] Whatever the differences among the nationalities, the degree of participation in these celebrations, and the mass sales of souvenirs and memorabilia of the emperor and his family, were constant reminders of the devotion of a large part of the empire's subjects to the person of the emperor and to the supranational empire that he symbolized. Portraits of Franz Joseph, to be found everywhere throughout the empire, in schools and offices, in private homes, on everyday items such as cups and plates, had almost religious, icon-like status (Urbanitsch 2004: 121–29, 135; Unowsky 2011: 244–57).

The Habsburgs, at least the Austrian Habsburgs, have often been said to have been weak, militarily and economically, their policies hesitant and vacillating. The nineteenth-century Austrian dramatist Franz Grillparzer famously wrote in his play *Bruderzwist* (Brothers' quarrel) of "the half-trodden path, the half-finished act, delaying with halfway means," as being the curse of the House of Habsburg (Wandruszka 1964: 117). On that account the mainspring of their six-hundred-year survival is something of a mystery. Part of the answer has to do with their role in the international system—"the Austrian necessity." But another, probably more important, part has to do with the mystique of rule, and the Habsburg ability to exploit it to the full.

Nowhere was this mystique more evident than in the army. The army is everywhere in Habsburg culture, high and low. "Probably," says István Deák, "no armed force has entered into popular music, literature, and art as spiritedly as that of Austria-Hungary. Its gallant officers waltz across the stage and court handsome countesses; its ordinary soldiers sparkle with *bon mots*, polished boots, and good manners" (Deák 1990: 213). The paradox is that the Habsburg Empire was in many ways a very unmilitaristic empire, unwilling to be drawn into war and anxious to come to terms as soon as possible. The concept of the *Clementia Austriaca*—the "inherited disposition to mercy, benevolence, and leniency," the "native Austrian mildness and clemency"—so frequently invoked down the centuries in Habsburg orders, edicts, and other official documents, had a real meaning and effect (Wandruszka 1964: 130).

The army was not so much a war machine as a social institution, one that expressed the Habsburg spirit and aspiration in the clearest and fullest possible way. While not very well designed for winning wars abroad, it was highly successful at maintaining order at home, as much by its cultural example as by any show of military force. It was a unique supranational institution, with a code of honor, a cultivation of manners, a set of rituals, and an ethos of ethnic and religious tolerance that set the standard for the whole of Habsburg society. This is what is portrayed so brilliantly in Joseph Roth's novel *The Radetzky March* (1932), for all its dissection of the irrationality and precariousness of the system that came apart in the First World War. In more practical terms, it was the supranational army that saved the monarchy in the revolutions of 1848. Quite rightly Grillparzer wrote of Field Marshal Joseph Wenzel Count Radetzky, victor of Custozza, that "In deinem Lager ist Österreich" (Austria is to be found in your camp); and the theme of a popular song sung by the soldiers returning from Custoza provided Johann Strauss the Elder with the inspiration for his *Radetzky March*, which became almost a second national anthem in the empire, and a nostalgic reminder after it had gone (it is always played in the traditional New Year's Concert in Vienna) (Beller 2011: 126).

István Deák (1990) has persuasively shown the extent to which the officer corps of the Habsburg army acted as "the guardian of the multinational monarchy," especially in the difficult years 1848–1918. Even when—and perhaps because—its social base widened, toward the end of the nineteenth century, it developed an esprit de corps and commitment to the empire second to none (Kann 1991c). The army was multiethnic, multiconfessional, and multinational to an extent not paralleled in other empires (even the Ottoman, which though ethnically mixed required conversion to Islam for a military career). While German was the language of command, communication between officers and the rank and file was carried on in a multiplicity of languages—there were at least ten major ones—and a Habsburg officer was required to learn the language of his men (Stone 1966: 100). Relations among officers of all nationalities were exceptionally close, symbolized by the use of the *du* form of address normally reserved for families and intimates. Remarkably Jews, the object of much anti-Semitism in the upper ranks of other armies, were treated on an equal basis with other nationalities in the Habsburg officer corps, being allowed, for instance, to defend their "honor" by the traditional method of the duel (Deák 1990: 133; Stone 1966: 99; Urbanitsch 2004: 116, 134–35).[19]

The attitude toward the Jews was representative of the treatment of nationalities more generally in the Habsburg army. Practical considerations—levels of skill and education, traditions—dictated the distribution of ethnic groups among the various branches of the military, so that the cavalry recruited more heavily among Magyars, Poles, Ruthenes, and Czechs, the infantry more among Romanians, the artillery more among Germans and Slovenes. But in general a military career was open to all the nationalities. It is true that Germans, Magyars, Poles, and Czechs are overrepresented among both the reserve and career officers, but this seems to reflect unequal levels of education rather than ethnic bias—as is clear from the high proportion of Jews in the officer corps. Moreover, as we have seen, "passing," as Germans or Magyars, was relatively easy and could be advantageous, so that many officers could have had Croat, Slovene, Romanian, or Ruthene roots (Deák 1990: 181). "Throughout its history," says Deák, "the Habsburg army was publicly and actively opposed to any manifestation of nationalism. . . . The fact is that an enormous number of Joint Army officers had, for all intents and purposes, no nationality. . . . At all times they were taught to view any expression of national sentiment as unbecoming an officer or even as treasonous" (Deák 1990: 183–84; cf. Jászi [1929] 1961: 141–48; Stone 1966: 97; Kann [1957] 1973: 8, 180, 1991c: 225–35; Wheatcroft 1996: 277–78).

What applied to the Habsburg officer corps applied to the other main pillar of the multinational empire, the bureaucracy, as well as to the principal ministers, advisers, and military commanders of the monarchy. Here too are to be found—echoing the practice of the Spanish Habsburgs—representatives of practically all the national groups within the empire, and not infrequently some from without.[20] The most notable "outsider" was the Habsburg hero Prince Eugene of Savoy. Refused a commission by Louis XIV in the land of his birth, France, he entered Habsburg service and went on to win glory and popular acclaim in the wars against the Ottomans, and in the War of the Spanish Succession against his former countrymen, the French. "In entire Austrian history," writes Robert Kann, "there exists perhaps no more supranational and cosmopolitan figure than this man, probably the empire's greatest soldier. A personality composed of German, French and Italian elements, the

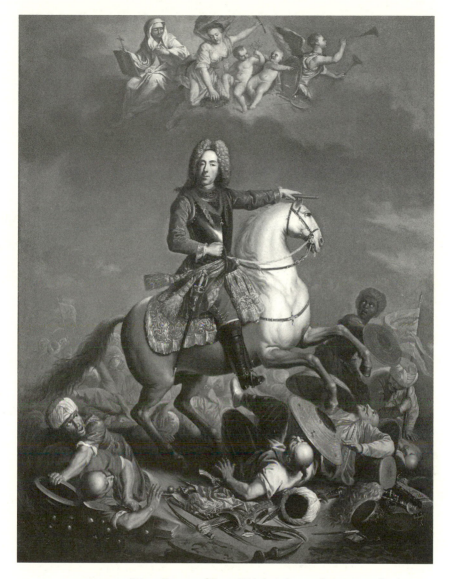

FIGURE 4.4. Prince Eugene of Savoy, Habsburg hero as "conqueror of
the Turks." Portrait, German School (eighteenth century). Deutsches
Historisches Museum, Berlin, Germany/Bridgeman Images.

prince was the most spectacular champion of the grandeur of the House of
Habsburg"—and a popular hero, to boot (Kann [1957] 1973: 178–79). Franz
Werfel calls Eugene "the finest example" of the "*gelertner Oesterreicher*," the
Austrian made, not born, which he sees as expressing the true imperial idea
of Austria (1937: 36).

Germans of course are to be found aplenty, though they too did not always come from the Habsburg lands. The outstanding example of this is Clemens von Metternich, from Koblenz in the Rhineland, who became the long-lasting chancellor of the (Austrian) emperors Francis I and Ferdinand I. Friedrich von Gentz, a Prussian from Breslau, was another convert to the "Austrian idea," serving alongside Metternich at the Congress of Vienna and supplying through his elegant writings powerful support for the Habsburg dynasty. As with all "state-bearing" peoples in imperial polities, Germans had to be careful to stress not their Germanness, but rather their identities as imperial servants (Judson 2016: 298). Joseph II's shortsighted attempt at Germanization was also short-lived, as later Habsburgs strove to eliminate all expressions of nationalism, including that of the Germans, from the multinational empire.[21]

Despite Hungary's history of maintaining a certain sense of separateness from the rest of the Habsburg lands, Hungarians, the "second people" of the empire, also flourished, not simply in dominating local institutions in Hungary but also more widely in the imperial administration and army. The grand families, the Esterhazys, the Károlyis, the Batthyánys, are to be found everywhere, as with Károly Batthyany, the Habsburg general who went on to become tutor to the archduke Joseph, later Joseph II (who deeply offended Hungarian sensibilities with his "Germanizing" policies). From within Hungary, but himself a Slovak, was Adam Franz Kollár court librarian and adviser to Maria Theresa; also prominent, at the highest level of diplomacy, was the bibliophile Count Károly Reviczky, Joseph II's ambassador in London and Warsaw. In the nineteenth century the two counts Julius Andrássy, father and son, continued this tradition of diplomatic service to the empire, the latter as foreign minister. In 1921 the younger Andrássy even attempted to restore the monarchy, and was imprisoned for it. Then there were the Hungarian generals, János Pálffy, Ferenc Nádasdy, and András Hadik, as well as Károly Batthyany. The army indeed became one of the principal channels though which Hungarians could make their way up the imperial hierarchy—Hadik, for instance, became successively president of the Imperial War Council, governor of Transylvania, and then governor of Galicia. Such Hungarians did not necessarily give up on their Hungarianness, anymore than, say, Scots on their Scottishness in the British Empire; they combined, as "overlapping, even complementary, sentiments," "solid Austrian loyalty" with the upholding of Hungary's traditional liberties and customs (Evans 2006: 32).

Bohemians, together with Moravians, played an even greater part in the running of the empire. This is at first sight surprising, given the resounding defeat of the largely Protestant Bohemian nobility at the Battle of the White Mountain in 1620, and the subsequent victory of the Catholic Counter-Reformation in Bohemia. But that very occurrence produced a strong pro-Habsburg force, in the reconstituted Bohemian nobility, made up in good part of foreigners (over 50 percent of Bohemia's landed wealth changed hands). And there were Austrian families, or families of Austrian descent, who established themselves strongly in Bohemia—the Dietrichsteins, the Liechtensteins, the Eggenbergs, the Althans, the Harrachs—playing a kind of bridging role. At the same time many of the old Bohemian families managed to survive and thrive, by dint of converting to Catholicism and affirming loyalty to the Habsburgs (Evans 2006: 86–90). Most famous of these was Albrecht von Waldstein, better known as Wallenstein, scion of an impoverished Czech Protestant noble family who was brought up a Catholic and had a meteoric rise in the imperial army, ending up as duke of Friedland and Mecklenburg and prince of Sagan. But there were other old Czech families who played prominent roles in the imperial administration: Martinic and Slavata, Lobkowitz and Czernin, Kinsky and Sternberg, Kolowrat, Nostitz, and Schlick. "But for the hubris of Wallenstein and his Czech friends . . . the preponderance of traditional families would have been yet greater" (Evans 2006: 87).

From Moravia came Wenzel Anton Kaunitz, for forty years chief counselor to Maria Theresa and Joseph II; also the famous educator and promoter of Austrian state patriotism, Joseph von Sonnenfels, son of a Jewish rabbi from Berlin who had migrated to Moravia and converted to Catholicism. In the nineteenth century the spread of Bohemians among the highest levels of the administration continued: "Wherever we look in the Austrian government of this period, we find Bohemians" (Evans 2006: 95, 197). Best known perhaps is Count Franz Anton Kolowrat-Liebsteinsky, head of the Staatsrat, the State Council, and Metternich's great rival in the reign of Francis I (Sked 2001: 29–31). And despite the rise of Czech nationalism in the nineteenth century, the Bohemians remained among the firmest supporters of the Habsburg Monarchy—one of them even declaring, as we shall see, that the Habsburg Empire would have had to be invented had it not already existed. R.J.W. Evans points out that the saviors of the Habsburg Empire in the revolutions of 1848–49 were two Bohemian generals—Prince Alfred Windischgrätz and Count Joseph Wenzel Radetzky—and a Bohemian statesman, Prince Felix Schwarzenberg (Evans 2006: 97; cf. Sked 2001: 228).[22]

As with other multinational empires, the Habsburg Empire developed an imperial service class that, while not unaffected by historic differences and the newer nationalist currents, saw itself as standing above these divisions and differences in its devotion to the dynasty and the imperial idea—which of course also provided it with an identity and an interest. Its members would have understood perfectly the emperor Francis I's impatient query, when told that someone was "a patriot for Austria": "Yes, but is he a patriot for me?" (Taylor [1948] 1990: 25). They developed a common outlook and style of life that, drawn largely from the court, linked them across the empire's many regions and ethnicities (Johnston 1986: 184; Urbanitsch 2004: 137–38; Kuzmics and Axtmann 2007: 179–214). As such, says Robert Kann, "it proved sufficiently strong not only to contribute to the empire's maintenance for centuries but also to form patterns of Austrian imperial institutions and behavior which came to be seen as the basic pattern, the way of life, of Austrian man" (Kann [1957] 1973: 190; also 7–24). Throughout the empire, the manners, dress, speech, and tastes of the higher echelons of the military and bureaucracy became a model for other classes, the style that had to be adopted if one wished to rise in society. But, as with the Roman elite, race, ethnicity, or nation was no barrier.

The Austrian Idea

"Austrian man" might seem somewhat fanciful, though perhaps no more so than "Soviet man." But the "Austrian idea" certainly existed. Striving to ward off the challenge of a Prussian-led German nationalism, and acutely conscious of the multinational character of the empire, a series of writers and statesmen in the nineteenth century sought to elaborate a concept of "Austria"—in its widest signification, encompassing the whole empire—that would enable the various parts to cohere and find a common identity.

Typically it was not a native Austrian at all, but a displaced, formerly Protestant northerner turned Catholic, Friedrich Schlegel, who is credited with giving the first systematic exposition of the Austrian idea. In the wake of the dissolution of the Holy Roman Empire—a "German" empire—and the promulgation of an Austrian empire, Schlegel was employed by Metternich and the foreign minister, Count Stadion, to set out the principles of a specifically Austrian patriotism (Beller 2011: 109–10). In a series of lectures on modern history delivered in Vienna in 1810, Schlegel did exactly that, drawing upon the experience and ideals of Charles V and his Habsburg successors to counter the nationalist philosophy of history so influentially propounded by Herder and Hegel. The Habsburgs, Schlegel contended, had stood for European civilization as a whole, uniting east and west, north and south, German and Slav. They had fought for Christendom against the common enemy, the Turks; they had sought to unite the European powers in a common purpose, preferring peaceful settlement to armed violence (the *Clementia Austriaca*); they had forged good relations between the papacy and empire. Such were *die österreichischen Grundsätze*, the Austrian principles, on which the empire was based, and which stood against the forces of a narrow nationalism and chauvinism. In place of this nationalism Schlegel championed a "federal state ... that is itself a system of allied nations and states, as Austria was under Charles V" (in Timms 1991: 902–6).

In the midst of the 1848 revolutions, which convulsed the Habsburg Empire as much as they did most of the other major powers on the Continent, another famous statement of the Austrian idea was pronounced. This was in the response of the Czech historian František Palacký, when invited to join the delegates of the German National Assembly meeting in Frankfort. The delegates seem to have been astonished when Palacký declined, on the grounds that as a Czech he had no wish to join a German nation. Even more, he protested at the fact that "from all that has so far been publicly announced of your aims and purposes you irrevocably are, and will be, aiming to undermine Austria forever as an independent empire and to make its existence impossible—an empire whose preservation, integrity and consolidation is, and must be, a great and important matter not only for my own nation but for the whole of Europe, indeed for mankind and civilization itself" (in Kohn 1961: 119).

Palacký went on to say that he saw the Habsburg Empire as the necessary and perhaps only obstacle to the growing power of Russia, which though undoubtedly a Slav culture threatened the freedom and independence of the smaller Slav nations to the west. Austria, he declared in a famous statement that became almost a clarion call on behalf of the empire, "by nature and history is destined to be the bulwark and guardian of Europe against Asiatic elements of every kind.... If the Austrian state had not existed for ages, we would be obliged in the interests of Europe and even of mankind to endeavor to create it as fast as possible" (Kohn 1961: 120).

Palacký later despaired of getting the Habsburgs to reorganize the empire along the lines of a federal union of all the nationalities, his solution to the national question. His gloomy prophecy is often quoted: "We were before Austria; we shall be after her too" (Evans 2006: 98). But certainly up to the Compromise of 1867 he continued to express his firm belief that, "considering that by our own efforts we could scarcely create an independent sovereign state, we can preserve our historic-political entity, our particular nationality and culture, and finally, our economic life nowhere and in no way better than we can in Austria. . . . We have no hopes and no political perspectives beyond Austria." He looked to an Austrian government that should be "neither German, nor Magyar, nor Slav, nor Latin, but Austrian in a higher and general sense, that means on the basis of equal justice for all its members. . . . That more than three hundred years ago such different peoples have by free agreements formed the Austrian Empire, I regard as no small blessing of providence for all of them" (Kohn 1961: 51–53).

Hans Kohn (1961: 49–57) has shown that this position became the basic credo of most Slav groups in the empire in the nineteenth century. Even after the Compromise of 1867 had disappointed them, by making the Slavs dependent on German and Magyar leadership, they continued to work for the reform rather than the dissolution of the empire—a prospect that horrified nearly all of them (Sked 2001: 226–28; Cohen 2007). No one was more convinced of this than the Czech philosopher and sociologist Thomas Garrigue Masaryk. Masaryk later became the first president of an independent Czechoslovakia. This was an outcome he certainly did not desire for most of the time, until the collapse of the Habsburg Empire in the First World War made it seem inevitable (Gellner 1994: 115–23). Masaryk declared himself a faithful follower of Palacký, "my guide and master," and regretted Palacký's loss of faith in reform after the 1867 Compromise. Like Palacký, Masaryk regarded a strong Austria as an indispensable protective shield against the designs of both Russia and—increasingly—the new rising power of Germany. In his book of 1895, *The Czech Question*, he wrote that "I regard Palacký's idea of the Austrian state, in spite of all constitutional changes, as a still reliable guide. . . . I act according to his program when I express my political experiences in the words, that our policy cannot be successful if it is not supported by a true and strong interest in the fate of Austria, . . . by the cultural and political effort to work in harmony with the needs of our people for the advancement of the whole of Austria and its political administration" (Kohn 1961: 52). In 1909 he announced: "We want a federal Austria. We cannot be independent outside of Austria, next to powerful Germans, having Germans on our territory" (in Sked 2001: 228).

The Slavs were the most fervent supporters of the Austrian idea as a federation of equal nations within the framework of a strong Habsburg state. This followed naturally from their position as generally the most "subaltern" and subordinated groups. Even the Poles of Galicia, who like Poles elsewhere saw themselves as members of a "historic" nation and looked to the eventual resurrection of an independent Poland, regarded the Habsburg Empire as their

FIGURE 4.5. Street view of Lemberg/Lviv/Lvov, capital of Habsburg Galicia.
Poles and Ruthenians (Ukrainians) made up the majority of the population of
Galicia, but there were also many Jews in the cities. Library of Congress.

best protection against the Russian threat, of which they were deeply conscious following the brutal suppression of the Polish rising of 1863 in Russian-
dominated "Congress Poland." In 1868, following the Compromise, there were
effusive declarations of loyalty to the monarchy and of commitment to the
dualist settlement, "in accordance with which the Poles proved themselves the
staunchest pillar of the new political system" (Sked 2001: 228).

But Germans and Hungarians, the two dominant peoples in the empire,
also produced their versions of the Austrian idea. Both saw the need to
transform the empire, if it were to survive the challenges of nationalism and
competition from other powers—most notably, in the nineteenth century,
Prussia. Hungarians maintained a traditional suspicion of what they saw as
German aspirations to superiority in the empire—for them "Austrians" were
generally "Germans," a perception heightened during the Josephinian reforms
(Evans 1994, 2006: 137).[23] Nor did they show much respect for the claims of
the Slavs and Romanians within their half of the empire—despite the fact that
by the nineteenth century they were a minority (45 percent) within "historic"
Hungary (Evans 2006: 127; Cohen 2007: 262–64). But they were sufficiently
aware of their own interests, and the accomplishments of the Habsburgs in

rescuing them from "the Turkish captivity," to feel that commitment to the empire offered them the best chance of preserving their culture and power. In a remarkable anticipation of Palacký's declaration of 1848, the liberal Hungarian leader Miklós Wesselényi wrote in 1843:

> Subjection to this ruling house [the Habsburgs] is that tight bond linking the Hungarian to those peoples and to that element which alone are and can be in kinship of interest with him, and which are therefore his sole and natural allies. This circumstance is so important that if our national bonds and our current relationship, sanctified by the centuries, did not exist, and if we had not raised to our throne the imperial scions of the counts of Habsburg, now would be the time and the urgent necessity to so. These views and this belief must pass into our bloodstream and become part of the inner conviction of every Hungarian. (in Evans 1994: 27)

The revolution of 1848, here as elsewhere in the Habsburg lands, showed that serious differences existed as to the form that the empire should take. But the restored Habsburg rulers, under the young Franz Joseph and his ministers, Schwarzenberg and Bach, were as convinced as the revolutionaries that there was no going back to the old order (Taylor [1948] 1990: 84–90; Evans 2006: 268–72; Beller 2011: 130–33). Changes, accelerated by the loss of the Italian possessions in 1859 and 1866, and exclusion from Germany by Prussia in 1866, brought in the Compromise of 1867. This in effect gave Hungary "Home Rule" and a real say in the common affairs of the empire. After 1867 several Hungarians played key parts in Habsburg administration, diplomacy, and the military—Gyula Andrássy, Alajos Károlyi, Imre Széchényi, László Szőgyény, János Forgách, Lajos Benedek (Evans 2006: 207, 238–39, 249). Hungary seemed finally to have secured its position in the empire. The Austrian idea as conceived by the Slavs, in the form of a federation of equal nationalities, of course had no appeal. But the Austrian idea as a commitment to a multinational empire in which Hungarians played so central a part was one that self-interest by itself made compelling, and certainly can be said to have given the empire an extended lease of life (Kann 1991d: 216–17; cf. Sked 1981: 180–83, 2001: 191–202). Few Hungarians wished to go it alone, or even thought that possible. Just as the Slavs looked to the empire for their salvation, so—for very different reasons—did the Hungarians. For Hungary, whatever its past disputes with the monarchy, the collapse of the empire in 1918 presented it with the greatest tragedy of its history, greater even than the Turkish conquest of the sixteenth century. It is, in a real sense, still struggling to come to terms with it.

Austrian Germans, for much of the nineteenth century hostile to German nationalism, contributed in various ways to the Austrian idea, most important perhaps negatively, in *not* stressing the Germanness of the empire. They were often to be found, as for instance in the 1848 revolutions, as supporters of "Austro-Slavism," a movement that sought to save the empire by cementing an alliance of the monarchy with the Slav groups against the pretensions of both German and Hungarian nationalism (Okey 2002: 143–44; Brubaker et al. 2006: 62). In the 1880s and 1890s this doctrine was given some force under the long-serving Austrian prime minister Count Eduard Taaffe, who is famous for his statement that his policy for maintaining the monarchy was to keep all its nationalities "in a condition of even and well-modulated discontent." Taaffe, a German aristocrat of Irish origins, especially promoted Czech interests, bringing Czechs into the government, making Czech and German equal as languages of administration in the Bohemian lands, and founding a Czech university in Prague. But he also favored Poles and Croats, along with liberal Germans, in the pro-monarchy "iron-ring" coalition that he formed (Taylor [1948] 1990: 169–82; Sked 2001: 226–27; Okey 2002: 268–69). His dismissal, in 1893, can be counted a serious blow to attempts to find a suitable strategy for a multinational empire in an age of nationalism.

Austrian Germans offered other varieties of the Austrian idea, from the very top of Habsburg society. At about the same time as Metternich and Stadion were enlisting Schlegel to promote Austrian patriotism, and just as he was proclaiming himself, in 1804, emperor of Austria, the emperor Francis I gave support to his brother, the archduke John, in his attempt to elaborate an "Austrian identity." Archduke John, as part of this effort, promoted and financed the grand project of the Innsbruck scholar Joseph Hormayr to manufacture a national identity from the ancient Habsburg past, much of it mythologized. Hormayr first produced a *Handbook for a National History* (1810), and then followed this over the years with the twenty-volume *Austrian Plutarch*. In these works Hormayr—who was appointed official historiographer of the empire in 1816—offered in effect a comprehensive repertoire of facts, symbols, and ideas connected to the House of Habsburg for use by pro-Habsburg writers and artists, and which was indeed liberally drawn upon in the nineteenth century. They supplied, as Claudio Magris has observed, "an authentic patriotic almanac, embracing the totality of the happy Habsburg past, gathering together the greatest figures from the Austrian and Bohemian past in a kind of pantheon, as a source of edification and emulation" (in Wheatcroft 1996: 248; see also Wandruszka 1964: 165–67).

Even more extravagant, and again enthusiastically supported by the emperor, in this case Franz Joseph, was the scheme of his son the crown prince Rudolf. As Rudolf explained to his father at an audience in 1884:

> The Austro-Hungarian Monarchy still lacks a great ethnographic work which, founded on the most advanced scientific research of the present day, and embellished by the highly perfected artistic means of reproduction, shall while stimulating and instructing, present a comprehensive picture of our Fatherland and its race of peoples. . . . This work will show at home and abroad what a rich treasure of intellectual power this Monarchy possesses in the peoples of all her countries, and how these co-operate in a splendid achievement, which is bound to serve to develop the consciousness and power of the common Fatherland . . . and a united patriotism. By the growing recognition of the qualities and characteristics of the single ethnographic groups and of their mutual and material dependence, that feeling of solidarity which is to unite all the peoples of our Fatherland must be strengthened. (in Wheatcroft 1996: 279–80)

Money and official support were immediately provided for this enterprise, and, over a period of sixteen years, from 1886 to 1902, twenty-four volumes appeared. But the important thing, and what made them so successful as Habsburg propaganda, was that each section first appeared weekly, in paper covers, at a price that everyone could afford. This part-work format followed the pattern of the publication of novels and other works by popular authors, such as Charles Dickens in England. Lavishly illustrated, the sections covered history, society, topography. They were published simultaneously in Hungarian, in Budapest, and distributed all over the empire (Wheatcroft 1996: 280–81; Judson 2016: 327–28). By the time the first few volumes had appeared, Rudolf was dead, by his own hand, in the mysterious joint suicide at Mayerling in 1889. But something of his vision continued in the thinking of his successor as heir apparent, his cousin the archduke Franz Ferdinand, until he too died, at the hands of an assassin in Sarajevo in 1914.

The ideas of Archduke John and Crown Prince Rudolf represented two complementary ways of advancing the Austrian idea. In the mid-1860s the archduke Albert, nephew to Archduke John, offered another, more traditional version, in a ringing restatement of the dynastic principle. The Habsburgs would survive, he argued, only if they remained aloof and absolutely separate from their subjects, above all considerations of class and nationality. The army must never be encouraged to serve "the state," a "liberal and abstract concept," but "the *House* of Austria, as it were the embodiment of the fatherland, for which its members are supposed to bleed and die" (Wandruszka 1964: 170). Such a view appealed to the emperor Franz Joseph, but he also saw the need to fuse it with Josephinian ideas of service to the state, a mission to which he committed himself throughout the sixty-eight years of his reign.[24] His chosen motto was *viribus unitis*—"with united strength"—which expressed the idea of cooperation among the various nations of the Habsburg Empire, under the protection of the dynasty—not, indeed, very dissimilar to Palacký's view. What in any case united the "royal" contribution to debates about the empire's future was, in the first place, the idea that the dynasty itself must take the lead in promoting its vision of the empire, not leaving itself to be the prisoner of events; and second, that it would be fatal if it were to identify itself with any national cause or group. The multinational empire had to have a multinational philosophy.

This was, in effect, what was also argued from the other end of society: not so much by the workers and peasants themselves as by their self-styled representatives, the middle-class socialist intellectuals and politicians. Not that all socialists in the Habsburg lands felt the need to deal directly with the problems of the multinational empire. For some, as for many Marxists generally, the question of national cultures was an obfuscating one, since the proletariat was an international entity, transcending national boundaries and destined to supersede them altogether in the new—potentially global—socialist state. But for the group of thinkers that have come to be designated "Austro-Marxists," this was an unreal and unhelpful position. For them, in regarding the Habsburg Empire as a reactionary, class-based, state that needed to be swept away, orthodox socialists ran the risk of consigning the many small nations of the empire to the rule of the large nation-states on their flanks, Germany and Russia especially. For the moment at least, the Habsburg Empire might be the best protector of the smaller nations, the best "political shell," as Lenin might have put it, for defending their interests. It should not be abolished; but it would have to be reformed, even transformed.

The best-known Austro-Marxists, Karl Renner and Otto Bauer, accepted the legitimacy of the nation.[25] *Pace* conventional Marxism, the nation was not just an expression of bourgeois class interests. It was a historical, spiritual, and cultural entity worthy of preservation and promotion. But the nation was not the state, and the nation-state—the aspiration of most nationalists in the nineteenth century—was not necessarily its best or highest political expression. This set nation against nation, in a debilitating Hobbesian or Darwinian struggle for survival. The Habsburg Empire, perhaps uniquely, contained the germ of another, more promising and progressive, principle. This was the multinational state, best organized as a democratic federation of national communities, "a free association of nations," as Renner put it. Reinterpreting the ideal of "socialist internationalism," Bauer argued that in the future socialist state national differences—precious, historically formed, resources—would not disappear but would on the contrary be more important, more capable of expressing themselves. "It is not the leveling of national particularities, but the promoting of international unity within national diversity that can and must be the task of the International" (Bauer [1907, 1924] 2000: 18; see similarly Otto Neurath in Sandner 2005: 282).

Bauer warned the working classes of "the Danubian Empire" against putting their faith in the disintegration of the empire as the solution to their problems. That would simply allow in the "national imperialism" of Germany, Italy, and Russia, who would pick up the pieces.

> If a victorious imperialism occupies the Austrian territories, if it integrates the small nations into the great nation-states, a terrible national struggle will erupt here—between Germans and Czechs, Germans and Slovenes, Italians and Southern Slavs, Poles and Ruthenians—which will make all class struggles impossible for some time. . . . The Austrian workers cannot place their hopes in German, Italian, and Russian imperialism, which is the enemy of their brothers abroad and the victory of which would diminish their own power at home. The politics of nationalist imperialism cannot be the politics of the working class. [The workers] must pursue their class struggle on the terrain that is historically given. . . . The prime objective of the workers of all the nations of Austria cannot be the realization of the nation-state, but only that of national autonomy within the given state framework. If Austria continues to exist, it is national self-administration that will create the most favorable conditions for the class struggle of the Austrian working class. . . . National autonomy based on autonomous local administration is for the working class the law of the co-existence of the nations inhabiting this soil. (Bauer [1907, 1924] 2000: 403–4)

It followed that the socialists must support the Habsburg Empire against its enemies, while seeking at the same time to reform it from within. "Well into the period of the First World War," says Robert Kann, "Bauer considered the great multinational Austrian Empire a good basis of operation for the realization of his Socialist program" (Kann [1950] 1970, 2:168).

Artists and writers made their own contribution to the Austrian idea. In the course of the First World War, as the Habsburg Empire struggled to survive, the great Austrian poet and dramatist Hugo von Hofmannsthal came out with a ringing declaration of faith in "the Austrian Idea," as he called it in an essay of 1917. Hofmannsthal confessed his was a belated conversion. Like many other artists and intellectuals he had formerly played the game of satirizing and criticizing the empire as antiquated and anachronistic. He now realized that that had been a lazy and dangerous exercise. "One was gradually compelled," he wrote, "to regard this 'conglomerate', this 'bundle of nations', allegedly ruled by some sort of tyranny, as the revelation of a spiritual power and of a historic necessity" (in Le Rider 1994: 121). Far from being "the prison-house of nations," as liberal and radical rhetoric held, for Hofmannsthal the Habsburg Empire had come to enshrine the principles of tolerance, diversity, and humanity. The peculiar Austrian quality of *Schlamperei*, much derided as muddle and inefficiency, now appeared as an attitude of salutary and humane neglect, an unwillingness to press the letter of the law when it obviously offended against common decency and humanity. In an essay titled "The Schema of Prussians and Austrians," which also appeared in 1917, the "indecisive and emollient" Austrian was contrasted with the officious and overbearing Prussian, bent on keeping strictly to the rules regardless of their sense or effect (Johnston [1972] 1983: 22–23; Kuzmics and Axtmann 2007: 14, 179–80).

When Viktor Adler, the Austrian socialist, called Austria's government "ein durch Schlamperei gemildeter Absolutismus"—"absolutism tempered by *Schlamperei*"—he too meant it in an approving way, setting a humanizing Austrian *laissez-vivre* against a rigid Prussian authoritarianism (Johnston [1972] 1983: 22). Something similar was implied in Count Taaffe's adoption of *fortwursteln*—"muddling through, slogging on"—as a principle of Austrian government (Morton 1980: 159).[26] This was perhaps the riposte to Grillparzer's charge of the "half-trodden path, and the half-finished act," as the source of the Habsburgs' failure. For Hofmannsthal the Austrian idea on the contrary encompassed "reconciliation, synthesis, a bridge linking incompatibles." It was both "a frontier and a bulwark," protecting Europe from external threats, and a "fluid boundary," allowing the cross-movement of peoples and cultures eastward and westward, an interconnection of Germans, Latins, and Slavs. "This Europe that wants to shape itself anew," concluded Hofmannsthal, "needs an Austria: a structure of genuine elasticity, but a structure, a real organism, permeated by inward self-worship without which living forces cannot be bound together; it needs Austria to grasp the polymorphous East. Central Europe is a day-to-day practical concept, but in the loftiest sphere, for Europe, Austria is indispensable" (in Le Rider 1994: 122).

Hofmannsthal was a Jew, or at least of Jewish extraction; and Jews, as has often been said, were the most loyal of the Habsburgs subjects, the most committed to the Austrian idea (as they were to the Ottoman idea). In Vienna, Prague, Budapest, Cracow, Lemberg (Lvov/Lviv), and many of the other leading cities of the empire, Jews found an opportunity, unequaled elsewhere in Europe, to cultivate their intellectual, professional, and commercial lives.[27] Many educated Jews became assimilated, mostly into the German high culture of the empire, but also into Magyar, Czech, or Polish culture, depending on where they lived. Few renounced their Jewishness entirely, though some did, and several prominent figures converted to Catholicism. Anti-Semitism too certainly had its place, increasingly in the later nineteenth century (Schorske 1980: 116–80; John 1999: 59). But it was balanced and offset by a widespread attitude of tolerance at the very highest reaches of society, including the emperor Franz Joseph himself. When, in 1916, Franz Joseph died, Moritz Güdemann, the chief rabbi of Vienna, wrote in his diary: "A true *tzaddik* [righteous man] has departed this life, a patient hero, a man of peace in the midst of war. His memory will remain a blessing" (Rozenblit 2005: 1). For most Jews, says Marsha Rozenblit, Franz Joseph was "not only '*der gute, alte Kaiser*', he was the source of their legal equality, the guarantor of their legal rights, their protector from anti-Semitism. . . . All Jews espoused a fervent Habsburg state patriotism and devotion to the continuity of the *Gesamtstaat*" (Rozenblit 2005: 2–3, 13; cf. Schorske 1980: 129–30; Déak 1997: 137).

An astonishingly large proportion of the most famous intellectuals and artists of the later Habsburg Empire were Jewish or of Jewish origin—many of them, or their parents before them, had converted to Christianity. The list would include Wittgenstein, Husserl, Herzl, Adler (Viktor and Alfred), Kelsen, Freud, Mahler, Schnitzler, Schönberg, Hofmannsthal, Kraus, Buber, Broch, Roth, to name just the most famous (to which we should perhaps add the earlier Strauss family, Johann the Elder and Younger, despite Nazi attempts to Aryanize them). When the Habsburg Empire collapsed in 1918, Freud was devastated: "Austria-Hungary is no more. I do not want to live anywhere else. . . . I shall live on with the torso and imagine that it is the whole" (in Coetzee 2002: 18; see also Jones 1964: 645).

The novelist Joseph Roth was another Jewish intellectual who became increasingly convinced that the disappearance of the empire had been a disaster, both for the Jews and for Europe. Roth, a Galician Jew who converted to

Catholicism, was no uncritical apologist for the Habsburgs. In his novels *The Radetzky March* (1932) and its sequel, *The Emperor's Tomb* (1938), he exposed the many archaic, inefficient, and occasionally brutal aspects of the empire. But in his portraits of the Trotta family—the grandfather, the "Hero of Solferino," who had saved the emperor Franz Joseph's life on the battlefield, and is ennobled for it; the father, the district captain Baron von Trotta; and his son, Carl Joseph, an army officer—he showed the appeal of the empire and the strength of commitment of many of its subjects. When Carl Joseph seeks to be stationed in a Slovenian village—thereby returning to the Trottas' Slovenian roots—his father cautions him strongly against it:

> He himself, the district captain, had never wished to see his father's homeland. He was an Austrian, a servant and official of the Habsburgs, and his homeland was the Imperial Palace in Vienna. Had he entertained any political ideas about a useful reshaping of the great and multifarious empire, it would have suited him for all the crown lands to be merely large variegated forecourts of the Imperial Palace and all the nations in the monarchy to be the servants of the Habsburgs. He was a district captain. In his bailiwick he represented the Apostolic Majesty. He wore the gold collar, the cocked hat, and the sword. He did not wish to push a plow across the fertile Slovenian soil. The decisive letter to his son contained the words: *Fate has turned our family of frontier peasants into an Austrian dynasty. That is what we shall remain.* (Roth [1932] 1995: 125–26)

In his foreword to *The Radetzky March*—"the great poem of elegy to Habsburg Austria," says the novelist J. M. Coetzee—Roth wrote: "My most unforgettable experience was the war and the end of my fatherland, the only one that I have ever had: the Austro-Hungarian monarchy. I loved this fatherland. It permitted me to be a patriot and a citizen of the world at the same time, among all the Austrian peoples and also a German. I loved the virtues and merits of this fatherland, and today, when it is dead and gone, I even love its flaws and weaknesses" (in Coetzee 2002: 18). Dreading the *Anschluss* with Nazi Germany in 1938, on its very eve he desperately sought to meet the Austrian chancellor Kurt Schuschnigg, to talk him into supporting the restoration of the Habsburg Monarchy; and one of the last letters he wrote—he died in 1939—was to Count Degenfeld, the adjutant of the exiled Otto von Habsburg, in which Roth requests him to "give his Majesty my sincerest thanks, and assure him that I will of course obey any order he cares to give me" (Roth 2012: 528).[28]

"I'm more of a Magyar than a Czech or German, but above all I'm a citizen of the Austrian Empire, and only as such am I a Magyar." So wrote the Hungarian journalist Aurel Kecskemethy in his diary in 1856 (Evans 2006: 282). The Jews of the Habsburg Empire would have understood that sentiment perfectly. They too felt that they could most easily be Jewish by being loyal citizens of the empire. Gustav Mahler may have proclaimed, "I am thrice homeless, as a native of Bohemia in Austria, as an Austrian among Germans, and as a Jew throughout the world" (in Janik and Toulmin 1973: 109). But Mahler's Jewishness did not prevent him from becoming *Hofoperndirector*, musical director, at the Vienna Imperial Opera, the most coveted artistic post in the city, nor from being idolized by the Viennese public (Spiel 1987: 165–67). No more did their Jewish origins stand in the way of the critical and popular acclaim awarded to Schnitzler and Hofmannsthal (Schorske 1980: 3–23).

Jews, along with many others, had more than enough reason to grieve over the passing of the Habsburg Empire and the Austrian idea, in light of the horrors that awaited them in the 1930s and 1940s. Otto Bauer, publishing a new edition of his *The Question of Nationalities and Social Democracy* in 1924—the first edition had come out in 1907—was forced to admit that his hopes for a reformed Habsburg Empire, on federal principles, had come to naught. "The political program I advocated in 1907 as a solution to the Austro-Hungarian nationalities problem has been passed over by history" (Bauer [1907, 1924] 2000: 6). The First World War, the Russian Revolution, and the fall of the Habsburg Empire itself in 1918 had all nullified prewar schemes for reform. But Bauer was right to think that the book's central ideas, and the tradition it enshrined, from Schlegel to Hofmannsthal, by way of Palacký and Masaryk, remained relevant to the postwar world of competing and conflicting nation-states—and particularly to what he called "the awakening of the non-historical nations," those looked down upon by the "master nations" of Central and Eastern Europe.

Later thinkers have reverted to this tradition with almost equal fervor. The fate of Czechoslovakia and Poland, and of many of the other small states of Central Europe, both between and after the two world wars, seemed only to confirm the correctness of the basic insight of the need for a "third power" between Russia and Germany. It was restated, as the communist world embarked on reform (*perestroika*), by the Czech novelist Milan Kundera, in an essay of 1984 that got wide attention. Kundera referred explicitly to Palacký's "dream" of Central Europe as "a family of equal nations, each of which—treating the others with mutual respect and secure in the protection of a strong, unified state—would also cultivate its own individuality." He mourned the disappearance of the Habsburg Empire, and its failure to realize Palacký's dream. "The Austrian empire had the great opportunity of making Central Europe into a strong, unified state. But the Austrians . . . did not succeed in building a federation of equal nations, and their failure has been the misfortune of the whole of Europe. Dissatisfied, the other nations of Central Europe blew apart their empire in 1918, without realizing that, in spite of its inadequacies, it was irreplaceable. . . . . After the destruction of the Austrian empire, Central Europe lost its ramparts" (Kundera 1984: 33–34, 37; cf. Timms 1991: 909–10; Kumar 2001: 93).

Decline and Fall?

"An experimental institute for the end of the world" (*eine Versuchstation des Weltunterganges*) was how the satirist Karl Kraus described the Habsburg Empire at the time of the assassination of the Habsburg heir Franz Ferdinand at Sarajevo in June 1914 (McCagg 1992: 63). Scholars and commentators have been only too happy to follow this lead, adding the Habsburg Empire to the many litanies of imperial decline and demise that mark the literature of and about empire. A notable and influential example was Oscar Jászi's *The Dissolution of the Habsburg Monarchy*, first published in 1929. Jászi, a Hungarian who had been active in the early part of the century in failed attempts to reform the imperial system, saw his task as "describing the mass-psychological process of the disintegration of the Habsburg Monarchy and of the failure of the conscious elaboration of a common will" (Jászi [1929] 1961: v). It was Jászi who identified "the irreconcilable antagonism of the different nationalities" as the central problem of the empire, one it could never solve. The First World War, he urged, should not therefore be seen as the cause of the empire's fall "but only the final liquidation of the deep inner crisis of the monarchy" (Jászi [1929] 1961: 23; see also Kann 1980: xi; Cornwall 2002: 2–3).

This has been a long-standing view of the Habsburg Empire's condition and prospects in the nineteenth century (Deak 2014: 338–57). A Götterdämmerung-like quality hangs over many accounts (e.g., Namier 1962). If not quite like the "sick man" image of the Ottoman Empire, this view shared something of the same sense that the Habsburg Empire was more or less doomed to dissolution, incapable of resolving its many problems, above all those of nationality. As a ramshackle, multinational, dynastic empire, it came to be a byword for an antiquated and outmoded form of polity. Even R.J.W. Evans, known

FIGURE 4.6. The emperor Franz Joseph, who ruled the Habsburg lands for over fifty years (1848–1916). George Grantham Bain Collection, Library of Congress.

for countering orthodoxies, speaks of "the effete conservative autocracy into which the Habsburg Monarchy . . . declined after the Napoleonic wars" (Evans 2006: 108). The very figure of the long-reigning and long-suffering emperor Franz Joseph, with his stiff formality and respect for the old forms, seemed to symbolize the incurably archaic character of the empire. Was it not Franz Joseph himself who, shortly before his death in 1916, remarked that "I have been aware for a long time of how much an anomaly we are in the modern world" (in Wank 1997a: 48)?

It has not helped that in the nineteenth century the enemies of the Habsburg Empire were able to popularize the notion of the empire as "the prison of nations" (*Völkerkerker*), and that many countries made heroes of famous nationalist exiles such as the Hungarian Louis Kossuth and the

Italian Giuseppe Mazzini, both of whom had led risings against the empire. The downfall of the Habsburg Empire has indeed come to be regarded as a textbook example of the incompatibility of nationalism and empire, and of the necessary triumph of the former in the modern world.

A highly influential view of this kind was propounded by the British historian A.J.P. Taylor in his 1948 book, *The Habsburg Monarchy 1809–1918*. Dismissing all earlier views—including his own—as the "liberal illusion" that the Habsburg Empire might have survived had it had different leaders, or followed different policies, or been spared some foreign-policy misadventures, Taylor resolutely declared: "The conflict between a super-national [*sic*] dynastic state and the national principle had to be fought to the finish; and so, too, had the conflict between the master and subject nations. Inevitably, any concession came too late and was too little; and equally inevitably every concession produced more violent discontent. The national principle, once launched, had to work itself out to its conclusion" (Taylor [1948] 1990: 9; for a later view see Taylor 1967; cf. Namier 1962; John 1999: 20).

It has to be said at once that practically all recent research and rethinking has radically revised and in many cases rejected this traditional view (see, e.g., Wessel 2011; Unowsky 2011; Deak 2014: 357–61). The fall of the Habsburg Empire was no more inevitable than that of any of the other European empires, many of which survived the "bonfire of empires" that occurred during and after the First World War. The problems of the empire were not in any marked way different from those of the other dynastic land empires, and in some ways were easier to manage than those of the overseas empires of the British and the French, with their many non-Western populations and non-Western cultures. Above all it was not nationalism, whether of the "master" or the "subject" nations, that destroyed the empire; it was other empires, and the bitter and protracted war that they became embroiled in, that brought about the demise of the Habsburg Empire in 1918.[29]

All nineteenth-century empires experienced crises of one kind or another, as we have seen in the case of the Ottomans, and as we shall see again in the case of the Russian and other empires. All felt the strains of managing entities as complex and convoluted as multinational and far-flung empires—far more complex than integrated, relatively homogeneous nation-states. One might say that such crises and strains are endemic to empires: one reason why it is normal to find their statesmen and intellectuals frequently wringing their hands about the empire's future, and uttering gloomy prognostications that later, when the empires disappear, are read back as prophetic diagnoses. It is always easy to be wise after the event. The fact that the Habsburg Empire fell in 1918 is taken as evidence that it had to fall, that its failure was inscribed in the history of the preceding century, if not earlier. Never mind that practically no one, on the eve of the First World War, wanted it to fail or even, in the case of its bitterest enemies, expected it to fall.

The fact is that the story of the Habsburg Empire in the nineteenth century can be as easily read as one of strength and success as it can one of weakness and failure (cf. Wandruszka 1964: xx; Deak 2014: 361–79; Judson 2016: 1–15). Riding the storms of the Napoleonic Wars and the 1848 revolutions, the empire regrouped under Franz Joseph and his advisers (not least members of his own family). Even the most serious reversals, as in the loss of the Italian lands in 1859 and defeat by Prussia in 1866, were the occasion for constructive reassessment, leading to the Compromise of 1867 and the Dual Monarchy. This certainly prolonged the life of the empire, and might have been capable of further modification had it not been for the First World War (Stourzh 1992: 17–20). Moreover, there were compensations in the Balkans, giving a new twist and a new possible future for the empire—making the Slavs a "third state" of a triple monarchy?—as the Ottomans retreated (Eisenmann 1910: 198; Kann 1977; Sked 2001: 247–51).

For all their discontents, Czechs, Slovaks, Slovenians, Croatians, Serbians, Bosnian Muslims, Poles, Ruthenians, and Romanians felt that they had more to lose without the empire than with it. Germans and Hungarians of course felt most comfortable within it as, for different reasons, did such groups as the Jews. We should think of the fates that befell many of these groups after 1918 before we judge too harshly their condition under the empire. War is a great test of public opinion and loyalty, and by that criterion the Habsburg Empire comes off rather well, according to all testimony. Norman Stone writes:

> On mobilization in 1914, the peoples of the Monarchy responded with a quite unexpected enthusiasm, even the Czechs giving no cause for complaint. . . . In fact the nationality agitation that had distinguished Austro-Hungarian politics before 1914 vanished almost completely in 1914. . . . It was not until 1916 that discontent began to assume alarming proportions, and not until 1917 that the 'lesser peoples' began to fumble for solutions outside the Monarchy. By 1918 the peoples were exposed to an intolerable strain. (Stone 1966: 103)[30]

"The Empire fell because it lost a major war" (Sked 2001: 301). This is a view that is gaining increasing popularity among students of the Habsburg Empire (e.g., Unowsky 2011: 237–38; Zückert 2011: 517; Deak 2014: 379, 2015: 261–74). This is not to ignore long-term trends or problems, which in the end could have brought down the Habsburg Empire as much as in the case of any other empire, none of which survives indefinitely. It is merely to say that in 1914 there was no reason to think that the empire could not survive barring some unexpected disaster (Kann [1966] 2011: 205). That disaster indeed supervened, in the form of a protracted and exhausting war that found Austria on the losing side and subjected it to crippling strains (Cornwall 2002).

If we look back briefly over the development of the empire in the nineteenth century, there are many positive achievements to report. Contrary to received views of the empire's economic backwardness, scholars now emphasize the relatively quick pace of change and the high degree of industrialization that took place especially in the second half of the nineteenth century. Development was uneven—by 1914 Czechoslovakia alone contributed 56 percent of Austro-Hungarian national output, and there were backward pockets such as Galicia and Bukovina—but so it was in almost all the Western economies of the nineteenth century, including the United States. In 1913, Austria-Hungary's share of total European GNP was 10.1 percent, about the same as France, and throughout the nineteenth century Austria remained the fourth-ranked European economic power, after Britain, Germany, and France. As Michael Mann says, "the Habsburg economy was a capitalist success" (1993: 333; see also 262–64, 333–36).[31]

Politically too the empire looked to many people in the early twentieth century to be relatively healthy and to be on the way to overcoming the many problems that had plagued it previously. "Civil society," that array of non-state organizations and associations concerned with "public opinion," was in a thriving state, with an especially lively daily and periodical press (Cohen 2007). Many organizations were empire-wide, such as the Imperial League of Secondary School Associations, or at least multinational, as with the League of Austrian Women's Associations. Class too could override national differences, shown most evidently in the rise of trade unionism and socialist parties in the early 1900s (Berenger 1997: 245–47; Okey 2002: 336–42). After 1848 a revitalized bureaucracy, including a substantial number of "new men" from all parts of the empire, accomplished a significant overhaul and modernization of the empire's central administration. Working with active and resourceful municipal governments, and largely bypassing the provincial diets and other traditional strongholds of the local aristocracy, it led the way in the creation of a modern constitutional state—albeit not a "national" one—that allowed for the creation of most of the rights and freedoms emerging in other Western societies (Deak 2015; Judson 2016: 336–63).

The arrangements of the 1867 Compromise seemed to be working, with significant concessions to the Slavs and Romanians, who rightly had felt left out. The electoral reform of 1907, pushed through by Franz Joseph, brought in universal male suffrage in Austria—with the promise of its extension to Hungary—and substantially reduced the inequalities in representation among the various national groups, with Germans now actually for the first time being in a minority in the Reichsrat (Okey 2002: 349–50). Writing in 1910, the French scholar Louis Eisenmann, one of the most knowledgeable students of recent Habsburg history, concluded that the empire, having surmounted several crises, was now remarkably strong and resilient.

> On December 2, 1908, Francis Joseph I celebrated the sixtieth anniversary of his accession to the throne. On the occasion of his Jubilee (December, 1898), Europe had viewed with fear and distrust the future of the monarchy, which seemed inevitably doomed to dissolution at the death of Francis Joseph. But ten years have elapsed since then, and the prognostications are wholly different. The acute crisis has been dispelled solely by the internal forces of the monarchy. The external dangers, that is to say, Pangermanism and Panslavism, appear much less serious today than at the time. Pangermanism has been swept aside by universal suffrage, and the Panslavonic feeling is growing weaker. . . . There is still a violent struggle between the nationalities, but the inevitable solution is in sight. The union between Austria and Hungary has, in reality, been strengthened by the new Compromise and the new Eastern policy. It seems as though all the Austrian, Hungarian, and Austro-Hungarian questions could be settled from within. It is in this that the progress consists; herein lies the great security for the future. (Eisenmann 1910: 212)

Eisenmann went on to attribute a good deal of the credit for this "far-reaching and peaceful transformation" to the emperor Franz Joseph, with his "wisdom, self-control, moderation, tact, and freedom from prejudice." Much, he said, will depend on his successor. "But fifty years of national and constitutional life have endowed the peoples of the monarchy with the strength to enforce their wishes side by side with those of their sovereign, and, if necessary, in opposition to him. They are of age, and can control their own destinies if they wish to do so. . . . They have come to realise the common interest which keeps them united in the monarchy and in time they will become conscious of the strength by means of which they can govern it in accordance with their own interests. The monarchy no longer rests on the power of the dynastic tie alone, but also on their conscious desire for union. Herein lies its great internal change; herein lies its mighty new strength, this is the great, the enormous result of the reign of Francis Joseph" (Eisenmann 1910: 212).

It is an extraordinary peroration, at variance with much of the doom-laden utterances of those years and, especially, since. But it seems to rest on solid foundations, the more so for being written by a scholar who a few years earlier had offered a highly critical account of the 1867 Compromise and who could in no way be regarded as an unabashed propagandist for the Habsburg cause. Moreover, when the cataclysm came, when war broke out in 1914, the Habsburg army, like the Ottoman, proved not just loyal and reliable but also a surprisingly efficient fighting force. "All authorities are agreed that it remained a praiseworthy and effective fighting machine until the summer of 1918, with even the South Slavs fighting for the most part to the end. It was not therefore overwhelmed by the nationality question" (Sked 2001: 266; cf. Zückert 2011: 510). It also survived staggering casualties: of the eight million men enlisted, over a million were killed and more than a million and a half captured or missing. Taken with other losses, "we must conclude that well over half of those in service were lost to the army" (Deák 1990: 192–93).

Two things in addition stand out in the war record of the Habsburg army: the loyalty right to the end of national groups—Slavs, Romanians, and Italians—that were supposedly on the side of the Habsburgs' enemies; and the fact that of all the great powers, the Habsburg Monarchy had since the 1870s spent the least on the military in proportion to its population—"a quarter of Russian or German expenditure, a third of British or French, and less even than Italian" (Taylor [1948] 1990: 247; cf. Stone 1966: 96, 103; Sked 2001: 266–67; Zückert 2011: 516). Both facts speak eloquently of the degree of dedication to the empire that still existed among nearly all national groups, and of the determination of the rulers to preserve, with their limited military strength, the monarchy in something of a recognizable form. That neither was in the end able to save the empire does not mean that it was not savable. It is important to note in this context that right down to early 1918 none of the principal Allies, Britain and the United States especially, desired the breakup of the Habsburg Empire. The tenth of President Woodrow Wilson's Fourteen Points of January 1918 explicitly stated that "the peoples of Austria-Hungary . . . should be accorded the freest opportunity of autonomous development"—not national independence. Only later did Wilson accept that such an outcome might be necessary, in the changed circumstances of the time (Namier 1962: 184, 188; Cornwall 2002: 177–78).

Much of what was traditionally said about the Habsburg Empire in its later years comprised backward readings from the situation after 1918. The Habsburg Empire did break up; successor states—Czechoslovakia, Yugoslavia, Poland—largely based on the nationalities of the empire did emerge. *Ergo* these national states were always there, waiting to be born, and the source of a persistent and ultimately fatal weakness in the empire's structure. This is the familiar "Sleeping Princess" story, a story of nationalist historiography and nationalist propaganda, and to be distrusted as such stories must be. No empire has a remit to exist for ever. The Habsburg Empire, in various forms, lasted for nearly six hundred years. The causes of its ultimate downfall were complex; but the nationalities problem was only one of them, and probably not the most important.

There was another reason why the later Habsburg Empire came to be presented as decadent and ripe for dissolution. After 1918 a rump "German Austria" sought desperately for some sort of identity. For many Austrian Germans, with the loss of their own empire, only absorption in a "Greater Germany," a new German Empire, seemed to offer any meaningful solution (Bruckmüller 1993: 198, 219, 2003: 304–11). A purely "Austrian" identity seemed, at that point, to make no sense: what would it consist of? The attractions of a resurgent Germany, under the rule of a renegade Austrian, Adolf Hitler (born near Linz), were only too evident. In 1938 Austrians greeted the *Anschluss* with Germany with near-universal acclaim. With this, Austrian Germans—like the other nationalities in the old Habsburg Empire—could pretend to themselves that this had always been their destiny, that the empire had clouded and obstructed that. For them too, as for the other nationalities, it made sense to present the Habsburg Empire in an unflattering light, as an artificial and "unnatural" agglomeration of disparate parts, waiting for the opportunity to split into its natural components.[32]

Only with the catastrophe of the Nazi regime, and total defeat in 1945, did Austrians wake up to the need to think again about their identity. In that sense, as Steven Beller has said, "only since 1945 have Austrians seriously tried to construct a national identity separate from that of the Germans" (Beller 2011: 1). By all accounts, they have been reasonably successful (Bruckmüller 1993: 199, 221). But they have done so against a background of a buried history that, time and again, resurfaces to trouble the new identity they have tried to construct for themselves. Like all imperial peoples, they cannot so easily turn their backs on their imperial past.

5

The Russian and Soviet Empires

The mistake we have been making for many decades is that we still have not admitted to ourselves that since the time of Peter the Great and Catherine the Great there has been no such thing as Russia: there has been only the Russian Empire.

—SERGEI WITTE (1910) (IN HOSKING 1998A: 479)

The dilemma of nineteenth-century Russian nationalism . . . consists in this—that it could only with difficulty, if at all, view the tsarist state as the embodiment of the national purpose, as the necessary instrument and expression of national goals and values, while the state, for its part, looked upon every autonomous expression of nationalism with fear and suspicion.

—HANS ROGGER (1962: 253)

The Soviet Union was an indissoluble part of Russian history, yet it had destroyed much of Russia. . . . It was both Russian and anti-Russian. That was the fundamental dilemma.

—GEOFFREY HOSKING (2006: 347)

A Tale of Two Empires

It is possible, and perhaps revealing, to tell the story of the Russian Empire backward, from the vantage point of its reincarnation as the Soviet Union. The Soviet Union recovered practically all the territory of the former tsarist empire. Like the tsarist empire, it announced a global mission, in its case cast not in the terms of religion but in those of a militantly atheist creed. As with the tsarist empire, the principal carriers of the new mission were the Russians, the dominant as well as the largest group within both empires. There were obvious differences between the two Russian empires, especially in the international context—the rise of the United States for one, the threat from a resurgent Germany for another. But many observers, both Russians and others, were also struck by the similarities and the continuities. For the Russian philosopher Nikolai Berdyaev ([1947] 1992: 263), the Soviet Union was simply the latest expression of the long-standing belief that Russia was the "third Rome," in succession to Rome and Byzantium, with a universal mission comparable to the Christian missions of the first two empires. For others, especially in the West, the similarities lay more in the fact that the Soviet Union was, despite its protestations, simply an empire, like its tsarist predecessor, with the same imperial drives and ambitions. It should be seen, and analyzed, as one actor in a world of competing empires.

The overlap and continuities meant that the Soviet Union also inherited many of the problems of the old tsarist empire. How to deal with the many non-Russian nationalities within its borders? Were they to be allowed their own cultures and a relatively high degree of autonomy, or were they to be "Russified" and attempts made at assimilation? And what of the Russians themselves? What was their role in the empire? Should they trumpet the superiority of their culture and their claim to be the guiding force in the empire? Or should they, as did most other dominant ethnic groups in empires, play down their ethnic identity in the interests of advancing the imperial cause and managing a multinational empire? At different times both impulses came to the fore, the one never entirely displacing the other.

So there might be a case for starting with the Soviet Union and working backward. Sometimes it can be illuminating to consider the less recent from the perspective of the more recent, on the grounds that over time certain features, certain questions, can be seen in a clearer light. That, for instance, is what Karl Löwith brilliantly showed in his *The Meaning of History* (1949), which begins with Hegel and Marx and traces their preoccupations and perceptions back to the Bible. This will not be the procedure followed here, partly to keep symmetry with the other chapters, partly because a traditional chronological approach still seems best even in the Russian case. But it is helpful nevertheless to state the continuities at the outset, to show the profound connections between what might be considered the two faces, or two installments, of the Russian Empire.

MAP 5.1. The Russian Empire, 1886

The Making of the Russian Empire

Some people see not just two but four, perhaps even five, empires in Russia's history (Longworth 2006; cf. Berdyaev [1937] 1960: 7, [1947] 1992: 21). There is first the Kievan Empire, the empire of Kievan Rus, (c. 900 CE–1240). This was an affair of Vikings ("Varangians"), Slavs, Balts, Finns, and others, ruled by the dynasty of Riurik, legendary Viking leader of the Rus to whom the Slav tribes and others subordinated themselves.[1] By the mid-tenth century Slavs and Vikings had merged, to create a predominantly Slavic language and culture with its center at Kiev, strategically placed on the Middle Dnieper with access to the Black Sea and Constantinople (Franklin and Shepard 1996: 141). "At its very inception, then, Rus was multi-ethnic, and the implications for later Russian history are not negligible" (Milner-Gulland 1999: 55).

More a federation than a unitary state, always precarious and repeatedly threatened by steppe nomads, Kievan Rus nevertheless managed to hold together for over two centuries. It developed strong trading links with the Baltic countries and Byzantium, and was one of the main axes of trade with the East. In the twelfth century, owing as much to the growth of wealthy and independent cities as to internal dissension, it began to fragment. It was finally destroyed in the mid-thirteenth century by the most formidable of the steppe nomads, the Mongols.

Before that, a fundamental and far-reaching development had taken place in the tenth century when, under Byzantine influence, first the princess Olga and then more decisively her grandson Prince Vladimir converted—the traditional date is 988—to Christianity and made it the state religion. Vladimir's marriage to Anna, sister of the Byzantine emperor Basil, sealed the connection; his son Iaroslav built the magnificent cathedral of St. Sophia in Kiev—modeled on its namesake in Constantinople—as a symbol of the Christian city and realm. The Byzantine inheritance, in religion, art, architecture, law, and concepts of rule, was to have profound and long-lasting effects on Russian history. Russia's written language, the Cyrillic script, was itself a Byzantine invention, the work of the ninth-century Macedonian monks Sts. Cyril and Methodios. "The Christian culture of the Rus . . . was formed in the Byzantine image, as a likeness—an icon—of the Byzantine prototype" (Franklin and Shepard 1996: 210; cf. Milner-Gulland 1999: 73–74; Pipes [1974] 1995: 223–26).

More controversially, a century and a half of Mongol (or Tatar) rule also influenced Russian developments. Delegating much authority to the Russian grand princes (such as Alexander Nevskii of Vladimir, hero of victories over the Swedes and the Teutonic Knights), the Mongols helped in the unification of Russia and in particular the spread and strengthening of the Russian Orthodox Church, whose authority they supported (Kivelson 1997: 642; Hosking 2012: 57). It was during this period that monasteries (one of whose products was the great icon painter Andrei Rublev) became important instruments of Russian culture (Pipes [1974] 1995: 226–27; Longworth 2006: 49–51).

It was once common—especially among Russians—to attribute also to the Mongols a legacy of "oriental despotism" in Russia, and a host of other barbaric "Asiatic" practices (Pipes [1974] 1995: 56–57, 74–76; Stone, Podbolotov, and Yasar 2004: 28). That is less often heard now; Europe has plenty of authoritarian traditions of its own to provide models, not least the Byzantine civilization that was formative in early Russian development. But the Mongols undoubtedly contributed much to Russian civilization, not just in political and ecclesiastical centralization but also in such areas as trade and markets, and in the development of systems of communication (Pipes [1974] 1995: 203–5; Kivelson 1997: 642–43; Figes 2002: 366–75; Riasanovsky 2005: 62–69).

Russian victory over the Tatars at the Battle of Kulikovo (1380) began the push-back that eventually overthrew Mongol rule (though it was to be another century before Russians no longer acknowledged the authority of the Golden Horde). Leading the "gathering of the lands of Rus" was the new city of Moscow. Moscow was formerly a backward part of the principality of Vladimir-Moscow but, blessed with a hinterland suitable for agriculture and occupying a central position on Russia's great network of rivers and portages, it had grown in size and wealth to rival Novgorod, Tver, and Vladimir. In 1325, under Ivan I, prince of Moscow and later grand prince of Vladimir and "All Russia," the Metropolitanate of Kiev moved permanently to Moscow, henceforth making Moscow the cornerstone of the Russian Church and the spiritual center of Russia. Amid warring princes, it was the Church that acted as a unifying force and promoted Moscow's primacy. It was the Church's monks and monasteries, established in the "wilderness" following the example of the famed hermit Sergius (Sergii of Radonezh), that took the lead in Moscow's colonizing mission (Longworth 2006: 58–61; Milner-Gulland 1999: 109–10; Hosking 2012: 72–78).

The second Russian Empire can accordingly be called the Muscovite Empire (c. 1400–1605). It was fundamentally the creation of two grand princes, Ivan III ("the Great") (1462–1505) and Ivan IV ("the Terrible") (1533–84). In 1478 Ivan III subjugated Novgorod, the largest of the rival Russian states and itself something of an empire, in its rule over various non-Russian ethnic groups. It has been said in fact that it was the conquest of Novgorod that "finally imparted a multi-ethnic character to the Grand Duchy of Moscow," which up till then had been mainly Russian (Kappeler 2001: 16; Martin 1988: 26–29). It has also been argued that the wholesale expropriation of the aristocracy and merchant class of Novgorod, and the creation of a military service system on their lands, introduced a new element of authoritarianism and centralization that was to have profound effects on the whole development of the Muscovite Empire (Lieven 2001: 240). Ivan III also embarked on a number of ventures that similarly carried unmistakable imperial overtones. In 1472 he married Zoe Palaeologue, the niece of the last Byzantine emperor, and so initiated the movement that was to culminate with the proclamation of Moscow as the "Third Rome." Ivan III also adopted as his insignia the double-headed eagle, symbol of the Roman Empire, which with successive modifications—the last in 1883—announced Russia's claims to be "a world power, dominating both East and West" (Hellbirg-Hirn 1998: 17; see also Riasanovsky 2005: 65).

To complete this signaling of imperial ambitions, Ivan's son, Vasilii III (1505–33), to the consternation of conservatives in 1525 shaved off his beard, in imitation of the Caesars of old (Longworth 2006: 86). It was to Vasilii too that the monk Filofei (Philotheus of Pskov) addressed his famous letter of 1523 (?), in which he declared that "all the empires of Christendom are united . . . in thine, for two Romes have fallen, the third stands, and there will be no fourth" (Hosking 2012: 103). The meaning of this pronouncement has been much debated, as also its implications for Russian imperialism.[2] But there can be no doubting the central message that, following the fall of Rome and

Byzantium, the torch of Christianity had passed to Russia, whose holy duty it now was to defend and promote the Christian cause (if necessary against the pretensions of the Roman Catholic Church).

It could hardly escape anyone's attention that Russia itself had just been liberated from Mongol rule, thus becoming providentially placed to take on the Byzantine mantle (Lieven 2001: 238). Moreover, the prophecy also contained a warning: if the grand prince of Moscow failed to pursue this mission, there would be no further chance—"there will be no fourth"—and the world would end (Bushkovitch 1986: 358). Such was the apocalyptic mood—strong also in the West at this time—in the wake of the fall of Constantinople and the growing divisions within Christianity itself (Luther's Ninety-five Theses were posted in 1517). Russia's destiny was marked out for it. That such a fateful mission had to be tempered by a pragmatic consideration for the sensibilities of the non-Christian, predominantly Muslim, subjects of the empire—a modifying feature of all imperial rule—did not prevent it from being a powerful unifying ideology, one that could take a number of forms, including secular ones.

Nothing could have seemed a more complete fulfillment of that sacred mission than Ivan IV's conquest of Kazan in 1552. That might also have seemed a fitting achievement for the first Russian ruler to be styled tsar (Caesar) or emperor, as Ivan IV was by express permission of the patriarch of Constantinople, the acknowledged supreme head of the Orthodox Christian Church (Hosking 2012: 131).[3] The Russian tsar now had the responsibility, as well as the authority, to establish the empire of Christendom to the fullest extent possible—to "bring all the barbarian peoples under his power," as it was declared in the investiture ceremony at his coronation in 1547 (Cherniavsky 1975: 124–26; Longworth 2006: 87). The "gathering of the lands of Rus"—Novgorod, Tver, Pskov, Smolensk—had all involved fellow Christians, now brought into the Muscovite fold. Kazan was different. Now it commenced the "gathering of the lands of the Golden Horde." Andreas Kappeler dates the history of Russia as a multiethnic empire from its conquest. The conquest, he says, "was an unparalleled step in the history of the Muscovite state. . . . The Khanate of Kazan was the first independent polity to come under Russian rule which possessed a historical tradition, dynastic legitimacy and an upper class which not only spoke a different language but also belonged to a different world religion and civilization, Islam" (Kappeler 2001: 14, 21; cf. Huttenbach 1988a; Lieven 2001: 231; Hosking 2012: 117).

Ivan IV's reign (1533–84) does indeed seem to mark a new departure, a new quality that for many scholars makes it the true beginning of Russian

FIGURE 5.1. Tsar Ivan the Terrible, conqueror of Kazan. Portrait (1897) by Victor Mikhailovich Vasnetsov. Tretyakov Gallery, Moscow, Russia/Bridgeman Images.

imperialism (e.g., Hosking 1998a: 3; Longworth 2006: 87). It is shown partly in the creation of new instruments of autocratic rule—the *streltsy*, a crack force of musketeers, and more notoriously the black-cowled *oprichniki*, the "men apart," Ivan's personal band of trusted special agents, organized and disciplined on quasi-monastic lines and used for terrorizing his enemies. But most of all the new mood is seen in a new expansiveness, a drive to take Russia to distant regions and to incorporate different peoples. Hard on the heels of Kazan came the capture of the Khanate of Astrakhan (1556), and with it the gateway to the southern steppes and Central Asia. Astrakhan also gave access to the Caucasus and its mountain peoples. Russia now entered on its fateful Caucasian entanglements, symbolized by Ivan's marriage in 1561 to a daughter of the Circassian prince Temriuk. The conquests of Kazan and Astrakhan therefore can truly be seen as epochal events in Russia's imperial history. Before that Russia had been a Slavic, Christian, and European state. "As result of its victories along the Volga, Muscovy broke out of these confines and became both a Eurasian body politic and a multicultural society" (Huttenbach 1988a: 68).

Russia's advance guard and colonizers in the new southern frontier lands were the Cossacks, a group of irregular fighting men made up of Tatars, Russians, Lithuanians, and Poles. The Cossacks were unruly and independent, passionately attached to their *volia* (liberty). They provided the leadership for the two greatest peasant rebellions in Russian history, those of Stepan (Stenka) Razin (1670–71) and Emelian Pugachev (1773–75). Nevertheless, they proved formidable agents of the march of empire. It was the Cossacks who were used to overcome the resistance of Siberian tribes in the latter part of Ivan's reign, and so set Russia on the path of one of its most momentous colonizing ventures (Huttenbach 1988b: 77–80; Kappeler 2001: 34, 49–50). In the next century Cossacks were to spearhead Russia's rapid advance across the immense Siberian landmass to the Pacific Ocean.

The seventeenth century, with the dying out of the Riurikovich dynasty and long-drawn-out succession struggles, brought turmoil in the Russian lands. A series of pretenders to the throne convulsed Russia for decades in risings and civil war. There were invasions by Poland and Sweden, which came close to dismembering Russia. Moscow was occupied by Polish troops in 1610; Novgorod fell to the Swedes (Longworth 2006: 117–26). This was the era, the "time of troubles," so vividly captured in Mussorgsky's great operas *Boris Godunov* (1872) and the unfinished *Khovanshchina*.[4] Everything turned on who controlled the *streltsy*, the musketeers, who, like the Roman Praetorian Guard of old or the Janissaries in the Ottoman Empire, made and unmade tsars. The election of Mikhail Romanov as tsar in 1613 by no means ended the troubles, despite the fact that the Romanovs finally prevailed to give their name to Russia's third empire (1613–1917), the greatest and longest lasting. Not until the rise of Peter the Great could the Romanovs feel at all secure on the throne.

Among many challenges, the most serious and far-reaching was the Great Schism in the Orthodox Church, between the reformers led by the patriarch Nikon and those who came to be labeled Old Believers. The reformers wished to introduce changes in liturgy and scriptures based on Byzantine practices, so that the Russian Church could move closer to the Byzantine one. With the latter captive to the Turks, this would lend strength to the Russian Church's claim to the leadership of the entire Eastern Christian ecumene. The move was helped by the fact that in 1591 the metropolitan see of Moscow had been elevated to the status of an independent Patriarchate, enhancing its power and prestige and making it now a more equal partner to the state.

The Old Believers viewed Nikon's reforms as a sacrilegious rejection of old Russian ways and a dangerous move toward Western ecclesiastical models. Tsar Aleksei, after some hesitation, supported Nikon, thus allying church and state against an increasingly disaffected group of Old Believers. The schism was to have profound repercussions over the centuries. The Old Believers remained stubbornly unreconciled. Moving mostly to remote regions of the north, often suffering persecution, they came to form a community within a community, a "parallel society" seeking to keep alive certain old practices and beliefs in contradistinction to the official ones. They became an inspiration to, and occasionally adherents of, many radical movements right up to the early twentieth century, many of which were not religious in nature but chimed with the Old Believers' way of life.

The Old Believers were not a mere sect; over the following two centuries something like a quarter of the Great Russian population were said to be Old Believers. Here were two Russias, or two ideals of Russia: one distinctively imperial, seeing in the Orthodox Church a means of advancing Russia's claims to be the protector of all Christians, in all lands; the other turning its back on church and state and looking for salvation in the "land"—especially in the villages—and the people. The divergence between these two ways of seeing Russia's mission was to reappear in various guises for many years to come, not least in the debate between Westernizers and Slavophiles in the later nineteenth century. It was also one of the ways in which the differences between national and imperial aspirations revealed themselves, the one looking back to distinctively Russian "national" traditions, the other stressing Russia's world-historical role as a Eurasian power (Hellberg-Hirn 1998: 90–93; Milner-Gulland 1999: 119–26; Hosking 1998s: 64–74, 2012: 165–74).

Despite, or perhaps because of, the troubles, Russian expansion continued apace in the seventeenth century. The great conquest of these years was the vast territory of Siberia. Siberia is the Russian equivalent of Western European conquest and colonization of the New World across the Atlantic. It began, in the mid-sixteenth century, a mere half century or so after Iberians and others had begun to carry European civilization across the oceans (Huttenbach 1988b:70; Bassin 1999: 61–62). Given the persistence of Siberia in Russia after the breakup of the Soviet Union, Russian conquest of this region can even be said to have been more long-lasting, and to have had greater consequences, than the colonial efforts of its Western European neighbors. Moreover, with the great exploitation of Siberian oil and gas in the twentieth century, Siberia might bid fair to be considered "the jewel in Russia's imperial crown" (Lieven 2001: 224; see also Breyfogle, Schrader, and Sunderland. 2007: 21–37 and passim).

With the collapse of Mongol power to the east of the Urals, a motley group of Cossacks, traders, trappers, runaway serfs, and adventurers of all sorts engaged in a steady but relentless movement across the Siberian flatlands, drawn above all by the quest for furs that were in such high demand at Western courts (Slezkine 1994: 11–45; Bassin 1999: 19–20; Etkind 2011: 72–90). The weak and disunited Siberian tribes were bought off or crushed. But mostly their institutions were left intact, with the Russian state mainly interested in collecting the fur tribute, *iasak*, from the elders of the tribes. Moreover, there was much intermingling and intermarrying of Russian settlers with the local populations, especially with the conversion of the tribal peoples to Orthodoxy. In this way, says Emanuel Sarkisyanz, the Russian Empire showed that it had "an ideological and not a biological criterion of identity. The criterion for belonging to the imperium was profession of Orthodox faith, not race or birth" (Sarkisyanz 1974: 73; see also Slezkine 1994: 42–45).

Siberia, *Sibir'*, came to occupy a powerful position in the Russian imagination. From a land of bounty, abounding in the riches of mink, sable, and ermine, it became, as the fur trade declined in the late eighteenth and early nineteenth centuries, "a vast wasteland," a harsh and unforgiving realm that was set apart for exiles. It also for Russians marked the place where "Asia" began, the region of savages and infidels whose taming and conversion became Russia's "civilizing mission" in the East. By the same token, Russia's Asiatic face, its position between East and West, might give it the edge over the West and counter Western assumptions of superiority. "Going native," in the Russian Empire, never acquired the quality of disparagement that it generally did in the Western empires, nor did "Orientalism," as characterized by Edward Said, impose the same negative features on the East. "We must," wrote Dostoevsky in 1881, "cast aside our servile fear that Europe will call us Asiatic barbarians, and say that we are more Asian than European" (Figes 2002: 415; see also 377–84, 415–20; Bassin 1991; Slezkine 1994: 47–92; Lieven 2001: 217–20).

Empire without Bounds

Peter the Great (1682–1725) was the real architect of Russia's third empire, the empire of the Romanovs. Surviving bloody conflicts, including a major *streltsy* rising, during the regency of his half sister Sophia, he consolidated his rule after 1696. It was Peter who made Russia a great power, fit to take its place among the European great powers and to attract their courtship. Peter studied Western European achievements closely, and made numerous trips to Western countries, most notably Holland in 1697–98. Like Atatürk in Turkey in the early twentieth century, Peter decided that Russia would become powerful only if it learned from the West. The great symbol of this was the new Russian capital of St. Petersburg on the Neva, Russia's "window on Europe."[5]

The move of the court from Moscow to St. Petersburg (in 1710) was not a renunciation of Russian heritage, nor of its Eurasian character, as heir to the Golden Horde. But it was a recognition that Russia had a lot of catching up with the West to do, especially in science and technology, and more generally in the fields of education and learning. To that end Peter founded a School of Mathematics and Navigation and other schools, such as the elite secondary schools known as the Cadet Corps, which "became the nursery of a whole distinct *dvorianski* [gentry] way of life, centered on school, regiment, state service, and landed estates" (Hosking 2012: 207). He opened Russia's first public library and its first museum. He laid the foundations for Russia's first university, which opened in Moscow in 1755. He established an Academy of Sciences, modeled on London's Royal Society, to promote research at the highest levels. He set up printing presses and encouraged book publishing; and the first Russian newspaper appeared in Moscow in 1703. "With an autocratic hand / He daringly sowed enlightenment," sang the great Russian poet Alexander Pushkin of Peter's accomplishment.[6]

A reshaping of the aristocracy was central to Peter's design. He suppressed the *streltsy*, who had become the main tool of the aristocratic factions. He

FIGURE 5.2. Peter the Great, the great Westernizer, who built the
city of St. Petersburg. Portrait (1838) by Hippolyte (Paul) Delaroche.
Hamburger Kunsthalle, Hamburg, Germany/Bridgeman Images.

amalgamated all ranks of nobles into a single estate, the *shliakhetstvo* (later
renamed the more familiar *dvorianstvo*), and created a Table of Ranks that
made state service a condition of membership and advancement. Already a
service nobility, the Russian aristocracy became even more so under Peter,
a character that was to last until the end of the empire (Pipes [1974] 1995:

124–25). Peter also brought in Western dress and manners, including the requirement for beardlessness among the nobility (merchants and peasants were exempted). The aristocracy was encouraged to learn French, the language of international diplomacy and generally of *politesse*, and to travel abroad. By 1725 there were twelve permanent diplomatic missions established in various European capitals, and Russian aristocrats began to be regular presences at the fashionable receptions and salons of the European aristocracy in Paris, Vienna, Berlin, London (Etkind 2011: 102; Hosking 2012: 183, 205).

The empire continued to expand in Peter's reign. His greatest triumph was the defeat of Sweden, Russia's formidable and longtime antagonist in the Baltic. A decisive victory at the Battle of Poltava (1709) led ultimately to the Treaty of Nystad (1721), at which Russia gained control of most of Sweden's Baltic provinces, Estonia, Livonia, and part of Finland. Peter consolidated this with the building of a great naval base at Kronstadt in the Gulf of Finland. Russia now had a powerful navy and full access to the Baltic, a vital strategic and trading artery. It became one of the great Northern Powers, complementing its expansion eastward and southward.

Peter's failures in other directions, notably in the Crimea, were made good by his successors, especially Catherine II ("the Great") (1762–96). In the course of the Russo-Turkish War of 1768–74, Russia (in 1771) established a protectorate over the Khanate of Crimea, displacing Ottoman overlordship. In 1783 the Crimea was annexed and formally incorporated into the Russian Empire. In addition the Treaty of Küçük Kaynarca (1774), which ended the Russo-Turkish War, gave Russia the right to keep its warships on the Black Sea and to send its commercial shipping through the straits to the Mediterranean. The treaty also, in somewhat ambiguous terms, recognized Russia as "protector" of the Orthodox subjects of the Ottoman Empire—a fateful clause that in later years Russians interpreted as giving them the right of intervention in the affairs of the Ottoman Empire on behalf of Orthodox Christians (Finkel 2007: 378).

Conquest of the Crimea represented the climax of Russia's southward expansion. The empire now ran from the Baltic to the Black Sea; while access to the Mediterranean, though for the time permitted only to merchant vessels, opened up vistas of a Mediterranean empire that Russia was fully prepared to contemplate. Ambitions went even further. Count Grigorii Potemkin, governor of the Crimea—newly renamed "New Russia"—and a favorite of Catherine the Great's, dreamed of raising the Balkan Christians against the Ottomans and of reestablishing the Byzantine Empire under Russian tutelage

(Hosking 2012: 233). The support of the Greek rebels against Ottoman rule in the 1820s was partly a reflection of this goal, though its success was always unlikely given the determination of the Western powers to limit Russian ambitions in the Black Sea region.

Nevertheless, Russian advance along the Black Sea coast continued. Following a further war with the Ottomans (1787–91), Russia gained additional territory and was able to lay the foundations of the great port city of Odessa in 1792. Moving up from the Black Sea, Russia in 1806–12 incorporated Bessarabia and, following the Greek War of Independence, in 1828–29, established a protectorate over the Danubian principalities of Moldavia and Wallachia—in both cases at the expense of the Ottomans. Russian designs on the Black Sea and the Balkans, bringing potential conflict with the British and the Habsburgs in addition to the Ottomans, were clear; the "Eastern Question" was born.

With the conquest of the Khanate of Crimea, together with the earlier conquests of Kazan, Astrakhan, and other Tatar territories, Russia had now definitively established itself as the imperial successor to the Golden Horde. But it had much grander aims, in both eastward and westward directions. Westward its main victories were over its great enemies of earlier times, Sweden and Poland-Lithuania. Under Peter, as we have seen, Russia detached the Baltic provinces—Livonia and Estonia—from Sweden. In 1808–9 Sweden also lost Finland to Russia. Earlier, in the seventeenth century, profiting from the revolt of the hetman Bohdan Khmelnytsky and the Dnepr Cossacks against Polish rule, Russia in 1667 incorporated the greater part of Ukraine. For Russians this represented no more than the liberation of their eastern Slav brothers—the "Little Russians"—from the Polish yoke, and the return of some of the most historic "lands of Rus" (including Kiev) to the Russian fold. Many Ukrainians then and since have seen it differently, as an initial agreement among equals that turned into a form of subordination and suppression of Ukrainian identity. The issue haunted relationships between the two peoples (or two cohorts of just one, according to the Russians) right up to the dissolution of the Soviet Union, and beyond.[7]

Poland's loss of Ukraine was nothing compared to what happened to it in the eighteenth century: its progressive dismemberment in the partitions of 1772, 1793, and 1795. Once again Russia justified its share of the spoils—Lithuania and Belorussia, together with what remained of Ukraine and Livonia—in terms of the "gathering of the lands of Rus," many of which had been under the "alien" rule of Poland. Since most of the population of the new territories were not Poles, Russia could speak of a reunification "of the lands and towns which had once belonged to the Russian Empire, had been populated by their fellow Slavs and illuminated by the orthodox Christian faith" (in Kappeler 2001: 80).

Russia was also the principal beneficiary, so far as Poland was concerned, of the new arrangements for Poland following Napoleon's defeat in 1815, inheriting the lion's share of Napoleon's creation, the Duchy of Poland, formed mainly out of the Austrian and Prussian spoils in the partitions of Poland. Russia now possessed not just the Polish borderlands but most of its core, now reestablished as the Kingdom of Poland within the Russian Empire. Since, unlike the borderlands, where a Polish nobility ruled over mostly Ukrainian and Belorussian peasants, the core lands were predominantly Polish throughout, Russia had given itself a new Polish question, one that was now domestic rather than international. Particularly after the defeat of the Polish revolts of 1830–31 and 1863–64, Polish aspirations were to become a source of constant anxiety in the region, affecting as they did Poles in adjoining territories such as Lithuania (LeDonne 1997: 70–80; Weeks 2001).

Russia's westward expansion in the seventeenth and eighteenth centuries was accompanied by equally far-reaching moves toward the east and southeast. As successor to the Golden Horde, Russia now had access to the Caucasus and the lands beyond. Here it came up against claims made by the Ottoman and Safavid empires. But these were perhaps the least of the problems in that region. Inhospitable mountainous terrain, more than fifty warlike tribes—Chechens, Circassians, Kabardinians, Ingushetians, Ossetians, Abkhazians, and others—and religious differences between Christians and Muslims, and within both confessions, made (and continue to make) the Caucasian region a nightmare for states seeking to conquer it and establish orderly rule there.[8]

Russia's first true success in this treacherous area came in Transcaucasia, the region beyond the Caucasus. Here were the more settled people of Georgia, which had a long history of statehood—ended, as with Russia, by the Mongols—and was largely Orthodox in religion. Under the energetic direction of Prince Potemkin, pursuing his goal of stripping the Ottoman Empire of all its Christian territories, Russia established a protectorate over Georgia in 1783. In 1800, in the midst of succession struggles and in the face of Iranian and Ottoman claims, Russia annexed Georgia and brought it administratively within the Russian Empire.

Success also came with two other Transcaucasian peoples, the Christian Armenians and the Turkic-speaking Muslims later called Azerbaidzhanis. Both of these, like the Georgians, were settled peoples with state traditions, but they were widely dispersed throughout the region, and their historic lands were divided between the Ottoman and the Iranian empires. Following the Russo-Iranian War of 1804–13, the khanates in the northern part of Azerbaidzhan were incorporated into the Russian Empire; another war with Persia brought, in 1828, the eastern khanates of Armenia within the Russian fold (larger groups of Armenians, however, continued to live under the Ottomans, in eastern Anatolia). The Armenians, like the Georgians, could be represented as captive Christians living under the Islamic yoke; the flood of Armenians into Russian Armenia from the Iranian and Ottoman empires was some testimony to this view of Russians as liberators (Kappeler 2001: 175, 178). With the Muslim Azerbaidzhanis this argument of course could not be made; here the "civilizing mission" of the Russians, bringing light to the barbarian East, became the standard justification, as it was to be for later Asiatic conquests.

In the middle and later nineteenth century it was the turn of the "Inner Asian" peoples of the steppe to be embraced by the Russian bear. Once more Russia could see this as part of "the gathering of the lands of the Golden Horde," in its role as successor to Tatar rule. Operating from the forward base of Orenburg, established in 1734, the vast area of the Kazakh Khanate was the first to be absorbed, from the late eighteenth to the mid-nineteenth century. As with Siberia, Cossacks provided the first colonists, but Russian and Ukrainian farmers were also encouraged to settle there, and by the late nineteenth century hundreds of thousands of settlers from European Russia were occupying the fertile pastures of northern Kazakhstan, forcing the nomadic Kazakhs to the drier and less hospitable areas in the south (Donnelly 1988: 204–6). The Bashkirs of the southern Urals too, over whom the Russian state had exercised uncertain control since the seventeenth century, were in the first half of the nineteenth century brought more firmly within the imperial administration (Donnelly 1988: 191–96; Steinwedel 2007).

Peter the Great believed that the Kazakhs were "the key and gate to all the Asian countries and lands," and so it proved (Donnelly 1988: 203). In the second half of the nineteenth century it was the fate of the Uzbeks, Tadzhiks, and Turkmen to be subdued and incorporated into the Russian Empire. Compared to the Caucasus, conquest here was relatively easy, achieved with small forces and few casualties (MacKenzie 1988: 231). The great Silk Road cities of Central Asia—Bukhara, Samarkand, Tashkent—all came under Russian rule, though by this time they had long lost their luster. Strategic as much as economic considerations, as well as the always-important spur of prestige, played their part in this expansion (MacKenzie 1988: 211; Lieven 2001: 210–11).

Russians saw Central Asia as a battleground for the three imperial powers of Russia, China, and Britain. Occupying Central Asia put pressure on the British in India, as did the struggle for Afghanistan; it was at this time that the "Great Game," the subject of Rudyard Kipling's famous novel *Kim*, was being played out between Russia and Britain. Whether Russia actually had designs on India is unclear (though the Russian general Skobelev is reputed to have said, "Give me 100,000 camels and I will conquer India").[9] But the British certainly thought so, which is the more important thing. Since Russia had shown a clear interest in acquiring Sinkiang and Manchuria from the Chinese, why think that Russia would be satisfied with Central Asia? Just as the United States felt it had a "manifest destiny" to occupy all the lands between the Atlantic and the Pacific on the North American continent, so too many Russians felt it was their destiny, and perhaps even their duty, to occupy the whole Eurasian landmass east of the Urals (Becker 1986: 42; Bassin 1999: 27). The founding of Vladivostok—"Ruler of the East"—in 1860 was a clear declaration of intent, accompanied as it was by a transfer of China's Amur and Maritime provinces to Russia.

Following China's defeat in the Sino-Japanese War (1894–95) Russia saw the opportunity for further Asian advance, a prospect additionally stimulated by the decision in 1891 to build a trans-Siberian railway. A strong position was established within Korea (1896–98), exploiting the Japanese threat to the country. But the real goal was China's Manchuria, into which Russia steadily inserted itself in the 1890s. In 1897 Dairen and Port Arthur were ceded to Russia, and between 1900 and 1905, following the Boxer Rising, the whole of Manchuria was occupied. Only defeat in the Russo-Japanese War (1904–5) put a stop to these East Asian designs. But a Russian Eurasian ideology had been born, whether it took the form of a belief in Russia's civilizing mission in the East or of a view of Russia's actual Eurasian character, as a country as much Asian as European.[10]

In 1864 the Russian foreign minister Gorchakov gave an acute analysis of the situation from the Russian point of view, in which he explicitly drew the parallel with the United States and other Western powers:

> The situation of Russia in Middle Asia is that of all civilized states which come into contact with semi-savage and itinerant ethnic groups without a structured social organization. In such a case the interest in the security of one's borders and in trade relations always makes it imperative that the civilized state should have a certain authority over its neighbours, who as a result of their wild and impetuous customs are very disconcerting.

Gorchakov went on to show how one step in the process of intervention led on to another, as the newly settled lands in their turn came to the unwelcome attention of other unruly people on their borders. An inexorable logic led on to further conquests to secure the earlier ones. For "the state has to decide between two alternatives. Either it must give up this unceasing work and surrender its borders to continual disorder . . . or it must penetrate further and further into the wild lands. . . . This has been the fate of all states which have come up against this situation. The United States in America, France in Africa, Holland in its colonies, Britain in eastern India—all were drawn less by ambition and more by necessity along this path forwards on which it is very difficult to stop once one has started" (in Kappeler 2001: 194; cf. Raeff 1971: 25; MacKenzie 1988: 212).

We shall return later to this remarkably clear and bold analysis, both in general and in relation specifically to Russia's treatment of its Central Asian peoples. But in rounding out this account of the growth of Russia's empire we need to note finally its penetration beyond Eurasia, across the Bering Straits and down the west coast of America. In itself, this was a relatively short-lived episode (Vinkovetsky 2011). Attracted especially by Alaskan furs, Russians from the beginning of the nineteenth century began to establish settlements in Alaska and the Aleutian Islands. By 1806 they had already reached the border with Spanish California, and in 1812 built a fort at Bodega Bay, about one hundred kilometers north of San Francisco. Opposition from Britain and America, the rapid depletion of fur-hunting grounds, and in consequence a declining number of Russian settlers led Russia to sell Alaska and the Aleutians to the United States in 1867 for the paltry sum of 7.2 million dollars. Russia was to remain a Eurasian power.

Russia's Alaskan settlement, and its abandonment, have been the subject of much fascinating counterfactual speculation (what if Russia had stayed in North America . . . ?). From our point of view what it best illustrates is the dynamism of Russian imperialism over several centuries. There seemed no bounds to Russian expansion. Russia poured itself out in all directions, west, east, north, south. True, it remained largely continental, and the oceans in the end set limits—self-imposed, as in China?—to Russia's growth. But in Europe and Asia at least its ambitions seemed infinite, to the alarm not just of traditional rivals such as the Ottomans, the Persians, and the Chinese, but now also the Habsburgs, the British, the French, the Americans. The great nineteenth-century Russian historian Vasilii Kliuchevsky once said that Russia is "a country that colonizes itself." There are a number of possible applications of this famous remark, as we shall soon see. But one that seems clear is that Russia grew with its empire, that it is unthinkable without empire, that to be Russian is to be imperial. That of course poses great problems when Russia loses its empire, tsarist or Soviet.

"A Country That Colonizes Itself"

At its peak, in the early twentieth century, the Russian Empire was the largest land empire in world history, and second only to the British Empire overall.[11] But "its combination of size and duration is unique in world history, since it has outlasted by far the other large empires" (Taagepera 1988: 1). Britain might eventually have constructed the world's largest empire; but Russia was the world's largest empire for about 300 years, Britain only for about 100 years (Taagepera 1978a: 125). In an ingenious calculation of what he calls the "time integral of area"—a measure of the combined size-duration effect—the political scientist Rein Taagepera has shown that it is 65 million square-kilometer-centuries for Russia, 45 for the British and post-Mongol Chinese, and between 30 and 20 for Rome, Baghdad, Han China, Sassanid Persia, and the Mongol Empire. "When one takes into account both size and duration of empires, Russia comes by far ahead of the British and Mongol empires . . . and also of the Roman and Sassanid empires. . . . As far as the impact of an empire depends on how much land it controls for many centuries, Muscovy-Russia-USSR already hold the record in world history" (Taagepera 1988: 4–6).

We have traced Russia's steady expansion, from the "gathering of the lands of Rus," completed by the mid-fifteenth century, to its conquest of Kazan in 1552 and the subsequent "gathering of the lands of the Golden Horde." By 1905 Russia had reached more or less its maximum point of expansion, its empire stretching from the Baltic to the Pacific and from the Arctic to the Black Sea. Its successor, the Soviet Union—Russia's *fourth* empire—never went beyond that, though remarkably despite early losses it recovered and held on to nearly all the old tsarist territories (Taagepera 1988: 3).

What was this Russian Empire—whether we consider it as two, four, or even five (the fifth, Philip Longworth and others have suggested, being the one currently in President Putin's mind's eye: Longworth 2006: ix; Beissinger 2008: 1; Etkind 2011: 4)? One thing that is clear is its immense lability, mobility, and fluidity. Unlike other empires, it did not have an obvious or permanent center. Over its thousand-year history the empire's center moved from Novgorod to Kiev to Vladimir to Moscow to St. Petersburg and back again to Moscow. Russians have a saying, "Novgorod is our father, Kiev our mother, Moscow our heart, Petersburg our head"—a comforting organic metaphor that conceals the disconcerting instability of the main organ, the head (Hellberg-Hirn 1998: 35–37). It is almost like the later Roman Empire, when the imperial center was wherever the emperor happened to be for the time. Certainly there is nothing in the Russian case to compare with the stability and long-standing status of Rome, Constantinople/Istanbul, Vienna, London, or Paris as the metropolitan centers of their empires (though the early Chinese Empire shows a similar indifference to a long-established capital).

It was therefore not so traumatic that, in the midst of the struggle against Napoleon in 1812, General Kutuzov should order a withdrawal from Moscow, abandoning it to the French. As he said to Tsar Alexander I, "so long as Your Imperial Majesty's army is intact . . . the loss of Moscow is not the loss of our fatherland" (Longworth 2006: 194). Earlier, in the seventeenth century, Moscow had been occupied by Poles and Swedes, but the empire had remained a going concern. Capitals had their place in the empire, symbolically and spiritually, but they were peculiarly dispensable and at times marginal. As Kliuchevsky said of the establishment of St. Petersburg, "in Russia, the centre is at the periphery" (in Etkind 2011: 97). Peter the Great could exchange Moscow for St. Petersburg—built on newly colonized soil, a "foreigner in its own fatherland," as Gogol put it—as readily as Lenin could exchange St. Petersburg for Moscow (and Putin, as a Petersburger, has occasionally hinted at returning the capital to St. Petersburg). Even the frequent and ready change of names suggests this instability. St. Petersburg transmogrified early into Petersburg; in 1914 it became Petrograd, in 1924 Leningrad; in 1991 it moved back to St. Petersburg; and for much of the time it has popularly been called simply Peter (Brodsky 1987: 71, 84). It is not surprising that in the writings of Gogol, Dostoyevsky, and Biely, St. Petersburg should carry an abstract, hallucinatory character, as of a place not quite real (Berman 1983: 173–286; Hellbirg-Hern 1998: 40–51).

In fact a peculiarity of the Russian Empire is the difficulty of distinguishing, in the conventional way, between metropole and colony. As we have seen (chapter 1), all land empires to some extent have this feature, as compared with overseas empires. But the Russian case shows this to an almost exceptional degree, as compared with land empires such as the Ottoman and Habsburg. Scholars have been driven to describing the Russian Empire as "a periphery without a metropole," one where the line separating the two has become so unstable and fuzzy as almost to disappear (Semyonov, Mogilner, and

Gerasimov 2013: 54; cf. Lieven 2001: 226; Tolz 2001: 2). This could be misleading if taken too literally; at the very least there was a dominant ethnicity—the
Russians—forming some sort of "core" in relation to a series of peripheries.
But the exaggeration is instructive. It indicates the particular form of Russia's imperial development, as a series of waves that redounded back on the
center and threatened to engulf it, to make it part of its own "colonial" creation. One might also almost see the Russian nesting doll, the *matrioshka*, as
an apt symbol of this kind of empire: after each doll has been taken out, one
after the other, there is nothing left at the center, no "core." Yuri Slezkine has
described the consternation of eighteenth-century travelers and ethnogra-
phers when attempting to distinguish Russia and Russians from the plethora
of new peoples and territories acquired by the empire: "Much of the 'sacred'
heartland seemed to consist of borderlands" (Slezkine 1997: 50). An empire of
borderlands: that is not a bad description of the Russian Empire.

A promising way to understand this process is through the idea of "internal
colonization." This has in one form become familiar to Western scholars, at the
very least since Michael Hechter's illuminating study of the United Kingdom
as a case of "internal colonialism" (Hechter [1975] 1999). But what is especially
relevant to our question is the use and development of the concept by Russians themselves, in the writings of some of their most distinguished historians
and commentators.

It was the Moscow historian Sergei Soloviev (1820–79) who first articulated
the concept in the form that was popularized by his students, most notably
Vasilii Kliuchevsky.[12] In his mid-nineteenth-century history of early Russia,
Soloviev wrote, "Russia is a vast, virgin country, which was waiting to be populated, waiting for its history to begin: therefore ancient Russian history is the
history of a country that colonizes itself." Soloviev was well aware that this
distinguished Russian development from that of the more familiar form of
overseas colonization. "This country was not a colony that was separated from
the metropolitan land by oceans: the heart of the state's life was situated in this
very country. . . . While the needs and functions of the state were increasing,
the country did not lose her self-colonizing character" (in Etkind 2011: 62–63).

Soloviev, perhaps influenced by the desire to make modern Russia look
more like contemporary European empires, restricted the self-colonization
concept to Russia's medieval history. His disciple Kliuchevsky, in lectures published in book form in 1904, took a further, bolder, step. Kliuchevsky repeated
Soloviev's formulation almost word for word (even though most people attribute the saying to Kliuchevsky): "The history of Russia is the history of a

country that colonizes itself. The space of this colonization widened along with the territory of the state." But then Kliuchevsky added significantly, "This centuries-long movement has continued until the current moment." For Kliuchevsky, there was no separation of ancient and modern imperialism, at least as far as Russia was concerned. From the earliest settlements in Siberia in the Middle Ages to the absorption of the Crimea, the Caucasus, and Central Asia in the nineteenth century, Kliuchevsky saw a seamless process of conquest and colonization. "The colonization of the country is the single most important fact of Russia's history," stated Kliuchevsky; from the Middle Ages to the modern era, the standard periods of Russian history are nothing but "the major moments of colonization" (in Etkind 2011: 67).[13]

The one constant in Russia's empire is the expansive movement itself. Russia might shrink or even be conquered—as in the twelfth and thirteenth centuries under the Mongols, in the seventeenth century under assault from Poles and Swedes, in the early nineteenth century following Napoleon's invasion, in 1917 with the collapse of the tsarist empire, in the Second World War under Hitler's onslaught. But it always seems to bounce back and reestablish the empire. This was most clearly the case after 1917; but it has been true for the earlier periods as well. It is this that makes many people feel that Russia's imperial story is by no means over with the collapse of the Soviet Union in 1991 (e.g., Hosking 2012: 4). Russia has been there before; it is still the largest country in the world, with vast resources of gas, oil, coal, gold, and diamonds; many of its neighbors have historic ties that in the right circumstances might lead them back to the Russian fold. The "end of empire" is no more certain in the Russian case than in the world more generally, despite repeated statements to the contrary.

What did Soloviev and Kliuchevsky mean by calling Russia a "country that colonizes itself"? In one sense, perhaps the dominant one in their minds, they seem to mean what most contemporary scholars today mean by internal colonization.[14] That is, their account of Russian development might be similar to Hechter's view of the United Kingdom as formed by the process whereby the English "colonized" the adjacent territories of the Welsh, the Irish, and the Scots—"the Celtic fringe"—and integrated their peoples into a unified state (Hechter [1975] 1999). The Russian case might also seem to be paralleled by the development of the United States through its "moving frontier": the great nineteenth-century westward movement that, as famously described by Frederick Jackson Turner (1920), played a central part in the making of the American nation as well as imparting a "frontier mentality" to the American

national character (Bassin 1993). Such an understanding is suggested by Soloviev's gloss that "because of this [Russia's self-colonizing character] there
was a constant powerful movement of population across enormous spaces";
and Kliuchevsky's similar remark that "the sphere of this colonization widened with the territory of the state" (Bassin 1993: 498). In all these cases the
principal idea is that the state and its culture resulted from a constant and
ever-widening process of expansion, in which neighboring lands and peoples
were conquered, colonized, and absorbed into the evolving state and society.
Whether those peoples were fully assimilated or simply integrated, with a considerable degree of autonomy, remains a variable matter. What is important
is the character of the state as a "colonial state," one whose very principle of
existence is dependent on a process of colonial expansion that is, in theory at
least, unbounded.

This type of internal colonialism is in reality the foundation of many so-
called nation-states, where the fact of such earlier colonization is obscured
by a later nationalist ideology that portrays them as the creation and embodiment of one particular nation. In that sense, many nations are "miniempires,"
empires in disguise (see chapter 1). But just as it is helpful, at least in principle, to distinguish empires from nation-states, so it is helpful to distinguish
internal colonialism from the more familiar form of colonization in which
states acquire colonies often remote from themselves in space and culture—
the case, for instance, with most Western overseas empires. Internal colonialism in this sense is evidently a feature not just of many nation-states but of
all land empires, the Ottoman and Habsburg as much as the Russian. In all
these cases the very state undertaking the colonial enterprise is itself a colonial
creation, the creation of a dominant ethnicity that may—as in the case of the
Germans in the Habsburg Empire—be an actual minority. There may be differences of degree—Russia certainly appears an extreme case—but generally
land empires share the same feature of a blurring of the distinction between
colonizing and colonized, a tendency for one to collapse into the other, so
that it becomes after a certain point difficult to separate the two. Exactly who
is doing the colonizing becomes a moot point when the supposed "metropolitan" state is itself constantly being reconstituted by the "peripheries" in
the process of colonization.

This primary sense of internal colonialism carries an implication that is
often hinted at but not usually articulated and developed; and it gives rise
to a somewhat different meaning of internal colonialism, or at least draws
attention to a frequently neglected aspect. It is one thing to characterize the

state as formed by colonialism; it is another matter to trace the impact of this on the "state-bearing" people themselves, the ones in whose name—in this case, the Russians—the empire is created. This is a case where the term "self-colonization" might be more accurate than "internal colonization." For what it points to is the way in which the imperial people are shaped by the acts of colonization that they themselves carry out, the effect of which is to make them in many ways as much *colonial subjects* as the other groups that they subjugate. They become in other words the object as much as the subject of the colonizing process; they, the ostensible colonizers, are themselves colonized.

We shall see in more detail later how this process works, and with what consequences. In general, though, we can say that internal colonization, or self-colonization, quite often makes the imperial people the victims as much as the beneficiaries of the colonial enterprise. Ostensibly the dominant people, the ones who give their name to the empire, they can find that this leads to a degree of enforced self-restraint, even to a form of "reverse discrimination," that puts them at a relative disadvantage compared to the peoples of the "periphery," the peoples subject to their colonization. In the interests of the empire as a whole, their own national identity may have to be suppressed or downplayed; their own institutions may remain undeveloped or merged with imperial institutions in which they may find it hard to see themselves reflected; eventually they may come to feel that the empire is no longer theirs, or that they no longer control it. Something of this kind has happened to all imperial peoples—the Romans, the Turks, the Spaniards, the Austrian Germans, the Russians, the English, and—though perhaps least of all—the French. Empire in their case is a mixed blessing. Proud of their creation, and having no formal existence apart from it, they may nevertheless increasingly come to feel alienated from it, as a power that has absorbed all their energies but is delivering diminishing returns, in their case at least. Commitment begins to wane, though accompanied by a melancholic sense that, without empire, things might be even worse for them—for what are they without it? It is such a mixture of pride, concern, and anxiety that is conveyed with such force and subtlety in *The Radetzky March* (1932), Joseph Roth's superb novel of empire.

To understand the Russian Empire, we need to look at both aspects of the process of self-colonization. We need to examine first the Russian imperial state, as it was formed by internal colonialism. This involves looking at the people who ran the state, who they were and how they saw their task. It means also examining their attitudes and policies toward the various peoples of the empire, not excluding of course the Russians themselves, the titular imperial nationality. Like all empires, the Russian Empire was a multiethnic and multinational empire; management of this diversity was and is a key task of all empires.

We need, second, to consider the Russian people, as both a ruling and a subject nation. They gave their name to the empire, "the Russian Empire." How far was it theirs? To what extent did they claim ownership? How much did it contribute to their sense of themselves, their identity as a people? What did it mean to be Russian in the era of empire? This will take us into a consideration of "Russian nationalism," which as a concept can seem as strange and unnatural as "English nationalism."

The Imperial State and Its Peoples

Since the sixteenth century, the Russian state and its territory have been officially known as *Rossiya*, wrongly but popularly thought to be a Latinate derivation from the medieval *Rus*. When Peter the Great was declared "emperor of Russia" in the early eighteenth century—a title that was added to the older and more familiar "tsar," which continued in use—it was Rossiya that was claimed as his realm. This was intended to show, among other things, that the Russian Empire, Rossiyskaia Imperiya, fashioned by Peter the Great "was not exclusively Great Russian in its composition" (Raeff 1971: 22; Milner-Gulland 1999: 1; Tolz 2001: 158).

The ancient *Rus*, as in "the lands of Rus," did not disappear, making frequent appearances in poetical and rhetorical language, and at times of national crisis (cf. "England" for "Britain" in similar uses). It has also continued in popular use throughout Russian history. In any case its persistence was guaranteed by the fact that it gave rise to the name of the Russian people, as *russky*. *Russky*, the term for ethnic Russians, stands alongside *rossiysky*, citizens of the Russian state, not all of whom are necessarily of Russian origin. "The difference," says Geoffrey Hosking, "is as important as that between 'English' and 'British', or—in some ways an even closer parallel—between 'Turkish' and 'Ottoman'" (Hosking 2006: 7; cf. Kristof 1967: 244–45; Cherniavsky 1969: 119–20; Brooks 1985: 219).

Russia may be unusual in having two words for national membership; but the situation this reflects is by no means uncommon and indeed, as Hosking indicates and as we have already seen in the cases of the Ottoman and Habsburg empires, occurs in nearly all empires. In nearly all empires there is a distinction between the imperial state—and the territory it controls—and the peoples of the empire, including the people that constitute the dominant ethnicity. The distinction may not always be clear or conscious in the case of the dominant ethnicity—certainly not as clear as it is to other ethnic groups in the empire. In the Russian case, this was particularly marked during the Soviet period, when "Russian" was regularly substituted for "Soviet" by both natives and outsiders (cf. "English" for "British" in Great Britain). But by late Soviet times Russians were very conscious that they were not simply Soviet; and during the imperial period, the period of the tsarist Russian Empire, the distinction between *russky* and *rossiysky* was clear to most Russians. It could become the basis of a feeling of distance and separation, even of alienation, from the Russian state. It has indeed been a frequent claim that "people" and "empire"—or nation and state—were radically distinct in the Russian Empire, and that much of its history can be understood only on that basis (e.g., Rogger 1962; Pipes [1974] 1995, Hosking 1998a).

We shall consider these claims later in this chapter. First, though, what was the ethnic composition of the Russian Empire? How "Russian" was the Russian Empire? In the early eighteenth century, ethnic Russians (as defined by language) made up just over 70 percent of the population of the empire. Ukrainians made up just under 13 percent, and Belorussians 2.4 percent. Of the remaining 15 percent, Baltic peoples (Latvians, Estonians, Lithuanians, Finns, Germans, Swedes) made up just over 4 percent, and Muslim groups (Tatars, Bashkirs, Nogai, and others) also just over 4 percent. The final 6–7 percent were made up of Christianized groups such as the Chuvash and Mordvins of Kazan, and the animist Siberian tribes, such as the Iakuts, Ostiaks, and Buriats. Given the propensity of the Russians to treat Ukrainians ("Little Russians") and Belorussians ("White Russians") as fundamentally Russian, the Russian Empire in the early eighteenth century was predominantly Russian— depending on definition, between three-quarters and more than four-fifths Russian (Rywkin 1988: xv; Kappeler 2001: 115–17, 395–99).

By the eve of the First World War, with the massive expansion of the empire in the eighteenth and nineteenth centuries, ethnic Russians were now a minority—just under 45 percent. Ukrainians now made up 18 percent, and Belorussians 4 percent. The great new addition was the Poles, who now constituted over 6 percent of the empire. Jews, mostly in Lithuania, Ukraine, and Belorussia, now also formed 4.2 percent. Georgians made up 1 percent, and Germans 1.4 percent. Baltic groups—minus the Germans—remained steady at 4 percent. Muslim groups, on the other hand, with the conquest of the Caucasian and Central Asian tribes—Chechens, Ossetians, Kazakhs, Kirghiz,

Uzbeks, Tadjiks, Turkmen—together with the Azeri Turks, had more than tripled their representation, from 4 to 15 percent—the largest non-Orthodox group in the empire, though highly diffuse and differentiated (Rywkin 1988: xv; Kappeler 2001: 285–86, 395–99; Crews 2006: 13–14).

Russians certainly still made up a larger proportion of their empire than Turks in the Ottoman or Germans in the Habsburg empires; if Ukrainians and Belorussians are added, they amounted to two-thirds. The Orthodox Church also continued to dominate, with 71 percent of the population being Orthodox of some kind. Moreover, the empire still remained predominantly European, the more so with the addition of the Polish lands. But there is no doubt that in the course of two centuries the Russian Empire had become vastly more multiethnic and multiconfessional. The second religion of the empire was no longer Roman Catholicism but Islam (14 percent). Next came Catholics (9 percent), Jews (4.3 percent), Lutherans (2.7 percent), Armenian Gregorians (0.9 percent). (Kappeler 2001: 286, 396). The question of the "Russianness" of the empire was bound to have become more complicated, more challenging, requiring sensitivity to the cultures and faiths of others. Conversion to Ortho-doxy could and would be promoted, often energetically; but it was clear that Catholic Poles and Lithuanians, Protestant Finns and Germans, and Muslims of all stripes would also have to be accommodated—not to mention Jews and Armenians with their own distinctive religions.

How did the empire manage its non-Russian peoples? (We will consider the Russians themselves separately.) Up to the mid-nineteenth century, the general rule—the result as much of practicalities as of considered policy—was to preserve as far as possible the structures and institutions preceding Russian absorption into the empire. In the north and west, with Finland, the Baltic provinces, Lithuania, Belorussia, and parts of Ukraine, a thin stratum of Russian administrators, military garrisons, and settlers lived amid populations strongly divided by class and ethnicity. In Finland Swedes lorded it over the majority Finns; in Estonia and Livonia, the Baltic German nobility dominated the Latvians and Estonians; in Belorussia, Lithuania, and Ukraine "on the right bank of the Dnepr" (the provinces of Kiev, Volhynia, Podolia), a Polish or Polonized aristocracy ruled over Belorussian, Lithuanian, Ukrainian, and Latvian peasants. The situation was one, in other words, where non-Russian elites were allowed to continue dominating the lower-class peasants who lived mostly in conditions of serfdom and who were divided by ethnicity both from the elites and from each other. From a governmental point of view this had the doubly advantageous effect of commanding the loyalty of the elites and of letting them take on much of the burden of social control in their areas. It also enabled the imperial government to exploit the many differences of ethnicity in the region, acting as both mediator and, where it suited them, champions of "oppressed" groups against their local overlords (e.g., Lithuanian peasants against Polish landlords) (Kappeler 2001: 119–20).

In other spheres too the imperial government followed a policy of tolerating the old ways in this region. In the Polish lands annexed to the Russian Empire after the partitions of 1772, 1793, and 1795, not only did the authorities leave untouched the relation between the Polish landowning nobility and their peasants, they also allowed a Polonization of these territories through the development of schools and universities in which the language of instruction was Polish, overriding other languages such as the Lithuanian and Ukrainian. The "Lithuanian Statute"—the civil and criminal code of the old Polish-Lithuanian Commonwealth—continued to be applied in these provinces, and Polish remained the dominant language in the administration. No attempt was made either to interfere with the religious beliefs of the inhabitants. The Poles and Lithuanians were allowed to practice their Catholicism; the Ukrainian and Ruthenian peasants were able to continue their adherence to the Uniate Church (Raeff 1971: 31–32; Kappeler 2001: 78–84; Miller and Dobilov 2011: 426–27).

Even the formation of the "Kingdom of Poland," a Napoleonic creation inherited by the tsarist state after 1815, and incorporating most of the territory of the former Duchy of Warsaw, did not initially change this situation. Until 1830 the kingdom had its own constitution, with Polish as the official language, and a Polish army with Polish uniforms and Polish as the language of command. The Polish administration had full budgetary control of the kingdom, subject only to the final authority of the tsar as king of Poland. Under Alexander I, the hope even began to grow among the Polish nobility that the tsar would be the liberator of Poland, uniting the Kingdom of Poland with the kresy, the Polish lands lost during the partitions. It did nothing to dampen these hopes that Alexander's chief adviser and confidant at this time was the liberal Polish nobleman Adam Czartoryski (LeDonne 1997: 71–72; Kappeler 2001: 85–89).

Things began to change in the later years of Alexander's reign, and also as a result of the Decembrist rising (1825) that coincided with the beginning of the reign of Nicholas I, and that revealed connections with Polish conspirators. Nevertheless, Nicholas still declared that he tried "to be as good a Pole as he was a Russian." He was fluent in the Polish language, and at his coronation as king of Poland in Warsaw in 1829 he swore to uphold the Polish constitution (Miller and Dobilov 2011: 430). What brought about a dramatic change in imperial attitude and policy was the failed Polish uprising of 1830–31. The Polish constitution was abolished and its territories annexed to the empire. The Polish army was disbanded and merged with the Russian army. Thousands of soldiers were exiled to Siberia or the Caucasus (Miller and Dobilov 2011: 434–36).

Nevertheless, the Kingdom of Poland was not abolished, and though the Polish language was restricted in official use, Poles were encouraged to learn Russian and join the imperial civil service. At Kiev University, which replaced that of Vilna in 1834, the majority of students were Poles studying in Russian, often with Polish professors. By the 1850s Poles made up 6 percent of the central imperial bureaucracy and dominated the ministries demanding specialized or technical knowledge. In the climate of reform created by defeat in the Crimean War, attempts were made to conciliate the Polish nobility. The nobility was once more allowed to take up state service in their own provinces. A certain amount of Polish-language education was restored in the schools and institutions of higher education. An attempt was made, through the Agrarian Society set up in Warsaw and run by Polish nobility, to regulate relations between Polish landlords and their peasants. The government wished to prove its goodwill toward the Polish nobility and to reward it for its loyalty in recent decades. In 1861 Alexander II signed an edict that would have restored Polish institutions of higher education and allowed for elected local administrations in the Polish kingdom (Miller and Dobilov 2011: 438–42; Kappeler 2001: 249–50, 252–53).

The Polish uprising of 1863, far more threatening than that of 1830, ended this search for a new accommodation with the Polish nobility, even though many Poles initially opposed the uprising. With the crushing of the rebellion, the Kingdom of Poland was abolished and its lands brought within the general administrative structure of the empire, as the "Vistula province." Poles were debarred from serving in the Polish or western provinces (though not in the central bureaucracy in St. Petersburg). The Higher School in Warsaw became Warsaw University, with Russian professors and Russian as the exclusive language of instruction. There was a concerted attack on the Catholic Church, with the closure of many monasteries, the confiscation of all the Church's property, and the establishment of an office in St. Petersburg to supervise the clergy (Miller and Dobilov 2011: 443–49; Löwe 2000: 69–71).

Nevertheless, despite the magnitude of the 1863 rebellion, no serious attempt was made to suppress Polish culture and the Polish language in the core Polish region, the old Kingdom of Poland. Only in the western provinces was a systematic campaign carried out against Polish culture, for fear of the Polonizing effects on a region that had historically been dominated by Poland and where the Polish or Polonized nobility still held sway. In Lithuania, the largely Catholic Lithuanians were thought of as "potential Poles," and the authorities went out of their way to suppress the Polish language and Polish publications among them (Weeks 2001: 99–104). The Lithuanians, on the other hand, were not regarded as a potential nation and therefore not seen as a threat to the empire. It became an article of faith that Lithuania had always been Russian, part of "Western Rus," and that the Poles had unjustly occupied it. In the late nineteenth century, as a means of offsetting Polish influences, Russian officials indeed encouraged Lithuanian culture, as for instance in the use of Lithuanian in church services and the printing of Lithuanian publications in the Latin (rather than Cyrillic) script. Lithuanians, it was thought, despite their Catholicism, would gradually and peacefully assimilate into the clearly superior Russian culture.

Theodore Weeks remarks in this context on "the elastic, 'imagined' character of Russian nationhood, which at times could stretch to include non-Slavic Lithuanians" (2001: 114). It is not clear that "Russian nationhood" is the right or best term here, especially as little attempt was made to "Russify" the Lithuanian population (Weeks 2001: 104–7). Better perhaps to see the Lithuanian case as part of a typical imperial strategy of divide and rule. The Russian government's main concern was to keep the peace and maintain the integrity of the empire, not to turn all its inhabitants into Russians. Polish nationalism became a threat to the empire; Lithuanian nationalism did not, or at least was not perceived as such, and so there was no need to suppress the Lithuanian language or religion (though, again typically, stimulation of Lithuanian culture as a counterweight to Polish had the unintended effect of bringing into being a Lithuanian national movement). As Weeks himself says, "not faith or nationality but loyalty [to the tsar] was the true criterion for inclusion in the 'Russian family'" (Weeks 2001: 107).

This seems the key point. A fundamental conservatism marked the Russian Empire throughout. Only in the 1860s and 1870s, following the weaknesses revealed by the Crimean War, was there a Russian Tanzimat, an attempt at far-reaching reform, with the emancipation of the serfs, reform of the legal system, and the introduction of the *zemstva*, the organs of elected local administration. The reform movement rapidly foundered on the shoals of the Polish uprising and the rise of a revolutionary movement within Russia itself, in the form of populism and terrorism. Another attempt was made after another defeat, in the Russo-Japanese War of 1904–5. This too led to revolution, the revolution of 1905; and the constitutional experiment halfheartedly tried following the suppression of that revolution ended with the First World War and the descent into imperial breakdown. Compared, say, to the Ottoman and Habsburg empires, the tsarist empire that was overthrown in 1917 shows a remarkable degree of continuity, at least since the time of Peter the Great. There was less fundamental, structural, change in the Russian Empire throughout the last two hundred years of its history than occurred in any of the other major empires that we are considering in this book.

That does not of course mean no change whatsoever; nor was there a single consistent policy pursued throughout, or a single administrative system for the whole empire, anymore than would be the case in any empire with so heterogeneous and far-flung a population. But so far as possible the Russian Empire aimed at keeping things as they were, as the best means of preserving the empire. When a new territory was acquired, the inhabitants usually kept the same status as they had had before, and were simply incorporated into the Russian estate system, the *sosloviia*. "A Georgian noble owning land and serfs was given a Russian aristocratic title and allowed to keep his land and serfs; a Tatar merchant was entered into one of the Russian merchant guilds and retained trading rights in his city of residence; a Ukrainian serf remained a serf under Russian rule" (Geraci 2009: 247). Even after the reforms of Alexander II, which aimed at a greater integration of the empire's population, the estate system was in the main retained, for fear that abolishing it would undermine the control of the traditional elites. Modernization, moreover, always carried the danger that it would educate and empower not just Russians but, perhaps even more, non-Russian minorities, who would make increasing demands for group rights and greater autonomy (Löwe 2000: 77).

In general it was easier to pursue a policy of preservation in relation to the empire's western, European, territories. Here were in the main long-established, settled communities, with strong institutions of rule. They were regarded as a valuable source of ideas and skills that were more likely to be forthcoming the less existing practices were tampered with. We have seen this policy applied to the Kingdom of Poland, until the government's hand was forced by the 1830 and 1863 risings. It was even clearer in the case of the Baltic provinces of Estonia and Livonia, conquered from Sweden under Peter the Great. These were turned into two provinces of the Russian Empire, governed by governors-general who were largely drawn from the ranks of the traditional governing class in the region, the Baltic Germans. The customary privileges of the nobility and the towns were confirmed; German continued to be language of the courts and administration; the German university of Dorpat was a powerful mainstay of Germanic culture; no attempt was made to interfere with the Lutheran faith of the bulk of the inhabitants. Not the least of their attractions indeed was that their Lutheranism made them powerful allies of the tsarist state against the Catholicism in the region, particularly that of the Poles.

Despite occasional bouts of interference from St. Petersburg, the Baltic provinces remained until the end of the nineteenth century almost model examples of the indirect rule favored by the government; in return they became, as the future Alexander III put it in 1880, "the most loyal, trustworthy, and civilized provinces of the Empire, which have provided the most able and trustworthy forces and men" (in Armstrong 1978: 92). They gave the least trouble of any provinces in the empire; and their ruling group, the Baltic German nobility, remained to the end among the tsar's most loyal and most supportive subjects, employed by him at the highest levels of the civil and military administration. When war broke out with Germany in 1914, despite attacks on provincial autonomy toward the end of the nineteenth century virtually all the Russian Germans remained loyal to the empire, and continued so up to the time of the 1917 revolution (Armstrong 1978: 95–96; see also Haltzel 1977; Kappeler 2001: 71–75).

The Swedish and Swedicized elite of the Grand Duchy of Finland, annexed in 1809 following some earlier periods of occupation, showed a similar dedication and loyalty to the Russian tsar throughout the nineteenth century. Finland if anything had even more autonomy than the Baltic provinces; its situation has frequently been compared to that of the Kingdom of Poland between 1815 and 1830. It had its own parliament, administration, and law courts, all staffed by Finns (though Swedish was the language of administration and education, absorbed by all Finns who made an official career). It kept its own religion, Lutheranism, and even a small army of its own. Its only formal link with Russia was through a governor-general appointed by the tsar. In 1812 Russia even reunited with the duchy the Finnish territories known as Old Finland, possessed by Russia since the early eighteenth century. No wonder that the Finnish upper class, enjoying more autonomy than it had done under Sweden, was content with Russian rule. Under Russian rule Finland developed economically and culturally. It moved its capital and university from Abo (Turku) to Helsingfors (Helsinki), on the Gulf of Finland facing St. Petersburg, and opened itself favorably to the influence of the Russian capital. As with the Baltic Germans, the Finnish aristocracy supplied numerous members to the civil and military administration of the empire. "Thus the Swedish-speaking elite in Finland . . . became a model partner for the Russian government" (Kappeler 2001: 98; cf. Hosking 1998a: 37–38).

With the Ukraine—the most populous "non-Russian" part of the empire—the autonomy granted to the other European provinces appeared to the Russians to be superfluous, since—as with Belorussia—Ukrainians and the Ukrainian language were seen as essentially Russian (Rogger 1983: 184; Slocum 1998: 188; Tolz 2001: 198). More consequentially, a good number of the Ukrainian nobility and intelligentsia were themselves uncertain of a distinct Ukrainian identity, following long periods during which Ukraine was under first Mongol, then Polish rule, before being (re)absorbed by Russia in the seventeenth and eighteenth centuries The uncertainty is reflected in the very names given to the people who came to be called Ukrainians. In the Habsburg Empire they were "Ruthenians," in the Russian Empire "Little Russians." Ukrainian national identity, as with many others in Europe and elsewhere, was invented by Ukrainian intellectuals in the mid-nineteenth century. "The independent Ukrainian state of 1917 was heir neither to the seventeenth century Cossack Hetmanate nor Sich, much less to Kievan-Rus; thus the essence of Ukrainian statehood had to repeatedly reinvent itself" (Prizel 1998: 301).

The subordination of Ukraine to Russia did not imply merely a one-way flow of influence and power. In the seventeenth century the Ukrainian Orthodox Church led the way in theology and Church leadership, and Nikon's reforms were highly indebted to Ukrainian scholars and clerics. Ukrainians were also responsible for introducing important elements of Western humanism into Russia, together with the arts of the baroque. "One may justifiably assert that the Ruthenians [i.e., Ukrainians] brought the modern age to Russia" (Torke 2003: 106; cf. Prizel 1998: 159; Tolz 2001: 211). Between 1700 and 1762 more than 60 percent of bishops consecrated in the Russian Orthodox Church were Ukrainians (Kappeler 2001: 135). Moreover, following the union with "left-bank" (eastern) Ukraine in 1654 the Russian state for a time allowed the traditional Ukrainian authority, the Hetmanate, considerable autonomy. The Cossack elite, the *starshyna*, was able to hold on to its privileges, including its hold over the peasants, similar to those of the Polish *szlachta* with which it had previously been equated.

What destroyed this arrangement was the action of Hetman Ivan Mazepa in going over to Sweden against Peter the Great in the Great Northern War. With the defeat of Sweden at Poltava in 1709 Ukraine's fate was sealed. Increasingly weakened, the Hetmanate was abolished in 1782. In return for the introduction of serfdom in the Ukraine, the Cossack nobility threw in its lot with the Russian state and indeed became one of its staunchest upholders. The Ukrainian Orthodox Church became an agent of Russification in the region (Prizel 1998: 305; Löwe 2000: 59–60). Ukrainian writers such as Nikolai Gogol were acclaimed as stars of the Russian literary firmament. Many Russified Ukrainians achieved high positions in the Russian bureaucracy and military. The Russians' condescending description of Ukrainians as "Little Russians," and Ukrainian as a peasant dialect of Russian, gained a measure of plausibility as Ukraine was reduced in the course of the nineteenth century to a backward rural area of the Russian Empire, the more so as the vast majority of Ukrainians were peasants.

For Russians, most of Ukraine had simply been the southern part of Kievan Rus, Russia's own ancestor, and hence a permanent part of Russia's patrimony. It had no destiny apart from Russia. Most Ukrainians came to agree; indeed it was Ukrainians, even more than Russians, who in the nineteenth century most fully developed the idea of the unity of the East Slavs, making Ukrainian and Russian one culture (Prizel 1998: 310; Tolz 2001: 211–12). Ukrainians sometimes saw their future in a union of all the Slavs, in Pan-Slavism, rather than specifically within Russia alone. But in any case a powerful movement of acculturation took place in response to the strength and vitality of Russian culture in the second half of the nineteenth century; against this the Ukrainian language and culture had little to offer (Rogger 1983: 183–86; Prizel 1998: 311; Kappeler 1992: 111, 121–22, 125–26).

With varying degrees of accommodation, and for varying periods of time, Poles, Lithuanians, Latvians, Estonians, Germans, Finns, Swedes, Belorussians, and Ukrainians found their place within the Russian Empire. So too did the Georgians, who shared with the Russians the Orthodox faith and who served the empire in numerous capacities, most notably in the person of Prince Bagration, hero of the 1812 war against Napoleon. The rights of the Georgian nobility were confirmed, and their upper ranks were co-opted into the Russian nobility. With the Armenians too there were many points of contact, though their Apostolic Gregorian Church differed significantly from the Orthodox—and from most other—varieties of Christianity. But Armenians regarded the tsar as their protector against the Ottoman Empire, within whose domains many of their coreligionists resided. The tsarist regime confirmed the autonomy and privileges of the Armenian Church and its monasteries, and the katholikos of Echmiadzin, the spiritual head of all Armenians, was recognized as the leader of the Armenians in Russia. Like the Georgians, numerous

Armenians found their way into the Russian army and bureaucracy. But even more important, and more valuable to the empire, were Armenian mercantile skills and connections, which the tsarist government did much to encourage and promote. As with other "mobilized diaspora groups," Armenians came to perform valuable commercial functions within the empire, especially in maintaining trading connections with the East (Kappeler 2001: 171–78; Armstrong 1976).

Muslims and Jews

These were of course all Christian groups. In an age—which lasted more or less to the end of the tsarist empire—in which religion was the main badge of identity and the main constituent of membership in society, it was clearly easier to integrate non-Russian groups that shared the same basic religion as the Russians (though we should not underestimate the difficulty, and the achievement, of accommodating religious rivals such as the Protestants and Catholics with which Orthodoxy fought many battles, as did they among themselves). But what of the non-Christian subjects of the empire—in particular the Muslims and the Jews? It has been common to see these groups as experiencing particular difficulties, compounded of prejudice against peoples of alien faiths and the sense that they would prove the most recalcitrant to assimilation (Löwe 2000: 53–54). In addition there was in the case of the Muslims a suspicion as to their loyalties, given that the spiritual leader of Islam, the caliph, was the sultan of one of the empire's main antagonists, the Ottoman Empire.

Since Russia's 20 million Muslim subjects—the largest non-Orthodox group in the empire, 15 percent of the population—exceeded the number of the Ottoman Empire's Muslims (around 14 million) during the same period, there appeared every reason to be concerned at collusive and concerted action, especially in the latter part of the nineteenth century. Pan-Islamism and especially Pan-Turkism were influential in Russia at this time, one of the founders of Pan-Turkism, Yusuf Akçura, actually being a Volga Tatar from Kazan (Geraci 2001: 277–78). Muslims, the Ministry of the Interior warned in 1893, must be watched for signs of sympathy with the "idea of a world-wide Muslim kingdom with the sultan at the head," and for evidence that they "pray for the former, and not for the Sovereign Emperor" (Crews 2003: 50). Even the reform movement among Muslims at the end of the nineteenth century— the *jadid* movement—whose aim was to make Muslims more fitted to play a fuller part in the social and institutional life of the empire, was regarded with

FIGURE 5.3. Muslims in Kazan. Edward Tracy Turnerelli, 1854.

suspicion. Might this not strengthen the Muslim community and make it more assertive, more difficult to control (Geraci 2001: 265–73; Findley 2005: 152–54; Campbell 2007: 328–31)?

In the early Muscovite period, Muslims in the Russian Empire had indeed suffered much prejudice and persecution. The conquest of the Khanate of Kazan by Ivan the Terrible "took the form of a crusade against Islam," both an act of revenge for Russian subjection to the Mongols and a campaign of conversion of the heathen (Kappeler 2001: 26–72). The male population of Kazan was put to death; mosques were razed and Christian churches constructed in their place; the khan and other high-ranking Tatars were deported and forcibly baptized; Russian missionaries went out to convert Muslims and other non-Christians (Geraci 2001: 15–18). Later, in the course of the conquest of the Caucasus and of Central Asia, there were bitter and bloody conflicts with mostly Muslim tribal and nomadic groups. Russia seemed to be repeating the pattern of the West, of an all-out war between Islam and Christianity. Muslims, it appeared, were fated to be *inorodtsy*, foreign or alien people whose destiny was either to disappear or to be absorbed in the Russian people (Becker 1986; Slocum 1998).

That did not in fact happen. Though the category of *inorodtsy*, especially in popular use, gradually expanded to comprehend all non-Russian peoples, in its earlier uses it referred primarily to backward, nonsedentary populations of the kind that inhabited Siberia and the steppes. It did not refer to peoples of historic religions and high civilization, as clearly characterized Muslims, whatever Russian hostility toward them. For long therefore Muslims, especially those of the Volga region, were not classified as *inorodtsy*, a term that was given official status only in 1822 as a juridical category comprising "various 'eastern' peoples, mostly nomadic or semi-nomadic Siberian natives, whose way of life was based on herding, hunting or fishing" (Slocum 1998: 174, 185; Geraci 2001: 31). Later, in 1835, Jews were designated *inorodtsy*, a clear indication that they were seen very differently from Muslims, despite their sedentary way of life and generally European milieu. When, in the early twentieth century, the term *inorodtsy* was hijacked by Russian nationalists, Muslims could be regarded as *inorodtsy*; but so too—in the view of the ethnographer Lev Shternberg in 1910—could Poles, Germans, Georgians, Armenians, even Ukrainians who, though "blood brothers of the Great Russians," have "the audacity to speak in their own Little Russian dialect" (in Slocum 1998: 189). In this classification is reflected the growing importance of language as a marker of identity; but it never replaced religion, and despite a growing uneasiness about Muslim loyalties it was uncommon for Muslims to be classified as *inorodtsy*.

Early attempts at large-scale conversion of Muslims had limited success. Conversion was always possible, indeed desirable, but the tsarist state from a relatively early date abandoned mass proselytization or forcible conversion of Muslims. Under Peter the Great, it is true, renewed efforts were made at proselytization, and conversion to Orthodoxy was made a condition of entering the ranks of the service nobility—a condition that had not been imposed on Tatar nobles in the Muscovite period. Hundreds of mosques in Kazan were destroyed (Löwe 2000: 54; Geraci 2001: 19–20).

But Peter's successors recognized the inadvisability of this strategy and rapidly halted the anti-Muslim campaign. A decisive turn of policy came when Catherine the Great, deeply influenced by Enlightenment ideas, declared a regime of general religious toleration. She halted all Orthodox missionary activity and closed the Office for New Converts. For Muslims she created the Muslim Ecclesiastical Administration (the Orenburg muftiate), headed by a mufti appointed by St. Petersburg. The tsarist government came to see the organization of the Orthodox Church, governed by the Holy Synod, as a model for regulating all non-Orthodox religions, even ones where it went against their traditions. Thus Muslims, with their highly decentralized communities and absence of official clergy, were made to accept a centralized, hierarchical authority backed up by the tsarist government. The muftiate was responsible for registering all Muslim "parishes," regulating the appointment of mullahs as "clergy," and supervising religious schools. In this way the government hoped to quell internal disputes and establish an "orthodox" Muslim creed, parallel to that of Christian Orthodoxy. The whole Muslim world would be policed by an officially recognized clerical hierarchy (Crews 2006: 52–91; Löwe 2000: 55–58; Geraci 2001: 21–22; Steinwedel 2007: 99–102).

But one should not take this arrangement as reflecting a policy of "isolating" the Muslim communities, leaving them to their own devices and self-regulation. As Robert Crews has shown, the tsarist authorities took a view of religion as the central mechanism of regulation and control in the whole society. This applied to non-Christian as much as Christian religions. All religion was a force for "stability, discipline, and order" (Crews 2003: 54, 2006: 1–30). Tsarist subjects were not allowed to declare themselves "without a confession" (*konfessionslos*); everyone had to be enrolled in a religious community, supervised by an officially sanctioned hierarchy. Orthodoxy, the state religion, was of course the best; but any religion was better than none, and all religions contributed to the moral and social order. The state saw it as desirable to establish a common system of belief and practice, free as far as possible from doctrinal disputes and sectarianism. Hence the policy of "tolerating" different religions entailed not a passive withdrawal or attitude of indifference but active intervention and constant monitoring of all aspects of social life, from the most public to the most private and intimate. "In the tradition of the 'well-ordered police state' (*Polizeistaat*), the regime became directly involved in the regulation of central aspects of religious life in nearly every community" (Crews 2003: 57).

It is striking that even when Muslims converted to Orthodoxy, the state did not sit back as if content with a job well done. Backsliding among converted Muslims was proverbial; Muslim missionaries from the Ottoman Empire, especially in border areas, could be persuasive. Hence the importance of "the Ilminsky system," the brainchild of the Kazan educator Nikolai Ilminsky and his work at the Kazan Theological Academy, founded in 1842. Ilminsky was only incidentally concerned with missionary activity, the other main concern of the academy. To him what mattered most was that converts should understand thoroughly and, as it were, inwardly the meaning of the religion they had converted to. That would be the best way of making and keeping them good Christians, and incidentally models to others in the communities in which they lived. To that end Ilminsky chose and trained teachers from within the non-Christian communities in the region—Tatar, Chuvash, Cheremis,

Mordvin. The Christian scriptures were translated into their native languages. Armed with these, and teaching in the native languages, the graduates of the Kazan Academy were able to staff the many schools set up for the purpose of instructing converts in the principles of Christianity. The success of the method was such that it was widely imitated over the whole empire, backed in its later years by the formidable procurator-general of the Holy Synod, K. P. Pobedonostsev (Kreindler 1977: 93–95; Geraci 2001: 47–85).[15]

What the Ilminsky system brings out is the sheer pragmatism of the empire's attitudes toward its non-Russian subjects, one continued by its Soviet successor.[16] There were certainly bouts of crusading enthusiasm, and the Orthodox Church remained throughout hostile toward the government's policies of toleration and accommodation, still more toward what they saw as the dangers of the Ilminsky system. But in general the tsarist government remained committed to the view that conversion to Orthodoxy should be voluntary, and that in any case the government's purpose would best be served by shoring up all major religions, as the surest guarantors of morality and good order. When, under Nicholas I, new legal codes declared Orthodox Christianity "the preeminent and predominant" faith of the empire, they also very deliberately supported other religions on the grounds that "all peoples inhabiting Russia praise Almighty God in different languages according to the creed and confession of their forefathers, blessing the reign of the Russian Monarchs, and praying to the Creator of the universe for the increase of the prosperity and strengthening of the power of the Empire" (Crews 2003: 59).

Even Nicholas's minister of education, Count Sergei Uvarov, when in 1833 he formulated the notorious doctrine of "official nationality" as "Orthodoxy, Autocracy, and Nationality," did not mean to exclude or disparage other religions. In the first draft of his proclamation Orthodoxy was not even mentioned at all; the focus instead was on "traditional" or "national" religion. "It was because of the fact that [Orthodoxy] was a traditional and the prevailing religion that it was valuable to Uvarov," says Alexei Miller. Uvarov spoke of the "government's duty to defend the dominant church" in relation not only to Orthodoxy, but also to other established religions (Miller 2008: 141). For much of the time the secular authorities disregarded the concern of the Orthodox Church with the growth of the Muslim religion within the empire; they "did not regard the religious question as a problem of the state and therefore were not inclined to participate in a religious struggle against Islam. . . . 'To avoid disturbances among Muslims' was the primary consideration that often directed Russian policies towards Islam" (Campbell 2007: 342–43; cf. Brower 1997: 119).

In response Muslims, as with the other non-Russian groups we have considered, sought to the end to better their position within the empire, rather than outside it. In meetings of the Duma in 1908 and 1909, Tatar deputies, seeking to remove disabilities affecting Muslims, again and again declared themselves as "loyal and true sons of Russia," agreed that Russian should be the state language, and committed themselves to the "unity" of the Russian lands. What they sought was cultural autonomy within the empire (Geraci 2001: 272). How little Muslim groups desired independence—rather than equal rights—from Russia was shown in 1914 when Muslims proclaimed their devotion to the fatherland and Muslim deputies in the Duma vowed to fight for Russia's honor and integrity (Rogger 1983: 198). Being Muslim and being Tatar, it is clear, were perfectly compatible with being Russian, insofar at least as this was understood in civic and not in ethnic terms.

Was that also possible for the Jews of the empire? The trajectory of Jewish history in the empire might seem to be the opposite of that of the Muslims: instead of rejection to (qualified) acceptance, it moves from relative acceptance to increasing exclusion, or at least increasing hostility toward them. "Relative" is perhaps the key word; Jews had never been exactly welcome in Russia; this alienation perhaps stemmed from the sixteenth century when the Orthodox Church stamped out the "Judaizer" heresy and Jews were banned from entering Moscow, a ban that lasted until the second half of the eighteenth century (Miller 2008: 93). But in the eighteenth century Jews were recognized for their mercantile skills, and were allowed to settle in certain parts of the empire, especially New Russia. They remained few in number, however, until the Polish partitions, which brought large numbers of Jews into the Russian Empire.

The Polish partitions transformed the situation of the Jews in Russia. From being a small number they increased to over 5 million by the end of the nineteenth century, forming 4 percent of the empire's population in the 1897 census (between 1881 and 1914 nearly 2 million emigrated, reducing their proportion to just over 3 percent). In the space of a few decades at the end of the eighteenth century, together with the addition of the Jews of Bessarabia (1812) and those of Congress Poland (1815), Russia turned from a country with hardly any Jews into one that had the largest number of Jews of any country in the world—more than half of all European Jews. The "Jewish question" was placed firmly on the agenda (Klier 1986; Miller 2008: 98).

The period from the late eighteenth to the mid-nineteenth century is generally regarded as a "golden age" for Russian Jewry. Their situation improved
markedly compared to what it had been under the Polish-Lithuanian Commonwealth, where Jews suffered severe disabilities (some of which continued
in the new Kingdom of Poland, largely run by Poles at least until 1830). A
decree of 1782 made a clean sweep of all Polish laws discriminating against
Jews; and a further decree of 1785 declared that "the people of the Jewish law
[faith] have already entered, by virtue of Her Majesty's edicts, into a state
equal to that of the others." "At that moment in time," says Alexei Miller, "the
legal situation of Jews in the Russian Empire was better than anywhere else in
Europe" (Miller 2008: 96; cf. Klier 1989: 124–26).

If Jews suffered restrictions under Nicholas I—the "Russian Haman," he
has been called, aiming at the total conversion of the Jews (Klier 2001: 96)—
so too did other groups, Christian ones included, especially after the Polish
revolution of 1830. Another Polish revolution, that of 1863, also partly halted
another hopeful period for the Jews, following the "Great Reforms" of the
1850s and 1860s initiated by Alexander II, which made significant concessions
to the Jews (Klier 1995: 152–58; Lieven 2001: 209). But what is perhaps more
remarkable is the degree of progress in Jewish emancipation in the 1860s and
1870s, despite the climate of suspicion following the 1863 rising. It was noted
that Jews had not supported the Poles during the rising but had remained loyal
to the tsar. Why should not the Jews continue to be peacefully integrated into
Russian society (Klier 1995: 153–57)? Jews shared in the new protections and
opportunities created by the great reforms of the 1860s, following the emancipation of the serfs. Restrictions of various kinds remained; but the reforms
opened up new avenues for Jews in Russian society.

Among the opportunities eagerly seized were those of education. Jewish students began to take up an increasing number of places in the newly
expanded *gymnasia* (selective grammar schools) and universities. In 1853 Jewish students made up 1.3 percent of the total *gymnasium* body; in 1880 they
were 12 percent of the total, and in the Pale of Settlement 19 percent. In the
universities the proportion of Jewish students moved from 0.5 percent of the
total in 1840, and 3 percent in 1865, to over 14 percent by 1886 (Slezkine 2004:
124; Miller 2008: 115; generally, Nathans 2002: 201–56). These figures were
of course out of all proportion to the 4 percent of the empire's population
constituted by Jews.

The impact of these changes was readily seen when, in the 1860s and 1870s,
the right to live outside the Pale was granted to an increasing number of Jews.

By 1897 there were 35,000 Jews living legally in the capital, St. Petersburg, and an equal number living illegally (though since 1880 these had been amnestied by the Ministry of the Interior). Both in the Pale and outside, Jews came to make up a disproportionate number of professionals, above all in law and medicine—55 percent of lawyers in St. Petersburg, 52 percent of dentists, 17 percent of doctors. With this degree of mobility, geographical and social, it is hard not to agree with Alexei Miller that "in the 1860s and 1870s the political conditions were ripe for abolishing the Pale of Settlement" (Miller 2008: 117; see also Klier 1989: 134; Slezkine 2004: 125).

Jewish participation in commerce, industry, and the arts was also pressing toward a position that would approximate that of the Jews in the Habsburg Empire. Jewish bankers and contractors played a leading part in the industrialization of Russia that took place in the late nineteenth century. "By the outbreak of the Great War," says Yuri Slezkine, "the tsar's Jewish subjects were well on their way to replacing the Germans as Russia's model moderns (the way they had done in much of East-Central Europe" (Slezkine 2004: 123; cf. Nathans 2002: 376–79). In the arts too Jews blossomed, Odessa producing a stream of world-class musicians (especially violinists and pianists such as Mischa Elman and Jascha Heifetz), Kiev and Vitebsk artists such as Marc Chagall and El Lissitzky, Grodno the great stage designer Leon Bakst (Lev Rozenberg). From Kibartai in Lithuania came Isaak Levitan, "the most beloved of all Russian landscape painters" (Slezkine 2004: 126).

Most of these educated Jews had moved out of their Jewish communities and adopted the Russian language and Russian culture, as did an increasing number of other Jewish professionals. Some, as is well known, found themselves attracted to the radical intelligentsia and the revolutionary parties that were developing at this time—something that could be, and would be, used against Jews in general when circumstances demanded it (Slezkine 2004: 150, 155; Haberer 1995: 256–57; Miller 2008: 123). But these were a minority of educated Jews, most of whom sought to make middle-class careers in an increasingly open Russian society. These were not so much Russian Jews as Jewish Russians, Jews who had assimilated voluntarily—though most were secular and did not adopt the Orthodoxy of the majority Russians. They were of course a small number by comparison with the Jewish masses in the towns and shtetls, where indeed a revitalization of Jewish culture and religion was taking place in the late nineteenth century. In such bodies as the socialist Jewish Bund there was an increasing demand for the recognition of the Jews as a nation within a federal Russia. Political Zionism too—opposed by the

Bund—began to gain a following in the Jewish community (Rogger 1983: 203–4; Kappeler 2001: 271–72; Slezkine 2004: 140–55).

It is against this background of mobility and opportunity that we need to consider the pogroms and persecutions that marked the period from the early 1880s to the early 1900s. This is a story that has been frequently told: the pogroms of 1881, 1903, and 1905, the fabrication of the *Protocols of the Elders of Zion*, the trial of the Jewish clerk Mendel Beilis for the ritual murder of a Christian youth, and several new discriminatory measures against Jews. Several things need to be said about this. The period of violence was highly compressed; there were no pogroms after 1906. The discriminatory measures were not primarily the result of racial anti-Semitism, which if anything was less developed in Russia than in other parts of Europe. The tsarist authorities were not responsible for the pogroms, which were popular outbursts conditioned often by local factors; though local authorities and police often stood by and intervened tardily (Rogger 1983: 201–6; Hosking 1998a: 390–96; Kappeler 2001: 267–73).

There was certainly strong hostility toward Jews at the very top of society, in the persons of the tsars Alexander III and especially Nicholas II. This attitude was shared and promoted by some of their key advisers and ministers, such as Konstantin Pobedonostsev, Dmitrii Tolstoi, and Viacheslav Plehve, minister of the interior. At the same time their views were opposed by ministers such as Sergei Witte and Petr Stolypin and many in the ministry of finance, who saw the Jews as valuable agents of the industrialization and modernization of Russia they were anxious to promote (Hosking 1998a: 392–93). Such figures argued for further emancipation of the Jews, and ensured for instance that Jews were represented in the new Duma that was established after the 1905 revolution (Kappeler 2001: 270, 342; Miller 2008: 124–25).

In much writing about the Jews in Russia there has been a tendency to consider them "a special case" and to single them out as creating a particularly difficult problem of integration in the multiethnic and multiconfessional empire. This is put down, on the one hand, to a particularly virulent strain of anti-Semitism in Russian culture, and, on the other, to the rigidity and obstinacy of the Jews in clinging to their old culture and religion (e.g., Hellbirg-Hirn 1998: 181). Neither of these stereotypes seems warranted by the evidence. Anti-Semitism in Russia seems no worse than in other Christian countries; and, given the opportunity as they were in the second half of the nineteenth century, Jews were no less eager than other groups to move into the mainstream of Russian life. The problem indeed, as many have commented, was that Jews were too eager to join in the new currents that were flowing through Russian society, and too successful in doing so. Their success in business in particular aroused the jealousy of other groups, Russian and non-Russian; while for Russian conservatives such as Pobedonostsev Jews seemed to embody all that was worst about the new modern world of industry and finance, which they saw as undermining the traditional moral and social order (Rogger 1983: 201; Kappeler 2001: 271; Slezkine 2004: 155–65; Miller 2008: 121–22). Jews became the convenient scapegoats, in Russia as well as elsewhere, for the problems thrown up by the rapid modernization that was taking place throughout Europe at the time. Hence the force and occasional violence of the backlash against them, which led to nearly 2 million Jews emigrating from Russia between 1881 and 1914. Their fates in other parts of Europe were to be far worse.

"Russification" and Russian Nationalism

Jews were not the only group to be targeted by the Russian government in the late nineteenth century. The same thing happened to other non-Russian groups, and indeed in a certain sense to Russians themselves. There seemed at this time to be a widespread movement of "Russification" taking place, subsequently interpreted as the rise of a strong strand of Russian nationalism. Russia, it is claimed, despite its character as a multinational empire, experienced in these years the same wave of nationalism as was washing over most countries in Europe. The result was a systematic attempt to make the empire Russian, to root out as far as possible non-Russian languages and cultures and to give the empire a more clearly and distinctively Russian cast (e.g., Kaspe 2007: 465–88).

"Russification" and "Russian nationalism" are, however, not the same thing and can indeed point in different directions.[17] Russification has sometimes been "administrative," concerned basically with the political integration of non-Russian groups into the Russian state, sometimes "cultural," an attempt to assimilate non-Russians to Russian culture and civilization. Only in the later nineteenth century, it has been claimed, was cultural Russification "a conscious policy backed by the full force of the state" (Becker 1986: 26; cf. Thaden 1990c). Robert Geraci proposes a continuum, "at one end of which was a model of the empire as a culturally homogeneous nation-state.... At the other end was a resolutely non-national, multicultural empire that imposed no change of identity on its subjects." He suggests that few people opted for either of these extremes, and that attitudes and policies were typically a mixture, as suggested by the several terms for cultural integration used in the tsarist era: "Christianization" (*khristianizatsia*), "assimilation" (*assimilatsiia*), "rapprochement" (*slizhenie*), "fusion" (*sliianie*), "civilization" (*tsivilizatsiia*), as well as "Russification" (*obrusenie*) (Geraci 2001: 9; cf. Jersild 2000: 542n19; Tolz 2005: 132–33, 135). Russification, it is clear, is by no means an unambiguous process and, like nationalism, should perhaps be referred to in the plural, as "russifications" (Miller 2008: 45–65).

For most scholars, "Russification" has meant primarily the policies of the tsarist government toward its non-Russian subjects in the closing decades of the nineteenth century. There is also general agreement that these policies aimed at cultural Russification, as understood for instance by Becker: that is, the process of making non-Russians shed their non-Russian identities and become as far as possible Russian in language and culture. While it might be admitted that these policies were also about civic and political incorporation, the focus has always been on what was seen as a novel and radical attempt to turn non-Russians into Russians. The parallels might be the Germanizing policies of Joseph II in the Habsburg Empire in the late eighteenth century, or the Magyarizing policies in the Hungarian half of the Habsburg Empire in the late nineteenth century, or indeed the ways in which "peasants became Frenchmen," in Eugen Weber's (1976) classic account.

The Russian state, as we have seen, had long resisted Russification in this sense. It had practiced an "arm's-length" approach to its non-Russian provinces, favoring where possible indirect rule through local elites. It had respected local rights and customs. It had not tried, in the main, to force Orthodoxy or the Russian language on non-Russians. Compared to its Western neighbors, the Russian Orthodox Church was never a vigorous proselytizer; when it tried, it was often reined in by the state (Geraci and Khodarkovsky 2001: 6–7). Conversion was welcome, and often necessary for achievement at the highest levels of state employment. But, apart from the earliest days following the conquest of the Tatars, it was rarely forced. In the case of the Volga Tatars, their Muslim religion was indeed seen as useful to the tsarist state, in enabling them to act as a bridge to their Muslim coreligionists in Central Asia (Starr 1978: 18).

In return for their cooperation and loyalty, the Russian state opened its ranks to non-Russian elites, co-opting them into its nobility and enrolling them in state service. Others, such as Armenian, Greek, and Jewish merchants, were also at various times given special privileges and encouragement to contribute to the wealth of the empire. Such a pattern seems to have suited the Russian Empire for much of its history, as it did other empires. As Frederick

Starr says, "to maintain the empire was an end in itself, the chief objective of Russian political life. This was far more important than the spread of Russian values, religion, customs, or language within the empire" (Starr 1978: 31; cf. Raeff 1971: 29; Steinwedel 2007: 98).

Did this policy change in the nineteenth century? It has been customary to argue that it did, that for various reasons the Russian state turned to an active policy of cultural Russification in the second half of the nineteenth century (Raeff 1971: 38–40; Rodkiewicz 1998: 13–14, 269; Carrère d'Encausse 1992: 216). This, it has further been claimed, complemented and was perhaps inspired by the rise of a new Russian nationalism in this period, conflicting with and overriding the older traditions of imperial rule. Russia, it is argued, was not immune to the powerful movement of nationalism sweeping over Europe as a whole. This affected not just the subject but also the ruling peoples in all multinational empires.[18]

What was the impact of Russian nationalism in this period? How far were policies of Russification carried out? Clearly attempts were not made to Russify everyone, certainly not to the same extent. No attempt was made to Russify the Jews, for instance, partly because they were already Russifying too fast for the comfort of many native Russians, partly because influential sections of Russian opinion came to see them as incurably alien. Nor were there deliberate policies of Russification in relation to most Muslim groups. In the case of the *inorodtsy* Muslims, the Muslims of the Caucasus, Transcaucasia, and Central Asia, it was assumed—as with the native Siberians—that over time they would lose their backward and barbarous customs and accept the superior Russian culture. Russification would occur as it were by stealth (Becker 1986, 1991; Brower 1997: 122; Hosking 1998a: 388–89).

Another strategy, equally opposed to cultural Russification, was to cultivate local cultures and identities—"native homelands"—as "the building blocks for the creation of a pan-Russian identity," a fusion of local and national on the German *Heimat* model (Tolz 2005: 144). In this view Muslim identity, just like Buriat or Kalmyk identity, was not opposed to but complemented a larger Russian identity, as a civic, multiethnic nation. The goal was not cultural uniformity but a uniform "citizenship," *grazhjdanstvennost*, which implied acceptance of certain standards of morality and civility. In "Russia's Orient," cultural Russification was seen by most Russian Orientalists and many local administrators as a threat to the building of the nation along these lines. "Forced Russification," as one of them argued, only "frightened the natives away from borrowing Russian customs." This was an idea that also swayed the architects of the Soviet Union's "indigenization" policies of the 1920s (Yaroshevski 1997: 59–61; Jersild 1997: 101–9; Brower 1997: 131; Tolz 2005: 141–49).

With the Volga Tatars, the Ilminsky system concentrated not on conversion but on securing the firmer adherence of the Muslims already converted to Orthodoxy. In this it met with considerable success. This could be regarded— and was so regarded by certain supporters, such as Pobedonostsev and the education minister Dmitrii Tolstoi—as Russification of a kind (Kaspe 2007: 475–76). But since its whole point was to employ native languages rather than Russian, Russian nationalists saw it as going the other way, as dangerously encouraging nationalist aspirations among non-Russians (Kappeler 2001: 263; Seton-Watson 1986: 22). Russification here was at the very least double-edged, and certainly cannot be counted a simple gain for Russian nationalism.

In Georgia and Bessarabia there were various measures of Russification in the later nineteenth century, mostly aimed at increasing the authority and influence of the Russian Orthodox Church. This was accompanied by an attempt to suppress the Romanian language in Bessarabia, and the Georgian language in Georgia—attempts generally held to have been unsuccessful. In any case Russification had long been going on among Georgians and Bessarabians. Russia was widely seen as their protector and liberator from the Ottoman Empire. Their shared Orthodoxy made them natural allies of Russians. There was no need for heavy Russification.

Things were different with the Armenians, whose Christian Gregorian Church had enjoyed a privileged position for much of the nineteenth century. They now came under attack, largely as a result of the rise of Armenian nationalism in the neighboring Ottoman Empire, and Russian fears of contagion. In the popular press Armenians came to be portrayed in the same manner as Jews, as exploiters, parasites, and potential traitors. In 1885 Armenian schools were closed or their curricula changed to strengthen Russian influence. In 1903 the properties of the Armenian Church were confiscated. These moves created strong anti-Russian feeling and led to attacks on Russian officials. In response the government recalled the governor-general, Prince Golitsyn, and replaced him by a more conciliatory figure, Count I. I. Vorontsov-Dashkov. After the 1905 revolution the confiscation decree was rescinded and most of the discriminatory measures removed. Russification had done little to bring about assimilation; its main effect was to damage the long-standing Russophilia of the Armenians, and to do the very thing that was feared, contribute to the rise of Armenian nationalism within Russia (Hosking 1998a: 386–88). Nevertheless, when Russia went to war against the Ottoman Empire in 1914,

Armenians rallied to the Russian cause, caring far more about the fate of their fellow Armenians in the Ottoman Empire than about their own, relatively secure, existence in Russia (Rogger 1983: 194–96; Kappeler 2001: 266–67).

When one surveys the evidence, it rapidly becomes clear that what is generally referred to as Russification in these years applies mainly to the western borderlands of the empire (cf. Becker 1986: 26, 43; Seton-Watson 1986: 21–22). It is also not difficult to see why that might be the case. It was there—not in the south and east—that the Russian government saw the principal threats to the security and integrity of the empire. Chief among these was Polish nationalism, and more generally Polish influence in a region historically dominated by Poles and Polish culture (Rodkiewicz 1998: 16–18). Secondarily there was German and Finnish nationalism, the former of particular concern with the rise of a powerful Germany that in the late nineteenth century challenged Russia in the Balkans and elsewhere.

The failed Polish rebellion was, as we have seen, the spur to a whole series of anti-Polish measures in the Kingdom of Poland, including its demotion to a province, the Vistula province. There were attacks on the Catholic Church, and the Polish language was heavily restricted in educational institutions (though not in the Church), to be replaced by Russian (Hosking 1998a: 376–78). But if this was intended as "cultural Russification," it was largely unsuccessful. Polish culture might be repressed, but that did not mean its replacement by Russian culture. The Polish language and religion survived, and Poles made much of the economic opportunities afforded by the integrated empire. Renouncing insurrection, Polish leaders strove to restore their autonomy within the empire—a goal at least partially achieved in the liberal reforms following the 1905 revolution. In 1914 the Polish members of the Duma and the National Democratic Party of Roman Dmowski rejected the separatist aims of Josef Piłsudski's Polish Socialist Party and proclaimed their loyalty to the empire in its hour of need (Rogger 1983: 187–89).

In the western provinces, the Polish language and the Catholic Church were more severely dealt with, in an attempt to lessen Polish influence on the mainly peasant Ukrainians, Belorussians, and Lithuanians. These groups were not themselves seen as threatening to Russian interests. National consciousness was low among them; and Russians regarded them all—even the Catholic Lithuanians—as part of historic Rus, and organically part of Russia. The banning of their languages, and the promotion of Russian, was not so much in response to the rise of Ukrainian, Belorussian, or Lithuanian nationalism—negligible at this point—as an attack on Polish cultural domination in the area.

The Poles were seen as being behind the movement for cultural revival among these peoples, as an anti-Russian device; repressing that movement was seen as a way of putting down the Poles.[19]

Just as Ukrainians, Lithuanians, and Belorussians felt they had more to fear from their Polish landlords than from the Russian state, so Finns, Estonians, and Latvians were more concerned with domination by Swedes and Germans than with Russian repression or Russification. This is why, in the case of the Estonians and Latvians in the Baltic provinces, Russification was welcomed as a counter to German culture and influence. In the first half of the nineteenth century the Orthodox Church had had considerable success in converting Estonians and Latvians. The peasants of the Baltic provinces had been emancipated in 1816–19—nearly fifty years before their Russian counterparts—and through their self-governing rural communities had begun to cultivate the native languages and cultures. This movement received encouragement from some Russian officials and publicists, such as the Slavophile Iurii Samarin, concerned to oppose the Germanizing tendencies spread by the Baltic German elites (Armstrong 1978: 84–85).

Conversions were stopped after the midcentury; but the municipal reforms of 1870 were extended to the Baltic provinces, weakening German control, and under Alexander III a more sustained effort at Russification was resumed. Much of this was welcomed by the newly developing Estonian intelligentsia, which in 1881 sent a delegation to Alexander III calling for the extension of the reformed Russian system to the Baltic provinces (Raun 1977: 127–29). The reformed Russian legal system was introduced in 1889, along with the Russian police system. The Russian language was made compulsory in schools and universities, and at the higher levels of the administration. The German university of Dorpat was closed and reopened as the Russian university of Iurev. Restrictions were placed on the Lutheran churches, and there were renewed efforts at conversion to Orthodoxy (Hosking 1998a: 382–84).

The Estonian and Latvian intelligentsia hailed many of these measures as benefiting them at the expense of the German nobility (Raeff 1971: 33; Thaden 1990d: 224, 227). Even the introduction of Russian was seen as an improvement over the German that had previously been the requirement in education and administration. A Russian education, in the Russian language, was the precondition for the "incredible career success" of Estonians, who increased their proportion of the local bureaucracy from less than 2 percent in 1871 to over 50 percent in 1897 (Miller 2008: 51). But Estonians and Latvians were disappointed at the lack of support for native languages, especially in the educational system. They were disappointed too that the *zemstvo* system was not introduced into the Baltic provinces, out of governmental concern that it would be used against the Baltic Germans. In the event the Russian government found it had created too politically conscious an Estonian and Latvian educated class. In the 1905 revolution, Baltic peasants and workers under its influence fought against both German landlords and Russian soldiers. Shaken by these events, the Russian government halted its Russification measures after 1905 and closed ranks with the Baltic Germans, who had stayed loyal throughout despite attempts to undermine their power. At the same time it permitted many developments in Estonian and Latvian languages and culture, thereby, as in Lithuania and elsewhere, giving these groups a new sense of national identity that they were to exploit during the chaos of the First World War.[20]

Russification in the Baltic provinces—aimed at weakening the Baltic Germans as well as continuing the process of administrative centralization—was therefore very different from Russification in the Polish lands. So too was Russification in Finland. Here too the main driving force seems to have been the urge to bring Finland more in line with the other provinces of the empire, to standardize and centralize the government of the empire. Finland had since its annexation in 1809 enjoyed a greater degree of autonomy than any other part of the empire. Its Swedish or Swedicized upper class dominated the affairs of the province, secure in their control of all the major institutions of politics and culture. Their dominance was further increased by Alexander II. The Finnish Diet was given new powers, and Finland was allowed its own currency, separate from the rouble. In 1878 Finland received its own army. The reforms of the 1860s were not extended to Finland, further preserving the Swedish elite's power.

Things began to change, but not until the 1890s, when the measures applied to other parts of the empire finally came to be applied to Finland. In 1899 Nicholas II issued a manifesto that curtailed the Finnish Diet's rights as regards matters "of general imperial concern." A conscription law was introduced that amounted to merging the separate Finnish army into the Russian one. Russian was made the language of the upper levels of the administration. Finland lost its independent postal service (Thaden 1990d: 225–27; Hosking 1998a: 380–81).

Many of these anti-Finnish measures were due to the governor-general of the province, N. I. Bobrikov, who viewed Finnish autonomy as an anomaly and Finnish separatism a threat. As in the Baltic provinces the Russian government

attempted to use the differences between the Finnish peasants and their Swedish masters as a means to putting pressure on the Finnish elites. But Bobrikov's
heavy-handed manner of rule antagonized all groups. His assassination by a
Finnish student in 1904 provoked a change of direction by the Russian government, especially, once more, in the wake of the 1905 revolution. The Finnish
Diet was put on a stronger basis, with an expanded electoral base and wide
powers. The conscription law was rescinded. Finns sat in the Duma and the
State Council. But Finns once more came under scrutiny, for their suspected
German sympathies and the fact that Finland's autonomy made it a convenient
place of refuge for Russian radicals fleeing the Russian police. Once more,
under Stolypin, attempts were made to restrict Finland's autonomy and to
integrate it more uniformly into the imperial administration. The outbreak of
war in 1914 meant that few of these new measures could be put into effect; but
they led to a hardening of separatist attitudes, which found their culmination
in Finland's independence in 1918 (Rogger 1983: 189–91; Kappeler 2001: 260–
61; Wortman 2006: 370).

"Few scholars," says Theodore Weeks, "would now endorse the rather crude
thesis that the Russian government aimed to wipe out all non-Russian cultures
and replace them with Russian culture and the Orthodox religion" (Weeks
2001: 96; cf. Kappeler 2001: 274). Vera Tolz calls such "widely-held views" of
Russification "a myth with little substance" (Tolz 2001: 8; see also 174–77).
But, crudely put or not, one does indeed still frequently find the claim, and
not simply by nonspecialists, that Russification was a sustained and deliberate
policy carried out by the tsarist government in the late nineteenth century.[21]
The implication also is that this policy marked a break with previous policies of
toleration and the preservation of traditional forms of rule in the non-Russian
territories.

We have seen how misleading such a view is. There was certainly a development of Russian nationalism in the nineteenth century, as there was in practically every other European country. Some groups wished to make the Russian
multiethnic empire more like a nation-state, in which Russian would naturally
be the dominant and defining culture. The problem was that Russian nationalists could not agree on what this Russianness might mean. Should it mean a
stress on Slavic culture, as the Slavophiles insisted?. In that case Pan-Slavism
was the more logical form to follow rather than a narrow Russian nationalism.
If, however, the "Westernizers" were correct, then, as the ex-Marxist and Pan-
Slavist Peter Struve complained, their cosmopolitanism and infatuation with
Western values distanced them from the majority of their fellow countrymen

and made it difficult for their nationalism to become the basis of a national
state (Rogger 1962: 254). There was a further possibility, that Russia should be
seen not as European but as Eurasian, which again suggested a different reading of the national character and the national destiny ("Yes, we are Scythians,
Yes Asians we are!" sang Alexander Blok in 1917).

We shall consider "Russianness" further in the next section. Here what
needs to be stressed are the limits and distortions of the Russification thesis.
There was no sustained, systematic policy of Russification at any time during
the tsarist period, up to and including the late nineteenth and early twentieth
centuries. Whatever the opinion of Russian nationalists, most tsars and tsarist statesmen saw that the application of the nationalist principle would be
destructive of the empire whose preservation was their main concern (Lieven
2001: 275). Of all the later tsars, only Alexander III (1881–94) seems to have
believed seriously in Russification and made efforts to promote it.[22] Alexander II (1855–81) and Nicholas II (1894–1917) both saw its dangers, and either
resisted its pressures or acted to undo whatever measures had been taken in
that direction. If Russifying currents can be discerned in the later part of the
nineteenth century—and there is no doubt they can be—then they were
irregular, inconstant, frequently inconsistent, and largely unsuccessful (Seton-
Watson 1986: 21–22; Löwe 2000: 75–80). Nationalist groups were frustrated
in their efforts to make the state respond to their demands. "Dynastic imperial patriotism inhibited the spread of ethnic national consciousness," further
limited by the split between the educated intelligentsia and the mainly peasant
class, for whom Russian nationalism held little appeal (Kappeler 2001: 243;
cf. Hosking 1998a: 397; Miller 2008: 55). Russia remained until 1917 a mainly
estate-based, *soslovie*, society, in which horizontal ties of class and status overrode the vertical ties of a common nationhood. Even factory workers were
fitted into the *soslovie* system (Morrison 2012: 337).[23] What linked the estates
was loyalty to the tsar and empire, not to the nation.

We need to remember in any case how relatively short the period of Russification was, and the particular context of the Russifying drive. Nearly all the
important Russifying measures took place in the two decades from the early
1880s. This was the period that began with the assassination of Alexander II in
1881 and ended with the revolution of 1905. It also saw the rise of a revolutionary and terrorist movement, which claimed not only Alexander II but also
Viacheslav Plehve, minister of the interior, in 1904 (and later, in 1911, Peter
Stolypin, the prime minister). There were nationalist movements in the non-
Russian provinces that were encouraged by the rise of nationalism elsewhere,

and that had the potentiality to link up with conationals outside the empire. There was the new and threatening power of a united Germany, and fears of the effects of German nationalism on Germans within the Russian Empire (Armstrong 1978: 91; Miller 2008: 22; Carter 2010: 73). There was the shock of the defeat in the Russo-Japanese War of 1904–5, which dashed the more ambitious of Russia's Far Eastern hopes.

All these developments were bound to create a climate of fear and anxiety, a sense that the empire needed to rethink and reorganize itself, much as the Habsburgs and Ottomans were doing at about the same time, and for similar reasons. One response was the promotion of industrialization and moderniza-tion, which made rapid strides in the later nineteenth century. The other was a further degree of rationalization and centralization in the administration of the empire, continuing a process that had begun with Peter the Great and Catherine the Great in the eighteenth century. What one saw at the end of the nineteenth century therefore was not so much cultural as administrative Russification (cf. Rogger 1983: 182). This had, as in the past, the capacity to arouse opposition among the various groups who felt their power and influ-ence threatened. But it was not an attempt to make the empire Russian in any ethnic sense.

The attempt at cultural Russification, such as it was—the imposition of the Russian language, the suppression of non-Russian cultures—was mostly abandoned after the 1905 revolution, and many of the most significant Rus-sifying measures were revoked. In April 1905 the government issued a toler-ance edict that, while affirming the primary status of the Orthodox Church, abolished discrimination against non-Orthodox religions. Most of the pro-hibitions against non-Russian languages were removed. In October the government issued a manifesto guaranteeing civil rights and freedoms, and permitting national organizations and national meetings. All nationalities were invited to elect representatives to the new Duma, and with the excep-tion of the Finns most did so, so that in the first Duma non-Russian deputies made up almost a half of the membership (Kappeler 2001: 334, 341). There were the predictable reversals and inconsistencies of policy in the years lead-ing up to the First World War, but no attempt to return to anything resem-bling a concerted policy of Russification, whose dangers were now only too apparent. The most compelling testimony to the success of this approach was that until 1918, and despite the opportunities offered by the turbulence of the war, only two groups, the Poles and the Finns, made demands for separation from the Russian state (Sarkisyanz 1974: 71). Other nationalities strove for a greater degree of autonomy and equality, but they sought to do so within the empire, not outside it. To the end of its existence the Russian Empire—like the Habsburg—managed to retain the loyalty of the vast bulk of its members, Christians, Muslims, Jews.

Russians and Russianness in the Empire

How Russian was the Russian Empire? How far did it reflect the identity, interests, and purposes of the dominant ethnic group in the empire? Russians, as we have seen, were a clear majority of the empire at the beginning of the eighteenth century, and at the end of the nineteenth century were still far and away the largest ethnic group, making up 44 percent of the population. Officially, since Ukrainians (Little Russians) and Belorussians (White Russians) were not recognized as separate groups, Russians in fact made up two-thirds of the population. Either way their proportion was much greater than that of the dominant ethnic groups, the Germans and the Turks, in the Habsburg and Ottoman empires.

The Russian language and the Russian Orthodox Church were preeminent in the empire. Other languages and religions were tolerated for most of the time, and conversion to Orthodoxy was never consistently pursued as a policy. But knowledge of the Russian language was well-nigh indispensable for a career in state service, and conversion to Orthodoxy certainly smoothed one's way. Increasingly, in the nineteenth century, a knowledge of Russian literature and culture also became necessary for acceptance in the upper circles of society in St. Petersburg and Moscow, and thereby the opportunity for advancement up the official ranks.

Impressed by these and similar considerations, some scholars have seen the Russian Empire as reflecting Russian identity, and even Russian nationalism, from an early date. For Liah Greenfeld, Catherine the Great, despite her German provenance, was "a convinced nationalist" who strove to advance the interests of the Russian people, and who repeatedly invoked "the Russian nation" (*otechestvo*) in her pronouncements (Greenfeld 1992: 201–2). The story is then one of an increasingly virulent ethnic and authoritarian Russian nationalism, born of *ressentiment*—"the existential envy of the West"—capturing and characterizing the state. The Soviet Union simply continued this pattern (Greenfeld 1992: 250, 261, 270–71).

Few scholars go as far as Greenfeld in her identification of the Russian Empire with the Russian nation. But there is certainly a tendency, not found in studies of most other empires, to see the Russian Empire as simply the Russian nation writ large (a tendency that extends to a similar view of the Soviet Empire). Partly this is because Russians themselves often did so, in the spirit of what Lenin and the Bolsheviks later chastised as "Great Russian chauvinism." One influential strand of opinion of this kind was nineteenth-century Russian historiography—the works of Nikolai Karamzin, Mikhail Pogodin, Sergei Soloviev, Vasilii Kliuchevsky, and others. This, despite its vivid awareness of the multiethnic and indeed colonial history of the Russian state, tended to present it as converging on Western models of the unitary and culturally homogeneous nation-state. Russian expansion—necessary for Russia's security, and to enable it to carry out its civilizing mission in the East—had indeed incorporated many non-Russian peoples and cultures; but their destiny was, either voluntarily or coercively, to be assimilated in Russian civilization (Saunders 1982; Becker 1986: 43; Tolz 2001: 155–81).

If this was an important strand of thought, then it seems to have had singularly little impact on the rulers of the empire. Tsars and their ministers, though occasionally indulging in bouts of Russification, mostly were acutely aware of the multiethnic and indeed multinational character of the empire. Nationalism, whether of Russians or non-Russians, was regarded, as it has been by most imperial statesmen, as a direct threat to the empire, perhaps the greatest it faced as the power of nationalism grew in the nineteenth century (Sakharov 1998: 8–13). Here the separation of state and society, which many have seen as the long-standing source of Russia's problems, may actually have contributed to the longevity of the Russian Empire. The autocratic tsarist administration, largely removed from popular influence and pressure, was able to steer its own course. To have adopted nationalism, to have tried to make the state a nation-state, conforming to the Russian nation, would have risked dissolving the empire. To the end the tsarist state resisted that temptation, and was rewarded by the loyalty of most of its subjects, Russian and non-Russian alike. It was not nationalism that brought down the Russian Empire in 1917, anymore than in the case of the Habsburg or even the Ottoman empires. It was the First World War that destroyed the Russian state, as it did in so many other cases; nationalism picked up the pieces where it could, as did the Bolsheviks in Russia (and promptly recommenced the empire).

Nothing more clearly shows the nonnational character of the Russian state than the character of its ruling elite. This remained, right down to the end of the empire, uncompromisingly multinational. The Russian state, as it expanded, simply incorporated the ruling classes of the annexed or conquered territories into the estates of its own ruling class, the *dvorianstvo*. This made entry into the ruling group relatively easy. "Anyone from the upper levels of the conquered societies, by taking up service, could acquire the rank (*chin*) which would put him on a footing of equality, or at least provide this opportunity for his children, with his Russian counterpart within the framework of the dominant 'Establishment'" (Raeff 1971: 34; cf. Wortman 2011: 267). For these families, Russification was natural and voluntary. Race was no barrier (as it was to be in the British and French empires), as was shown by the Tatar and Asiatic origins of many aristocratic families (Steinwedel 2007: 98). But nor too was religion. Conversion to Orthodoxy was, in most cases, required for the highest positions in the administration, but not for many of those at the lower levels, especially in the provinces. Many agents of the Kazan office (*kazanskii prikaz*), for instance, were Muslim (Rywkin 1988: 14).

But even at the highest levels Orthodoxy was not always insisted on. The best example is the Baltic German nobility, who kept their Lutheran religion while occupying key positions in the tsarist military and bureaucracy. They learned Russian but retained also their German language and culture, which they employed in their role as leaders in the Baltic provinces (Raeff 1971: 35). Their formative institutions were not just the German university of Dorpat but also the elite secondary schools in St. Petersburg, the Tsarkoe Selo Lycée (later the Alexander Lycée) and the Imperial School of Jurisprudence. To these, together with the upper-class preparatory schools in the capital, they freely sent their sons where they mingled and merged with the scions of the Russian aristocracy. While generally retaining their Lutheranism, the Baltic nobles saw little to complain of in Orthodoxy, and had no difficulty with sons and daughters who married Russians and converted to Orthodoxy (Armstrong 1978: 71–72).

"There is no doubt," says John Armstrong, "that a large portion of the top elite of the tsarist elite—the high officers of the court, the military, and the civil service—were Germans. The most reasonable estimates run from 18 per cent to more than 33 per cent for the late eighteenth and nineteenth centuries." Germans were particularly strong in the Ministry of Foreign Affairs (Minindel)— even as late as 1915, when the empire was at war with Germany, 16 of 53 top officials in the Minindel were Germans (Armstrong 1978: 75, 88; Kappeler 2001: 300; Bushkovitch 2003: 145, 153–54). Their wide connections with Western European courts and families made them particularly suitable as ambassadors and diplomats. For instance, "for 93 of the 105 years between 1812 and 1917 Baltic noblemen represented the Tsar at the Court of St. James" (Haltzel 1977: 149).

FIGURE 5.4. General K. P. von Kaufman, a leading "Baltic baron,"
and first governor-general of Central Asia. Library of Congress.

Other illustrious German names in the Russian civil service include the diplomats Baron von Meyendorff and Count Alexander Keyserling; Alexander von
Benckendorff, the first head of the Third Section under Nicholas I; Count Karl
Lieven, minister of education; Count Constantin von der Pahlen, minister of
justice from 1867 to 1878; Nikolai von Bunge, minister of finance from 1881 to
1887. In the military there was General K. P. von Kaufman, the great conqueror
and first governor-general of Central Asia (MacKenzie 1988: 219–28). The loyalty and commitment of the Baltic Germans to the empire, even during the
trying times of "Russification" in the late nineteenth century, were legendary
(Pipes [1974] 1995: 1; Hosking 1998a: 160–61).

The prominence of Baltic Germans in the higher echelons of the Russian
military and bureaucracy was exceptional perhaps only in degree. From the
very beginning of the expansion of the empire, with the conquests of Kazan

and Astrakhan, upper class non-Russians had been freely inscribed in the ranks of the Russian *dvorianstvo* (Lieven 2001: 250). First, in the sixteenth and seventeenth centuries, came the Tatar nobles, in the next century Georgian and Bashkir nobles, Ukrainian Cossack "elders," Baltic barons, Swedish nobles, Polish *szlachta*, and Caucasian princes. Prominent examples include Prince Charkasski, of Kazan Tatar origin, adviser to Peter the Great; General Alexander Suvorov, of Swedish descent, Catherine the Great's most successful general; Prince Pyotr Bagration, from Georgia, hero of the 1812 Battle of Borodino; Count Adam Czartoryski, Polish nobleman and confidant of Alexander I; Count Mikhail Loris-Melikov, of Armenian-Georgian family, minister of the interior under Alexander II (Jersild 1997: 104–5; Steinwedel 2007: 98).

Nor were these the only "foreigners" to join the *dvorianstvo*. Throughout its history the tsarist government felt free to confer nobility on Irish, Scots, French, Italian, and other Western Europeans who were invited to Russia and who rendered service to the state. It has been calculated that of the 2,867 civil servants occupying the top ranks during the imperial period (1700–1917), 1,079 or 37.6 percent were of foreign nationality; in the middle of the nineteenth century Lutherans alone held 15 percent of the highest posts in the central administration. "No other nobility was so open to the inflow of aliens or so lacking in deep native roots" (Pipes [1974] 1995: 182; cf. Starr 1978: 17–18; Kappeler 2001: 103–4, 124–41, 151–53; 300–302). What is particularly striking is that, despite the increase in the number of educated Russians, and the occasional Russifying tendencies, the multinational character of the Russian elite remained intact to the very end of the empire. "Until the First World War the tsarist government adhered to its principles, which were to value loyalty, specialist knowledge and noble descent more highly than religion or ethnic origins" (Kappeler 2001: 302).

Not only was the Russian aristocracy "foreign"; so too was the monarchy, at least since Peter the Great and symbolically even before. To be sure, most European monarchies are foreign, the British no less than the Russian. Nearly all drew upon the ready supply of princes and princesses provided by the German states in the eighteenth and nineteenth centuries. All Russian tsars after Peter, and following his example, had foreign, mostly German wives (and there were of course two German empresses, the two Catherines). The wives took Russian names and converted to Orthodoxy, but they generally retained a great affection for their families and cultures of origin and often maintained strong contacts with them. Both they and their husbands consorted regularly with the German, Danish, and British royal families with which they were connected. Alexander III and his Danish wife, Dagmaar (Marie), sister of the Danish king, made yearly visits to the Danish court (where they often met their British cousins); and a favorite spot for Nicholas II and his German wife, Alix (Alexandra), was Alix's family home at Hesse-Darmstadt, though neither did they neglect the families or the family residences of Alix's grandmother, Queen Victoria of England. "Almost nothing about the Romanovs was 'Russian,'" says Miranda Carter. "Their lives were those of Westernized aristocrats. Their court etiquette was German, their parks and palaces were neoclassical, their home comforts English. Even by blood they were barely Russian at all, the product of endless marriages into German royal families" (Carter 2010: 70). It has been said that "the Romanovs of later years were, from a genealogical point of view, probably 9/10 German rather than Russian" (Hellbirg-Hern 1998: 78n12; see also Carter 2010: xiv).

The association of "foreignness" with monarchy went further in Russia than elsewhere. Most dynasties of foreign origin, such as the Hanoverians in England, sought to play down their foreign origins, and to "nativize" themselves as much as possible, at least from the mid-eighteenth century onward (Hobsbawm 1987: 149). Russian tsars on the contrary sought to emphasize their foreignness, to establish a distance and a separation between themselves and the people they ruled. Ivan IV even denied being Russian, and prided himself on his genealogical link with the first Roman emperor, Augustus. Ivan III's adoption of the title "tsar" was a claim to take on the Byzantine mantle; when Peter was declared "emperor" this assimilated Russia more to Western European models of empire, though they too claimed Roman inspiration (Wortman 2006: 9–10, 21–39). But the point was always the same, to look outside Russia for the symbols and sources of legitimation, to show that "royalty is the foreigner" (Hellberg-Hirn 1998: 69). "The animating myths of Russian monarchy from the fifteenth to the late nineteenth century associated the ruler and the elite with foreign images of political power" (Wortman 2006: 1; cf. Wortman 2011: 266–68; Cherniavsky 1969: 42).

Again, many of the monarchies of early modern Europe claimed foreign origins, the Trojans/Romans being favorites with them as well. But by the eighteenth century they had mostly dropped this practice. "The distinguishing feature of Russian monarchy," says Richard Wortman, "was the persistence of a pattern of appropriation of symbols and images from abroad long after it ceased to be the practice in Europe." Coronation rites, court rituals, official ceremonies, art, and architecture hammered home the message (Wortman 2006: 2).

We should remember in this context how readily in the eighteenth and nineteenth centuries the Russian court and aristocracy took to German and French, making them the languages of choice as much at home as in the public sphere. Russian was something to be used with servants and the common people. In later years, especially under the influence of Nicholas and Alexandra, English was added to the foreign languages common at court and among the upper classes (Hellberg-Hirn 1998: 69; Carter 2010: 66, 133). Foreignness—sometimes exotic, though mostly drawn from the Western lexicon—was a central theme of the "scenarios of power" designed and staged at public ceremonies.

> The open, and often flamboyant displays of Byzantine or Western culture accentuated the inferior quality of the native population, who lived outside the heroic history of the ruling dynasty. The ceremonies of power—the coronation, the European advent, the court fête, and the parade—elevated the monarch in settings resembling distant realms: they were spectacular demonstrations of otherness, confirming the foreign and therefore exalted and sovereign character of the ruler and the elite. (Wortman 2006: 411)[24]

Under Alexander III and Nicholas II, an attempt was undertaken to make the Russian monarchy more Russian, to associate it more closely with the Russian people (Wortman 2006: 245–409; cf. Tolz 2001: 100–101). In the wake of the assassination of Alexander II in 1881, it was felt that the monarchy had lost touch with the common people. For the sake of its future it needed to do more to show that it reflected the values and traditions of the "real" Russia, Russia as it had existed before the Westernizing reforms of Peter the Great. A powerful influence here was Konstantin Pobedonostsev, tutor to both Alexander and Nicholas. Pobedonostsev was also, successively, a senator, a member of the Council of State, and the director-general of the Holy Synod of the Russian Orthodox Church. As statesman and confidant of the tsars, he was in a strong position to urge a new direction on the Russian monarchy and empire. Pobedonostsev was convinced that with Peter Russia had taken the wrong turn. The move to embrace Western modernization and rationalism had been fatal. Alexander II's liberal reforms had also been dangerous and damaging. The need now was to return to the Russia of the seventeenth century, with its traditions of autocracy and Orthodoxy (Walicki 1979: 297–300).

Hence it was that in this period there were significant currents of Russification in relation to non-Russians, and numerous statements of what "true Russianness" was, most of it in a conservative mode. Hence the "Slavophiles" tended to be favored, as against the "Westernizers." The peasantry and their communal institutions were invoked as the foundation of Russian society. The Cossacks were given elevated status, as representing the cardinal Russian virtue of loyal and devoted service to the tsar. Beards were now allowed and indeed encouraged, as symbolizing the virility of old Russia. There were now frequent references to "Holy Russia," the "Russian Soul (*russkaia dusha*)," the traditions of ancient Rus and Muscovy. At his coronation in the Assumption Cathedral in Moscow, Alexander III was hailed as "a truly Russian tsar, of Moscow and all Rus" (Wortman 2006: 276).

Moscow, against "alien" Petersburg, was reasserted as the sacred center of Russian culture and symbol of the unity between tsar and people. The primacy of Orthodoxy was reemphasized, and Orthodoxy seen as the bearer of the Russian national spirit. The doctrine of "Moscow the Third Rome"—reasserted in the coronation cantata written for Alexander III—found resonance not simply in Russia's "civilizing mission" in the East but also in its allotted task to support and if necessary free oppressed Orthodox subjects everywhere.

These tropes and themes were eminently suitable for the construction of an imperial ideology, an ideology of "imperial nationalism" that while recognizing the leading role of Russians and Russian culture did so in the context of an imperial mission. But how fitted were they for a truly *nationalist* ideology, one that elevated Russians above all others and, if it acknowledged non-Russians at all, did so by regarding them as alien and inferior, destined to be absorbed in Russian culture or expelled? Not very well, it turns out—which is why the concept of "Russian nationalism," at this time at least, is almost as eccentric and improbable as that of "English nationalism" for the same period.

Take "Holy Russia," an idea with a long life; it was still being invoked by Russian soldiers on the battlefields of the First World War (Cherniavsky 1969: 222). "Holy Russia" was established in the seventeenth century, as Michael Cherniavsky has shown, as "a popular epithet expressing a popular ideology." It symbolized the Orthodox Russian people as an entity distinct from the state; official discourse rarely referred to it. "Holy Russia"—often written as one word, as in the "holyrussian land," *sviatorusskaia zemlia*—was thus a concept separate from and potentially opposed to the state. It was popular with Old Believers, who rejected the post-Petrine state as the work of the Antichrist Peter and refused to have anything to do with it. If Russian thought, as many believe, tends toward anarchism, then "Holy Russia" made an important contribution in that direction. "Holy Russia" expressed the (ideal) character of the Russian people as an eternal essence, without reference to any particular political embodiment. "The way in which the epithet was used in popular folksongs and epics did not prescribe the political form of Russian society; that is to say, Russia could be 'Holy Russia' whether there was a tsar or not" (Cherniavsky 1969: 115; cf. Tolz 2001: 79).

According to "Holy Russia," the character of the Russian people was Orthodox. That was what defined Russianness. To be Russian was to be Orthodox. Cossacks—made up of Tatars, Poles, and Lithuanians—could invoke "Holy Russia" because they were Orthodox and hence Russian. So too could converted Germans, Finns, Jews, and Muslims. Race and ethnicity were no barrier to becoming Russian. The folk *lubok* literature contains many examples of outsiders converting to Orthodoxy and so becoming members of the Russian community. In these stories, conversion to Orthodoxy and swearing allegiance to the tsar are enough to make one Russian. A particularly popular theme is romance between an Oriental and a Russian suitor or bride, with conversion of the lover to Orthodoxy and full acceptance thereby into Russian society. In several cases there is not even a change in behavior; conversion is all that is required. Conversion, says Jeffrey Brooks, was "more a national than a religious experience. . . . The conversion to Orthodoxy signaled the change in status from alien to Russian" (Brooks 1985: 216, 220; cf. Slezkine 1997: 32). As late as the 1870s the Slavophile Ivan Aksakov could argue that "a Jew, a Catholic or a Muslim can be a Russian subject, but cannot be a Russian. In contrast, in the eyes of ethnic Russians, anyone who has converted to Orthodoxy can be a Russian" (in Tolz 2001: 193).

"The Russian soul is an Orthodox one," says Michael Cherniavsky; "in fact no other characterization of a Russian is necessary, and the synonym 'Russian' and 'Orthodox' rings a familiar note for us" (Cherniavsky 1969: 123; cf. Hellberg-Hirn 1998: 101–3; Lieven 2001: 236–37; Figes 2002: 300–301). Among the peasants to be Russian was to be *krestiane-khristiane* (peasants-Christians)—effectively the same word—or *pravslavnye* (orthodox) (Figes 2002: 376). Acknowledging this, within months of the emancipation of the serfs in 1861 the Holy Synod arranged for the canonization of St. Tikhon of Zadonsk, "the people's saint." Russian peasants in their hundreds of thousands flocked to his shrine as a way both of expressing their gratitude to the tsar-liberator, Alexander II, and of reconfirming their joint identity with him as Orthodox (Chulos 2000: 33–40).

But neither "Holy Russia" nor Orthodoxy could prove very serviceable to ideas of Russian nationhood, not at least as found in nationalist thinking. In the case of the former, the disjunction of "Holy Russia" from the state, and even possible opposition to it, made it impossible to achieve that union of state and nation that is the goal of all nationalism. A disturbing wedge was interposed between state and nation that suggested different and perhaps incompatible destinies for the two. The distinction mirrored that between *Rus* and *Rossiia*, between the people and the state. "To be of *Rus'* was to be an Orthodox, a Christian, to indicate one's status in eternity; to be of *Rossiia*, was to be of the political state. What we seem to have here are two different Russias, each expressing a different myth: the common and popular '*Rus'*,' material carrier of 'Holy Russia,' and '*Rossiia*,' the political state, ruled by the *Imperator Vserossiiskii* [emperor of all Russia]" (Chernivasky 1969: 120). *Rossiia*, the empire, could incorporate *Rus*, the Russian people, and even give it a leading role; but *Rus* could never be *Rossiia*, the whole empire, and at various times might be as much its victims as other subject nationalities.

Orthodoxy could certainly be associated with the empire, and for much of the time was indeed the state religion. But that too indicated the difficulty of making Orthodoxy the hallmark of a specifically Russian nationalism. If "Holy Russia" was less than the empire, Orthodoxy was more than it, flowed beyond its bounds. For Orthodoxy was shared by many peoples—not just by the "Little Russians" and "White Russians" within the empire, together with converts from other religions, but by many groups outside it. Crucially there were the Greeks, the senior Orthodox people by virtue of antiquity, and founders of the very creed by which the Russian people came to define themselves. Byzantium was the acknowledged font of Orthodoxy and revered in Russian culture; even after it succumbed to the Ottomans, allowing Russia to claim the leadership of the Orthodox Church, Greek Orthodoxy remained a powerful influence, as was shown in the Great Schism of the seventeenth century. Many of the early Moscow metropolitans were Greeks, as were some of its greatest icon painters, such as Theophanos. Then too there were the other Orthodox subjects of the Ottomans in the Balkans—Bulgarians, Bosnians, Serbs, Macedonians, and others. Russia had a declared obligation to free its oppressed coreligionists. Like all great religions, Orthodoxy was ultimately universalistic; it was ill-suited to becoming the basis of a merely national identity. When Patriarch Nikon, in a reproof to the "nativism" of the Old Believers, declared that "I am a Russian but my faith is Greek," he was affirming the impossibility of a purely national understanding of Orthodoxy (Berdyaev [1947] 1992: 31; Stremooukhoff 1970: 119). If Orthodoxy was indeed to be the Russian creed, it could be so only as part of an imperial commitment to bring into one ecumenical community all Orthodox believers.

That indeed was precisely the mission that was marked out for Russia in the doctrine of "Moscow the Third Rome." In 1393 Anthony, patriarch of Constantinople, had reproved the pretensions of Grand Duke Vasilii I of Moscow to be head of the Church, declaring that "it is impossible for the Christians to have the Church without having the Emperor, because the Empire and the Church constitute one unity and one community" (Stremooukhoff 1970: 110). That emperor was of course the Byzantine emperor, resident in Constantinople. With the fall of Constantinople in 1453, and with it the Byzantine Empire, this opinion of the Greeks could now be turned against them. The fall of Constantinople was attributed by the Russian Church to just retribution for Greek "treason" in reuniting with the Roman Church at the Council of Ferrara-Florence in 1438–39. The imperial throne and the imperial city were now vacant. Into that vacuum stepped the Russian tsar as the new defender of the Orthodox faith and new ruler of the Orthodox ecumene; so too Moscow as the imperial city, sacred center of the Orthodox Church. With the conquest of the Balkans by the Ottomans, and with it the subjection of the major Orthodox communities, there simply were no other contenders. Russia remained the only free Orthodox community in the world. It was Russia's duty, according to the Greek doctrine itself, to provide the emperor without whom the Orthodox Church would be fatally incomplete.

In 1492 Zosimus, metropolitan of Moscow, pronounced Ivan III "the new Emperor Constantine of the new Constantinople—Moscow." This appears to be the first statement in which the Russian tsar is proclaimed the emperor and Moscow the imperial city (Stremooukhoff 1970: 113). It was Filofei (Philotheus), a monk from Pskov, who in a letter of c. 1523 to Vasilii III added the idea of the succession of the three Romes, and the messianic prophecy (and warning) that Moscow would be the last: "two Romes have fallen, the third stands; there will not be a fourth; thy Christian empire . . . will not pass to others" (Stremooukhoff 1970: 115).[25]

There have been many interpretations of Filofei's prophecy. But whatever the intention, the doctrine of Moscow the Third Rome could hardly be of much use to Russian nationalists—again, except in the terms of "imperial" or "missionary" nationalism. For what it enjoined and justified was not the task of the Russian nation qua nation but of Russia as an empire, as the "third Rome," continuing the providentially ordained mission of the first two Romes as the agency of Christianity and civilization in the world. Such an imperial conception could lead, as it did, to Russia's ambitions in the Balkans, as the protector and potential liberator of the Orthodox subjects of the Ottoman

Empire; it could lead, especially in Pan-Slavic visions, to Russian hopes to retake Constantinople itself for the Christians, and reestablish the Byzantine Empire—but "under the wing of the Russian eagle" (Walicki 1979: 114, 292). It could also justify Russia's *drang nach Osten*, its drive to the East, as the power that was bringing Christianity and civilization to pagans and infidels in the Asiatic lands. This was what was involved in the *translatio* and *renovatio* of empire embodied in the doctrine of the three Romes. Nothing like it could ever be applied to a (mere) nation-state.

To the end the Russian Empire was a Christian empire, and Orthodoxy was always a defining feature of its self-conception (Kristof 1967: 244–46; Brooks 1985: 217). To be Russian was to be first and foremost Orthodox, and those who did not convert, however elevated their position, were made to feel it. All empires have a mission, and Orthodoxy—the protection and spread of it—fairly sums up that of the Russian Empire. A notion of the "civilizing mission," particularly in relation to the East, could accompany and at times partly displace this, or at least shift the emphasis. But secular goals never displaced religious ones so long as the empire lasted. This was particularly clear in the life and thought of the last emperor, Nicholas II, with his ostentatious family piety and his concern for religious sites and ceremonies (Wortman 2006: 347–60).

But the very halfheartedness of the Russification policies of Nicholas's reign, as of those of his predecessors, indicates the limits to which in practice one can pursue the imperial mission. What matters in the end is the strength and survival of the empire itself, for only then is it in any position to achieve its goals. As a multinational empire, Russia like other empires had of necessity to balance its missionary goals against the requirements of imperial management. There has to be a degree of self-restraint and of self-denying ordinances. As we have seen, the Russian state restrained the proselytizing propensities of the Orthodox Church and practiced a considerable degree of toleration of other faiths and other traditions. The same pragmatism made it turn a deaf ear to most of the more extreme demands of Russian nationalism, except where these could be seen to coincide with imperial interests. In areas as different as Finland, the Baltic provinces, Poland, and the region of the Volga Tatars, pressures for forced Russification were resisted not out of respect for some version of "multiculturalism"—Russian culture was clearly seen as superior, and would no doubt win out in the end—but because to succumb to them would have been impolitic, damaging to the security of the empire. Imperial missions reach their limits in imperial realities, and imperial realism.

Slavophiles and Westernizers

The Slavophiles reveal with equal clarity the difficulty of maintaining the boundary between nation and empire, and the frequent crossing from one to the other. What starts off as an attempt to define the national "soul" ends up as Pan-Slavism, the ultimate union of all the Slavs. In any case the principal concern of the Slavophiles was not to define a specifically Russian, ethnic, nation (Prizel 1998: 163; cf. Sarkisyanz 1974: 57). Their antagonists were the "Westernizers," and their animus was directed against all the Westernizing trends that had so deeply affected Russian society, and especially the Russian elite, since the time of Peter the Great. If Peter was not quite the Antichrist that he was to the Old Believers, he at any rate bore responsibility for introducing the Western rationalism and materialism that were undermining the traditional Slavic sensibility and spirituality. His "alien" city, Petersburg, symbolized the new forces that were destroying Russia. It had displaced the ancient capital Moscow, the spiritual center of traditional Russian life.

Slavophiles, as represented by their most influential theorists, Ivan Kireevskii, Aleksei Khomiakov, and Konstantin Aksakov, stressed the religion of Orthodoxy as the source of Slavic strength and of its greatest virtues.[26] Orthodoxy had remained true to the original Christian ideals. Western Christianity by contrast had been poisoned by classical rationalism, which had led many in the direction of atheism. Orthodoxy had preserved the collective, communal character of the Church; the Western churches had succumbed to the fragmentation and individualism that were reflected in all their other institutions. Slavic communalism was also represented in the village commune, the *obshchina*, and the *artel* (cooperative), governed by the traditional authority of the *mir*, the council of elders. *Sobornost*, "conciliarism" or community, was the hallmark of Russian society as against the possessive individualism of the West. "Society was held together by what was primarily a moral bond—a bond of convictions—that united the entire land of Rus' into one great *mir*, a nationwide community of faith, land, and custom" (Walicki 1979: 96).

The Slavophiles found room for the state but only if it restricted itself to the "external" affairs of society, to law, war, and "high politics." It had no right, or need, to interfere in the "inner" life of the people, the sphere governed by religion, tradition, and customs. There was no need for a parliament or constitution, as demanded by the Westernizers; consultation through the historic *zemskii sobor*, the "Assembly of the Land"—which should be revived—was a sufficient means for the tsar to be informed about the concerns of his loyal

subjects. The bond between ruler and ruled was one of trust, not of legal contract. The Russian state, since Peter, had illegitimately and disastrously intervened bureaucratically in the life of the village. The result was to create a great
divide between state and society, between the Westernized elite and the *narod*,
the ordinary Russian people. Westernized Russians, claimed Khomiakov, had
become "colonizers in their own country" (Walicki 1979: 99).

The Slavophiles found a sympathetic response among several leading
statesmen, including Konstantin Pobedonostsev and Tsars Alexander III and
Nicholas II. But the "conservative utopia" of the Slavophiles (Walicki 1975)
came up against the practicalities and realities of imperial rule. *Sobornost* was
acceptable so long as it did not include a call for the restoration of the *zemskii
sobor*, against which Slavophile demand Pobedonostsev strongly, and successfully, counseled Alexander III (Walicki 1979: 299; Hosking 1998a: 373–74;
Wortman 2006: 272). Pan-Slavism too, under the influence of Ivan Aksakov
(Konstantin's brother), was attractive to a government with designs on the
Balkans. It responded to the call of their fellow Slav Bulgarians and Bosnians
in their risings of 1875–76 against the Ottoman Empire, resulting in the Russo-
Turkish War of 1877–78 (Hunczak 1974: 103–4). But statesmen such as Pobedonostsev quickly realized the dangers of pursuing the Pan-Slavic dream too
far (Kristof 1967: 248; Lieven 2001: 247). Pan-Slavism, as practical politics,
showed its limits at the Congress of Berlin in 1878, when Russia accepted its
responsibilities as a great power among other great powers and renounced the
gains made in the Treaty of San Stefano (Hosking 1998a: 371–73).

Pan-Slavism revealed, even more clearly than other varieties, that Slavophilism and Russian nationalism made very uncomfortable bedfellows. Pan-
Slavism was evidently an imperial doctrine, as in Nikolai Danilevsky's project
for "the full political liberation of all the Slav peoples and the formation of a
Pan-Slav Union under the hegemony of Russia" (in Kohn 1962: 196). But even
if Russians should take the lead, they would be one group of Slavs among others. The Slavophiles varied in their focus on different groups of Slavs, some
restricting it more or less exclusively to Russians, some including all the East
Slavs, some reaching out to all Slavs, which meant including not just the South
Slavs of the Balkans, many of whom were Orthodox, but in some versions
also the West Slavs, which meant including Catholic Poles and Czechs (Miller
2008: 21–22).

There were reasonable grounds for Pan-Slavism, in related Slavonic languages and certain other common cultural features. But so too there were for
the Teutonic or Latin nations, without anyone seriously proposing—until

perhaps Hitler's Aryanism—that they were or could form one nation. Pan-Slavism in fact had started not among the Russians but among the Czechs and Slovaks. It is generally thought to have commenced with the famous cycle of poems of 1824, *Slávy Dcera* (The daughter of Slava) by the Czech Jan Kollár, who called for the cultural and literary solidarity of all Slavs. But this did not necessarily entail political unity, least of all under Russian rule. Many of the leading Polish and Czech scholars and spokesmen, such as the Polish poet Adam Mickiewicz, the Czech historian František Palacký, and the Czech journalist Karel Havlíček, vehemently and eloquently rejected Russian claims to be the leader and unifier of all Slavs (Kohn 1962: 69–90). Russia for them was a greater threat than Austria or even Hungary and Germany, and Russian Pan-Slavism concealed Russian imperial ambitions. Russians, said Havlíček, "have started everywhere to say and write Slav instead of Russian, so that later they will again be able to say Russian instead of Slav" (in Kohn 1962: 88; see also Sarkisyanz 1974: 63–66; Hunczak 1974: 84–88; Hosking 1998a: 370).

Slavophilism could never escape the contradictions of its doctrines. Was it racial or religious, cultural or ethnic, national or imperial? The answers to these questions led to a host of different strategies. But Slavophilism was never in any case primarily a political program. It was really a movement of spiritual and cultural renewal, powerful and creative in many spheres, as shown above all in the writings of Fedor Dostoevsky and even Alexander Herzen. In this it aspired to go beyond the nation, the Russian nation as much as any other, and to identify itself with the fate of humanity as a whole. E. H. Carr writes that "the conception that Russia was not merely a nation among nations, but had a unique mission to transcend nationality by becoming the archetype of universal humanity, became a central tenet of the Slavophil creed." Thus Konstantin Aksakov could write in the 1850s, "The Russian nation is not a nation, it is humanity; it is a nation only because it is surrounded by other nations having exclusive national essences, and its humanity therefore appears as nationality." For Dostoevsky the poet Pushkin was great not because he was Russian but because he was the prototype of the "all-man"; and Russia was important not for itself but because it was the "god-bearing nation" (Carr 1956: 371; see also Hosking 1998a: 368–69).

The "Westernizers" too were primarily moralists, as seen above all in their acknowledged leader, Vissarion Belinsky. They opposed much of what the Slavophiles stood for, autocracy and Orthodoxy especially, but also any expressions of narrow nationalism. Fundamentally they took upon themselves the Enlightenment quest for truth and justice. For them the Russia of their day obstructed the path of both, and they labored to clear it (Berlin 1979: 150–85). Nationalism would have been of no help to them in this, for nationalism requires of nations that they have a history, and for the Westernizers Russia did not have one, not a serviceable one at any rate.

Here the Westernizers followed the lead of Petr Chaadayev, whose "Philosophical Letter Written to a Lady" of 1836 was described by Alexander Herzen as "a shot that rang out in the dark night; it forced us all to awaken" (Walicki 1979: 88). Russia's tragedy, wrote Chaadayev, is that "we do not belong to any of the great families of mankind. We are not part of the Occident, nor are we part of the Orient; and we don't have the traditions of the one or of the other. Since we are placed somewhat outside of the times, the universal education of mankind has not reached us." When Peter the Great began the education of Russians, he had no national traditions to draw upon. "Peter the Great found only a blank page when he came to power, and with a strong hand he wrote on it the words *Europe* and *Occident*: from that time on we were part of Europe and of the Occident." But "don't be mistaken about it: no matter how enormous the genius of this man and the energy of his will, his work was possible only in the heart of a nation whose past history did not imperiously lay down the road it had to follow, whose traditions did not have the power to create its future, whose memories could be erased with impunity by an audacious legislator. We were so obedient to the voice of a prince who led us to a new life because our previous experience apparently did not give us any legitimate grounds for resistance" (in Kohn 1962: 39, 53).

The task remained to complete Peter's work. But a narrow or boastful nationalism would be no help in this. Repelled by what he saw as the expression of this spirit at the time of the Crimean War, Chaadayev wrote: "We knew that Russia was great and powerful, with much promise for the future. But . . . we were far from imagining that Russia represented some abstract principle comprising the definite solution of the social problem, that she by herself constituted a world apart . . . that she had a special mission of absorbing all the Slav peoples in her bosom, and of bringing about the regeneration of mankind." With evident reference to the Slavophiles, he expressed profound regret that "the so-called national sentiment had grown to a state of real monomania among our new class of learned men" (in Kohn 1962: 37).

The Westernizers, following Chaadayev, accepted that the lack of a usable past meant constructing a future out of elements drawn from elsewhere, from the West. Nationalism was ruled out by this very premise. Belinsky, the most influential of the Westernizers after Chaadayev, also praised Peter the Great for freeing Russia from "Asian barbarism," and even more Catherine II for spreading the European Enlightenment in Russia and awakening the Russian mind through her policies of education. As a result, "we are today the pupils and no longer the zealots of Europeanism; we no longer wish to be either Frenchmen, or Englishmen, or Germans; we want to be Russians in the European spirit." The ultimate goal was "the utter penetration of our *narodnost* [nationality] by Europe" (in Kohn 1962: 128).

But to do so, to make Russians Europeans, was to make Russians not nationalists but cosmopolitans, like the novelist Ivan Turgenev, or the host of educated Russians who were drawn to the international socialism of the French and German thinkers. Or there could be creative syntheses, as in the work of Alexander Herzen, drawing on native strengths but also the thought and experience of Western Europe (Lampert 1957: 171–259; Berlin 1979: 186–209; Tolz 2001: 93–99). Principally the targets of the Westernizers were the ignorance, servility, and obscurantism spread by the autocracy and the Church. As such, they prized destruction over creation, in the belief that what Russia most needed at the present time were not constructive schemes of reform but the unseating of old beliefs and prejudices. That is why Belinsky praised the eighteenth century above all, when "the guillotine chopped off the heads of aristocrats, priests, and other enemies of God, Reason, and Humanity." "My God," he declared, "is negation! In history my heroes are the destroyers of the old—Luther, Voltaire, the Encyclopedists, the Terrorists, Byron" (in Kohn 1962: 130).

The nation the Westernizers hoped to form was not one built on the inherited traditions of the past but a completely new creation, one that might indeed make Russians proud of themselves in the eyes of Europeans but in the spirit of Enlightenment rationalism and cosmopolitanism, not of native Russian chauvinism. The "great idea of national individuality," said Belinsky, had to give way "to a still greater idea of humanity. The nations are beginning to realize that they are members of the great family of mankind. They are beginning to share with each other in the spirit of brotherhood the spiritual treasures of their nationality. . . . Today only weak and narrow minds can think that the successes of humanity can harm the successes of nationality and that we need Chinese walls to safeguard nationality." Belinsky had nothing but scorn for those "haters of Europeanism" who hold up to "the educated (Westernized) members of Russian society . . . the unkempt, dirty masses as an example of unspoiled Russian nationality worthy of imitation. . . . Nationality is not a homespun coat, bast slippers, cheap vodka, or sour cabbage." Russia, he said, "sees her salvation not in mysticism, asceticism, or pietism, but in the success of civilization, enlightenment, and humanity" (in Kohn 1962: 131–23, 135–36; cf. Carr 1956: 376; Berlin 1979: 158, 172–73; Walicki 1979: 140–41).

Imperial Nationalism: Nation and Empire

"A Russian," said Dostoevsky, "is not only a European, he is also an Asiatic. Moreover, our hopes may belong more to Asia than to Europe. In our future destiny it is perhaps Asia that would offer us the final solution" (in Hellberg-Hirn 1998: 227). Belinsky, conceding that the Slavophiles had a point in criticizing some aspects of "Russian Europeanism," accepted their view that "there is some sort of duality in Russian life and consequently a lack of moral unity [which] deprives us of a clearly defined national character such as distinguishes, to their credit, all the European nations; this makes a kind of nonesuch out of us, well able to think in French, German, and English, but unable to think in Russian.... To think in Russian is much more difficult, because the Russian to himself is still a riddle, and the significance and destiny of his native land, where everything is embryonic and incipient and nothing is determinate, fully evolved, and formed, are likewise a riddle to him" (in Kohn 1962: 134–35).

It is significant that both a Slavophile and a Westernizer agree that there is something peculiar about Russian nationality, that it points in different directions, West and East, that it remains a "riddle" owing to its incomplete or distorted development. This was accepted even by those such as Nicolai Danilevsky who argued against the view "of an alleged lack of unity in the Russian state, because there are in it, maybe, about a hundred peoples of different nationalities." What was forgotten was that "all this diversity disappears before the preponderance of the Russian race—qualitatively and quantitatively." It was Russia's duty, as the only surviving independent Slav state, to liberate her "racial brothers," and to do this "she must steel them and herself in the spirit of independence and Pan-Slav consciousness" (in Kohn 1962: 202–3, 210).

Danilevsky's position revealed all the contradictions of the Slavophile view of Russian national identity. To save itself, and to be itself, Russia had to save all Slavs, which meant an imperial war against the Ottomans, probably also the Habsburgs, and perhaps even the Hohenzollerns. The Slavophile poet Fedor Tyuchev spoke frankly of "the indispensable fulfillment of Russia as the Slavonic Empire," the prelude and necessary condition of the restoration of the unity of Christendom on "Greco-Slavonic" foundations. This meant in effect the reestablishment of the Byzantine Empire under Russian auspices, a persistent theme of the Slavophiles. But it could also be linked with a deeper theme, the messianic belief in Russia's destiny to regenerate the world. The creation of the Slavonic Empire, the recovery of Constantinople, would according to Tyuchev transform Russia itself into something new, something greater than empire. "She will have become herself, and yet she will be associated with so many other elements which will complement and transform her that her very name will be changed. She will no longer be an empire but a world" (in Kohn 1962: 92–93; see also Kristof 1967: 248; Bassin 1999: 45–49).

This is a very strange form of nationalism, as normally understood. Conceivably a Russian nation could have been consolidated around the idea of a Slav core, and that as we have seen was one tendency in the later nineteenth century. But we have also seen the limits of those ideas and policies, and the realization that to press them too far would undo the empire. Even if Russianness could be equated with the Slavs—all of them? some of them?—there remained the many non-Slavs in the empire, who by the end of the nineteenth century amounted to nearly a third of the empire's population. There were some, such as the extreme nationalist Mikhail Katkov, who proposed lopping these non-Slav elements off, and making the Russian Empire more purely Russian, even to the exclusion of the other Eastern Slavs. This was "Great Russian chauvinism" with a vengeance (Tolz 2001: 172; Hosking 1998a: 375). But it remained a minority view even within the conservative camp, and seems never to have been taken seriously by Russian tsars or their advisers, even under Alexander III, the most nationalist—the only nationalist—of the tsars (Miller 2008: 165, 177n15). "On the cultural level (church-building, court festivals), [the government] paid a certain tribute to 'Russianness', but its policies were couched in terms that held to the statist and dynastic concept of Russia" (Bushkovitch 2003: 157).

Nation and empire, *Rus* and *Rossiya*, remained opposing and alternative points of reference in the nineteenth century, and beyond (cf. Prizel 1998: 164–65). To espouse one was to suppress or threaten the other. The nation might, as Eric Hobsbawm puts it, have become "the new civic religion of states" (Hobsbawm 1987: 149). But all efforts to enroll the national principle in the service of the state had to tread with extreme care if the preservation of the empire were the main concern. This was as true for Russia as it was for the Ottomans, the Habsburgs, the British, and other imperial peoples. Too strong an identification of any one nation, even and especially the dominant one, with the state was to risk the empire's stability and survival. In the end, despite their

FIGURE 5.5. Tsar Nicholas I, exponent of "official nationality." Portrait (1852) by Franz
Kruger. State Hermitage Museum, St. Petersburg, Russia/Bridgeman Images.

many overlaps and similarities, empires and nation-states did point in different
directions (see chapter 1).

That this was recognized by Russian statesmen is shown clearly in the exercise of the principle of "official nationality" that was, with suitable caution,
used by Russian statesmen at various times in the nineteenth century. "Official
nationality" was the term given to the policies of Nicholas I by the liberal historian A. N. Pypin in 1875. Thereafter it passed into general currency as a gloss
on the triadic formula "Orthodoxy (*pravoslavie*), Autocracy (*samoderzhavie*),

and Nationality" (*narodnost*)," formulated in 1833 as the watchword of the regime by Nicholas I's minister of education, Count Sergei Uvarov. While Pypin himself had no doubt that the formula reflected a strong embrace of Russian nationalism, most scholars, as with "Russification" in general, have come to be more skeptical (Miller 2008: 139–54).

The term "nationality" in the triad "Orthodoxy, Autocracy, and National-ity" seemed almost calculated to create ambiguity. The term used was *narod-nost*, from *narod* or people. For Belinsky and others concerned with the kind of nationhood they saw in the West, this was very different from *natsionalnost*, from *natsiia*, a nation. There is, said Belinsky, "a difference between a nation in its natural, immediate, and patriarchal state, and this same nation in the rational movement of its historical development" (Walicki 1979: 136; cf. Dixon 1998: 155–56; Steinwedel 2000: 73–75). What Uvarov and the regime—like the Slavophiles—invoked was the conservative, "immediate," principle of the *narod*, not the fully fledged principle of the *natsiia* as enunciated by the French Revolution (Tolz 2001: 78–79, 85–86). The Populists, the *narodniki*, drew on this as much as did the proponents of "official nationality," showing its extreme flexibility, the many uses to which it could be put (Knight 2000). In the doctrine of "official nationality," *narodnost* expressed a desire to link the tsar to the people, who were vaguely but familiarly invoked, not to proclaim that Russia was a state based on a nation (the principle of modern national-ism). Nationality remained couched in the terms of traditional dynasticism. "Official Nationality was the negation of ethnicity" (Knight 2000: 56).[27]

"Official nationality" is a fitting expression of the relation between nation and empire in nineteenth-century Russia. It is clear that it puts nation in the service of empire, not the other way round. Empire remained the overriding concern of all rulers and their advisers to the end of the dynasty (Weeks 1996: 12–13; Rowley 2000; Bushkovitch 2003). Nationalism, whether of Russians or non-Russians, was a threat to this enterprise. Nationalism arose as a power-ful ideology in nineteenth-century Europe, and Russia was not immune to it. Alongside the nationalisms of non-Russians in the empire, a strand of Russian nationalism did develop. But it never managed to capture the state, nor most of the Russian intelligentsia, for whom it remained too narrow and restrictive (Kristof 1967: 248; Hosking 1998a: 397; Tolz 2001: 103; Miller 2008: 165).

The Russians were clearly the dominant group in the empire, both in num-bers and in influence. The Russian state conspicuously avoided identifying itself too closely with them because it was a multinational state with a multi-national ruling class. Russian might be the dominant language of the empire, and Russian literature, art, and music the most esteemed cultural forms. Everyone admired Pushkin, Tolstoy, Dostoevsky, Mussorgsky, Tchaikovsky, Glinka. The empire was a vehicle for diffusing this culture across vast spaces. But Russians were not simply the carriers of a national culture (if that is indeed the right expression, given its many sources from different parts of the empire as well as from Western Europe). They were also the carriers of principles and projects with universal reach. For most of the time the chief one of these was Orthodoxy, seen as the pure form of Christianity that would redeem and unite all the others. As with all major religions, this could never take purely national form. Its goal was the messianic transformation of the whole world, not the spiritual salvation of a particular people. But a people could conceive it as their divinely ordained task or mission to accomplish this purpose. This could link nation and empire, a people and its universal mission.

"Imperial nationalism" is the term I used earlier (chapter 1) to express the link between an empire and its national carrier. The danger is that this may make us put the stress more on the nationalism than on the empire. That would be a mistake. Imperial nationalism is present where a nation—not always consciously—gets its sense of itself and its purpose in the world by becoming the vehicle of a principle that is larger than itself, typically in an empire with a "world-historical" or universalist mission. National states too, or at least some of them, conceive of themselves as having missions. Hence another term for imperial nationalism might be "missionary nationalism" (see chapter 1; and cf. Bassin 1999: 13, 15, 274–76). But this is not nationalism in the usual sense. In many respects it is the opposite of nationalism. The nation that is the national carrier—the "state-bearing" nation—must not stress a distinctive national identity that separates it from the other peoples of the empire. That would threaten the integrity, perhaps even the survival, of the empire. The role of the state-bearing nation is to be the quiet, even self-effacing, carrier of the imperial mission, taking pride in its achievement in creating an entity with a reach and a purpose far beyond that of the typical nation-state.

That was the place of the Russians in the Russian Empire. The empire—unlike the case of the Ottomans or the Habsburgs—might nominally be identified with them, as the Russian Empire, rather than with the ruling dynasty, the Romanovs. But that should not lead us to think that it existed for them solely or even principally. They might even come to think of themselves as its victims, as much as or even more than the non-Russians in the empire. That was to become a theme of Russian nationalists later, in the Soviet period; in the tsarist period there is more pride than pity in the special role marked out for Russians.

Geoffrey Hosking quotes the contemporary cultural historian Georgii Gachev: "*Rus'* was the victim of *Rossiia*." It is the leitmotiv of his own work, *People and Empire, 1552–1917* (1998a). The theme of this book, he says, "is how *Rossiia* obstructed the flowering of *Rus'*, or, if you prefer, how the building of an empire impeded the formation of a nation." Nineteenth-century Russian thinkers agonized over the problem of Russian national identity, feeling it undeveloped by comparison with the West. Hosking thinks they were right to be so preoccupied, and so concerned. "I believe the Russians are right, and that a fractured and underdeveloped nationhood has been their principal historical burden in the last two centuries or so, continuing throughout the period of the Soviet Union and persisting beyond its fall."[28]

Truly, there was no great development of Russian nationalism in the nineteenth century, for good reasons to do with the nature of the multiethnic empire. The puzzle lies in the faulting of the Russian Empire for its failure to produce nationalism, as if that were the only and inevitable solution to the problems faced by the empire. Hosking and others like him seem to subscribe to the common opinion that empires in the nineteenth-century world were in some sense "anachronistic," premodern formations that had somehow survived into the era of modernity. The form most suited to modernity was the nation-state; in failing to become a nation-state, Russia had signed its own death warrant.[29]

This ignores the fact that in the nineteenth century—and beyond—empire not only thrived but was indeed the expression sought by nearly all the major European powers (and arguably the United States as well) (Kumar 2010). Why should an empire, in a world of empires, seek to nurture a nationalism of which it would be the first victim? Russia's main rivals and competitors were all empires—the Ottomans, the Habsburgs, the British, the French, even the Germans. All faced the challenge of nationalism, and all, with greater or lesser success, sought to deflect or suppress it. For Russia to have tried to develop nationalism would have been tantamount to proclaiming that it was renouncing empire—and its great power status—and trying to reduce itself to something like Hungary or Serbia (cf. Knight 2000: 59–60). Even had that been possible, in the absence of any clear sense of the Russian nation, it is hard to see why any Russian statesman should have aspired to it.

In the debacle of the First World War and the Russian Revolution of 1917, competing definitions of Russianness warred with each other, in this case

1. ESTONIAN S.S.R
2. LATVIAN S.S.R.
3. LITHUANIAN S.S.R.
4. BELORUSSIAN S.S.R.
5. MOLDAVIAN S.S.R.

Arctic Ocean   *Arctic Ocean*

RUSSIAN SOVIET FEDERATIVE SOCIALIST REPUBLIC   Magadan

Tallinn
1.   Leningrad
2.   ★ Moscow   • Novosibirsk
3.
4.   ★ Kiev   ★ Astana
UKRAINIAN S.S.R   KAZAHK S.S.R
5.
Black Sea   Bishkek
           Baku   UZBEK   KIRGHIZ S.S.R
                   S.S.R
           TURKMEN   TAJIK S.S.R
Mediterranean   S.S.R   *Pacific
Sea*   Ocean*
        AZERBAIJAN S.S.R.
        ARMENIAN S.S.R.
        GEORGIAN S.S.R.

MAP 5.2. The Soviet Union, 1989

literally, in bloody and protracted conflict. Eventually what took the place of the old tsarist empire was not a Russian nation-state but a new empire, the Soviet Empire. Russian nationalism, it seemed, would still have to bide its time.

The Soviet Union: The Return of Empire

In retrospect the Soviet Union can be seen as a relatively short-lived experiment, of some seventy years. That does not mean, though, that it was doomed to die, by some internal principle of decay. In many ways it was extraordinarily successful. Its death was due more to failure in international competition, especially with the West, than to any fatal flaw in its social and political structure. As a result it remains uncertain whether the communism of the Soviet Union was an impossibility in the modern world or whether, given more time, it might have proved a true alternative to Western capitalism (not necessarily in classic Marxist form).

From the point of view of our concerns, however, what is most striking about the Soviet Union is not rupture but continuity. Specifically it is the reconstruction of empire, after a brief period of breakdown in which the future of the Russian state was very much in doubt (Geyer 1986: 53–55). Following the Bolshevik Revolution, in the course of the Civil War (1918–21) the new Soviet regime rapidly recovered most of the lost Russian lands and reestablished the empire more or less within the borders of the old tsarist empire. The principle exceptions were Poland, the Baltic provinces (Lithuania, Latvia, and Estonia), and Finland. Following the Ribbentrop-Molotov Pact of 1940, the Baltic republics were recovered, as was Bessarabia (Moldova). In addition the Soviet Union gained a section of Poland—which became western Ukraine—that had never been part of the tsarist empire; neither too was the Königsberg/Kaliningrad region of East Prussia which the Soviet Union also took at the end of the war. Moreover, after the war the Soviet Union also had an "informal empire" (the "Soviet bloc") in Eastern Europe, in its self-proclaimed role as patron of the new communist states formed under its aegis and whose client status it enforced if need be (as in 1956 and 1968). Nor should one ignore the many communist parties across the world that looked to the Soviet Union as the "fatherland of the international proletariat" and center of the new civilization, and gave it their fervent support. From 1945 the Soviet Union was indeed a world empire, on a scale that surpassed the dreams of all but a few Pan-Slavists of the past.

The Soviet Union of course never called itself an empire. Empire and imperialism were, in principle, anathema to it, as they were to all parties of the left (Geyer 1986: 52; Beissinger 1995: 149–50; Martin 2001: 19). Part of its sense of itself was indeed its decisive rejection of the old Russian Empire, seen as a cover for "Great Russian chauvinism." "Empire"—"the Soviet Empire"—was the term used of it by its enemies, especially in the West (Suny 2001: 23). For some indeed it was the "last empire," a hangover from tsarist times and a relic of the age of empires (e.g., Conquest 1986). The Soviet Union replied in kind, by speaking of "the American Empire" and in general of Western imperialism, including the covert or "neocolonial" imperialism practiced after the Western empires were formally wound down. "Empire" became a dirty word in the course of the twentieth century, especially after the Second World War. All political entities were quick to deny it in their own case (Beissinger 1995: 152, 156–57; Suny 1995: 189).

Nevertheless, after the Soviet Union broke up in 1991, Russians and other Eastern Europeans were quick to join their Western brethren in speaking of "the Soviet Empire." Former Soviet nations announced that they had been "colonies" of the Soviet Empire; Russia itself declared that it too had been a colony, despite appearances (Hirsch 2005: 3–4). The concept became a commonplace of international symposia and conferences, in which the "Soviet Empire" was routinely compared with other empires, Russian, Habsburg, Ottoman.[30] In the past twenty years, one could almost say that "the Soviet Empire" has become the standard way of referring to the Soviet Union, and "empire" has become the main conceptual tool for analyzing it (Beissinger 2006: 294–95).[31] Almost no one discusses it in its own terms, as an anti-imperial union of socialist republics.

There may in time be a reaction to this; the Soviet Union may turn out to have been a different kind of animal after all, not readily susceptible to analysis on past models, including that of empires.[32] But for the time being it does seem plausible and helpful to consider it as a species of empire. It is particularly convincing to see it as a reassertion and reinvigoration of the specifically Russian imperial tradition, a continuation of the Russian Empire "by other means." This too has been a common theme, from the earliest years of the Soviet recovery of the old tsarist lands.[33]

There were differences, of course. The new empire was no longer called the Russian Empire; it was the Union of Soviet Socialist Republics (USSR). Even more than of old, Russia was not the whole empire but formally simply one republic among the fifteen that constituted the multinational USSR. More strikingly still, the "world-historical" mission of the Soviet Union was spelled out with a specificity and a clarity that would have embarrassed the old tsarist officials, even if some of the intelligentsia were less restrained. The USSR loudly, formally, and frequently committed itself to the goal of the world revolution of the proletariat and the construction of a worldwide socialist society. For the Bolsheviks, says E. H. Carr, "the revolution which they made in Russia was conceived by them not primarily as a Russian revolution, but as the first step in a European or world-wide revolution; as an exclusively Russian phenomenon, it had for them no meaning, no validity and no chance of survival" (Carr 1956: 358).

The Soviet Union's role was to provide a model, a foretaste, of the coming world society, and to aid to the utmost limit of its power the realization of that goal. In 1919 it established the Communist International (the Comintern), the "Third International," following the demise of the Second in 1914. As a federation of socialist parties from all over the world, the Comintern dedicated itself to world revolution and the victory of the international proletariat. Moscow would lead the way, Moscow the Third Rome, Moscow the capital of the Third International (Agursky 1987; Duncan 2000: 48–61). Stalin's foreign minister, Viacheslav Molotov, once spoke rhapsodically of "the great historical destiny and fateful mission of the Russian people—the destiny about which Dostoyevsky wrote: the heart of Russia, more than that of any other nation, is predestined to be the universal, all-embracing humanitarian union of nations" (in Lieven 2001: 295). As with tsarist Russia, the messianic theme could surface repeatedly in the Soviet era: "Upon the Russian revolution," wrote Nikolai Berdyaev, "shines the reflected light of the Apocalypse" ([1937] 1960: 132; cf. Flenley 1996: 231). But never, even with the adoption of "Socialism in One Country," was it thought that Russia was anything other than the standard-bearer for world revolution and world communism.

No ideology could have been more hostile to nationalism, widely stigmatized by socialists as "bourgeois," and seen as a device used by ruling classes to blinker the proletariat and lure it into a deceptive sense of equal partnership in the nation. Even more than the tsarist empire, the Soviet Union proclaimed its hostility to the national principle and trumpeted its internationalism. The paradox is that this same Soviet Union was responsible for promoting nationality on a massive scale, finally even bringing into being that reluctant creature, Russian nationalism. The tsarist empire has been accused of ignoring nationality and so bringing about its own downfall. The Soviet Union, with some exaggeration, might stand accused of being too favorable to the principle of nationality, and so hastening if not causing its own demise. None of this was expected of course, and it was certainly not the result of a conscious intent (Brubaker 1996: 32). Nevertheless, the Soviet Union, stigmatized as "the prison of peoples" as much as the old Russian (and Habsburg) Empire, did more to stimulate national feeling and nationalism than did any of the policies of the old empire.

Nationalities and the National Question in the Soviet Union

Like the tsarist empire, the Soviet Empire covered one-sixth of the earth's land surface, second in size only to the British Empire. Like the tsarist empire the Soviet Empire contained more than 100 nations and nationalities. In 1989, 22 of these nations had more than a million members each, and 55 had more than 100,000 members. Ukrainians (15.46 percent)—the largest non-Russian group, as in the tsarist empire—and Belorussians (3.51 percent) made up about the same proportions as under the tsarist regime, as did most other non-Russian groups. The principal exceptions were Poles and Jews, whose proportions dropped from 6 and 4 percent, respectively, to less than 1 percent in both cases. The biggest change came with the doubling of the Central Asian proportion—Kazakhs, Uzbeks, Tadzhiks, Turkmen, and others—from about 6 percent in 1897 to over 12 percent in 1989, mostly owing to natural increase (Kaiser 1994: 30–31; Kappeler 2001: 397–99; Hirsch 2005: 320–23).

The relation of Russia to the Soviet Union was structurally similar to that of Russia to the tsarist empire. That is, Russia and Russians dominated, to an even greater extent than formerly. The Russian Republic (RSFSR) made up 90 percent of the Union's territory and 72 percent of its population. Not all of its people were ethnic Russians of course, though the proportion increased from 73.4 percent in 1926 to 82.6 percent by 1979 (Simon 1991: 376). In terms of the total population of the Soviet Union, ethnic Russians made up 50.8 percent in 1989, as compared with 44.3 percent in the last years of the tsarist empire (Kappeler 2001: 397). Thus ethnic Russians, even without "Little" and "White" Russians, were an absolute majority, if only just, for the whole life of the Soviet Union. This was significant, given that with the development of Ukrainian and to a lesser extent Belorussian national consciousness, and the recognition of Ukraine and Belarus as separate union republics, it was less easy for Great Russians to make the traditional assumption that all could be counted as ethnic Russians. It was equally telling that it was Ukraine's declaration of independence in July 1990 that heralded the breakup of the Soviet Union.

In relation to the nationalities, the Russian Revolution wished to make a complete break with the tsarist past. There was to be no oppression of the nationalities, no new "prison of peoples." The Bolsheviks inveighed repeatedly against the "Great Russian chauvinism" of the tsarist era, the domination of non-Russians (including Ukrainians and Belorussians) by Great Russians. The Soviet Union was conceived as a federation of nationalities, with Russia just one of the nationalities. According to all the constitutions of the Soviet Union—from the 1922 Union Treaty to the last, the Constitution of 1977— "the union republics were voluntary participants in a confederation of sovereign states. Each of the fifteen union republics retained a number of rights which were said to guarantee their sovereign status, including their own constitutions, flags and anthems, the right to enter into foreign relations, to coin money and, perhaps the most important, the right to self-determination, up to and including secession" (Kaiser 1994: 342; cf. Martin 2001: 13–14). In practice many of these rights were not and probably could not be exercised, especially owing to the fact that at every level of government and administration state institutions were shadowed by Communist Party organs, whose headquarters were unmistakably Moscow Central. Nevertheless, the symbolism of these rights remained throughout of great importance; they were indeed to form the constitutional basis of the disintegration of the Soviet Union in 1991.

But despite this concession to national aspirations the Soviet Union could not of course condone nationalism. "Marxism," declared Lenin, "is irreconcilable with nationalism, even the 'fairest', 'purest', most refined and civilized. Instead of nationalism of every kind, Marxism advances internationalism, the amalgamation of all nations in the higher unity that is growing under our eyes" (Lenin 1962: 33). The Soviet Union was avowedly committed to an internationalist goal, the achievement of world socialism; and nationalism—the desire to "fence off all the nations from each other by means of a special state institution"—was seen as a prime weapon in the armory of the bourgeoisie to prevent its attainment. In principle socialism and nationalism remained bitter antagonists. How, then, to accommodate the just demands of the national groups, formerly oppressed by Great Russians, in the Soviet Union?

The intellectual solution was one of those dialectical schemas beloved of Marxist thinkers (Fedyshyn 1980: 152; Kaiser 1994: 97; Martin 2001: 5–6). Following Lenin, Soviet theoreticians of "the national question" offered as the *thesis* the idea that there is first a "flowering" (*rastsvet*) of nations in the early stages of capitalism. The *antithesis* to this is provided by the "drawing together" (*sblizheniye*) of nations as capitalism matures. From this development emerges the *synthesis*, the solution of the national question through the ultimate merger (*sliyaniye*) of all nations into one socialist community. For, declared Lenin, "the aim of socialism is not only to abolish the division of mankind into small states and all segregation of nations, not only to draw the nations together, but to merge them" (Lenin 1962: 176; see also 21–23, 74–75).

Lenin laid out his main ideas on the national question in 1913–16, that is, before the Bolshevik Revolution of 1917; with some modifications they were adopted and developed by Stalin and others in writings both before and after the revolution.[34] There were two problems faced by the new Soviet state. One was that the hoped-for socialist revolutions in the advanced capitalist societies failed to materialize. The Soviet Union would have to go it alone. But the doctrine of "socialism in one country" meant that the dialectical scheme laid out by Lenin would have to be adapted to the new situation. One conclusion was that the synthesis, the merger of all peoples, would have to occur first in the Soviet Union, in the creation of a single Soviet people, rather than in a worldwide socialist community envisaged by Marx and most Marxists (including initially Lenin).

The second problem related to the "backwardness" of the Soviet Union, a legacy of the tsarist period. The tendency of capitalism to "obliterate national distinctions" applied to the mature period of capitalism. Hence it was to be found mostly in the advanced capitalist nations; Lenin was fond of pointing to the United States, with its "Americanization" of diverse immigrant communities, as a prime example of that. But the Soviet Union, as a country that was economically backward, had not yet reached that point. The nations that constituted it existed at many different stages of development, from primitive Siberian tribes and Caucasian mountain peoples to advanced urban societies in the European parts of the USSR. Hence, in the enforced and accelerated "catching-up" with the West, there would have to be a strategy of "social engineering" to bring about the equalization of national groups as a first step toward their eventual merging in a common Soviet identity.

Here a second idea of Lenin's offered a smooth theoretical path forward. Lenin had argued that every modern nation is composed of "two nations," one socialist, one bourgeois, though in the conditions of capitalist society they were unequally represented. "There are two nations in every modern nation. . . . There are two national cultures in every national culture. . . . Every national culture contains elements, even if not developed, of democratic and socialist culture, for in every nation there are toiling and exploited masses, whose living conditions inevitably give rise to the ideology of democracy and socialism. But every nation also has a bourgeois . . . culture—and not only in the shape of 'elements', but in the shape of the *dominant* culture." The task of the "world working-class movement" was to "take from every national culture only its democratic and socialist elements," first as a "counter-balance to bourgeois culture," but ultimately for the fashioning of a whole new socialist culture that would do away with nations entirely (Lenin 1962: 30, 16–17).

This thinking became the basis of the oft-repeated formula, first coined by Stalin, of "socialist in content, national in form" (Stalin [1934] 1975: 391). It was an acknowledgment that in the conditions of Soviet society, many nations still remained underdeveloped and would need help to bolster their national cultures and institutions. In Soviet thinking, nations still remained important, as forms of attachment and integration. But how then, asked Stalin rhetorically, was this to be squared with the attainment of socialism? "How is the building of national culture, the development of schools and courses in the native languages, and the training of cadres from the local people, to be reconciled with the building of proletarian culture? Is there not an irreconcilable contradiction here? Of course not!"

> We are building proletarian culture. That is absolutely true. But it is also true that proletarian culture, which is socialist in content, assumes different forms and modes of expression among the different peoples who are drawn into the building of socialism, depending upon differences in language,

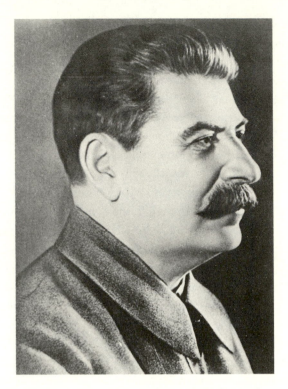

FIGURE 5.6. Joseph Stalin, architect of Soviet nationality policies. Library of Congress.

manner of life, and so forth. Proletarian in content, national in form—such is the universal culture towards which socialism is proceeding. Proletarian culture does not abolish national culture, it gives it content. On the other hand, national culture does not abolish proletarian culture, it gives it form. (Stalin [1934] 1975: 308; see also Hirsch 2005: 268–70)

In this formulation, Stalin appears to accept the persistence of "national forms" even as socialism is developed into a "universal culture," at least so long as this takes place within the confines of the Soviet Union alone. They would not of course be like bourgeois nations, with their class contradictions, but rather "socialist nations," linked together in a common "friendship of peoples." In a report of 1930 he denounced as a "deviation towards Great-Russian chauvinism" the view that, "since, with the victory of socialism, the nations must merge into one and their national languages must be transformed into a single common language, the time has come to abolish national differences and to abandon the policy of promoting the development of the national cultures of the formerly oppressed peoples." Lenin, he reminded these deviators, "never said that national differences must disappear and that national languages must merge into one common language within the borders of a *single* state *before the victory* of socialism *on a world scale*." Up to that point, in order to help "the laboring masses of the non–Great Russian peoples to catch up with Central Russia, which has gone in front," it was necessary to "develop and strengthen among them courts, administration, economic and government bodies functioning in their native languages and staffed with local people familiar with the manner of life and mentality of the local inhabitants." It was also necessary to develop among them "press, schools, theatres, clubs, and cultural and educational institutions in general, functioning in the native languages." None of this was in contradiction to the "dictatorship of the proletariat," for under such a system national culture is "culture that is *socialist* in content and national in form, having the object of educating the masses in the spirit of socialism and internationalism." Indeed, declared Stalin, the building of socialism and the development of national cultures go hand in hand. "The period of the dictatorship of the proletariat and of the building of socialism in the USSR is a period of the *flowering* of national cultures that are *socialist* in content and national in form; for, under the Soviet system, the nations themselves are not the ordinary 'modern' nations, but *socialist* nations, just as in their content their national cultures are not the ordinary bourgeois cultures, but *socialist* cultures" (Stalin [1934] 1975: 386–87, 390–92; see also Simon 1991: 136–38; Martin 2001: 245–49; Hirsch 2005: 267).

As commissar of nationalities from 1917 to 1924, and even more so when he took over supreme directorship of the Soviet Union after Lenin's death in 1924, Stalin was in a powerful position to carry out nationality policies based on these ideas. During the 1920s and 1930s, there was a wide-ranging and comprehensive program of *korenizatsiia*, or "indigenization." As Yuri Slezkine puts it, "'the world's first state of workers and peasants' was the world's first state to institutionalize ethnoterritorial federalism, classify all citizens according to their biological nationalities and formally prescribe preferential treatment of certain ethnically defined populations" (Slezkine [1994] 1996: 204). For Terry Martin, the Soviet Union became an "affirmative action empire" (Martin 2001: 12–20, 341).

Scholars have shown to what a remarkable extent this program was actually achieved in practice. In the interests of developing the previously "oppressed nations," and reining in the "mindless Russian chauvinism" (*rusotiapstvo*) of Great Russians and others, in the 1920s and 1930s there was a deliberate, state-sponsored policy of supporting native language culture and education, and in appointing local people to state and party institutions. In the twelve Union republics (increased to fifteen in 1940), organized on the basis of their "titular" nationality—Ukrainians, Belorussians, Georgians, Armenians, Azerbaidzhanis, Uzbeks, and the like—as well as to a lesser extent in the "autonomous republics" and "autonomous oblasts," the language of the titular nationality became the official language, and local people came to staff most of the state and party organs. Though Russian was encouraged and usually taught as a second language, teaching in most educational institutions was primarily in the native languages. Through centrally conducted research, more than forty non-Russian written languages were created, mostly new. Never mind that "vernacularization" was to some extent an arbitrary affair, with a particular dialect of the titular nationality chosen to be developed as the literary language (cf. Tuscan as the official language of the newly unified Italy in the nineteenth century). Never mind too that the titular nationality had itself sometimes—as in the case of several Central Asian groups, such as the Uzbeks—to be invented as a "nation" (Martin 2001: 402; cf. Khalid 2006). The point was rather the determination and consistency with which the Soviet state pursued *korenizatsiia*, and the fact that, linked to the modernization policies of the Soviet state, "*korenizatsiia* policies achieved impressive results, and international equalization, if not yet outright equality, occurred during the 1920s and 1930s" (Kaiser 1994: 134).[35]

Equalization of nationalities through *korenizatsiia* was meant to lead to greater commitment to the Soviet system, and as a step on the way to the absorption of the different nations in a common Soviet people. Ironically, though perhaps not altogether surprisingly, it had almost the opposite effect. Instead of merging the peoples, it rather consolidated them as distinct nations, hardening the sense of boundaries and establishing powerful indigenous elites in the republics. The more development occurred, the more urbanization, industrialization, and social mobility took place, the more the gains went to indigenes at the cost of nonindigenes (Kaiser 1994: 125, 135; Suny 1989: 282; Khalid 2007: 129–30).

Concerned at what it saw as the growth of "local nationalism" in some of the republics, in the late 1930s the Soviet state pulled back on its comprehensive policies of *korenizatsiia* (Martin 2001: 344–93). But what took its place was not so much "Russification," as some have claimed, as "Sovietization."[36] In March 1938 Stalin imposed mandatory Russian language instruction in all non-Russian schools (though native language instruction also continued), and at the same time tried to curtail the use of non-Russian languages in administration. But this was not because he had reversed his views on Great Russian chauvinism. It was in order to promote modernization and, so he hoped, the gradual "withering away" of nations, which had always been the ultimate aim of *korenizatsiia* ("national in form, socialist in content"). "The measure was implemented," says Peter Blitstein, "not because Russian was the language of the ruling nation of the state, but because a common language was necessary for the effective functioning of a modern economy, polity, and military" (2006: 290).[37] Russian was the obvious lingua franca of the Soviet Union, the best means to achieve that "higher culture" and economic progress that were the ultimate goals of the system. As Stalin put it, justifying the Russian language decree, "in the conditions of a multinational state such as the USSR, knowledge of the Russian language should be a powerful means for communication and contact among the peoples of the USSR, enabling their further economic and cultural growth. . . . [It will] help the further perfecting of the technical and scientific knowledge of national cadres. . . . [I]t is a necessary condition for the successful performance of military service in the Red Army by all citizens" (in Martin 2001: 459; see also Slezkine [1994] 1996: 223, 2000: 231; Blitstein 2001: 255–58).

A more cautious state-led strategy of *korenizatsiia* in fact continued even in the late 1930s and 1940s; it returned more strongly after Stalin's death, continuing until the 1980s.[38] But even more important now was "*korenizatsiia* from below," as rapid geographic and social mobility led to a further strengthening of national boundaries. With the entrenchment of local indigenous elites, every aspect of development could work to the benefit of indigenes, who were given preferential treatment in employment and promotion in the new industries and in the expansion of training and education. International equalization might be occurring, but it was at the expense of intranational equalization. Ethnicity and nationality, against all official doctrine, came to be entrenched, emblazoned as they were on internal passports and many other documents— birth and marriage certificates, for instance—required by the Soviet state.[39]

Soviet statesmen continued to think, or at least to speak, as if nevertheless the goal of a single Soviet community was being attained. By bringing out and developing the "democratic and socialist" elements contained in all national cultures, the point was being reached where the national shell could be discarded (Hirsch 2005: 311–19). *Homo Sovieticus*, Soviet man, was in the process of replacing all the different and divisive nationalities (Fedyshyn 1980; Rasiak 1980). The preamble to the 1977 Constitution declared that this historic aim had indeed been achieved: "A new historical community of people—the Soviet people—has come into being on the basis of the drawing together of all classes and social strata and the juridical and actual equality of all nations and nationalities and their fraternal cooperation" (Kaiser 1994: 344). As late as 1988, Mikhail Gorbachev was declaring his conviction that the Soviet peoples all belonged to "one large international family," as evinced by their "Soviet patriotism" (Kaiser 1994: 152; Dunlop 1997: 33–34).

The events of the 1980s and 1990s were to cast severe doubts on this claim, at least insofar as it suggested the decline of nationalist feeling and the adoption of a common Soviet identity. There was greater truth in the view that there had been a fundamental equalization of the nationalities, in their economic, social, cultural, and even political conditions. However, by a mechanism that Alexis de Tocqueville was the first to identify, this equalization, representing as it did an improvement in the conditions of many of the non-Russian nations, far from bringing about a decline in national attachment actually and paradoxically enhanced it. The more developed the nations were, the more uniform the patterns of urbanization, industrialization, and social mobility across the whole Soviet Union, the more pronounced became the nationalism of the non-Russian peoples and the more emboldened they were to express their aspirations. There was a kind of historical ingratitude in this that was not lost on the Russian people, who as the majority nation naturally and rightly claimed some credit for the progress that had been achieved. In response they began to formulate—perhaps for the first time ever, as a mass phenomenon— their own nationalism (Flenley 1996: 235–46).

In 1990, as Gorbachev strove to hold together the Soviet Union, the Russian nationalists under Boris Yeltsin finally—and against Gorbachev's wishes—got their own Communist Party, Komsomol, KGB, MVD, radio and television station, Academy of Sciences, trade union organization, and other trappings of a "normal" Union republic. On the eve of the breakup of the Soviet Union, the RSFSR had finally achieved equal status to the other republics (Dunlop 1997: 34). The Soviet Union might have been able to survive the nationalism of other peoples; but how easy would it be to confront the nationalism of the Russians themselves?

The Russians: Victims of Empire?

In 1994, returning to Russia after a nearly twenty-year exile in the United States, the novelist Alexander Solzhenitsyn published a long essay, *The Russian Question at the End of the Twentieth Century*.[40] In a synoptic review of Russian history, he castigated all Russian rulers from the time of Peter the Great through to the communist leadership of the Soviet Union for neglecting Russia and the Russian people. None of these rulers, he charged, had seen that it was "harmful . . . for the dominant nation in a state to create a multiethnic empire" ([1994] 1995: 38). In a distinctly Slavophile mode, he saw the Russian state as an alien body imposed on the native Russian people. In pursuit of imperial glory, and in a misguided attempt to prove themselves in the eyes of Western nations, they had engaged in costly and bloody foreign adventures that had brought terrible suffering to the Russian people and wrought long-term damage to Russian society. "That the Soviet Empire was not only unnecessary for us [the Russians], but ruinous," was Solzhenitsyn's verdict on the whole Soviet experiment, as it was on the empire created by the tsars ([1994] 1995: 88).

Nor did this sad story end with the collapse of the Soviet Union in 1991. For thanks to its policies—following those of the tsars—of encouraging Russian migration across the whole expanse of its empire, there were now the 25 million ethnic Russians—18 percent of all Russians, "the largest diaspora in the world by far"—who found themselves in the "near-abroad," marooned in the newly independent states formed out of the former Soviet republics. Taken with the disastrous economic policies of the 1990s, and the wholesale plundering of state property by the ex-Communist *nomenklatura*, his people were living through "the Great Russian Catastrophe" ([1994] 1995: 104).

Solzhenitsyn was by no means the only one who in these years saw Russians as among the principal victims of the Soviet Empire (Brubaker 1996: 52; Flenley 1996: 234; Rowley 1997: 321). Boris Yeltsin, who seized the reins of Russian nationalism and took Russia out of the Soviet Union, spoke bitterly of the "Marxist experiment" that was tried out on the Russian people: "Instead of some country in Africa, they began this experiment with us," which has "pushed us off the path the world's civilized countries have taken" (in Kumar 2001: 171). Opinion polls in December 1991 showed that a majority of Russians favored the dissolution of the Soviet Union and the creation of an independent Russia—a marked shift in opinion from only a few years previously (Dunlop 1997: 42–45; Beissinger 2006: 295).

The irony of this was not lost on anyone. Russia was supposedly the dominant nation in the Soviet Union, as it had been in the tsarist empire. It was easily the richest, largest, and most populous unit. Its language was widely accepted as the lingua franca of the multinational Soviet Empire. After some hesitation, its culture—the culture of Pushkin, Tolstoy, Dostoyevsky—was celebrated throughout the Soviet Union. It was strongly represented in the Soviet leadership—Stalin was the only non-Russian to hold the top office throughout its history, and Russians dominated most of the policy-making bodies in the USSR (Rywkin 1980: 182, 185; Medish 1980: 193; Brubaker 1996: 42). Russians were clearly "the first among equals." How could it be that they could become, or see themselves as, *victims* of empire?

The Russians were not of course the first or only imperial people to think of themselves as having suffered from their position of superiority. The same thought has affected the "state-bearing nations" of most European empires— Castilians, Austrian Germans, Turks, English, French. It even occurred to the Romans of the later Roman Empire. Of course there is an element of speciousness in this. The ruling people do generally impart their character to the empire they have created and sustain. It is, in the broadest sense, "their empire," even where, as in the Soviet Union, they do not give their name to it. But as we have noted several times, they generally have to repress their own identity, and their own claims, in the interests of the management of the empire and its general well-being. That can easily lead some of their members to feel that, of all the nations of the empire, theirs has been singled out for discriminatory treatment—that they are the victims of "positive" or "reverse discrimination," "affirmative action" on behalf of others and against them. *Because* they are the dominant nation, they must subordinate themselves to the needs and desires of others.

The Russian sense of bearing the brunt of "reverse discrimination" goes back a long way, present as much in the tsarist as the Soviet Empire. "O Tsar, bestow upon your own people what you have already granted the Poles and Finns" was a popular Russian mock-prayer from the early nineteenth century onward (Pearson 1989: 102). The 80 percent of the Russian population who were peasants felt their relative deprivation particularly keenly. Peasants on crown-owned lands, who fared better than those on the lands of the nobility, were mostly non-Russians. Serfdom was general in the central Russian lands, but there was no serfdom in Finland, Central Asia, or the Far East. Peasants in Poland (1807) and the Baltic provinces (1816–19) were emancipated decades before Russian peasants were freed (1861), and on far better terms. And in an attempt to counter the influence of the Polish landowning class, peasants in Belorussia, western Ukraine, and Lithuania were treated better than their Russian counterparts (Kaiser 1994: 49). This was "internal colonialism" with a vengeance. Dominic Lieven goes so far as to compare the position of Russian peasants to that of the native, non-European, peoples of Europe's overseas empires (Lieven 2001: 257; cf. Etkind 2011: 124–28; Kappeler 2001: 124–25; Morrison 2012: 338).

The Soviet Union's radical policies of *korenizatsiia*, indigenization, were bound to create similar feelings of neglect and disparagement on the part of the Russian population. Lenin's and Stalin's fear and distrust of "Great Russian chauvinism" were real and enduring. The Bolshevik theoretician Nikolai Bukharin stated the official position clearly: "As the former Great Power nation, we [Russians] should indulge the nationalist aspirations [of the non-Russians] and place ourselves in an unequal position, in the sense of making still greater concessions to the national current. Only by such a policy, when we place ourselves artificially in a position lower in comparisons with others, only by such a price can we purchase for ourselves the trust of the formerly oppressed nations." Quoting this, Terry Martin comments: "Soviet policy did indeed call for Russian sacrifice in the realm of nationalities policy: majority Russian territory was assigned to non-Russian republics; Russians had to accept ambitious Affirmative Action programs for non-Russians; they were asked to learn non-Russian languages; and traditional Russian culture was stigmatized as a culture of oppression" (Martin 2001: 17).

The Russian nation, says Martin, "was always the Soviet Union's awkward nationality, too large to ignore but likewise too formidable to give the same institutional status as the Soviet Union's other major nationalities" (2001: 395; cf. Dunlop 1997: 29). Throughout the Soviet period, Russians lacked many of the key institutions possessed by the other titular nations. While there were Ukrainian, Belorussian, Armenian, Uzbek, and other "national" communist parties, there was no Russian Communist Party ("We didn't forget," Stalin's foreign secretary Viacheslav Molotov once said, "there was just no place for it"). There was no separate Russian Ministry of Foreign Affairs, unlike the case with other republics. There was no Russian Academy of Sciences to set besides all the other national academies of sciences (there was a Soviet Academy of Sciences in Moscow). All the other Union republics had their own national radio and TV organizations; Russia had none. Television and radio broadcasting in the RSFSR was directly managed by the USSR Council of Ministers' State Committee for TV and Radio (Rywkin 1980: 179). When in the enthusiasm for the promotion of national cultures in the 1930s, scientific research institutes of national culture were set up in the national republics—there were over forty by 1936—none was provided for Russian national culture. Russia had to make do with the calculatedly named All-Union Scientific Research Institute of National Culture set up in Moscow in 1934 (Martin 2001: 445).

Territorially too Russia was the "awkward nation." Unlike all the other Soviet Socialist Republics, the RSFSR did not have its own capital—Moscow doubled as its capital and that of the USSR as a whole. It was even difficult to decide what constituted Russian territory, comparable to the territories of the other Union republics. The RSFSR was huge but it was also amorphous. It contained many ethnic groups—around a hundred—apart from ethnic Russians. It was in fact, uniquely in the USSR, not a national but a *federated* republic—the "Russia-wide (*Rossiiskaia*) Soviet Federated Socialist Republic," hence a kind of microcosm of the multinational Soviet Union itself. "Significantly," says Francine Hirsch, "neither the party nor Narkomnats [People's Commissariat for the Affairs of the Nationalities] ever seriously discussed giving 'the Great Russians' their own ethnoterritorial unit. To do so would have been gratuitous; the working assumption was that the Russians, as the state-bearing people of the former Russian Empire and the most dominant nation of the Russian Soviet Federation, did not need their own ethnoterritorial unit. All of the territories that remained outside the official ethnoterritorial units were understood to be 'Russian' by default" (Hirsch 2005: 69). As Yuri Slezkine puts it, "the Russian nationality was developed, dominant and thus irrelevant. The Russian territory was 'unmarked' and, in effect, consisted of those lands that had not been claimed by the non-Russians known as 'nationals'" (Slezkine [1994] 1996: 210). Russian territory was residual, "empty," space—as unfilled with content as the Russian nation itself, which had to see itself merged with the larger entity of the Soviet Union, just as earlier it had to submerge its identity in the Russian Empire.

That was indeed the story over and over again. Russians were everywhere and nowhere. Russia did not need its own institutions because it was somehow, inevitably and insensibly, bound up with all institutions of the Soviet Union. Soviet institutions were surrogates for Russian institutions. This could be seen as both a loss and a gain. It was a loss insofar as Russia was not given the opportunity to develop its own national consciousness—a serious obstacle to its future development, according to outside scholars such as Geoffrey Hosking, as we have seen, as well as to native Russian commentators such as Solzhenitsyn. It was a gain insofar as, as Michael Rywkin puts it, the RSFSR could regard itself "as synonymous with a USSR to which other republics are just appendages" (1980: 179). Just as the English confuse English and British, so it has been common for Russians as well as others to confuse Russian and Soviet.[41] For them Soviet institutions were vehicles for their own identities and interests as much as they might be for some greater, all-union, identity and interest. Or rather, for Russians the two might be just two sides of the same coin. To promote the Soviet Union was to promote Russia, and vice versa.

Moscow might be the capital of the multinational Soviet Union but it was also the historic center of "Mother Russia."

The conflation of national and imperial could be a source of pride to the Russians in the Soviet Union as much as it was to them in the tsarist empire. It could confer on them that "missionary nationalism" that is so common a feature of all dominant or "state-bearing" nations in empires. In the case of the Soviet Union, the adoption of the mission was the easier for the fact that it expressed the official, repeatedly declared ideology of the Soviet state. The Soviet Union existed to establish a world community of socialism and so liberate humanity from its chains. Russia and Russians of necessity, by virtue of their size and numbers, and the dominance of their culture, would have to play the leading role in achieving that goal of universal freedom (cf. Flenley 1996: 231; Dunlop 1997: 31; Khalid 2007: 128). Even if some Russians, at various times and in varying numbers, doubted the possibility of reaching that goal, there was pride enough to be gained from being the chief actor in a world-transforming venture. Whether or not it could change the whole world, to challenge the hegemony of the United States, to pit communism against capitalism and so ignite revolutionary conflicts the world over, gave the Soviet Union a role and a standing in the world denied to most nations. Set besides that, national identity—if the question even arose—might seem a price worth paying.

That was not always the view of course; and increasingly, in the "era of stagnation" of the late 1960s and the 1970s, as the socialist vision faded, voices began to be raised calling upon Russians to look to their own interests, as other nations in the Soviet Union were looking to theirs. Solzhenitsyn's writings of the 1970s began the critique that he developed more fully in the 1990s; and some of the *samizdat* literature of those years also, as in the journal *Veche*, deplored the Russian people's loss of dignity, self-respect, and greatness.[42] There had been earlier concerns of this kind as well. In the 1930s policies of indigenization had provoked protests from Russian party members who felt that Russians were being unfairly discriminated against. Concern was expressed at the lack of specifically Russian institutions, compared to other republics. There was a sense that Russia's great contribution to the revolution, and the "brotherly help" offered to the more "backward" non-Russian nations, had not been recognized. There was resentment too at the transfer of Russian territory to non-Russian republics (Martin 2001: 271, 400–401, 445, 454).

Partly in response to this, there was a certain rehabilitation of Russian culture in the 1930s, and a reversal of the extreme hostility to traditional Russian culture shown in the early years of the regime. Pushkin was proclaimed "the great Russian poet," but that at the same time made him the poet for "the toilers of all nationalities," and indeed the "national poet" of the whole Soviet Union (Martin 2001: 456, 461; Hosking 2006: 178). Russia was declared to be "first among equals" in the general "friendship of the peoples" prevailing in the Soviet Union. Russian culture and the Russian language were promoted in the schools and universities, with textbooks emphasizing Russia's past struggles and its leading role in the Russian Revolution (Martin 2001: 432–61; Brandenberger 2001: 275; Hosking 2006: 148–59).

The high point of this celebration of Russianness, by general agreement, was during the "Great Fatherland War" of 1941–45. It was during this war that Stalin made his famous speeches, for instance that of November 1941, in praise of "the great Russian nation—the nation of Plekhanov and Lenin, of Belinsky and Chernyshevsky, of Pushkin and Tolstoy, of Gorki and Chekhov, of Glinka and Tchaikovsky, of Sechernov and Pavlov, of Suvorov and Kutuzov!" (Rees 1998: 88). At the end of the war, at a banquet in the Kremlin on May 24, 1945, in honor of Soviet military commanders, Stalin declared: "I drink above all to the health of the Russian people, because it is the outstanding nation among all the nations which make up the Soviet Union. I drink to the health of the Russian people because in this war it has deserved general recognition as the driving force among the peoples of the Soviet Union" (Brandenberger 2001: 287; Hosking 2006: 211).

Scholars have rightly cautioned against seeing these Second World War speeches, and Stalin's later policies generally, as representing the triumph of Russian nationalism and the conversion of the Soviet Union into something like a (Russian) nation-state. Even those who, like Terry Martin, see the rehabilitation of Russian culture as an important development after the 1930s, declare firmly that "the Soviet Union was not a nation-state," and that "no attempt was ever made . . . to turn the Soviet Union into a Russian nation-state" (Martin 2001: 461; cf. Rasiak 1980: 161; Brubaker 1996: 28–29; Slezkine 2000: 233; Suny 2001: 26). Certainly in the conditions of the world war, with Russian cities such as Stalingrad, Leningrad, and Moscow enduring terrible hardships, it was not surprising that the Soviet leadership should appeal to patriotic themes drawn from Russian culture and history. Particularly inspiring would be those great figures who defended Russia in critical times. "May you," declared Stalin in a speech in Red Square on November 7, 1941, "be inspired in this war by the heroic figures of our great ancestors, Alexander Nevsky, Dimitri Donskoi, Kuzma Minin, Dimitri Pozharsky, Alexander Suvorov, Michael Kutuzov!" (Rees 1998: 89; see also Brandenberger 2001: 277–79).

But even then, even in the midst of the "Great Patriotic War," it was never clear whether it was Russian or Soviet patriotism that was being promoted and celebrated (Kohn 1971: 58; Brandenberger 2001: 288). Even Stalin's rapprochement with the Russian Orthodox Church during the war was designed not to appeal to Russian patriotism but to make the Church serve as a rallying force for all Orthodox believers in the region and, after the war, for the Orthodox community worldwide—"a kind of Orthodox International, headed by the Moscow Patriarch, as a rival to the Vatican" (Hosking 2006: 246; cf. Rywkin 1980: 183). Moreover, after the war a determined effort was made to merge Russian and Soviet, "*russkoe, rossiskoe, sovetskoe,*" and to promote the idea and reality of the "Soviet people," *sovetskii narod.* Nikita Khrushchev and Leonid Brezhnev both put themselves energetically behind such a program, the latter in the early 1970s launching an elaborate and highly publicized campaign to promote the idea of "The Soviet People—A New Historic Community of Persons" (Fedyshyn 1980: 151; Rasiak 1980: 159; Flenley 1996: 229, 233–34). As we have seen, the 1977 Constitution proclaimed that such an entity had in fact come into being. Nor was this simply official rhetoric. Soviet patriotism, as Adeeb Khalid says, "had real content based on common patterns of education and mobilization, participation in the Soviet economy and Soviet rituals, and, for men, conscription in the Soviet army" (Khalid 2007: 135). If Eugen Weber is right in his account of the making of French national identity, had it been given more time it is not impossible that the Soviet Union—as perhaps Yugoslavia—might have been able to forge a common Soviet identity.

The promotion of a supraethnic ideal such as the Soviet people was particularly important in the conditions of the new international Cold War. Russian nationalism would have been no use in this war, rather a hindrance, and was accordingly discouraged. What became particularly pronounced was anti-Westernism, and this demanded an all-Union response and as far as possible an all-Union identity. It was East versus West, communism versus capitalism, the USSR versus the United States, the Warsaw Pact countries versus NATO. This was a global conflict, a conflict of global actors. It demanded civilizations, not nation-states. Nationalism could be used, as it was in Third World liberation struggles, but it was in principle—as recognized from the outset by Lenin and Stalin, following Marx—antithetical to the task the Soviet Union had set itself. "For the leading force in the international communist movement to adopt an outright nationalist position would have been unthinkable and untenable" (Rees 1998: 100; cf. Hosking 2006: 230–36).

In the end Russian nationalism remained a weak and "essentially contested" thing. Just as in the tsarist empire, where Russians were expected to carry the burden of rule without asserting their own nationality, so in the Soviet Union Russians as the "state-bearing nation" were forced to restrict the cultivation and expression of their own nationhood (while promoting that of others). Empire and nation, Soviet and Russian, were too much mixed together, too difficult to separate, even more perhaps than in the case of the eponymous Russian Empire. In the "communal apartment" that was the USSR, every nationality but the Russians had a room of its own. "In the center of the Soviet apartment there was a large and amorphous space not clearly defined as a room, unmarked by national paraphernalia, unclaimed by 'its own' nation and inhabited by a very large number of austere but increasingly sensitive proletarians" (Slezkine [1994] 1996: 217). Lurking in the corridors and kitchen, ubiquitous but curiously lost, the Russians could peer into the rooms inhabited by increasingly self-conscious nationalities but lacked the credentials to lay claim to their own. If we think this is anomalous in a period in which the nation-state is supposed to have achieved dominance, we should remember that for much of the time the Soviet Union was in existence the English were also having the same difficulty in separating themselves from their empire and in developing a distinct English national consciousness. The Russian case is by no means unique—most imperial peoples in the twentieth century have experienced much the same difficulties.

The challenge becomes of course most acute after the end of empire. The disintegration of the Soviet Empire confronted Russians, even more than other nations of the former Soviet Union, with pressing questions: Who are we? What is our identity and how do we promote it? Can Russia indeed ever be a "normal" nation-state? As the central element for hundreds of years of a succession of empires, all its experience has been imperial. How does one learn to be a nation-state in a matter of a few years? Within days of proclaiming that the USSR no longer existed, the Russian government of Boris Yeltsin adopted the double-headed eagle, the old symbol of the tsarist empire, as the state emblem of the new Russian Federation. The preamble to the new constitution introduced in 1993 proclaimed, "We, the multi-national people of the Russian Federation. . . ." Although ethnic Russians make up 82 percent of the Russian Federation, some 25 million Russians live outside it (Dixon 1996: 47). Not all of this is unique to Russia—most so-called nation-states are multinational or multiethnic, and many have large diasporas living in other states. But given Russia's long imperial past, stretching back over five centuries, the difficulties of creating something like a viable nation-state become especially formidable. Russia might like to think of itself today as a "great power" rather than an "imperial power," but "within the post-Soviet context . . . the distinction between the legitimate pursuit of [national] state interests and empire-building is entirely nebulous and likely to remain so."[43]

Under Vladimir Putin's long reign, indeed, a new tsar seems to have seated himself on the Russian throne. In August 2008, Russia established a protectorate over the former Soviet territories of Abkhazia and South Ossetia, detaching them from an independent Georgia. It also continues to prop up the "Pridnestrovian Moldavian Republic" (Transnistria), refusing to accept it as an integral part an independent Moldova. In March 2014 Russia annexed the Crimea, declaring it a Russian territory that just unfortunately happened to have been left in Ukraine when that country became independent in 1991. The fate of east Ukraine, and of the country as a whole, hung in the balance. In all these former Soviet territories, opinion polls show that the majority of the population—and not just ethnic Russians—trust the Russian leadership more than their own and would be happy to be absorbed in the Russian Federation (Toal and O'Loughlin 2014). Putin is on record as having declared that the breakup of the Soviet Union was "the greatest geopolitical catastrophe of the [twentieth] century," and "a genuine tragedy" for the Russian people (Beissinger 2008: 3). There will be no new Soviet Union; but the engines of empire seem once more to have started up.

6

The British Empire

How an archipelago of rainy islands off the north-west coast of Europe came
to rule the world is one of the fundamental questions not just of British but of
world history.

—NIALL FERGUSON (2004: XI)

I know no example of it, either in ancient or modern history. No Caesar or
Charlemagne ever presided over a dominion so peculiar.

—BENJAMIN DISRAELI ON THE BRITISH EMPIRE,
SPEECH IN THE HOUSE OF LORDS, APRIL 8, 1878
(IN KOEBNER AND SCHMIDT 1964: 136)

Paradox! The most insular people in the world managed to establish the
largest empire the world has ever seen. No, not paradox. Insularity, like
empire-building, requires superb self-confidence, a conviction of one's moral
superiority.

—PAUL SCOTT, A DIVISION OF THE SPOILS
(THE RAJ QUARTET) ([1975] 1977: 106)

Overseas and Overland Empires

The empires we have been considering in the last three chapters—the Ottoman, Habsburg, and Russian empires—were primarily land empires. Each of
these grew by the expansion of the center from a core outward, as it took in
contiguous lands and incorporated them in its rule. The geographical proximity of metropole and periphery meant that, characteristically, not just the
physical but the cultural and social distance between the two was not as great
as in overseas empires. This might lead some observers and commentators

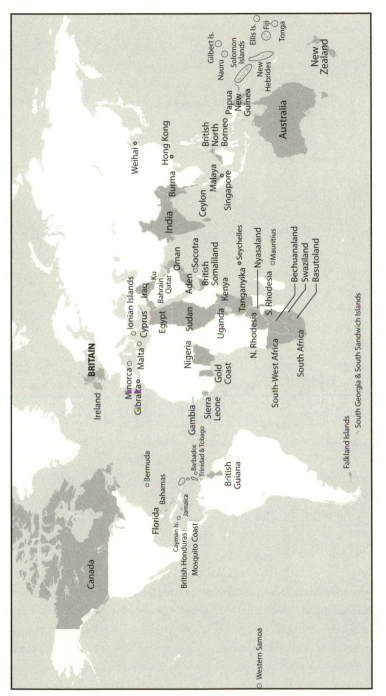

MAP 6.1. The British Empire at its greatest extent, c. 1920

The map is labeled with the following places:

Western Samoa

Canada

Mosquito Coast
British Honduras
Cayman Is.
Jamaica
Florida
Bahamas
Bermuda

British Guiana
Trinidad & Tobago
Barbados
Gambia
Sierra Leone
Gold Coast
Nigeria

Falkland Islands
South Georgia & South Sandwich Islands

Ireland
BRITAIN
Minorca
Gibraltar
Malta
Ionian Islands
Cyprus
Egypt
Sudan

Iraq
Ku
Bahrain
Qatar
Oman
Aden
British Somaliland
Socotra
Uganda
Kenya
N. Rhodesia
S. Rhodesia
Tanganyika
Nyasaland
Seychelles
Mauritius
South-West Africa
South Africa
Bechuanaland
Swaziland
Basutoland

Weihai
India
Burma
Hong Kong
Ceylon
Malaya
Singapore
British North Borneo
Papua New Guinea

Australia

New Hebrides
Solomon Islands
Nauru
Gilbert Is.
Ellis Is.
Fiji
Tonga

New Zealand

to treat the empire almost like a nation-state, as we saw in the case of some nineteenth-century Russian historians. This was wrong—an expression more perhaps of aspiration than of reality. In no case were the Ottoman, Habsburg, or Russian empires like nation-states; the rise of nationalism, that of the dominant ethnicity as much that of other groups, signaled the demise of empire, not its realization. But the relative nearness of metropole and periphery, the difficulty sometimes of separating the two, meant that relations between the dominant ethnicities and others could be very different from what was generally the case in overseas empires.

All empires aim at universality, land empires as much overseas empires. Size and contiguity do not change that. Compared to modern empires the Roman Empire was relatively small, but that it no way diminished its claim to universality—so powerful indeed that it was handed on to the modern empires as one of the principal elements of the Roman legacy. The Ottoman Empire wished to universalize Islam, the Habsburgs Catholicism, the Russians Orthodoxy. All empires, of whatever size and character, think they have found the truth of the world, and they wish to spread that truth worldwide, to make of the world one ecumene.

But size, especially as expressed in character, can make a difference to claims of universality. It can affect their credibility. The Russian Empire was large, but it was restricted to the Eurasian landmass. Apart from a brief foray into North America, it did not attempt to spread its rule beyond its Eurasian home. Similarly with the Ottomans and the Austrian Habsburgs—despite occasional impulses they too restricted themselves to contiguous landmasses. They might conceive their mission in universal terms, but without a worldwide presence how likely was it to be accomplished? Islam became the second-largest religion in the world, but it took the combined efforts of several empires, not just that of the Ottomans, to achieve it. Catholicism did spread worldwide, but not much of that can be attributed to the Austrian Habsburgs (though the Spanish Habsburgs, with their overseas empire, played a major part). And how likely was it that Orthodoxy would be established in Africa or Latin America without a Russian presence there? Even the Soviet Union, despite its self-proclaimed role as the center of the world socialist revolution, was unable to break out of its landlocked enclosure and had to settle eventually for "Socialism in One Country."[1]

The overseas empires were among the largest in the world. That was true of the overseas empire of the Spanish Habsburgs, as well as of the Portuguese, Dutch, British, and French empires. But more important than the actual size was their character. Unlike the land empires, these were empires whose imprint was truly global. They established themselves on practically every continent and in every quarter of the globe. Their impact was worldwide, as was their legacy. Unlike the land empires, they could aim to make their missions universal in a more than a symbolic way. Through their religion, their language, their laws, their settling with their own peoples whole sections of the globe, they aimed to make their universal mission a concrete, institutionalized, reality. There really could be a Spanish, a British, or a French world, in more than just name.

The European overseas empires were something new in the history of empires. There had been vast, continent-spanning empires before, as with the empire of Alexander the Great. The short-lived Mongol Empire of Genghis Khan was actually the largest the world has ever known. Even the fact of being an overseas empire was not new, if we include the Phoenician and the Athenian empires. But the scale and spread of the European overseas empires were unprecedented. Within an astonishingly short period of time, starting in the fifteenth century, they established themselves all over the world, in the process discovering and colonizing continents known previously only to the indigenous inhabitants. The European overseas empires became a fact of world history in a way that had not been true even of the greatest empires of the past, such as that of Alexander. The world that exists today is in good part the creation of the European overseas empires.

This and the next chapter consider the two largest overseas empires, the British and the French. There are some interesting parallels between them, as well of course as differences. The same is true if they are compared with the Spanish Empire, the other overseas empire discussed—rather more briefly—in this book. But the parallels between them and the Spanish case are fewer. Here the difference of historical time is critical. Both the British and French empires reached their peak a long time after the Spanish Empire had declined. This does not prevent comparison, but it sets limits to what can be gained by it. The world in which the British and French empires grew—mostly in the eighteenth and nineteenth centuries—was vastly different from the early modern world of the Spanish Empire. For one thing, the Spanish (along with the Portuguese) had been pioneers in overseas empires, and both the French and the British learned from their experience. This did not necessarily make the British and the French better imperialists, but it affected their behavior, for better or worse.

But more important were the changes in technology and communications that transformed the relations between the metropole and the peripheries. Between the Spanish and the French and British empires lay the Industrial

Revolution, and with it the development of the railway, the steamship, the electric telegraph, the Gatling gun, and a host of other new inventions and innovations. This gave the British and the French many new tools of imperial rule; but by the same token it gave those very tools to their enemies, both within and beyond their empires. Add to that the rise of new anti-imperial ideologies such as nationalism and socialism, and one can see that the British and French were operating in an environment very different from that of the sixteenth-century Spanish and Portuguese. We can thus understand why the British and French empires deviated significantly from the patterns of early modern imperial rule.

The World's Largest Empire: How "Peculiar"?

The British Empire grew to be the largest ever in world history (Taagepera 1978a). At its height, after the First Word War, it occupied a quarter of the world's landmass and incorporated nearly a quarter of the world's population—more than three times the size of the French Empire, its nearest rival among the overseas empires (Ferguson 2004: 240–41). The Russian Empire might have lasted longer as the world's largest, but in its global reach it never matched the British, and in any case as the world's largest it was overtaken by the British by the early nineteenth century.

The English were the dominant ethnicity, the "state-bearing people," of the British Empire. The English in fact can claim—if somewhat embarrassingly these days—to be among the most imperial people in the world, if not *the* most imperial, even more than the Russians and equaled only perhaps by the Romans. For long before they constructed the British overseas empire, they had already, nearer home, created "the first English empire" (Davies 2000). Already in the tenth century the chronicler Aethelweard was declaring that "Britain is now called England, thereby assuming the name of the victors," and early in the eleventh century the English king Edward the Confessor, reversing the terminology, laid claim to be *rex totius Britanniae*—king of all Britain. After the Norman Conquest of 1066 these claims were rapidly made a concrete reality, with the conquest of Wales and Ireland and the near conquest of Scotland (union with which was finally forced in 1707). A "United Kingdom of Great Britain and Ireland" was in being by the early nineteenth century—the completion of centuries of English conquest of its "near abroad," and the creation of an "inner empire," "the British Empire in Europe," dominated by England (Kumar 2003: 60–88, 180; cf. Hirst 2012).

This early existence as an imperial people created the characteristic problem for all imperial peoples, how do we define ourselves in relation to our empire? Who are *we*, by comparison with the other peoples in the empire, who generally have a surer sense of who *they* are? The answer, as we have seen in other cases, was normally to merge one's national identity with an imperial one, to lose oneself in the empire as one's greater, grander, and more important home. So too the English, in their "land empire" of Great Britain, came to redefine themselves as Britons, or rather to conflate English and British identities, so that often when they said "English," they meant British, and when they talked about "the British way of life," they often filled it with English content (Kumar 2003: 1–17; Colley [1992] 1994). Like the Russians and other imperial peoples, the English found it hard to separate nation and empire.

Our concern here is mainly with the British overseas empire, the "outer empire," not the inner, domestic one. But it is important to bear in mind that the English had been an imperial people well before they expanded overseas. Their imperial identity had been formed before, in the sixteenth century, they began the overseas colonization and conquest that over the next two centuries brought them a world empire. The British identity, emerging from the conquest and unification of Britain, was further solidified by overseas empire, so that the empire was as British as the United Kingdom that made it.

The British Empire overseas was a continuation of the English/British Empire at home; the British identity that was constructed in the homelands was available for elaboration and export abroad (cf. Spain in the linking of the *reconquista* in the peninsula with the conquest and settlement of the Americas). This was the theme of one of the most important works on the British Empire, Sir John Seeley's *The Expansion of England* (1883). It was encapsulated in the concept of "Greater Britain," considered below. As expressed by one of its leading exponents, C. P. Lucas, it took the view that "Great Britain repeated its own story on an immense scale, and widened into a Commonwealth, all the vital elements of which had already existed, in embryo or in active life, in the Old Country" (in Lee 2004: 129). This attractive vision had its problems, and its limitations; but it expressed a fundamental truth about the British Empire and the way it was seen by many people in both the home country and the colonies.

An intermediate term between the two empires is offered by Ireland, often declared, following Friedrich Engels, to be England's "first colony" (Marx and Engels 1972: 83). Since Ireland was conquered and colonized in the twelfth century, it clearly belongs to the first wave of English imperialism. There was a second wave of plantations—including those in the province of Ulster—and a second conquest in the late sixteenth century and the first half of the seventeenth: at precisely the time that the English were beginning their first overseas settlements in North America. The coincidence in time of these two processes, and certain similarities in the manner of colonization, naturally prompt many people to see a connection between them. Ireland seems to belong to both the first empire and the second, overseas, iteration. "Ireland," says Niall Ferguson, "was the experimental laboratory of British colonization and Ulster was the prototype plantation" (Ferguson 2004: 57).[2]

No one can doubt that Ireland, along with Wales, belongs to the "first English empire." It was a key element in the process of internal colonialism whereby the United Kingdom was created (Hechter [1975] 1999). But how far should it also be seen as belonging to the second English/British empire, the overseas empire? How far was Ireland a colony, "another India for the English," as the Irish Earl of Thomond put it in the seventeenth century (Ohlmeyer 2006: 26)? This was the analogy beloved of a whole generation of Irish nationalists, as well as English and other radicals such as Karl Marx and Friedrich Engels. It has also in recent years been popular among Irish historians and cultural theorists.

There were many reasons for finding the parallels plausible. In Ireland there was an "alien" ruling class, especially after the seventeenth century in the form of the Protestant "Ascendancy." There were local collaborators—Catholic as well as Protestant—as in other British colonies. There was the wholesale introduction of English laws and English administration. There was the introduction of the English language, the "language of the oppressor," and the suppression of the native Celtic. Following the English Reformation, there was the persecution of Catholicism, the religion of the majority of the Irish, and the imposition of the Anglican Church of Ireland as the Established Church. There was the expropriation of native lands, and the plantation of "outsiders," Scots and English, with customs and religions different from those of the natives. There were restrictions on direct Irish trade with the colonies, similar to those imposed on the American colonies. There was the frequent, racially charged, portrayal of the Irish as backward and barbaric. There was even the fact that some of the same people responsible for English policies in Ireland—most noticeably Humphrey Gilbert, Walter Raleigh, and William Penn—went on to play prominent roles in the early English settlements in Virginia, Maryland, and elsewhere. Towering above all these, in many ways, is the catastrophic Irish famine of the 1840s, seen as comparable to the Bengal famine of 1942, and like that one blamed on Ireland's colonial rulers. Add to this the highly imperial image of a lieutenant-governor ruling, on behalf of the crown, from Dublin Castle, and one seems to have a clear picture of Ireland as an oppressed and exploited colony of a classic kind.[3]

But as many have suggested, there are good grounds for questioning this conclusion. It is one thing, and a reasonable one, to consider Ireland as part of England's land empire. That would allow us, contrary to a common view, to see for instance the geographical proximity of Ireland to England as no grounds for refusing to think of the relationship in imperial terms. As we have seen with the Russians in relation to the Tatars, proximity to the imperial nation is no barrier to conquest of a colonial kind—if anything, it prompts and even appears to necessitate it. The strongest and most enduring reason for England's determination to take and to hold on to Ireland was its concern not to allow its enemies—successively the Spanish and the French, later the Germans—a back door for a possible invasion of British territory (Bartlett 2006: 61). For vital security reasons, over and above any other considerations, Ireland had to be incorporated as an "internal colony" of the English empire.

But in relation to the idea of Ireland as part of the overseas empire, geographical propinquity does matter. The amount of constant to-ing and fro-ing between Ireland and mainland Britain is highly unusual in the relation between metropole and periphery; so too is the settlement of hundreds of thousands of Irish in British cities, such as Liverpool, London, and Glasgow—a "reverse colonization," if one wants to see it that way.[4] Other well-known features of Ireland's position point to the difficulties of seeing it as a classic colony. Until 1801, Ireland was a separate kingdom (though sharing a monarch with the English and Scottish) with its own Parliament at Dublin. After the Union of 1801, Ireland like Scotland became an integral part of the metropolitan core of the empire. One hundred Irish MPs—several of them Catholics after the Emancipation of 1829—sat in the Westminster Parliament, and in the latter part of the nineteenth century often held the balance of power between the two main parties in the House of Commons. Economically and socially, the Anglo-Irish gentry became an integral part of the British ruling class, and Anglo-Irish literature—Swift, Berkeley, Burke, Wilde, Yeats, Shaw, and others—became a vital component of British culture. Nor does the Irish economy seem to fit the colonial model of an exploited, underdeveloped economy—in the later nineteenth century especially, both Irish agriculture and Irish industry benefited from the British and imperial connection, and Britain's balance of trade with Ireland favored the Irish. Even more tellingly numerous Irish—both

Protestants and Catholics—shared in the management of the British Empire, as administrators, soldiers, settlers, missionaries, merchants, doctors and educators. None of this sounds like the condition of the classic colony.[5]

Certainly Ireland seems to occupy a most peculiar status in "the British world," a point brought home vividly when, after Irish independence in 1921 and even more after Ireland seceded from the Commonwealth in 1949, Irish citizens were allowed to travel freely, to work, and even to vote in Britain. The Irish, in other words, unlike newly independent Commonwealth nations, were to enjoy on equal terms all the rights of citizens of the United Kingdom and its colonies: a most extraordinary position for an "ex-colony" that—alone in the Commonwealth—had remained stubbornly neutral during the Second World War, and that immediately after it, declaring itself a republic, withdrew even from membership of the British Commonwealth of Nations (Hansen 2000: 44–48).

Ireland may be thought an oddity in the British Empire; but for many people the British Empire is full of such oddities. In recent years there has been an increasing tendency to emphasize the higgledy-piggledy nature of the empire, the heterogeneity of its parts, the haphazard way it was put together. John Darwin observes that the word "imperialism" had no settled meaning in nineteenth- and twentieth-century Britain "partly because the British *imperium* was so bafflingly diverse. For the real British Empire was not just a bloc of territories to rule. It was a colossal jigsaw of dependencies and protectorates, settlement colonies and 'spheres of influence', trucial states and treaty-ports, enclaves and entrepots, gunboats and garrisons, shipping lanes and coaling stations, cable routes and airways, consulates and concessions, infrastructures and investments, barren rocks and bases. How it actually worked or was held together, even how they acquired it, was a mystery to even the cleverest of its rulers. . . . They had no English name for this crazy construct: the closest they came was a dog-Latin tag, the Pax Britannica" (Darwin 2005: 6). In a later full-scale treatment Darwin eschewed the term "the British Empire" altogether. Instead, following Adam Smith's declaration that the British Empire "has hitherto been not an empire, but the project of an empire," he called his book *The Empire Project* (Darwin 2009: 25). As if to hammer home the point, the next book was called *Unfinished Empire*, and again stressed "the improvised and provisional character" of the British Empire, the fact that it was "always an empire-in-making, indeed an empire scarcely half-made" (2012: xii).[6]

Darwin's view here chimes with one of the most famous observations on the growth of the British Empire, Sir John Seeley's celebrated remark of 1883 that "we seem, as it were, to have conquered and peopled half the world in a fit of absence of mind" (Seeley [1883] 1971: 12). Though not always acknowledging it, several prominent scholars in recent years have followed Seeley in emphasizing the unplanned, unintended, and unacknowledged character of the British Empire. Bill Nasson, for instance, talks of the empire as "a peculiarly mangled creation, seemingly pieced together almost accidentally from disparate strips of the globe," and "lacking any consistent pattern of co-ordinated empire construction" (Nasson 2006: 11). Like Topsy, it seems, the British empire just "growed." It might seem to others the greatest empire the world had ever seen, but to the British themselves it remained something mysterious and unfathomable.

That very lack of self-consciousness, that sense of something not quite understood or grasped, could lead to a feeling of insecurity and vulnerability. Linda Colley has suggested that contemporaries were acutely aware of Britain's small size in relation both to its competitors—France, Russia, the Ottoman Empire, later Germany and the United States—and to its own vast empire, and correspondingly afraid that its hold on empire was precarious and transient. "Greater Britain, that is the possessions of the British people over the sea," declared the geographer G. H. Johnson in 1902, "is one hundred and twenty-five times the size of Great Britain." "Because its core was so constrained," says Colley, "and because it depended on maritime power, Britain's empire was always overstretched, often superficial, and likely to be limited in duration" (Colley [2002] 2004: 378). Maya Jasanoff similarly highlights the "cracks and insecurities" in British power. She suggests that the triumphalism implicit in the idea of the "white man's burden" was to some extent "a piece of wishful thinking, a way of justifying and compensating for . . . the fundamental vulnerabilities and contradictions embedded in British imperial rule" (2005: 8, 11; cf. Deudney 2001: 192–93; Price 2008: 6–7, 57, 344).

If the British Empire was not the swaggering power it sometimes seemed to itself and others, it also perhaps did not figure as powerfully in the consciousness of the British people as one might have expected. It is not always remembered that what prompted Seeley's famous remark about England's absentminded imperialism was his acute awareness of the characteristic "indifference which we show towards this mighty phenomenon of the diffusion of our race and the expansion of our state." We did not, says Seeley, "allow it to affect our imagination or in any degree to change our ways of thinking; nor have we even now ceased to think of ourselves as simply a race inhabiting an island off the northern coast of the Continent of Europe" (Seeley

[1883] 1971: 12–13). A host of frustrated commentators, from John Stuart Mill to BBC officials during the Second World War, have similarly lamented the ignorance and indifference of the general population toward the empire. "We must unfortunately explain to these d——d fools why we want an Empire," expostulated Lord Milner in 1906. Even among those who should have cared, it was apparently difficult to arouse an interest in the empire. The House of Commons, it was frequently remarked, emptied when imperial matters came up for discussion.[7]

The climax—for the moment—of this strand of thinking about the empire might be said to be Bernard Porter's *The Absent-Minded Imperialists* (2004b). With its deliberate echo of Seeley, though going far beyond him, Porter sought to show that for nearly the whole of its history most British people knew little, cared less, and were in almost all important ways untouched by empire. A handful of upper- and upper-middle-class people—those who actually ran the empire—were interested and involved, but for the rest what mattered most were domestic concerns, such as work and the family. The British Empire, in other words, was "a class act." "So long as a minority of men (and their female helpmeets) was committed enough to actually ruling it, the rest of the population could be left to concentrate on other things. The empire made no great material demands on most people, at least none that they were aware of, and did not need their support or even their interest. All that was required was a minimum of apathy" (Porter 2004b: 307; see also 2008).

The views of Porter and others are salutary in reminding us that we cannot take for granted that the British Empire, for all its evident presence in the world, loomed large in the popular imagination. It is also valuable in questioning the sometimes mechanical assumptions of postcolonial scholars that the empire's impact on the metropolitan society—in the British as in other cases—*must* have been as profound and pervasive as it was on the populations of the colonial peripheries. These things have to be shown, by whatever empirical means are to hand; and if the evidence is not there, or is thin, then it is right to challenge the postcolonial theorists (who, with reference to their leader Edward Said, Porter provocatively terms "Saidists").

As it happens, there has been a stream of publications in recent years by major scholars of the British Empire aiming to show, in detailed monographs or wide-ranging inquiries, that the effects of the empire on British society, past and present, have been deep and long-lasting. Porter is aware of many of these, and it is in fact to counter their claims that he conducted his study.[8] But whatever our view of these works—by no means all or even most by card-carrying postcolonialists—or of Porter's response, it is simply wrong to think that there is no evidence to examine, that the argument for the impact of the British Empire on British society rests on mere assertion or unsupported assumption. That position is as dogmatic and uninformed as the opposite claim that empire can be found everywhere, in every nook and cranny of British society.

There is a further consideration. "Empiricism," in some of its more obvious forms, can be a crude thing. A reliance on opinion polls, for instance, or tests of the population's knowledge of this or that aspect of empire, are poor ways of assessing impact and influence (Thompson 2005: 207–9). Even an examination of the place of the empire in school and college syllabuses, or its presence in popular culture (both central to Porter's study), does not necessarily tell us much about whether or how the empire might affect consciousness and behavior. One does not have to be an extreme structuralist, or a psychoanalyst, to think that cultures and ideologies work in different ways and at arguably deeper levels. The whole point about an ideology, after all, is that it is disguised, that we are the last people to know that it is working on us. The structures of ideology, at the most rarefied level of social and political belief as well as the more mundane level of everyday life, operate mostly "behind our backs." We should remember that there is "banal imperialism" as much, and acting in much the same ways, as "banal nationalism," both working beneath the level of consciousness (Kumar 2012a: 298–304).

A similar caveat needs to be uttered regarding the declarations of Darwin and others that the British Empire was peculiarly disorganized and vulnerable. What empire has not thought of itself as woefully irregular, and struggled to bring order and reason into its discordant structures?[9] What empire has not felt fear and anxiety about its stability and continuance? One might almost say that such expressions of concern are defining qualities of empires (Robert Musil's sardonic account of the ramshackle nature of the Habsburg Empire comes particularly to mind). Most empires grow by the opportunistic exploitation of chance circumstances, rather than through some master plan (Hitler's short-lived empire perhaps indicates the fate of those who work to a master plan). Most fear that a change of circumstances will weaken or undermine them.

For all the strength of the recent historiography of the British Empire, a conspicuous weakness has been a lack of a comparative focus. The British Empire is so grand a spectacle, so global in its reach, that it is understandable that few have felt able to tackle it in a comparative manner.[10] But as a result claims are made about the British Empire that simply do not stand up in a comparative framework. All empires are different, all unique in their own ways. But they also share certain characteristic properties and problems, certain ways of seeing themselves and being seen. The British Empire was a far-flung, unwieldy assemblage of disparate parts. It was an unfinished, always evolving "project." Almost from the start, it feared for its future. All this can be said of all empires. All are more or less disorganized, all change, all express at regular intervals anxiety and concern about the health and stability of the empire ("decline and fall" is written in the master script of all empires). The British Empire may have been the world's largest empire; but size did not exempt it from empire's way.

An Empire of Parts

Like the Russian Empire, the British Empire can be seen to have gone through successive incarnations. And just as the Russian Empire gave way to the Soviet, so the English empire gave way to the British. Equally the confusion, among both natives and outsiders, as to what was Russian and what was Soviet was matched by a similar confusion as to what was English and what British. Russians dominated in their empires throughout, as did the English in their empires. But for the English as for the Russians that dominance brought with it a radical uncertainty, or perhaps better indifference, as to their own specific identity as a nation. For some that has been seen as the price paid for empire, for others perhaps a blessed inheritance (as mitigating the evils of nationalism). But certainly, compared, say, to their Irish, Welsh, and Scottish neighbors, the English throughout the imperial period were inclined to ignore or play down questions as to their own national identity, as unfitting for an imperial people. As with the Russians, the question was inevitably to surface with considerable force after the end of empire.

Ged Martin (1972: 562) asks, "Was there a British empire at all?" raising the question of how we should describe and analyze so large and heterogeneous a complex. A common answer, combining both chronological and geographical features, has been to identify a series of British empires. There was the "First British Empire," based largely on the North American and Caribbean colonies, and lasting roughly from the late sixteenth century to the loss of the American colonies in 1783. There then followed a "Second British Empire," focused especially on India and the "white colonies" of Canada, Australia, New Zealand, and South Africa. In 1927 the historian and statesman Alfred Zimmern proposed that a "Third British Empire," now known as "The British

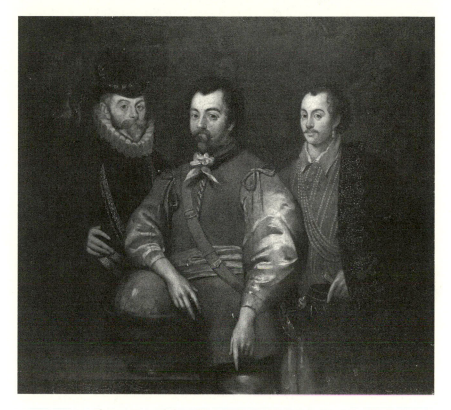

FIGURE 6.1. Thomas Cavendish, Sir Francis Drake and Sir John Hawkins, Elizabethan
buccaneers and early English overseas explorers. Stimulated Elizabethan attempts
to colonize America. © National Maritime Museum, Greenwich, London.

Commonwealth of Nations," had come into existence since the First World
War. It was based on the dominion principle, the increasing equality of all parts
of the empire in its rule. The new designation—the British Commonwealth—
had surfaced just before the war began; it had been popularized during the
war in speeches by the South African statesman General Jan Smuts; it made
its formal entry in the Irish Treaty of 1921, setting up the Irish Free State as a
dominion within the British Commonwealth of Nations (Zimmern 1927: 3).

Zimmern's concept of the "Third Empire" has found favor with a number of recent scholars (e.g., Darwin 1999; Sinha 2014). But many reservations
have been expressed about the conventional division between the First and
the Second Empire, and generally about the whole idea of a succession of
empires. There is first the ignoring of the "First English Empire," the medieval
empire constructed by the Anglo-Normans as they overran Wales and Ireland

in the eleventh and twelfth centuries. There seems, as we have noted, a clear connection—mediated particularly by Ireland—between that empire and the supposedly "First British Empire" built up overseas in the West Indies and North America in the sixteenth and seventeenth centuries. So the "First British Empire" was not the *first* empire made by the English.

Moreover, to what extent was that first overseas empire *British*? James VI and I, king of Scotland, England, and Ireland, might have declared himself king of "Great Britain," but that designation was rejected by the English and Scottish parliaments and was of limited currency—and reality—throughout the seventeenth century. Only with the parliamentary union with Scotland in 1707 did "Great Britain" come into being, becoming the United Kingdom of Great Britain and Ireland following the parliamentary union with Ireland in 1801. So the so-called First British Empire was disconcertingly first an *English* empire (despite the participation of many Scots, Welsh, and Irish) and only later, in the eighteenth century, a *British* empire. The overlap between English and British continues, as in so many other contexts, to sow confusion.

Even if we accept the designations and distinctions of First and Second empires, there is the problem of the continuity between them. The distinction makes sense only on the understanding that the loss of the American colonies represented a fundamental break, and a fundamental reorientation, in the history of the British Empire. The British, it is argued, after a decent lapse of time during which they licked their wounds and rethought the whole project of empire, turned their attention away from the Atlantic and looked eastward toward Asia and southward toward the Pacific.

This notion, of a fundamental break, has come under sustained attack in recent years from a number of prominent historians (e.g., Bayly 1989; Marshall 2007). There was, it is argued, rather a fundamental continuity, both in time and in the ideas and assumptions concerning the nature of the British Empire. The first, "Western," empire was not succeeded by a second, "Eastern," empire. At the very time, during and after the Seven Years' War (1756–63), that the British government was attempting to reorder and tighten its administration of the North American colonies, the East India Company was laying the foundations of British rule in Bengal, the springboard for the expansion of that rule to the whole of India. Equally, the earlier idea of the British Empire as an "empire of the seas," an empire "Protestant, commercial, maritime and free," as contrasted with despotic rule in the Spanish and French empires (Armitage 2000: 142–43, 193), was now powerfully complemented by a sense of the importance of a territorial empire that had to be properly administered by the metropolitan power.

The "free English" of the North American colonies might go their own way, but the British now ruled extensive territories containing Native Americans, Australian Aborigines, French Canadians, and Asian Indians—none of whom were Protestant, British, or free, according to standard British notions (Marshall 2007: 7, 160–61). New forms of imperial government would have to be devised. Rome, rather than Greece, might have to become the model for the British Empire; or at the very least Roman-style centralization, and not simply the autonomous Greek colony, might have to play an important part in the future governance of the empire (Kumar 2012b). In the years 1780 to 1830 there was, says Christopher Bayly, "an imperial revolution in government." A whole new proconsular style of imperial rule came into being, "loyalist, royalist, aristocratic, militarist," with strong Roman overtones (Bayly 1989: 116–21, 160, 194, 250; Gould 1999: 485).

Most challenging to traditional ways of defining and periodizing the British Empire has been the idea of the "informal empire," a view put forward most influentially in an article of 1953, "The Imperialism of Free Trade," by the imperial historians John Gallagher and Ronald Robinson. Gallagher and Robinson argued against the long-standing practice of treating the British Empire only through its formal possessions, "those colonies coloured red on the map." That, they said, was "rather like judging the size and character of icebergs solely from the parts above the water-line" (Gallagher and Robinson 1953: 1). One effect of this was to give undue prominence to the period after 1880, when the British and others added greatly to their formal empires around the world, especially in the "scramble for Africa." Both imperialists such as Seeley and anti-imperialists such as Hobson and Lenin were agreed in their (mistaken) emphasis on this period. It is linked to their view that mid-Victorian Britain was indifferent or hostile to empire, mainly because of the triumph of free-trade ideas and the conviction that colonies were an unnecessary and wasteful burden. When, in the last quarter of the nineteenth century, free-trade ideas came under attack, so—in the conventional account—empire resurfaced as a desirable and perhaps necessary thing.

But, argued Gallagher and Robinson, even if we consider only the formal empire, the idea of decades of indifference in the middle years of the century does not stand up to scrutiny. "Between 1841 and 1851 Great Britain occupied or annexed New Zealand, the Gold Coast, Labuan, Natal, the Punjab, Sind and Hong Kong. In the next twenty years British control was asserted over Berar,

Oudh, Lower Burma and Kowloon, over Lagos and the neighbourhood of Sierra Leone, over Basutoland, Griqualand and the Transvaal; and new colonies were established in Queensland and British Columbia" (Gallagher and Robinson 1953: 2–3). If the British government and British public opinion really were against empire in this period, then such widespread acquisitions need to be explained. "Fits of absence of mind" is one explanation but not a very convincing one.

But for Gallagher and Robinson what is an even more serious objection to the conventional view is its ignoring of the great growth in the "informal empire" in this period and indeed throughout the nineteenth century. By this they mean the exercise of British "paramountcy"—predominant British power and influence—without the formal annexation of territories. British industrialization and British expansion in the nineteenth century needed markets and suppliers, and fundamentally it did not matter if these were secured through formal or informal means. Obviously informal means were on the whole less costly and did not involve direct and possibly troublesome administration. Hence where the opportunity offered, as in Argentina, Brazil, and other parts of Latin America, they were preferred. But where such techniques did not or could not work, as in India or Southeast Asia, the British government had no qualms, even in the so-called period of indifference, about asserting formal control. The important thing was securing the environment for the growth and expansion of the British economy and more generally making the world accessible and hospitable to British goods, ideas, and people. Such a dual strategy proved triumphantly successful in the nineteenth century.

> By informal means if possible, or by formal annexations when necessary, British paramountcy was steadily upheld. . . . The fact that informal techniques were more often sufficient . . . in the circumstances of the mid-century than in the later period when the foreign challenge to British supremacy intensified, should not be allowed to disguise the basic continuity of policy. Throughout, British governments worked to establish and maintain British paramountcy by whatever means best suited the circumstances of their diverse regions of interest. (Gallagher and Robinson 1953: 3, 12)

The stress on the informal empire has proved enormously influential in recent scholarship, and there is no doubting that Gallagher and Robinson provoked a serious rethinking about British—and other—imperial history and policy.[11] They have particularly strengthened the argument for continuity, which can be cast back to the eighteenth century, erasing the distinction between a First and a Second British Empire. It can also be taken forward to the twentieth century, questioning the idea of a Third Empire as representing some new principle (for the dominion concept clearly has its roots in the nineteenth century). But in other respects the concept of the informal empire raises great difficulties of analysis. It is one thing to study territories under formal rule, with their constitutions, administrations, armies, and rule of governance. These are relatively bounded systems. But how does one measure power and influence without such structures and boundaries? How compare the British impact, say, on Argentina with that on India? There is no denying that the British established a powerful presence in nineteenth-century Argentina, but is it really comparable to British power in India, or Canada, or Australia?[12] The techniques of power and influence, unsupported by formal rule, seem remarkably different. They appear to demand a different kind of analysis (cf. Baumgart 1982: 6–7).

That at any rate is the conviction of the reflections on the British Empire that follow, which will restrict themselves to the formal empire. Formal and informal empire are different things, and while it is no doubt important to have pointed to similarities and stressed the connections between them, that does not entail treating them alike and subjecting them to the same mode of analysis. Something similar perhaps can be said about the thesis of continuity. It is a powerful riposte to more traditional accounts, and it must be taken into account where relevant (as for instance in considering British economic relations worldwide). But there may still be good heuristic reasons, to make particular emphases and to draw attention to significant differences, for distinguishing between a First, Second, and even Third empires. There was change in the British Empire, as in all empires, but not all changes were equal in importance.

This said, it will be convenient—again following traditional accounts—to divide the British Empire into three main parts.[13] There were first the "colonies of settlement," later (after 1907) officially referred to as "the dominions," more colloquially as "the white dominions." These were the regions of the empire where British and other white Europeans settled, usually displacing either completely or in good part the original indigenous inhabitants. The North American colonies of what later became the United States were of this kind. So too were Newfoundland (merged with Canada after the Second World War), Canada, Australia, and New Zealand. South Africa belonged to this group, though distinguished by the fact that it was shared by two opposing European groups, Dutch and British, and crucially also by the fact that the indigenous

FIGURE 6.2. Francis Hayman, *Robert Clive and Mir Jaffir after the Battle of Plassey, 1757* (c. 1760). Clive's conquest of Bengal laid the foundations of British rule in India. The epigraph to the painting reads: "Power Exerted/Conquest Obtained/Mercy Shown." © National Portrait Gallery, London.

black population was not displaced but continued to be the majority. Southern Rhodesia after 1923 enjoyed dominion-like status but was never formally considered a dominion. Ireland was also, after the formation of the Irish Free State in 1921, a dominion, though often choosing not to act like one, eventually leaving the British Commonwealth in 1949.

The second part of the empire was represented by India. "India" was much more than the India we know today, more like "Greater India." It was the center of a "miniempire" or "subempire" that for most of the time included not just Burma but whole regions "east of Suez," from Aden to Burma. Within its ambit at various times were also coastal East Africa and the "Straits Settlements" of the Malayan peninsula. Technically, and perhaps fittingly, only India had an emperor or empress, a title conferred on Queen Victoria by Benjamin Disraeli when in 1876 he made her "empress of India." The usual style for the British monarch after Victoria was king-emperor (there were no queens before

Elizabeth II's accession in 1953), reflecting the fact that the monarch was an emperor in India but a king elsewhere in the empire (cf. Austrian *königlich-kaiserlich*). British public opinion in the mid-Victorian age was sensitive about empire. For them it smacked of the authoritarian character of Napoleon III's Second Empire, as well as the despotism of the Roman Empire. Disraeli was reluctantly forced to restrict the title to India (Koebner and Schmidt 1964: 117–23; Parry 2001: 168–69, 173).

The third part of the empire, sometimes referred to as "the Colonial Empire" because it mostly came under the Colonial Office—was something of a ragbag. It was effectively everything that was *not* the dominions and India. The Colonial Empire consisted primarily of crown colonies and protectorates. These included the West Indian colonies, as well as most of the African colonies and (after 1937) such possessions as Aden. The Colonial Empire, the most heterogeneous section of the empire, adds greatly to the difficulty of generalizing about "the British Empire." But some parts, the West Indian and African colonies especially, figured importantly in the imperial imagination as well as imperial policy; they most certainly cannot be ignored in any attempt to assess the impact of empire on British identities.

"Greater Britain" and the Dominions

It was one of the most fundamental assumptions of the peoples of the dominions that they were and remained British (Cole 1971). This was also true for most people in Britain itself: the view that Australians, New Zealanders, Canadians, and South Africans of British birth or descent were simply British people overseas, "kith and kin," extensions of their own families and neighbors. Canterbury, New Zealand, was as English as Canterbury, Kent. The Australian statesman Sir Henry Parkes expressed the prevailing dominion view when he spoke of "the crimson thread of kinship which runs through us all (Cole 1971: 169; cf. Hyam 1999: 58). It was a view with a remarkably long life, from the early nineteenth century right through to the mid-twentieth century, even after most of the dominions had achieved self-government and effective independence.[14]

In 1866–67, the rising statesman Sir Charles Wentworth Dilke "followed England around the world." Journeying in America, New Zealand, Australia, India, and parts of the Mediterranean, he found himself everywhere in "English-speaking or in English-governing lands." He was struck by "the grandeur of our race, already girdling the earth, which it is destined, perhaps, eventually to overspread." And he coined a term that was to have considerable currency. "If two small islands are by courtesy styled 'Great', America, Australia, India, must form 'Greater Britain'" (Dilke 1869: vi–vii).

"Greater Britain," it has increasingly come to be recognized, played a large part in the discourse of late nineteenth- and early twentieth-century Britain. But its meanings were multiple and sometimes—perhaps deliberately— ambiguous. Did it mean the British Empire, in all its parts? Did it simply mean the "white dominions," the settlement colonies to which the British had migrated and in which in most cases had come to constitute the majority population? Or did it mean the whole English-speaking world, the "Anglosphere" or "Anglo-world"? United in advocacy of "Greater Britain," its proponents were often divided on whom or what to include. Particularly problematic were those two great entities America—the United States—and India. Was either or both part of Greater Britain?[15]

Dilke himself had no doubts that both the United States and India were part of Greater Britain. "Through America, England is speaking to the world" (1869: 230). The inclusion of America in a worldwide English-speaking "Anglo-world" was common in the powerful movement of "Anglo-Saxonism" that swept both England and America in the late nineteenth century (Horsman 1981; Brundage and Cosgrove 2007: 137–63; Young 2008: 177–95). The Americans were once part of the British Empire. Through an unfortunate family disagreement, they had departed to form their own state. But increasingly in the nineteenth century they had once more grown closer to Britain, recognizing a basic similarity of outlook and interests (Belich 2009: 479–82). No longer as subjects or dependents but as equal partners they once more formed a part of the great Anglo-Saxon family that was encircling the globe. "We are a part, and a great part, of the Greater Britain which seems so plainly destined to dominate the planet," declared the *New York Times*, on the occasion of Queen Victoria's Diamond Jubilee in 1897 (in Morris [1968] 1980a: 28). It was a sentiment that found a heartfelt echo among English thinkers and statesmen, fully aware of the mighty second "Anglo metropolis" that was developing on the other side of the Atlantic (Belich 2009: 68–70).

India, with its old civilization and majority Hindu population, fitted less easily into the concept of Greater Britain. But Dilke at least believed that, since Indian civilization had irreparably decayed, Indians were ready to receive the culture and civilization of England. Like Macaulay, Dilke argued that the teaching of the English language and English literature was the first and indispensable step toward "Englishing" the Indians and preparing them for self-rule (Dilke 1869: 543–49). Indians were "our fellow-subjects," under the same

FIGURE 6.3. John Everett Millais, *The North-West Passage: It Might be Done
and England Should Do It* (1874). This painting was immensely popular in
Victorian England as exemplifying British imperial heroism and manly endeavor,
especially in the wake of the tragic expedition of Sir John Franklin (1845) in
search of the Northwest passage. Private Collection/Bridgeman Images.

queen; it should be the concern of the British government to turn them into
"our fellow-men," and so an integral part of Greater Britain (1869: 560). In a
later contribution he expressed himself even more emphatically: "However
extraordinary may be the progress, however marvellous the future, either of
Australasia or of Canada, India ought always to be first in our minds when we
are thinking of Greater Britain" (1899: 17).

It should be remembered that this inclusion of India in British or European
civilization was not so unusual or eccentric. The great eighteenth-century Orientalist William Jones had demonstrated a shared "Indo-European" linguistic
past that made Britons and Indians "distant cousins"; the British Empire, Jones
felt, could be a vehicle for a family reunification (Koditschek 2011: 60). Max
Müller, the dominant Orientalist of the mid-Victorian period, waxed lyrical over
this discovery of a common Indo-European past. "Two worlds, separated for
thousands of years, have been re-united as by a magical spell, and we feel rich in

a past that may well be the pride of our noble Aryan family. . . . The East is ours, we are its heirs, and claim by right our share in its inheritance" (Müller [1876] 2003: 242). "India," he wrote elsewhere, "is not, as you may imagine, a distant, strange, or, at the very utmost, a curious country. India for the future belongs to Europe, it has its place in the Indo-European world, it has its place in our own history" (in R. Mantena 2010: 55–56). It was common, among Orientalists both Indian and European, to compare the great Indian epics, the *Mahabharata* and the *Ramayana*, with the revered Homeric epics, the *Iliad* and the *Odyssey*—often to suggest derivations and parallels between them. Some of the most famous thinkers and poets of the nineteenth-century "Bengali Renaissance"—such as Henry Louis Vivian Derozio and Michael Madhusudan Dutt—drew freely upon European, especially classical, history and literature to create joint Indo-European epics, and to urge the case for an Anglo-Indian future. There was, on the part of both Indians and British, a fascination with Alexander the Great, and the sense that the British in India were treading in his footsteps, attempting to establish a cosmopolitan empire that drew upon both Eastern and Western traditions (Hagerman 2009; Vasunia 2013: 33–115, 239–52, 301–33).

Some such as Thomas Macaulay looked not back to a common Eurasian past but to a common future in which Indians—or at least a significant part of them—would be assimilated into British civilization. This was the message of his famous (or infamous) "Minute on Indian Education" (1835), when he advocated the formation of "a class who may be interpreters between us and the millions whom we govern; a class of persons, Indian in blood and colour, but English in taste, in opinions, in morals, and in intellect" (Macaulay [1835] 2003: 237). The Anglicization of India was the route to integrating India in the British Empire. Just a few years later, Macaulay's brother-in-law, Charles Trevelyan, colonial administrator in India and future civil service reformer, put forward a similar vision. Just as the Romans civilized the nations of Europe, so the British would civilize the Indians—a comparison that was to become very popular. "The Indians will, I hope, soon stand in the same position towards us in which we once stood towards the Romans " (in R. Mantena 2010: 60–61). It needs to be stressed that such a vision was not unattractive to many prominent Indians as well, such as Rammohun Roy, Rabindranath Tagore, and Dadabhai Naoroji (the first Indian to be elected to the British Parliament); nor has it ceased to be nostalgically recalled.[16]

But the inclusion of India was resoundingly rejected by the thinker who perhaps gave the idea of "Greater Britain" its greatest currency and influence: the historian Sir John Seeley. Perhaps this was in part a reflection of the more sombre mood that followed the Indian Mutiny of 1857, and the sense of a greater divide between Indians and British than had existed before.[17] In his book *The Expansion of England* ([1883] 1971)—"the bible of Greater Britain" (Bell 2007: 150)—Seeley was prepared to give some place in Greater Britain to the United States, since they had once formed part of the British Empire and, even after independence, continued to be closely linked to Britain by the ties of blood and common culture. Indeed, he claimed, "there is no other example in history of two states related to each other as England and the United States are related." Despite their separation, "the United States are to us almost as good as a colony; our people can emigrate thither without sacrificing their language or chief institutions or habits" ([1883] 1971: 50, 119–20).

But chiefly for Seeley the United States was important to Britain as a model of empire. For it showed that size and variety were no barrier to the construction of a great state, one moreover in which—unlike the empires of old—liberty could be preserved and society prosper. As such it could show Britain, whose empire as yet lacked any theoretical or systemic basis, the way forward. Under the old colonial system England had regarded its colonies as possessions, to be used for its own benefit. That ultimately was the cause of the American Revolution and the loss of the American colonies. What was now needed, and what the United States clearly indicated, was a new conception of empire, a new understanding of the relation between the mother country and its colonial offshoots.

> If the colonies are not . . . possessions of England, then they must be part of England; and we must adopt this view in earnest. We must cease altogether to say that England is an island [*sic*] off the north western coast of Europe, that it has an area of 120,000 square miles and a population of thirty odd millions. We must cease to think that emigrants, when they go to colonies, leave England or are lost to England. We must cease to think that the history of England is the history of the Parliament that sits at Westminster, and that affairs which are not discussed there cannot belong to English history. When we have accustomed ourselves to contemplate the whole Empire together and call it all England, we shall see that here too is a United States. Here too is a great homogeneous people, one in blood, language, religion and laws, but dispersed over a boundless space. ([1883] 1971: 126; see also 134–35)[18]

A singularity of Seeley's position was that for him the British Empire was "not an Empire at all in the ordinary sense of the word. It does not consist of a congeries of nations held together by force, but in the main of one nation, as much as if it were no Empire but an ordinary state" ([1883] 1971: 44; see also 233). This did not stop Seeley discussing the empire in many of the same terms employed by others in the debates on the character and destiny of the British Empire. For one thing he committed himself to the idea of "Greater Britain" and was one of its most fervent advocates in public. He was also a strong supporter of the view that the British Empire could and should be turned into an "Imperial Federation," the example of the United States always before him ([1883] 1971: 18, 62). But he was perhaps more outspoken even than Dilke in treating the empire as a single nationality, "a vast English nation." Before the age of steam and electricity, the dispersal of its parts in distant corners of the globe prevented a clear awareness of the "strong natural bonds of race and religion" that held together this extended nation. But "as soon as distance is abolished by science . . . so soon Greater Britain starts up not only a reality but a robust reality" ([1883] 1971: 63; cf. Deudney 2001: 191).

So Greater Britain "is not properly, *if we exclude India from consideration*, an Empire at all" ([1883] 1971: 63). But there was the rub. Where did India, "the jewel in the crown" after all, fit into the scheme of things? For Seeley, there was no future for India in Greater Britain, and correspondingly no future for Greater Britain if it had to include India. For the British Empire, as conventionally understood, consisted for him of two fundamentally different parts. There was the "Colonial Empire," the settlement colonies that together with Britain made up "Greater Britain." They were united with the home country by the ties of blood and held together, like all states, by the community of race, religion, and interest. The second part consisted of the "Indian Empire," whose people are for the most part "of alien race and religion, and are bound to us only by the tie of conquest." Their place in the future of the empire was highly questionable. Hence, concluded Seeley, "when we inquire into the Greater Britain of the future we ought to think much more of our Colonial than of our Indian Empire" ([1883] 1971: 14–15; see also Bell 2007: 8–10, 171–81).

But what kind of an empire would the British Empire be without India? Was the British Empire after all no more than an extension of Britain, a diffusion of British nationality? Was the British Empire, in other words, no more than an expanded nation-state? That seems clearly to have been Seeley's view. Hence the statement that, if we leave out India, the Colonial Empire—"Greater Britain"—need not really be considered an empire at all.

This was a profoundly disturbing conclusion to many thinkers and statesmen, for whom India was in many ways the centerpiece of Britain's imperial enterprise. More than just a compensation for the loss of the American colonies, it put Britain at the center of world history. It was Britain following in the footsteps of Alexander, the ruler who had attempted to unite East and West and make of them one ecumene. One of the reasons why the historian Edward Freeman—who otherwise was sympathetic to the idea of Greater Britain—opposed the movement for imperial federation was that most of its proponents found no place in it for India. "India, so present to every mind in every other argument, India, the choicest flower of the Empire, the brightest jewel in the Imperial Crown . . . seems suddenly to be forgotten" (Freeman 1886: 140).[19] For Freeman, Greater Britain without India (or, as Dilke had argued, the United States) was impossible. At the same time, like Seeley, he recognized the differences between India and the colonies of settlement. Its assimilation into the common English-speaking civilization of Greater Britain was thus highly problematic (Freeman 1886: 41–43).

David Deudney has said that "Greater Britain was a vision of national ide-alism, of sentiment working against the grain of the material constraints and opportunities of the twentieth century" (2001: 203). That seems to play down the role of "sentiment" unduly. Empires, including the British Empire, are as much, perhaps more, a matter of sentiment as they are of material interests. The power of the Greater Britain idea was precisely its appeal to the sentiment of a common British heritage and culture, the ideal of a common British citi-zenship spanning the oceans. As such it commanded widespread support, at all levels of society, throughout the settlement colonies. Its effect could be seen in many measures of public policy, both at home and in the colonies. It could increasingly be seen in the direction of emigration and investment, altering previous trends, as we shall see.

But undoubtedly Freeman had put his finger on its weakest spot. Not only was there India; as the empire expanded in the later nineteenth century to take in wide swaths of Africa, increasingly the British Empire, if it were to survive, had to take account of the millions of the crown's subjects that were not of British origin or of British culture. In the end the circle was squared by invok-ing another model of empire than that of the homogeneous, culturally similar, entity of Greater Britain. The Roman Empire had been a great multicultural and multinational polity. Might that not be a model for an expanded Greater Britain, one that allowed for the plurality of Britain's far-flung and variegated empire? Such increasingly became the conviction in the latter part of the nine-teenth century, as the movement for imperial federation, based on the more restricted concept of Greater Britain, faltered in the face of the realities of the British Empire.[20]

India in the British Empire

Unlike many other commentators of the time, Seeley did not disparage Indian civilization, which he knew to be of great antiquity and creativity. But that was in the past, and that was the problem. Compared with the settlement colonies, "which have no past and an unbounded future," India is "all past and, I may almost say, no future." India is mired in "superstition, fatalism, polygamy, the most primitive priestcraft, the most primitive despotism" ([1883] 1971: 140–41). "Two races could scarcely be more alien from each other than the English and the Hindus. . . . Their traditions do not touch ours at any point. Their religion is further removed from our own even than Mohammedanism" ([1883] 1971: 147).

Britain, Seeley admitted, has a great responsibility in managing the vast Indian Empire. In part 2 of *The Expansion of England* Seeley gives an incisive and thoroughly dispassionate account of British rule in India, an analysis that can still be drawn upon with profit.[21] He showed clearly that British rule depended on Indian support, passive or otherwise, and that Indians could indeed be considered corulers of their own country, at least as far as self-supporting taxation, routine administration, law enforcement, and service in the armed forces were concerned.[22] But the British found India in a state of "wild anarchy," and for the foreseeable future must remain in order to bring it to a condition in which it would be able to govern itself. "A time may conceivably come when it may be necessary to leave India to herself, but for the present it is necessary to govern her as if we were to govern her for ever" ([1883] 1971: 154; see also 241).

The idea of a kind of trusteeship of India—and other non-European colonies—was a common one among "liberal imperialists" such as Macaulay and J. S. Mill. It formed part of the dominant "stadial" view of human development whereby those societies that were at a more "advanced" stage of development had the right—and even the duty—to govern others. But it had to be in the interest of those others, and it was justified only insofar as the goal was eventual self-government, when those societies under the tutelage of the colonial power had achieved the appropriate level of civilization. This was the essence of the European "civilizing mission" (Mehta 1999; Pitts 2005).

The inclusion of India in the empire is clearly for Seeley a necessity, perhaps a burdensome one, rather than a matter of celebration. India does not feature in his vision of the long-term future of Greater Britain. In this he reflected, as well as powerfully influenced, a strong strand of thinking about the empire among British liberals. One such, the famous classicist and prominent intellectual Gilbert Murray, resoundingly echoed Seeley when he wrote in 1900 that "British Empire" is a misleading term. "'Empire' is the rule of one nation over other nations. We hold empire over India, over Soudan; we do not hold empire over Canada or Australia. Free Canada and free Australia are grander evidences of England's greatness and solider elements in her strength than all those tropical provinces which she has won as conqueror and holds as foreign despot. The word 'empire' has blurred this great distinction" (Murray, Hirst, and Hammond 1900: xv).[23] For Murray, as for most liberals, the health of Greater Britain depended on Britain's shedding its Oriental empire.

But Victorian England's most famous poet, the poet laureate Alfred Lord Tennyson, begged to differ. For him India and the Eastern empire were Britain's glory, the greatest testimony and the strongest claim for Britain to be considered the true legatee of Rome. He scorned those who wished to loose the colonies, to leave Britain "some third-rate isle half-lost among her seas." He praised "Our ocean-empire with her boundless homes / For ever-broadening England, and her throne / In our vast Orient" ("To the Queen," *Idylls of the King*, 1872). In an ode written for the opening of the Indian and Colonial Exhibition of 1886, he hailed the "gifts from every British zone," and appealed for "Britain's myriad voices" to be welded "into one imperial whole." Like Rome as seen by Virgil, Britain's mission in Tennyson's eyes was ecumenical; its destiny, as the "mightiest of all peoples under heaven," was to be the teacher of mankind and the metropolis of a world empire (Kiernan 1982). Britain could no more ignore—still less give up—India than Rome could Spain or Syria.

Tennyson was a fervent admirer of Virgil, for him the greatest of the classical poets, and he was partly instrumental in the rehabilitation of Virgil in the later part of the nineteenth century. In the eighteenth and early nineteenth centuries, Virgil's reputation had suffered by comparison with Homer's, much of that having to do with Virgil's close association with the Augustan Principate, and the sense that it was Augustus who had extinguished Roman republican liberty. Greece, not Rome, was what the romantics such as Keats, Shelley, and Byron worshipped and praised. The admiration for Greece continued with George Grote, the great historian of Greece, the liberal leader (and Homer scholar) William Gladstone, and later liberals such as W. E. Forster, John Morley, Gilbert Murray, and Alfred Zimmern. For them, the Greek style of colonization, in which peoples of Greek origin and culture set up their own autonomous communities while retaining a sense of kinship with the metropolis, was the best model for Greater Britain (Kumar 2012b: 87–91; Vasunia 2013: 252–53, 302–16).

Fears of "Caesarism," and the contamination of domestic liberties by despotic practices abroad, as was held to have happened in the Roman Empire, continued to haunt the British imagination throughout the nineteenth century (Betts 1971: 153–54; Taylor 1991: 13–14; Matikkala 2011). India, and the Eastern empire generally, seemed to pose a particular threat in this respect. "England in the East is not the England that we know," warned Dilke. "Flousy Britannia, with her anchor and ship, becomes a mysterious Oriental despotism, ruling a sixth of the human race" (1869: 550). Nevertheless, Dilke saw many good reasons for Britain to be in India, and many good things that it was doing.

In any case in the second half of the nineteenth century India had begun to impress itself on the British imagination and British policy with increasing urgency. Following the Indian Mutiny of 1857, the British government took over the administration of India from the East India Company and set about establishing British rule on a firmer, more systematized, footing. In 1877 Benjamin Disraeli, the most imperially minded of British statesmen, had Queen Victoria proclaimed empress of India. Although Victoria herself never visited India, elaborate ceremonies in her name began to be a part of normal British rule in India. The Imperial Assemblage of 1877, announcing Victoria to the Indians as Kaiser-i-Hind, with its extravagance and theatricality became the model for a whole succession of displays of imperial grandeur and opportunities for Indian princes to show their loyalty (Cohn 1983). The queen's Golden (1887) and Diamond (1897) Jubilees provided similar occasions for the display of pomp and circumstance. The climax of this sequence of celebrations might well be held to be the Delhi Durbar of 1911, a durbar of "unprecedented scale and magnificence," attended by the king-emperor George V himself and his queen, in the presence of over 100,000 spectators who watched as the ceremonially dressed Indian princes one by one paid homage to their imperial rulers. All these events were fully covered by the British newspapers—in the case of the 1911 durbar by newsreel cameramen as well—thus bringing India vividly to the attention of the British public at home (Cohn 1983: 208; James 1998: 320–21).

Equally publicized was the move of the capital from Calcutta to the old Mughal capital of Delhi in 1911, and the construction of a "New Delhi" by Edwin Lutyens and Herbert Baker in a design that carefully blended classical European and Indian traditions. Nothing could have made clearer the claim by the British that they were now the successors to the Mughals, and had become as much part of the fabric of Indian life as had previous rulers. A British Empire without India became increasingly unimaginable—the more so, perhaps, in that the buildings of New Delhi not only referred to India's past but consciously echoed those constructed elsewhere in the empire (notably South Africa) and so emphasized the unity of the empire as a whole (Metcalf 2005; Vasunia 2013: 172–76).

Symbolism was only one aspect of the new importance given to India. In 1875 Disraeli purchased for Britain a majority shareholding in the Suez Canal Company. He made it clear that his concern was the security of India and the Eastern possessions, and that for him the empire was not two divisions—the Colonial and the Eastern—but one and indivisible. In the debate on the purchase in the House of Commons he declared roundly that "this was a purchase which was necessary to maintain the Empire" (in Koebner and Schmidt 1964: 116). At a stroke India became infinitely nearer to Britain: voyages by steamship to India now took three weeks instead of three months around the Cape of Good Hope.

India's strategic importance was now greatly enhanced. It became "the second centre of British world power" (Darwin 2009: 181). Securing the Suez Canal, as ensuring the traffic of men and goods to India, became the linchpin of British policy in Africa and the Middle East. It was to protect the canal that Britain intervened in Egypt in 1882 and found itself—reluctantly—Egypt's overseer for the next half century. Similar anxieties—to keep control of the Cape and the sea route to India—governed Britain's South African policy in the last decades of the nineteenth century (Robinson and Gallagher [1961] 1981; Darwin 2009: 241–42). Geopolitically as well as symbolically, India came to occupy a central place in the empire. Whatever the hopes, and fears, of the Seeleyites, for most people in the later nineteenth and early twentieth centuries the British Empire without India became increasingly hard to imagine.

Lord Curzon, former viceroy of India, was only one of the powerful voices raised to protest at the exclusion of India from schemes of imperial federation and tariff reform at the turn of the century. He was particularly incensed at the way this ignored India's huge contribution, in men and resources, to the war effort during the Boer War. For Curzon, the empire without India would be fatally weakened, economically, militarily, and culturally. At an address in Edinburgh in 1909 titled "The Place of India in the Empire," he warned against the tendency to treat India as "lying somewhat outside the main congeries of States and communities that compose the Empire, to regard it, so to speak, as a magnificent jewelled pendant hanging from the imperial collar, but capable of being detached there from without making any difference to its symmetry or strength." He pointed out, with a wealth of examples, that India was "the determining influence of every considerable movement in British power to the east and south of the Mediterranean," and that any attempt to detach it would bring about the unraveling of empire. "When India is gone and the great Colonies have gone, do you suppose we can stop there? Your ports and coaling stations . . . your Crown Colonies and protectorates will go too" (in Grainger 1986: 196; see also Thompson 2000: 33, 1997: 151–52; Moore 1999: 443). The event seemed to prove him right. Was it no more than simply historical accident that the departure of India from the empire in 1948 should herald the almost total dissolution of the rest of the empire in the next two decades? To give up on India, it seems, was indeed to give up on empire (cf. Brown 1999: 421–22).

Rome in the British Empire

In a memoir of 1899 written when he was over seventy, Robert Cust, a former member of the Indian Civil Service, recalled that "when gradually, though not yet thirty years of age, I found myself helping to rule Millions in their hundreds of towns and thousands of villages, the lines of Virgil came back to me:

> Tu regere imperio populos, Romane, memento;
> Hae tibi erunt artes; pacisque imponere morem,
> Pacere subjectis, et debellare superbos.

(IN VASUNIA 2013: 252)

Cust was by no means the only one to have thought of these famous lines from book 6 of Virgil's *Aeneid* during his time in India (for translation see chapter 2, above). It was repeatedly quoted by higher-ranking administrators, military officers, and professional men sent out to rule India's millions. It reminds us of two things: the importance of the classics in the background and training of the imperial administrators; and, connected to that, the ease with which comparisons between the British and the Roman empires came to mind.[24]

The classics—always an important part of the education of the British as of all European ruling classes—increased in importance when, from 1855, entry into the Indian Civil Service was thrown open to competitive examinations. Under the influence of such well-known proponents of the classics as Macaulay and Benjamin Jowett, master of Balliol College, Oxford, knowledge of Greek and Latin was made central to the examination. Not surprisingly students from Oxford and Cambridge fared best—best of all those who studied "Greats" (the Greek and Latin classics) at Oxford, better still at Balliol College. Study of the classics, it was thought, was the best training in character and comprehension for those who would be in charge of the millions of British subjects worldwide—especially, perhaps, in the case of those peoples of very different customs and cultures from the native British (Larson 1999: 197–207; Majeed 1999; Vasunia 2013: 203–35). Since entry into the Indian Civil Service became the aspiration of the best and brightest in Britain—salaries and prestige were among the highest in the land, far outshining most careers at home—the luster of the ICS was yet another way in which India established itself in the English imagination in the later nineteenth century (Grainger 1986: 133; Moore 1999: 429–30).

With the classics came the renewed significance of Virgil, and of Rome. Homer and the Greeks were not overthrown—particularly among literary scholars—but for statesmen and political thinkers it was Rome and the Roman Empire that seemed to offer the most suitable objects for reflection.[25] With the increasing importance of India, with the "scramble for Africa" in the 1880s and 1890s, the British Empire was ever more multinational and multicultural, ever more in need of guidance as to how to manage such a diverse entity. That had been Rome's challenge too; and for many British thinkers of the nineteenth century, schooled as they were in the classics, it was natural to draw upon the experience of Rome for possible lessons that could be applied to the British Empire. "Rome," as Rama Mantena says, "provided the imperial framework to imagine the meeting of different cultures within a single political unit" (2010: 60; cf. Hagerman 2013: 62). "Greater Britain" and the Greek model continued to have their advocates; but in their restricted form, applied only to the white colonies, they could not serve the purposes of an empire whose non-European elements increased with every passing year.

The turn—or return—to Rome can be dated to the midcentury, starting perhaps with the famous speech in which Lord Palmerston, defending what many took to be his high-handed action in the Don Pacifico affair, declared that the crucial question was "whether, as the Roman, in days of old, held himself free from indignity when he could say *Civis Romanus sum*; so also a British subject, in whatever land he may be, shall feel confident that the watchful eye and the strong arm of England, will protect him against injustice and wrong" (in Vance 1997: 226).[26] Citizenship featured as a constant theme in the comparisons of the British and Roman empires. A favorite quotation was from Claudian, on Rome's wise policy of "summoning those she has defeated to share her citizenship and drawing together distant races with bonds of affection" (see chapter 2, above, and Kumar 2012b: 94). British statesmen aimed to imitate the emperor Caracalla and to make all British subjects equal citizens of the empire. Ironically it was only on the eve of the empire's demise, in the British Nationality Act of 1948, that Britain came near to fulfilling that promise. But late or not in its realization, and as imperfectly as it was practiced, the ideal of a common imperial citizenship, and the pride and protection that came with it, remained among the central points of comparison between the Roman and the British empires (Brunt 1965: 270–74). The parallels were often stated: *pax Romana, pax Britannica; civis Romanus, civis Britannicus.*

In 1869 Sir Charles Adderley, a former under-secretary for the colonies, wrote a critical review of government policy in which he distinguished between the "Grecian elements" in the British Empire—the increasingly self-governing colonies of British descent—and the "Roman elements," those non-European parts that were more or less despotically governed. In line with many liberals, he feared the effects of the "Roman" influence on domestic politics, and argued that the empire should consist as soon as possible of only the self-governing dominions (Koebner and Schmidt 1964: 91–93; Betts 1971: 154). This was a view, with its Greek-Roman contrast, that was adopted by many proponents of Greater Britain; it was given an additional twist by Gilbert Murray when he argued that "at home England is Greek, in the empire she is Roman" (in Jenkyns 1981: 337).

Replying to Adderley's criticism of the administration in which he had recently been prime minister, Lord John Russell also drew upon classical parallels, but to make a quite different point. This was not the time, he argued, to think of shedding any of Britain's imperial possessions, to make the empire more "Greek" and less "Roman." The world was becoming a world of great states, great powers. Britain was faced with competition from France, Germany, Russia, the United States, all of whom were bent on building up their territories.

> There was a time when we might have stood alone as the United Kingdom of England, Scotland, and Ireland. That time has passed. We conquered and peopled Canada, we took possession of the whole of Australia, Van Dieman's Land and New Zealand. We have annexed India to the Crown. There is no going back. *"Tu regere imperio populos, Romane, memento."* (in Koebner and Schmidt 1964: 94)

Britain, as Thomas Carlyle had announced in the 1840s, was the new Rome, the British the new Romans. Russell's ringing endorsement of the "Roman" principle, capped by a quotation from Virgil, tallied well with the increasingly imperialist temperament of British opinion in the later nineteenth century, for all the fears and anxieties expressed by a number of radicals and liberals (Parry 2001: 175; Matikkala 2011: 98–99, 109–18). Seeking to assuage the fears of those who felt that empire, as at Rome, would lead to corruption and loss of liberty, Benjamin Disraeli, employing a popular misquotation from Taci-tus's *Agricola*, assured his audience at London's Guildhall in November 1879 that the *pax Britannica* would mean peace and freedom. "I know [the British] will not be beguiled into believing that in maintaining their Empire they may forfeit their liberties. One of the greatest Romans, when asked what were his politics, replied *Imperium et Libertas*. That would not make a bad programme for a British Ministry" (in Vance 1997: 230–31; on the misquotation, see Cramb [1900] 1915: 13–14; Bradley 2010b: 139–40).

Disraeli might have added that Tacitus in his *Agricola*, even when he famously denounced empire, showed what great benefits Roman rule had conferred on the Britons. Tacitus might put anti-imperial sentiments in the mouth of a rebel leader—a rhetorical device in any case common in Roman literature—but he also emphasized Rome's civilizing impact on Britain, espe-cially under Agricola's governorship. The *Agricola* was favorite reading in Victorian and Edwardian times; and statues of Agricola adorned Manchester Town Hall and the Roman baths at Bath. Agricola could be hailed not simply as a Roman who brought the arts of civilization to Britain—as powerfully stated earlier by David Hume in his popular *History of England* (1757–62)—but as in a sense also British, the "parent" and originator of Britain's own rise to imperial greatness, with a destiny similar to Rome's. As Rome had civilized Britain and Europe, so the British would civilize India and other realms that lacked the ideas and institutions of the modern West (Bradley 2010b: 131–57).

For many writers, what Rome stood for—following the example of Alexander—was cosmopolitanism and ecumenism. It was this that Charles Dilke had in mind when, in a similar vein to Tennyson, he contended that "the possession of 'colonies' tends to preserve us from the curse of small island countries, the dwarfing of mind which would otherwise make us Guernsey a little magnified" (1869: 398; cf. Joseph Chamberlain in Grainger 1986: 216).[27] Empire as a counter to provincialism was always one of its attractions. Dilke might appeal to a "greater Saxondom" as the theater of this larger awareness, but for others this was too restricted and in any case unrealistic. There was a sense in which, despite all their protestations, the proponents of Greater Britain could sound like Little Englanders. The reality was that Britain possessed a far-flung, global empire that included peoples of many races and nationalities. This was a challenge, but for many it was also a matter of pride and a cause for celebration. Ruler of the world's largest empire, with a variety that matched if not surpassed that of Rome, Britain now stood unequivocally as Rome's successor. Like Rome, Britain too had "empire without end"; like Rome it too had a civilizing mission in the world. It was with such a conviction that George Curzon, on the eve of his investiture as viceroy of India in 1898, could speak of how he and his contemporaries were led "to contemplate the pomp and the majesty, the law and the living influence, of the Empire of Rome" (in Hagerman 2013: 36).

The virtues of Rome, and what it might teach the British about empire, constituted the underlying theme of one of the most popular publications of the nineteenth century, Macaulay's *Lays of Ancient Rome* (1842). As an old India hand, and an ardent believer in the civilizing effects of the classics—hence the importance, as we have seen, he attached to them in the examinations for the Indian Civil Service—Macaulay was well placed to see the British Empire in the image of Rome.[28] Introducing the *Lays*, he picked out the virtues—"fortitude, temperance, veracity, spirit to resist oppression, respect for legitimate authority, ardent patriotism"—that had allowed Rome to create its great empire. The classics that formed the backbone of the education of the English governing classes were similarly, he thought, imparting these characteristics to the young men who studied them and learned the history of Rome. Men who understood the Roman Empire, and were shaped by its culture, would be the best suited to govern the British Empire. After the Indian Mutiny of 1857, and the recognition of the need to reorder imperial rule, Macaulay's *Lays* increased its popularity tenfold, becoming, as Robert Sullivan says, something like "a surrogate national epic" (2009: 258; see also Edwards 1999c; Hagerman 2013: 44–45). It portrayed the imperial character suited to the rule of nations of varied cultures and customs, not simply of those linked by kith and kin to the homeland.

Those who found in Rome a positive example of empire and of its effects did not, of course, always have it their own way. The inheritance of Gibbon—the fears of the corrupting effects of empire, its propensity to erode liberties at home—continued strong in the nineteenth century, even though the theme of the inevitable decline of empire was to some extent countered and overcome (Dowling 1985). We shall consider this more in the next section. Here we should note, as a last instance of the importance of Rome to the British Empire, a series of systematic comparisons carried out by a group of prominent scholars and statesmen in the early years of the twentieth century. These include the Earl of Cromer's *Ancient and Modern Imperialism* (1910), Sir C. P. Lucas's *Greater Rome and Greater Britain* (1912), and James Bryce's *The Ancient Roman Empire and the British Empire in India* ([1901] 1914). These were the works, we should stress, not simply of eminent scholars addressing fellow specialists, but of individuals as much at home in the world of politics as in that of the academy. Evelyn Baring, First Earl of Cromer, served in India, was commissioner of the public debt in Egypt, and for a quarter of a century, as consulgeneral (1883–1907), was the virtual ruler of that country. Sir Charles Lucas was an Oxford classicist who became head of the dominions department of the Colonial Office and later fellow of All Souls College, Oxford. James, later Viscount, Bryce was a well-known lawyer and historian who served in the Liberal administrations of Gladstone, Roseberry, and Campbell Bannerman; from 1907 to 1913 he was British ambassador to Washington. The works of these authors were widely noted and discussed. They were contributions to a public debate, many of whose participants would have had the same classical—and class—background as they.[29]

All three writers shared Cromer's conviction that, "if it be true that history is philosophy teaching by example, some useful lessons are to be learnt" from the Roman example of empire (1910: 14). They were also in general agreement with Bryce's view of the globalizing, civilizing, effects of both the Roman and the British empires. "As Rome was the principal agent [of world civilization] in the earlier, so has England been in the later effort. England has sent her language, her commerce, her laws and institutions forth from herself over an even wider and more populous area than that whose races were moulded into new forms by the laws and institutions of Rome" ([1901] 1914: 4). What also struck all these thinkers forcefully—as it had Dilke and Seeley—was the extent to which, owing to the immense speeding up of transport and communications brought about by the railway, the steamship, and the electric telegraph, the spread of English civilization had been quicker and more widespread than in the Roman case. Modern science and technology had unified the British Empire in a way not possible for the Romans (Lucas 1912: 35–48; Bryce [1901] 1914: 2–3. See also Bell 2007: 63–91; Deudney 2001).

So the English or British were Romans, only as it were more so. But the comparison also brought home some striking differences from Rome. The size and diversity of the British Empire were, all agreed, infinitely greater than in the Roman case. Lucas noted that "one British Province alone (Canada)" was "about double the size of the whole Roman Empire" (1912: 61). Cromer compared the 410 million subjects of the British Empire—"constituting about one-fifth of the population of the globe"—with the not more than 100 million people in the Roman Empire at the time of its greatest extent (1910: 18). But it was not just in numbers that the difference lay; it was more in the character of the population. Cromer estimated that out of a total population of 410 million in the empire, Europeans (including those in the United Kingdom itself) amounted to no more than about 55 million people. Of the remainder 305 million were Indians and other Asiatics, and 48 million Africans. This, for Cromer, was the great challenge. "The great Imperial problem of the future is to what extent some 350 millions of the British subjects, who are aliens to us in race, religion, language, manners, and customs, are to govern themselves, or are to be governed by us" (1910: 18). Or, as Lucas put it, the British Empire—unlike the Roman—was in reality "two Empires," one made up of the white dominions, the other centered on India (1912: 131–55). How to keep such disparate parts together?

Bryce saw this question as one marking a fundamental difference between the Roman and British empires. Rome had also governed a large number of diverse peoples. But over time it had merged with those peoples, so that eventually individuals from provinces as far afield as Spain and Syria were attaining to the highest offices in the state, including the imperial throne itself. "In the end, Rome ceases to have any history of her own, except an architectural history, so completely is she merged in her Empire" ([1901] 1914: 70–71; cf. Cromer 1910: 73; Lucas 1912: 94). Such a fusion is much more problematic in the British case, especially as regards India. "In the case of England there is a dissimilarity which makes fusion of her people with the peoples of India impossible" ([1901] 1914: 59; cf. Cromer 1910: 72–77; Lucas 1912: 77–78).

Seeley, as we have seen, had faced this problem squarely and decided that Greater Britain ultimately could not include India. Bryce, Cromer, and Lucas agreed that, whether or not the white settler colonies went their own way, they would still be bound to Britain by ties of race and culture. In that sense they would always be British, always belong in some sense to what was increasingly being called the British "commonwealth of nations." But, unlike Seeley, for these three thinkers it was hard to imagine the British Empire without India. India was too important to the empire, ever more so in the early twentieth century as competition intensified among the great powers, all on the lookout for territories to take from each other. Hence, for all the difficulties it entailed, for the foreseeable future India would and must be an integral part of the empire. This was as much for the good of the Indians as it was for the strength and security of the empire. Cromer was as usual the most forthright in his expression: "It will be well for England, better for India, and best of all for the cause of progressive civilization in general, if it be clearly understood from the outset that, however liberal may be the concessions that have now been made, and which at any future time may be made, we have not the smallest intention of abandoning our Indian possessions, and that it is highly improbable that any such intention will be entertained by our posterity" (1910: 126–27; cf. Lucas 1912: 176–78; Bryce [1901] 1914: 73–78).

The task was indeed a formidable one, but once again Rome provided the inspiration, if not in this instance the actual example. Like the Romans, said Lucas, "the English have shown in a marked degree constructive genius"; one could trust to "the British instinct" for the continuation of empire as a force for progress and betterment in the world (1912: 170). Rome had once been the instrument of that progress; in a far-reaching *translatio imperii* it was now Britain, on a far greater and grander scale, that had taken up the torch. As Thomas Carlyle had put it in 1840, "the stream of World-History has altered its complexion; Romans are dead out, English are come in" ([1840] 1971: 202).

Debating Empire: Decline and Fall?

In 1897 England's poet of empire, Rudyard Kipling, offered his "Recessional." There was a note of alarm, and anxiety. "Far-called, our navies melt away; / On dune and headland sinks the fire: / Lo, all of our pomp of yesterday / Is one with Nineveh and Tyre!"

The title of the poem suggested an ending, a withdrawal, as with the recessional hymn sung by clergy at the end of a service. But there was in truth no repudiation of empire here, more a call for continued reflection on its purpose and justification, and a warning of the dangers of forgetting what empire was for—"Lest we forget!" That Kipling had not given up on empire was clear from the poem written just two years later, "The White Man's Burden," when—in the wake of the Spanish-American War—he appealed to the Americans to take over from the Spanish the imperial mission in the Pacific. Once again what was called for was sacrifice and a stern commitment to duty on the part of the imperial people: "In patience to abide, / To veil the threat of terror / And check the show of pride. . . . / To seek another's profit / And work another's gain . . . / Fill full the mouth of Famine / And bid the sickness cease." That the subject peoples might not see the good that was being done was only to be expected ("The blame of those ye better, / The hate of those ye guard"). But it was the white man's duty to endure such ingratitude and persist in the task, because "By all ye cry or whisper / By all ye leave or do / The silent, sullen peoples / Shall weigh your Gods and you."

The early 1900s witnessed an intense and wide-ranging debate about the current condition and future prospects of the British Empire.[30] Powerful and resplendent as it undoubtedly was, there was cause to be concerned about its health and security. Since the shock of the Indian Mutiny of 1857, there had been a series of highly publicized reversals and crises in nearly all the regions of the empire (Burroughs 1999: 172–96; MacKenzie 1999a: 280–82; Porter 2004a: 81–100). In New Zealand there had been the 1860 Maori insurrection, put down only after three years of hard fighting and continuing sporadically for a further ten years. In Jamaica there was the Morant's Bay rising of 1865, brutally suppressed and the cause of bitter divisions in opinion back home (one could call it Britain's "Dreyfus affair"). Fearful of Russian designs on India via Afghanistan, Britain intervened in 1878, only to find itself in the midst of a debacle in which the British envoy in Kabul was murdered and hundreds of Afghans hanged in retaliation (a reprise of the even more disastrous invasion of Afghanistan in 1839–42). None of this ensured that the Afghan emirs would choose the right (British) side in the "Great Game" between British and Russians.

Nor was there just Russia, expanding gigantically across Central Asia, to consider. There was the new rising power of Germany, recently united and looking to find its rightful place in the sun. Despite Bismarck's caution, Germany made a vigorous bid for empire in Africa and elsewhere—not to mention displacing the British in the affections of the Ottomans in the later nineteenth century. After 1870 France too, recovering from the humiliation of 1870–71, sought compensation for its weakness in Europe in empire abroad, in Africa and Southeast Asia. Britain found itself, as in the eighteenth century, confronting a power with imperial pretensions equal to its own. Then there was the United States—part of Greater Britain for some, and not directly challenging Britain for overseas possessions. But the United States was clearly a formidable rival in all other respects, an economic titan that threatened British hegemony in global markets. On all sides Britain felt the breath of a cold wind, and worried about its ability to hold on to its position of world leadership, and to its world empire. "The weary Titan staggers under the too vast orb of its fate," was Joseph Chamberlain's much-quoted comment of 1902, expressing the widespread sense of unease (Hyam 1999: 50; see also Thornton 1968 [1959]: 71–77; Porter 2004a: 124–37).

New challenges, growing in strength at the end of the nineteenth century, came from the empire's subject peoples. Starting in India in the 1880s, when the Indian National Congress was founded (1885), anticolonial nationalism came into its own, and slowly though unevenly spread throughout the empire. For a while it even affected the white dominions, chafing at British control and what they sometimes saw as high-handed British action, as for instance during the Boer War (Eddy and Schreuder 1988). Irish nationalism, which can in some ways be regarded as the parent of anticolonial nationalism in the British Empire—certainly there were strong ties among Irish, Indian, and Afrikaner nationalists—experienced a resurgence in the later nineteenth century and for the next few decades presented the British government with one of its most painful and intractable challenges. Anticolonial nationalism was a direct export of European nationalism, and in many ways a creation of the European empires themselves. There was no case where, unaided, such nationalism brought down the European empires. It took massive wars between the empires to do that, in the First and Second World Wars (Kumar 2012b). But, chiming as it did with some of the most powerful currents in the West, anticolonial nationalism added to the growing problems of the British as of other empires.

For Britain, it was Africa, into which Britain was reluctantly but ineluctably drawn in the last two decades of the nineteenth century, that most clearly dramatized the predicament of empire. It was here that the British public came to see most vividly the costs and penalties of holding on to the empire. General Charles Gordon's death at Khartoum in 1885 made him a popular hero of the empire, but it also brought home the horror and perils of empire. In 1898 came the Fashoda crisis in the Sudan, epitomizing the French-British struggle for dominance in northeast Africa and almost precipitating a war between Britain and France. Further south were the long-drawn-out wars with the Xhosa and the Zulus, including the crushing defeat of British forces by Zulu tribesmen at Isandhlwana in 1879.

Above all there was the Boer War (1899–1902) between British and Afrikaners. More than anything else it was the Boer War that called into question Britain's purpose in its empire, and exposed shortcomings that threatened its future. Britain's scorched-earth policy, the farm burnings, the concentration camps, later the use of Chinese coolie labor in the mines, all were widely reported and discussed at home; all caused bitter divisions. As Lord Rosebery, the Liberal leader, wrote in a letter to the *Times*, the differences between supporters and opponents of the war "is not simply on the war, but is a sincere, fundamental, and incurable antagonism of principle with regard to the Empire" (in Thornton [1959] 1968: 124). The protracted character of the war, the methods used, and the inconclusive outcome all were profoundly disquieting. "The fact that the mightiest Empire ever known took four years, lost thousands of lives, and spent millions of pounds subduing 'a little people, few but apt in the field' was a great shock" (Green 1999: 361). Chamberlain, Milner, and other imperialists took the view that a fundamental rethinking and reorganization of the empire was an urgent necessity. Liberals were more inclined to think that the war had shown the immorality and undesirability of empire.[31]

In an angry outburst against the way the British dealt with the Boer repub-lics, in one of the last things he wrote, the sociologist Herbert Spencer—famous not just in Britain but throughout Europe and beyond—denounced British "Imperialism" as a form of "slavery." But the slavery was not just that of the victims; it was that of the conquerors themselves. He wished to show of an imperial society "that in proportion as liberty is diminished in the societies over which it rules, liberty is diminished within its own organization. . . . [A] society which enslaves other societies enslaves itself" (1902: 159–60, 162). The idea that empire corrupts and inevitably comes back home as despotism had been a popular theme of the radicals throughout the nineteenth century (Tay-lor 1991). It became a common expression in the opposition to the Boer War, nowhere more than in the work, J. A. Hobson's *Imperialism* (1902), that did the most to discredit imperialism in the early years of the twentieth century. Hob-son drew a direct parallel between the "moneyed oligarchy" that came to rule Rome and the one which he thought was responsible for modern imperialism, and warned of the like consequences, a moral and material enfeeblement of the state (Hobson [1902, 1938] 1988: 366).

But, at the height of the Boer War and just two years before Hobson, the classicist and historian J. A. Cramb had published his almost equally influen-tial *The Origins and Destiny of Imperial Britain* (1900), a work that was espe-cially popular in the dominions and the United States (Grainger 1986: 188–91). For Cramb the war represented a conflict between two great principles: that of "Nationality"—espoused by the Boers—and that of "Empire," for which the British fought, and which was "the vital principle of the future" ([1900] 1915: 100–101). Like Hobson Cramb also referred to Rome, but to draw almost the opposite lesson, Rome as a great force for civilization in the world. So Britain, he wrote in rhapsodical terms, "is laying the foundations of States unborn,

FIGURE 6.4. Thomas Jones Barker, *The Secret of England's Greatness* (1863). The painting illustrates the popular anecdote that when asked by the envoy of an African prince how it was that Britain had become so powerful in the world, Queen Victoria presented him with a Bible for the prince, saying, "Tell the Prince that this is the secret of England's greatness." The painting toured Britain and Ireland with great success. Christianity was always part of the "civilizing mission" of the British Empire, especially in Africa. National Portrait Gallery, London, UK/Photo© Stefano Baldini/Bridgeman Images.

civilizations undreamed till now, as Rome in the days of Tacitus was laying the foundations of States and civilizations unknown" ([1900] 1915: 231).

Picking up a theme that became common in the comparisons of the British and Roman empires, Cramb argued that decline was not built into the destiny of all empires, that Britain could avoid the fate of Rome and other ancient empires, and was indeed by the principle of its rule likely to do so. The British Empire, he wrote, "is built upon a design more liberal even than that of Athens or the Rome of the Antonines. Britain conquers, but by the testimony of men of all races who have found refuge within her confines, she conquers less for herself than for humanity" ([1900] 1915: 100). Hence there was no conflict between patriotism and imperialism; for, as Lord Rosebery put it, imperialism is "the larger patriotism" (in Matikkala 2011: 95).

This was a time, we should remember, when Bryce, Cromer, and Lucas were also making their comparisons between the British and Roman empires, and like Cramb seeing in the British case an achievement that was likely to outrank Rome's, and to ensure a longer lease of life, if not avoid decline altogether. We have been accustomed, from much of the recent literature, to write off the British Empire from the time of the early twentieth century onward, to see everywhere the signs of decadence and more or less imminent demise. Not only does that make mysterious its continued existence for another fifty years or more. It also ignores the plentiful evidence of the continued vitality of the empire, and a growing, not lessening, belief in its mission in the world. What it also passes over is the continuing evolution of the empire, and the fundamental rethinking as to its future that took place in the years before and after the First World War. The British Empire, it was argued, could and would survive; but it might need to change its form in order to do so.

In the early decades of the twentieth century, a vast and ambitious policy of "education in empire" was conducted by a determined group of imperialists, among them C. P. Lucas, Hugh Egerton, A. P Newton, L. S. Amery, Sidney Low, and W. Pember Reeves. Many of these occupied senior academic positions—Lucas was a fellow of All Souls College, Oxford, Egerton the first Beit Professor of Colonial History at Oxford, Newton the first Rhodes Professor of Imperial History at London University, Pember Reeves the first director of the London School of Economics. Through a stream of publications, and with the aid of organizations such as the Royal Colonial Institute, the Victoria League, and the League of the Empire, this group sought to promote, in schools, universities, workingmen's colleges, and even public venues such as the Albert Hall, an understanding of the empire, and of the vital role it was playing in the betterment of the world (Greenlee 1976, 1979; Grainger 1986: 190–92; Lee 2004).

What was particularly important was that, though most of them acknowledged their indebtedness to Seeley, they refused to accept the restriction of Greater Britain to the white settler colonies. The British Empire was something greater than that, "a great and beneficial organism," wrote Lucas, "unique alike in kind and extent, the result of growth to which no parallel can be found" (in Greenlee 1976: 274). In such an entity, which Lucas also likened to a great family, there was room for diversity as well as unity. Each part of the empire, however different its customs and culture from that of the metropolis, had its particular quality to contribute. Asia and Africa were as much part of this empire as Canada and Australia. What bound them together was membership of the same imperial family. Like children, even if when they grew up they went their own way, they would still be bound to the parent stock by the ties of affection and loyalty (Greenlee 1976: 276).

In a number of publications, John MacKenzie has argued persuasively that the early decades of the twentieth century, far from showing the marks of a widespread pessimism and disenchantment with empire, rather indicate that empire was growing in popularity, among the home population at least.[32] Proponents of empire now had a wide range of new technologies of mass communication—the mass-circulation daily press, cinema, and radio—to go alongside the more traditional means of disseminating empire. The annual Christmas Day broadcasts by the monarch to the empire, begun in 1932, were an immediate success, listened to by millions throughout the empire. In the same year the BBC opened its Empire Service, broadcasting on a regular basis to the whole empire, and employing the services of broadcasters from all over the empire. Earlier the great Empire Exhibition at Wembley in 1924–25, attended by over seventeen million people, gave the infant BBC, broadcasting live from the exhibition, its first opportunity to establish itself as the voice of the nation. Under the firm guidance of Lord Reith, the BBC's first director-general, the BBC committed itself to playing a central role in promoting understanding and support for the empire.

Empire Day (May 24), informally launched in 1904 and made official in 1916, became in the 1920s and 1930s an established and widely observed holiday, with public concerts and radio broadcasts, including an address by the prime minister. The "cinema of empire," with films such as *The Charge of the Light Brigade* (1936), *Sanders of the River* (1935), *Four Feathers* (1939), and *Gunga Din* (1939), was almost wholly celebratory. Often these films were based upon the stories of popular writers such as G. A. Henty, Edgar Wallace, John Buchan, and "Sapper," who used the empire as the setting for the daring actions of their heroes (MacDonald 1994: 205–31). Kitchener, the hero of Omdurman (1898), remained an emblematic figure of imperial glory in the 1920s and 1930s. The same period also saw the romanticization and idealization of the First World War hero T. E. Lawrence, "Lawrence of Arabia," as the tortured intellectual turned imperial warrior.

Then there was the work of the Empire Marketing Board, which made imperial produce—tea from Ceylon, cocoa from the Gold Coast, butter from New Zealand—familiar items in British households. Empire could not have been made more material, not to say corporeal. Switching consumer habits away from foreign imports—Argentine beef, Californian tinned fruit—could be done, the board felt, only by "bringing the Empire alive." It was a testimony

FIGURE 6.5. *Imperial Federation: Map of the World Showing the Extent of the British Empire in 1886.* Frequently reproduced, Walter Crane's map artfully supported

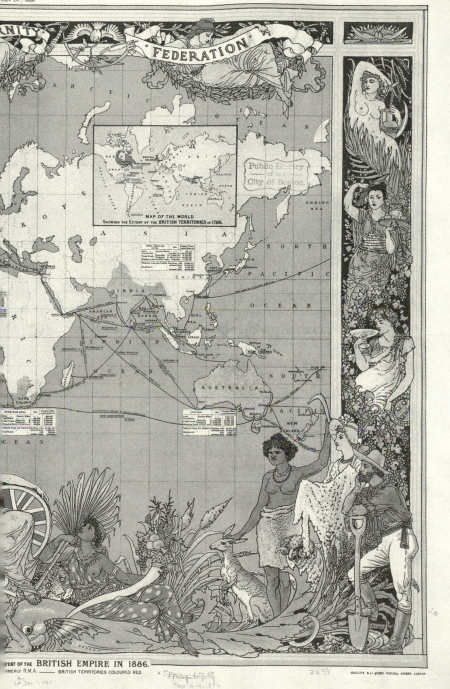

the case for imperial federation in the 1880s. Map reproduction courtesy of the Norman B. Leventhal Map Center at the Boston Public Library.

to the continuing force of an imperial "Britannic" identity that the slogan "Buy British" was recognized, and promoted, as interchangeable with "Buy Empire Goods." The EMB's film unit, under John Grierson, developed a legendary reputation for the quality and impact of its documentary productions, many concerned with publicizing food production in different parts of the empire. The EMB in fact was not just concerned with the short-term goal of getting British consumers to buy empire goods. A team of brilliant publicists and propagandists took it upon themselves to promote the empire as such, emphasizing its great size and correspondingly abundant resources (the "resources of a quarter of the world," as the Prince of Wales put it in a broadcast for the EMB). Through books, pamphlets, posters, films, lectures, and exhibitions, in schools, railway stations, road junctions, the EMB hammered home, with "conspicuous success," a simple and frequently repeated message, of "the values and virtues of the Empire" (Constantine 1986: 215).

One might add, as a last example of the popularity and vitality of imperial sentiment in this period up to the Second World War, the remarkable growth and spread of the Boy Scout and Girl Guide movement. Founded by R.S.S. Baden-Powell, hero of the siege of Mafeking (1899–1900) during the Boer War, the Scout and Guide movement was a conscious response to the concern about the health of British society and the British Empire that had surfaced so insistently during and immediately after the Boer War. Baden-Powell's handbook, *Scouting for Boys* (1908), both drew upon and sought to offset the fears expressed in the popular, anonymously published book—the author was Elliott Mills—*The Decline and Fall of the British Empire* (1905). Moreover, unlike those contemporaries whose thinking about empire focused very much on the empire of "kith and kin," the empire of the white dominions, Baden-Powell's concept of membership and belonging extended to all the regions of the empire, India as much as South Africa or Canada. "A Scout is a brother . . . no matter to what country, class or creed the other may belong," ran the Fourth Law of Scouting. In the great international jamboree camps of Scouts in the interwar period were to be found Scouts from every corner of the empire. Scouting and Guiding for Baden-Powell not only cut across domestic divisions of class and religion; "it could also be presented as genuinely imperial, an effective creative cement for the emerging commonwealth of nations, itself presented as a living embodiment of Scouting's multi-racial ideals" (Warren 1986: 241). By the early 1930s there were a million and a half Scouts and half a million Guides throughout the empire—326,000 Scouts in India alone, where the government of India after initial hesitation put itself behind the movement (Warren 1986: 249).

For Baden-Powell, character—its right making and performing—was the key to empire. Character was best formed on the frontier rather than in the city, he argued, a view that not surprisingly endeared him to many people in the dominions, though of course not there only ("frontier life" could be found in the English countryside as well as on the veld) (MacDonald 1993). Thus world Scouting could survive the decline of empire after the Second World War, unified by the cult of the camp and the outdoors (Warren 1986: 252–53). Character was indeed a strong theme of many writers on empire in the early decades of the twentieth century. For them there was a "fundamentally symbiotic relationship" between empire and character, character bringing about empire and being in its turn fortified by it (Cain 2007: 255, 263, 269; Bivona 1998: 99–130). A favorite way of treating the subject was to examine, as exemplars, the lives and actions of some of the great empire-builders and heroes of empire, such as John and Henry Lawrence of the Punjab, Lord Gordon of Khartoum, Frederick Courtney Selous—the original of Rider Haggard's Allan Quatermain—and Sir Frederick Lugard in Africa (Tidrick 1992). Fears of decadence and degeneration were certainly strongly expressed at the fin de siècle, not least in the revelations of physical unfitness among the men called upon to fight in the Boer War (Pick 1989: 189–221). But, both in that war and in the First World War, as well as in a series of larger-than-life imperial proconsuls—Cromer and Kitchener in Egypt and the Sudan, Curzon in India, Milner and Lugard in Africa—there were examples enough of empire-building character to balance the fears that the race had lost its ability to rule (Grainger 1986: 134–39, 182–218; Cain 2007).

A. P. Thornton expresses a common view when he says that, owing to the Boer War, "the imperial idea suffered a contraction, a loss of moral content, from which it never completely recovered. . . . The British Empire survived, indeed was augmented by, the South African War; but its dynamic for self-confident expansion was dead" ([1959] 1968: 125; cf. Porter 1982: 128). Everything we have considered above—and further below—tells against this view. The evidence indicates that, despite the trauma both of the Boer War and the First World War, confidence and support for empire were not fundamentally shaken. British society continued to see itself in imperial terms, and to project to the world the image of its empire as a civilizing force.

If anything, the importance of the empire to the British increased during the First World War and its aftermath (Lloyd 1996: 276–79; Holland 1999; Marshall 2001: 76–84; Porter 2004a: 227–39). One indication of this was the return of "imperialists" such as Curzon and Milner to power and influence, with senior positions in Lloyd George's War Cabinet. The dominions too were

FIGURE 6.6. John Singer Sargent, *Sir Frank Swettenham* (1904). Swettenham
was high commissioner for the Malay States and governor of the Straits
Settlements. Sargent presents him as the archetypal imperial civil servant,
with the trappings almost of royalty. © National Portrait Gallery, London.

given representation in London, and dominion premiers invited to special
meetings of a new body, the Imperial War Cabinet. The South African general
Jan Smuts, highly regarded in Britain, served in the War Cabinet and as an
official representative at the Paris Peace Conference after the war, together
with other dominion premiers. There were regular Imperial Conferences

throughout the war—from 1917 including India—and at the Peace Conference the British were represented by the British Empire, not by the United
Kingdom (Zimmern 1927: 29–30; Darwin 1999: 68). In 1921 the British prime
minister Lloyd George said that "there was a time when Downing Street
controlled the Empire; today the Empire is in charge of Downing Street" (in
Marshall 2001: 83). This was hyperbole; but it expressed a real truth about
the heightened significance of the empire brought on by the war. We fought
the war, wrote Leo Amery later, "as a united Commonwealth and Empire,
and in the course of it achieved a greater measure of effective Imperial unity
than statesmanship had ever contemplated before, or has achieved since" (in
Grainger 1986: 323).

Moreover, the empire's contribution to the war effort was not lost on the
British public. It was made clear that this was an imperial, not a national, war,
a war in which the empire fought as a unity. The empire was the source not just
of men but of vital supplies of food and raw materials (partly because of which
food supplies in Britain did not run out, as they did in Germany). But it was
the human contribution that above all brought home the imperial dimension
of the war. In all about 2.5 million colonials fought for the empire. Canada
sent 630,000 troops; Australia—despite rejecting conscription—415,000, all
volunteers; New Zealand sent 130,000—nearly 20 percent of the adult male
population. The bravery and sacrifice of the Australian and New Zealand
(Anzac) troops in the ill-fated Gallipoli expedition of 1915 won widespread
sympathy in Britain no less than in Australia and New Zealand (even if it
also stimulated Australian nationalism and considerable anti-British feeling).
Despite Afrikaner opposition, South Africa contributed 195,000 men, including 44,000 black South Africans; British West and East Africa, 62,000 troops,
mostly black (Holland 1999: 117; Marshall 2001: 78–79; Martin and Kline 2001:
270–71; Thompson 2003).

India, as befitting its size and its central strategic role in the empire, sent
nearly 1.5 million men, who served in nearly all the main theaters of the war,
from France to the Middle East. Gandhi spoke for many Indians when he
declared, "We are, above all, British citizens of the Great British Empire. Fighting
as the British are at present in the righteous cause for the good and glory of
human dignity and civilization . . . our duty is clear: to do our best to support
the British, to fight with our life and property" (in Burbank and Cooper 2010:
375; cf. Albertini 1969: 19).[33] India got its reward in the Montagu Declaration
of 1917, which spoke of "the gradual development of self-governing institutions with a view to the progressive realization of responsible government in

India as an integral part of the British Empire" (Porter 2004a: 233; Holland 1999: 122–24; Brown 1999: 430). The ambiguity of the promise disappointed some Indian nationalists; but what is perhaps more remarkable is the fact that throughout the great conflict of the war, neither in India nor elsewhere was there any serious opposition to fighting with Britain as part of one entity, the British Empire. Unlike the case of the Second World War, there were almost no attempts to exploit Britain's difficulties in the form of nationalist risings or mass campaigns of noncooperation. That this did happen in the case of Ireland—with the Easter Rising of 1916—only goes to confirm the sense that Ireland was always the odd man out in the empire.

The First World War not only reinforced imperial solidarity; it also extended the physical bounds of empire. As a result of the peace settlement, Britain gained a new empire—in fact if not in name—in the Middle East, in the form of the League of Nations mandates of Iraq, Palestine, and Trans-Jordan (Egypt had formally been declared a British protectorate in 1914, and though this was renounced in 1922, effective British control remained until well after the Second World War). A treaty with Iran also secured Britain's dominance there. Curzon, who as foreign secretary presided over this immense extension of British power in the Middle East, must have felt satisfied that he had finally obtained for Britain what he had always hoped for, control of the band of territory between the Mediterranean and India. Britain also got the lion's share of the German colonies, notably Tanganyika and German South-West Africa, and the Pacific islands of New Guinea and Samoa. With the new acquisitions in East Africa, Britain now had the uninterrupted swath of territory from the Cape to Cairo that Rhodes had striven for. The British Empire, in 1920, now stood at its fullest extent, occupying a quarter of the world's land surface and incorporating a quarter of the world's population: the largest empire the world had ever seen. "Far from beginning a long decline, the British empire seemed to be much more secure in 1920 than it had been in 1900."[34]

There were other, equally solid, indications that the empire, far from being in a state of decline, was actually becoming more significant and more central to its members. One was in the area of trade and investment. During the nineteenth century the empire, though more important to Britain than their overseas possessions were to other European empires, was not the major theater of trade and investment. Exports to the empire between 1814 and 1914 stayed relatively steady at between 30 percent (1814) and 35 percent (1914), with India and the white settlement colonies steadily rising in importance and the West Indies sharply declining. Imports—mostly in food and raw materials—from the empire were lower still, never being more than a quarter and sometimes falling to a fifth of all imports between 1850 and the First World War. Overseas investment followed the same pattern, with nearly two-thirds of all foreign investment going to regions outside the empire (the empire took 38 percent between the 1860s and 1914). In the era of free trade, whether for trade or investment it was mainly Western Europe, the United States, and South America, not the British colonies, that promised the biggest rewards and best returns; similarly for many vital imports Britain depended on nonimperial sources.[35]

Emigration tells a similar story, with the United States again the great draw. For most of the nineteenth century, with some fluctuations, the United States was the favorite destination for more than two-thirds of all British emigrants. The remaining third were mostly attracted to the other white settler societies, Canada, Australasia, and South Africa. The "Anglo-world" was therefore the main draw for emigrants, but it was a former colony, not the existing ones, that seemed to offer the greatest opportunities to the ordinary British (unmoved by the vitriolic attacks on the United States by prominent visitors such as Charles Dickens).[36]

Things changed dramatically in the period following the First World War. The average of British exports to the empire rose from 35 percent in 1909–13 to 37.2 percent in the later 1920s and to 41.3 percent between 1934 and 1938. After the Second World War the figure rose even higher, to 48 percent of all British exports. The shift in imports from the empire was even more marked: from an average of 26.9 percent in 1909–13 to 32.9 percent in the later 1920s and 41.2 percent between 1934 and 1938. Here too there was a further increase after the Second World War: imports from the empire to Britain were 45 percent of the total in 1948 and 48.3 percent in 1954 (Fieldhouse 1999: 98–103). What is clear from these trends is that the increase in the economic importance of the empire, though undoubtedly accelerated by the adoption of imperial preference in the Ottawa agreement of 1932, preceded that measure. In the international climate after 1918, together with the strains caused by the Great Depression of 1929, for both Britain and its colonies the empire seemed increasingly to offer a haven of security, a protective enclave in the midst of an increasingly turbulent world. Now that Britain's global supremacy was no more, its markets less assured, the empire became more, not less, important to it—and it to the colonies (Kennedy 1983: 206, 211; Porter 2004a: 252–53).

The trend in British overseas investment showed this even more clearly, reflecting a sea change in its pattern. Whereas before the First World War about two-thirds of all overseas investment went outside the empire, this pattern was precisely reversed in the interwar period. By 1929 more than two-thirds of all new capital issues were within the empire, and by 1938 more than four-fifths. As with overseas trade, after the Second World War the empire became even more important for British capital markets, at least until the early 1960s (Fieldhouse 1999: 97, 105; Darwin 1999: 71–72).

Migration too reflected the increasing salience of empire in the first half of the twentieth century (Murdoch 2004: 111–15). Empire destinations, sought by barely a third of British emigrants at the end of the nineteenth century, rose to four-fifths of all emigrants by 1946 and continued at that level until the early 1960s. Nor did this represent any significant drop in the total number of emigrants over the period (Constantine 1999: 167). Moreover, the movement of people in this period was not just from the metropolis to the peripheries, but also increasingly between sections of the empire, and involving not just unskilled workers but artisans, clerical workers, technicians, and professionals. The growing urban centers of Toronto, Melbourne, and Johannesburg provided plenty of opportunities for skilled and qualified workers of all kinds, in schools, hospitals, and new universities. And for those Oxbridge graduates crowded out of the Indian Civil Service by its increasing Indianization, there was now an attractive alternative in a newly invigorated Colonial Service, especially in the African colonies. Though never fully closed or entirely coherent, it seems plausible to argue that "in the twentieth century the British Empire-Commonwealth operated as an integrated labour market, which shifted around the labour and skills required to service especially the producing and consuming needs of the Imperial metropolis" (Constantine 1999: 181).

In his sparkling and celebrated book, *Parkinson's Law, or the Pursuit of Progress* (1961), C. Northcote Parkinson enunciated the principle that whole societies, as much as individual organizations, tended to make the most elaborate plans and attempted to fulfill the most ambitious schemes just as they were beginning their decline. "Perfection of planning is a symptom of decay," he averred; "perfection is finality, and finality is death." Among many examples he singled out the new Indian capital of New Delhi, the intention to build which was announced by George V at the Delhi Durbar of 1911. "Sir Edward Lutyens then proceeded to draw up plans for a British Versailles, splendid in conception, comprehensive in detail, masterly in design, and overpowering in scale." But every stage of the building was accompanied by one or more indications that British rule in India was coming to its end. The first viceroy to move into the newly completed viceregal palace was Lord Irwin, in 1929, "the year in which the Indian Congress demanded independence, the year in which the Round Table conference opened, the year before the Civil Disobedience campaign began." All subsequent phases of the building of New Delhi were attended by similar manifestations of Indian resolution, Britain's declining power, and its intention to withdraw from India. "What was finally achieved was no more and no less than a mausoleum" (Parkinson 1961: 96–99).

There is much to be said in favor of this lively account, which certainly contains the kernel of a general truth. But applied to the British Empire in the early twentieth century it is highly misleading. Specifically in the case of India there was no intention of withdrawing, nor did Indian nationalists expect or even in many cases want Britain to do so. In general, despite the enormous strains produced by the Boer War and the First World War, despite the challenge of strong nationalist movements in Ireland, India, Egypt, and elsewhere in the Middle East, despite a certain amount of anti-imperial sentiment at home, the British Empire not only survived but in many ways can be said to have been strengthened by these trials. The members of the empire drew closer together. The ties between them were consolidated, economically, socially, and culturally. At home the empire was given more publicity, was more widely promoted, and attracted more attention than ever before in its history (Marshall 2001: 81–82).

At some level perhaps, and mainly in retrospect, the fact that the empire did acquire such prominence in the consciousness of the British at this time, the fact also that this was when the empire achieved its fullest territorial extent, might lend some plausibility to Parkinson's "law" (and to Hegel's observation that the owl of Minerva flies only at dusk). At its height it is almost inevitable that an empire should betray that hubris which, poetically at least, might herald its downfall, its tragic peripeteia. But poetry is not history; nor should we let the fact that the British Empire came to an end in the second half of the twentieth century distort our understanding of its condition and prospects in the first half of the century.

There is a tenacious and widely held view that the European overseas empires began a slow but inexorable decline after the First World War. Probably it was influenced by the crash of the land empires in that war, the breakup of the Ottoman, Habsburg, and Romanov empires. Somehow empires, all empires, were supposed to have had their day, to belong to the past. Such a view, as we have seen (chapter 1, above) is profoundly mistaken. But it continues to be voiced by many commentators on and historians of the British

Empire (e.g., Porter 2004a: 251–55, 346–47). Despite the evidence of recovery after the First World War, despite the strengthening and solidification of the empire as revealed in statistics of trade, investment, and migration, despite the evidence of a widespread culture of empire, at home and overseas, for some people the empire *must* have been in a state of decline. It is written in the script of empire that it must decline and fall, and since the British Empire was wound up after the Second World War, the seeds of that dissolution must have been sown much earlier, most likely during and after the First World War—if not indeed earlier still, with the Boer War.

But to date the downfall of empire half a century before it happens is a peculiar way of considering its history. Should we see the seeds of the loss of the American colonies, the "First British Empire," somewhere in the trends and events of the early 1700s? Perhaps one can, but it would be a highly unconvincing exercise. A similar anticipation and foreshortening, as we have seen, is common in the accounts of the Ottoman and Habsburg empires. Whether in those cases, or in those of the First and Second British Empires, a teleology is imposed that is severely distorting of the actual histories of those empires. All living things must die, but that does not mean that we have to dwell on their death at every stage of their lives.

"There is a general notion," writes John Gallagher, "that the empire rose, flourished, declined, fell, and that in its fall lay its fulfilment. But this is a sentimental view, arising from a banal teleology. In fact, the movement towards decline was reversible and sometimes was reversed. So far from showing some steady trend towards decolonization, the period between 1919 and 1945 might be described as the decline and the rise of the British empire" (1982: 86; cf. Darwin 1999: 66).[37] But while decline seems the wrong description, change after 1918 there certainly was. It was indeed change of a kind that had been urged for several decades preceding the First World War. In the thinking of both right and left, in the ideas of the liberals and the Fabians as much as Chamberlain and his followers in the Conservative Party, there was a conviction that the empire needed tightening up, that there would have to be a renegotiation of the relations among its parts. Talk of the empire as a "Commonwealth of Nations" had already become routine in the Imperial Conferences that began in 1907, with the dominion and British prime ministers sitting as equals.[38] Imperial preference, though resoundingly defeated by the electorate in 1906, resurfaced during the First World War and, in the turmoil of the postwar period, increasingly came to be accepted as necessary and desirable for both Britain and its empire (Louis 1999a: 12).

Cynically one could argue that this was a case of changing everything so that everything should stay the same. Certainly the changes proposed were meant to save and strengthen the empire. But they were more than cosmetic, more than simply conciliatory gestures toward the dominions and the other colonies. They were intended to preserve the empire by accepting that there must be a fundamental change in the way the different members regarded each other, and in the character of the relations among them. In a speech— with echoes of Seeley—in Birmingham in 1905, Chamberlain declared that "the British Empire is not an Empire in the sense in which that term has been applied before. The British Colonies are no longer Colonies in the sense in which that term was originally applied to them. . . . We are sister States in which the mother country by virtue of her age, by virtue of all that has been done in the past, may claim to be first, but only first among equals" (in Green 1999: 356). The empire was indeed a family, as so frequently claimed; but as in all families there are times when members need to clarify and perhaps rethink their relationship.

A "Third British Empire"

At the 1917 Imperial Conference, a resolution was passed calling for the "full recognition of the Dominions as autonomous nations of an Imperial Commonwealth, and of India as an important portion of the same." It further declared that these nations, "while thoroughly preserving all existing powers of self government and complete control of domestic affairs," had a further right to "an adequate voice in foreign policy and in foreign relations," and to "continuous consultation in all important matters of common imperial concern" (in Zimmern 1927: 30).

Another Imperial Conference, in 1926, restated this position even more firmly. In the Balfour Report issued by the conference it was affirmed that Great Britain and the dominions "are autonomous Communities within the British Empire, equal in status, in no way subordinate one to another in any aspect of their domestic or external affairs, though united by a common allegiance to the Crown, and freely associated as members of the British Commonwealth of Nations." It was made clear that this position was not to be interpreted solely in terms of prohibitions and the principle of noninterference in each other's affairs. "The British Empire is not founded upon negations. It depends essentially, if not formally, on positive ideals. Free institutions are its life-blood. Free co-operation is its instrument. Peace, security, and progress are among its objects." These goals were among the "common causes" that linked all members of the empire, and for which they willingly cooperated (in Zimmern 1927: 41–42; see also Darwin 1999: 68–69).

For Sir Alfred Zimmern, classicist and statesman, these two conferences stated the central principles of what in 1927 he called the "Third British Empire." There were, he admitted, earlier pointers to these principles, going right back to the 1791 Constitutional Act for Canada and, especially, the famous Durham Report of 1839. He was also aware that the concept of the "Commonwealth of Nations" had been enunciated by a number of thinkers and statesmen in the early years of the century. But it was only during and after the First World War, he felt, that pressure of circumstances and developments in the empire had brought these principles to fruition, to the full realization by thinkers and statesmen that the empire had evolved into a new form, comparable to the shift that had accompanied the movement from the First to the Second Empire in the eighteenth century. In a strong echo of Chamberlain's speech of 1905, which questioned the traditional terminology of empire, Zimmern declared that "the British Empire of 1914 has become a British Entente, a group of states, each independent and with full control over its policy, but bound together by cordial feelings and by arrangements for mutual consultation at more or less regular intervals" (1927: 44–45). The Third British Empire represented the move from subjecthood to citizenship, from dependency to equality.

There was a clear element of idealism in this claim, likewise in the further claim that, in its operation and principles—especially the idea of trusteeship—the British Empire anticipated the League of Nations (Zimmern 1927: 87–90). But there was real practical experience behind the claim. Zimmern, along with fellow members of the "Round Table" group of imperialists—Lionel Curtis, Philip Kerr, Edward Grigg, Reginald Coupland—had been centrally involved in the thinking and planning of the League of Nations; and during the Second World War they were again to be active in the advocacy and planning for the United Nations. In these endeavors they linked themselves to Jan Smuts, twice South African premier, a senior statesman of great prestige in Britain, and like them a passionate believer in the British Commonwealth. What all shared was a view of the international community as in all essential respects continuing the work of the British Empire and indeed as something of a surrogate for it. The Commonwealth, said Smuts, already contains "the elements of the future World Government," and could lead the way to it (Mazower 2009: 37; see also Morefield 2007: 360–61).

For Zimmern the classicist, author of the best-selling *The Greek Common-wealth* (1911), here would be the British Empire offering to the world something of the high quality of civilization and moral leadership that Athens had provided for the ancient world. Whatever happened to the actual British Empire, the Idea—in the Hegelian sense—of the empire would live on in a higher embodiment, in the League of Nations and the United Nations (More-field 2005, 2007: 346–54; Mazower 2009: 66–103). This was no doubt heady stuff for many, not used to Hegelian idealism (despite the powerful example of T. H. Green). But it was an idea and an ideal espoused and promoted by a powerful and influential group of well-placed intellectuals and men of affairs in the first half of the twentieth century (Rich 1990: 54–69; May 2001).

In advocating the idea of a Third British Empire, Zimmern was clear that it could not follow the route marked out by Seeley and most of the Greater Britain enthusiasts. It could not, that is, exclude India and the other non-European parts of the empire. Philip Kerr spoke for many in the Round Table group when he had argued in 1912 that "if we manage to create in India a self-governing, responsible dominion, and if India, when it is responsible and self-governing, elects to remain within the British Empire, we shall have solved the greatest difficulty which presents itself in the world today" (in Rich 1990: 58–59). When the Round Table spoke of the Commonwealth, they meant the whole of the empire, not just the white self-governing dominions. "For the Round Table's founders, the term 'Commonwealth' implied a community of peoples moving at different stages and different speeds towards self-government, while remaining a single unit in international affairs" (May 2001: 47).

Zimmern considered the race question to be "the most urgent problem of our time," and one the British Empire had to face. "For the British empire, on a majority vote, is not a white empire but a coloured empire. Hitherto, the whites have borne rule; but if the Third Empire is to be a Commonwealth of Nations, based on the idea of equal partnership, we must discover how to transform the relationship of prestige . . . into a more equal co-operation for common ends" (1927: 91–92). Zimmern felt that, of all the powers, the British were the best fitted by their history and tradition to respond to the challenge of multiracial states. Unlike the states of continental Europe, and increasingly elsewhere in the world, the British had not espoused the doctrine of nationality, nor the dangerous and narrow equation of state and nation that came with it. Great Britain itself, he pointed out, was not a national but a multinational state, the union of English, Welsh, Scots, and Irish under a single government. The British Commonwealth was an outgrowth and continuation of that tradition. "So far from associating and confusing government with nationality it has recognized that the whole art of government consists in bringing different kinds of people, different nations, different groups, different religions, different cultures, under a single law, under what we call the 'Pax Britannica'" (1927: 144).

Zimmern was stern with Seeley for titling his book on the British Empire *The Expansion of England*. "The British Empire is not, and has never been thought of as, an English Empire. Nobody ever speaks of the English Empire" (1927: 148). Nor should it even be thought of as Greater Britain, in the manner of Dilke. Zimmern referred back to the Quebec Act of 1774, which committed Britain to recognizing the culture and institutions of the French-speaking people of British North America. "The Act committed us once and for all in our overseas Empire against the policy of an English Empire. It committed us to tolerance of non-English and even non-British institutions, as the word British was understood at that time. The British Empire, as a result of the Quebec Act, was set on a course under which it could neither become an expansion of England nor a Greater Britain." Britain did not have and should not have "an Anglo-centric empire." The ties binding its parts would be strengthened, not diminished, by the encouragement of "cultural self-determination" within each community. The empire was not English—that was a purely cultural thing, for the English themselves—but British in the political, "nationally colourless," sense that had developed with the expansion of empire (1927: 150–51, 155–56; cf. Amery 1944: 10). National diversity within a shared political and economic space would go a long way toward ensuring that the "Commonwealth of Nations will live on as an enduring partnership in common tasks and common hopes" (1927: 158).

Zimmern's confidence in empire was not so unusual at the time, contrary to many received impressions. Britain was by no means eccentric or alone in the 1920s and 1930s in thinking that the world was still a world of empires, and that whatever changes might have to be made the future would still be one dominated by empires. Nationalism, in the form of Wilsonian self-determination, might be the official ideology of the time, and the League of Nations might struggle to uphold the principle. But the reality was an international order—or disorder—in which empires were still the major players and those that did not have empires sought to acquire them (Pedersen 2015). Not only did the British Empire expand after the First World War, but the French too pressed forward vigorously, in Syria, Lebanon, and Morocco. "Greater France" was becoming greater still. The Dutch, Belgians, and Portuguese tightened up metropolitan control of their empires and instituted far-reaching administrative reforms. The Russians reestablished their empire in the form of the Soviet Union, giving it a new lease of life. Germany, deprived of its overseas empire in 1919, under the Nazis showed a clear determination to acquire a new one in Europe. Italy under Mussolini embarked on re-creating the Roman Empire, beginning with the African empire in Somalia, Libya, and Ethiopia. In the Far East, Japan was fast creating a large Asian empire, rivaling and threatening the European empires (as well as the United States, another power of imperial dimensions). Empire, it might be thought, far from being consigned to the dustbin of history, was very much alive and thriving.

Addressing the common view that the interwar war period saw a retreat from empire and a loss of confidence in empire's future, John Darwin says, "At a time when colonial empires seemed so much a part of the natural order, it would be surprising to find that British imperial policy was geared to the dismantling of the largest and richest colonial system of all" (1980: 658; cf. Lloyd 1996: 282). The Balfour Report of 1926 was not, as often seen, "a conscious act of decolonization," but aimed at "the enhancement of dominion status as a device for frustrating the separatist tendencies at work in Canada, South Africa and Ireland." The policy-makers were confident that "the force of cultural, economic and strategic inter-dependence would overwhelm the sectional nationalisms that threatened imperial unity" (Darwin 1980: 667; see also 1999: 69).

For Darwin, to this extent following Zimmern, such a view was by no means naive or unrealistic. The dominion idea could form the basis of the "Third British Empire" because it "rested upon a remarkable foundation of cultural self-confidence. Although it had been shaken by war and depression, in the inter-war years a shared belief among British communities around the world in the supreme attractiveness of their institutions, ethos, literary culture, and forms of civility remained extraordinarily pervasive" (1999: 86). Once more the rearview mirror, reading the world of the 1960s back into the 1930s, has distorted the reality of the life of the British Empire in the period before the Second World War. In many ways, compared to the anxieties of the earlier part of the century, one might almost say that it was in this period that the British Empire reached the highest point of its confidence, if not of its power. Its culture encompassed a large part of the world, most of whose people expected British culture to continue to be part of their own culture, whatever the political future. In Britain itself, as we have seen, the interwar period saw what was perhaps the most intensive as well as extensive development of imperial culture in the empire's history. It would have been difficult for anyone, however critical of the workings of the empire, to imagine the future without it.

In fact it is clear that British statesmen had no intention of dismantling the imperial system, and that a remarkable consensus existed in Britain that, whatever reforms might be necessary, the empire remained a central and essential part of Britain's future, as well as that of the colonies. That conviction continued also to inform the thinking of most people in the colonies, going alongside the understanding that self-rule—achieved or sought—would be the condition of their membership of the empire. Even Ireland, separated from Britain in 1921 after a bitter civil war, remained a dominion within the British Commonwealth. For the dominions in general, the declarations of the Imperial Conferences of 1917, 1926, and 1930 were formally realized in the Statute of Westminster of 1931, which gave the dominions—Ireland, Australia, New Zealand, Canada, and South Africa—full control over not just their domestic affairs but also their relations with other nations, free of British parliamentary control (Barker 1941: 97–100). That this was not meant as a step toward the disintegration of the empire was made clear by the Ottawa agreement of the next year, the fulfillment of the movement toward imperial preference and empire free trade that had started with Chamberlain thirty years before. The empire had to change, but that was in order to strengthen it, not to prepare it for its demise.

The same attitude can be observed in relation to India. The Imperial Conference of 1917 had acknowledged that India, though not a dominion, was "an important portion" of the "Imperial Commonwealth." John Darwin observes that India's "geopolitical significance as a vast zone of stability under British supervision remained in the 1920s and 1930s as great as before 1914; and her separation from Britain appeared no less incompatible with the survival of the imperial system in any recognizable form" (1980: 673). At the same time it was clear to the British that concessions had to be made in the face of the growing pressure for more Indian involvement in the government of the country.

The Montagu Declaration of 1917 seemed to hold out the promise of dominion status for India in the not-too-distant future, and the measures taken over the next two decades gave every indication that this goal might be realized. The Government of India Acts of 1919 and 1935 enlarged the legislatures both at the center, in Delhi, and in the provincial capitals, making elected Indians a majority and giving them a large measure of control over finance as well as a powerful voice in matters of policy. From 1919 Indian ministers, in the system known as "dyarchy," directly controlled many aspects of provincial government; in

1935 dyarchy was introduced into the central administration as well and the provinces were given full autonomy and self-government. At the same time there was a sharp increase in the number of Indians in the Indian Civil Service, the "steel frame" of imperial rule. In 1905 only 5 percent of the ICS was Indian; by 1929 that proportion had arisen to nearly a third (367 Indians to 894 Europeans) (Brown 1999: 423–25, 430; Louis 1999a: 7).[39] Indian nationalists of course continued to press for more concessions, and the Congress Party formally rejected the 1935 act. But many Indians as well as many officials in London saw the act as a stepping-stone to full dominion status: an interpretation fully in line with the dramatic statement by the viceroy Lord Irwin in 1929 that dominionhood was indeed the Raj's goal for India (Brown 1999: 430; Gallagher and Seal 1981: 406–7; Darwin 1999: 79).

None of this was intended as a prelude to full Indian independence. As Judith Brown says, "despite the powerful 'myth' of an orderly transfer of power as the natural culmination of the Montagu declaration, it is evident that constitutional reforms in 1919 and 1935 were devices to re-establish Empire on surer foundations of Indian alliance rather than the manoeuvres of a beneficent Imperial demolition squad" (1999: 437–38; cf. Darwin 1980: 677). A similar story can be told of Egypt, a country long regarded by the British as strategically central to the whole empire east of Suez. The protectorate declared in 1914 was, under pressure from nationalists, abrogated in 1922. But this did not mean a retreat from British control, which was reimposed by the informal but highly effective methods employed by Cromer as consul-general from the 1880s onward. Not until the arrival of Nasser in the 1950s was British direction of Egyptian affairs seriously disrupted (Darwin 1980: 668–72). Thus, whether we consider the dominions, India, or Egypt, we find the same story of mending rather than ending, the attempt not to wind up the empire but to put it on a new, surer, footing. "Dominion equality, Egyptian 'independence', and provincial autonomy in India were all designed to knock out the props which, so it appeared, had supported the upsurge of anti-British nationalism in the aftermath of the war. By the same token, they were to equip British influence with a streamlined efficiency" (Darwin 1980: 678; cf. Gallagher 1982).

The strains imposed by the Second World War were to disrupt the pattern of relatively orderly evolution "from Empire to Commonwealth." In the case of India, Judith Brown wonders what might have happened had the war not occurred. "For in 1938–39 it seemed that the reforms were working well, satisfying Indian political aspirations, and driving India surely on the road to a greater unity between British and princely India and to Dominion Status. . . .

The war changed all this" (1999: 435–36). The same was to happen elsewhere in the empire. The empire had weathered the storms of the Boer War and the First World War. By 1931 the dominions had been rewarded for their support in those wars, and continued expressions of loyalty, by the grant of more or less full independence within the empire. If any wished to leave, as the Irish did in 1949, there was nothing that Britain could have done to stop them. But most had no desire to leave, and in the Second World War were once more on hand with generous support in the form of men and materials (the Irish again partially excepted). In the rest of the empire, in Africa and the Middle East, colonial nationalism could occasionally create disturbances and disrupt the routines of administration. In Egypt and Palestine the conflicts could be particularly severe. But nowhere did they constitute a serious threat to British rule (Kennedy 1983: 207–8). Writing of British policy-makers in the 1930s, John Darwin notes that "the eventuality they dreaded was not the revolt of the colonial masses but the irruption of Britain's imperial rivals into their ill-defended empire" (1980: 679). This was to be the major impact of the Second World War—a war more global than the first, more exhausting and greedy of resources, one in which new powers with their own imperial ambitions burst upon the scene. Only then did Britain come to feel that its hold on empire was precarious, and that it might no longer be able to justify the effort involved in preserving it.

The Second World War: "Apotheosis of Empire"

In the final volume of Paul Scott's *Raj Quartet*, his sequence of end-of-empire novels, one of the central figures, Guy Perron, reflects on England's relation to India. "For at least a hundred years India has formed part of England's idea of herself." Perron sees a shift beginning to occur around the early part of the century, "certainly since 1918." From that time dates an increasing sense that it is Britain's moral duty to let go of India. "The part played since then by India in the English idea of Englishness has been that of something we feel it does us no credit to have. Our idea about ourselves will not now accommodate any idea about India except the idea of returning it to the Indians in order to prove that we are English and have demonstrably English ideas" (Scott [1975] 1977: 105). These reflections occur on the morrow of the Labour Party's victory in the 1945 election, and the commitment to Indian independence as soon as possible.

We have seen that this dates an acceptance of Indian independence, on the part of Indians as much as British, too early. It took the jolt of the Second

World War to hasten the process—and that too makes it seem part of a preconceived plan, which it was not. When Indian independence came in 1947, it was rushed, badly—indeed hardly—thought out, and with appalling consequences, both short- and long-term (some of which, in the partition riots, Scott shows graphically in *A Division of the Spoils*, the last volume in the quartet). Insofar as Perron reflects Scott's view, this is a retrospective rationalization of the manner in which India achieved independence. It makes it seem as if over a longish period Britain gradually came to feel that it was immoral to hang on to India, and so—governed by "English ideas"— gracefully handed over power to the Indians. In fact that was not in the minds of any except a few Indian nationalists on the eve of the Second World War. The war, as wars tend to, not only concentrated minds and speeded up developments barely discernible before it, but also introduced new exigencies and urgencies that brought about new directions and outcomes, many of them unanticipated and unwelcome. This was true not just for India but for the empire as a whole.

The Second World War was in fact fought—though that was not of course its only goal—to preserve, not give up, the British Empire. That was certainly the view of the British war leader Winston Churchill, who famously declared in 1942 that "I have not become the King's First Minister in order to preside over the liquidation of the British Empire. . . . I am proud to be a member of that vast commonwealth and society of nations and communities gathered in and around the ancient British monarchy, without which the good cause might well have perished from the face of the earth" (in Amery 1944: 19). For Churchill the fight against fascism and the preservation of the empire were intrinsically linked, for the empire stood for everything the fascists hated and wished to suppress. In his very first speech as prime minister in 1940 he declared that the aim of his government was simply "victory—victory at all costs . . . for without victory there is no survival," and that also meant there would be "no survival of the British Empire; no survival for all that the British Empire has stood for; no survival for the urge and impulse of the ages, that mankind will move forward towards his goal." After the disaster at Dunkirk in June 1940 he declared that "even if, which I do not for a moment believe, this Island or a large part of it were subjugated and starving, then our Empire beyond the seas, armed and guarded by the British Fleet, would carry on the struggle" (in Clarke 2008: 5–6).[40]

Three years later, in a speech of 1943, Churchill explained why he felt his faith in the empire had been vindicated. At Dunkirk, he said, Britain had had its back to the wall; it would have been the ideal moment, had they wished it, for the colonies to break free of the British Empire and settle with the "the conquering Nazi and Fascist power." "But what happened? It was proved that the bonds which unite us, though supple and elastic, are stronger than the tensest steel. . . . In that dark, terrific, and also glorious hour we received from all parts of His Majesty's Dominions, from the greatest to the smallest, from the strongest and from the weakest . . . the assurance that we would all go down or come through together" (in Porter 2004a: 291). It was observed at the time that these expressions of support came not just from the self-governing dominions but also from the dependent colonies—those who might be supposed to have had the more reason to seize the opportunity to abandon the imperial ship and seek the protection of the fascist powers.

Churchill was not alone in seeing the war as a struggle for empire as much as one against aggression and fascism, nor in regarding the two as twin aspects of the same conflict. There were a host of prominent men in the wartime government—Lord Lloyd, Brendan Bracken, Lord Beaverbrook, Field Marshal Jan Smuts, Leo Amery—who shared his passionate commitment to the empire as, in the words of Lord Rosebery frequently quoted in these years, "the greatest secular agency for good known to mankind" (e.g., Amery 1944: 18; Ashley Jackson 2006: 7–9). Its defeat, they thought, would be a defeat not just for the British people but for the hopes of all humanity. Amery, Churchill's secretary of state for India, in 1944 stated his firm belief "that the British Empire and Commonwealth is not only the essential framework within which and through which each of its members can best defend its own freedom, best expand its resources, and best build up its social well-being, but also the best instrument by which it can contribute to the peace and prosperity of the world. . . . In fact, to paraphrase Pitt, it will be up to the British Commonwealth after this war, as during it, to continue to save itself by its own exertions and to save the world by its example" (Amery 1944: v–vi; see also Louis 1992).

Amery accepted that the words "Empire" and "Commonwealth" had become interchangeable, but continued to press the case for "Empire," on the grounds that "the word 'Empire' not only brings out the idea of unity comprising infinite variety, but also that of responsibility for peace and good government, of trusteeship towards the weak and backward" (1944: 5). For Amery "the essence of the British Imperial tradition" was toleration—"toleration in all that concerns religion, language, or race." The English might have been the creators, as they have been the main bearers, of that tradition; but they have no monopoly of it. "Scots and Irish, French-Canadian and Afrikaner, Moslem and Hindu, have carried forward, and, each in his own way, enriched the British tradition as they have contributed to the strength of the British Empire" (1944: 10). This was indeed a message appropriate to the moment, when the whole empire, in all its variety, was engaged in a life-and-death struggle with the Axis powers, whose principle of racial purity and superiority seemed the diametrical opposite of this.

In the early years of the war, the classicist and political scientist Ernest Barker made his own contribution to the war effort in the form of a little book, *The Ideas and Ideals of the British Empire* (1941). For Barker the British Empire was unique among empires, almost "a contradiction in terms, a living paradox," in its attempt to promote liberty and responsible government among peoples of many different cultures and at vastly different stages of development. It was "empire without *imperium*, an empire which has preferred the opposite principle of *libertas*" (1941: 8). In relation particularly to the colonial or "dependent empire" it had a "double trust," or what Lord Lugard, famous theorist of "Indirect Rule," called a "dual mandate": as Lugard put it, Great Britain "has her task, as trustee, on the one hand for the advancement of subject races, and on the other hand for the development of material resources for the benefit of mankind" (in Barker 1941: 146). Witnessing as he did in the first few months of the war "the spontaneous offerings of men as well as money from all parts of the empire . . . to aid Great Britain in her struggle," Barker felt reassured that Britain was sufficiently discharging its trust and engaging the loyalty and commitment of people from all over the empire (1941: 163). Like Churchill and Amery, Barker was certain that the fight for the British Empire was also a fight on behalf of humanity (Stapleton 1994: 186–97).

One can be skeptical of these highly idealized portrayals of the British Empire. What cannot be denied is that, as Barker noted, the empire did respond wholeheartedly to Britain's appeal for help in the Second World War. Keith Jeffery speaks of the "extraordinary acceptance and even enthusiasm for the war effort across the Empire" (1999: 307; cf. Thornton [1959] 1968: 360–63). The response was if anything even more impressive than during the First World War. India contributed two and half million troops; Canada over a million, Australia just under a million, New Zealand a quarter of a million. South Africa, divided as in the First World War, nevertheless under Smuts's direction committed itself to the war effort and sent nearly half a million men to fight for the empire. Only Ireland in the Commonwealth remained neutral, but that did not stop 43,000 Irishmen volunteering for war service. Further, 374,000 Africans were recruited into the armed forces, as were over 6,400 West Indians (many more worked in auxiliary roles). Together the colonial contribution more than matched the six and a half million troops from Britain itself—a significantly greater proportion than during the First World War (Jeffery 1999: 308; Ashley Jackson 2006: 45–46). What is more, and unlike the First World War, with the exception of India all the dominions financed their own war effort. Nor was there any of the carping or criticism that had been directed at some of the colonial contingents in the First World War. In the Second World War praise for the performance and bravery of the colonial troops was loud, heartfelt, and virtually unanimous (Ashley Jackson 2006: 526).

The empire suffered some severe reversals, of course. Worst were in Asia at the hands of the Japanese, in 1941–42. Within months of the attack on Pearl Harbor, the Japanese had taken Hong Kong. With the fall of France in 1940 and a complaisant Vichy regime established in Indochina, the Japanese had a clear path across Southeast Asia. Malaya fell to them, then—most humiliatingly—Singapore, then Burma. India seemed next, the more vulnerable for the withdrawal of Congress support for the war effort, in the "Quit India" movement (though Gandhi, as in the First World War, expressed support for the war, saying that he viewed it "with an English heart"). Even more than with the defeat of Russia by Japan in the early years of the century, the myth of European invincibility was shattered. Colonial populations everywhere saw their European masters—British, French, Dutch—humbled by an Asian power. The Japanese made the most of their role as "liberators" of millions of fellow Asians from Western rule. They aided and abetted nationalist movements across the region, enlisting them in their fight against the Europeans. Many a future postcolonial leader was made by the Japanese— underlining the point that it was not nationalism that defeated the European empires but other empires.

But the British Empire survived, at least for the time. The Japanese advance in Burma was halted—mostly by Indian troops—at the Battle of Imphal (March–June 1944). India was saved. At the end of the war Britain recovered all its lost possessions, and even added to them, at least temporarily. Not only did it recover the colonies lost to the Japanese; British military administrations were established in former Italian Somaliland, Libya, Madagascar, Sicily, and Syria. During the war southern Iran was also taken to forestall a German invasion. Ashley Jackson reminds us that "it is more accurate to describe the British Empire as being at its greatest territorial extent not in the wake of its post–First World War gains but in 1945" (2006: 5).

The Second World War indeed, as Keith Jeffery says, "saw the apotheosis of the British Empire" (1999: 326; cf. Thornton [1959] 1968: 362). The "Home Front" and the overseas empire were drawn together as never before. To ensure this, lest there be any doubts or misgivings, a concerted, officially backed program of propaganda and information was orchestrated on a vast scale. If a "Britannic identity" was one of the unifying marks of the empire, the Second World War saw Britishness reach a new peak and intensity of expression (Kumar 2003: 233–38; Mandler 2006: 187–95). It was a Britishness, seen as a shared property, that was widely diffused and deliberately conferred on all the regions and subjects of the empire, through such media as the BBC's Empire Service, the Colonial Film Unit, and the royal Christmas broadcasts to the empire. The British actor Leslie Howard—a virtual compendium of the best British qualities—through his films and broadcasts was a particularly appealing and effective carrier of British values to all corners of the empire. Newsreels in Britain showed Australian, Canadian, New Zealander, South African, Indian, and West Indian servicemen relaxing in British cities as well as fighting in the war zones. Films such as *49th Parallel* (1941) showed the multinational empire in action against the threat of the Nazi "New World Order." The common theme was that of the empire united in defense of a particular way of life, faced with a threat to its very existence. The common image was that of "one great family," as George V said in his Christmas broadcast of 1941, "the family of the British commonwealth and Empire." There was a calculated stress on the ordinary people of the empire, the men and women in the fields and factories as well as at the front. The spirit of the "people's war" at home was complemented by that of the "people's empire" at large (Webster 2007: 19–54; Kumar 2012a: 316–17).

The idea that all this imperial unity was but a show, a pretense, that masked fatal weaknesses is often expressed (as often as the "inexorable decline" of empire is dated from Edwardian times, or 1918, or the 1860s, or at some other date that is said to show the unmistakable signs of decline). But if it was a show, what a show! In any case, there is no evidence that the empire on the eve of the Second World War was in worse shape than at some earlier period when it might be claimed to have been at its height. The Statute of Westminster of 1931 had set relations between Britain and the dominions on a firmer footing than ever before. The India Act of 1935 had all but promised India dominion status, and satisfied a good deal of Indian opinion. There were problems in Palestine—when had there not been?—and other parts of the Middle Eastern empire, but none that tough policing had been unable to handle. In the

"Colonial Empire" of the dependencies there were nationalist movements, as there were in all the European empires, but none that seriously threatened British rule (Porter 2004a: 277).

No more convincing is the view that the Second World War "artificially" and as it were unnaturally prolonged the life of the empire. That assumes that the empire was on the point of collapse before the war, for which there is no evidence. John Gallagher has said that "the period between 1941 and 1945 has striking resemblances to the period between 1916 and 1922," and that as with the earlier conflict the Second World War "considerably strengthened the empire" (1982: 139). That seems to square with all that we know about attitudes toward empire, both in Britain and overseas, during the war. The reversals—especially in Southeast Asia—no doubt gave comfort to the empire's enemies (Subhas Chandra Bose's Indian National Army is the best-known expression of this). But by the same token they also strengthened the resolve to fight on, and fight on alongside Britain the colonies did, despite huge losses. Similarly, though the offer of immediate dominion status to India, in the Cripps Mission of 1942, was rejected by the Congress leadership, it once more reaffirmed Britain's intention to bring India up to the constitutional level of the other self-governing dominions. This was indeed proclaimed as the goal for the empire as a whole. In 1943 Oliver Stanley, secretary of state for the colonies, told the House of Commons that the British government was "pledged to guide Colonial people along the road to self-government within the framework of the British Empire" (in Jeffery 1999: 321). While this would mostly have to wait until the war ended, moves in that direction were made even in wartime. In 1943 Ceylon and Malta were promised internal self-government. In 1944 Jamaica was granted full internal self-government, with a House of Representatives elected by universal adult suffrage. There were also new constitutions for Trinidad, British Guiana, the Gold Coast, and Nigeria, with Legislative Councils allowing for elected majority control (Porter 2004a: 296). The British Empire was, it seemed, indeed on the move again, on course to reestablish itself after the war more firmly on the basis of "Third British Empire" principles. There was no talk, or intention, of giving it up.

End of Empire—or Empire by Other Means?

The end, when it came, was sudden, almost brutal, certainly disconcerting. "In 1945 the independence of India could be seen on the horizon, but no one would have guessed that within the next two decades the British Empire would be in a state of dissolution" (Louis 1999b: 331; cf. Hopkins 2008: 228). Just two years after the end of the war, India attained its full independence, at the same time being partitioned into two states, India and Pakistan. Burma, previously governed as a part of India, became independent in 1948 and elected to leave the Commonwealth. In the same year Ceylon (renamed Sri Lanka) also gained its independence, and Britain withdrew from Palestine, leaving a legacy of bitter division between Jews and Arabs.

There was greater reluctance—indeed initially no intention—to give up the empire in Africa, Southeast Asia, the Mediterranean and the Middle East. Major colonial wars were fought in Malaya (1948–58), Kenya (1952–56), and Cyprus (1954–59). None of these were as bloody as the colonial wars fought by the French in Algeria and Vietnam, or the Dutch in Indonesia, or the Belgians in the Congo. But they were messy and ugly enough to give the lie to those who think that the British Empire ended painlessly and easily. There were plenty of people who felt that it was irresponsible as well as contrary to British interests to concede too readily to nationalist demands. What had happened in India and Pakistan was not a reassuring precedent. Such people—who included Churchill and Anthony Eden, his successor as prime minister—were prepared to fight to keep what remained of the empire.

But the failure and humiliation of the Suez adventure in 1956, when Britain and France went to war with Gamal Nasser's Egypt in a fruitless attempt to hold on to the Suez Canal, persuaded many that Britain no longer had the strength or backing necessary to hold on to empire. Above all was the critical loss of American support following the Suez debacle, in the resolution of which America had played a key role. "Suez made plain for all to see that Britain was doomed both as a colonial power and as a world power unless she acted in concert with the United States" (Louis 1999b: 342). The Middle East having gone, Eden's successor as prime minister, Harold Macmillan, together with his colonial secretary Iain Macleod, briskly wound up the empire in most of Africa and the West Indies in a few astonishing years, from 1957 to 1966.[41] Singapore also went, in 1963, and Aden in 1967. In January 1968 the Labour government announced that it would be withdrawing all forces east of Suez by 1971 (Darwin 1988: 293–96; Hyam 2006: 393–97). This announcement has rightly always been seen as decisive, for symbolic as much as strategic reasons. For over a century it had been an article of faith that there could never, for Britain, be a meaningful empire without an effective presence east of Suez. That was now to cease. In making the announcement the prime minister Harold Wilson showed that he recognized its epochal significance by invoking Kipling's "Recessional"—"The tumult and the shouting die; / The Captains and the Kings depart"—and quoting it in the House of Commons (Hyam 2006: 397). "For anyone looking for a firm date to mark the end of the British empire, 12 January 1968 fits the bill better than most" (Porter 2004a: 322). There were some loose ends—Hong Kong was not handed back to the Chinese until 1997—and an imperial war or two still to fight (such as for the Falklands in the 1980s), but as far as the formal empire is concerned 1968 does seem to mark the end of a four-hundred-year-old story.

This is not the place for a detailed discussion of how and why the empire came to an end. Material and moral forces, in a complex interaction, were more or less equally involved, as in all cases of this kind.[42] What is more important, from the point of view of our present concerns, is to stress for how long and to what extent the British tried to sustain their hold on empire, to prolong it despite the need to shed parts of it. The scholarly consensus now increasingly sees decolonization not so much as the death as "the continuation of empire by other means" (Darwin 1986: 42). The exigencies of the postwar period— war weariness, financial exhaustion, pressure from the United States, promises made to nationalist groups during the war—forced Britain to give up, more speedily than originally envisaged in many cases, important parts of the empire. But that by no means meant that Britain gave up on empire, or simply abdicated its imperial role. The hope rather was that, by the usual mix of formal and informal empire, Britain would be able to retain its position as a great power in the world, relying on the support of its allies and Britain's traditional influence over its colonies, even when they became formally independent (Darwin 1984; Louis and Robinson 1994). In the end that turned out to be impossible. Britain came to accept its reduced position in the world, and to look nearer home, to Europe, for its future. What is more striking, however, is both the strength of the belief that Britain could and should continue to be a world power, and the length of time during which it was able to sustain that belief in the changed conditions of the postwar world. Central to that endeavor was the empire, though one that had—as in the past—to undergo substantial change.

The Labour Government that succeed Churchill's coalition government in 1945 had no more intention of giving up the empire, and the great power status that came with it, than had Churchill and the Conservatives. That was the settled conviction of the leading Labour statesmen, the prime minister Clement Atlee, the foreign secretary Ernest Bevin, the chancellor of the exchequer Stafford Cripps, and many others on the front bench (Louis 1999b: 333). Bevin in particular had a grandiose scheme, in the context of the Cold War, for a

"Western Union" in which the British Empire would be the key element in the defense of Western civilization. There was no need for Britain's great power status to shrink in the face of the United States and the USSR. "It should," he declared in 1948, "be possible to develop our own power and influence equal to that of the United States of America and the USSR. We have the material resources in the Colonial Empire, if we develop them, and by giving a spiritual lead now, we should be able to carry out our task in a way which will show clearly that we are not subservient to the United States of America or to the Soviet Union" (in Hyam 2006: 137–38).

The anticolonialism championed by some on the left—though not mostly among the ranks of Labour—had not been popular during the war and was no more popular after it (Howe 1993: 82–142). There was indeed a remarkable bipartisan consensus, at least among the political elite, on the value of the empire and the need to continue it (Porter 2004a: 297–98; Ashley Jackson 2006: 526–30; Hyam 2006: 94–95). Moreover, the general public in Britain, though as always rather vague about the details of empire, continued to feel pride in it and to support it as the basis of British prestige in the world. The wartime theme of "the people's empire" continued in the popular culture of the postwar period. The term "Commonwealth," as the more acceptable, "democratic," term, increasingly replaced "empire" in popular as well as official discourse. The *Sunday Times*, going one better than Alfred Zimmern, in 1947 even proclaimed a "Fourth British Empire of independent peoples freely associated," much what people had come to understand by the expression "the British Commonwealth of Nations." This popular image of empire reached something of a climax in the great procession of representatives from the whole empire at the coronation of Elizabeth II in 1953. "The 'people's empire' promoted in Coronation year emphasized the ideal of a multiracial community of equal nations that would maintain Britishness as a global identity through transforming and modernizing its imperial dimension" (Webster 2007: 8; see also 55–56, 92–118).

For some commentators, such as the scholar W. K. Hancock, the Commonwealth was indeed the Aristotelian *telos* of empire, the end toward which it had been tending, if not always consciously, for the whole of its existence. It was the final reconciliation of *imperium* and *libertas* (Hyam 2006: 71). The accession of India and Pakistan, even though republics, to the Commonwealth in 1948 was regarded as of pivotal importance to its future—"the greatest opportunity ever offered to the Empire," in the words of Lord Mountbatten, last viceroy of India (Louis 1999b: 336). In recognition of this the term "dominion" was dropped and the "British" removed from what was now simply, and more equally, the "Commonwealth of Nations" (McIntyre 1999: 696). India's acceptance paved the way for most of the former colonies in Asia and Africa, the majority of which became republics, to join the Commonwealth in the next two decades. This might not quite be the cozy club of the mainly white dominions of the prewar era (an organization that by 1997 had fifty-four members—larger than the United Nations itself in 1945—was hardly likely to be). But just as the empire had prepared the way for the League of Nations, so the Commonwealth would complement what the United Nations was attempting to do in the world at large after 1945. The old empire had given birth to the new Commonwealth; but the ties forged during the earlier phase were expected to remain, and to allow Britain to continue to do what it fervently believed was good in the world. The veteran liberal imperialist Ernest Barker expressed such a view when he wrote to his friend Alfred Zimmern, now installed on the other side of the Atlantic, "To me . . . the hope of the world is the continuance of our Commonwealth as the great sane *via media* power of the world" (in Stapleton 1994: 192).

As the Commonwealth came to reformulate the relations between its members—becoming now in reality and no longer simply in aspiration a multiracial community—its economic importance to its members also increased, surpassing the volume of trade and investment that, as we have seen, grew significantly in the interwar years. Imports from the empire grew from 39.5 percent on the eve of the war to 49 percent in 1950–54, and were still 47 percent in 1955–59. Exports to the empire jumped from 49 percent before the war to 57.5 percent in 1946–49, and remained at over 50 percent in 1950–59. Exports of capital, as before, were higher still, 65 percent going to the empire between 1950 and 1954, and remaining at 60 percent between 1958 and 1960 (Porter 2004a: 306–7). While for some these figures might reflect a growing weakness in the British economy, as British products were shouldered out of the wider global economy, they also make clear the increased salience of the empire, both as a protected source for necessary imports and as an outlet for British goods and capital. In an increasingly competitive environment, the empire seemed, at least economically, necessary to Britain as never before. By the same token many of the colonial economies came to be linked even more closely to that of the metropolis (which was why British entry into the European Common Market was seen by many of them as a betrayal).

Particularly important to the British economy were certain vital imports from the tropical colonies: metals (copper, tin, cobalt, gold, uranium), vegetable products (rubber, palm oil), and foods (cocoa, coffee, groundnuts). As a result, and fulfilling promises made both before and during the war, the British after 1945 embarked on a vigorous and sustained program of development in the tropical colonies, especially in Africa. "The same Labour Government which had liquidated most of British Asia," says John Gallagher, "went on to animate part of British Africa. Africa would be the surrogate for India, more docile, more malleable, more pious" (1982: 146; cf. Hyam 2006: 95, 130–36). Africa had been neglected before the war; now, properly managed and developed, it seemed the place where the British might find the resources for a wide-ranging renewal of empire.

In some ways the most radical of all the measures taken after the war to strengthen imperial ties was the British Nationality Act of 1948. Common citizenship, as the bond of solidarity among all classes, had been a major theme of both official propaganda and popular culture in Britain during the Second World War. It had also been a long-standing promise held out to the other peoples of the empire, though in many cases slow in its fulfillment. Now, partly in recognition of the all-out effort by the whole empire in the war, the British government at last delivered on that promise. At a stroke all members of the empire—all inhabitants of the dominions and dependencies, as well as of former colonies, such as India, which had joined the Commonwealth—were made equal subjects of the crown, with the right to live and work in the United Kingdom. While each dominion was left free to create its own citizenship laws, the United Kingdom, as the "Mother Country," made it clear that all subjects of the empire were equal in its eyes, and that it remained the center to which all members would be drawn. As the attorney general Sir Hartley Shawcross stressed, the Nationality Act's "whole purpose is to maintain the common status, and with it the metropolitan tradition that this country is the homeland of the Commonwealth." The image of the family, common in the war, was once more drawn upon: the conception of an "all-pervading common status, or nationality," said Lord Chancellor Jowitt, was "the mark of something which differentiates the family from mere friends" (in Paul 1997: 16–17). Critics of the act were concerned at what seemed its excessive liberality with regard to immigration, and warned of trouble in store for the future. But no one at the time doubted that the act represented an extraordinary declaration of faith in the British Empire, and the hope and the expectation that, thus transformed, it could continue its life well into the future.

That hope depended, in the end, not just on the willingness of the populations of the empire to accede to the reshaped empire, but on the international climate at large and the attitude of the major international players. In the case of the British Empire that meant mostly America. Britain ended the war heavily dependent on American financial aid and in the decades thereafter found itself bound to its transatlantic partner in all important decisions of defense and foreign policy. America had a traditional dislike of empire, the British as much as any other, and under Franklin Roosevelt had declared on more than one occasion its determination to wind up the European empires after the end of the war. But with the onset of the Cold War, and the succession of Harry Truman to the US presidency, the American attitude changed. "In the American mind anti-Communism always prevailed over anti-imperialism, and this gave the British Empire . . . an extended lease of life" (Louis 1999b: 330). Now it seemed useful to deploy the European empires, especially the far-flung British and French empires with their strategically placed naval bases and army garrisons, as the means to counter communist influence and pro-Soviet anticolonial movements throughout the world. The European empires became "proxies" for American control; the Americans "acted as sleeping partners in the British and French empires," operating behind the scenes and letting the Europeans do much of the heavy lifting (Louis and Robinson 1994: 472). Some have even thought of this as a kind of "outsourced," informal, American Empire, riding on the backs of the European empires and to all intents and purposes controlling their development—a new application of the "informal" principle practiced by Britain in the nineteenth century (Go 2011: 136–45).

However we conceive it, it is clear that American support was yet another reason why the British had reason to think that they could continue in their imperial way. They could even contemplate with equanimity the independence of former colonies, so long as they remained within the Commonwealth and so long as it was possible to establish complaisant nationalist leaders in the new states. This would allow for the continued operation of influence, and for the maintenance of the key military bases needed to preserve Britain as a world power (Darwin 1984: 199; Louis and Robinson 1994: 487). Here again was the recognition of the old principle, going back to the "Third Empire" of the 1920s, that everything must change for everything to remain the same.

Whether all this was based on an illusion, whether, as increasingly proved the case, it was always going to be difficult to keep the newly independent nations—even those within the Commonwealth—within the British, or at least Anglo-American fold, is not our principal concern here. What matters is the belief, shared by so many of the commentators and policy-makers for more than two decades after the Second World War, that the imperial story was by no means over, that the British Empire in some form would and should survive. In the unpropitious climate of the postwar period, when nationalism and anticolonialism seemed to be sweeping forward to an unstoppable victory, this remains a remarkable testimony to the centuries-old British—and especially perhaps English—faith that they were a people made for empire, and could scarcely imagine themselves without one.

"Why did the British Empire last so long?" asks Paul Kennedy (1983) in an engaging essay. He gives a number of reasons, but one that he singles out for particular attention is the political culture of the British elite over a very long period. This he characterizes as "the dislike of extremes, the appeal to reasoned argument, the belief in the rationality of politics and the necessity of compromise" (1983: 216). These may seem modest virtues, and perhaps leave out some important and not so attractive features that may also have been necessary to gain and hold on to empire. But they do seem to contain a modicum of truth, and go some way toward explaining why the British were able to keep their empire for so many centuries. It also for Kennedy helps to explain why "its decline and fall was a reasonably gentle process, at times slightly inglorious and involving a certain loss of face, but also avoiding the cataclysm and chaos and domestic fissures which attended the fall of the Roman Empire, the collapse of the Third Reich, or, on a lesser scale, the end of the Portuguese Empire" (1983: 217). Many others have concurred with this view, adding the examples of the bloody ending of the French, Dutch, and Belgian empires to this comparison and contrast with the British case (see, e.g., Spruyt 2005).

But it seems necessary to add something more to this account of why the British were able to create the world's largest empire and to hold on to it for so long. Rather like the other ruling peoples we have been considering in this book—the Ottoman Turks, the Russians, the Austrians—there was the British faith in and commitment to empire, a feeling that it was Britain's destiny in the world to be an imperial power and to do with that power something good and great. We have, in other words, here as in the other cases we have discussed, to think of Britain's sense of mission, as the carrier variously or together of "Christianity, commerce, and civilization," to cite the trinity hallowed by the likes of the famous missionary David Livingstone. No account of long-lasting empire can leave out the fact of mission, because without mission there is no empire.

After the formal end of the empire in the late 1960s, it became the fashion among some people to claim that the empire had never really mattered to the

British people, at least not to most of them, and that it had left little legacy among them. A particularly egregious example was the Conservative politician Enoch Powell, once a passionate imperialist but later, as members of the empire in increasing numbers came to exercise their right to enter Britain, an equally fervent opponent of all that he thought the empire had come to stand for. In Powell's case the response took the form of virtually denying the existence of the empire. "The myth of the British Empire is one of the most extraordinary paradoxes in political history," he stated. "During the whole of the period in which Britain is imagined to have been creating her empire, she was not only unconscious of doing any such thing, but positively sure she was not" (Powell 1969: 247). This echo of Seeley—but with a meaning the opposite of Seeley's—has been heard, less forcefully put but equally unconvincingly, in more scholarly circles (e.g., Porter 2004b).

Whatever one thinks of these claims, the one thing they seem to point to unambiguously is that the empire has not gone away, and indeed continues to show its active presence if only by its ability to trouble people. The very act of denial betrays, by its force, a lively persistence. There is in fact plenty of evidence around to show that the empire, as with most of the European empires, has left behind a powerful and wide-ranging afterlife (see, e.g., Ward 2001; Thompson 2012). The British Empire may be dead; but its ghost continues to haunt the British imagination—and not just the British.

7

The French Empire

"IMPERIAL NATION-STATE"

One cannot be a great power if one stays in one's own backyard.

—JULES FERRY, LE TONKIN ET LA MÈRE PATRIE,
1890 (IN BRUNSCHWIG 1966: 84)

France is almost the only nation that has come close to resolving the problem of administering foreign races: she does not destroy them, as other nations all too often do; she knows better than anyone how to assimilate them.

—ALFRED RAMBOUD, LA FRANCE COLONIAL,
1886 (IN BAYCROFT 2004: 150)

France, by its geographic position, the extent of its territory, its fertility, has always been in the first rank of continental powers. The land is the national theater of her power and glory. Maritime commerce is but an appendage to her existence; the sea has never excited, nor will it ever excite, those national sympathies and that sort of filial respect that navigating or commercial peoples have for it. Maritime enterprises will never attract attention in France nor gain the help or wealth or talent.

—ALEXIS DE TOCQUEVILLE, "SOME IDEAS
ABOUT WHAT PREVENTS THE FRENCH FROM
HAVING GOOD COLONIES" ([1833] 2001: 1)

Empire as Nation

The French are at once the most and the least imperialist of people. They are imperialist because they believed that they should establish their presence throughout the world, that France should have a world empire. But at the

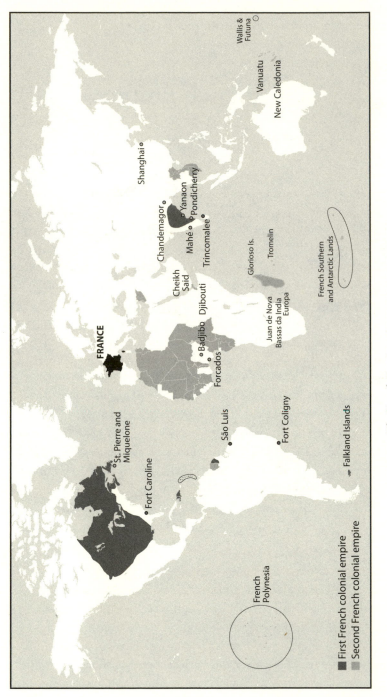

MAP 7.1. The French Empire at its greatest extent, c. 1920

Wallis &
Futuna

Vanuatu

New Caledonia

Shanghai

Yanaon
Chandernagor
Pondicherry
Mahé
Trincomalee

Glorioso Is.
Tromelin

French Southern
and Antarctic Lands

Cheikh
Saïd

Djibouti

Badjibo
Forcados

Juan de Nova
Bassas da India
Europa

FRANCE

St. Pierre and
Miquelone

Fort Caroline

São Luis

Fort Coligny

Falkland Islands

French
Polynesia

First French colonial empire

Second French colonial empire

same time they believed that the world's civilization should be distinctively French, that the French nation should stamp its character on the world. At one time that was bound up with the idea of France as God's chosen nation, charged with the mission of spreading Catholicism and royalism throughout the world. Later, after the French Revolution, rationality, republicanism, and secularism characterized the French imperial mission. But in whichever form, as compared with other empires, the French come nearest to the fusion of empire and nation, the understanding of the empire as "the nation writ large" (see chapter 1, above). Not for them—as for the Ottomans, the Habsburgs, and most other imperial peoples—the acceptance of the irreducibly plural and multinational character of empire. For the French, the French Empire was first and foremost French, marked by the qualities that distinguished the French as a nation. Hence Gary Wilder's use of the hybrid term "the French imperial nation-state" to describe both France and its empire seems peculiarly apt.[1]

It has been common, in the literature on nationalism, to regard France as the archetypal nation-state. In one sense that is absurd, and reflects the usual tendency of scholars cultivating one field not to glance over the hedge to see what their colleagues are up to in another. The French have been as imperial for as long as the English, especially if—as we have seen with the English—we regard the formation of France itself ("the Hexagon") as imperial. By the early twentieth century the French had the second-largest empire in the world, behind only the British. If we do not immediately—as we do with the Romans, the Russians, and the British—think of empire when we think of the French, that cannot be because they did not have an empire, and, like the British, more than one.

But it is nevertheless a pardonable error not to think initially of the French in imperial terms. They themselves have been so insistent on the quintessentially French—national—character of their empire that they have blinded others to the usual features associated with imperial rule. Not that their non-European subjects could possibly be unaware of those, as they showed in the extreme violence with which, in some regions at least, they threw off French rule. But to European observers and commentators what seemed more obvious was the French focus on the construction and maintenance of a viable nation-state. Given the series of revolutions and periodic crises that shook the French state in the nineteenth and twentieth centuries, it was inevitable that much thought and effort would have to go into domestic affairs, as statesmen grappled with the problem of national solidarity and national cohesion (the preoccupation of much nineteenth-century French social thought). At least four major revolutions and five republics since 1789, catastrophic military defeat on at least three occasions: how could the French not be obsessed with questions of national survival and national pride?

We need to consider the French Empire within this nationalizing perspective. Certainly there are many other things to say about the empire, and we shall consider those as well. No general account of empire can ignore the French case. But as compared with the other empires we have considered, the difference in the French case is the extent to which the French strove to make their empire an extension of themselves, of their culture and identity. The usual suppression of the ruling people's nationalism and national identity, common to most forms of imperial rule, was less marked in the French case. Often the opposite occurred: there was an expression of strong nationalism and a conviction that French culture had much to teach the world. The world would be better for being French. Hence the importance in the French case— again as compared with others—of the idea of assimilation. There were many varieties of this, and often a great distance between ideal and practice. But fundamentally it remained a governing idea for much of French imperial history. Whereas the Ottomans and the Habsburgs and even the British would accept and even promote difference, for the French it seemed inconceivable that, once exposed to French culture, everyone would not wish to share in that culture to the fullest extent possible, to become, in a word, French.

There was a further reason why the distance between nation and empire did not seem so great in the French case, why there might be a tendency to elide them, at least in the modern period. During the course of the Great French Revolution, the French nation defined itself in peculiarly universalistic terms. In their Declaration of the Rights of Man and of the Citizen, in their espousal of the goals of liberty, equality, and fraternity, in their enthronement of Reason as the supreme standard by which all must be judged: the French characterized themselves in terms that were eminently suitable for empire. The universality of French nationhood could easily be transposed to the universality of empire. What was good for the French nation was precisely what would be good for humankind as a whole: the reign of reason and liberty, the forms and attitudes of French republicanism. The civilizing mission that was launched in relation to the French people themselves during the course of the French Revolution could, by a fairly easy extension, be applied to the world at large. It could form the justifying ideology of the French Empire, the same universalism doing duty for both nation and empire. France, *la grande nation*, and Greater France, *la plus grande France*, had an overlap and a continuity unusual in overseas empires, where the distance—in all senses—between metropole and colony is commonly quite considerable. In that sense the French overseas empire comes closer to the model of the land empires, where metropole and colony can merge insensibly into each other. That cannot truly be said to have happened in the French case, partly because the French people themselves did not settle in their empire in any great numbers, unlike, say, the British in their empire. The difference between French and "natives"—most of whom were African and Asian—was too obvious to be ignored. But it was one of the many ways in which the French Empire was distinguished from others—both land and overseas empires—that, despite this, nation and empire could still occupy the same ideological space. Alfred Ramboud, writing in 1886, could see this is as a distinctively French achievement: "Only France, until now, has had the courage to think of the metropole and the colonies as forming one single homeland, one state" (in Baycroft 2004: 150).

France's Many Empires

Like the English and British, the French have been the creators of multiple empires. The first was, like the English, medieval and early modern. This was, again like the English, a land empire, the "inner empire" of the Hexagon, built up over many centuries by the French kings. The French nation-state, like the English/British, has all the hallmarks of the "miniempire," the empire in miniature (see chapter 1). France achieved nationhood by a process of conquest launched by the Capetian kings from their base in the Île-de-France. One by one they forcibly incorporated Brittany, Burgundy, Languedoc, Normandy, Gascony, Aquitaine, Provence, and several other once proud and independent principalities of the Carolingian successor kingdoms of West Francia, East Francia, and Lotharingia. It took several hundred years, and the suppression of many internal rebellions, for the French kings to weld together the disparate territories of their "inner empire" (Collins 1995).

Even the great centralizing influence of the French Revolution still left much to be done, at least in the countryside where the majority of the people lived. According to Eugen Weber (1976), it was only in the late nineteenth century that the process seriously began of turning peasants of many tongues and disparate traditions into Frenchmen and Frenchwomen. Rogers Brubaker points out that the idea of *la mission civilisatrice*, usually applied to justify France's overseas empire, initially had reference to the civilizing mission of the French state in relation to its own domestic inhabitants. This "internal *mission civilisatrice"* was to be carried out by the *instituteurs*, the schoolteach-ers, "whose mission was to *institute* the nation" (Brubaker 1992: 11). As Eugen Weber says, "the famous hexagon [i.e., France in its current form] can itself be seen as a colonial empire shaped over the centuries: a complex of territories conquered, annexed, and integrated in a political and administrative whole, many of them with strongly developed national or regional personalities, some of them with traditions that were specifically un- or anti-French" (Weber 1976: 485; see also Kuzio 2002: 32; Quinn 2002: 109; Baycroft 2004: 149–51).[2]

While France was creating its first "imperial nation-state," it was also con-structing its first overseas empire in the North Atlantic in the sixteenth and seventeenth centuries (Aldrich 1996: 10–19; Quinn 2002: 11–65; Hart 2004: 188–92). As with the English, the abortive search—in the French case by Giovanni da Verrazzano and Jacques Cartier—for a Northwest passage to the East led to the French settlements on the St. Lawrence River that later became Québec (1608) and Montréal (1642). This was "New France," domi-nated by the cod-fishing industry and the fur trade that became the basis of the economic prosperity of French Atlantic ports such as Bordeaux, Saint-Malo, Rouen, Dieppe, and Honfleur.

From New France, French traders and explorers ventured beyond the Great Lakes southward along the Mississippi River all the way to its outlet in the Gulf of Mexico. New Orleans was founded in 1718. The French province of Louisiana encompassed a vast tract on either side of the Mississippi, about five times the size of continental France.

French colonial enterprise also showed itself in the Caribbean. French set-tlements were established in Guadeloupe (1635) and Martinique (1635), and in the 1630s France strengthened its hold on Saint-Domingue (the eastern side of Hispaniola). In 1612 French Guiana (Guyane) was first settled, making it France's oldest continuous overseas possession (it is still French), though also one of its most notorious, as the site of the penal colony of Devil's Island from 1852 to 1937 (one of whose best-known inmates was Captain Dreyfus). Guiana was never a success as a colony; but the other West Indian colonies prospered with the development of the sugar trade, cultivated mostly by slaves. By 1700 there were over 44,000 people (of whom 30,000 were slaves) in the French West Indies; in New France (Canada) there were barely 10,000 (Quinn 2002: 56).

France did not restrict itself to the Atlantic; it had Asian ambitions too. In 1664 the French East India Company was founded, and bases were established in India at Pondicherry (1674) and Chandernagore (1684). The French also settled the Indian Ocean islands of Île de Bourbon (now Réunion) and Île de France (now Mauritius)—important stepping-stones on the route to Asia.

At the beginning of the eighteenth century, France seemed firmly established on its imperial course—more firmly perhaps than its main rival, Britain. "Much of North America, including the vast expanses of New France and part of the American heartland, belonged to the French Overseas Empire in the 18th century, and from it poured the wealth of the Canadian fur trade. In the West Indies the sugar industry burgeoned and, with it, the demand for African slaves. In East Asia the brief but real prospect of a French India made France a major presence on the subcontinent" (Quinn 2002: 67). By the end of the century, most of this was gone. France had lost Canada and India. Saint-Domingue—at one time the richest possession in the whole Caribbean—had erupted in rebellion (1791), and in 1804 became the independent state of Haiti. In 1803 the vast Louisiana territory was sold to the new United States. After three centuries of overseas expansion, France's overseas empire was reduced to a handful of small Caribbean islands and a few African and Asian trading stations. How had that happened?

The answer can almost be put in one word: Britain. It was the English/British who had competed with France in the North Atlantic, and it was the newly united kingdom of Great Britain and Ireland that after 1707 bested France in almost every theater of the globe. Britain was at war with France for a good part of the eighteenth century and in most of the encounters came out on top. Most important was the Seven Years' War (1756–63), often called the "First World War." Here Britain defeated France in North America, India, and the Caribbean. France's first overseas empire was more or less wiped out, to Britain's benefit. At the Treaty of Paris (1763), France ceded New France (Canada) and the whole section of Louisiana east of the Mississippi (until 1803 the rest of Louisiana went to Spain in compensation for Florida, which went to Britain). France also lost some of its Caribbean colonies, but managed to cling on to Martinique, Guadeloupe, and Saint-Domingue. By siding with the colonists against Britain in the American War of Independence, France even managed to regain some of its possessions, such as Senegal and Tobago. But these were small crumbs of comfort for the almost total loss of empire.

Rivalry with Britain for global power and influence has to be seen as one of the principal forces driving France's imperial ambitions in the eighteenth and nineteenth centuries. For much of the seventeenth century France, while constructing a large overseas empire, had also been the dominant power in Europe. Long before the English, as far back as the fourteenth century, the

French had declared themselves the "elect nation," favored by God among all peoples. Popes at various times gave papal sanction to this concept (Strayer 1971: 313). This sense of a special, divinely ordained, mission had sustained the French kings through all the trials and ordeals—the Fronde, the Wars of Religion—of the sixteenth and early seventeenth centuries. In the second half of the seventeenth century, under the "Sun King," Louis XIV, that promise seemed on the point of fulfillment. The French state had vastly expanded its boundaries and—it seemed to its anxious neighbors—was poised to take over the whole of the Continent. The French established themselves more firmly in North America and gained a foothold in India. Power and glory radiated from the magnificent new palace at Versailles (Goubert 1970; Hart 2008: 112–18).

Momentarily checked by the Dutch and British in the War of the Spanish Succession (1702–13), France resumed its bid for world power in the eighteenth century (Jones 2003). It was aided in this quest by the fact that France had become, in the eyes of many, the shining light of European civilization, setting the standards and becoming the model for all other European countries, if not the world. French was the language of most European courts and aristocracies (including the Russian). French thought and the French thinkers of the Enlightenment were admired and courted everywhere. It was indeed the French who invented the very concept of "civilization" and the "civilizing process"—French civilization being of course taken as the defining example (Febvre 1973).

French reverses and rebuffs, especially at the hands of the British, were therefore especially wounding to the national pride. A strong strain of French "Anglophobia" developed in the second half of the eighteenth century, to which the British responded in kind with their own brand of "Francophobia" (Acomb 1950; Newman 1987; Bell 2003: 78–106). Britain's loss of its American colonies was of course greeted with great satisfaction in France, which enthusiastically welcomed the American heroes Benjamin Franklin and Thomas Jefferson as well as Tom Paine, the Briton who had done the most to aid the American cause. Voltaire and Montesquieu might praise British freedom and its constitutional arrangements; but for most French Britain was the enemy, the country that constantly thwarted French ambitions (Tombs and Tombs 2007).

Liah Greenfeld has argued that the principle of nationalism in the modern world has been *ressentiment*—as she puts it, following Nietzsche, "a psychological state resulting from suppressed feelings of envy and hatred (existential envy) and the impossibility of satisfying these feelings" (1992: 15). As a general rule, Greenfeld clearly overstates this factor, but she is on stronger grounds in seeing it at work in the French case (Greenfeld 1992: 177–84; see also Kumar 2003: 89–120). It was not, however, that nebulous thing "English nationalism" that the French attempted to imitate, nor was it the English idea of the nation that inspired them (if anything, in the case of nationalism, the influence was all in the opposite direction). What caused *ressentiment* in eighteenth- and nineteenth-century France were the repeated triumphs of British *imperialism*, and the seeming impossibility of thwarting or matching it. Again and again, wherever and whenever they encountered the British—in North America, the Caribbean, India, Africa—the French found themselves either defeated or frustrated in their designs. For a nation accustomed to thinking of itself as *la grande nation*, the center and cynosure of European civilization, the repeated humiliation at the hands of a power that had only recently arrived on the world stage was especially galling. Eventually the French did rebuild their overseas empire, making it the second-largest in the world. But there was the rub; France was not used to being second, especially when the first place was secured by the rival that it had fought—mostly unsuccessfully—for over a hundred years.

It was, it seems, in the course of the Hundred Years' War (1337–1453) between France and England that the idea, if not exactly the phrase, of "perfidious Albion"—*la perfide Albion, Albion perfide, le perfide anglais*—was first announced in France. But its real career was not to come until the eighteenth and nineteenth centuries. Used by the French themselves at various times in the eighteenth century—and borrowed by others angered by Britain's behavior, such as Prussia after its abandonment by Britain at the close of the Seven Years' War—it achieved something like official national status during the French Revolution and the Napoleonic empire. Both Robespierre and Napoleon, in their official capacities, assiduously promoted the expression in their anti-British propaganda. With Napoleon's Europe-wide empire, the expression was diffused throughout Europe, becoming available for use by anyone resentful of Britain's rising world power in the nineteenth century. But throughout the nineteenth century it was the French who, as Britain's main rival for empire, felt most called upon to employ the expression against their frustratingly successful antagonist (Schmidt 1953).

The French Napoleonic Empire

Having lost their first overseas empire, the French almost immediately set about constructing their second land empire (if the first be taken to be the Hexagon itself). Its name is indelibly associated with Napoleon Bonaparte, first as a general under the Directory (1795–99), then as First Consul under the Consulate (1799–1804), and finally, from 1804, as the self-styled and self-crowned "emperor of the French" (a title made the more significant by Napoleon's abolition of the Holy Roman Empire in 1806 and his marriage in 1810 to Maria-Louise, daughter of the Habsburg emperor—thus proclaiming Napoleon as legatee of the venerable Holy Roman Empire). Thus was established what came to be called the "First Empire" (1804–15), to be succeeded later by the Second Empire (1852–70) of Napoleon's nephew, Louis Napoleon Bonaparte, as Napoleon III.

The Napoleonic empire was, in the end, almost wholly a continental land empire This was not because Napoleon, fervent admirer of Alexander the Great, did not have ambitions beyond Europe. The French conquest of Egypt (1798–1801), short-lived as it turned out to be, was meant to inaugurate a great Eastern empire, to drive the British out of India and reestablish French influence and power in Asia. The British, under Admiral Horatio Nelson, put an end to this dream at the "Battle of the Nile" (Aboukir Bay) (1798), once more thwarting French imperial designs.[3] But French interest and influence in Egypt were lasting, continuing throughout the nineteenth century until—once more and finally—the British eclipsed them in the 1880s and 1890s. Napoleon himself was fascinated by Egyptian culture and religion, parading himself in Islamic costume, setting in motion a vast program of research and documentation on Egypt, and carting off many Egyptian antiquities to Paris. He was acutely conscious that Alexander the Great had conquered Egypt at exactly the same age, twenty-nine, as he, and aspired to set his cultural imprint on the region in just the way Alexander had. His disappointment at his failure was deep and lasting (Englund 2004: 136; Jasanoff 2005: 117–48; Cole 2007).

Napoleon's other attempts to create an overseas empire were equally unsuccessful. Blocked in the East, he aspired to create a new French Empire in the West, by reviving French power in North America and the Caribbean. The newly restored Louisiana Territory was to be the linchpin of an empire linked to Saint-Domingue and the other Caribbean colonies. But the unexpected return of war with Britain in 1803 dashed these hopes, leading to the sale of Louisiana to the United States in 1803 for $15 million—the bargain of the century. Meanwhile Napoleon's reimposition of slavery in Saint-Domingue had—despite the capture of Toussaint L'Ouverture—brought about renewed black rebellion, resulting in Haitian independence in 1804. French attempts to reconstruct their Atlantic empire had led to the creation of the first independent black state in the Western hemisphere: an inspiration to others in the years to come. Napoleon's reaction to this loss as well as to other failures in the region is well-known: "Damn sugar, damn coffee, damn colonies!" (Quinn 2002: 77).

After Napoleon's defeat in 1815, France was stripped of many of its few remaining overseas possessions. It lost the Île de France (Mauritius), the Seychelles, and a number of the smaller Caribbean islands. But Guadeloupe and Martinique were restored to it, and it held on to Guyane, Réunion (the post-revolutionary name for the Île de Bourbon), the rich cod islands of St. Pierre and Miquelon—still French today—off the Newfoundland coast, its five trading posts (*comtoirs*) in India (Pondicherry, Mahé, Chandernagore, Yanaon, and Karikal), and the island of Gorée and the city of Saint-Louis in Senegal (Aldrich 1996: 20). These—later referred to as the *vieilles colonies*, the "old colonies," to distinguish them from the new colonies acquired after 1830—were small pickings indeed, compared to France's once-thriving overseas empire. Meanwhile, despite the loss of the American colonies, Britain was reorganizing Canada, strengthening its hold on India, and developing new colonies in Australia, New Zealand, and South Africa. The comparison could not fail to be bitter to the French, on top of their defeat by an alliance mainly led and funded by their great rival.

But if Napoleon failed in his bid to found an overseas empire, he was spectacularly successful in establishing a European empire. Napoleon's *Grand Empire*, like most empires, was a hodgepodge of territories linked in different ways to the person of the emperor. But by 1812 it included practically all the lands constituting the contemporary European Union, and, through alliance, for a while even including Russia. Napoleon's "Continental System," formed as a result of British blockade of French foreign trade, was an early and remarkably successful instance of a European Economic Community. The Napoleonic empire was the greatest European empire since Charlemagne's, with which it was often compared. But equally common were comparisons with Rome's empire, and Napoleon with Caesar. Napoleon had not been able to match Alexander the Great's exploits in creating an empire that linked two worlds, East and West. But he had at least equaled if not excelled the achievements of the Roman emperors (Englund 2004: 332–39).

The Roman parallel is especially instructive in understanding what was perhaps the most important legacy of the Napoleonic empire: the French "civilizing mission," *la mission civilisatrice*. This was not of course the first time that the French had linked their empire to the civilizing mission. Since the Middle Ages, first in relation to the territories adjacent to the core area of the

Île-de-France—the "inner empire"—then in relation to the overseas empire, French kings had seen it as their mission to diffuse French civilization to the world. Primarily this meant at this time Catholic Christianity and the institutions of French absolutism (Stanbridge 1997). As always this was conceived in universalistic terms: just as with the Roman or British empires, the French imperial rulers thought they had discovered what was best for the world as a whole.

The French Revolution dramatically and decisively ended the possibility of conceiving the French imperial mission in these terms. Church, king, priests, aristocrats: all were bloodily rejected. In their place were installed "the people" and "the nation." Monarchy became republic. Subjects became citizens. Reason replaced religion (or became the new "civil religion"). Equality and fraternity replaced privilege and hierarchy. France was still the teacher to the world, even more so than before. But the lesson was now very different. "French civilization" carried a different stamp. Its civilizing mission had to change accordingly.

This was Napoleon's accomplishment. The importance of the Napoleonic empire in French imperial history was that it marked an almost total transformation of the idea of the French imperial mission—from royalism and Catholicism to republicanism and secularism. For his detractors, at the time and since, Napoleon may have been thought to have corrupted, even undermined, the message of the French Revolution. Empire and dictatorship seemed to have little to do with "liberty, equality, and fraternity." But in longer-term perspective he can be seen to have in many ways consolidated the achievements of the Revolution (Woolf 1992: 95–98; see also Woolf 1989). The Napoleonic Code incorporated many of the legal and administrative changes introduced by the Revolution. It became the basis of the legal systems adopted by many of the states of Napoleon's empire, even after they regained their independence. The slogans of the Revolution—and its anthem, "La Marseillaise"—were carried by Napoleon's armies to every corner of the European continent, inspiring its inhabitants to seek the necessary changes within their own societies, and, by an ironic but not unfamiliar twist, giving them the ideological ammunition to rise up against their French masters themselves. The French civilizing mission took on a new, thoroughly modern, character. It now promised the world not religion and royalty but reason and republicanism—achieved, if necessary, by revolutionary means.

Maya Jasanoff has expressed very well how profoundly these new developments changed not just French conceptions of themselves but also the nature of the century-long struggle between France and Britain for global supremacy.

Earlier conflicts had pitted British liberty, British Protestantism, and British-style monarchy against the perceived despotism of French absolutism and Catholicism. From 1793, however, the clash was no longer between two different models of crown, church, and state; it was between two drastically opposing visions of society. In British eyes, this was a struggle to defend the familiar social order against the kingless, godless, egalitarian republicanism of the Reign of Terror. To the French revolutionaries, the conflict pitted reason, equality, and liberty against religion, privilege and tyranny. The strength of these ideological convictions made the Revolutionary-Napoleonic Wars stand in relation to the Seven Years War in something like the way World War II later would to World War I. The Seven Years War had been fought for power, land and security; now Britain and France were fighting to defend and extend their very ways of life. (2005: 118–19)

The French mission may have changed its character and content; but there were still continuities with the earlier empire that indicated how any later efforts at empire would be conceived and executed. Even more than the case with the earlier empire, and far more than in the case of England/Britain, the new civilizing mission was linked more firmly than ever with the nation. It was after all one of the most notable accomplishments of the French Revolution to invent the very notion of "the nation" in its modern sense, and in doing so to formulate the doctrine of nationalism (Brubaker 1992: 35–49). The French were the first modern nation; they showed the rest of the world what it was like to be a nation. If, like many other nation-states, France was also imperial, it was almost inevitable that the empire would carry the stamp of the nation to an even greater degree than in other cases. The French revolutionary nation, through its citizen armies, through the conquests of Napoleon, had carried its idea of itself to every corner of Europe, and beyond, to South America, the Caribbean, the Middle East. It had defined itself in revolutionary terms, as republican and free. If, as to its critics, it would appear paradoxical and even contradictory that such a nation could create and have an empire, nevertheless when it did so that empire was bound to be deeply marked by the signs of French national identity. *La Grande Empire*, like other French empires before and to come, was still an extension of *la Grande Nation*, the French nation-state writ large.

There were other features that made the association of nation and empire unusually close in the French case. The first was the widespread failure of most of the private chartered companies set up to develop the overseas empire. The

French West India Company, set up by Colbert in 1664 to manage France's Caribbean colonies, limped along for a decade before failing and being replaced by direct state rule. The French East India Company, also launched in 1664, fared a little better, but never managed to do more than establish a few trading posts in India (compare the British East India Company, which ruled India for over a century, or the success of the Dutch East India Company in the East Indies). Other companies—like the Compagnie de Cap Vert de Senegal, de la Chine, des Indes, des Indes Orientales, du Cap Nord—were short-lived failures. Part of their problem was French insistence on close governmental control, stifling local initiative (Quinn 2002: 44). Whatever the reason, the French overseas empire, from an early date, was of necessity a state-sponsored venture, directly regulated from Paris (Stanbridge 1997). Once the state, following the Revolution, became a nation-state, it was more or less inevitable that any new empire that was formed would be subject to the same pattern of centralized control, but reflecting now the character of the newly fashioned nation.

There was a further feature that had an enduring effect on the character of the French colonial empire. That was the difficulty of persuading the French themselves to travel overseas and settle in the French colonies. At the end of the seventeenth century, New France had barely 10,000 French settlers, compared to over 20,000 British further south in the American colonies. This pattern continued into the eighteenth century. By the mid-eighteenth century, there were more than two million British settlers on America's eastern seaboard. By contrast, the French had only about 70,000 people spread thinly along a wide arc from the St. Lawrence River though the Great Lakes to the Mississippi River Valley. Only Quebec and New Orleans, 1,500 miles apart, were cities of any size (Quinn 2002: 52, 68).

French reluctance to move and settle abroad—despite repeated pressure from the government and many schemes of state assistance—has been traced to France's relatively small population throughout the eighteenth and nineteenth centuries, linked to the widespread availability of land and the relative prosperity of the French peasantry (as Alexis de Tocqueville pointed out in *L'Ancien Régime et la Révolution*, 1856). There was, in other words, little "push" from the motherland, little inducement to risk one's life and fortune in parts of the world with often uncongenial climates and strange diseases (Aldrich 1996: 138–39). With a soaring population in the nineteenth century, and the ravages of industrialization, the British on the contrary poured out of the British Isles, peopling Australasia and South Africa as well as adding vastly to the population of North America (both Canada and the United States). France's population in the nineteenth century stubbornly refused to rise, to the despair of its statesmen and publicists. In 1870 the population was 36 million. By 1911 it had reached only 39 million, a growth of only 8.6 percent since 1870. In the same period Germany's population grew from 41 million to 65 million, an increase of 60 percent; and the United Kingdom—with a land area much smaller than France's—increased from 29 million to nearly 45 million. France's yearly rate of growth, at 0.3 percent, was the lowest in the whole of Europe (Conklin, Fishman, and Zaretsky 2015: 76; Livi-Baci 1992: 139; Quinn 2002: 110).

Pour sauver un petite France, il faut avoir une grande France—"to save a small France there must be a greater France." Such was an oft-repeated sentiment in the years before the First World War, in the face of what was seen as a disastrously low birthrate. French women in particular were urged to help save the French race by creating an "overseas France." In the end, in the late nineteenth century, reasonable concentrations of ethnic French were built up in some of the North African colonies, especially Algeria and Morocco. But overall the numbers of overseas French remained dismally low throughout the period of the empire from the 1870s to the 1950s. "France has colonies but no colonists," quipped Otto von Bismarck.

On the eve of the First World War there were only 700,000 French living abroad in the colonies, 500,000 of them in Algeria alone (where they were a bare majority in a European population containing many Italians, Spaniards, and Maltese). Sometimes the French were in a minority even among Europeans: in Tunisia in 1911 there were 88,000 Italians but only 46,000 French (there were also 11,000 Maltese). In Morocco in 1914 the French made up a bare majority—53 percent of a European population of 48,000—the rest being Spanish and Italian. In French Indochina there were only 24,000 French among an indigenous population of 16 million. French communities in the sub-Saharan African colonies made up an even smaller proportion of the total population. At its height, after the First World War when it included the League of Nations mandates, the French overseas empire encompassed over 12 million square kilometers and 65 million overseas inhabitants. This made it the second-largest empire in the world after the British (which was three times the size of the French and contained seven times as many people). But the number of overseas French never exceeded 1,475,000 persons (Aldrich 1996: 144–45; Quinn 2002: 114, 183, 210; Ferguson 2004: 240–41; Frémeaux 2007: 157).

Unlike "Greater Britain," "Greater France," it is clear, was defined more by territory than by the presence of significant numbers of people from the

BRITAIN

FRANCE

MAP 7.2. The British and French empires compared, 1920

homeland. There was no real equivalent to the British "white dominions" in Greater France, no Australia or Canada with their millions of Britons. The nearest thing were the *colons* of Algeria or Morocco, an embattled minority in a much larger indigenous population, closer, say, to South Africa or Kenya in the British Empire, and like those colonies as problematic for the home government as for the majority population.

The Second Overseas Empire

It has been persuasively argued—by Maya Jasanoff, among others—that there was considerable continuity between the first, old regime, French overseas empire, and the second, the one that began with the conquest of Algiers in 1830. French hopes continued in India, as they sought and made alliances with various anti-British Indian princes, notably Tipu Sultan of Mysore. The romance of the East continued to draw French statesmen and savants. The French had retained their interest in Egypt in particular, following Napoleon's withdrawal, as shown for instance in the collecting activities of Bernardino Drovetti and Jean-François Champollion in the 1820s. Since his appointment as pasha of Egypt by the Ottomans in 1805, the French too had courted and supported the ambitious and energetic Muhammad Ali. British opposition to a renewed French presence in Egypt meant that there was no hope of the French reasserting themselves politically there, at least for the time being; and in any case Muhammad Ali, closely advised by the French consuls Mathieu de Lesseps and Drovetti, was a kind of French surrogate. But there was Algeria; and the French assault on Algiers can therefore be seen as a continuation of French designs on Egypt and more generally North Africa and the Middle East. "The turn to North Africa was anchored in France's long history of involvement in the region, and in Egypt in particular. Arguably, France would never have moved to conquer Algeria had it not already established itself in Egypt" (Jasanoff 2005: 286; and see generally 211–306).

In French eyes there was always something special about Algeria, so close to France's Mediterranean coast. Interest in the country dated back to the sixteenth century, when the French established a trading base there, the Bastion de France, and trading relations had continued thereafter. The Bastion was an entrepôt for the import to France of exotic goods from Africa and the Middle East—gold, spices, ostrich plumes (Aldrich 1996: 24). The exoticism and romance of Algeria and other North African countries, so frequently exploited by French painters such as Eugène Delacroix and writers such as

Gustave Flaubert, had deep roots. Jasanoff comments that "Algeria was to the modern French Empire something like what India was to the British: the Eastern colony most closely tied to France, its first won and hardest lost" (2005: 286; see also Gildea 2009: 222–24).

The conquest of Algeria was nevertheless a long-drawn-out, brutal, and bloody affair, marked by the heroic resistance of Abd el-Kader and the vengeful suppressions of General Bugeaud. Ten percent of the population of Algeria is said to have died in the fighting. Only in 1847 was Abd el-Kader forced to surrender, and only in 1871 was French control of Algeria finally secured. Even then Algeria continued to be ruled by the military, as it had been since 1830; a civilian administration was installed only in 1879 (Aldrich 1996: 25–28; Quinn 2002: 121–27; Kiser 2009).

But Algeria remained for long a lone outpost of the new French Empire. It is this that lends support to the idea that, although indeed there are continuities, in many ways Algeria marks a new beginning, a recommencement of empire, after the massive losses, in North America and India, of the eighteenth century (Andrew and Kanya-Forstner 1988). The British First and Second Empires seem more closely connected, by the continuing British presence in North America (Canada), as well as the early conquests by Clive and Hastings in India, which overlapped with and compensated for the loss of the American colonies. In France in the early nineteenth century, following Napoleon's failure to reestablish an overseas empire, there was almost nothing left of the first overseas empire. The defeat of Tipu Sultan ended France's last hopes of restoring its influence in India. The sale of Louisiana to the United States wound up its North American empire. A few West Indian islands, a few specks in the Indian Ocean: that was virtually the French overseas empire before the conquest of Algeria. After that there was no further looking to India or North America. The new French Empire would be African, beginning with North Africa. It would also be Asian, but no longer South Asian; it was further east, to Southeast and East Asia that the French turned their eyes in the nineteenth century.

The period between the 1830s and 1870s certainly is not bereft of imperial ventures. But the general picture is one of quiescence, a turning away from the grand imperial ambitions of the kings and emperors of the past. A restoration in 1815, a revolution in 1830, a new regime—the "bourgeois monarchy" of Louis-Philippe: France felt it best to devote itself to internal matters, above all to economic and commercial development. "Enrichissez-vous," declared Louis-Philippe's chief minister, François Guizot, to his fellow countrymen. That was infinitely preferable to the pursuit of empire. In a speech to the

National Assembly in 1842 Guizot explained why he was opposed to old-style colonialism, and why what France needed were not colonies but simply "support stations" (*points d'appui* or *points de reláche*) around the world for its commerce.

> I am inclined to believe, in general, that it is little befitting the policy and genius of France to essay new and great colonial establishments at a great distance from our territory and, for their sake, to engage in long struggles either against natives of these countries or against other powers. What is appropriate for France, what is indispensable, is to possess at points on the globe which are destined to become great centres of commerce, sure and strong maritime stations to serve as a support for our commerce, where the fleet can obtain provisions and find a safe harbor. (in Aldrich 1996: 94; see also Andrew and Kanya-Forstner 1988: 10, 15)

Richard Cobden, the great opponent of colonies in Britain at this time, would have found plenty to approve of in this philosophy. But whereas in Britain opinion soon began to swing the other way, or at least accept that there was a case for empire, Guizot's view represented a strong strand of thinking about overseas empire that resonated throughout the nineteenth century in France. Even after 1871, when, for various reasons, empire returned to the agenda, many in France remained convinced that it was a dangerous distraction, that France had far more important things to do at home and in Europe than to get entangled with overseas possessions. Even more than has been claimed for Britain, the French in the nineteenth century were "reluctant imperialists."

There were indeed some episodes, between the initial conquest of Algiers in 1830 and the resumption of empire under the Third Republic after 1871, of an imperial kind. When Muhammad Ali declared his independence of the Ottoman Empire in 1838, he was supported by the French, who saw an opportunity for France to gain an important foothold in Egypt. The British, under the direction of the foreign secretary Viscount Palmerston, quickly and decisively put a stop to all this, forcing Muhammad Ali to restore Ottoman rule and indicating to the French that any action on their part would result in war with Britain. The British had supported Greek independence, but were not prepared to allow any further weakening of the Ottoman Empire, especially if the beneficiaries were the French (Jasanoff 2005: 301–3; Gildea 2009: 221–22). Once more the British stood in the way of French imperial aspirations.

Not surprisingly, there were also imperial episodes during the "Second Empire" of Louis-Napoleon Bonaparte, Napoleon III (1852–70). Not only did these relate to Europe—the vague hopes of pushing the French borders to the Rhine, the championing of Polish independence, the help given to the Italians against the Habsburgs, all of which aroused suspicions of French imperial designs, especially as the Italian war led to the French annexation of Nice and Savoy. There were also important overseas ventures, the most significant of which were the annexation of Cochinchina and the establishment of a protectorate over Cambodia between 1862 and 1867. The pacification of Algeria continued, with Napoleon, in imitation of his uncle, declaring that "I am equally the Emperor of the Arabs as of the French" (in Quinn 2002: 125). In Senegal, the French engineering officer Louis Faidherbe between 1854 and 1865 did much to extend and strengthen French control. He established the three-tiered system of local administration that became the model for the whole of French Africa, and founded the famous Tirailleurs Sénégalais (Senegalese Infantry) that—drawing on troops from many parts of French West Africa—provided the backbone of the colonial contribution to the French war effort in the two world wars of the twentieth century (Cobban 1961: 174; Andrew and Kanya-Forstner 1988: 11; Quinn 2002: 155–56).

Less consequentially, and having something of the character of a fantastic dream about it, was what seems to have been a halfhearted attempt to restore a French presence in the Americas. Using the opportunity offered by a debt-collecting Anglo-French expedition to Mexico in 1862, Napoleon III committed French troops to the region and induced the Mexican government of President Juárez to offer the Mexican crown to the archduke Ferdinand Maximilian, younger brother of the Habsburg emperor Franz Joseph. Maximilian ruled as emperor of Mexico for a few troubled years, before being abandoned by the French, and seized and shot by Mexican rebels in 1867 (Cobban 1961: 180–82; Bérenger 1997: 273; Cunningham 2001).

Napoleon III's aims and ambitions have always puzzled historians. While in exile, living in various European capitals, he presented himself as a "man of destiny," called upon to finish the work begun by his illustrious uncle, the first Napoleon. His *Des Ideés napoléoniennes* (1839) outlined vague and vast plans for a world united on the national principle, living in peace and harmony. He committed himself to undoing the Treaty of Vienna of 1815, which he considered had unfairly handed Europe over to a few reactionary powers, Britain, Russia, Austria. Had they taken these ideas seriously, the European powers would have had good reason to be alarmed.

Once installed in power, the man of destiny acted with a much greater degree of circumspection and caution than his earlier posturing might have suggested. Protesting that "L'Empire, c'est la Paix," he put much of his energy into furthering France's economic and social development. Paris was transformed under the prefect of the Seine, the Alsatian Protestant Baron Haussmann. The country was covered with railways. Important banks were founded, and the foreign commerce of France greatly expanded. Napoleon surrounded himself with Saint-Simonians, encouraging the endeavors of such innovators as Ferdinand de Lesseps with his daring project of a Suez Canal, begun in 1859. Determined not to repeat the mistake of his uncle in antagonizing Great Britain, he joined with Britain in the Crimean War and in the punitive expedition to Peking in 1860 at the end of Britain's Second Opium War with China. Against the opposition of French industrialists, in 1860 he negotiated the Cobden Free Trade treaty with Britain, thus inaugurating a period of free trade between the countries that greatly furthered French industrial development (Cobban 1961: 175–77; Parry 2001: 149, 156–62).

At the same time, he continued to arouse European suspicions as to his intentions by his policies in regard to Poland, Italy, and other "oppressed nationalities." He showed constant interest in the idea of France's "natural frontiers," and the acquisition of the Rhineland in pursuit of that aim. Echoes of earlier Napoleonic ambitions were too often worryingly present. Britain in particular, especially under the premiership of Lord Palmerston, remained deeply suspicious of the emperor's intentions, even to the point of fearing a French invasion of Britain. Even the Suez Canal aroused fears, as restarting French ambitions in Egypt (Parry 2001: 148–49).

In the end the collapse of Napoleon's empire as a result of the Franco-Prussian War threw a shadow over the whole Second Empire. French politicians and intellectuals vied with each other in denigrating it and its leader. Napoleon was portrayed as a rogue and a buffoon, the subject of merciless caricatures. The cartoons of Daumier ("Ratapoil"), the writings of Victor Hugo (*Châtiments*) and Émile Zola (the Rougon-Macquart novels) were hugely influential in portraying the empire as vulgar and corrupt, the plaything of greedy financiers and scheming prostitutes.[4] The very word "empire," associated with the Second Empire, developed negative and opprobrious overtones, making it a shunned expression not just in France but elsewhere, as in Britain and Germany (Koebner and Schmidt 1964: 1–26; Parry 2001: 169–73).

It was in fact the Franco-Prussian War of 1870–71, and its consequences, that radically changed French attitudes toward empire. The period from the conquest of Algeria in 1830 to the foundation of the Third Republic in 1871 was one of intermittent overseas ventures—some of which turned out to be important—but no sustained effort and, it appeared, no strong public interest in reviving empire after the failure of the first overseas empire and that of the first Napoleon. The revolution of 1830, another revolution in 1848, a Second Republic, a Second Empire: France seemed to have enough domestic problems not to have the time and energy for overseas concerns. Throughout its European neighbors watched France closely, on the lookout for any signs of the old adventurism, ready to act decisively, as they did during the Egyptian crisis of 1840.

The crushing defeat of France by Prussia in 1871, and the consolidation of a powerful united Germany on its eastern flank, might have made it appear that France would be even less inclined than formerly to think of empire, whether in Europe or overseas. How could it do so when faced by such devastating losses and such domestic turmoil? The Franco-Prussian War was immediately succeeded by the rising of the Parisian workers and the establishment of the Paris Commune in 1871. The Commune was put down bloodily by the French government of Adolphe Thiers, which had removed itself for safekeeping to Versailles. Something like 20,000–30,000 Communards were killed in the fighting, many of them in summary executions by Thiers's troops. It was the worst defeat of the French working class in the nineteenth century, perhaps its worst ever. The Third Republic was founded on a disastrous defeat by a foreign enemy; but it was also founded on the blood of its own citizens, at its own hands. The crushing of the Paris Commune gave rise to just one of the many bitter social and ideological divisions that beset the Third Republic from its inception and that only ceased, at least to some degree, during another bloodbath, that of the First World War. Only in that war did the nation really seem united, perhaps for the first time since 1871.

The concerns of domestic stability and order might be considered one factor inhibiting imperial ambitions (though of course one cannot discount empire as a time-honored distraction from domestic problems). But what to contemporaries appeared an even greater obstacle was the predicament France found itself in as a result of the Prussian victory. In the peace settlement of 1871, France was forced to cede the two great and prosperous provinces of Alsace and Lorraine to Germany, added to which was a huge indemnity of five million francs, to be secured by the presence of a German occupying army until the sum was paid (something the French never forgot or forgave, as they showed at Versailles—the scene of their 1871 disgrace—in 1918). Here was humiliation and loss on a gigantic scale. Nothing could be more important, it seemed to many, than to reverse that loss and avenge that humiliation. All other concerns—including and especially perhaps the pursuit of overseas empire—would have to be subordinated to this urgent and overriding aim.[5]

In this precarious situation, the pursuit of empire might seem highly unpromising. And yet, in an astonishingly short period of time, mainly from the 1880s to the 1900s, the French rebuilt their overseas empire on a vast scale, in the end making it the second-largest in the world.[6] Nothing comes from nothing, of course, and the acquisitions of that short period were built on a series of contacts and involvements that went back in some cases to the sixteenth century (e.g., with Gorée and Saint-Louis in Senegal). Traders, explorers, and missionaries, as with the other European empires, blazed the way. But intermittent encounters, attended with many failures and reverses, are not the same as empire. Even with the conquest of Algiers in 1830, it took another forty years for the pacification of the country and its secure possession. The same was true in most of the other areas where the French established some sort of presence before 1870, in Indochina, the Pacific, and the Indian Ocean. Empire had to wait, in the main, for the Third Republic.

North Africa—the Maghreb—was always in many ways the heart of the French Empire, with Algeria as its centerpiece. Algeria was declared a department—split into three—of the French Republic in 1848, but only with the coming of a civilian administration in 1879 did that become a reality. Algeria became the base for further expansion, eastward and westward. In 1881 France established a "protectorate" over Tunisia, one of many such in the French Empire. In practice, whether or not it led to formal annexation, the distinction between protectorates and colonies was insignificant (the same was true of the formally "mandated territories" of Syria and Lebanon in the French Empire after the First World War).

Morocco was a much less easy matter than Tunisia. The French incursion was spearheaded in 1903 by a French officer, Louis Hubert Lyautey, who was to become the most famous of the French colonial administrators. In a pattern to be followed in several other colonies, Lyautey ignored orders from Paris to withdraw. But, unlike Tunisia, Morocco was a fiendishly complicated international problem, with Britain, Germany, Spain, and Italy all making claims to influence there. The French government, pressed by Lyautey, moved with extreme caution. There were two "Moroccan crises," in 1905 and 1911, that almost brought the European powers to war. In 1907 French troops sacked Casablanca, destroying much of the city and killing over a thousand of its inhabitants. Eventually, by buying off Germany with a piece of the French Congo, and reassuring the British that France accepted British preeminence

FIGURE 7.1. Marechal Louis Hubert Lyautey, commissary-general of Morocco
(1912–25), where he successfully practiced some of the principles of
"associationism" ("Vex not tradition, leave custom be") and influentially
pursued the "dual city" policies of colonial urbanism. Lyautey also organized
the great Colonial Exhibition of 1931. Library of Congress.

in Egypt, France was able to establish a protectorate over Morocco in 1912.
Lyautey was made resident-general, with extensive powers (Aldrich 1996: 31–
35; Quinn 2002: 129–31).

Africa south of the Sahara also came into the French orbit in these years
of the 1880s and 1890s. French West Africa (Afrique Occidentale Française,
AOF) began with the consolidation of French influence and the establishment

of French rule in the earlier coastal settlements of Senegal, Guinea, Dahomey (Benin), and Côte d'Ivoire. It continued with exploration and conquest in the interior of Central Africa, adding Upper Volta (Burkina Faso), Soudan (Mali)—where the fabled Tombouctou (Timbuktu) was conquered—and Niger to French West Africa. Niger, a vast though largely arid area, was important to the French mainly as a strategic center linking North and Central Africa, and, it was hoped, West and East Africa. The latter dream was shattered in the famous Fashoda Incident of 1898.[7] Captain Jean-Baptiste Marchand, leading a French expedition from the French Congo into the Sudan, encountered the British forces under Lord Kitchener marching south from the Upper Sudan, a region that the British had already claimed as successors to the Ottomans in Egypt. They met at Fashoda, on the Upper Nile in a remote corner of the Sudan, four hundred miles south of Khartoum. The British were determined to hold on to the Sudan and the Upper Nile, to safeguard their recently established protectorate over Egypt. In France, convulsed by the Dreyfus affair, the French right called for a war with England. But the French government would not take such a step. Marchand was ordered to withdraw. In an agreement with Britain in 1899, France kept its extensive new possessions west of the River Nile but renounced claims to any further territory in the Nile valley. Thus was ended any hopes of a continuous French Empire in Central Africa stretching from Dakar in the west to Djibouti and French Somaliland on the Red Sea. The last two remained France's only small, lonely, outposts in the east. The British were left in a strong position to pursue their own dream of a continuous African empire stretching from north to south, from Cairo to the Cape of Good Hope. Once more the old enemy, the British, had not just stood between the French and their imperial ambitions, but had demonstrated the superior strength of Britain's imperial drive.

The acquisition of Mauritania, like Niger vast—twice the size of metropolitan France—but nine-tenths desert, was again mostly driven by strategic motives, in helping to link up the other territories of French West Africa and forestall other foreign presences. It also gave France a bridge to its North African territories, Morocco and Algeria. After the First World War, France added the mandated territory of Togo, taken from the Germans, to its West African empire.

Another mandated territory, Cameroon, also taken from the Germans, was added to the other main complex of France's African empire, French Equatorial Africa (Afrique Equatoriale Française, AEF). The AEF is indelibly associated with the name of the explorer Pierre Savorgnan de Brazza, known to the French as Stanley and Livingstone are known to the British (Brunschwig 1966: 43–49; Murphy [1948] 1968: 95–102; Aldrich 1996: 51–55). Journeying up the Ogooué River—which he mistakenly thought was a branch of the Congo River—Brazza reached an area near the Congo River where in 1882 he negotiated a treaty with Makoko, chief of the Batéké peoples, granting France a generous slice of territory in the region. This treaty—though greeted with skepticism even in France and initially rejected by the other European powers—was confirmed by the Berlin Conference of 1884, and formed the basis of the French colony of Moyen-Congo (its chief city, founded by Brazza, came to bear his name, Brazzaville).

Between 1886 and 1898 Brazza was commissioner-general of French Equatorial Africa, during which time much of the rest of the complex was added. The additions included Gabon, Oubangui-Chari (now the Central African Republic), and Chad. Like Niger and Mauritania, Chad was huge but arid and economically unpromising. It remained mostly military territory. At the beginning of the twentieth century there were only twenty Europeans living there. Generally French Equatorial Africa was, as compared with French West Africa, poorer, less developed, less well-known, and less well-regarded, the Cinderella of France's African empire. In some ways it symbolized what was perhaps the most striking feature of the French Empire, at least until the period after the First World War: the relative unimportance of the economic factor, and the corresponding importance of military, strategic, and prestige considerations.

Africa was one part, the major one in terms of territory, of the French overseas empire. On the other side of the world the French constructed the second main part of their new overseas empire, in Southeast Asia. The principal rival, here as in Africa, was the British. The British had driven the French out of India. They had taken Burma, and were pressing on Siam. Further east they had taken Malaya, and established the strategic port city of Singapore (1819). In the two Opium Wars (1839–42 and 1856–60) Britain had put great pressure on China, annexing Hong Kong and winning important trading concessions in Canton (Guangzhou), Shanghai, and elsewhere. Where were the French to turn? What spaces in the East were left for them to occupy (the Dutch still successfully holding on to the East Indies)?

As with Africa, the French first moved into areas with which they had had historic relations. French missionaries had been active in Indochina since the 1600s, and in the eighteenth century the French East India Company, employing the good contacts of the French priests, negotiated a treaty with the Vietnamese emperor giving France trading privileges. Successive Vietnamese rulers alternated between protecting and persecuting Catholics. But the priests were resourceful and resilient and, supported by the pope, in the 1830s and 1840s French Catholics became the leading missionaries in East Asia.

It was in fact persecution of Catholic priests in the 1850s that led to French intervention in Indochina. In 1859 Saigon was occupied, and between 1862 and 1867 the French annexed Cochinchina and established a protectorate over Cambodia. But little followed for some time after that, especially in the aftermath of the Franco-Prussian War. It was not until 1883 that protector-ates were established over the two other Vietnamese provinces, Annam and Tonkin. In 1887 French Indochina was created under a Government-General, incorporating the colony of Cochinchina and the protectorates of Annam, Tonkin, and Cambodia. In 1897 Laos was also incorporated in Indochina as a protectorate. As with North Africa, the distinction between protectorates and colonies seemed not to matter much in practice: all were run as colonies (Brunschwig 1966: 59–61; Aldrich 1996: 108). It had taken nearly forty years, but finally France had secured for itself a populous and extensive empire in Southeast Asia.

What did this empire, and its counterpart in Africa, mean to the French? What, given the evident reluctance of the earlier period, had motivated its acquisition, and in such a rush at the end of the nineteenth century? What ideas and ideals guided the French in their rule of empire? How did the French compare with other ruling peoples?

An Empire of Power and Prestige

On July 28, 1885, Jules Ferry, recently thrown out of office, in a speech in the Chamber of Deputies defended his colonial policy in what has come to be regarded as one of the most important statements of French thinking about its colonies in the years 1871–1914. Ferry, as minister of education from 1879 to 1881, had presided over a far-reaching program of secularization of the whole French educational system. Together with his ally Léon Gambetta (prime minister from 1881 to 1882), he represented one of the most uncompromis-ing strands of republicanism in French political life in the decades following the establishment of the Third Republic in 1871. Influenced by Paul Leroy-Beaulieu's much-discussed *De la colonisation chez les peuples moderns* (1874), he championed French colonialism against the powerful opposition of both left and right. It was during his first ministry, of 1880–81, that a protectorate was established over Tunisia, against the protests of many deputies. In his second

FIGURE 7.2. Jules Ferry, leading advocate of French imperialism
under the Third Republic. Portrait by French photographer. Private
Collection/© Bianchetti/Leemage/Bridgeman Images.

ministry, of 1883–85, he pursued his colonial policy even more vigorously, in
Africa and Indochina. It was as a result of a temporary reverse of French fortunes in Tonkin that he was forced to resign in 1885, hounded from office by
cries in the Chamber of "Tonkin-Ferry." In his speech of July 28, following his
resignation, he not only defended his actions in Indochina but offered a whole
rationale for French colonialism.[8]

Ferry first outlined—hewing very close to Leroy-Beaulieu's discussion, and
anticipating Hobson's famous analysis in *Imperialism* (1902)—the economic
reasons for having colonies. "Colonial policy is the daughter of industrial
policy." Countries like France, which depended on exports, needed outlets,

and "to create a colony is to provide an outlet." Like other advanced industrial countries, France also needed to invest its surplus capital abroad, and colonies again provide suitable sites for such activity. Economic control of colonies would also mean political control: "Provided the colonial link is maintained between the mother country, which is the producer country, and the colonies it has founded, economic dominance will accompany, and to some extent will be subject to, political dominance."

Ferry's second argument for colonies related to "the humanitarian and civilizing side of the question," the *mission civilisatrice*. His position was stark: "The superior races have rights over the inferior races. . . . [They] have a right because they have a duty. They have a duty to civilize the inferior races." Ferry was as firm about the duties as about the rights. These included restraining the activities of European traders and settlers, combating slavery and the slave trade, and bringing the benefits of a "material and moral order"—Western government, education, medicine, morals—to the indigenous population. Without the civilizing mission, Western possession of colonies was unjustified.

Ferry's third point, which brought out the full force of his rhetorical skills, was political: France needed colonies so that it could take its rightful place among the great powers of the world. He rejected the view, expressed by some deputies, that colonies could be thought of as "compensation in the East for the caution and self-containment which are at the moment imposed on us in Europe." That would be to belittle the scale of the tragedy that France had suffered. "There can be no compensation, none whatever, for the disasters we have suffered."

The real question in the face of this disaster, said Ferry, was whether it was going to paralyze France and prevent it from acting upon its best interests as a great European power. Are French governments to "let themselves be so absorbed by contemplating this incurable wound that they play no part in what is going on around them? Are they going to remain just as spectators and allow peoples other than ourselves to establish themselves in Tunisia, allow peoples other than ourselves to police the mouth of the Red River. . . . Are they going to leave it to others to dispute the mastery of the regions of equatorial Africa? Are they going to leave it to others to decide the affairs of Egypt which, from so many points of view, are in reality French affairs?"

Ferry drew attention to the changing face of Europe and the world, the rise of new powers that competed with France and could also be threats to its prosperity, perhaps even its survival.

In Europe as it now exists, in this competitive continent where we can see so many rivals increasing in stature around us. . . . In a Europe, or rather in a world, which is so constructed, a policy of containment or abstention is nothing other than the broad road leading to decadence! In this period in which we are living, the greatness of nations is due exclusively to the activities they develop. . . . To radiate without acting, without taking part in the affairs of the world, to stand on one side from all European combinations and to regard any expansion towards Africa and the Far East as a snare and a rash adventure—this is a policy which, if pursued by a great nation, would, I assure you, result in abdication in less time than you could think. It would mean that we should cease to be a first-rate power and become a third- or fourth-rate power instead. Neither I, nor I imagine anyone here, can envisage such a destiny for our country. France must put itself in a position where it can do what others are doing. A policy of colonial expansion is being engaged in by all the European powers. We must do likewise. If we do not, then we shall meet the fate . . . which has overtaken other nations which played a great role on the world's stage three centuries ago but which today, for all their power and greatness in the past, are now third- or fourth-rate powers. . . .

France cannot just be a free country; she must also be a great country, exercising on the destinies of Europe all the influence that belongs to her. She must spread that influence throughout the world, carrying wherever she can her language, her customs, her flag, her arms, her spirit.[9]

In a small book published five years after this speech, *Le Tonkin et la mère patrie* (1890), Ferry returned to the themes of the speech, repeating that "colonial policy is the offspring of industrialization." But once more economic arguments are joined to political ones. "One cannot," declared Ferry, "be a great power if one stays in one's own backyard." He applauded recent French acquisitions overseas and defended a bold and expansionist colonial policy. Against the usual demurs, he vehemently denied that colonial expansion was distracting the French people from getting their revenge on Germany for the humiliations of 1871. The time for dealing with Germany would come. For the moment the urgent thing was not to lose out in the competition for influence and power in the world. "Are we going to allow unrestrained chauvinism and short-term views to drive French policy into a dead end; and are we going to be so obsessed with the blue line of the Vosges that we allow everything about us to be done, agreed and resolved without our concurrence?" Already Italy in

Tunisia, Germany in Cochinchina, England in Tonkin were taking advantage of French hesitations and vacillations. Ferry expressed his fears of "another treaty of 1763"—the Treaty of Paris that concluded the Seven Years' War, and by which France lost nearly all its possessions in North America and India (Brunschwig 1966: 82–85; see also Baumgart 1982: 40–41).

In stressing the economic value of colonies, Ferry was reflecting a fairly common view of the time, one that culminated in Hobson's famous *Imperialism* and that was then developed by Lenin and other Marxists. But not only has that view frequently been criticized at the general level—European colonies, it has been argued, did not pay[10]—it is also apparent that it is weakest in the case of France in particular, at least for the period up to the First World War. Not only did the French not rush to people the colonies, showing in fact a decided reluctance to leave France; French financiers, investors, and industrialists also seem to have been curiously indifferent to their colonies, showing for much of the time a clear preference for other, non-French, outlets and opportunities.

The figures speak clearly on this. Of France's total external trade (imports and exports) between 1882–86 and 1909–13, trade with the colonies was responsible for only 5.71 percent at the beginning of the period and 10.2 percent at the end—a "negligible amount" in either case, as Henri Brunschwig says, especially considering that France's foreign trade made up only a small proportion of its total internal and external trade. One should compare this with Britain's figure of 30 percent of its foreign trade being trade with its colonies in this period (see previous chapter). Foreign investment similarly went far more to projects in the Ottoman Empire, southeastern Europe, Russia, and South America than to France's own colonies. In 1900, 71.1 percent of France's foreign capital was invested in Europe, 25 percent in Russia alone. Only 5.3 percent went to the French colonies. By 1914 there was more overseas investment—the European proportion dropped to 61.1 percent—but still only 8.8 percent in the French colonies. Like the British, only considerably more so, for the French trade and investment for much of the time conspicuously failed to follow the flag, or even to anticipate it. Only in North Africa—trade with which exceeded trade with all the other colonies put together—was there a significant degree of trade and investment.[11]

Brunschwig notes that, despite Ferry's strong invocation of the economic motive for empire in his speech of July 28, 1885, "it was his political peroration which earned him the Chamber's applause when he sat down" (1966: 81). In this it was the Chamber, rather than Ferry, that may be said to have best sensed the true public feeling about empire, though of course Ferry was passionate enough about the political reasons for empire. It is true that all empires are at bottom political, whatever the other motives involved. They demand a commitment that is impossible without the political will to create and the political skill to maintain them. But some empires are, as it were, more political than others. The French Empire is unusual in the extent to which it was almost wholly political, almost wholly the result of a gigantic effort to express and promote national goals.

The political drive to empire has to be traced back to France's terrible defeat in the Franco-Prussian War of 1870–71. It is impossible to exaggerate the national trauma caused by this event. After the capture and surrender of Napoleon III at the Battle of Sedan on September 2, 1870, Bismarck demanded that France cede Alsace and Lorraine to Prussia and pay an indemnity equivalent to the amount that the first Napoleon had imposed on Prussia after its defeat at Jena (1806). It was a crushing demand, both morally and materially. "You want to destroy France!" exclaimed a distraught Jules Favre, the foreign minister of the new republic, in a meeting with the unrelenting Bismarck. The great scholar Ernest Renan wrote on September 15, 1870: "A weakened and humiliated France would be incapable of survival. The loss of Alsace and Lorraine would mean the end of France" (in Schivelbusch 2004: 110). The French fought on desperately, but after General Bazaine's defeat at Metz on October 28, 1870, the game was up. The newly formed German Empire duly acquired the great and prosperous provinces, and France had to face the consequences (Gildea 2009: 229–39).

Loss in national war was followed immediately by divisive class war, the rising of the Parisian workers and the formation of the Paris Commune of 1870–71. This too was a searing experience, most notably in the manner of its suppression, which left an enduring legacy of bitterness on the left. Rarely can a new regime have begun its life as unpromisingly as did the Third Republic. "One half of the population wants to strangle the other," wrote Flaubert, "and the other has the same desire" (in Gildea 2009: 244). Years later, on the eve of another great war and another humiliation for France at the hands of Germany, Charles de Gaulle thus described France's condition after the trials of 1870–71:

An immense disaster, a peace of despair, griefs that nothing could console, the state without foundations, no army save the soldiers returning from enemy prison-camps, two provinces snatched away, an indemnity of billions to pay, the victor occupying a quarter of the territory, the capital running with the blood of a civil war, Europe cold or disdainful: such were the conditions in which a defeated France resumed her march toward her destiny. (in Ousby 2003: 113)[12]

The remarkable thing is that, despite this, the Third Republic held together, lasting until 1940, making it the longest-lasting of all five French republics so far (though the fifth, now over fifty years old, may well surpass it) (Ousby 2003: 128–35). A fitful consensus was regained and maintained, despite multiple crises of which Boulangism and the Dreyfus affair were the most serious. Secularization achieved some sort of fulfillment, with the separation of church and state in 1906. To some extent the left and the right canceled each other out, leaving moderate republicans in power for much of the time. Above all, largely through imperial expansion, France regained its status as a great power, vying with Britain for global possessions, and courted by the other great powers of Europe.

But the growth of the French Empire, impressive as it was, had to contend from the outset with a powerful strand of opinion that considered colonies a waste of energies and a distraction from the main task that all French patriots must embrace: the recovery of the lost provinces of Alsace and Lorraine, and revenge against Germany for the humiliation of 1870–71 (Schivelbusch 2004: 128–39). For much of the past two hundred years, France's main rival and frequent enemy had been Britain. Rivalry with Britain remained and, as in the past, was one of the forces behind French imperial ambitions in the second half of the nineteenth century. Nor did the possibility of actual war between France and Britain entirely end—certainly not in the eyes of the British—as was shown during the Fashoda crisis of 1898. But now French foreign policy had to take into account a formidable new rival on the continent: the rising power of a united Germany. From now on French policy, whether it related to domestic security or to France's international position, would have to have one eye on the old enemy to the west, Britain, and the other on the new threat to the east, its continental neighbor Germany. The French Empire would remain one of *ressentiment*, but the *ressentiment* would now be directed as much as, and perhaps more, at Germany as at Britain.

The new German Empire was certainly a formidable challenge. It far surpassed France in population and had a much healthier birthrate. Industrially it soon surpassed France and came to challenge the great industrial powers of Great Britain and the United States. Militarily it had proved its superiority in three striking victories of recent years: over Denmark in 1864, over the

Habsburg Empire in 1866, and, most spectacularly, over France in 1870–71. It was now clearly the dominant military power on the Continent. It had stripped France of two of its most populous and prosperous provinces and imposed other humiliations on it. In the early 1900s it challenged French aspirations in Morocco, bringing the two countries close to war and reviving all the anti-German feeling of earlier decades. *Revanche*, revenge, against Germany had to be the watchword of any patriotic party in France. All else—including the pursuit of overseas empire—had to be subordinated to that overriding goal.

The colonialists, the proponents of empire, never forgot, and were never allowed to forget, that if they pressed the cause of empire, they had to respond to this call for revenge and recovery. They had to show that, even if not directly, the construction of a global French Empire would to some extent at least offset the loss, by restoring France's dignity and power. They had to be careful of using words such as "consolation" or "compensation"—we have seen Ferry passionately rejecting them. These seemed to suggest second-rate or second-best strategies. "I had two sisters and you are offering me two domestic servants" was the acid riposte of the deputy Paul Déroulède to the suggestion that African colonies might compensate for the loss of Alsace and Lorraine (Aldrich 1996: 100). "The breach in the Vosges can never be filled with the desert sands of Africa and the mud of Asia" was another contemptuous response of the anticolonialists to the idea of consolation (Schivelbusch 2004: 181).

Nevertheless, given that there was little chance of dealing with Germany in the immediate future, the colonialists had something of a trump card. Nothing, as Ferry said, could truly compensate for the losses of 1871; the reckoning must come at some point in the future. But something could be done in the meantime to restore France's reputation and standing in the world. France could once more build up its empire, to rival that of the greatest states, and by doing so prove that it was still one of the great powers of the world. That too would make it more prepared to embark on the task that all agreed was primary. As the cabinet minister Paul Bert put it in 1885, responding to the accusation that the government was seeking to substitute a colonial empire for Alsace-Lorraine, "a substitute is as unimaginable as a consolation. But if the colonies cannot serve as a replacement for Alsace-Lorraine, they could be a means of bolstering national energy so that when the time is ripe we can win back the two provinces" (in Schivelbusch 2004: 180; see also Gildea 2009: 410–19).

That was the message of the work that launched the colonial movement in France, Paul Leroy-Beaulieu's *De la colonisation chez les peuples modernes* of 1874. It was a work written, as Raoul Girardet says, in the immediate wake, and with full awareness, of "la grande meurtrissure," the great wound, of 1871. Successful colonization, the building of a great empire, would help to heal that wound. Leroy-Beaulieu wrote in glowing terms of the significance of colonization, the way it allowed a nation to imprint its civilization on the world.

> La colonisation est la force expansive d'un peuple, c'est sa puissance de reproduction, c'est sa dilatation et sa multiplication à travers les espaces; c'est la soumission de l'univers ou d'une vaste partie à sa langue, à ses moeurs, à ses idées et à ses lois. Un peuple qui colonise c'est un peuple qui jette les assises de sa grandeur dans l'avenir et de sa suprématie future. . . . Le peuple qui colonise le plus est le premier peuple, s'il ne l'est pas aujourd'hui, il le sera demain. (in Girardet 1972: 55–56; see also Murphy [1948] 1968: 137–38)

"The people who colonize the most are the first people": that became the inspiration and rallying cry of the group that become known as the *parti colonial*, the colonial party or colonial lobby, the people and organizations that pressed the case for colonies in the 1880s and 1890s.[13] Jules Ferry had been very persuaded by Leroy-Beaulieu's arguments for colonies, as he showed in his 1885 speech. Once out of office he continued his activities informally, becoming a kind of elder statesman to a number of figures who took up the cause of colonial expansion. Many of these were in highly influential positions. They included Gabriel Hanotaux and Théophile Delcassé, both of whom were at various times foreign ministers in the government. There were famous explorers, such as Brazza, Joseph Gallieni, and Jean-Baptiste Marchand, colonial theorists such as Joseph Chailley-Bert, Saint-Simonian visionaries such as Ferdinand de Lesseps. Many of these were regular participants in the meetings of the Paris Geographical Society, which under the directorship of Prosper Chasseloup-Laubat achieved great prominence and influence, attracting public servants, military men, and clerics as well as scholars and explorers. The colonial party also included leading military figures such as Generals Archinard and Lyautey, and prominent businessmen such as Prince d'Arenberg, president of the Suez Canal Company and the Paris-Lyon-Mediterranean Railway, and Charles Roux, president of the shipping line the Compagnie Générale Transatlantique. Financiers were also well represented, as for instance Emile Mercet, president of the Comptoir national d'escompte, and André Lebon, president of the Algerian, Malagasy, and Syrian land banks, and also at various times a deputy and minister for commerce and industry.

It was generally accepted that the leading figure in the colonial party was Eugène Etienne. Born in Oran, Algeria, in 1844, he brought to French politics

something of the frontier mentality of the French Algerians and a passionate devotion to the French Empire. He was deeply affected by the disaster of
1870, and committed himself to restoring France's honor and prestige. As a
deputy for Oran in the Chamber from 1881, he quickly established himself as
a powerful advocate of the cause championed by Léon Gambetta and Jules
Ferry, both of whom were close friends and of whom he regarded himself
as a protégé (it was Etienne that Gambetta requested be with him when he
lay dying in 1882). He remained a deputy for Oran until 1919, after which he
was a French senator until his death in 1921. But he was also at various times
an under-secretary of state for the colonies, minister of the interior, minister
of war, and for twenty years vice president of the Chamber of Deputies. He
was a prolific writer on colonial affairs and founded a newspaper, *La Dépêche
colonial*. Not content with those activities, he involved himself in business
enterprises, being president of the Paris omnibus company as well as of a construction company active in the colonies. In this linking of politics, journalism,
and business, Etienne well represented the constellation of interests that made
up the colonial lobby (Andrew and Kanya-Forstner 1971: 114–15, 121, 127–28;
Cooke 1973: passim; Aldrich 1996: 101–2).

Etienne was the founder of the *groupe colonial* in the Chamber, giving the
colonial party a parliamentary base. By 1902 almost a third of the deputies in
the Chamber belonged to the group, which held frequent joint meetings with
a similar group of senators. They were united, they said, "par le désir d'assurer
la force et la grandeur de la France coloniale et extérieure" (Brunschwig 1966:
107). Between 1894 and 1899 five of the seven ministers for the colonies came
from this group. The *groupe colonial* was among the best organized and most
successful of the parliamentary pressure groups. It was the moving force
behind the attempt to reestablish French power in Egypt, culminating in the
Fashoda crisis. With that reverse, it promoted the alternative strategy of leaving Egypt to the British and getting British agreement to French supremacy in
Morocco: an aim achieved in the Entente Cordiale of 1905, to Etienne's great
satisfaction (Brunschwig 1966: 118–19; see also Andrew and Kanya-Forstner
1971: 108, 111–16, 122–25; Schivelbusch 2004: 186).

But the *parti colonial* was never a formal political party, and never depended
solely on parliamentary or ministerial pressure. It included a variety of groups
and individuals, both inside and outside parliament. What united them, and
the common cause for which they worked, was promotion of the French
Empire and propaganda on its behalf to dispel the skepticism and hostility of
opponents and doubters. Informal groups of explorers, geographers, military

officers, and parliamentarians met regularly and frequently at banquets to coordinate strategy. There were committees for practically every individual colony: the Committee for French Africa (one of whose founders was Arenberg), the Committee for Madagascar (chaired by Etienne), the Committee for French Asia (founded by Etienne), the Committee for French Morocco, the Committee for French Oceania. They held lectures, awarded prizes, and sponsored exhibitions. They published journals dealing with the life of the colonies, and highlighting achievements of administrators and settlers. They lobbied ministers and business organizations. A particularly effective pressure group was the French Colonial Union, founded in 1893, which brought together representatives of more than four hundred French companies "having an interest in the colonies." The editor of its influential periodical, the *Quinzaine Coloniale*, was the prominent colonial theorist Joseph Chailley-Bert, particularly associated with the idea of *mise en valeur des colonies*, the rational development of the natural and human resources of the colonies for the mutual benefit of their inhabitants and those of the mother country.[14]

What was the real influence of the colonial party? How much did it affect government policy? To what extent did it create a public opinion favorable to empire? "Two characteristics of the *parti colonial* stand out above all others: its diminutive size and its enormous influence" (Andrew and Kanya-Forstner 1971: 126; 1988: 26–28; cf. Brunschwig 1966: 117). Before 1914 the colonialists numbered probably no more than 10,000 people. They were loosely organized and could not speak with one voice on any particular issue. Although agreed on the importance of empire, they were divided between Africanists and Orientalists. They were faced with a largely apathetic public and fiercely opposed by parties on the right and left, who constantly threw the charge of betrayal—betrayal of the lost provinces of Alsace and Lorraine, betrayal of the need to humble Germany—against them. That was a charge they had to answer.

But their opponents—on both the left and the right—were even more divided and weakened. General Boulanger's rightist challenge to the republic, the Dreyfus affair, the bitter conflicts over secularization, all put right and left at each other's throats. Their common opposition to colonies could never be articulated in a set of principles that overrode their more fundamental differences. Moreover, the colonialists had a unifying force in the towering figure of Eugène Etienne, for over two decades a dominant influence in French colonial policy. "His leadership made the *parti colonial* one of the most powerful pressure groups in the history of the Third Republic" (Andrew and Kanya-Forstner 1971: 127). Thanks to the persistent pressure and propaganda of the colonialists, by the First World War France had a great African empire, a more or less continuous tract linking all their territories in the north and west. They also had a large and populous empire in the east, in Southeast Asia, one that could allow France to hold up its head against the might of British power in the region, and also receive a generous share of the concessions forced upon the Chinese.

What was even more important for the success of the colonialists, despite their small numbers, was that they were able to play the same card that their opponents threw down at them: the cause of nationalism. The right in particular accused the colonialists of betraying the nation. By looking beyond Europe, they were distracting attention from France's continental interests and the need to rebuild French power in the face of Germany. Imperialism and nationalism here were portrayed as alternative and to a good extent antagonistic strategies.

The colonialists turned this argument against the right, and also those on the left who in good part accepted it. It was clearly impossible, in the circumstances in which France found itself after 1871, to think of going to war against Germany in order to recover the lost provinces. Not only would that have sounded alarm bells all over Europe—France up to its old adventurist tricks— but the French army was in no position to take on the Germans. Nor, even more perhaps, when it came to Fashoda, was there any stomach for a war with Britain, despite the agitation stirred up by the right at the time. In relation to neither Britain nor Germany, France's two main rivals, did it seem feasible to assert France's national interest by direct confrontation in Europe.

But that left the rivalry to be displaced outside Europe, to the world at large. It was in the competition for empire that France could rebuild its strength and prove itself once again one of the world's great powers. "The people who colonize the most are the first people." Here was a way for France once again to become *la grande nation*, the country that, as in the eighteenth century, set the standard of civilization for the world. The *mission civilisatrice*, earlier directed by the French kings toward the French people themselves, and by the first Napoleon toward fellow Europeans, could now be carried out on a far grander scale in the whole wide world. France would take its civilization to Africa, Asia, the Pacific. What could be a nobler cause for a nation? How could the nationalists accuse the colonialists of betraying the cause of the nation? In the French Empire the nation would see itself projected on the greatest possible screen, the French language, French culture, French institutions made the model for the world.

By about 1890, says Wolfgang Schivelbusch, one sees a decisive weakening of the anticolonialist force in French politics and culture. "A kind of role reversal had taken place: the national mission had been transposed from *revanche* to colonialism. The latter had always been cast as the servant to the former, but now brimming with newly won self-confidence, colonialism boldly announced itself as indispensable to the nation's revitalization. Instead of having to justify its every initiative as a means toward the ultimate end of *revanche*, colonialism had become legitimate on its own terms" (2004: 182; see also Andrew and Kanya-Forstner 1988: 23–24).

Moreover—and here too the colonialists were skillful—empire could be achieved without direct confrontation or armed conflict with any of the major European powers. French governments for the whole period from 1871 to 1914, despite the many international crises, always drew back when the possibility of war became real. That was what happened with Britain at Fashoda, and it is what happened with Germany in the Moroccan crises of the 1900s. The French second overseas empire was constructed with a great deal of violence so far as non-Europeans—Arabs, Africans, Indochinese—were concerned, but with remarkably little as regards Europeans. The French were careful not to tread too heavily on the toes of their main European rivals. Africa was shared out among Europeans at various international conferences. The French Empire in Southeast Asia was not regarded as a particular threat by any of the main European powers, and where friction arose, as over Siam, that too was peacefully settled between the British and French. In relation to the great prize of China, France joined with Britain, Germany, Russia, and the United States in more or less amicably carving out independent spheres of influence (only the Japanese sounded a discordant note—a warning for the future).

Power and prestige, not profit and production, were the hallmark of the French Empire before 1914. Imperialism was driven by nationalism. France never spoke of giving up its colonies, "for colonial policy was never regarded as a purely economic matter. Imperialism, born of nationalism, remained nationalist" (Brunschwig 1966: 89; see also 182–83; cf. Schivelbusch 2004: 178; Andrew and Kanya-Forstner 1988: 19). This was of course the same nationalism that, for the opponents of empire, should have kept France engaged exclusively in its own backyard, on the European continent. But "one cannot become a great power if one stays in one's backyard," not, at least, if one's room to maneuver is so severely limited there. The colonialists took the *tricouleur* abroad, and had it flying in Algiers, Tangiers, Brazzaville, Saigon, and Hanoi. What was lost on the Rhine was regained on the Niger, the Congo, the Mekong, the Red River. When in 1914, in spite of all, the Europeans did once more engage in war among themselves, "the million men mobilized by the Empire proved its worth as the *reservoir d'énergie nationale*" (Andrew and Kanya-Forstner 1971: 128). The bravery and sacrifice of the Tirailleurs Séné-galais redounded to French national pride.

There is finally, in the matter of French motives for empire, one further consideration. The empire was to an unusual extent the creation of military men: soldiers and sailors (Betts 1961: 109–20; Andrew and Kanya-Fortsner 1988: 12–15). It was the military that most keenly felt the humiliation of 1870–71. It was the officers above all who felt, and were blamed for, the crushing defeats. General Bazaine, who surrendered at Metz, was publicly vilified, charged with high treason, and condemned to death (he managed to escape). Gambetta commented on the conviction, "With this, France has taken its first step on the road to honor, justice, and *revanche*" (in Schivel-busch 2004: 120).

For the military, denied at least for the time being the possibility of regain-ing their honor on the battlefields of Europe, the empire offered an alternative and expansive stage on which they could rebuild their identity and image. In the sands of the Sahara and the jungles of Indochina they would wipe out the shame of 1870–71. Moreover, they felt keenly that it fell to them above all to undertake the task, that they had both the greatest need and the best oppor-tunities. Frequently they acted on their own initiative, either not seeking or disregarding the orders of their civilian superiors in Paris. "One should burn instructions so as to avoid the temptation of reading them," declared General Bugeaud, under whom "military insubordination was raised to the level of an art." Not only did he pursue his own way in Algeria; in 1844 he invaded Morocco in direct violation of his orders. Louis Faidherbe acted similarly in Senegal, as did Admiral Dupetit-Thouars in the annexation of Tahiti in 1843, Admiral Bonard in forcing the Vietnamese government to cede the three east-ern provinces of Cochinchina to France in 1862, and Admiral La Grandière in completing the conquest of Cochinchina in 1867 (Andrew and Kanya-Forstner 1988: 13–14).

Traders and missionaries had been, as in the case of the British Empire, active agents of empire. Geographers and explorers had promoted it. But, as compared with the British case, it was the military who stood out above all. "It was," says Ronald Robinson, "the military, far more than the geographers and intellectuals, who felt the need to restore the national honour; for them it was a professional need; it was they who stood to gain most, in decorations, promotion and glory, from a set of brilliant victories on colonial fields, and they who had the best opportunities—in the institutional set-up and confused, atomized politics of Paris—to carry the flag forward. The French colonel with one hand on his Gatling and the other on the proofs of his next book was no myth. His British opposite number had no such chances since the Company's days in India" (in Brunschwig 1966: x; see also 16–17, 164–65).

The British had their military heroes, of course, many of them linked to empire: Clive in India, Wolfe in Canada, Nelson on the Nile and at Trafalgar, Gordon and Kitchener in the Sudan. But apart from Clive their fame came from purely military victories. What was peculiar about the role of the military in the French case was the extent to which soldiers were administrators, explorers, theorists, and commentators on empire. Generals Bugeaud in Algeria, Faidherbe in Senegal, Archinard in Soudan, Gallieni in Indochina and Madagascar, above all Lyautey in Morocco, were famous as much for their styles of administration and their writings as for their military success. General Mangin wrote influentially on *la force noire*, France's African troops that would make up for the shortfall of French soldiers and would carry French civilization into the heart of Africa. Though Captain Marchand failed in the quest to make the Sudan French, his journey to Fashoda was closely followed and he was acclaimed as a national hero after the event. Lieutenant Francis Garnier did not just explore the Mekong River and prepare the way for the French takeover of Tonkin; he wrote a best-selling account of his expedition and the prospects for the French Empire in the East.[15]

From 1815 to 1882, the French colonies, with the exception of Algeria, were administered by the Ministry of the Navy and the Colonies. Algeria itself came under the War Ministry until 1870. Only in 1882 was an under-secretaryship of the colonies created, and only in 1894 did the colonies get their own Ministry of the Colonies. Colonial administrators were often naval and army officers, trained in the military academies. Only in 1889 was the Ecole Coloniale founded, to train senior administrators (Brunschwig 1966: 194). This history was a fair reflection of the way the colonies had been acquired, administered, and conceived. The military saw the empire as in many ways their empire, an empire for France, of course, but one that was entrusted to their peculiar care. In many countries the military are seen as representatives of the nation and guardians of the national honor. That does not always mean, though, that they are identified with the empire.[16] Businessmen such as Cecil Rhodes, George Goldie, William Jardine, and James Matheson, missionaries such as David Livingstone, visionaries such as Lawrence of Arabia—these are at least in the

British case better-known imperial heroes than military men. In France businessmen are conspicuous by their absence in the pantheon of imperial heroes; their place is taken by soldiers.

The military, in the aftermath of 1871, felt called upon to undertake the task of rebuilding the nation, of reclaiming its dignity and strengthening its power. At the same time it sought to restore its own morale. Empire was the means of doing so in both cases. The success of this strategy might be said to have been shown in the First World War, when the generals—many of whom, like Mangin, had been active in the colonies—led the French army to a joint victory of the Allies over the old enemy, Germany, and rescued the lost provinces of Alsace and Lorraine. The part played in this by the colonial troops—especially the famed Tirailleurs Sénégalais—was not lost on the French population. In the First World War empire and nation were seen as two branches of the same French family; and it was the military who appeared as both the creators and the best expression of this unity.

Civilization, Assimilation, Association

At a banquet held by the French Colonial Union in March 1910, Martial Merlin, the governor-general of French Equatorial Africa, gave a remarkably full and frank account of what had driven French colonialism in the recent period, and what it hoped to achieve.

> After the disaster of 1870, we had to draw in ourselves and, for a time, cease to concern ourselves with European affairs. But, as we are far from finished as a race, whatever some pessimists say, after a few years of self-containment we felt the need to act. As our freedom in Europe was limited, we went to distant countries; and then came the beginnings of that marvellous colonial epoch which, a few years later, put us in all parts of the world on a footing of equality with Britain, the colonial power par excellence, and far ahead of that power which defeated us in 1870 but which is still far behind us in the colonial field.
>
> We went to new territories. We went there by virtue of the right of a civilized, fully developed race to occupy territories which have been left fallow by backward peoples who are plunged in barbarism and unable to develop the wealth of their land ... [B]ut, when we exercise this right, we at the same moment are charged with a duty towards [these peoples], and this duty we must never for one instant forget. (in Brunschwig 1966: 170–71)

Of all the empires considered in this book, the French was the one that put the greatest stress on its civilizing mission—the *mission civilisatrice*, whose common use in its French form by other Europeans itself indicates that France in some sense claimed a patent on the term. In this the French were very conscious of continuing what, centuries ago, the Roman Empire had begun. Just as the Romans had civilized Gaul, so the descendants of the Gauls would carry that civilizing mission across the globe. As with Rome the elements of that mission would be language, culture, institutions, and citizenship. And as the civilizing mission in the Roman Empire meant in effect Romanization, so the civilizing mission in the French Empire meant Frenchification—*francisation*—or Gallicization: in a word, "assimilation" in some sense (Belmessous 2013).

At a meeting of the Congrès Colonial Internationale de Paris in July–August 1889, the social psychologist Gustave Le Bon launched a swingeing attack on policies of "assimilation" and French hopes of civilizing "savages," "barbarians," and "inferior races." One "must consider as dangerous chimeras all our ideas of assimilating or Frenchifying any inferior people. Leave to the natives their customs, their institutions, their laws" (Betts 1961: 68). In response Frank Puaux, a member of the Superior Colonial Council, quietly reminded the participants of the Roman example.

> Suppose that if on the conquest of Gaul, some savant of that time had maintained that the Gauls should be left in barbarism; that singular philanthropist might have been heeded. Would we be here today, if the Romans had followed this counsel? Do not forget, Messieurs, that we have become what we are because a people of superior civilization communicated their light, their arts, and their laws to our ancestors. Have we the right to keep this rich heritage for ourselves? Can we refuse to do today for others what the Romans did for us nearly two thousand years ago? (in M. D. Lewis 1962: 140)

The British—often drawing the same parallel—also wished to export their civilization, and did so more or less wholly and successfully within the white dominions, where Europeans were in a majority. In the nonwhite parts of their empire, in Asia and Africa, they proceeded with greater caution. Political and legal institutions were implanted, and English became more or the less the official language of the colony. But especially in the later part of the nineteenth century, the British became less convinced of the possibility or desirability of imposing a full-fledged British (*sc.* English) culture on populations that had, in many cases, long traditions of their own of very different civilizations and cultures. This was particularly true in places such as India, especially after the Mutiny, but it was also true of the African colonies, where the concept of "indirect rule" was first fully worked out, and where respect for local traditions and traditional authorities governed policy for much of the time. While it would be wrong to say that there was no tradition of "assimilation" in British colonial policy—Macaulay's "Minute on Indian Education" partly stands as a powerful refutation of that view—it seems fair to say that gradually but steadily British opinion retreated from the idea of making the world British in the sense of producing fully Anglicized natives of non-European origin.

It would be equally wrong to see the French as having adopted policies diametrically opposed to those of Britain. Policies of full-blooded assimilation were never accepted by all shades of political opinion in France, and in some cases were vigorously rejected. But it seems right to say that throughout its colonial history France leaned more in the direction of assimilation than any other alternatives (cf. Belmessous 2013: 1–12). Once more that sprang from the close identification of nation and empire in the French case. If the empire was a direct expression and extension of the French nation, if it served to glorify France, then how could it better do this than by being a magnification, on a global scale, of French culture and civilization? And since the French were convinced of the superiority of their civilization, what else could the civilizing mission mean than the attempt to make the world French—to make the empire a showcase for the glories of French civilization? That surely too was the lesson of the Roman Empire, an exemplar constantly in the mind of French colonialists even though they never sought to match its cosmopolitanism. "Greater France" was, like "Greater Britain," the nation writ large. But unlike Britain with its dominions or Rome with its provinces, the admixture of nonnational elements in the case of the French Empire was severely diluted. Paris dominated the French Empire in a way that neither Rome nor London did in the case of their empires.

All empires strive to replicate themselves to some extent. Roman provincial towns in Gaul, Spain, and Britain carried the stamp, in their layout and architecture, of the principal features of Rome itself and the Italian cities. The British too created "little Englands," and occasionally "little Scotlands" and "little Irelands," in different parts of their empire, though mostly where there were large contingents of Europeans, as in South Africa, Canada, and Australia. But it has often been remarked how much more completely the French sought to replicate themselves in their empire, the more remarkable in that the bulk of the French Empire was tropical, in Africa and Asia, and that the European presence in the empire remained relatively slight. Frederick Quinn, an American diplomat with postings throughout the former French Empire, records a visit to Upper Volta (Burkina Faso) just after its independence.

> Administrative hierarchies, uniforms, decorations, and ceremonies replicated those in France. A *café au lait* and *croissant* became a universal breakfast, *sapins de Noël* appeared in the tropics and sub-Sahara for Christmas day, lilies of the valley and labor demonstrations were part of May 1, and the year climaxed with the annual Bastille Day celebration.

Further postings showed the same pattern, "the way France tried to create a total presence in its overseas empire."

> Stationery, type fonts, and sizes of letters were the same everywhere, and buildings looked as if they had come from a central design office in Paris, albeit with Arabic or Oriental twists. What struck me most was how the geographic layout of French colonial cities and even the smallest, most isolated outposts reflected imperial ideas. The *cercle* was always on the choicest ground, with trees planted around it, and wide roads leading off in every direction, pointing to the colonial capital and France itself. Avenue Binger, Rue de Strasbourg, Place Foch, Avenue de Dakar—somehow the empire was tied together in one master architectural plan of global dimensions. (Quinn 2002: xv)[17]

The colonial city did not destroy all remnants of the ancient buildings and urban traditions where they existed, as in North Africa and Indochina. Here the typical form was the "dual city," as defined and refined particularly by Hubert Lyautey in Morocco. There was the modern French city—the *ville nouvelle*—and side by side the old "native city," with its ancient alleyways, markets, mosques, temples, and the like. The Europeans lived mostly in the modern city and the natives in the old city. But it was clear where the power and prestige lay, and also what was in store in the future. The apparent blending of "tradition" and "modernity" concealed the overall imperial purpose of "civilizing" the inhabitants. "Traditional forms were utilized in an effort to downplay resistance while mitigating the more disruptive aspects of modernization. Traditionalism and modernism thus formed a unified urban policy" (Wright 1997: 339). As long as the empire lasted, the destiny of the colony was to become increasingly French—administratively, culturally, economically—though no

FIGURE 7.3. St. Joseph's Cathedral, Hanoi. A good example of the French desire to re-create French culture throughout their empire. © Marcyan079/Dreamstime.com.

doubt picturesque remains of the old cultures would still be there, rather like the Place des Vosges and Montmartre in Paris.

"By 1895," says Alice Conklin, "the *mission civilisatrice* had become the official ideology of the Third Republic's vast empire" (1997: 11). The geographical societies, writers such as Leroy-Beaulieu, politicians such as Ferry, the mixed body of the *parti colonial*, all had powerfully established the idea in the French mind (though not without considerable dissent from both left and right). School textbooks reinforced the message of France's right and duty to educate mankind, as in the great days of the *philosophes*, and to bring it up to the level of French civilization. But what did it mean to civilize? And if civilizing was tantamount to assimilating—making the world in the image of France—what precisely was meant by assimilation? What did it entail and what, if any, were its limits?

The basic terms of the civilizing mission were drawn from the lexicon of the French Revolution (Betts 1961: 30–32; Miller 1994). By the 1880s the republican tradition of the French Revolution—shorn of its troubling association with the Terror and mob rule—had become the official ideology of the

Third Republic (Hobsbawm 1984: 269–73; Gildea 1994: 34–42; Hazareesingh 1994: 80–89). The Fall of the Bastille on July 14 had become a national holiday. The *tricouleur* had become the state flag. "La Marseillaise" had become the national anthem. Monuments to Marianne, the graceful female symbol of the republic, were to be found in the central squares of every small town and village in France. The revolutionary ideals of liberty, equality, and fraternity were emblazoned on official buildings—town halls, museums, schools—throughout France.

The civilizing mission meant the carrying of these ideas and ideals to every corner of the globe. One aspect reflected the ideas of the Enlightenment, and the enthronement of Reason as the guiding principle of human conduct and social organization. Another was more connected to nineteenth-century ideas of Progress, particularly the material and mental betterment of humanity (as expressed particularly in the concept of *mise en valeur*). French civilization, the civilization of the Third Republic, was seen to have espoused these principles, to have made of them its lodestar.

In its stress on the French revolutionary heritage as embodied in the Third Republic, the civilizing mission necessarily gave precedence to materialism, rationalism, and secularism over older imperial aims associated with the spread of religion, especially Catholicism. This did not mean that missionaries and religious institutions did not play an important part in the French colonies. On the contrary missionaries were very active, and in the case of Indochina were the main reason why France was there in the first place. Just as in the metropolis itself, so in the colonies religious parties and doctrines continued to struggle for power and influence throughout much of the life of the Third Republic (Daughton 2006; White and Daughton 2012). But following the bitter conflicts of the Dreyfus affair, and the discrediting of the upper echelons of church and army, it became very clear that the secular forces had gained the upper hand, as symbolized by the separation of church and state in 1905 (Gildea 2009: 337–60). The civilizing mission was henceforward even more strongly defined in the terms of the secular, anticlerical, tradition of the first French republic.

Alice Conklin, noting the pervasiveness of this republican ideology in the thinking and policies of colonial administrators, has summarized the theme of the *mission civilisatrice* under the idea of "mastery": mastery not so much of other peoples—though of course this might be necessary—but more "mastery of nature, including the human body, and mastery of what can be called 'social behavior.' . . . To be civilized was to be free from specific forms of tyranny: the tyranny of the elements over man, of disease over health, of instinct over reason, of ignorance over knowledge and of despotism over liberty. Mastery in all these realms was integral to France's self-definition under the Third Republic" (1997: 5–6). What was proposed for the citizens of the mother country was also to be administered in the colonies, with the necessary adjustments of speed and timing appropriate to local conditions. But as so often in the case of empires, it was frequently easier to state these aims, and to attempt bold schemes of implementation, in the colonies than in the metropolis. The civilizing mission—with its disruptive attack on old traditions and institutions—was often less clear to French peasants at home than it was to the peasants and pastoralists of Indochina and the Soudan.

At different times, and in different places, different aspects of the mission would be emphasized, political and cultural here, economic and developmental there. There would also be debates on how far it would be desirable, and to what extent possible, to turn Africans and Asians into Frenchmen and Frenchwomen. Much of this has been discussed under the headings of "assimilation" and "association" in French colonial theory and policy. These relate to the various possible meanings of the civilizing process. Assimilation, in all its varieties, assumed that the way to civilize the native non-Europeans of the French Empire was to make them as alike as possible to the metropolitan French. To civilize was to Gallicize. This, it is claimed, was the first idea of French colonialism (Betts 1961: 8).[18] At a later stage, it is argued, this idea gave way to the idea of association. As put by Raymond Betts, the authoritative exponent of this account, the shift meant that "rather than attempt to absorb the native societies administratively and culturally into the French nation, France was to pursue a more flexible policy which would emphasize retention of local institutions and which would make the native an associate in the colonial enterprise" (1961: vii). As many have pointed out, in at least one interpretation the idea of association came close to imitating the policy of "indirect rule" advocated by Lord Lugard and others in the context of the British Empire (e.g., Deschamps [1963] 1994).

The idea of a "succession" of modes of imperial rule has plausibly been disputed by many (e.g., Conklin 1997: 75–211, 305n2; Lebovics 1994: 69n26; Belmessous 2013: 119–204). Partly this is because both "assimilation" and "association" were multifaceted and carried several meanings, such that at different times and in different places one might see greater emphasis on one rather than the other but rarely a replacement of one by the other (Lewis 1962; Lebovics 1994: 80–81n40). "Assimilation" could mean mainly political and administrative integration, with deputies being elected from the colonies to sit in the French parliament, citizenship gradually being extended to all France's imperial subjects, and French laws being applied equally and evenly in the colonies as well as the metropolis. Thus would be fulfilled one of the aims of the First Republic, when under the Directory it declared that "the French Republic is one and indivisible. . . . The Colonies are an integral part and therefore subject to the same laws" (in Deschamps 1994: 169).

Assimilation could also mean a more intensely cultural and psychological type of integration, an attempt to produce black and brown Frenchmen and Frenchwomen as near to the European originals as possible. It is rare to find direct statements of this goal in official pronouncements, but plenty of material in the writings of both French theorists and subjects of the empire indicates that this was indeed often an implicit goal. Again this can be seen as a legacy of the First Republic, where the attempt was made, for instance, to turn "Jews into Frenchmen" (Kates 1989; Miller 1994; Hazareesingh 1994: 73). It was what was seen as a largely successful venture in that direction—the production of thoroughly acculturated natives, subjectively infused with the culture of their conquerors—that provoked Frantz Fanon's passionate protest, *The Wretched of the Earth* (1961). Fanon, a native of Martinique who had practiced as a psychiatrist in Algeria, was appalled at the extent to which French colonialism had produced willing accomplices of the system, and felt that only an act of purging violence could cleanse the victims of the poison of their colonialist mentality.

Association, in its turn, was never really an attempt to remake French colonial policy on the British model of "indirect rule," despite official nods in that direction. Lord Lugard, the great theorist of indirect rule, was firm about that. "The French system," he asserted, "proceeds on the hypothesis that the colonies are an integral part of France, and their inhabitants Frenchmen" (1965: 228). The French never allowed local chiefs and traditional authorities the degree of discretion and autonomy granted them by British rulers. Nothing could be clearer than the forthright statement by the governor-general of French West Africa, Joost van Vollenhoven, generally regarded as one of the chief exponents of associationism. "There are not two authorities in the circle, French authority and native authority; there is only one. Only the *commandant* of the circle commands, he alone is responsible. . . . The native chief is only an instrument, an auxiliary . . . the native chief never speaks in his own name, but always in the name of the *commandant* of the circle and by formal or tacit delegation from the letter" (in Conklin 1997: 182–83).

Writing of the two French African federations in the early decades of the twentieth century, Michael Crowder says that "generally the French system of administration deliberately sapped the traditional powers of the chiefs in the interest of uniformity of the administrative system." In French colonial policy the overall goal of assimilation survived "despite its official abandonment in favour of a *politique d'association*" ([1964] 1994: 183–86). The aim of creating French citizens out of natives was never abandoned; it is just that it was now seen as likely to be a more protracted process than previously thought. A high degree of administrative centralization continued, at odds with the declared policy of associating native chiefs with colonial rule. The *mission civilisatrice* continued apace, as reflected in the policies and practices especially of education. "Children spoke in French from the day they entered school" (Crowder [1964] 1994: 187). Unlike the British case, no concession was made to teaching in the vernacular.

In terms of administration, little attempt was made to attend to the differences and particularities of different colonial territories (compare the British in Africa). The same administrative organization was imposed on all territories. One result of this was that there was little incentive for administrators to learn the native languages and study the local cultures—again the contrast with the British is telling in this respect. By the same token, this meant an educated native could rise higher in the administrative hierarchy than was generally possible in the British case. To a greater degree than in the British case, at least in Africa, the French approach to colonialism meant the creation of a highly Frenchified native elite, as much at home in Paris as in their native territory. The British anthropologist Lucy Mair, writing about French Africa in 1936, was struck by the difference in status of the *évolués*, the educated natives, and their British counterparts.

> The assumption which governs the whole attitude of France towards native development is that French civilization is necessarily the best and need only be presented to the intelligent African for him to adopt it. Once he has done so, no avenue is to be closed to him. If he proves himself capable of assimilating French education, he may enter any profession, may rise to the dignity of Under-Secretary for the Colonies, and will be received as an equal by French society. This attitude towards the educated native arouses the bitter envy of his counterpart in neighboring British colonies. (in Crowder [1964] 1994: 186; see also Wilder 2005: 149–200)

To Hubert Deschamps, governor of the French Ivory Coast in the 1930s, the term "association" was a "hypocritical expression." "The word 'association' seemed to affirm the existence of a contract between the dominating power and its subjects, whereas it really conjured up the idea of the association that exists between a man and his horse" ([1963] 1994: 170). Association, in other words, was a disguised form of assimilation. The only problem for Deschamps, a confirmed assimilationist who believed in the universalist ideas of the Enlightenment and the French Revolution, was that the official rhetoric and halfhearted policies of association distracted from the proper task of turning the colonies into full-scale replicas of the mother country. When that attempt was at last consciously and systematically made, after the Second World War, it came too late to bear fruit.

The idea of association was most fully developed in the book by Jules Harmand *Domination et colonisation* (1910). Harmand rejected the idea of assimilation as "utopian," "based on a preconceived faith in the equality of all men and their rapid perfectibility." But it was clear even in Harmand's account that association was rather differently conceived from what seemed the parallel idea of British indirect rule. Association would "preserve with unshakeable firmness all the rights of domination. . . . It does not aim to prepare for the realization of an equality which cannot be possible, but to establish a certain equivalence or compensation of reciprocal services." There was no question but that "the colonies should be made for the metropolis, for the many and diverse advantages which it can derive from them." When he argued that "an Annamite, a Negro, an Arab" could not become a Frenchman by "the adoption of certain European habits, the knowledge of the language and literature of the conqueror," the warning was uttered mainly because he feared that such an attempt at acculturation would only make the native "an enemy better armed against us. Wisdom tells us not to forget the lessons of Santo Domingo" (in Lewis 1962: 148–49; see also Betts 1961: 122, 144–45).

It seems clear that Harmand regarded assimilation not so much as impossible as undesirable, for its possible consequences in raising up an assimilated elite that would turn French ideas of republican liberty—as did Toussaint L'Ouverture in Saint-Domingue—against its colonial rulers. In any case whatever the theory, in practice the distinction between assimilation and association became decidedly blurred in the early part of the twentieth century. For instance in 1917, during the high tide of associationism, the French Chamber of Deputies passed a resolution in which it affirmed France's determination "to pursue ever more effectively towards the colonial peoples its generous policy of association [sic] which will continue to assure their progressive incorporation in the national unity and will strengthen the ever closer union of all the territories over which flies the flag of France." This was not really so different in spirit from the clearly assimilationist purpose of the resolution passed at the Congrès Colonial National of December 1889, which declared that "in all the overseas lands under French authority, the efforts of colonization should propagate among the natives the language, the methods of work, and, progressively, the spirit and the civilization of France." In both cases, as Lewis says, "Gallicization was permitted to stand as the ultimate goal" (Lewis 1962: 143, 150; see also Lorcin 1995: 7–8; Conklin 1997: 248; Belmessous 2013: 119–204).

It seems fair to say, at least by comparison with the other empires in this book, that of all the European empires the French was the one most enamored of the goal of assimilation. That followed more or less logically from the French belief, expressed most clearly in the eighteenth century and sealed by the universalism of the French Revolution, that it was the French who had discovered the secret of civilization, and that it was their bounden duty to offer the fruits of this discovery to the rest of humanity. To become French, to be like the French, seemed to them not an imposition but a liberation. To colonize the world was to civilize it—which is to say, to make it French. As Christopher Miller has said, "assimilation could be summed up as the notion that French civilization is the best civilization, but it is not exclusive to any race or even nationality. Frenchness can be taught and learned; the royal road to civilization is the French language, whose actual materiality is taken as an embodiment of values and skills. The subliminal message of assimilation is: You can be equal to me, provided that you become identical to me" (1994: 115–16). To Hubert Deschamps, assimilation, a long-standing tendency of the French people at home and abroad, was "the Revolution of 1789 sneaking into Africa rather late on tiptoe" ([1963] 1994: 172).

Assimilation was the goal; what were the means? Here differences of culture and of tradition meant that in practice assimilation was necessarily a fitful, halting, and radically incomplete project. Martin Lewis has said that "what was wrong with 'assimilation' was not that it was illogical, unrealistic, or impossible, but rather that no serious effort was ever made to carry it out" (1962: 153). Hubert Deschamps admits that the effort was made too late, and partly blames the misguided policies of association for this. Giving the Lugard Lecture in Brussels in 1963, he drew attention to his own writings of the 1930s, when as an administrator he pleaded—against the associationists—that we "should not waste our forces by maintaining an outmoded past, but rather ... set ourselves through education to laying the foundation for a modern future." "We all realized this only in 1945," he says, "and a mere fifteen years of formation were not sufficient. It is not the fault of the Africans, but our own for we developed too late an ultimate policy goal" ([1963] 1994: 178). By 1945 the forces of native nationalism, created largely by the empires themselves, had become too strong to resist.

The difficulties turned mainly on the question of citizenship. French administration and French laws were readily transmitted to the colonies. That aspect of assimilation—political and legal integration—was fairly easily accomplished, at least with respect to the European subjects (Saada 2013: 329). The question was who had the right of participation in a system that was meant to mirror the egalitarian, republican regime of the metropolis. Universal suffrage for males had been introduced in 1848, in the Second Republic, and was confirmed by the Third Republic. How far could it also be extended to the colonies? To what extent could citizenship be universal—and, if not, why not? On what grounds could a republic conceived in the universalist image of 1789 deny to its non-European subjects what had been granted to the inhabitants of the metropolis? If the Roman Empire, comparisons with which were popular among the colonialists, had been able, in the emperor Caracalla's famous Constitutio Antoniana of 212 CE, to extend citizenship to all its subjects, why not the French, its glorious successor?

There was a difference here between the "old colonies"—Guadeloupe, Martinique, Guiana, Réunion, Mauritius, Pondicherry—and the newer ones acquired in the "second French overseas empire" begun with the conquest of Algiers in 1830. In the older colonies, with the exception of some such as the Indian ones, the indigenous inhabitants had nearly all been wiped out, by conquest and by European diseases. The imperial power had in effect a clean slate to work on, which it proceeded to do with imported slaves, indentured laborers—Indian, Chinese, and others—and Europeans. Policies of assimilation could be applied with least resistance here; there were few indigenous traditions or institutions that stood in the way. With the definitive abolition of slavery by the Second Republic in 1848, the work of turning subjects into citizens could begin in the old colonies. This was a slow and uneven process, but it reached some sort of conclusion when the majority of the old colonies became overseas departments (*départements d'outre-mer*) in 1946. A similar set of policies in relation to the Pacific colonies—New Caledonia, French Polynesia, the Commores Islands, and some others—led to their being declared overseas territories (*territoires d'outre-mer*), a somewhat looser form of connection with metropolitan France. Though mostly nineteenth-century acquisitions, and so part of the newer empire, they shared with the old colonies a relative absence of, or very sparse, native populations, and so were easier to assimilate. It is mainly as a result of these policies of incorporation and assimilation, without the countervailing force of indigenous populations and institutions, that these colonies have to this day remained as part of France.

Formally, the French Empire was almost as heterogeneous as the British, with its possessions divided into departments, colonies, protectorates, and other administrative forms. It was also common to distinguish between settler colonies (*colonies de peuplement*), and "colonies of exploitation" (*colonies d'exploitation*), colonies that were mainly regarded from an economic point of view, as a source of natural resources and as a market for French manufactured goods. All this meant considerable variety in legal forms and administrative apparatuses among the possessions. There was also—as in the British case—no one government department overseeing all the colonies. Algeria, for instance, considered as part of metropolitan France, came under the Ministry of the Interior. Most of the possessions in sub-Saharan Africa, Asia, and the Pacific came under the new Ministry of the Colonies created in 1894. Formally the protectorates, such as Tunisia and Morocco, as well as Tonkin, Amman, and Laos (but not Cochinchina, a colony) came under the Ministry of Foreign Affairs. So too did the mandated territories of Syria, Lebanon, Togo, and the Cameroons administered by France after the First World War.

In practice, it is generally agreed, these divisions mattered less in the French case than in the British. Philosophies of assimilation and association, though often having their origins in particular parts of the empire, tended to be applied more or less universally. The different departments of state rarely felt constrained by their formal areas of responsibility—the Ministry of Foreign Affairs for instance, as one of the most senior and prestigious ministries, often intervened in the affairs of colonies formally administered by the new and more junior Ministry of the Colonies. While, as with the British case, it is dangerous to generalize about the whole empire, generalizations are not wholly misleading and can illuminate general trends. This is particularly so in the French case, which like the Spanish practiced a high degree of centralization, making the ideas and policies emanating from the metropolis especially consequential.

The French certainly recognized difference in their empire (a term that, in its unitary sense, became popular in France only relatively late, in the early twentieth century, and was particularly influenced by the heroic role of imperial subjects in the two world wars). Evolutionary social science was all the rage over all of Western Europe in the late nineteenth century, and the French participated fully in it, through the work of Gustave Le Bon, Lucien

Lévy-Bruhl, and others (Betts 1961: 59–89). In terms of the French Empire, this meant recognizing a "civilizational hierarchy," with the Europeans at the top, the Vietnamese (because of their ancient, Chinese-inspired, civilization) second, Algerians (Berbers and Arabs) next, sub-Saharan Africans beneath them, and at the bottom the "savage" Kanaks of New Caledonia and other Polynesian and Melanesian peoples. Depending on their place in the hierarchy, greater or lesser degrees of administrative autonomy could be granted to the different native populations (Saada 2013: 326–27).

The same or similar perceptions affected the extension of citizenship. Though citizenship as an eventual goal was held out to all inhabitants of the empire, for much of the time there was a clearly recognized distinction between "citizens" and "subjects" (Saada 2012: 95–115; Cooper 2014: 6–7, 13–18). Though all imperial subjects were French "nationals"—legally part of the French state and subject to its sovereignty—not all were full "citizens," with the political and legal rights conferred by this status. Over the course of the nineteenth century, in the metropolis the distinction between "national" and "citizen" gradually became blurred, with nationality conferring all or most of the rights of citizenship (Saada 2012: 98–99).

But such a merging was slow to develop in the colonies. Most Europeans were citizens, and citizenship was also made available to non-Europeans on the basis of certain conditions and qualifications. But the number of non-European citizens remained relatively small until the Second World War.[19] One consequence was that large parts of the colonial population were subject to the special provisions of the *code de l'indigénat* (indigenous penal code), a separate system of laws and jurisdiction for noncitizens that aimed both to support customary law and at the same time closely control (or "discipline") the native population. It was the *indigénat* that was the principal symbol of the gulf separating subject and citizen, and seemingly the most glaring example of the affront to the republican principle of equality of all French nationals (Aldrich 1996: 213–14; Belmessous 2013: 148–49).

We have to see though that, contradictory and iniquitous as it has seemed to some, the existence of separate categories of citizen and subject was closely bound up with the overriding goal of assimilation (Shepard 2008: 20–39). For instance in Algeria, where the *indigénat* was first developed, the separate code was justified on the grounds that, because it was based on customary laws and adjudicated in most cases by native authorities, it was intended to uphold the "religion, mores, marriage customs, and family organization" of the natives *as requested by them* in the 1830 treaty of capitulation (Saada 2012: 100). It reflected, in other words, an early example of the principle of association—and was so justified, for instance, by Alexis de Tocqueville, who wrote in 1847 that "it is not along the road of our European civilization that they [the indigenous Algerians] must, for the present, be pushed, but in the direction proper to them" (2001: 142).

The system of separate laws and jurisdictions, it appears, was meant as a *temporary*, provisional, expedient, to allow the "civilizing process" to do its work, to the point where the native population was ready to enter fully into not just the rights but also the duties and obligations of citizenship. Jules Ferry, an ardent assimilationist, argued that "surely, assimilation in its absolute sense, is the work of centuries, but the civilizing work which consists in uplifting the native, in extending to him a hand, is the daily work of a great nation" (in Belmessous 2013: 149; see also Baycroft 2008: 157). Assimilation was a gradual process, to be accomplished by daily effort and a steady application of measures to this end. It was the ultimate goal; in the meantime, for pragmatic reasons if no other, respect and recognition were due to native laws and customs, at least as concerned personal, domestic, matters.

This was fully in accordance with the understanding of the French "civilizing mission," and was not so different from the idea of colonial "trusteeship" as developed by British liberals such as John Stuart Mill. It was consistent with most of the legal judgments and declarations of the nineteenth century, where the application of the separate laws principle was justified on the grounds that for the time being it would be wrong to override the traditional customs and beliefs of the native population. "Why should the code of Gia Long, a learned monument to Chinese civilization, not be as good for the Annamites as the Civil Code is for the French?" (in Saada 2012: 107).

It was in fact always possible, in principle, for any subject of the empire to become a citizen. A senate decree of 1865, drawn up in relation to Algeria and after 1880 extended to the other colonies, stated that any native could "upon request be granted the rights of citizenship, in which case he would be subject to the civil and political laws of France" (in Saada 2012: 100–101). Like all naturalization laws everywhere, the grant of citizenship was conditional on the fulfillment of certain requirements. These included knowing the French language, and accepting the basic norms and conventions of French civilization, such as those having to do with the system of marriage and divorce. In this way citizenship was linked to certain notions of "civility," obviously derived from European and especially French practices (Saada 2012: 111–15).

Not all natives sought citizenship or saw it as necessarily beneficial. To accept citizenship meant giving up traditional practices—such as polygamy—and being subject to French laws and courts rather than local laws and traditional authorities. This, as much as French prejudices and reluctance, partly explains why citizenship was so slow to develop in the colonies (Aldrich 1996: 212–13; Belmessous 2013: 139–40). But it was not thought inherently impossible for natives to be acculturated and assimilated, and indeed a significant number did so. It was in many ways easier for a native to become French than for one in the British Empire to become English. Racism operated in both empires, as throughout the European world; but it seems clear that it operated to a lesser degree in the French than the English case.[20]

There was not therefore a system of permanent legal apartheid, as conceived by the white South African regime in the twentieth century, and as sometimes presented as an example of the racist ideology of the French Empire (e.g., Saada 2013: 335). Existing practices fitted in with the perception that, particularly in the case of peoples such as the Arabs and the Vietnamese, there were strong, preexisting civilizations whose force and appeal had to be respected—if only for reasons of expediency. In time, and with the power of the French state and the French educational system behind them, the superior culture and civilization of France would assert themselves in the minds and hearts of the natives, and they would be ready to take their place as full citizens of France. Just such a process, it was argued in the renewed debate about citizenship in the 1880s, was actually taking place in France itself, especially through the agency of the school and service in the army. The successful defense of the tradition of *ius soli* citizenship rested on the view that it was entirely possible for foreigners to be assimilated, just as was happening to French peasants still in the process of being "civilized" into full-scale republican citizens. "Internal and external assimilation were sociologically identical: if school and army could turn 'peasants into Frenchmen,' they could turn native-born foreigners into Frenchmen in the same way" (Brubaker 1992: 108–9; see also Weber 1976; Weil 2008: 30–53; Shepard 2008: 13). Much the same applied to foreigners abroad, the natives in the empire. When, at long last, French citizenship was extended to all subjects of the empire in the Lamine-Guèye law of 1946, it was such a view that finally triumphed (Aldrich 1996: 281; Cooper 2014: 26–60).

Algeria in the Empire

Fresh from his American journey and the triumph of *Democracy in America* (1835), the young Alexis de Tocqueville turned his attention to Algeria, the French conquest of which had begun with the capture of Algiers in 1830. When

FIGURE 7.4. Harbor and Admiralty, Algiers. The European section
of the city, the *ville nouvelle*, sharply demarcated from the "native"
city of mosques and markets. Library of Congress.

many of his countrymen—we have seen Guizot on this, previously—were
dubious about recommencing empire, Tocqueville became convinced that
it was above all through colonial ventures that France would reunite the fractured nation and regain the honor and respect it was due in the eyes of Europe
(Tocqueville 2001: xiv; Pitts 2005: 204–39; Veugelers 2010: 351). Algeria was
the beginning. "I have no doubt," he declared in 1837, "that we shall be able to
raise a great monument to our country's glory on the African coast" (Tocqueville 2001: 24).

Tocqueville was equally convinced that Algeria should not be a "colony
of exploitation" only, on the model of British India, but rather a colony of
settlement, one as thoroughly Europeanized as possible. There should not be
"domination without colonization": "the great end that France must set itself
[is] the establishment of European society in Africa" (2001: 61–63, 122). Like
the ancient Greek colonies in the Mediterranean, or the municipalities of the
Roman Empire, the aim should be to populate Algeria with Frenchmen and
Frenchwomen and to make Algeria "a perfect image of [its] homeland" (2001:

110). Ultimately the intent should be to colonize Algeria so intensively that the line dividing it from the metropolis would be erased. "We should set out to create, not a colony properly speaking in Algeria, but rather the extension of France itself across the Mediterranean" (2001: 161).

Tocqueville's imperialism has troubled some people, who see it as being at variance with the liberal sentiments expressed by the author of *Democracy in America* (see, e.g., Richter 1963). But "liberal imperialism," the imperialism of J. S. Mill and other liberals as much as Tocqueville, has come to be recognized as a fairly familiar phenomenon in nineteenth-century Europe (Mehta 1999; Pitts 2005). Whatever his reservations about the methods of conquest, Tocqueville accepted the civilizing mission of the European societies. France, with the universalism of the French Revolution as its guide, had more to offer than most. Algeria would be the laboratory of the new French Empire.

What Tocqueville also early recognized was that Algeria would be a very special part of the French Empire, occupying a unique status. Its proximity to France, the fact that it was the first colony of the new overseas empire and in that sense launched France's new and successful bid for empire, made it appear increasingly important in the eyes of the French. Its incorporation into the metropolitan administration in 1848, as three departments, with its citizens (mostly European) enjoying full political rights, exemplified its exceptional position; until 1946 no other colony was formally part of metropolitan France.

In the wake of the defeat of 1871 and the loss of Alsace-Lorraine, Algeria acquired a new importance. Many of the emigrants to Algeria came from the lost province, fleeing German rule. In 1871 the bishop of Algeria, Charles Lavigerie, addressed them directly, offering them "la France africaine" as "a home no less French than the one you have lost. It awaits you, and its love is as great as your misfortune" (in Schivelbusch 2004: 183). The author Augustine Fouillée who, under the pseudonym G. Bruno, had published the immensely popular children's book *Le Tour de La France par deux enfants* (1877), followed this up with another novel based on emigrants from Alsace-Lorraine, *Les Enfants de Marcel* (1887). In this almost equally popular novel, which became like the earlier one firmly established in the primary schools, the Alsatian family reestablishes itself in Algeria and prospers there. The grandmother apostrophizes this "Blessed land": "You have become almost as precious to me as the motherland. After so many trials and tribulations, my children owe you their safety, their happiness, and their health. When my time has come, I will take my final rest in your soil without regrets, my new Alsace" (translated from Girardet 1972: 183–84).

Algeria, in fact, got caught up in the whole concern with national regeneration, following the humiliation of 1871. It was the linchpin of the new program
of colonial expansion that was launched under the Third Republic. A good
part of Leroy-Beaulieu's influential book *De la colonisation chez les peuples
modernes* (1874) was devoted to Algeria, "which has for France," he declared,
"a supreme importance worthy of her past" (in Murphy [1948] 1968: 144; cf.
Conklin 1997: 19–22). "Because of its psychological and geographical proximity," says Schivelbusch, "Algeria would become the main forge in the production of myths for the whole colonial enterprise. The 'desert sands of Africa',
dismissed so disparagingly by the anticolonialists, began in the regeneration
rhetoric of the 1890s to represent a place of preservation, renewal, discipline,
and masculinization (*virilisation*)" (Schivelbusch 2004: 183).

Algeria, as we have seen, is sometimes referred to as the jewel in the French
imperial crown, by analogy and comparison with India in the British Empire
(e.g., Jasanoff 2005: 286). Jewel in the crown it certainly was, if we are to go on
the many heartfelt and passionate statements about its significance by French
writers and statesmen throughout the nineteenth century. Algeria, whether as
a curse or a blessing, remains burned in the French collective memory (Lorcin
2006). But the comparison with India in the British Empire may be misleading, at least in certain respects. India certainly occupied a very special place in
the British "imaginary" of empire. But there was never any significant European settler community there: people, many of them born there, for whom
India was their home. There were soldiers, civil servants, engineers, educators,
missionaries, traders. Their exit from India after 1948 was personally difficult
for a number of them, and has produced a rich literature of memoirs and fiction. But it never amounted to anything like the trauma that confronted Europeans in Algeria when the tie with France was severed in 1962. If a comparison
with the British Empire is sought, rather than India we should rather look to
South and East Africa, with their strong and numerous British communities.[21]
For them the break with Britain was almost as painful as that with France for
the European Algerians.

By the early 1900s there were over a million European Algerians—French,
Italian, Spanish, Maltese, Jewish—making up about a tenth of the population
of French Algeria (a little less than the proportion of the black population in
the contemporary United States). For them the idea that they were French,
that Algeria was French, that it was an integral part of France, was a central
tenet of their credo and the defining element in their identity. Right up to
the late 1950s this was a view shared by practically all shades of opinion in

France.[22] In the midst of the crisis of the Fourth Republic, Charles de Gaulle, backed by the French army and the Algerian *colons*, was summoned from retirement in 1958 to save the republic and prevent a slide into civil war. He seemed firmly behind the cause of *l'Algérie française*. To the consternation of the *colons* he abandoned them and rapidly, between 1958 and 1962, moved toward the granting of Algerian independence.

This abandonment seemed nothing less than treason in the eyes of the *colons*. They frequently reminded their compatriots in the metropole that, in France's darkest hour, under a Vichy regime and German occupation, it was from Algeria, freed from the Vichy state by the Allies in November 1942, that the Free French under General de Gaulle had launched their bid to liberate metropolitan France. The regiments of the Army of Africa stationed in Algeria had been made up of a majority of Muslims. In singing, in 1962, "We are the Africans / we return from afar / to save the Fatherland," the Algerians who opposed Algerian independence were appealing to that moment when all Algerians—both "European" and "Muslim"—were united in defense of France, and who by their very actions were demonstrating that Algeria was inextricably part of France (Shepard 2008: 118; see also Frémeaux 2007: 169).

Too often the feelings and actions of the European Algerians have been presented as simply the expressions of embittered and fanatical right-wingers espousing fascist and racist views. Certainly the violence and savagery on the part of some of the *colons*, such as the members of the paramilitary Organisation de l'armée secrète, cannot be denied or excused (though in fairness their opponents in the largely Arab Front de Libération Nationale [FLN] gave as good as they got). But as Todd Shepard has shown so well, this was far from the whole story. The European Algerians could and did point to a whole history of republican ideas, and of French commitment to Algeria as an integral party of the "one and indivisible" France, in making their protest against what they saw as a sellout by the metropolitan state. The cutting-off of Algeria, as an independent state, was indeed the only example in its history in which the French state had voluntarily given up what was undeniably one of its constituent territories (the other colonies had not shared in Algeria's unique constitutional status). De Gaulle and his allies had to go to considerable lengths, in terms of constitutional ingenuity, to do what they did. In the process they managed to present the *colons* as the enemies of the republic, so disguising that what they in effect were doing was dismembering the republic in the higher interest of preserving metropolitan France. The price was a political system, in the Fifth Republic, giving unprecedented power to the president and severely curtailing that of the legislature (Shepard 2008: 101–35).

The Algerian-born novelist Albert Camus, winner of the Nobel Prize for Literature in 1957, stands as a poignant and powerful example of the feelings of the *colons*. No one could accuse him of reactionary or racist views. He stood, as he still does, as a beacon of integrity and intellectual independence. During the Algerian War of Independence, from 1954 to his death in 1960, he was caught in the cross fire between the proponents of *Algérie française* and their opponents, the FLN and their left-wing allies in metropolitan France. He was unsparing in his condemnation of the violence on both sides. He appealed repeatedly for a truce and for an Algeria that would include all races and all religions, for "a future in which France, wholeheartedly embracing its tradition of liberty, does justice to all the communities of Algeria without discrimination in favor of one or another" (in Messud 2013: 56; see also Judt 1998: 116–21).

But, despite the pressure from his friends on the left as the conflict intensified, he could not abandon Algeria, could not abandon the people among whom he had been born and the land that had been the source of his creativity as a writer. In his posthumously published autobiographical novel, *The First Man* (1994), he showed vividly how central his early years in Algeria had been to his whole development as a writer, how he had been shaped not just by family and school there but also by the very physical features of the country, its landscape and climate. In it he lays claim to an identity that is distinctively Algerian, however much that has also been shaped by French culture. When, as the atrocities on both sides mounted, and many were coming to feel that an independent Algeria was the only solution, Camus insisted that France could not just leave Algeria to its fate in the hands of the Muslim majority. "She cannot, because she could never agree to throw one million, two hundred thousand Frenchmen into the sea" (in Messud 2013: 56). He rejected the idea that the French of Algeria were somehow alien interlopers, who should leave the land to its native inhabitants, the Arabs. He pointed out that the majority of French Algerians, like himself, had been born in Algeria. They too should be considered natives, *originaires*. "At present the Arabs do not alone make up all of Algeria. The size and seniority of the French settlement, in particular, are enough to create a problem that cannot be compared to anything in history. The Algerian French are likewise, and in the strongest meaning of the word, natives" (in Prochaska 1990: xvii).

In 1957, at a press conference in Stockholm following his acceptance of the Nobel Prize, Camus was asked by an Algerian student about his attitude toward the Algerian War, then at its height. His much-quoted (and as frequently misquoted) response was this: "People are now planting bombs in the tramways of Algiers. My mother might be on one of those tramways. If that is justice, then I prefer my mother" (in Messud 2013: 58; for another version, see Judt 1998: 131). In the version quoted by David Prochaska—"if I had to choose between justice and my mother, I would choose my mother"—justice is identified with an independent Algeria and the mother with *Algérie française* (Prochaska 1990: xvii). That is misleading insofar as for Camus true justice would be served by the recognition of the rightful claims of both groups, Arabs and Europeans, to the exclusion of neither. But it is accurate at least in its recognition of the succoring role of French Algeria in Camus's development. As Claire Messud, herself an Algerian-born novelist, has said, "if France was Camus's father, Algeria was his mother; and for their adoring son, no divorce could be countenanced" (Messud 2013: 58).

Were Camus's hopes and aspirations so unrealistic? Was Algeria fated to become independent, under the rule of a Muslim majority and with no real place for non-Muslims? That became the belief of many in France in the later years of the Algerian conflict, convinced that "the tide of History" ("winds of change" in the British version) was moving inexorably toward decolonization, and that French and Arabs could never mix. They thereby reversed what had been an equally strong belief up till then that Algeria must remain French (Shepard 2008: 55–81). Others too drew general lessons from the French example about the impossibility of a multicultural nation of the kind envisaged by Camus (e.g., Thody 1985: 13).

The fact is that Europeans in Algeria were not the only ones who held out hope that the disparate populations, admittedly unequal in development and differing in many ways in culture and customs, might nevertheless be able to coexist and even perhaps to converge. Such an outlook was shared by significant groups of Arab intellectuals—mostly *évolués* and *assimilés*—in the period between the two world wars. Particularly prominent was the group known as the Jeunes Algériens, inspired by the modernizing ideologies of the Young Tunisians and, behind them, the Young Turks. For these thinkers, the future of Algeria could only be in a "Greater France," with French ideas and institutions creating the modern culture that was the condition of survival and progress in the contemporary world. The aim, as one of them, L. Tahrat, put it in 1927, was the creation of a new community out of two peoples, a unique people "specifically Algerian but of French culture" (in Belmessous 2013: 161; generally, 160–200; see also Shepard 2008: 28–38).

Saliha Belmessous, who has given us the fullest study of this group, comments that "whereas assimilation was, in the nineteenth century, the main objective of the French state in Algeria, it had become a century later, and especially during the inter-war years, the political programme of the large majority of the indigenous intelligentsia" (2013: 167). Algeria is not of course the whole French Empire, and in many ways cannot be regarded as a representative colony. There was always something special about it in French eyes. But it was partly that that gave the hope to the indigenous people that something new might come out of the experiment, something in which they could share. It was a hope by no means restricted to Algeria or the Maghreb generally. Indigenous elites, the *évolués* of the other colonies in sub-Saharan Africa, Indochina, the Caribbean, and the Pacific, also at various times expressed their belief in a Greater France that would incorporate on equal terms all its peoples (Wilder 2005).

This faith was severely tested by the experience of the Second World War and in particular the policies of the Vichy regime. By 1943 Ferhat Abbas, previously a leading member of the Jeunes Algériens and a fervent assimilationist, was proclaiming the failure of assimilation and calling for an independent Algeria, though still within the framework of a French federation (Belmessous 2013: 195–96). Nationalist movements throughout Asia were given a huge boost by Japanese triumphs over the European empires. It was apparent that the French Empire, like the British, if it were to survive at all would have to change its ways.

La Plus Grande France: Apotheosis

As with the British Empire, and once again going against much received opinion about the condition of the European empires after the First World War, the interwar period can be seen as one in which the French Empire reached new heights and attained a new level of self-confidence. Almost nowhere were there calls for the end of empire—as opposed to reforms—and few signs that empire had exhausted its potential. The idea that the French Empire, like the British, would have all but disappeared by the early 1960s is one that would have astonished French even more than British commentators in the 1920s and 1930s. "The period from 1918 to 1940," says Robert Aldrich, "was the 'golden age' of French colonial empire" (1996: 114). For Raoul Girardet it represented "l'apothéose de la plus grande France": "never did the colonial idea arouse among the public more interest, more enthusiasm, more fervor" (1972: 176; and generally 175–99; see also Wilder 2005: 24–40).

As with Britain, the role of the empire in the titanic struggle of the First World War was only too obvious, and the lessons were not lost on the French public. The participation of Africans, in the Tirailleurs Sénégalais, made a particularly strong impression: 171,000 of them fought in the war, over 30,000 of whom were killed—the largest number of casualties among the colonial conscripts. "The heroism of the *tirailleurs sénégalais* during the war helped change stereotypes of Africans, the jungle savage replaced by the smiling, brave soldier willing to sacrifice his life for France" (Aldrich 1996: 223; see also Andrew and Kanya-Forstner 1971: 128; Betts 1978: 90–91). Altogether over 800,000 conscripts, from different parts of the empire, fought in the war; the 78,000 casualties among them amounted to 15 percent of the 1.4 million French losses (Quinn 2002: 186–87). Nothing succeeds quite like war, especially one on the scale of the First World War, in concentrating the national mind and making it aware of its strengths and weaknesses. The empire indeed appeared indispensable to France's greatness and security.

Again as with Britain France also came out of the war with a considerably extended empire. From the ruins of the Ottoman Empire it received Syria and Lebanon as League of Nations mandates; from Germany, also as mandates, came Togo and Cameroon. Most important, perhaps, it received back, also from Germany, the lost provinces of Alsace and Lorraine, bringing into the country 1.7 million men and women, a much-needed boost to a society that not only suffered from population stagnation but had lost over a million soldiers in the war (Jones 1999: 248). The minister for the colonies, Albert Sarraut, spoke in 1923 of "a greater France, no longer relying for its security on 40 million, but on 100 million people, and able to seek all its basic provisions from a unified domain twenty times bigger than the mother country" (in Frémeaux 2007: 168–69; see also Wilder 2005: 30–31). At over 11 million square kilometers it was the world's second-largest colonial empire, its reach as global as Britain's, its language and culture influencing millions.

The war and its aftermath greatly enhanced the importance of empire in the public mind. "Indeed," says Raymond Betts, "it was in the interwar period that the terms 'empire' and 'France Overseas' entered the popular vocabulary, thus indicating that the overseas possessions had been structured in the French mind somewhat as they were in reality" (1978: 90). Again and again one heard the refrain that, as was put by Leon Archimbaud in his book *La plus grande France* (1928), "our colonies are indispensable to us, and . . . without them, France would no longer be France" (in Wilder 2005: 32). It was during this period that French schoolchildren learned about the heroic actions and

SECRÉTARIAT AUX COLONIES SERVICE D'INFORMATION

TROIS COULEURS
UN DRAPEAU
UN EMPIRE

FIGURE 7.5. Eric Castel, *Trois Couleurs*. First World War poster proclaiming
the unity of the empire and a common patriotism across the different races.
Interestingly, the metropolitan (European) French themselves are not
included. Private Collection/Archives Charmet/Bridgeman Images.

great achievements of men like Pierre Savorgnan de Brazza, Marshal Joseph
Gallieni, and Marshal Hubert Lyautey. Newspapers and advertisements made
lavish use of the exotic costumes, colors, and products from the colonial lands.
One of the most famous advertisements was that for the chocolate drink Bana-
nia, which featured a laughing Senegalese soldier, another for Sati coffee with
its African woman. A "cinema of empire" developed, making use of the exotic

locales but also emphasizing the romance of empire. Lecturers carried the story of empire around the provinces (Frémeaux 2007: 169; Goerg 2002: 92–97). The parallels with Britain in this period, with its own popularization of empire, are remarkably strong.

Strongest of all, perhaps, was the great Colonial Exhibition of 1931 in Paris, which more than matched that at Wembley in 1924. This occurred, as Robert Aldrich says, "when French colonialism reached its apogee," and was "an unprecedented celebration of Greater France and the civilizing mission of France" (1996: 261). Organized by the great imperialist Marshal Lyautey, the exhibition drew over eight million visitors, from France and overseas. There they could see a full-scale, faithful reproduction of the great Cambodian temple of Angkor Wat, another one of the imposing mud-brick fortress at Djenné in West Africa, the great Tour de Bucrânes from Madagascar, spouting fountains from a Moroccan palace, a Sudanese mosque, Tunisian markets, silk makers from Indochina.[23] The exhibition aimed to show the benefits of French rule in the colonies: how, the visitors' guide explained, "our protection . . . delivered millions of men, women and children from the nightmare of slavery and death." Introducing the guide, Lyautey enjoined: "You must find in this exhibition, along with the lessons of the past, the lessons of the present and above all lessons for the future. You must leave the exhibition resolved always to do better, grander, broader and more versatile feats for Greater France" (in Aldrich 1996: 261). The pedagogic purpose of the exhibition was underlined in an interview in which Lyautey explained that "the French have to become more and more convinced to the marrow of their bones that the whole nation must line up behind its colonies, and that our future lies overseas" (in Lebovics 1994: 53). Paul Reynaud, the colonial minister, in opening the exhibition, also wished to stress that "the empire is the result of a perspective and policies that were part of France throughout all its history. . . . Colonization is the essential vehicle of civilization"—French, of course (in Quinn 2002: 205).

The mood of exhilaration and uplift was reflected in many of the publications on the colonies in the interwar period. Introducing an authoritative collection on the history of the colonies, Gabriel Hanotaux, himself the author of a six-volume history, wrote in 1929: "The history of France is not truly complete if it does not include the history of French colonisation and French expansion in the world. France has always tried to extend itself outwards. In doing so from age immemorial, it has not responded to an egoistic instinct, not even to an appetite for conquest, but a singular need to know men and the world, to propagate, to found, to create" (in Aldrich 1996: 4).

A whole "colonial literature" developed in these years, with authors—many of them army officers—popularizing colonial life in Algeria, Morocco, black Africa, Indochina. As with a similar British genre, fiction writers also found the colonies a suitably exotic setting for tales of heroism and adventure (Girardet 1972: 238–46; Baycroft 2008: 160–61). For the French public, "the colonial fact ceased to be a vague entity and became a familiar reality. The colonial presence began to be felt more and more in the interior of the national consciousness. It tended more and more to be integrated into the whole fabric of the moral life of contemporary France" (Girardet 1972: 185).

A fair reflection of this—the normalization of empire and its acceptance by the mass of the population—is the weakness of the anticolonial movement in metropolitan France in this period. There were dissident voices, of course, particularly among artists and writers, such as André Gide. The socialists and especially the newly founded Communist Party took the lead in opposing what they saw as many forms of abuse and exploitation in the colonies. But it is significant how few of them supported anticolonial movements in the colonies or called for France's withdrawal from its empire. Even the Communists, the most consistent hard-liners in the 1920s and early 1930s, changed their attitude when the Comintern adopted a Popular Front policy in 1936. Now the watchword was cooperation with the socialists, who were committed to the preservation of the empire and indeed believed in France's *mission civilisatrice*.

This was true even of erstwhile critics of empire, such as Georges Clemenceau and Léon Blum. In 1925 Blum, recently made leader of the Socialist Party, declared that "we are too imbued with the love of our country to disavow the expansion of French thought and French civilization. . . . We recognise the right and even the duty of superior races to draw unto them those which have not arrived at the same level of culture"—a classic statement of the *mission civilisatrice* (in Aldrich 1996: 115; see also Derrick 2002: 54–64). When leader of the Popular Front government in 1936, Blum endorsed Maurice Viollette's proposal to extend the vote to some 25,000 Algerian *évolués*, and announced bold plans to reform the French colonial system with a view to bettering the conditions of the indigenous populations. But the Viollette proposal failed, and the other hopes for reforms ended with the fall of Blum's government in 1937. If reform of the empire was to come about—and it did—it would need other levers than socialist good intentions.

A further indication of the growing importance of the empire to France in this period was economic. We have seen the relative insignificance of the colonies to the French economy in the period before 1914. After the First World

War, and for reasons very similar to those that brought about greater economic integration between Britain and its colonies in the interwar period—the disruption caused by the war, the Great Depression of 1929, the growing climate of international insecurity—France and its colonies grew closer together economically. In 1913 the colonies accounted for only 10 percent of France's foreign trade, and were well behind Russia and Latin America for French overseas investment. By 1933 the colonies accounted for 27 percent of France's foreign trade (23 percent of French imports and 33 percent of its exports), making the empire France's premier trading partner; it would remain so until 1960 (Girardet 1972: 180).

During the Depression years France's dependence on its empire increased, particularly in certain areas and for certain crucial resources. Algeria alone took 45 percent of France's exports and furnished 40 percent of its imports during the 1930s. Nearly all of France's imports of agricultural products came from the empire, many, such as tea, rice, and corn, from Indochina. Indochina was also the main source of rubber, of which France had increasing need, and other raw materials such as coal and tin. By 1938, 53 percent of Indochina's exports went to France, and France accounted for 57 percent of Indochina's imports (comparable figures for 1911–30 were 20 percent and 30 percent, respectively). A similar change can be observed in investment patterns. After 1918 the empire became the leading destination for French investment, by the late 1920s accounting for between 30 and 40 percent of all overseas investment. Large French banks, such as the Banque d'Afrique Occidentale, and large commercial companies, such as Compagnie française de l'Afrique occidentale, dominated the economic life of the colonies (Aldrich 1996: 118, 188–98; Wilder 2005: 26–27). The future was beginning to look increasingly similar to Britain's "Third Empire" of the 1930s, with its imperial economy and its Commonwealth idea.

Here too there was a French parallel, with ideas of imperial federation beginning to be aired in the interwar period. Unlike the situation in Britain, however, the most significant proposals were coming not from within the metropolis, or, at least, not from the native French, but from a group of évolués who, in Paris and in their homelands, engaged in a spirited discussion of the future of the French Empire and their place within it. The leading lights here were Blaise Diagne, a Senegalese from Gorée, who in 1914 became the first elected black member of the French National Assembly and in 1931 the first African ever to be appointed under-secretary of state for the colonies; Léopold Sédar Senghor, also Senegalese and also a deputy in the French National

FIGURE 7.6. Léopold Sédar Senghor, a leading theorist of *négritude* who became a deputy in the French National Assembly and later first president of an independent Senegal. Photo © AGIP/Bridgeman Images.

Assembly (and later first president of an independent Senegal); Aimé Césaire from Martinique, like Senghor a deputy and poet and with him one of the leading theorists of the cultural movement of *négritude*; Léon-Gontran Damas, from Guiana, along with Senghor and Césaire generally regarded as among the most accomplished of the *négritude* poets (Atlan and Jézéquel 2002; Wilder 2005: 149–294; 2009).

These African and Caribbean intellectuals varied considerably in their political outlook, Diagne the more conservative, Senghor and Césaire more radical. What united them, however, was the belief in "colonial emancipation without national independence" (Wilder 2009: 104). They were eloquent in elaborating the distinctiveness of African culture, and in presenting in their work the images, sounds, and rhythms of the indigenous cultures. Assimilation should not mean homogenization, the reduction to a single French culture. Nevertheless, they were convinced—as much as Ferhat Abbas—of the advantages of a French education and generally of partaking in the inheritance of French republican culture. They themselves were after all the products of that very process; and it was with the tools of French intellectual culture that they developed the idea of *négritude* (Wilder 2005: 149–57). They did not reject French culture and French civilization: indeed they embraced them as providing the scaffolding for a new type of culture that could emerge within the French Empire.

This was the burden of the famous speech to the United Nations delivered by Senghor on October 3, 1950, as a member of the French delegation. Defending French policies in the UN trust territories of Togo and the Cameroon, and more generally in Africa, he drew attention to his own origins in African peasant culture, and how, without rejecting the strengths of that inheritance, he had been able through his French education and experience to add immeasurably to it. The future lay in drawing on the perspectives of both the (African) peasant and the (French) intellectual, in producing a *métissage* (cross-fertilization) of both *négritude* and classical French humanism (Atlan and Jézéquel 2002: 109–13). As he had put it earlier, in an essay of 1945, the ultimate goal must be "a moral and intellectual fertilization, a spiritual grafting. In other words an assimilation that allowed association, but an assimilation conducted by the natives" (in Belmessous 2013: 199).

This was not so very far from certain interpretations of assimilation, as expressed in the past. Assimilation could mean political integration without cultural homogenization; the stress now on diversity within the overarching unity of the empire squared with many general cultural tendencies in the twentieth century, including the rediscovery of "the primitive" in twentieth-century art (Lebovics 1994: 94). At any rate there was no basic incompatibility between the aspirations of Senghor, Césaire, and other *évolués* and the call for a more enlightened, "humanist," empire that came from certain French thinkers and statesmen such as Albert Sarraut and Octave Homberg in the interwar period (Wilder 2005: 76–117). The stress now was on *la mise en valeur*, the need to develop the colonies in the interests of the natives as much as those of the metropolis. If this were done there would be no reason to fear for the future of the empire. In his widely read book *La France des cinq parties du monde* (1927) Homberg, a banker and businessman, elaborated the idea of "total France," a Greater France that while allowing for diversity still was organized around a single principle.

The goal . . . is to attach the colonies to the metropole as solidly as possible—to work to cement the unity of this total France. Just as formerly the policy of our sovereigns was to combine diverse provinces . . . into a French unity, today the Republic should, respecting the diversity of faraway colonies, integrate them entirely into our national life, to the point where this "France of all the continents" with the same blood, beats to the same rhythm in the same heart. (in Wilder 2005: 32)

The Agony of Exit

The French have often been portrayed as reluctant imperialists, even more than the British as portrayed by John Seeley and Bernard Porter.[24] Unlike the British, with the exception of some parts of the Maghreb few French people were willing to migrate and settle in the colonies. A sample survey of 1945, the first ever taken in relation to the empire, appeared to show the French uninterested in, even hostile to, empire (de Gantes 2002: 15). Unlike the British at the time, who despite their ignorance of it still seemed to take pride in their empire, one might be inclined to think that the French were ready to bid their empire goodbye and good riddance.

Polls, as so often, mislead. They can also show wildly fluctuating attitudes, the responses to transient public moods or the pressures of the present moment. A later poll, taken in 1949, showed that 84 percent of the population—77 percent "strongly"—considered it in the country's best interest to have colonies (Lebovics 1994: 93; Aldrich 1996: 283; Frémeaux 2007: 169). Certainly so far as the educated French were concerned—politicians, publicists, civil servants, writers, intellectuals, military officers—the empire became more, not less, important as the twentieth century progressed. After 1945 a determined effort was made to reform it, to put it on a firmer footing and make its existence more permanent.

In the end those efforts failed. But almost to the end the French fought grimly to hold on to their empire. This was not primarily because of the French settlers in Algeria, Indochina, and elsewhere. Unlike the British case, French colonialism was not really about settlement, not really about planting colonies. It was more a case of classic imperialism, the expansion of the French state and the French nation in the interest of power and prestige. If British colonialism can sometimes be compared to Greek colonization, French colonialism seems nearer the Roman model, in which French culture and civilization were to be spread more by "civilizing" the natives than by planting Frenchmen and Frenchwomen among them. Algeria had over a million European settlers, Indochina around 40,000 by 1945. This difference mattered but not as much as one might think. Algeria and Indochina were the two jewels in the imperial crown. Their losses were in both cases severe blows to French prestige and power in the world. That was why they were fought over so bitterly.

Once more, though, we should beware of abbreviating the process, of assuming that it was all over with empire after 1945. As with Britain, though for somewhat different reasons, the Second World War hastened certain developments that, sometimes mooted before the war, were now rapidly put into effect. They were designed to strengthen and prolong empire, not give it up. The effort was made easier by the fact that once more, as in 1914–18, no one could be unaware of the enormous contribution of the empire to the war effort. In 1940, colonial troops made up about 10 percent of the total French fighting force. After France's defeat, colonial troops made up an even greater proportion of the Free French fighting under de Gaulle. The liberation of Algeria and Morocco by the Allies in 1942 provided the Free French with a bridgehead for the assault on the Germans and the Vichy regime. In 1944, out of 633,000 Free French soldiers, about 60 percent were "natives" from the colonies; French *pied noirs* from Algeria made up most of the remaining 40 percent (Frémeaux 2007: 169). "France's honor was saved by its empire" (Cooper 2014: 8). Gaston Monnerville, a deputy from Guiana, declared to the Consultative Assembly on May 25, 1945, a few days after Germany's surrender, that "without the Empire, France today would merely be a liberated country. Thanks to its Empire, France is a victorious country (*un pays vainqueur*)" (in Girardet 1972: 281; see also Marshall 1973: 208–9).

Nevertheless, the war had inflicted serious blows on the empire. France's defeat by Germany in 1940—the second humiliation in less than a century—dented the idea of France's invincibility in the eyes of its colonial subjects. Perhaps even more serious were the reverses in the East, with Japan occupying Indochina and proclaiming to the whole world that the European empires could be vanquished by an Asian power. Anticolonial forces all gained an enormous boost from the Japanese success, not to mention moral encouragement and material support (Albertini 1969: 26–29). The racism and intolerance of the Vichy regime further tarnished France's reputation, putting in question the republican values that had been at the center of France's political identity since 1871, and which had furnished the main elements of its *mission civilisatrice* in the empire.

The opponents of Vichy, aware that something urgently had to be done if France's empire were to survive the peace, acted even before the fighting was over. In 1943 de Gaulle set up a provisional government in the now-liberated Algiers and in 1944 invited administrators from all the African colonies to a conference at Brazzaville, presided over by Félix Eboué, the black governor-general of French Equatorial Africa. The conference was to discuss necessary changes to the constitution of the empire. The final declaration of the conference left no doubt that what was intended was reform, not abolition, of the empire. "The ends of the civilizing work accomplished by France in the colonies exclude any idea of autonomy, all possibility of evolution outside the French bloc of the Empire; the eventual constitution, even in a distant future, of *self government* [given in English in the text] is denied" (in Smith 1978: 73; see also Aldrich 1996: 280; Marshall 1973: 102–15).

But the Brazzaville Conference at the same time made it clear that the development of the colonies was of paramount concern in the interests of both the colonies themselves and the metropole. "France places not only her honor but her interests in having the colonies endowed with their own prosperity, and access to the riches of all that bears the French name is the most certain measure of our country's return to grandeur" (in Marshall 1973: 110). It also acknowledged that the indigenous peoples of the colonies must be given a greater part in the government of their societies, and that a certain measure of decentralization would be necessary. The burning question of citizenship was raised but not answered—certainly not to the satisfaction of the indigenous leaders, who were not invited to the conference. They continued to press; and events were on their side. Indochina precipitated the more radical action. In 1945 the Japanese occupied Indochina and threw their support behind Ho Chi Minh's Viet Minh, with its demand for total independence from France. In response de Gaulle's government issued a declaration that became in effect a template for a new French Empire—now to be called the "French Union."

The Indochinese Federation forms with France and other parts of the community a "French Union" whose external interests will be represented by France. Indochina will enjoy, within this union, a liberty of its own. The inhabitants of this Indochinese Federation will be Indochinese citizens and citizens of the French Union. In these terms, and without discrimination of race, religion, or origin and given equality of merit, they will have access to all federal positions and employment in Indochina and in the Union. (in Cooper 2014: 30)

There were ambiguities here too, especially in relation to the old issue of citizenship. But still the general direction was clear. In 1946 de Gaulle stated that "the future of the 110 million men and women who live under our flag is an organization of federative form" (in Cooper 2014: 1; see also 44–45). Just as the British Empire was becoming the British Commonwealth of Nations, so the French Empire envisaged its future in the form of an imperial federation, with a relatively high degree of internal autonomy for its parts. Now too indigenous voices could not be kept out. At the National Constituent Assembly of 1945–46, summoned to draw up a constitution for the new Fourth Republic, the deputies included some of the best-known and most articulate *évolués*. Senghor, Césaire, and Abbas were there; so too was Félix Houphouët-Boigny of Côte d'Ivoire, like Senghor and Abbas a future president of an independent state. There was also Lamine Guèye from Senegal. It was Lamine Guèye who gave his name to the law of May 7, 1946, that turned all French "subjects" of the empire into French "citizens." Like the British in the nationality law of 1948, the French finally delivered on the long-standing promise to make all members of the empire into full French citizens. It was particularly fitting that it was a Senegalese who should introduce the law, as it was the "Senegalese model" of 1916—full citizenship without the requirement that the individual should give up "personal status"— that was adopted in the Lamine Guèye law (Cooper 2014: 8). What Ferhat Abbas, what many others had striven for all these years, citizenship without the condition that one abandoned one's ancestral religion and other aspects of personal and family life, now in the postwar years was made into a reality.

Contemplating the changes discussed in these years, Robert Delavignette, an official in the Ministry for the Colonies, wrote in 1945: "Empire, French Federation, Imperial Community, French Union: we see in the variations of vocabulary only a groping step by which we try to capture and fix very new relationships that need to be presented together in spirit. There are no more colonies in the old sense of the word. There is even no more colonial empire considered in relation to the metropole and as an object different from the metropole. . . . France no longer has an Empire, she is an Empire" (in Cooper 2014: 38, 54). More than one deputy in the National Constituent Assembly quoted those words as they voted the citizenship law. Here, if it were true, was the dream of "Greater France" realized: the 110 million inhabitants of the empire, Europeans, Africans, Asians, all equal parts of the same family, the French Union, "the Republic, one and indivisible."

That was what seemed to be implied in the preamble to the constitution of the Fourth Republic, adopted in October 1946, which established the French

Union. It stated that France "forms with the overseas peoples a Union founded on equality of rights and duties, without distinction of race or religion" (in Aldrich 1996: 281; see also Smith 1978: 74). There were ambiguities and contradictions in the citizenship law of 1946 that, between then and 1958, the French government under pressure from nationalists attempted to resolve (Marshall 1973: 215–72; Cooper 2014). In the 1958 constitution of the new Fifth Republic, citizenship—in an attempt especially to assuage Algerian feeling—was granted unequivocally to all adult men and women in the new "French Community."

Political changes were not the only ones that seemed to suggest a closer union between metropole and colonies in the future. Economic ones too, continuing developments begun before the war, pointed in the same direction. The Compagnie française de l'Afrique occidentale dominated the business life of black Africa even more than before the war. Despite the civil war raging in Indochina, the Banque de l'Indochine continued to do business in the region, right up to the communist victory in Vietnam in 1975. Trading relations between France and its colonies also continued to get stronger: in 1952, 42 percent of France's exports went to its empire, the highest ever (Aldrich 1996: 197; Thomas, Moore, and Butler 2008: 159–61). The parallels with Britain, once more, are striking. After the Second World War, the empire seemed more, not less, necessary, to the economic well-being of the metropole.

The empire mattered to the French. That was why they fought so bitterly to hang on to it, especially in the two areas, Algeria and Indochina, that they regarded as essential to its continuance. There was no question of peacefully handing power to the nationalists, as somehow the rightful legatees of French power. Two long-drawn-out colonial wars, in Vietnam from 1946 to 1954, and in Algeria from 1954 to 1962, were necessary before the French conceded that they could no longer hold on to their empire. They were defeated militarily in Vietnam, finally at Dien Bien Phu in 1954. With that ended French rule in the whole of Indochina. In the same year the Algerian revolt broke out, leading to a civil war marked by atrocities on both sides. The failure to resolve it led to the collapse of the Fourth Republic. Brought to power by the army in 1958, and publicly committing himself to the new "French Community" that, in the constitution of the Fifth Republic, replaced the French Union, by 1961 de Gaulle was announcing that the age of empire was past and France had to look to its future in Europe. Algeria had to go its own way (Shepard 2008: 73–77; Evans 2012).

With the loss of its two key colonies, there was no great enthusiasm to struggle to hold on to the remaining parts of the empire. The Indian *comptoirs* were promised to India in 1954, and the cession ratified in 1961. In 1956 Tunisia and Morocco received their independence. After 1958 it was the turn of sub-Saharan Africa. The constitution of the new French Community offered the overseas territories various options, including full independence. In 1958 only Guinea chose that option; by 1960 all the other sub-Saharan African territories had done so, and been allowed to. Part of the reasoning, in the case of these as of Tunisia and Morocco, was that France would continue to have a close association with the independent states, as seemed likely under the leadership of such men as Bourguiba, Senghor, and Houphouët-Boigny. A new "francophone community," matching the British Commonwealth, seemed a possible outcome, allowing France to continue to influence developments without formal rule.[25]

Was the end of empire inevitable? Was it written in "the tides of History," as claimed by de Gaulle and others after 1958? The answer is as elusive in the French case as in the British. Certainly anticolonial nationalism, relatively weak before the war, had accelerated tremendously during and after the Second World War, thanks largely to the activities of the Japanese and Chinese, and aided by the anticolonial attitudes of the American and Soviet governments (Smith 1978: 70–71). But it would be as wrong in the French as in the British case to posit some sort of inevitability to the demise of empire. In the years following the Second World War, few of the nationalists in the French Empire—Ho Chi Minh was something of an exception—called for an end to the French Empire and total independence for the native people. They continued to think that the best thing for the colonies was membership within a reformed empire, one that would give everyone an equal place and equal opportunities within a framework of equal citizenship. Only when that seemed unduly held up, and most of all when armed conflict hardened attitudes on both sides, did they begin to feel that independence might be the better and perhaps only option. Only retrospectively, and under the guidance of some sort of doctrine of historical determinism, was it possible to argue that there was a "logic" to the process of decolonization that signaled doom to all the European empires.

For their part France's rulers, and more generally its political class, had embraced empire more comprehensively by the time of the Second World War than at any time previously. To that extent the educative campaigns of the 1920s and 1930s had done their work well. On both left and right there was, as Tony Smith puts it, a "stubborn colonial consensus" on the need for empire as the means to regaining—after Vichy—France's honor and place in the world (Smith 1978: 80). Nor was that all. A whole generation of French-men and Frenchwomen had come to believe that Greater France existed for the good of the world as much as for the good of France. That did not inhibit criticism, as became particularly clear during the Vietnamese and Algerian wars of independence. But a majority of statesmen and intellectuals, including most of those on the left, saw mending, not ending, empire as the right way to proceed. They could find common cause with many of the intellectual and artistic leaders of the indigenous communities. For both, French civilization was something that still, as in the Enlightenment, as in 1789, had the capacity to inspire the world. When, by 1960, it had become clear that the empire could not hold together, not at least without intolerable force, it was still possible to hope that that civilization might exert its influence in the successor states.

Formally, at least, the European empires have passed. Does that mean also that empire has had its day? What might be its aftereffects, its legacy? What might be its new forms? A brief consideration of these questions seems in order, to round off this account of the rule of empires.

8

Epilogue

NATIONS AFTER EMPIRES

Here was a system of world-wide dimensions which only a few years earlier
still had a look of solidity and permanence to it and which had ordered—or
disrupted—the affairs of very large segments of mankind. . . . Is there any
other occasion on which so global and commanding a scheme of things was
swept away in so brief a time?

—RUPERT EMERSON (1969: 3)

The age of imperialism is dead and buried.

—WOLFGANG MOMMSEN (1982: 113)

The empires of our time were short-lived, but they have altered the world
forever; their passing away is their least significant feature.

—V. S. NAIPAUL, THE MIMIC MEN ([1967] 1985: 32)

COMPARED TO THOSE of the ancient world, the empires of the modern world
have had relatively brief lives. The Egyptian Empire lasted over three thousand
years, that of China over two thousand years. The successive Akkadian, Babylonian, and Assyrian empires in Mesopotamia lasted two thousand years. The
Roman Empire, which included the last two hundred years of the republic and
the thousand or so years after the fall of its Western half, can be said to have
lasted nearly two thousand years.

Of the modern empires, the Ottoman Empire had the longest continuous
existence, from the fifteenth to the early twentieth century—a period of over

five hundred years. The Russian Empire—including its Soviet extension—lasted from the sixteenth to the late twentieth century, almost as long as the Ottoman, but with a clear break in between. The House of Habsburg ruled two empires, Spanish and Austrian, which together lasted almost as long as the Russian Empire, though there was not the same continuity as between the tsarist and the Soviet empires. The British Empire began in the late sixteenth century and ended in the mid-twentieth, but also experienced something of a break in the late eighteenth century. The French Empire certainly began as early as the others, in the sixteenth century, but the almost total loss of its first empire in the eighteenth century meant that France effectively had to begin again in the nineteenth, losing it again not much more than a century later.

At any rate it is clear that the life of modern empires has to be measured in centuries—around five hundred years for most—rather than millennia, as with several of the ancient empires. Does this matter? Did modern empires have less impact on the world than the ancient ones? Clearly not. The Roman Empire may have thought of itself as the *orbis terrarum*, the world; the Chinese Empire may have thought of itself as the Middle Kingdom, the center of the earth. But in neither case was their reach truly global (though Alexander's short-lived empire came close). That is what distinguishes the European empires, at least the overseas ones, the Spanish, Portuguese, Dutch, British, and French empires. Even the land empires of the Ottomans, the Russians, and the Habsburgs operated within a globalizing world created by their European rivals. In their thinking, as well as in their strategy, they had to take into account the global forces unleashed by the overseas empires. In the Crimean War, for instance, fought by Ottomans, Russians, British, and French, land and overseas interests and outlooks intersected in complex ways—as was to be the case again, this time on a truly global scale, in the First and Second World Wars.

It was not simply that the European empires had to think and act globally. There was also the fact of the new organizational and technological forces that gave them world supremacy and that they diffused throughout the world. European armies and navies, European weaponry and military organization, European industry and forms of transport and communication—railways and steamships, electric telegraph and cable—all gave Europeans a commanding lead over other cultures, some of them, such as the Chinese, that had once led in nearly all these fields. The challenge was out: adapt and adopt European ways or face impotence and backwardness. Most chose to Westernize, even if, like the Japanese and Chinese, they found their own way, drawing on the resources of their own cultures, of doing so.

But if, for the past two centuries or so, European empires remade the world, what is the consequence of their demise? What happens when, in a formal sense at least, European empires are no more? The world may have been substantially Europeanized or Westernized by them, but how do European societies come to terms with the fact that they are no longer running that world, or large sections of it? What is the impact on their sense of themselves? What happens when empires—finally, and much later than generally acknowledged—become nation-states?

"Decolonization"—the loss or abandonment of colonies—is a term coined in relation to the overseas empires, and is not usually applied to the land empires, but it can serve as a useful term for both. In all cases it was painful, even traumatic, whatever the obvious differences between them.[1] In the first place it was often painful for the nonmetropolitan subjects of the empires, even though they were the notional beneficiaries in the form of independent nation-states. They can be said to have been marked by their severance from empire as much as the populations of the metropolitan powers. There have been many accounts of this from the viewpoint of the non-European subjects of empire, ranging from the bitter denunciation of Frantz Fanon's *The Wretched of the Earth* (1961) to the nostalgic lament of Nirad Chaudhuri's *Autobiography of an Unknown Indian* (1951). One common observation is that, under new native elites, the subjects of the newly independent states were not necessarily better off than they had been under the old empires. Another is that the old imperial rulers continued to exercise considerable power over the new nations, this time through informal rather than formal means ("neocolonialism").

Our concern here is the impact of empire, and of its loss, on the ruling peoples. The land empires collapsed in war and revolution, mostly in the First World War. Out of the Ottoman Empire came the new nation-state of Turkey, shorn of its Greek and Armenian population. Under Mustafa Kemal, "Atatürk," it embarked on a radical program of modernization and Westernization. Turks were to become like their counterparts in the modern West: secular, scientific, industrial. The outcome of this ambitious effort is still uncertain, but one effect has been to produce a backlash in the form of a revival of Islam—one of the many examples of "the empire striking back." Going with this has been a certain "Ottomania," a decided revival of interest among Turkish scholars and intellectuals—after decades of official neglect—as to what the Ottoman Empire stood for, and what may have been lost with its demise. Turkey's importance in the region, and the existence of various Turkic cultures on its borderlands—many of them from the former Soviet Union—have led some to dream, once again, of a Greater Turkey that would encompass more than the inhabitants of the Turkish nation-state. That this might exclude membership of the European Union, for long an official aim, is a prospect that they face with equanimity.

Out of the Austro-Hungarian Empire came, apart from a host of independent states formed by the subject peoples, the independent states of the former ruling peoples, the Austrians and the Hungarians. Both were severely truncated versions of their past imperial forms. Both experienced extreme difficulty in coming to terms with their radically diminished power and prestige. The Austrians settled, for a while, on membership in a new Greater Germany, until the disastrous consequence of that choice forced them to rethink their identity and their future. After 1945 they seemed content to see themselves as a small power in Central Europe, even, during the Cold War, as a sort of bridge between East and West. Habsburg nostalgia has been officially frowned on, though there is some pride, and some suggestion, that the European Union can be seen in some of its aspects as a resurrected Habsburg Empire.

Hungary too experienced great difficulties during the interwar period, succumbing to fascism and engaging on the side of the Nazis during the Second World War. After the war it became a communist country and part of the Soviet bloc. The end of communism in 1989 was hailed as a liberation, but Hungary's development since then, even as part of the European Union, has been far from reassuring. The ghosts of the past, in the form of anti-Semitism and authoritarianism, continue to haunt it. Unlike Austria, which seems to have found a reasonably comfortable niche within the European community of nations, Hungary still seems to be searching for an identity that would allow it to forget its former great power status as coruler of a great empire.

Of all the land empires, it is in Russia that the imperial past seems to loom most powerfully. Perhaps this is because the imperial experience lasted so long there, far longer than in the case of the other land empires. From the ruins of the tsarist empire Russians reconstructed a new empire, the Soviet Union, based on new principles. That lasted over seventy years, finally collapsing in 1991. Russia since that time, still the largest country in the world, with enormous resources, has struggled to find a new role and a new identity. Sometimes it has stressed Russian nationalism, but at other times it has expressed dissatisfaction with the restricted place—Russia as just one nation among others—this implies. Strands of Russian messianism, the conviction that Russia has a special mission in the world, continue to surface, helped by the revival of Russian Orthodoxy. The ideology of Eurasia, interpreted to mean that Russia is the core and ruling spirit of a vast landmass stretching from Russia to the Far East, has enjoyed a renaissance (Chamberlain 2015). Conflict with countries of the former Soviet Union, above all Ukraine, has suggested that Russia has not given up the hope of reassembling, in some form, a new Russian Empire. Under the long-lasting leadership of Vladimir Putin, all these tendencies seem at various times to have received official endorsement.

The overseas empires ended mostly in the 1950s and 1960s. Boosted by the First World War—unlike the land empires—they enjoyed something of a halcyon period in the 1920s and 1930s, despite the rumblings of discontent on the part of some subject peoples. The Second World War showed both their continuing importance to their rulers and, at the same time, their vulnerability in the eyes of their subject peoples. Despite energetic efforts at colonial development, and in wide-ranging political concessions, after the war, the empires unraveled in the late 1940s and 1950s.

The British, by the common consent of most scholars, let go of their empire with the least degree of violence and suffering (e.g., Smith 1978: 100). There was, as we have already noted, the legacy of the partition in India, which uprooted millions of people and was accompanied by thousands of deaths on both sides. The British must certainly bear some responsibility for this. There was also the obduracy of the British settlers in East Africa, which led to violent conflicts and a number of atrocities, mostly committed by the local white population. So the British withdrawal from empire can in no way be considered peaceful, let alone "graceful," as some in Britain were inclined to say. But by comparison with the French, Dutch, Portuguese, and Belgian empires, it seems fair to say that Britain got out of its empire with less violence and bloodshed than in those other cases.

But that does not mean that the loss of empire had less consequence for the British people than in those cases where it was a longer, more painful, process. It may even be that the relatively easy manner of exit made for a deeper impact than in those societies where the anger and hatred bred by crippling colonial wars led to a strong desire to bury the empire, to expunge it from the collective memory. The Dutch, the Belgians, and the Portuguese, at least, together with the Spanish, whose empire ended much earlier, do not seem to be much concerned these days with their empires, or the glory they once brought them.

For the British, the empire had always been so large a part of their collective identity that the effect of its loss was bound to be profound. For a while they pretended they didn't care, or even chose, in some cases, to regard the imperial past with disfavor, to see it as a shameful and discreditable episode in the country's history. Imperial history was not a popular subject in the universities in the 1960s and 1970s, among either students or their teachers. Expatriates, returning from the former British Empire, found themselves often the butt of humor and satire, not all of it good-natured.

This has changed markedly in recent years. Books and television programs about empire have proliferated. Imperial history has experienced a renaissance, with the five-volume *Oxford History of the British Empire* (1998–99) being as good an indicator as any of this. Sociologists and literary scholars have also turned with enthusiasm to the empire, seeking in it the source of many current attitudes and concerns (see, e.g., Ward 2001; Kwarteng 2012; Bailkin 2012).

Most marked, perhaps, is the attention paid to empire as the British wrestle with questions of national identity. The problem has been particularly acute for the English. They were the architects of empire, its guiding force. Others in the United Kingdom certainly played major roles, but when the empire disappeared, they were able to fall back on reasonably well-developed national identities, Scottish, Welsh, Irish. No such recourse was possible for the English, who had passed most of their history without the need for such an identity, suppressing it in the commitment to the wider enterprise of empire (Kumar 2003). The loss of the overseas empire has therefore posed a particularly acute challenge to them, the more so as, with threats of the breakup of the "inner empire" of the United Kingdom itself, they can no longer nestle so comfortably within the wider identity of Britishness (Kumar 2015).

The French, like the British, for a while after 1962 were disinclined to reflect on their empire. The Algerian War, in particular, had created a wound that they were anxious to cover over as quickly as possible. The best strategy seemed amnesia. "In 1962, most French institutions and people chose to purge their past and present of signs that empire mattered" (Shepard 2008: 272). Rather like Enoch Powell in the case of Britain, the French began to say that empire had been unnatural, had been a mistake, had distracted France from its historic role as a great European power whose proper theater of operations was Europe. Under de Gaulle in particular, France presented itself as the driving force of the European Community, drawing Germany into a partnership (and excluding Britain) to ensure that the Franco-German relationship would be at the core of the growing achievement of European unity.

In such a context memories of empire could only be an embarrassment, or worse. Put in charge of creating a new museum of colonial history in the

1990s, the Marseille historian Jean-Jacques Jordi recalled that, after decades of promoting the empire, from 1962 "everything that was a reminder of this colonial culture and this French presence was consigned to oblivion, treated with shame and sometimes hatred, and made taboo. . . . Colonisation, which took pride of place in French history in the 1930s, no longer had any place" (in Aldrich 2005: 329). The message of shame was rammed home in Gillo Ponte-corvo's acclaimed film *The Battle of Algiers* (1965), with its graphic depiction of scenes of torture by the French army. Initially denied distribution in France, from 1971 the French too were able see in the film what that almost-defining part of their empire had been like, and join in the general condemnation.

The very fact that a museum of colonial history was contemplated in the 1990s showed how far things had changed by then. In the 1960s, as part of the process of forgetting, the colonial museum in Paris had been transformed into a museum of African and Oceanic arts. Now, in 2007, the National Memorial of France Overseas (Mémorial national de la France Outre-Mer) was opened to triumphant fanfares in Marseille on the site of the great Colonial Exhibi-tion of 1906. Several other museums opened at this time, such as the Musée du Nouveau Monde and the Musée de la Compagnie des Indes, testified in addition to a renewed interest in France's early empire (Lebovics 2004: 143–77; Aldrich 2005: 328–34). Nicolas Sarkozy, campaigning for the presidency in February 2007, declared that "France should be proud of its past and stop this nonsense about repentance" (*New York Times*, October 17, 2007). When presi-dent he tried to have the teaching of French colonial history made compulsory in schools—with an accent on the positive contribution made by France to world civilization.

It was in 2007 too, and again suggesting the reversal of the tide of indiffer-ence, that the National Center of the History of Immigration (Cité nationale de l'histoire de l'immigration) opened its doors on the same site in the Bois de Vincennes as the Colonial Exhibition of 1931. The movement of many North African Muslims to France in the decades after the 1960s had confronted France not just with novel problems of integration, but—as in Britain—also with strong reminders of its empire, from which so many of the immigrants came. Here indeed was the "empire striking back," but also stimulating fresh inquiry into the meanings of empire and the significance of the imperial experience.

None of this of course means a return to celebration of the empire, certainly not in any simple way. It is more a recognition, not simply of the importance of empire in French history, but of its continuing impact even after formal empire has ended. Speaking of Algeria, for instance, the French sociologist Etienne Balibar declared in 1997 that "France today was made (and doubtless is still being made) in Algeria, with and against Algeria." The French nation, he argued, was "formed as part of the empire," and "the empire remains part of the nation for a long time after physical and juridical separation." France and Algeria were irreducibly part of each other, he affirmed, forming a "Franco-Algerian ensemble" in which any notion of a hard-and-fast "frontier" could not be maintained. This was a common condition of all the former European empires, Balibar held, an interpenetration of former colony and former empire (Balibar 1999: 162, 166–67).

It is clear that for France, as for Britain, the empire is back on the national agenda. The attempts to bury it have resulted in the usual consequences of repression, its return in sometimes troubling ways. But at least there is now the recognition that France's identity as a nation is bound up in some way with the fact that it also had an empire, that in fact it fused its identity in an "imperial nation-state." Confronting the imperial past is a necessity for understanding its present condition, and perhaps too its future.

The full story of the effects of the end of empire on the metropolitan populations—Turks, Austrians, Russians, British, and French—will have to await another time, and another book. But, by way of conclusion, one might ask, Is empire truly over? Is a whole era of world history—the "age of empires"—at an end ? Has—at last—the nation-state truly come into its own as not just the ideal but the actual form of collective belonging and identification? Have we finally, in the last fifty years, made the much-trumpeted transition "from empire to nation-state"?

Wolfgang Mommsen writes that "there can be little doubt that the ending of formal colonial rule by the Western powers with but few remnants of their former colonial possessions still intact is a crucial caesura in the history of mankind." But he immediately qualifies this by adding that this caesura "on closer inspection . . . evaporates to some extent" (1986: 333). Rupert Emerson too, an early and one of the best-known commentators on the epochal move from "empire to nation" ([1960] 1962), also nevertheless later felt drawn to raise the question "Have we now come to a turning point in history, or will the next throw of the global dice bring forth a new imperialism and a new colonialism?" (1969: 16).

What both writers—along with many other commentators—drew attention to were some fairly obvious features of the postcolonial world. There was first what was called the "neocolonialism" of the Western powers, whereby they sought to keep, and in most cases succeeded in keeping, their former colonies in a state of "dependency" through informal mechanisms of economic, political, and cultural power. Colonies might formally become independent states, the United Nations might repeatedly pass declarations against the reimposition of any form of colonialism, but the reality was the continuance, in a form that Gallagher and Robinson (1953) had influentially analyzed for an earlier period, of "informal empire" and Western dominance of much of the "Third World" of newly independent states.[2]

In the Third World the West shared the struggle for influence and control with the great new twentieth-century power of the Soviet Union. Since the main representative of the West was the United States, here too was a phenomenon that seemed severely to question the idea of the triumphant nation-state. For whatever they were, neither the Soviet Union nor the United States seemed to fit the conventional model of the nation-state. The Soviet Union was evidently the successor of the Russian tsarist empire, as even Russians were quick to say after its fall in 1991. Talk of "the Soviet Empire" is now commonplace. The debate over whether America is or ought to be thought of as an empire has raged for several decades, but most are prepared to agree that it has frequently acted very "imperially" and that its hegemonic power in the world for much of the time since the Second World War has conferred on it, willy-nilly, empire status.[3]

The Soviet Union has gone, but Russia as we have seen has shown new imperial tendencies. The United States is faced with formidable challenges but continues to exercise a worldwide economic and political role, and its military power is so far still unsurpassed. There is now also, in the early twenty-first century, the rise of China as a new superpower. China, like the United States, also fits very awkwardly into the category of nation-state. Its past, for more than two millennia, is decidedly imperial—it can in fact claim to have the longest continuous existence as an empire of all states. Now poised to become the world's largest economy, it has begun to spread its wings in the world, challenging its neighbors in East and Southeast Asia and establishing a powerful presence in Australasia, Africa, and South America. No more than the United States and the Soviet Union will it ever declare itself an empire: like them it claims, in its current (communist) form, to have been founded on anti-imperial and anticolonial principles. But like them too, the reality—at least as seen from the outside—might look more imperial than anything else comparable. The recent recovery—after decades of neglect or of outright rejection—of the Chinese past, the playing down of Marxism and Maoism, the rehabilitation of Confucianism and other traditional doctrines, all certainly seem to point in the direction of a linking up with China's imperial tradition rather than an avoidance of it.

There are many other indications in the contemporary world that the nation-state has not yet occupied center stage, and may never do so, despite what for so long has been destined for it by mainstream opinion. There is the impressive supranational experiment of the European Union: not a conventional empire, of course, but with features that have reminded at least one observer of the Holy Roman Empire (Lieven 2001: 86), and have prompted another to say that "Europe's future will not be able to do without borrowing from the imperial model" (Münkler 2007: 167; see also Zielonka 2006; Foster 2015). There is the United Nations and all its agencies, a permanent reminder that the nations of the world have committed themselves to a form of international regulation and supervision that constrains and limits, in principle at least, national sovereignty and national independence. There is a whole panoply of "international non-governmental organizations" (INGOS)—humanitarian groups such as Médecins Sans Frontières, environmental groups such as Greenpeace—which have come to constitute a kind of "global civil society" (Keane 2003) that complements and overlaps with the civil society organizations of national states. These too keep a watching brief on the nation-state, and can hold it up to the bar of international public opinion if it neglects its responsibilities or violates international norms. In exceptional cases—but these have been on the increase—national statesmen can be referred to the International Court of Justice at the Hague, or specially constituted International Criminal Tribunals, such as the one for the former Yugoslavia. In all these ways the future looks increasingly unlike one in which anything like the classic nation-state will be the predominant form.

There is a further element, one affecting particularly the European countries that had large overseas empires (but not only those). That is the movement to the metropolitan centers of large numbers of immigrants from former colonies, especially those in Asia, Africa, and the Caribbean. This was, Salman Rushdie wrote in relation to Britain, the "new Empire" within Britain, Britain's "last colony" (1992: 130). Attitudes on the part of both Europeans and the mainly non-European newcomers in their midst have been strongly marked by the experience of empire. Once more the nation-state struggles to regulate and control its population and its borders, to solidify national identities, to expunge if possible memories of empire. Once more the exercise proves futile, as the empire repeatedly breaks in and disrupts the order of the nation-state, forcing it to confront its past and to come to terms with the empire that has now come home to the European heartlands.

In their splendidly wide-ranging and stimulating survey *Empires in World History*, Jane Burbank and Frederick Cooper comment on the longevity of empire, as compared with the recently arrived nation-state. "The nation-state appears as a blip on the historical horizon, a state form that emerged recently from under imperial skies and whose hold on the world's political imagination may well prove partial or transitory." They ask: "Has the normality of empire come to an end? Is the only alternative the nation-state with its capacity for violence in the cause of homogeneous community? Or are there alternatives that can recognize diverse types of political association without insisting on uniformity or hierarchy? An attentive reading of the history of empires brings us face to face with extremes of violence and hubris, but also reminds us that sovereignty can be shared, layered, and transformed. The past is not a single path leading us to a predetermined future" (2010: 3, 22; see also 413–15, 458–59). This seems a wise and pertinent observation, one that has been echoed by several scholars in recent years (e.g., Kappeler 2001: 3). Empires, in their historic forms, may have had their day; but it is not at all clear that the desirable alternative is today's system of two hundred or so nation-states all claiming sovereignty and all tending toward ethnic uniformity. That seems a recipe for unending conflict, both within and between states. Empires, for all their faults, show us another way, a way of managing the diversity and differences that are now the inescapable fate of practically all so-called nation-states. That by itself seems sufficient grounds for continuing to study them, and to reflect on what they may be able to teach us.

NOTES

Chapter 1: The Idea of Empire

1. For these studies, see Hobson ([1902, 1938] 1988); Lenin ([1917] 1939); Schumpeter ([1919] 1974); Burnham ([1941] 1962); Neumann ([1944] 1966). There is a good survey in Mommsen (1982).

2. Hardt and Negri's *Empire* (2001) is a later version of this discussion of late global capitalism as a very amorphous "empire," bearing little relation to the historic empires.

3. In addition to the titles mentioned in this paragraph, a very selective list of significant publications on empire over the past two decades would include Alcock et al. (2001); Aldrich (2007); Burbank and Cooper (2010); Calhoun, Cooper, and Moore (2006); Cooper and Stoler (1997); Duverger (1980); Ferro (1997); Hobsbawm (1987); Kupchan (1994); Lustick (1993); Maier (2006); Miller and Rieber (2004); Motyl (2001); Muldoon (1999); Münkler (2007); Osterhammel ([1995] 2005); Pagden (1995, 2003, 2015); Parsons (2010); Snyder (1991), Steinmetz (2013). Central insights on empire are also contained in two works with a wider remit, Mann (1984) and especially Finer (1999).

One should also note the revival of studies of thinking about empire, what the great political and social theorists—Locke, Montesquieu, Burke, Diderot, Herder, Tocqueville, Mill—of the last two or three centuries had to say about empire. Notable examples here are Mehta (1999), Muthu (2003, 2014), Pitts (2005), and K. Mantena (2010).

Popular mass media treatments of empire have included Niall Ferguson's six-part television series *Empire*, broadcast on Britain's Channel 4 in January 2003, and Jeremy Paxman's BBC series on the British Empire in 2011 (published as *Empire*, 2012). One might also note the popularity of a number of recent films devoted to imperial themes, such as *Troy* (2004), *Alexander* (2004), and *Hero* (2002). The popular HBO television epic *Game of Thrones* is also replete with imperial references.

4. "Empire" and "imperialism," as concepts, need to be distinguished; the one is old, the other relatively recent. In the second half of the nineteenth century "imperialism" was coined—and suffered in the process—to describe the Second Empire of Napoleon III. Empire, by contrast, could connote noble aspirations and intentions. Later both empire and imperialism developed pejorative connotations. See on all this Koebner and Schmidt (1964). Already in 1919 Joseph Schumpeter ([1919] 1974: 71) was saying that "today . . . the very word 'imperialism' is applied only to the enemy, in a reproachful sense." On empire as "a term of abuse" today, see, e.g., Pagden (2003: xxi); Howe (2002a: 9, 22, 126). It may be that the "Empire

State" of New York is the only positive, or at least neutral, use of the term "empire" in its political sense today—an ironic twist given America's anti-imperial origins.

5. An example is John Gaddis (2004) who, declaring that empire is "as American as apple pie," argues that America has since its foundation thought and acted in imperial terms, and has no choice but to continue to do so. A similar argument is made by Niall Ferguson, who calls the United States "an empire in denial" (2005: 6), and urges it to take up its imperial mission more confidently and vigorously.

6. "Europe"—or at least the European Union—"as empire" is one such parallel that several have found instructive in recent years (e.g., Zielonka 2006; Foster 2015). For Charles Maier, empire gets its appeal from the recent rise of what he calls "extra-territoriality"—the loss of "the presumed identity between decision space and identity space" (Maier 2000: 820).

7. One is reminded here of Lord Acton's defense of the British and Austrian empires as bastions of liberty against the oppressive and exclusive principle of nationality, which, "by making the State and the nation commensurate with each other in theory, . . . reduces practically to a subject condition all other nationalities that may be within the boundary" (Acton [1862] 1996: 36).

8. See, e.g., Barkey and von Hagen (1997); Beissinger (2006); Dawisha and Parrott (1997); Hirsch (2005); Lieven (2001); Lundestad (1994); Martin (2001); Miller and Rieber (2004); Motyl (2001); Rudolf and Good (1992); Suny and Martin (2001). The Russian journal *Ab Imperio* is a good source for continuing discussions in this vein.

9. For some lively contributions, see Bacevich (2003); Calhoun, Cooper, and Moore (2006); Ferguson (2005); Gaddis (2004); Go (2008, 2011); Kagan (2004); Maier (2006); Mann (2003); Münkler (2007); Porter (2006); Roy (2004); Steinmetz (2005, 2013); Todd (2003); Wood (2005). All accounts stress that the idea of America as an empire is a venerable one—whether in terms of America's internal expansion across the continent or in terms of its policies toward other nations. John Pocock has pointed to "the paradox that the new republic, born of the revolt against empire, had a commitment to empire—and to empire of settlement—built into its structure in a way that the parent system never had" (Pocock 1985: 86; cf. Lichtheim 1974: 59–61; Muldoon 1999: 140–41). To a good extent this was linked to the view of America's "exceptionalism," on which see Tyrell (1991). For the view that America cannot really be considered an empire, see Walzer (2003), Pagden (2004), and King (2006), though Walzer gives cautious endorsement to "virtual empire."

10. "The lonely superpower" is Samuel Huntington's phrase (1999); the "new world disorder," Kenneth Jowitt's (1992).

11. For some preliminary thoughts on this, see Kumar (2012a).

12. Richardson notes (1991: 3) that originally, and in the strict sense, *imperium* was conferred not only, and not necessarily, by the people but by god: *imperium* has religious origins, as shown by the fact that an unelected official such as the dictator, after nomination by the consul, received his *imperium* through the taking of the auspices, which confirmed his acceptance by the god Jupiter. It was, argues Richardson, this sense of a divinely conferred, quasi-regal power, attached to an individual, that allowed *imperium* to be identified later with the rule of a single absolute *princeps* or *imperator* over his realm, the *imperium Romanum*.

13. For the history of the term *imperium* in the Middle Ages and the Renaissance, see Folz ([1953] 1969); Koebner (1961: 18–60); Muldoon (1999: 21–113). Koebner emphasizes the

importance of the Italian humanists in restoring the original Roman meaning of "lawful authority" to the term, thus allowing those states outside the Holy Roman Empire—which had more or less monopolized the concept of *imperium* during the Middle Ages—to declare themselves empires. But it says something for the still-continuing identification of empire with the Holy Roman Empire that Charles V, the ruler of huge overseas territories, was emperor only as the Holy Roman emperor; in relation to his Spanish possessions he was a monarch, as was his Spanish successor Philip II, ruler of more than twenty kingdoms (but not Holy Roman emperor). There was no "Spanish Empire," merely the "universal monarchy" of Spain; nor, for that matter, was there—until the nineteenth century—a "British Empire," properly so-called (Koebner 1961: 56; see also Muldoon 1999: 9, 114, 137). "Universal monarchy" was indeed the common (and not always pejorative) expression used to refer to what we might call the imperial ambitions of early modern rulers, such as Philip II of Spain and Louis XIV of France. "By the end of the sixteenth century . . . *monarchia universalis*—Universal Monarchy—had, in effect, come to replace *imperium* as a term for the continuing aspiration to supra-national authority" (Pagden 1995: 43).

14. Francis Bacon's essay "Of Empire" ([1625] 1906: 73–79) deals exclusively with the cares and concerns of kingship; there is no discussion of empire in our now commonly understood sense of an extensive territory. Even when, in another essay, " Of the True Greatness of Kingdoms and Estates" ([1625] 1906: 115–27), he speaks of the importance of sea power, and declares that "the battle of Actium decided the empire of the world," he is still using "empire" in the sense of "rule"; sea power is not the basis of a seaborne empire. The phrase "the empire of the sea"—taken from Virgil's *Aeneid*—was common at the time; Shakespeare uses it ("Sextus Pompeius . . . commands the empire of the sea," *Antony and Cleopatra*, 1.2). But the reference usually is to its role, as with Bacon, in conferring rule or dominance rather than as the springboard for constructing an overseas empire. On its later use, when it does come to be linked definitively to the British Empire overseas, see Koebner (1961: 77–105); Armitage (2000: 170–98).

15. A number of more recent scholars have been inclined to stress the dynamism and expansiveness of the period of empire, continuing the pattern begun under the republic (see, e.g., Brunt 1978, Lintott 1981). But as Anthony Pagden (2003: 21) points out, Rome at any rate showed very early that empires, though mostly monarchical, can also be republican and even democratic. This was demonstrated even earlier by the empire of fifth-century Athens, a democratic city-state. In modern times the empire of the French Third Republic is a good example; America may be another. See on this Lichtheim (1974: 87–88).

16. Andrew Lintott has said that "for Augustus the Roman empire was not only the whole world controlled by Rome: it was equivalent to the world itself. . . . Rome in fact essentially desired that her will should be obeyed by other nations—the fundamental concept behind the word *imperium*. . . . Jupiter's remark in *Aeneid* 1.279, 'imperium sine fine dedi', sums up the Roman attitude to the empire " (Lintott 1981: 53–54, 64; see also Brunt 1978: 161, 168–70; Veyne 1980: 121–22; Pagden 1995: 23; Woolf 2001: 317–18). Pagden (1995: 23) quotes Theodor Mommsen: "It was a familiar concept to the Romans that they were not only the first power on earth, they were also, in a sense, the only one." Lintott and Woolf show that this global, "multinational," concept of the Roman Empire—"empire as the power of one people over others" (Woolf 2001: 314; cf. Richardson 1991: 6)—was held by several earlier writers, notably Polybius

and Sallust; for the similar views of Cicero and Caesar, see Brunt (1978: 162–68). This was also the common view of the Roman Empire among early Christian writers such as Origen, Orosius, Jerome, and Augustine. It was linked to the theme that God had prepared the nations of the world for Christ by putting them all under one ruler, the Roman emperor. See Fanning (1991: 10–14); Muldoon (1999: 101–4); Swain (1940: 18–21).

17. See Koebner (1961: 60). The point at which the earlier meaning began to be superseded by the later one—though never entirely—is difficult to pin down, but the later seventeenth century is a good candidate. In addition to the French writer quoted (Gabriel Gérard, writing in 1718), Koebner quotes Sir William Temple, from an essay written in 1672: "A nation extended over vast tracts of land, and numbers of people, arrives in time at the ancient name of king-dom, or modern of empire" (Koebner 1961: 59). Temple is perhaps responding to the "ancient" use of the term "empire" that was to be found as recently as in Francis Bacon and James Har-rington; to that extent he is being self-consciously "modern" (Temple was on the side of the moderns in the famous late seventeenth-century quarrel of "the Ancients and the Moderns"). But he seems unaware that this meaning of empire was already familiar to the Romans, and in some form at least was kept alive by the Holy Roman Empire throughout the medieval period and beyond (see, e.g., Benson 1982: 383–84).

18. The original meaning comes out most often in metaphorical uses of "empire," as in the "empire of the seas," or the "empire of letters," or the "empire of the mind." In all these cases what is implied is a certain kind of commanding influence or authority rather than actual pos-session, the entities in question being almost self-evidently unpossessable by any one person or power (as was famously argued for the oceans of the world by Hugo Grotius in his *Mare Liberum* (1609).

19. On the Holy Roman Empire, and generally the idea of empire in the Middle Ages, see Koebner (1961: 18–43); Bloch (1967); Folz ([1953]1969); Ullmann (1979); Benson (1982: esp. 370–84); Muldoon (1999: 21–100); Moreland (2001); Heer (2002); Wilson (2016). On the later history, to 1806, see Wilson (1999); Evans, Schaich, and Wilson (2011); Whaley (2012).

20. Although for many medieval writers empire meant *the* Empire, the one and only (Holy) Roman Empire (East or West), the term *imperium* was used by or on behalf of a variety of me-dieval rulers, such as the group of Anglo-Saxon kings called *bretwaldas* as well as later Anglo-Saxon rulers such as Athelstan and Canute. Several Spanish kings of Léon and Castile in the eleventh, twelfth, and thirteenth centuries also styled themselves *imperator* (one, Alfonso X of Castile, even attempted to have himself declared Holy Roman emperor, when the pope de-posed Frederick II in 1245). In all these cases the kings appeared to think of themselves as "king of kings"—that is, they claimed overlordship over a number of territories that were themselves kingdoms (Folz [1953] 1969: 40–44, 53–58; Muldoon 1999: 53–58; see also Fanning 1991). In this way they reaffirmed the idea of empire as rule over a multiplicity of peoples. One might even say that many medieval kingdoms, such as that of the Angevins in England, were empires, even if they did not call themselves such. Henry II, after all, was not just king of England; he was also duke of Aquitaine, count of Anjou, and feudal overlord of the king of Scotland and the high king of Ireland. "If," says Muldoon, "we accept as a definition of empire, rule by force over several distinct peoples, it becomes clear that institutionally medieval Europe was a period in which virtually all attempts at large-scale governments were imperial in nature. . . . By almost any standard, medieval kingdoms were empires, as the territorial acquisitions of European

dynasties in the early modern world were empires in fact, even if the term empire was not employed to describe them" (Muldoon 1999: 63). For the "imperial" nature—centrally involving conquest and colonization—of medieval states, see also Bartlett (1994).

21. See further, on Rome's civilizing mission, chap. 2, below.

22. On the universalism of the Roman Empire, both in its classical and its later forms, such as the Holy Roman Empire, see Folz ([1953] 1969: 4–5, 108–11, 171–77); Bloch (1967: 31–32); Brunt (1978: 168–72); Veyne (1980); Pagden (1995: 19–28). A famous formulation of the theme of Rome's mission is in Virgil's *Aeneid* (bk. 6, 847–53): "Remember thou, O Roman, to rule the nations with thy sway—these shall be thine arts—to crown Peace with Law, to spare the humbled, and to tame in war the proud!" For Polybius's conception of "world history," and of Rome's "world empire" that makes such a history necessary, see Polybius (1979: 41–45).

23. The origin of the name Istanbul is the subject of much discussion. See further chap. 3, below.

24. Thinkers following Doyle include Howe (2002a: 30); M. Smith (2001: 129–32); Münkler (2007).

25. Finley singles out Koebner (1961) and Eisenstadt ([1963]) 1993) as influential examples of the tendency "to confuse empire with territorial state" (1978a :1). This does not seem quite fair in the case of Koebner, who shows very well the evolution of the concept of empire to mean rule over several peoples. Eisenstadt is perhaps a clearer case of the tendency, including as he does the states of "Absolutist Europe" in his general category of "centralized historical bureaucratic empires or states" (Eisenstadt [1963] 1993: 11).

26. There is a huge literature on the economic theories of imperialism associated particularly with Hobson and Lenin. For some good studies, see Owen and Sutcliffe (1972); see also Kiernan (1974); Etherington (1984). For critiques, see, e.g., Fieldhouse (1961); Landes (1961); Lichtheim (1974: 110–21); Mommsen (1982: 66–69).

27. Ferguson (2005: 169) similarly notes that "colonization"—"the establishment of new settlements by large and organized groups of migrants"—is "a process that predates recorded history," and is to be distinguished from empire—"the extension of one's civilization, usually by military force, to rule of other peoples." With "colonization" therefore there is no question of dependence on a metropolitan power, as with "colonialism" in Finley's sense, though Ferguson shows no inclination to follow Finley in distinguishing colonialism from imperialism. What we can have therefore, it seems, is colonies without colonialism, and empire without colonies or colonialism; but colonialism itself, with its relationship of dependence between metropole and colony, surely has to be called a species of empire, by most common definitions.

28. Some similarities to Finley's distinction—including, for instance, the disinclination to treat India as a colony—can be found in Seeley ([1883] 1971) and Hobson ([1902, 1938] 1988: 6–7). But there are also important differences. See further chap. 6, below.

29. Though not always: Russia's annexation of Crimea, in 2014, from the clearly independent state of Ukraine suggests that old-fashioned imperialism may still have a future, though Crimea's large Russian population provided the pretext.

30. This and the remaining sections in this chapter draw heavily upon my article "Nation-States as Empires, Empires as Nation-States" (Kumar 2010). In these sections I have used the conventional shorthand of "nations" for what should in most cases be "nation-states" (e.g.,

"United Nations"—an organization of nation-states). Where the distinction might be important I have indicated it.

31. I have similar objections to the discussion, which closely parallels Marx's and on which Marx draws, in Gorski (2000). See Kumar (2005); and for some powerful objections to the concept of "religious nationalism," see Brubaker (2015: 102–18).

32. Cf. Max Weber, who links the "prestige interests" of the great powers—which generally take the form of a drive toward imperial expansion—with "the legend of a providential 'mission,'" which he sees as a manifestation of "the idea of a nation." Just as with empire, then, "those to whom the representatives of the [national] idea zealously turned were expected to shoulder this mission" (Weber 1978: 925).

33. For these examples, see Kumar (2000) and the references therein. For a good discussion of the Christianizing mission, differently conceived, of the Spanish and British in the Americas, see Elliott (2006: 57–87, 184–218).

34. A characteristic expression of the Little Englanders was William Cobbett's: "It is my business, and the business of every Englishman, to take care of England, and England alone.... It is not our business to run about the world to look after people to set free; it is our business to look after ourselves" (in Gott 1989: 94).

Chapter 2: The Roman Empire

1. Edward Gibbon's view, that the Byzantine Empire existed for a thousand years "in a state of premature and perpetual decay" (Gibbon [1776–88] 1995: 2:237), was influential on generations of scholars, and remains popular even today among some commentators and the general public (cf. Lewis Mumford's remark that Byzantium "for a thousand years . . . made a virtue of arrested development" [Mumford 1961: 241]). But it is no longer held by historians of Byzantium, who on the contrary emphasize the vitality and creativity—in art and learning especially—of the empire, as well as its considerable political success in the region until the final centuries of its existence. See especially Herrin (2008); and, for a synthesis of recent work, see Treadgold (1997); Cameron (2006).

2. After the conquest of Constantinople the Ottomans adopted the star and crescent as their device. This was taken from the Byzantine coins that commemorated the saving of the city from Philip of Macedon in 340–339 BCE—through, it was believed, the intercession of the goddess Hecate, whose symbol it was.

3. See Lane Fox (1986: 372); Burn (1962: 204); Ray and Potts (2008); Hagerman (2009); Vasunia (2013: 33–115).

4. Very little is known for sure about Alexander. For recent scholarship, and the continuing disputes and controversies about him and his aims, see Lane Fox (1986); Bosworth (1993); Bosworth and Baynham (2000); Thomas (2007).

5. Some have thought that, in this account, Tarn was unduly influenced by his hopes first for the League of Nations and then the United Nations, and wished to present Alexander as the ancestor of both. For skeptical accounts of this view of Alexander, see Badian (1958) and Bosworth (1993: 160–61); for one more sympathetic to Tarn, see Lane Fox (1986: 417–29). It is worth noting that Hitler's admiration for Alexander was tempered by the view that he introduced "racial chaos" into his empire by encouraging intermarriage between Greeks and Asiatics (Scobie 1990: 20).

6. For the influence of these two addresses, see Oliver (1953: 981–82); Claudian ([c. 370–404 CE] 1922: 1:xix–xxiv); Cameron (1970: 349–89). Gibbon knew Aristides well, and quotes him a number of times in the first three chapters of book 1 of the *Decline* (e.g., Gibbon [1776–88] 1995: 1:64, 82); see also Schiavone (2000: 16–19). For quotations of Claudian in the nineteenth century, see, e.g., Lewis ([1841] 1891: 128n2, 129n1); for other examples see Cameron (1970: 448–50); Vance (1997: 233–34, 254); Koebner (1961: 15).

7. My account of Aristides is based on Oliver (1953); Bowie (1970); Sherwin-White (1973: 425–44); Nutton (1978); Schiavone (2000: 3–15). See also Ando (2000: 54–69 and passim); Edwards and Woolf (2003: 2–5). Oliver's study contains the full text, in both Greek and English, of Aristides's Roman oration.

8. For a discussion of this literary and artistic tradition, with some representative examples from Victorian England, see Vance (1997: 197–268). See also Edwards (1999b: chaps. 6–10). For the general idea of decline in the European intellectual tradition, in which of course Rome figured prominently, see Burke (1977).

9. On the general importance, for the elaboration of Rome's imperial ideology, of the Greek-educated "sophists, rhetoricians and litterateurs" from the eastern provinces of the empire, see Nutton (1978: 210); Sherwin-White (1973: 465–67, on Claudian). Educated Greeks came to see Rome as the legitimate successor to the Hellenistic kingdoms of the East, and to associate "Hellene" with "Roman"—a development, says Sherwin-White, that was "essential to the accomplishment of the unity of the Roman world" (1973: 428; see also Brunt 1990b: 269).

10. On Claudian generally see Cameron (1970), esp. 348–89 for his attitude toward Rome. Gibbon drily observes that "as Claudian appears to have indulged the most ample privilege of a poet, and a courtier, some criticism will be requisite to translate the language of fiction, or exaggeration, into the truth and simplicity of historical prose" (Gibbon [1776–88] 1995: 2:106). But he shows his admiration for the poet and draws liberally on him in his account of Stilicho, and of the state of the empire at this time (2:106–64). "Claudian," he states, "is read with pleasure in every country which has retained, or acquired, the knowledge of Latin," noting especially his reputation among Renaissance writers such as the courtier Balthazar Castiglione (2:163–64).

11. It was Augustine, writing in the immediate aftermath of the event, who first remarked on the "humble clemency" and "gentleness" of the barbarians in the sack of Rome, attributing this to their Christianity, and comparing it to the much more ferocious behavior of pagan Greeks and Romans (Augustine [413–27 CE] 1984: 10, 12). Peter Heather (2006: 227–29) calls Alaric's sack of Rome "one of the most civilized sacks of a city ever witnessed." Alaric's Visigoths were Christians—albeit Arians—and spared all of Rome's major Christian monuments, including the main basilicas of St. Peter and St. Paul. On Alaric's "artful moderation," and the respect he showed for the Christian religion in the sack of Rome, see also Gibbon ([1776–88] 1995: 2:167, 200–209). For the view that the sack of Rome was a relatively minor event in Rome's history, heralding not the end of empire but rather the weakness and failure of Alaric, see Goffart (2008: 879n65); for the wider significance in Rome's history, Ward-Perkins (2005: 16–17); Kelly (2009: 56–57).

12. For some, of course, "empire" and "civilization" were just a cover for Roman exploitation and enslavement of other peoples. "To plunder, butcher, steal, these things they misname empire: they make a desolation and they call it peace," as Tacitus puts it into the mouth of the

British rebel chief Calgacus (*Agricola*, 30). In the same work, describing the Britons' adoption of Roman ways, Tacitus jeers that "the naive natives called this part of their servitude, 'civilization'" (*Agricola*, 21) (both passages in Champion, 2004: 264, 276. See further on this chap. 6, below). There is no lack among contemporary scholars of a similar characterization and critique of Romanization and the civilizing mission: see, e.g., Hingley (2005) and, more moderately, Brunt (1978).

13. For Greek concepts of autochthony and the importance of purity of type, especially among the Athenians, see Isaac (2006: 109–33).

14. Cf. Gibbon: "The narrow policy of preserving, without any foreign mixture, the pure blood of the ancient citizens, had checked the fortunes, and hastened the ruin, of Athens and Sparta. The aspiring genius of Rome sacrificed vanity to ambition, and deemed it more prudent, as well as honourable, to adopt virtue and merit for her own wheresoever they were found, among slaves or strangers, enemies or barbarians" ([1776–88] 1995, 1:61).

15. The original and still most powerful account of Romanization is Mommsen ([1909] 1974). For more recent accounts, see Sherwin-White (1973: 399–437); Brunt (1990b); Laurence and Berry (1998); Macmullen (2000); Brown (2003: 45–58); Champion (2004: 214–77); Hingley (2005), Heather (2006: 32–45); Woolf (2012: 222–29). For particular studies, see Barton (1972), Africa; Ebel (1976) and Woolf (1998), Gaul; Syme (1958: 1–23) and Knapp (1977), Spain; Price (1984) and Sartre (2006), Asia Minor; Hingley (2000, 2008), Mattingly (2006), and Creighton (2006), Britain. For a wide-ranging study of the plurality of Roman identities, as seen by contemporary writers, see Dench (2005). For a subtle and sophisticated account of the *consensus* created in and by the empire, whereby Rome came to be recognized as the *communis patria* of all its inhabitants, citizens and noncitizens alike, see Ando (2000).

16. See Walbank (1972: 155); Miles (1990: 653); Laurence and Berry (1998); Woolf (1998: 208); Sartre (2006); Burns (2009: 55–58).

17. It needs to be remembered that for most of the history of the empire Greek remained the literary language, as well as the lingua franca, of the eastern half—especially of course after the fall of the Western empire in the fifth century. Still, as Brunt remarks, "in the end [Greeks] were to call themselves Rhomaioi. Romanization in sentiment triumphed at last" (1990b: 269). See also Woolf (1994); Dench (2005: 314–15); Gruen (1992: 31, 50–51).

18. In her recent history of Rome, Mary Beard has called Caracalla's decree "a revolutionary decision . . . the culmination of a process that had been going on for almost a millennium. . . . Caracalla in 212 CE completed a process that in Roman myth Romulus had started a thousand years earlier" (2015: 527). It may not be irrelevant to remember that Caracalla was one of the greatest admirers of Alexander, and in this initiative he may well have seen himself as carrying on the Alexandrian mission to unify the peoples of the world.

19. See, e.g., Syme (1958: 17); Brunt (1965: 270–78); Sherwin-White (1967); Walbank (1972); Jenkyns (1992a: 6–7); Woolf (1998: 238–41); Miles (1990); Geary (2002: 49–50); Dench (2005: 222–97). The principal exception to this view is Isaac (2006), who argues for what he calls the existence of "proto-racism" in antiquity. But he himself says that this antique proto-racism is very different from the "scientific racism" of the nineteenth and twentieth centuries. Moreover, he admits that, unlike the Greeks, the Romans were largely indifferent to ideas of race and explicitly accepted that other groups could be thoroughly Romanized, thus merging conquerors with conquered (2006: 192–93).

20. St. Augustine was to see this act of Romulus's as foreshadowing the creation of the heavenly city itself: for "the remission of sins, the promise which recruits the citizens for the Eternal Country, finds a kind of shadowy resemblance in that refuge of Romulus, where the offer of impunity for crimes of every kind collected a multitude which was to result in the foundation of the city of Rome" (Augustine [413–27 CE] 1984: 207).

21. See on this also Syme (1958: 3–9); Hopkins (1965: 13, 23); Brunt (1990b: 273–74); Sherwin-White (1973: 259–61); Edwards and Woolf (2003: 11).

22. It was the third-century African Church Father, Tertullian (c. 160–c. 225 CE), who gave the sharpest and most influential account of Roman immorality and idolatry, as contrasted with Christian virtues, and who urged Christians to separate themselves from pagan society . The renunciation of the world deepened with the monastic movement of the third century. See Rayner (1942: 118–19 and passim).

23. A similar carelessness as to context and overall purpose attends the common interpretation of the even more famous and frequently quoted passage, at the very end of the *Decline and Fall*, where Gibbon says that "in the preceding volumes of this History, I have described the triumph of barbarism and religion" (Gibbon[1776–88] 1995: 3:1068). But which barbarians and whose religion? It is generally thought that Gibbon is referring to the Germanic tribes and to Christianity, but John Pocock (1977: 118) has persuasively argued that in the context of the *History* as a whole, and given the fact that its last volumes deal with the Byzantine Empire and its overthrow by Islamic forces, Gibbon could just as well be referring to the Arabs and Islam.

24. As the early fifth-century Christian historian Orosius wrote, "When the city of Jerusalem had been overthrown . . . and the Jews wiped out, Titus, who had been ordained by the judgment of God to take vengeance for the blood of Lord Jesus Christ, in company with his father Vespasian shut the temple of Janus as a victor in triumphal procession" (in Lupher 2006: 38). David Lupher calls this the "locus classicus of this idea," though it had earlier also been expressed by Augustine ([413–27 CE] 1984: 211–12).

25. The Catholic Church, says Macaulay, "may still exist in undiminished vigour when some traveller from New Zealand shall, in the midst of a vast solitude, take his stand on a broken arch of London Bridge to sketch the ruins of St. Paul's" ([1840] 1907: 39). For Macaulay's complex attitude toward Catholicism, see Sullivan (2009: 206–29).

Chapter 3: The Ottoman Empire

1. Two recent works make this point very emphatically: Goffman (2002) and Faroqhi (2006). It is also implicit in much of the current rethinking about the character of the early Ottomans and the origins of their empire.

2. See, in order, Gibbons (1916); Köprülü ([1935] 1992); Wittek (1938). There are good accounts of the historiographical debates in Kafadar (1995: 9–59); Darling (2000: 133–38); Goffman (2002: 29–34); Lowry (2003: 5–31). See also Imber (2002: 120–22) for a general account of the *gazi* tradition in Ottoman rule—renewed, as he shows, as late as the nineteenth century.

3. In this section I have relied mainly on the following accounts of the early years of the Ottomans: Köprülü ([1935] 1992); Wittek (1938); Itzkowitz (1980: 3–36); Inalcik ([1973] 2000: 3–52); Kafadar (1995: 1–9, 122–50); Imber (2002: 1–30); Lowry (2003); Finkel (2007: 1–80). I

should also say that Arnold Toynbee's (1962–63, 2:150–54) masterly sketch of the early Ottomans, as a marcher people shaped by the "stimulus of pressures," holds up remarkably well in the light of more recent work.

4. Orthodox Christians had every reason to think that protection against the Latins might come more readily and more securely from the Ottomans than from the enfeebled Byzantines. In the last days of the Byzantine Empire a high official of the Orthodox Church declared that he would rather see the turban of the Turk rule in Constantinople than the Latin miter (Nicol 1967: 335; see also Clogg 1982: 191; Shaw 1976: 58–59).

5. On the origins and development of the *devshirme* system, see Inalcik ([1973] 2000: 77–80); Sugar ([1977] 1993: 55–59); Imber (2002: 134–42); Goffman (2002: 67–68); Finkel (2007: 28); Barkey (2008: 123–28). There is a vivid, detailed, description of the *devshirme* in Toynbee (1962–63, 3:32–44).

6. "Under the first sultans in Constantinople, the Orthodox Church preserved vast lands, and the Patriarch had the same badge of rank as the Grand Vizier, three horse-tails" (Stone, Podbolotov, and Yasar 2004: 29). Sugar remarks that "for all practical purposes the new powers conferred on it by Mehmed II made the church a state within a state" (Sugar [1977] 1993: 47). See also Clogg (1982: 185–87); Karpat (1982: 145).

7. The Ottomans may have saved the Orthodox Greeks, but in their fervent desire to associate themselves with the Roman Empire, they also proclaimed themselves descendants of the Trojans ("*Teucri*—Trojans" equals "*Turci*"—Turks), legendary ancestors of the Romans and old enemies of the Greeks. Thus in one aspect the Ottoman conquest of the Byzantines could be seen as the revenge of the Trojans-Romans for their defeat by the Greeks. See Spencer (1952); Kafadar (1995: 9). For the Romans' choice of Trojans, rather than Greeks, as their ancestors, see Gruen (1992: 6–51). One should remember, of course, that though the Byzantines were culturally Greek they saw themselves as *Romaioi*, Romans, continuing the Roman Empire.

8. From among a host of confirming statements, see, e.g., Seton-Watson (1964: 10); Lieven (2001: 133); Goffman and Stroop (2004: 144n26); Stone, Podbolotov, and Yasar (2004: 33); Findley (2005: 20). Serif Mardin sees the divide between Ottomans and Turks in terms of Robert Redfield's distinction between a "great" and a "little" culture. The "little culture" of the Turks, based on the clan and the peasant community, was never sufficiently integrated with the "great culture" of the educated, urbanized, cosmopolitan Ottomans. Right down to the nineteenth century Turks were "country bumpkins," as against the "smooth, Paris-oriented" Ottomans (Mardin 1969: 270–74).

9. "'Turk' as a nationalist category was a product of the 1908 Revolution. The Ottomans would have resisted the appellation 'Turkish', even though Europe insisted on it" (Aksan 1999: 121n54; see also Lewis 1968: 333).

10. On the basic social structure and administrative organization of the empire, see Inalcik ([1973] 2000: 65–69, 89–118); see also Inalcik (1993: 59–67, 1954: 112); Sugar ([1977] 1993: 31–44); Woodhead (1987: 27–37); Göçek (1993: 103–5). It is interesting to note, as an expression of the importance of the empire's European possessions to the Ottomans, that positions in Rumelia carried greater rank and prestige than those in Anatolia, with Africa coming third (Inalcik [1973] 2000: 106).

11. An excellent comparative history of Muslim empires is Dale (2010).

12. Braude and Lewis (1982b: 1–2). The quotation is from J. S. Furnivall, *Colonial Policy and Practice* (1957). For a similar view of Ottoman society, see Mazower (2005: 304); Quataert (2000: 181 and generally 172–83); Findley (2010: 64).

13. Karen Barkey compares the Ottomans favorably with the Habsburgs and Russians with respect to the toleration of diversity within their empires. This was because Islam and Christianity had different attitudes toward nonbelievers: "Islam had a script for how to deal with Jews and Christians, whereas Christianity . . . conducted itself as an exclusive religion with an organized body ideally unified with public authorities" (Barkey 2008: 153; cf. Goffman 2002: 9, 111–12). For an account that explains the differences in terms of relative state formation rather than ideology or culture, see Salzmann (2010).

14. See on this the essays by Kevork Bardakjian, Mark Epstein, Joseph Hacker, Kemal Karpat, and Richard Clogg in Braude and Lewis (1982a, 1:89–126, 141–69, 185–207). See also the classic account of the *millet* system by Gibb and Bowen (1950–57, vol. 1, pt. 2: 207–261), though note the cautionary remarks by Braude (1982) and Owen (1975) on Gibb and Bowen's treatment. See also Sugar ([1977] 1993: 44–49); Goffman (1994, 2002: 47, 170–72); Barkey (2008: 130–50), who concludes that "the centuries of Pax Ottomanica were relatively calm and free of ethnic or religious strife" (2008: 146).

15. Jews often expressed the view that the Ottomans had been sent providentially to save them from the Christians: "The Turk is called the Destroyer of Christianity and the Defender of the Jewish Faith," wrote an Istanbul Jew in the fifteenth century (Armstrong 1976: 398).

16. In theory non-Muslims could not enter the *askeri*, the empire's ruling class; in practice, from the very beginning, this rule was breached, with non-Muslims being able to purchase tax farms and other offices. In this way, for instance, Jews came to dominate Ottoman customs collection. Even foreigners sometimes could purchase Ottoman posts: for instance Henry Hyde, English consul of the Morea, became *voyvodalik* (local commander) and *bacdarlik* (customs officer) of Patras in the early seventeenth century (Goffman 1994: 147, 151–52).

17. For an account of the Armenian *millet*, and generally the role of Armenians in the empire, see the essays by Kevork Badarijan and Hagop Barsouminan in Braude and Lewis (1982a: 89–100, 171–84). See also Barkey (2008: 140–42). The Armenian Massacres—"Genocide," for some—of 1915 are of course the subject of intense historiographical and political controversy. All one might note here is that the context of war is very important: so too the very recent development of Turkish nationalism, in many respects reversing traditional Ottoman attitudes toward non-Muslim communities. For two recent contributions to the subject, see Göçek (2015) and Suny (2015).

18. "No doubt," says Caroline Finkel, "there were tears on both sides as such boys left home and family, but the youth-levy appears not to have aroused much resistance among the Christians subject to it—it almost seems that it may have been regarded as a legal duty owed to a legitimate monarch, rather than a tyrannical imposition" (Finkel 2007: 233).

19. Cf. Inalcik, who says that under Suleyman, "the Ottoman state, abandoning its historically developed eclectic character of a frontier state, became a rather worthy successor to the classical Islamic caliphate in its policies, institutions and culture" (1993: 72); similarly Barkey (2008: 70–71, 85–86).

20. See, on the Kizilbas risings, Inalcik ([1973] 2000: 194–97); Finkel (2007: 98–100); Barkey (2008: 175–78). On the east Anatolian nomads' discontent with the Ottomans, and their

turn toward Shiite Iran, see Lindner (1983: 105–12). It was always true that, at least well into the nineteenth century, the empire had more to fear from its Muslim heretics than from the "infidels," its Christian subjects (Goffman 2002: 23; Woodhead 1987: 32–33).

21. For the view that, as a result of the conquest of the Arab lands, and/or the rivalry with Safavid Iran, there is "the beginning of a more conservative Sharia-minded Ottoman state," see Inalcik (1993: 70–72, [1973] 2000: 34, 179–85); see also Finkel (2007: 110); Sugar ([1977] 1993: 252); Kafadar (1993: 42–44); Kunt (1982: 63–64); Imber (1995: 148, 2002: 121); Lieven (2001: 143–44); Barkey (2008: 70–71, 85–86, 102–4, 177–78). All stress, with varying degrees of emphasis, what Barkey calls "the consolidation of a Sunni Islamic identity" in this period.

22. See on these developments Naff (1977b); Quataert (2000: 75–81); Goffman (2002: 192–225); Finkel (2007: 369–71).

23. As Jennifer Pitts notes (2016), by the eighteenth century differences of religion were no longer thought to be central to interstate relations; hence in Western eyes it was not Islam—the "Turks" as "infidels"—that was an obstacle to relations between the Ottoman Empire and the West but, arguably at least, the political system of "oriental despotism."

24. See also, on the growth of Western-style education among the Ottoman elites, and generally on secularizing trends, Göçek (1996: 80–85); Lewis (1968: 53–73, 117–18).

25. Woodhead points outs that "despite the prominence given in literature and diplomatic to Ottoman guardianship of the holy cities, no sultan is known to have taken his religious duties so strictly as to have made the pilgrimage to Mecca"—a remarkable fact, as Donald Quataert observes (Woodhead 1987: 27n18; Quataert 2000: 97). For the conflict between secular and religious elites, see Naff (1977a: 6–7); Aksan (1999: 124); Cirakman (2001: 62).

26. For surveys and discussions of the literature of decline, see Lewis (1962); Itzkowitz (1980: 87–109); Woodhead (1987); Howard (1988); Hathaway (1996); Goffman (2002: 112–27); Finkel (2007: 188–90). Howard rightly makes the point that the "decline" literature, here as in other instances, was a literary genre, and should be read as such.

27. See the discussions of the idea of a Suleymanic "Golden Age" in Inalcik and Kafadar (1993); Kunt and Woodhead (1995). See also Itzkowitz (1980: 79); Woodhead (1987: 25–26), Howard (1988: 52–53, 64); Goffman (2002: 112–13, 229–30). An incisive rebuttal of the idea is Hathaway, who remarks that "a massive empire that lasted for over six centuries cannot have had an ideal moment and an ideal permutation by which the entire chronological and geographical span of the empire can be judged" (1996: 26).

28. For complaints about "harem politics," palace factionalism, and the "Sultanate of the Women," see Shaw (1976: 170); Itzkowitz (1980: 75); Inalcik ([1973] 2000: 60); Kafadar (1993: 46); Imber (2002: 87–96, 323); Goffman (2002: 124, 214); Finkel (2007: 196). An enlightening account of both the myth and the reality is Peirce (1993); see also Goffman (2002: 124–25).

29. For these developments see Naff (1977a: 8–9); Itzkowitz (1977: 22, 25–26); Inalcik (1977); Karpat (1982: 152–54); McGowan (1994); Göçek (1996: 60–65); Aksan (1999: 116, 124, 132–34); Barkey (2008: 197–263); Findley (2010: 28–31). The *sened-i ittifak*, says Itzkowitz, "is a political document designed to extract from the sultan his recognition of the new status and rights of the *ayan*. It is the opening gun of the constitutional struggle that would grip the Ottoman Empire in the nineteenth century and that would not be resolved until its destruction by Atatürk and the birth of the Turkish Republic" (1977: 26; see also Zürcher 1997: 31). Others have pointed to the fact that that the "Deed of Agreement" was made between the *ayans* and

the state, not the sultan. Mahmud II did not himself sign it. This left the sultan free to repudiate the pact, as is in effect what later sultans did (Findley 2010: 35–36).

30. See on this Itzkowitz (1962: 73–83); Naff (1977a: 3–4); Howard (1988: 73–77). The key works that transmitted the views of the Ottoman "decline" literature to Western scholars seem to have been Paul Rycaut, *The History of the Present State of the Ottoman Empire* (1688); Dimitrie Cantemir, *History of the Growth and Decay of the Othman Empire*, trans. N. Tindal (1734–35); Muradgea D'Ohsson, *Tableau générale de L'Empire othoman* (1787–1820); Josef von Hammer-Purgstall, *Geschichte des osmanischen Reichs* (1835).

31. There are strong statements of the thesis of decline in Gibb and Bowen (1950–57, vol. 1, pt. 1: esp. 215–16); Lewis (1958, 1968: 21–36); Toynbee (1962–63, 3:47); Shaw (1976: 169–216); Inalcik ([1973] 2000: 41–52); Kitsikis (1994: 85–101). More qualified statements are in Naff (1977a); Itzkowitz (1980: 87–108); McGowan (1994: esp. 639–45); Lieven (2001: 138–57, with interesting comparisons with Russia). Good critical discussions of the thesis are Owen (1975, 1977); Faroqhi (1994: esp. 552–73, 1995, 2006: 96–7, 213); Howard (1988); Goffman (2002: 112–27); Barkey (2008: 22–23, 197–204).

32. See on this Owen (1975: 107–8, 111); Naff (1977a: 9); Salzman (1993, 2004); Faroqhi (1994, 1995); Goffman (2002: 125); Quataert (2000: 46–50); Barkey (2008: 226–63). All authors make the point that "decentralization" cannot automatically be equated with decline, that in fact insofar as it took place, it can be seen as a creative adaptation to a more complex economic and political environment.

33. See on this interpretation of Lepanto and the North African struggles especially Hess (1972, 1978); see also Shaw (1976: 178–79); Itzkowitz (1980: 63–68); Lewis ([1982] 2001: 43–44); Goffman (2002: 158–61); Biceno (2003). For the conquest of Chios and Cyprus, Goffman (2002: 151–58); Biceno (2003: 182–202). It has now become commonplace to dismiss the significance of the Battle of Lepanto, at least from the perspective of the Ottomans: "a battle without strategic consequences," says Colin Imber (2002: 63); cf. Mantran (1980: 232); Goffman (2002: 189); Faroqhi (2006: 38). It seems to have been Voltaire who first questioned the significance of the victory at Lepanto, so much celebrated by the Christian powers, pointing out that "the Turks" retook Tunis in 1574 "without resistance," so that "the victory of Lepanto seemed rather to have been on the side of the Turks" (1901: 270–71). Fernand Braudel notes that "people have always found it surprising . . . that this unexpected victory should have had so few consequences," but argues that with it "the spell of Turkish supremacy had been broken," ending "a period of profound depression, . . . a genuine inferiority complex," on the part of Christendom (1975, 2:1088, 1103–4).

34. Daniel Goffman's comment on the decline debate seems highly apposite: "It makes good sense . . . to conceive the early modern Ottoman world broadly as a multi-faceted entity rather than narrowly as a state embarking on a long death march, to insist that rot in some of its components did not mean consuming decay, and may even have reflected brilliance onto other features of the state and society" (2002: 127).

35. For the Tanzimat, see Lewis (1968: 106–28); Welker (1968); Karpat (1972); Inalcik (1973); Zürcher (1997: 52–74); Quataert (2000: 61–68); Hanioglu (2008: 72–108); Findley (2010: 76–132).

36. On the reforms of Mahmud II, see Lewis (1968: 76–106); Zürcher (1997: 41–51); Hanioglu (2008: 60–71); Findley (2010: 39–44, 88–90).

37. On the Young Ottomans, see Mardin (1962); Lewis (1968: 154–74); Deringil (1993): Zürcher (1997: 71–74); Hanioglu (2008: 103–4); Findley (2010: 104–6, 123–32).

38. For the reign, and reassessments, of Abdulhamid II, see Lewis (1968: 175–209); Zürcher (1997: 80–94); Hanioglu (2008: 109–49); Fortna (2008); Findley (2010: 133–91).

39. Some scholars are beginning to cast doubt on this interpretation of the Tanzimat, and to note its Islamic features. See, e.g., Manneh (1994).

40. See on this Lewis (1968: 184–94); Deringil (1999: 46–50, 60–63); Zürcher (1997: 83); Quataert (2000: 82–83); Finkel (2007: 491–99); Hanioglu (2008: 142); Findley (2010: 139, 150, 168).

41. For a similar assessment, see Quataert (1994: 766); Zürcher (1997: 81); Hanioglu (2008: 125); Fortna (2008: 38); Findley (2010: 150).

42. For these debates, see Lewis (1968: 230–37, 323–61); Aksin (2007: 82–88); Hanioglu (2008: 138–49, 183–88, 210–11; 2011: 48–67, 130–59); Findley (2010: 194–206), Zürcher (2010: 95–123, 147–50, 213–35).

43. For a good brief account of Gökalp's thought, see Niyazi Berkes's "Translator's Introduction," in Gökalp (1959: 13–31); see also Lewis (1968: 350–51); Findley (2010: 236–38). For his influence on Mustafa Kemal—and the differences between them—see Hanioglu (2011: 64–65, 174–75); Zürcher (2010: 149–50). A full-scale study of Gökalp is Parla (1985).

44. On the continuing significance of Islam during the First World War and the ensuing resistance movement, see especially Zürcher (2010: 221–28, 271–84); see also Kayali (2008: 118, 122, 129).

45. The botched military coup of July 2016 was yet another example of these continuing fissures in Turkish society. The ferocity of the resulting repression is unlikely to do anything to end them.

Chapter 4: The Habsburg Empire

1. This is the title of the very good general account by Spiel (1987). There have been many other similar treatments of the culture of this period, some celebratory, nearly all tinged with an air of melancholy. More academic studies are Janik and Toulmin (1973); Schorske (1980); Johnston ([1972] 1983); Gellner (1998b). On Vienna as "the capital of the twentieth century," see also Francis (1985); Stourzh (1992: 4–9); Beller (2011: 169–77).

2. On the question of how far Spain's European possessions can be called an empire, see also Elliott (1970: 166–67, 2006: 120–22); Lynch (1991: 67–68); Kamen (2005: 243). "Composite" or "multiple" monarchy is one current favorite, on which see Elliott (1992).

3. The classic statement of decline is Hamilton ([1938] 1954). For a critical discussion, see Elliott (1989c, 1989d, 1989e); Kamen (1978); Parry ([1966] 1990: 229–50); Thompson (1998: 135–88).

4. See Pagden (1987: 65–70, 1990: 91–132); Lupher (2006: 325); Elliott (2006: 241).

5. On *limpieza de sangre*, see Elliott (1970: 220–24, 2006: 171); Lynch (1991: 36–38); Wheatcroft (1996: 161–64).

6. For these debates, see Parry (1940, [1966] 1990: 137–51); Pagden (1990: 13–36, 1995: 47–61, 91–102); MacLachlan (1991: 47–66); Lupher (2006); Elliott (2006: 69–78). Las Casas's passionate attacks on the Spanish settlers, especially as laid out in his *The Devastation of the Indies*

(1552), became the basis of the widely disseminated "Black Legend" of Spanish cruelty and authoritarianism that had such a long life in Protestant Europe.

7. Sicily was in fact given to the duke of Savoy, who exchanged it for Sardinia in 1718 (Bérenger 1997: 29).

8. See on the baroque as an imperial style Evans (1991: 443); see also Wandruszka (1964: 125–37); Wangermann (1973: 28–45); Ingrao (1994: 95–101, 120–26); Kuzmics and Axtmann (2007: 123–24).

9. The Habsburgs did not, however, give up on overseas trade and "informal empire," gradually in the nineteenth century building up the port city of Trieste as a the basis of a thriving trade with the Ottoman Empire and beyond, in Asia and Latin America. A key figure in this was the emperor Franz Joseph's brother Maximilian, whose later unhappy fate as the short-lived emperor of Mexico was very much bound up with his overseas imperial ambitions for the Habsburgs. The conventional idea of the Habsburg Empire as quintessentially a land empire, eschewing colonies and overseas ventures, may have to be revised. See especially Frank (2011); and see also Sauer (2007: 214–18); Judson (2016: 32, 113–15, 172).

10. As is common, unless specified I use the word "Austria" to stand for all the Habsburg lands, and as a convenient synonym for the Habsburg Empire (cf. Evans 1991: 157). I distinguish it from the Habsburg-headed Holy Roman Empire, which included rights and responsibilities in German lands not belonging to the Habsburgs. Also, though strictly speaking the term "Austrian Empire" emerged only with the proclamation of 1804, and the dissolution of the Holy Roman Empire in 1806, I follow Robert Kann and others in speaking of an Austrian or Habsburg Empire in the preceding centuries, stretching at least as far back as the union of the Habsburgs' hereditary lands and the crowns of Bohemia, Hungary, and Croatia in 1526–27 (see Kann 1980: xi and passim; for a demurral, Evans 1991: xiii). As with the Spanish monarchy, the "Austrian monarchy"—its formal title—clearly ruled an empire, in the usual understanding of that term, even before 1804. I discuss the various elements of the empire below.

11. The fullest account, and assessment, of Joseph II's accomplishments is now Beales (1987, 2009). For the various uses of "Josephinism"—liberal, radical, conservative, German nationalist—in the nineteenth century, see Wingfield (2007).

12. This is probably the place to remark that one of the best ways of understanding the later Habsburg Empire is through some wonderful works of literature—especially Jaroslav Hašek's *The Good Soldier Švejk* (1921), Robert Musil's *The Man without Qualities* (1930), and Joseph Roth's *The Radetzky March* (1932).The plays of Franz Grillparzer are also illuminating (on which see Kuzmics and Axtmann 2007: 265–84). So too of course are the novels of Franz Kafka, even though most of his works—*The Trial* (1925), *The Castle* (1926)—were published posthumously, and deal only obliquely with empire.

13. For the early history of the Habsburgs and the principal divisions of the Habsburg lands, see Wandruszka (1964: 1–77); Kann (1980: 1–24); Evans (1991: 157–308); Wheatcroft (1996: 1–68); Mametey (1995: 1–27); Fichtner (2003: 1–30); Beller (2011: 10–35).

14. For the nationalities in the Habsburg Empire, see Kohn (1961: 141–43); Kann ([1950] 1970, 1:29–332); Taylor ([1948] 1990: 25–38, 283–91); Deák (1990: 11–14); John (1999); Okey (2002: 12–25), Sked (2001: 334–35); Cornwall (2009). Figures relate mainly to the census of 1910, the last one taken. For a discussion specifically of the non-German groups, "the peoples of the Eastern Habsburg lands," see Kann and David (1984).

15. In the "Compromise" (Ausgleich) of 1867, which divided the empire as "Austria-Hungary" or the "Austro-Hungarian Empire," "Hungary" was the "Greater Hungary" that had existed since the sixteenth century, to which now Transylvania was added; but the "Austrian" half had no official name, being merely "the Kingdoms and Provinces represented in the Reichsrat," or sometimes Cisleithania—the lands on *this* side of the river Leitha separating the two countries. "Austria"—"constitutional Austria" as it was sometimes also called—was in effect everything else apart from Hungary—thus not just Austria (Upper and Lower, etc.) but also Bohemia, Moravia, Silesia, Galicia, Dalmatia, Bukovina, and the three "coastal provinces" of Gorica, Istria, and the free city of Trieste. After 1908 there were also Bosnia and Herzogovina (though formally these were common possessions of the "Dual Monarchy," not Austrian provinces, and in effect formed a "third part" of the empire). Only in 1917 were these lands recognized collectively as "Austria"—just before, of course, they split apart with the disintegration of the Habsburg Empire in 1918 (Okey 2002: 193).

As usual, Robert Musil has the best comment on the typically Habsburg complexity that followed the setting up of "Austria-Hungary." "It did not consist of an Austrian and a Hungarian part, as one might imagine, combined to form a unity, but of a whole and a part, namely of a Hungarian and Austro-Hungarian sense of nationhood; and the latter was at home in Austria, whereby the Austrian sense of nationhood actually became homeless. The Austrian himself was only to be found in Hungary, and there as an object of dislike; at home he called himself a citizen of the kingdoms and realms of the Austro-Hungarian Monarchy as represented in the Imperial Council, which means the same as an Austrian plus a Hungarian minus this Hungarian. . . . As a result, many people simply called themselves Czechs, Poles, Slovenes or Germans, and this is where that further decay began" (Musil [1930–32] 1979, 1:198–99; see also Stourzh 1992: 10–20).

16. The motto can be found on many religious and public buildings, a particularly striking one being on the west portal of the Domkirche—built by Frederick III—in Graz. It can also be seen on Frederick III's tomb in Vienna's St. Stephen's Cathedral. It has to be said that there are a number of interpretations of the initials A. E. I. O. U.—the one given is that stated by Frederick III himself.

17. Though Franz Joseph remained personally and firmly committed to the toleration of the other faiths in his empire—Protestantism, Islam, Judaism, Orthodoxy, Greek Catholic—and resisted all attempts to limit them (Unowsky 2001: 26; Judson 2016: 235–36).

18. Beller notes Karl Kraus's characteristically sour and satirical account of the 1908 jubilee, but even Kraus had to admit that it was a great success, that "the disorganization was so great that the thing actually worked" (Beller 2001: 59).

19. This supplies an important episode in Roth's *The Radetzky March*, where the Jewish *Regimentsarzt*, the regimental medical officer, Dr. Demant, does not hesitate to fight a duel with an aristocratic fellow officer who has insulted him with his anti-Semitic remarks (Roth [1932] 1995: 107–11). There was indeed "a unique relationship between a confessionally tolerant monarchy and the Jews, who were among its most loyal citizens" (Deák 1990: 172; cf. Stone 1966: 99; Urbanitsch 2004: 114–15; Judson 2016: 235).

20. Sources for these examples include especially Evans (2006), in various chapters. See also Wandruszka (1964: 2–3); Wangermann (1973: 61–63); Kann ([1957] 1973: 168–95); Bérenger (1994, 1997: passim); Okey (2002: 30–33).

21. Despite nineteenth-century attempts by German nationalists to claim Joseph II as one of their champions, Joseph's privileging of the German language—and that of his successors— had nothing to do with ethnicity and everything to do with efficiency. German was simply seen as the most suited to act as the "high language" of empire, "universal" in the way that Latin had been universal in the Middle Ages. Czech and Hungarian were "national" languages. German was not; it was simply the best language for education, communication, and administration. When in 1875 a university was founded in Czernowitz, in Bukovina, German was made the language of instruction on the grounds that "only German scholarship can claim universality," and that it would thus have "a universal meaning [for] the non-German sons of Bukovina" (Judson 2016: 79, 297–98, 322).

22. The roll call of nationalities in the service of the Habsburgs does not of course end there. See, for other groups, Evans (1991: 308). Wandruszka (1964: 2) remarks that "no other ruling family, throughout the centuries until the end of its power, was served by men of so many different European countries."

23. The compliment was returned in kind, as in Metternich's famous jibe that "Asia begins at the Landstrasse"—the road leading from Vienna toward Hungary (Evans 2006: 129).

24. In a striking portrait of the emperor, Louis Eisenmann, writing in 1910, concludes: "Assuredly, the existence of the monarchy does not depend on him alone; but, by his good qualities and his misfortunes he has undoubtedly strengthened the dynastic loyalty which is traditional in Austria. This man, not in virtue of any conspicuous intellectual gifts, but by his diligence, benevolence, and devotion to duty, will give his name to the epoch of which his reign, from 1859 onward, constitutes the unity" (Eisenmann 1910: 175). The "misfortunes" Eisenmann refers to include the death of the emperor's brother the archduke Maximilian, executed in 1867 by a Mexican firing squad; the suicide of his son Rudolf, together with Rudolf's mistress Marie Vetsera, at Mayerling in 1889; the death of his younger brother Karl Ludwig through drinking contaminated water in the Holy Land in 1896; the murder of his wife, Elisabeth, at the hands of an Italian anarchist in 1898 (the year of his Golden Jubilee as emperor). Later was to come the assassination of his nephew the archduke Franz Ferdinand and his wife Sophie at Sarajevo in 1914. Assuredly Franz Joseph needed to call upon all the reserves of stoicism that he was famous for. When news of the assassination at Sarajevo reached him, he "immediately enquired after the progress of the recently completed maneuvers" (Wandruszka 1964: 180; see also Morton 1980; Johnston [1972] 1983: 33–39). There is an unforgettable portrait of Franz Joseph, in his later years, in Werfel (1937: 18–33).

25. On the Austro-Marxists, see Kann ([1950] 1970: 2:154–78); Johnston ([1972] 1983: 99–111); Nimni (2000); Sandner (2005); Munck (2010).

26. *Fortwursteln* was a Viennese slang expression, variously translated as "getting by," "slogging on," "muddling through," "meandering along." For many it came to signify the typical Austrian character, as opposed especially to the Prussian type. The Austrian writer Franz Werfel saw the Austrian German language as a variety of German that with "its involutions and complications made it an admirable vehicle for veiling emotions, concealing intentions, and disguising intrigues. A detached style, attractive and disingenuous, it was ideal for facilitating, officially and privately, the time-honoured '*fortwursteln*'" (Werfel 1937: 34).

27. On Jews in the Habsburg Empire, see Janik and Toulmin (1973: 58–61); Johnston ([1972] 1983: 23–29, 357–61); Beller (1989, 2011: passim); Stourzh (1992: 7–9); Gellner (1998b: 30–66, 46–58, 100–106); Rozenblit (2005); Kuzmics and Axtmann (2007: 319–21).

28. On Joseph Roth's attitude toward the Habsburgs and the Habsburg Empire, see especially the letters in Roth (2012). See also Manger (1985); Le Rider (1994: 127); Coetzee (2002); Kuzmics and Axtmann (2007: 314–22); Hoffmann (2012); Raphael (2012).

29. The best account of this, with full references to the recent research, is Cohen (2007). Cf. also Bérenger (1997: 288, 296); Unowsky (2011: 237–38); Deak (2014: 365–67, 373–80); Judson (2016: 387–407). Sked firmly asserts: "It can be argued that there was no domestic or even foreign threat to its integrity until 1918" (Sked 2001: 6; see also 191). For the argument that it was the clash of empires, not the challenge of nationalism, that brought down the empires after the First (and Second) World War, see Kumar (2010).

30. There is now, contrary to earlier accounts—often written in terms of the nationalist historiography of the successor states after 1918—remarkable agreement on this view of the wartime support given to the empire. See Déak (1990: 199); Mann (1993: 347–50); Cornwall (2000: 16–39, 2002: 2–3); Sked (2001: 235–36, 301); Cohen (207: 242–43); Zückert (2011: 501). The view of a mass Czech "desertion" was a convenient fiction for both later German and Czech nationalists, and so the myth was perpetuated (Judson 2016: 406–7).

31. See also Good (1984); Bérenger (1997: 225–35, 257–59); Schulze (1997); Sked (2001: 202–6, 301, 310–12). From the late 1820s to the First World War, Austria's industrial sector grew at an annual rate of about 2.5 percent—comparable to all the leading economies of Europe (Schulze 1997: 296).

32. See, for a strong statement of this view, the article in the Viennese *Arbeiter-Zeitung* of November 3, 1918, "The End of the Military Monarchy," with its ridiculing of the Austrian "State Idea" (*Staatsidee*) and its "legend about the loyalties of all the nationalities" (in Namier 1962: 200–201).

Chapter 5: The Russian and Soviet Empires

1. Riurik and his people, who first appear in the much later *Primary Chronicle* (late eleventh century), have been for centuries the subject of passionate debate and controversy among Russian historians and publicists. For a survey see Etkind (2011: 45–60). For the current state of scholarly opinion, see Kivelson (1997: 636–39).

2. The origin of the idea of "Moscow the Third Rome" lies in the text *The Legend of the White Cowl*, allegedly found in the Vatican archives by the Russian Church's emissary Dmitrii Gerasimov and brought back by him to Moscow c. 1490. The text reads: "The ancient city of Rome has broken away from the glory and faith of Christ because of its pride and ambition. In the new Rome, which has been the city of Constantinople, the Christian faith will also perish through the violence of the sons of Hagar [i.e., Muslims]. In the third Rome, which will be the land of Rus, the Grace of the Holy Spirit will shine forth. Know then . . . that all Christians will finally unite into one Russian realm because of its Orthodoxy" (in Hosking 2012: 103; see also Stremooukhoff 1970: 113, 122n46). Some people think that the text was written by Gerasimov himself, to bolster the claims of the Church against the rising power of the tsar.

3. The title "tsar" had traditionally been applied by Russians to the khans of the Golden Horde, and some have supposed that in being styled "tsar" Ivan IV was claiming for the Moscow dynasty the imperial succession to the dynasty of the Chinghizides. This is certainly plausible; but Michael Cherniavsky, who makes this point, also argues this does not exclude the

claim in addition of a succession to the Byzantine Empire, as proclaimed in the doctrine of the Third Rome. Russian identity was always "playful," capable of taking on multiple forms at the same time (Cherniavsky 1975: 133; see also Pipes [1974] 1995: 74–76; Kivelson 1997: 643; Lieven 2001: 216; Figes 2002: 369; Riasanovsky 2005: 62–67).

4. The term the "time of troubles" was coined in relation to a specially disordered period (1598–1613), following the death of Feodor I up to the election of the first Romanov tsar. But it has been widely and justifiably applied to the whole seventeenth century, up to the time of Peter the Great's consolidation of his rule.

5. Commenting on this phrase, first used by a European visitor to Russia, the writer Joseph Brodsky says that Peter "didn't want to imitate Europe: he wanted Russia to *be* Europe, in much the same way as he was, at least partly, a European himself" (Brodsky 1987: 72). See also, especially on the Dutch as a model of European modernity, Etkind (2011: 97–101).

6. To which the composer Balakirev later darkly responded, "Peter the Great killed our native Russian life." Peter has always divided opinion. On the cultural changes, see Figes (2002: 4–13); Cracraft (2004); and for general accounts of Peter's reforms, Anisimov (1993); Tolz (2001: 23–66); Hosking (2012: 175–209). The best and most vivid portrait of Peter remains that of the nineteenth-century historian Vasilii Klyuchevsky (Klyuchevsky 1958).

7. On Russians and Ukrainians, see Seton-Watson (1986: 16–17); Horak (1988: 106–8); Prizel (1998: 158); Kappeler (2001: 61–69); Lieven (2001: 259–61).

8. On Russian experience in the Caucasus, see Atkin (1988: 141–63); Kappeler (2001: 179–85); Tolz (2001: 137–40); Figes (2002: 384–90); Longworth (2006: 200–203).

9. Kappeler (2001: 193); see also Sarkisyanz (1974: 48–49, 60–61); MacKenzie (1988: 225–31); Yapp (1987).

10. For Russian attitudes and policies toward the Far East see Chang (1974); Sarkisyanz (1974: 66–68); Becker (1986, 1991); LeDonne (1997: 178–215); Bassin (1999: 52–55, 278); Figes (2002: 414–15, 423–29). On Eurasianism see Lieven (2001: 219–20); Laruelle (2008).

11. The Mongol Empire of Genghis Khan was admittedly the largest land empire—and the second-largest empire ever—but its duration was short. Leaving that out, the British Empire was the world's largest empire, Russia next (Taagepera 1978a: 126).

12. For this account of Soloviev and Kliuchevsky I have drawn mainly upon Etkind (2011: 61–71); see also Becker (1986); Bassin (1993), Breyfogle, Schrader, and Sunderland (2007: 2–6).

13. There is an interesting parallel here—not by any means the only one between Russia and England—in the way John Seeley sees England as a nation formed by its colonial extensions, though in this case they are mostly overseas. See chap. 6, below.

14. Usefully surveyed by Etkind (2011: 6–8), who notes its use by a number of Russian writers of the nineteenth century, such as Afanasi Schapov, as well as more recent writers such as Hannah Arendt.

15. Isabelle Kreindler has plausibly argued that Ilminsky, who was a colleague of Lenin's father in Kazan, had a significant influence on Lenin's nationality policy. "Long before the Soviet formula, 'National in form, Socialist in Content' was coined, Il'minskii's approach, which centered on native languages, was defended—from Russian nationalist attacks—as one which stressed the 'Orthodox content' rather than the 'national form'" (Kreindler 1977: 87).

16. As stressed by Geraci (2001: 80–81); Thaden (1990c: 216); Löwe (2000: 73–74); Kaspe (2007: 475–76); Campbell (2007: 332).

17. On the various meanings of "Russification" (*obrusenie*), see Becker (1986); Pearson (1989: 88–94); Thaden (1990c: 211); Rodkiewicz (1998: 7–12); Miller (2008: 45–65).

18. Kappeler (2001: 213, 247); Hosking (1998a: 367); Jersild (2000: 542); Kaspe (2007: 465–86).

19. See Rogger (1983: 184–87); Rodkiewicz (1998); Prizel (1998: 166); Kappeler (2001: 224–28, 255–56).

20. On these developments among Latvians and Estonians, see Raun (1977: 132–43); Haltzel (1977: 150–56); Rogger (1983: 191–93); Thaden (1990d: 228); Kappeler (2001: 257–60).

21. For such claims, see for example Walicki (1979: 298); Rodkiewicz (1998); Wortman (2006: 283–84); Kaspe (2007: 470–76); Carter (2010: 72).

22. See Wortman (2006: 284–85, 2011: 276–77); Riasanovsky (2005: 185); Kaspe (2007: 483–85).

23. For the obstacles that the estate system put in the way of nationalism throughout the nineteenth century, see especially Burbank (2007a: 83–84). See also Burbank (2006, 2007b); Steinwedel (2000: 69–70); Dixon (1998: 155); Löwe (2000: 77).

24. Michael Cherniavsky discerns an enduring "playfulness," an openness to multiple options—Muscovite, Roman, Byzantine, Mongol—in Russian political culture and Russian national consciousness. He adds, 'Italian architects building the palaces and churches of the Kremlin; Greek-Byzantine diplomats; Italian and German gunners, German doctors; Persian gardens, medicine, and astrologers; Hungarian fashions, homosexuality and the dandy were also options which made up consciousness" (Cherniavsky 1975: 124).

25. As Paul Bushkovitch has observed, most commentators have interpreted Filofei's doctrine in an "optimistic" vein, as declaring Russia the last great world empire and conferring on it a messianic world mission to preserve and expand the Orthodox faith. There is also a "pessimistic interpretation: that if Russia should deviate from the true faith—and Filofei was troubled by such signs at the time, hence his warning—that would mean the fall of the last empire and the end of the world" (Bushkovitch 1986: 358–60). The optimistic meaning seems to have triumphed—in mainstream Russian thought at least—but the alternative meaning was always available to those (such as the Old Believers) alarmed at developments within the Russian Church (Stremooukhoff 1970: 119).

26. For the Slavophiles—and their opponents, the Westernizers—see especially Riasanovsky (1965); Berdyaev ([1937] 1960: 19–36); Walicki (1975; 1979: 92–114). A good selection of texts is Kohn (1962: 104–115, 191–211); Raeff (1966: 174–301); Leatherbarrow and Offord (1987: 61–107). Helpful discussions are in Carr (1956: 366–77); Hunczak (1974); Berlin (1979); Becker (1991: 53–58); Pipes ([1974] 1995: 265–69); Hellberg-Hirn (1998: 197–208); Hosking (1998a: 270–75, 368–74, 2012: 274–77); Prizel 1998: (160–66); Tolz (2001: 81–99); Figes (2002: 310–18). As is common in ideological discourse (cf. Whigs and Tories), the terms "Slavophilism" (*slavianofilstvo*) and "Westernism" (*zpadnichestvo*) were both originally coined as slurs by each other's opponents, only later becoming accepted as badges of identity by the two groups (Carr 1956: 368; Walicki 1979: 92).

27. There is now considerable agreement on this meaning of *narodnost* for the exponents of "official nationality." See Riasanovsky (1959: 124–66, 2005: 133–34, 141–43); Saunders (1982: 58–62); Bassin (1999: 38–40); Tolz (2001: 78); Stone, Podbolotov, and Yasar (2004: 32); Miller (2008: 142–46).

28. Hosking (1998a: xix–xx; see also 1998b); and cf. Szporluk (1997: 65–66); Dixon (1998: 159); Prizel (1998: 180–238, esp. 154–55, 178–79); Becker (2000); Rowley (2000: 32–33).

29. Nicholas Riasanovsky's wry comment on this view seems highly apposite: "It seems precipitous to find the best solution for imperial Russia in becoming a modern national state. Germany did just that, quickly and brilliantly, with the process eventuating in Hitler" (2005: 210). This seems a fair response to those, such as Dominic Lieven, who think that "the surest way to save an empire is to turn as much as possible of it into a nation," and that Russian elites sought to do this—unsuccessfully—in the last decades of tsarist rule (2001: 281–84).

30. See, e.g., Rudolph and Good (1992); Motyl (1992); Barkey and von Hagen (1997); Dawisha and Parrot (1997).

31. On this development see also Cohen (1996: 67–116, 151–66); Suny (2001: 27); Lieven (2001: 288–90); Hirsch (2005: 1–4); Beissinger (2006: 294–95); Khalid (2007: 113); Turoma and Waldstein (2013).

32. Or even if empire remains a useful analytical category, it might still be important to consider the ways in which the "Soviet Empire" differed from both the tsarist empire and the European overseas empires. See on this, variously, Geyer (1986); Beissinger (1995, 2008); Parrott (1997: 11–12); Szporluk (1997: 76–77); Kotkin (2001: 151–56); Suny (1995, 2001); Slezkine (2000); Lieven (2001: 293–309); Martin (2001: 15–20, 2002); Hirsch (2005: 164, 188). Martin (2001: 20) playfully offers "the Soviet Union as the Highest Stage of Imperialism," and Slezkine (2000) "Imperialism as the Highest Stage of Socialism."

33. See for example Berdyaev ([1937] 1960); Szporluk (1997: 76); Prizel (1998: 186–88); Hosking (2006: 83–85).

34. For Lenin and Stalin on the national question, see Lenin (1962), Stalin ([1934] 1975). Useful commentaries are Pipes (1964: 1–49); Kohn (1971: 43–54); Connor (1984: 28–66); Carrère d'Encausse (1992: 26–98); Slezkine ([1994] 1996: 204–10); Smith (1999: 7–28); Martin (2001: 1–27); Hirsch (2005: 24–61).

35. For the profound and lasting impact of *korenizatsiia* policies, see Simon (1991: 20–70); Kaiser (1994: 124–47); Slezkine ([1994] 1996: 214–16, 219–22); Brubaker (1996: 29–32); Martin (2001: 9–15, 75–207, 379–87); Payne (2001); Khalid (2006, 2007: 124–25). "No other state," says Rogers Brubaker (1996: 29), "has gone so far in sponsoring, codifying, institutionalizing, even (in some cases) inventing nationhood and nationality on the sub-state level, while at the same time doing nothing to institutionalize them on the level of the state as a whole."

36. For the claim that what took place, increasingly in the 1930s, was Russification, see Martin (2001: 269–72, 394–431, 451–60; see also Simon 1991: 150–52). For contrary views, emphasizing continuity of basic aims and policies, see Seton-Watson (1986: 28); Slezkine ([1994] 1996: 222–25); Blitstein (2001, 2006); Hirsch (2005: 8–9, 103, 267–68, 273–308).

37. This remarkably parallels the efforts of Joseph II to make German the official language of the Habsburg Empire, not in order to advance the claims of the German nation but because German was the most "advanced" and so most efficient language for administration (see chap. 4).

38. Kaiser (1994: 125, 147); Slezkine ([1994] 1996: 227–28); Martin (2001: 27, 372–93); Blitstein (2006: 290–91).

39. See on this Martin (2001: 449); see also Kaiser (1994: 247–48); Suny (1995: 190); Slezkine ([1994] 1996: 224–29); Brubaker (1996: 31); Hirsch (2005: 106, 146, 293–302, 324).

40. For an earlier effort in a similar vein, before he had returned to Russia and before the Soviet Union had broken up, see Solzhenitsyn ([1990] 1991). For these and the earlier writings of the 1970s, and generally on the character of Solzhenitsyn's Russian nationalism, see Barghoorn (1980: 61–63, 1986: 50–59; Rowley (1997); Dunlop (1983, 1997: 40–41).

41. See Fedyshyn (1980: 155); Guroff and Guroff (1994: 86–87); Brubaker (1996: 49, 51); Slezkine (2000: 233); Martin (2001: 457). It had been clear for long that Russians, unlike the titular peoples of other Union republics, did not regard the RSFSR as "their" republic, and did not particularly identify with it. For them the whole Soviet Union was their territory. In a survey of Russians in Moscow in 1987, 70 percent saw the whole Soviet Union as their "motherland," and only 14 percent identified with the RSFSR. Even as late as 1994, after the breakup of the Soviet Union, only just over half (54.1 percent) of Russians considered themselves citizens simply of Russia, while 10 percent continued to consider themselves citizens of the USSR (Flenley 1996: 234; Brubaker 1996: 50; Dunlop 1997: 55). One can interpret this as Great Russian chauvinism or as Soviet patriotism; the main point, however, is the conflation or confusion of Russian and Soviet identities.

42. For attempts to stimulate Russian national consciousness in the 1970s and 1980s, see Wimbush (1978); Barghoorn (1980, 1986); Rasiak (1980: 163–66); Dunlop (1983, 1993); Carter (1993); Dixon (1996: 56–60); Flenley (1996: 235–41); Rowley (1997: 321–23); Szporluk (1990: 12–14, 1998: 302–4); Prizel (1998: 201–11); Duncan (2000: 62–109); Hosking (2006: 338–71). All accounts stress that this was mainly a movement among sections of the intelligentsia; only in the later Gorbachev years was there anything like a popular response, and this was mainly in reaction to the nationalist movements in the non-Russian republics (e.g., Flenley 1996: 235–66, 238; Dixon 1996: 58).

43. Beissinger (1995: 167; cf. 2008: 6–7). See also Suny (1995: 193); Brubaker (1996: 47–48); Flenley (1996: 245–46); Dixon (1996: 60–62); Dunlop (1997: 50, 55–56); Khazanov (2003).

Chapter 6: The British Empire

1. China offers another good example of the limitations of land empires. Its decision, under the Ming dynasty, to destroy its oceangoing fleet and to renounce overseas territories meant that Confucianism, and Chinese civilization more generally, though highly influential remained restricted to the East Asian region.

2. Cf. Canny (1973: 596–98); Kenny (2006a: 7); Ohlmeyer (2006: 57); Nasson (2006: 25, 36).

3. For a broadly colonialist perspective, with suitable caveats as to Ireland's peculiarities, see Canny (1973, 2003); Ohlmeyer (2006); Alvin Jackson (2006); Cleary (2006); Gibney (2008). See also, on Irish precedents and prototypes for other British colonies, Cannadine (2001: 15, 45; McMahon 2006: 185). For a sustained critique of the model of colonialism, see Howe (2002b, 2006); see also, for critical discussion, Armitage (2000: 148–69); McDonough (2005); McMahon (2006: 185–89); Cleary (2007). It is interesting that the idea of Ireland as a colony—whether, as for the home-rulers, on the model of Canada, or, for the unionists, on the model of India—was a commonplace in the intense debates over Irish Home Rule in the 1880s (Dunne 1982: 154–73). A colonialist understanding clearly was not a monopoly of the radicals.

4. One might indeed also see the settlement in British cities of hundreds of thousands of Asians and West Indians—denizens of former British colonies—as a kind of "reverse

colonization," or perhaps as the empire "striking back." But this is a relatively recent phenomenon, compared to the hundreds of years in which the Irish have settled in Britain. Time does matter, in the extent to which one is considered "naturalized." It is perfectly conceivable that in the years to come black and brown British will be thought of as British nationals in the way the Irish—and Jews and Huguenots—came to be after initial resistance and hostility.

5. See on all this Morgan (1994); Jeffery (1996); Kumar (2003: 140–45); Bartlett (2006: 88); Kenny (2006b: 93–95, 102); Alvin Jackson (2006: 135).

6. See also, on the heterogeneity of the British Empire, Martin (1972: 562); Thompson (1997: 150); Burroughs (1999: 171); Ashley Jackson (2006: xi–xii); Cleary (2006: 253).

7. For complaints about the "lamentable ignorance" (the Earl of Meath, originator of the Empire Day movement), and the "ignorance, indifference and prejudice" (R. A. Rendell, assistant controller, BBC Overseas Service), of the British population regarding the empire, together with the indifference of MPs toward imperial matters, see Bodelson ([1924] 1960: 41–2); MacKenzie (1986: 231); Kendle (1997: 57); Nicholas (2003: 225–26); Gallagher (1982: 79); Darwin (1988: 229), Bell (2007: 31–32). H. G. Wells expressed a common view when in the First World War he declared that "nineteen people out of twenty, the lower class and the middle class, knew no more of the empire than they did of the Argentine Republic or the Italian Renaissance. It did not concern them" (in Porter 2004a: 273). Polls of the 1940s and 1950s showed the continuing ignorance of the British public concerning the empire: MacKenzie (2001: 28); Thompson (2005: 207–9); Kumar (2012a: 298–99).

8. As well as castigating the "Saidists," Porter also refers to "the MacKenzie school," to acknowledge the great influence of John MacKenzie's works in exploring the impact of empire on British society (e.g., MacKenzie 1984, 1986, 1999a, 1999b, 2001, 2011: 57–89). There are also the many publications—currently numbering over a hundred—in the series Studies in Imperialism, edited by MacKenzie for Manchester University Press, nearly all of which purport to show, in different ways and in various spheres, the effect of the British Empire on Britain itself as well as on the overseas territories. For a complete list of the series, and an assessment of their contribution, see Thompson (2014). See also, for varying accounts of the ways empire influenced British identity, culture, and society, Burton (2003: 1–23, 2011); Hall (2000, 2002); Hall and Rose (2006); Wilson (1998, 2003, 2004); Kumar (2000, 2003, 2012a); Thompson (2005, 2012); Gilroy (2004); Buettner (2004); Schwarz (2013). The area remains contentious, but no one can deny that there is now a rich and growing body of material to reflect on.

9. In a review of Darwin's *The Empire Project* (2009) Denis Judd pointed out that "by the same token we could discuss 'the Roman Empire project', or the 'Ottoman project', the 'Soviet project' or even the 'Third Reich project'" (2010: 22).

10. There are some stimulating "world histories" by certain major students of the British Empire—e.g., Bayly (2004), Darwin (2008)—but they do not try specifically to consider the British Empire in a comparative way. Those few who do tend to be scholars whose primary expertise is not in the British Empire—e.g., Lieven (2001), Go (2011).

11. See also the other major contribution by Robinson and Gallagher ([1961] 1981). For a good study of the working of the informal empire—in the case of Uruguay—see Winn (1976). The work of John Darwin is also self-confessedly heavily indebted to Gallagher and Robinson (2009: xii, 2012: 11–12). See also Cain and Hopkins (2002: 26–30). There are valuable discussions of Robinson and Gallagher's approach in Louis (1976).

12. James Belich's absorbing account of the "Anglo-World," while accepting some aspects of "informal empire," clearly shows its limits in the case of Argentina, whose economic decline is attributed in part to competition from the dominions within the British Empire and the preference of British customers for "British" meat and wheat. Britishness, conferred by membership of the British Empire, clearly mattered after all (Belich 2009: 536–40). For critical comments on the concept of informal empire, see also Porter (1999: 8–9); Lynn (1999: 115–20); Marshall (2001: 11–12).

13. For these divisions see Ashley Jackson (2006: xi–xiii); Marshall (2001: 34–51); Darwin (2009: 9–12). An early form of this tripartite division is Barker (1941: 8, 47–48). All attempts to divide up the empire in this way point to a multitude of anomalies, e.g., the position of Southern Rhodesia, technically a crown colony but run like a dominion; or Sudan, officially a "condominium" ruled jointly by the British and Egyptian governments, but in practice a British colony—though administered not by the Colonial Office but by the Foreign Office. Egypt itself was an anomaly, never formally a colony but ruled like one (and thus not like the "informal empire"). Darwin adds the "informal empire" to his divisions, thus complicating the picture even further.

14. Much of the discussion of the "Britishness" of the dominions has gone under the heading of "the British world." See especially Bridge and Fedorowich (2003); Buckner and Francis (2003); Darian-Smith, Grmshaw, and Macintyre (2007); Ward (2008); Darwin (2009: 144–79); Belich (2009); Bickers (2010); Magee and Thompson (2010); Fedorowich and Thompson (2013a, 2013b). There is considerable overlap between this contemporary concept of "the British world" and the Victorian idea of "Greater Britain," though the British world idea is firmer in its rejection of the inclusion of non-European parts of the British Empire in Asia and Africa. Both, though, often, as with Dilke, include America—e.g., Belich (2009).

15. For discussions of Greater Britain, see Doyle (1986: 257–305); Gould (1999: esp. 485–89); Deudney (2001); Lee (2004); Bell (2007: esp. 6–12, 93–119); Belich (2009: 456–73); Koditschek (2011); Vasunia (2013: 119–55).

16. See Koditschek (2011: 90–97, 263–313). For a passionate restatement of this view in our own times, see the works of Nirad C. Chaudhuri (e.g., 1990: esp. 773–80).

17. For the change of mood produced by the Mutiny, see Metcalf (1997: 43–44, 160–65); MacKenzie (1999a: 280–81); Burroughs (1999: 174–75); Baucom (1999: 100–134).

18. For a discussion of the place of the United States in ideas of Greater Britain and, even more, imperial federation, see Deudney (2001: 195–99); Bell (2007: 231–59). One consequence of the idea of an imperial federation was a revival of Adam Smith's proposal along these lines (Palen 2014; see also Benians 1925: 282–83).

19. John Morley too pointed out that those who "blew the imperial trumpet louder than other people . . . would banish India, which is the most stupendous part of the Empire—our best customer among other trifles—into the imperial back kitchen" (in Green 1999: 365). See also Matikkala (2011: 153–55).

20. For ideas of imperial federation, and the imperial federation movement, see Bodelson ([1924] 1960: 205–14); Kendle (1997: 37–57); Bell (2007: 92–119); Matikkala (2011: 150–58). As expressed by the Imperial Federation League, the movement for formal union of the empire in a federation was relatively short-lived (1884–93) and divided the imperialists; but the general idea went back to Adam Smith, and the demise of the league did not mean the end of several

schemes to unite the empire, politically and commercially (of which imperial preference was the best known and most successful). See, on what was called at the time "constructive imperialism," Green (1999), Porter (2004a: 186–91).

21. A. P. Thornton remarks that "much of the best part of Seeley's book contains his thought on the future of India" ([1959] 1968: 59). In that sense nothing can be more misleading and unhelpful than Eliga Gould's cavalier dismissal: "With its ethnic bombast and smug belief in the desirability of Britain's imperial project, Seeley's *Expansion of England* is too much a work of its day to be regarded as anything other than a primary text" (1999: 486).

22. It was this fact that formed the basis of the criticism, emanating from both British and Indian sources, that Britain was "draining" India, forcing it to cover all the costs not just of its own upkeep but also often of imperial adventures elsewhere, as in Afghanistan and Egypt (Matikkala 2011: 54–74).

23. Another way of expressing this difference was to distinguish between "empire" and "imperialism." Empire—as expressed in colonies such as Canada and Australia—could be a force for good; imperialism, which involved force and conquest over other, usually non-European peoples, as in India, was unjust and oppressive. For "empire without imperialism," see Matikkala (2011: 11–18, 145–58).

24. For wide-ranging collections of studies on the role of the classics in the British Empire, see Webster and Cooper (1996); Goff (2005); Bradley (2010a). See also Dowling (1985); Reid (1996); Freeman (1996); Larson (1999); Hingley (2000, 2001, 2008); Bell (2007: 207–30); Kumar (2012b). Specifically on the classics and the Indian empire, Hutchins (1967: 144–52); Majeed (1999); R. Mantena (2010); Vasunia (2013); Hagerman (2009, 2013).

25. For the turn to Virgil, and to Rome, see Faber (1966: 22–26); Jenkyns (1981: 333–37); Reid (1996: 3–4); Vance (1997: 141–43); Kumar (2012b: 91–96); Vasunia (2013: 252–78).

26. A. P. Thornton has called this statement "the first, and still the most famous, enunciation of a doctrine which two generations later was accepted as part of the *mystique* of the fully-developed imperial idea" ([1959]1968: 4–5).

27. And cf. W.E.H. Lecky in 1893: "An England reduced to the limits which the Manchester School would assign to it would be an England shorn of the chief elements of its dignity in the world" (in Matikkala 2011: 110).

28. How far the classics actually "civilized," and in general the role of the classics in forming character, both individual and national, was—and is—a contentious matter. For a good discussion of the various positions, see Hagerman (2013: 1–36); see also Larson (1999: 189); Adler (2008: 210).

29. For discussions of these and related authors, see Freeman (1996); Larson (1999: 218–21); Majeed (1999); Reid (1996: 7); Owen (2005: esp. 25–26, 378–79); Adler (2008: 194–205); Reisz (2010); Kumar (2012b: 96–100); Vasunia (2005, 2013: 140–55).

30. See on this debate Thornton ([1959] 1968: 57–122); Porter (1982); Darwin (1986); Hyam (1999: 49–53); Marshall (2001: 52–77).

31. For the debates and divisions thrown up by the Boer War, see Thornton ([1959] 1968: 121–73); Porter (1968, 1982); Greenlee (1976: 271–72); Green (1999: 361–62); Matikkala (2011: 50–52, 87–89). For a range of contemporary contributions, see Burton (2001: 285–329); Harlow and Carter (2003b: 629–708). Ronald Hyam calls the Boer War "the most important and divisive war of Empire since the loss of the American colonies" (1999: 50).

32. See MacKenzie (1984, 1986, 1999a, 1999b, 2011: 57–89). And see also note 8, above, for other publications of the "Manchester school." For skepticism as to the effects of this imperial propaganda—especially among the working people—see Porter (2004a: 273).

33. Indians took this appeal to heart: among colonial troops, they had the largest number of deaths, 62,056. Next came Australians (59,330), Canadians (56,639), New Zealanders (16,7111), and South Africans (7,121 whites and 2,000 or so blacks) (Porter 2004a: 229; Marshall 2001: 79 gives slightly higher figures in all cases).

34. Marshall (2001: 84). See also Kennedy (1983: 199); Lloyd (1996: 279–81); Porter (2004a: 239–42); Pedersen (2015: xv–xvii).

35. For these figures, see Cain (1999); Offer (1993, 1999); Fieldhouse (1999: 98–100); Dilley (2008: 102–3).

36. For the relative numbers of British migrants to the United States and the British Empire in the nineteenth century, see Cain (1999: 37); Louis (1999a: 14); Constantine (1999: 167); Martin and Kline (2001: 255); Murdoch (2004: 107); Fedorowich (2008: 71).

37. "Decline," as John Darwin notes, "is a treacherously ambiguous phrase in the history of empires" (1984: 187; see also 1986: 27). On the plethora of dates on which the alleged decline of the British Empire is said to have begun—1921, 1897, the 1860s, even the early nineteenth century—see Kennedy (1983: 202). Kennedy sees this "declinist" literature as "the imperial converse" of the "Whig interpretation of history": instead of steady but inevitable progress, there is steady but equally inevitable decline.

38. Lord Rosebery is credited with the first public utterance of the term "the commonwealth of nations," in reference to the British Empire, at a speech in Australia in 1884. It became common in the early 1900s among liberals and Fabians, as well as at the imperial conferences before the First World War. From about 1910 it was popularized by the Round Table group of imperialists led by Lionel Curtis (Morefield 2007: 329). A particularly important statement of its principles was in a speech by General Smuts in May 1917, where he spoke of the British Empire as "a dynamic and evolving system," metamorphosing now into "the Commonwealth of Nations" (in Kennedy 1983: 209).

39. By 1947 Indians had achieved more than parity with Europeans: that year there were 429 European and 510 Indian ICS officers (Brown 1999: 439). This partly reflected a decline in the attractiveness of a career in India to British graduates, who increasingly turned to the Colonial Service (Porter 2004a: 281).

40. When Churchill retired as prime minister in 1955, his final words as recorded in the cabinet minutes spoke of his hope of "weaving still more closely the threads which bound together the countries of the Commonwealth or, as he still preferred to call it, the Empire" (in Clarke 2008: 5).

41. For the details of this "revolution in colonial affairs" (Louis) between 1957 and 1966, see Darwin (1988: 244–78); Louis (1999b: 351–54); Porter (2004a: 320–21); Hyam (2006: 411–12). It was at this time, in a speech at Capetown in 1960, that Macmillan made his famous "wind of change" speech.

42. For good accounts of decolonization in Britain, see Darwin (1984, 1988, 1991); Louis and Robinson (1994); Louis (1999b); Hyam (2006); Hopkins (2008). Shorter accounts are in Lloyd (1996: 320–80); Chamberlain (1999: 15–69); Porter (2004a: 297–325); Stockwell (2006); Stockwell (2008b). For the first stage, to 1948, see the vivid account in Clarke (2008).

For the sorry story in Kenya, see Anderson (2005) and Elkins (2005). As always, there is a perceptive and highly readable account in Morris ([1978] 1980b).

Chapter 7: The French Empire

1. I should note that though I have taken the expression "imperial nation-state" from Wilder, I use it in a somewhat different way from him. For him it expresses a unity of principles—and of their "antinomies"—across both the French nation and its empire; for me it is more an expression of the empire as an extension of the nation. We both agree, though, on the unusual integration of empire and nation in the French case. See Wilder (2005: esp. 3–23); and see also Cooper (2007: 358), for the analogous idea that France is not so much a nation-state as an "empire state."

2. The idea that France is a nation formed by conquest was clear to Ernest Renan. He reminds us of that uncomfortable fact in the context of his famous observation that "forgetfulness, and I shall even say historical error, form an essential factor in the creation of a nation." The French, like all other nations, forget, and must forget, that "unity is ever achieved by brutality. The union of Northern and Southern France was the result of an extermination, and of a reign of terror that lasted for nearly a hundred years" (Renan [1882] 2001: 166).

3. Britain's defeat of France's major ally in India, Tipu Sultan of Mysore, along with the capture of his capital Seringapatam in 1799, was the parallel event, on the other side of the Indian Ocean, that ended French hopes of establishing an Indian empire. After his defeat in Egypt, Napoleon had hoped to march his army to the Red Sea where he would link up with envoys from Tipu Sultan; together they would wage war on the British in India. Napoleon's defeat at Acre (1799) by the joint forces of the Ottomans and the British put paid to those plans too (Jasanoff 2005: 123, 149–76).

4. For assessments of Napoleon III and the Second Empire, see Farmer (1960); Cobban (1961: 156–210); Zeldin (1973: 504–60); Smith (1991); Gildea (1994: 67–72, 117–18). It has proved hard to shake off the inglorious image presented so brilliantly by Daumier, Hugo, and Zola.

5. There are many accounts of the Franco-Prussian War and the Paris Commune of 1870–71: see, for brief but helpful accounts, Cobban (1961: 196–210); Schivelbusch (2004: 111–18); Ousby (2003: 113–22); Gildea (2009: 229–45). Horne (1965) is especially good on the Commune.

6. For the details see Betts (1978); Andrew and Kanya-Forstner (1988: 16–28); Aldrich (1996); Quinn (2002); Frémeaux (2007).

7. On the Fashoda Incident, see Taylor (1954: 381–83); Brown (1970); Cooke (1973: 81–97); Baumgart (1982: 63–68); Quinn (2002: 164–65).

8. For Ferry's thought and activities, see Cobban (1961: 220–22); Brunschwig (1966: 75–81); Girardet (1972: 80–88); Cooke (1973: 23–27); Baumgart (1982: 40–41, 70–71); Ozouf (2015). For Leroy-Beaulieu and his influence, Murphy ([1948] 1968: 103–75); Brunschwig (1966: 27–28); Girardet (1972: 53–57). Despite his hopes, Ferry, who was personally very unpopular in the Chamber, never regained power after 1885.

9. For Ferry's full speech of July 28, 1885, see Brunschwig (1966: 75–81); for the French original, see Girardet (1972: 82–86). See also Aldrich (1996: 97–100).

10. For good discussions of economic theories of imperialism, see Baumgart (1982: 91–135); Etherington (1984); Wolfe (1997).

11. On all this see Betts (1961: 134–35); Brunschwig (1966: viii–ix, 87–96); Baumgart (1982: 114–19, 127–29) Andrew and Kanya-Forstner (1988: 28); Aldrich (1996: 195–98). See also Kanya-Forstner (1972).

12. See also, in very similar terms, Gildea (2009: 244–45). The "national trauma" and the "culture of defeat" of these years are vividly described by Schivelbusch (2004: 103–87), who also shows how from the very fact of defeat were wrung the inspiration and resolve toward national regeneration; see also Ousby (2003: 113–35).

13. On the *parti colonial*, see Brunschwig (1966: 105–34); Andrew and Kanya-Forstner (1971); Cooke (1973: 52–68); Persell (1974); Baumgart (1982: 78–80); Aldrich (1996: 100–106). Agnes Murphy's important study ([1948] 1968) of the decade 1871–81 traces the role of the geographical societies, the explorers, and prominent theoreticians such as Leroy-Beaulieu, Gabriel Charmes, and the abbé Raboisson in preparing the way for the colonial movement of the 1880s and 1890s. On the important role of the geographical societies in the provinces, created principally in the 1870s and 1880s—in 1900 they had approximately seven times as many members as Paris—see Goerg (2002: 83–86).

14. On these activities see Brunschwig (1966: 120–34, 146–49); Betts (1961: 147–52); Persell (1974); Aldrich (1996: 171–77); Conklin (1997: 6–7).

15. For a vivid portrait of General Hubert Lyautey, the most famous of the soldier-administrators, see Singer (1991). See also, on Faidherbe, Gallieni, and Lyautey, Betts (1961: 109–20). On Garnier and the other soldier-explorers, see Murphy ([1948] 1968: 41–102); for Mangin and *la force noire*, Girardet (1972: 152–53).

16. That army was closely identified with the Habsburg Empire, as we have seen, and the same might be said of the Roman Empire. But in both cases we are dealing with armies that were as multinational as the empires they defended. The peculiarity in the French case is that it was very much a *national* army that took upon itself the imperial mission. The army engaged in empire as a matter of national prestige, and as a way of regaining its honor in the eyes of the French nation. Here once more we see the unusually close relation between nation and empire in the French case.

17. See also Ross and Telkamp (1985: 171–206); Prochaska (1990: 206–29); Wright (1991, 1997); Aldrich (1996: 232–33).

18. For the history of the idea of assimilation, which Raymond Betts traces back to Richelieu and the doctrine of religious conversion, see Betts (1961: 12–21); see also Belmessous (2013: esp. 1–12), who understands assimilation as "the integration of foreign societies into European cultures," under the banner of the civilizing mission.

19. Citizenship rights had been granted to the peoples of the "old colonies" of Gaudeloupe, Martinique, French Guiana, and Rénunion following the abolition of slavery throughout the empire in 1848. In the same year voting rights were given to the inhabitants of Senegal and France's Indian territories; in 1916 the Senegalese received full citizenship (Aldrich 1996: 212; Saada 2013: 333). The "Senegalese model"—in which citizenship was granted without the requirement that "personal status" be given up—acquired great importance in the measures for the extension of French citizenship to the natives of all the colonies after 1945 (Cooper 2014: x–xi, 8, 29).

20. This is of course a controversial issue; for a good discussion of race in French thought and practice, see Hargreaves (2007); for a comparison with Britain, see Favell (2001) and Bleich (2003).

21. See the helpful remarks on "settler colonialism," as a distinct type of colonialism, in Prochaska (1990: 1–28). This as clearly excludes the case of India as it includes that of Algeria (and such former colonies as Kenya, Rhodesia, and South Africa).

22. The unlikely bedfellows of Jean-Paul Sartre and Raymond Aron were the principal exception to this consensus; few shared their view until the last years of the Algerian conflict (Shepard 2008: 63–73). See also Girardet (1972: 335–65).

23. The fullest account of the 1931 exhibition is Hodeir and Pierre (1991); see also Girardet (1972: 175–76); Lebovics (1994: 51–97); Aldrich (1996: 261–64); Wilder (2005: 37–38); Jennings (2005: 702–5).

24. Betts (1961: 1–2); Goerg (2002: 82); Chafer and Sackur (2002: 1–9); Evans (2004: 2). Baycroft (2004: 153, 2008: 147–48, 161–62). But Baycroft also argues that at a deeper level the empire was all-pervasive in French culture. The whole discussion is strikingly similar to the British case: see chap. 6.

25. On the decolonization process of the 1940s and the 1950s, see Betts (1991); Ross (1995); Aldrich (1996: 266–306). The attitude of many of the new leaders was summed up in a speech made in 1959 by François Tombalbaye, soon to be the first president of the Republic of Chad, when he declared his "profound belief in the principles of democracy that France has taught us" (in Betts 1991: 126; see also Howe 2005: 596–97).

Chapter 8: Epilogue

1. The term "decolonization"—like *Tiers Mondisme*, "Third Worldism," with which it was connected—was popularized during the French debates of the 1950s, but it seems to have been coined by the German economist Moritz Bonn in the 1930s, and thence to have passed into scholarly usage in French and English (Shepard 2008: 5, 56, 72; Thomas, Moore, and Butler 2008: 2–3). For some good general accounts of European decolonization in the twentieth century, see Albertini (1969); Betts (2004); Chamberlain (1999); Holland (1985); Thomas, Moore, and Butler (2008). Duara (2004) includes important statements by the anticolonial leaders themselves. For theoretical and comparative approaches, see Smith (1978); Morris-Jones and Fischer (1980); Kahler (1984); Spruyt (2005); Shipway (2008). See also the valuable review essay by Howe (2005). A long-range perspective (1500–1987) is provided by Strang (1991).

2. For a good discussion of "neocolonialism" and "dependency" theory, with references to the main contributors, see Mommsen (1982: 113–41, 1986: 344–50).

3. On America as an empire, see the helpful chapters in Mommsen and Osterhammel (1986), Calhoun, Cooper, and Moore (2006), and Steinmetz (2013), all of which contain references to the extensive literature on the subject. See also Steinmetz (2005).

BIBLIOGRAPHY

Aasland, Aadne. 1996. "Russians outside Russia: The New Russian Diaspora." In Smith 1996: 477–97.

Abernethy, David B. 2000. *The Dynamics of Global Dominance: European Overseas Empires 1415–1980*. New Haven, CT: Yale University Press.

Acomb, Frances. 1950. *Anglophobia in France 1763–1789*. Durham, NC: Duke University Press.

Acton, John Emerich Edward Dalberg, First Baron. [1862] 1996. "Nationality." In *Mapping the Nation*, edited by Gopal Balakrishnan, 17–38. London: Verso.

Adas, Michael. 1998. "Imperialism and Colonialism in Comparative Perspective." *International History Review* 20 (2): 371–88.

Adler, Eric. 2008. "Late Victorian and Edwardian Views of Rome and the Nature of 'Defensive Imperialism.'" *International Journal of the Classical Tradition* 15 (2): 187–216.

Agursky, Mikhail. 1987. *The Third Rome: National Bolshevism in the USSR*. Boulder, CO: Westview Press.

Aksan, Virginia H. 1999. "Locating the Ottomans among Early Modern Empires." *Journal of Early Modern History* 3 (2): 103–34.

Aksin, Sina. 2007. *Turkey: From Empire to Revolutionary Republic*. Translated by Dexter H. Mursaloglu. London: Hurst and Co.

Albertini, Rudolf von. 1969. "The Impact of Two World Wars on the Decline of Colonialism." *Journal of Contemporary History* 4 (1): 17–35.

Alcock, Susan E., Terence N. D'Altroy, Kathleen D. Morrison, and Carla M. Sinopoli, eds. 2001. *Empires: Perspectives from Archaeology and History*. Cambridge: Cambridge University Press.

Aldrich, Robert. 1996. *Greater France: A History of French Overseas Expansion*. Houndmills, Basingstoke: Macmillan.

———. 2005. *Vestiges of the Colonial Empire in France: Monuments, Museums and Colonial Memories*. Houndmills, Basingstoke: Palgrave Macmillan.

———, ed. 2007. *The Age of Empires*. New York: Thames and Hudson.

Allworth, Edward, ed. 1971. *Soviet Nationality Problems*. New York: Columbia University Press.

———. 1980a. "Ambiguities in Russian Group Identity and Leadership of the RSFSR." In Allworth 1980b: 17–38.

———, ed. 1980b. *Ethnic Russia in the USSR: The Dilemma of Dominance*. New York: Pergamon Press.

———, ed. 1989. *Central Asia: 120 Years of Russian Rule*. Durham, NC: Duke University Press.

Alter, Peter. 1994. *Nationalism*. 2nd ed. London: Edward Arnold.

Amery, L. S. 1944. *The Framework of the Future*. Oxford: Oxford University Press.

Anderson, Benedict. 2006. *Imagined Communities: Reflection on the Origin and Spread of Nationalism*. 2nd rev. ed. London: Verso.

Anderson, David. 2005. *Histories of the Hanged: The Dirty War in Kenya and the End of Empire*. New York: W. W. Norton and Co.

Ando, Clifford. 2000. *Imperial Ideology and Provincial Loyalty in the Roman Empire*. Berkeley: University of California Press.

Andrew, C. M., and A. S. Kanya-Forstner. 1971. "The French 'Colonial Party': Its Composition, Aims and Influence, 1885–1914." *Historical Journal* 14 (1): 99–128.

———. 1988. "Centre and Periphery in the Making of the Second French Colonial Empire, 1815–1920." *Journal of Imperial and Commonwealth History* 16 (3): 9–34.

Anisimov, Evgenii V. 1993. *The Reforms of Peter the Great: Progress through Coercion in Russia*. Translated by John. T. Alexander. Armonk, NY: M. E. Sharpe.

Arendt, Hannah. 1958. *The Origins of Modern Totalitarianism*. 2nd ed. New York: Meridian Books.

Armitage, David, ed. 1998. *Theories of Empire, 1450–1800*. Aldershot, UK: Ashgate Publishing.

———. 2000. *The Ideological Origins of the British Empire*. Cambridge: Cambridge University Press.

Armstrong, John A. 1976. "Mobilized and Proletarian Diasporas." *American Political Science Review* 70 (2): 393–408.

———. 1978. "Mobilized Diaspora in Tsarist Russia: The Case of the Baltic Germans." In Azrael 1978: 63–104.

Arthurs, Joshua. 2012. *Excavating Modernity: The Roman Past in Fascist Italy*. Ithaca, NY: Cornell University Press.

Ashcroft, Bill, Gareth Griffiths, and Helen Tiffin, eds. 1995. *The Post-Colonial Studies Reader*. London: Routledge.

Atkin, Muriel 1988. "Russian Expansion in the Caucasus to 1813." In Rywkin 1988: 139–87.

Atlan, Catherine, and Jean-Hervé Jézéquel. 2002. "Alienation or Political Strategy? The Colonised Defend the Empire." In Chafer and Sackur 2002: 102–15.

Atlee, Clement. 1961. *Empire and Commonwealth*. Oxford: Oxford University Press.

Augustine, St. [413–27 CE] 1984. *Concerning the City of God against the Pagans*. Translated by Henry Bettenson. London: Penguin Books.

Azrael, Jeremy R., ed. 1978. *Soviet Nationality Policies and Practices*. New York: Praeger.

Bacevich, Andrew. 2003. *American Empire: The Realities and Consequences of U.S. Diplomacy*. Cambridge, MA: Harvard University Press.

Bacon, Francis. [1625] 1906. *Essays, or Counsels Civil and Moral*. Edited by Frederick Harrison. London: Blackie and Son.

Badian, E. 1958. "Alexander the Great and the Unity of Mankind." *Historia* 7 (4): 425–44.

Bailkin, Jordanna. 2012. *The Afterlife of Empire*. Berkeley: University of California Press.

Balibar, Etienne. 1999. "Algeria, France: One Nation or Two?" In *Giving Ground: The Politics of Propinquity*, edited by Joan Copjec and Michael Sorkin, 162–72. London: Verso.

Barghoorn, Frederick C. 1980. "Four Faces of Soviet Russian Ethnocentrism." In Allworth 1980b: 55–66.

———. 1986. "Russian Nationalism and Soviet Politics: Official and Unofficial Perspectives." In Conquest 1986: 30–77.

Barker, Ernest. 1941. *The Ideas and Ideals of the British Empire*. Cambridge: Cambridge University Press.

Barkey, Karen. 2008. *Empire of Difference: The Ottomans in Comparative Perspective*. Cambridge: Cambridge University Press.

Barkey, Karen, and Mark von Hagen, eds. 1997. *After Empire: Multiethnic Societies and Nation-Building. The Soviet Union and the Russian, Ottoman, and Habsburg Empires*. Boulder, CO: Westview Press.

Bartlett, Robert. 1994. *The Making of Europe: Conquest, Colonization and Cultural Change 950–1350*. London: Penguin Books.

Bartlett, Thomas. 2006. "Ireland, Empire, and Union, 1690–1801." In Kenney 2006c: 61–89.

Barton, I. M. 1972. *Africa in the Roman Empire*. Accra: Ghana Universities Press.

Bassin, Mark. 1991. "Inventing Siberia: Visions of the Russian East in the Early Nineteenth Century." *American Historical Review* 96 (3): 763–94.

———. 1993. "Turner, Solov'ev, and the 'Frontier Hypothesis': The Nationalist Signification of Open Spaces." *Journal of Modern History* 65 (3): 473–511.

———. 1999. *Imperial Visions: Nationalist Imagination and Geographical Expansion in the Russian Far East, 1840–1865*. Cambridge: Cambridge University Press.

Baucom, Ian. 1999. *Out of Place: Englishness, Empire, and the Locations of Identity*. Princeton, NJ: Princeton University Press.

Bauer, Otto. [1907, 1924] 2000. *The Question of Nationalities and Social Democracy*. Edited by Ephraim J. Nimni. Translated by Joseph O'Donnell. Minneapolis: University of Minnesota Press.

Baumgart, Winfried. 1982. *Imperialism: The Idea and Reality of British and French Colonial Expansion, 1880–1914*. Translated by Ben V. Mast. Oxford: Oxford University Press.

Baycroft, Timothy. 2004. "The Empire and the Nation: The Place of Colonial Images in the Republican Visions of the French Nation." In Evans 2004: 148–60.

———. 2008. *France*. London: Hodder Education.

Baycroft, Timothy, and Mark Hewitson, eds. 2009. *What Is a Nation? Europe 1789–1914*. Oxford: Oxford University Press.

Bayly, C. A. 1989. *Imperial Meridian: The British Empire and the World, 1780–1830*. London: Longman.

———. 2004. *The Birth of the Modern World 1780–1914: Global Connections and Comparisons*. Oxford: Blackwell.

Baynham, E. J. 2009. "Power, Passions, and Patrons: Alexander, Charles Le Brun, and Oliver Stone." In Heckel and Tritle 2009: 294–310.

Beales, Derek. 1987. *Joseph II*. Vol. 1, *In the Shadow of Maria Theresa*. Cambridge: Cambridge University Press.

———. 2009. *Joseph II*. Vol. 2, *Against the World, 1780–1790*. Cambridge: Cambridge University Press.

Beard, Mary. 2015. *S.P.Q.R.: A History of Ancient Rome*. New York: Liveright.

Becker, Seymour. 1986. "The Muslim East in Nineteenth-Century Russian Popular Historiography." *Central Asian Survey* 5 (3/4): 25–47.

———. 1991. "Russia between East and West: The Intelligentsia, Russian National Identity and the Asian Borderlands." *Central Asian Survey* 10 (4): 47–64.

————. 2000. "Russia and the Concept of Empire." *Ab Imperio* 3–4: 329–42.

Beissinger, Mark R. 1995 "The Persisting Ambiguity of Empire." *Post-Soviet Affairs* 11 (2): 149–84.

————. 2002. *Nationalist Mobilization and the Collapse of the Soviet State.* Cambridge: Cambridge University Press.

————. 2006. "Soviet Empire as 'Family Resemblance.'" *Slavic Review* 65 (2): 294–303.

————. 2008. "The Persistence of Empire in Eurasia." *NewsNet* 48 (1): 1–8.

Belich, James. 2009. *Replenishing the Earth: The Settler Revolution and the Rise of the Anglo-World, 1783–1939.* Oxford: Oxford University Press.

Bell, David. 2003. *The Cult of the Nation in France: Inventing Nationalism, 1680–1800.* Cambridge, MA: Harvard University Press.

Bell, Duncan. 2007. *The Idea of Greater Britain: Empire and the Future of World Order, 1860–1900.* Princeton, NJ: Princeton University Press.

Beller, Steven. 1989. *Vienna and the Jews, 1867–1938: A Cultural History.* Cambridge: Cambridge University Press.

————. 2001. "Kraus's Firework: State Consciousness Raising in the 1908 Jubilee Parade in Vienna and the Problem of Austrian Identity." In Bucur and Wingfield 2001: 46–71.

————. 2011. *A Concise History of Austria.* Cambridge: Cambridge University Press.

Belmessous, Saliha. 2013. *Assimilation and Empire: Uniformity in French and British Colonies, 1541–1954.* Oxford: Oxford University Press.

Benians, E. A. 1925. "Adam Smith's Project of an Empire." *Cambridge Historical Journal* 1 (3): 249–83.

Bennison, Amira K. 2002. "Muslim Universalism and Western Globalization." In *Globalization in World History*, edited by A. G. Hopkins, 74–97. London: Pimlico.

Benson, Robert L. 1982. "Political *Renovatio*: Two Models from Roman Antiquity." In *Renaissance and Renewal in the Twelfth Century*, edited by Robert L. Benson and Giles Constable, with Carol D. Lanham, 339–86. Cambridge, MA: Harvard University Press.

Berdyaev, Nicholas. [1937] 1960. *The Origin of Russian Communism.* Ann Arbor: University of Michigan Press.

————. [1947] 1992. *The Russian Idea.* Translated by R. M. French. Hudson, NY: Lindisfarne Press.

Bérenger, Jean. 1994. *A History of the Habsburg Empire 1273–1700.* Translated by C. A. Simpson. London: Longman.

————. 1997. *A History of the Habsburg Empire 1700–1918.* Translated by C. A. Simpson. London and New York: Longman.

Berezin, Mabel. 1997. *Making the Fascist Self: The Political Culture of Interwar Italy.* Ithaca, NY: Cornell University Press.

Berlin, Isaiah. 1979. *Russian Thinkers.* Harmondsworth: Penguin Books.

Berman, Marshall. 1983. *All That Is Solid Melts into Air: The Experience of Modernity.* London: Verso.

Bernal, Martin. 1987. *Black Athena: The Afroasiatic Roots of Classical Civilization.* Vol. 1, *The Fabrication of Ancient Greece 1785–1985.* New Brunswick, NJ: Rutgers University Press.

Betts, Raymond F. 1961. *Assimilation and Association in French Colonial Theory 1890–1914.* New York: Columbia University Press.

———. 1971. "The Allusion to Rome in British Imperialist Thought of the Late Nineteenth and Early Twentieth Centuries." *Victorian Studies* 15 (2): 149–59.

———. 1978. *Tricouleur: The French Overseas Empire.* London: Gordon and Cremonisi.

———. 1991. *France and Decolonisation 1900–1960.* Houndmills, Basingstoke: Macmillan.

———. 2004. *Decolonization.* 2nd ed. New York: Routledge.

Biceno, Hugh. 2003. *Crescent and Cross: The Battle of Lepanto 1571.* London: Cassell.

Bickers, Robert, ed. 2010. *Settlers and Expatriates: Britons over the Seas.* Oxford: Oxford University Press.

Birnbaum, Pierre. [1998] 2001. *The Idea of France.* Translated by M. B. DeBevoise. New York: Hill and Wang.

Bivona, Daniel. 1998. *British Imperial Literature, 1870–1940: Writing and the Administration of Empire.* Cambridge: Cambridge University Press.

Bleich, Erik. 2003. *Race Politics in Britain and France: Ideas and Policy-Making since the 1960s.* Cambridge: Cambridge University Press.

Blitstein, Peter A. 2001. "Nation-Building or Russification? Obligatory Russian Instruction in the Soviet Non-Russian School, 1938–1953." In Suny and Martin 2001: 253–74.

———. 2006. "Cultural Diversity and the Interwar Conjuncture: Soviet Nationality Policy in Its Comparative Context." *Slavic Review* 65 (2): 273–93.

Bloch, Marc. 1967. "The Empire and the Idea of Empire under the Hohenstaufen." In *Land and Work in Medieval Europe: Selected Papers by Marc Bloch,* translated by J. E. Anderson, 1–43. Berkeley: University of California Press.

Bodelsen, C. A. [1924] 1960. *Studies in Mid-Victorian Imperialism.* London: Heinemann.

Bodin, Jean. [1586] 1962. *The Six Bookes of a Commonweale.* Translated by Richard Knolles (1606). Edited by Kenneth Douglas McRae. Cambridge, MA: Harvard University Press.

Boerner, Peter, ed. 1986. *Concepts of National Identity: An Interdisciplinary Dialogue.* Baden-Baden: Nomos Verlagsgesellschaft.

Bosworth, A. B. 1993. *Conquest and Empire: The Reign of Alexander the Great.* Cambridge: Cambridge University Press.

Bosworth, A. B., and E. J. Baynham, eds. 2000. *Alexander the Great in Fact and Fiction.* Oxford: Oxford University Press.

Bosworth, C. E. 1982. "The Concept of *Dhimma* in Early Islam." In Braude and Lewis 1982a: 1:37–51.

Bowersock, G. W., John Clive, and Stephen R. Graubard, eds. 1977. *Edward Gibbon and the Decline and Fall of the Roman Empire.* Cambridge, MA: Harvard University Press.

Bowie, E. L. 1970. "Greeks and Their Past in the Second Sophistic." *Past and Present* 46: 3–41.

Bradley, Mark, ed. 2010a. *Classics and Imperialism in the British Empire.* Oxford: Oxford University Press.

———. 2010b. "Tacitus' *Agricola* and the Conquest of Britain: Representations of Empire in Victorian and Edwardian England." In Bradley 2010a: 123–57.

Brandenberger, David. 2001. "'. . . It Is Imperative to Advance Russian Nationalism as the First Priority': Debates within the Stalinist Ideological Establishment, 1941–1945." In Suny and Martin 2001: 275–99.

Braude, Benjamin. 1982. "Foundation Myths of the *Millet* System." In Braude and Lewis 1982a: 1:69–88.

Braude, Benjamin, and Bernard Lewis, eds. 1982a. *Christians and Jews in the Ottoman Empire: The Functioning of a Plural Society.* 2 vols. New York: Holmes and Meier.

———. 1982b. "Introduction." In Braude and Lewis 1982a: 1:1–34.

Braudel, Fernand. 1975. *The Mediterranean and the Mediterranean World in the Age of Philip II.* 2 vols. Translated from the French by Sian Reynolds. London: Fontana.

Bremmer, Ian, and Ray Taras, eds. 1997. *New States, New Politics: Building the Post-Soviet Nations.* Cambridge: Cambridge University Press.

Breuilly, John. 2000. "Nationalism and the History of Ideas." *Proceedings of the British Academy* 105: 187–223.

Breyfogle, Nicholas B., Abby Schrader, and Willard Sunderland, eds. 2007. *Peopling the Russian Periphery: Borderland Colonization in Eurasian History.* London: Routledge.

Bridge, Carl, and Kent Fedorowich, eds. 2003. *The British World: Diaspora, Culture and Identity.* London: Frank Cass.

Brodsky, Joseph. 1987. "A Guide to a Renamed City." In *Less than One: Selected Essays*, 69–94. London: Penguin Books.

Brooks, Jeffrey. 1985. *When Russia Learned to Read: Literacy and Popular Culture, 1861–1917.* Princeton, NJ: Princeton University Press.

Brower, Daniel R. 1997. "Islam and Ethnicity: Russian Colonial Policy in Turkestan." In Brower and Lazzerini 1997: 115–35.

Brower, Daniel R., and Edward J. Lazzerini, eds. 1997. *Russia's Orient: Imperial Borderlands and Peoples, 1700–1917.* Bloomington: Indiana University Press.

Brown, Judith M. 1999. "India." In Brown and Louis 1999: 421–46.

Brown, Judith M., and Wm. Roger Louis, eds. 1999. *The Oxford History of the British Empire.* Vol. 4, *The Twentieth Century.* Oxford: Oxford University Press.

Brown, Peter. 2003. *The Rise of Western Christendom.* 2nd ed. Malden, MA: Blackwell Publishing.

Brown, Roger Glenn. 1970. *Fashoda Reconsidered: The Impact of Domestic Politics on French Policy in Africa 1893–1898.* Baltimore: Johns Hopkins University Press.

Brubaker, Rogers. 1992. *Citizenship and Nationhood in France and Germany.* Cambridge, MA: Harvard University Press.

———. 1996. *Nationalism Reframed: Nationhood and the National Question in the New Europe.* Cambridge: Cambridge University Press.

———. 2015. *Grounds for Difference.* Cambridge, MA: Harvard University Press.

Brubaker, Rogers, Margit Feischmidt, Jon Fox, and Liana Grancea. 2006. *Nationalist Politics and Everyday Ethnicity in a Transylvanian Town.* Princeton, NJ: Princeton University Press.

Bruckmüller, Ernst. 1993. "The National Identity of the Austrians." In Teich and Porter 1993: 196–227.

———. 2003. *The Austrian Nation: Cultural Consciousness and Socio-Political Processes.* Translated by Lowell A. Bangerter. Riverside, CA: Ariadne Press.

Brundage, Anthony, and Richard A. Cosgrove. 2007. *The Great Tradition: Constitutional History and National Identity in Britain and the United States, 1870–1960.* Stanford, CA: Stanford University Press.

Brunschwig, Henri. 1966. *French Colonialism 1871–1914: Myths and Realities.* Translated by William Glanville Brown. Introduction by Ronald E. Robinson. New York: Frederick A. Praeger.

Brunt, P. A. 1965. "Reflections on British and Roman Imperialism." *Comparative Studies in Society and History* 7 (3): 267–88.

———. 1978. "Laus Imperii." In Garnsey and Whittaker 1978a: 159–91.

———. 1990a. *Roman Imperial Themes*. Oxford: Clarendon Press.

———. 1990b. "The Romanization of the Local Ruling Classes in the Roman Empire." In Brunt 1990a: 267–81.

———. 1990c. "Roman Imperial Illusions." In Brunt 1990a: 433–80.

Bryce, James. [1901] 1914. *The Ancient Roman Empire and the British Empire in India*, and *The Diffusion of Roman and English Law throughout the World: Two Historical Studies*. London: Oxford University Press.

Buckner, P., and D. Francis, eds. 2003. *Rediscovering the British World: Culture and Diaspora*. London: Taylor and Francis.

Bucur, Maria, and Nancy M. Wingfield, eds. 2001. *Staging the Past: The Politics of Commemoration in Habsburg Central Europe, 1848 to the Present*. West Lafayette, IN: Purdue University Press.

Buettner, Elizabeth. 2004. *Empire Families: Britons and Late Imperial India*. Oxford: Oxford University Press.

Burbank, Jane. 2006. "An Imperial Rights Regime: Law and Citizenship in the Russian Empire." *Kritika* 7 (3): 397–431.

———. 2007a. "The Rights of Difference: Law and Citizenship in the Russian Empire." In Stoler, McGranahan, and Perdue 2007: 77–111.

———. 2007b. "Thinking Like an Empire: Estate, Law, and Rights in the Early Twentieth Century." In Burbank, von Hagen, and Remnev 2007: 196–217.

Burbank, Jane, and Frederick Cooper. 2010. *Empires in World History: Power and the Politics of Difference*. Princeton, NJ: Princeton University Press.

Burbank, Jane, Mark von Hagen, and Anatolyi Remnev, eds. 2007. *Russian Empire: Space, People, Power, 1700–1930*. Bloomington: Indiana University Press.

Burke, Peter. 1977. "Tradition and Experience: The Idea of Decline from Bruni to Gibbon." In Bowersock, Clive, and Graubard 1977: 87–102.

Burn, A. R. 1962. *Alexander the Great and the Hellenistic World*. New ed. New York: Collier Books.

Burnham, James. [1941] 1962. *The Managerial Revolution*. Harmondsworth: Penguin Books.

Burns, Thomas S. 2009. *Rome and the Barbarians, 100 B.C.–A. D. 400*. Baltimore: Johns Hopkins University Press.

Burroughs, Peter. 1999. "Imperial Institutions and the Government of Empire." In Porter 1999: 170–97.

Burton, Antoinette, ed. 2001. *Politics and Empire in Victorian Britain: A Reader*. New York: Palgrave.

———, ed. 2003. *After the Imperial Turn: Thinking with and through the Nation*. Durham, NC: Duke University Press.

———. 2011. *Empire in Question: Reading, Writing, and Teaching British Imperialism*. Durham, NC: Duke University Press.

Bushkovitch, Paul. 1986. "The Formation of National Consciousness in Early Modern Russia." *Harvard Ukrainian Studies* 10 (3/4): 355–76.

———. 2003. "What Is Russia? Russian National Identity and the State, 1500–1917." In Kappeler et al. 2003: 144–61.

Cain, P. J. 1999. "Economics and Empire: The Metropolitan Context." In Porter 1999: 31–52.

———. 2007. "Empire and the Languages of Character and Virtue in Later Victorian and Edwardian England." *Modern Intellectual History* 4 (2): 249–73.

Cain, P. J., and A. G. Hopkins. 2002. *British Imperialism 1688–2000*. 2nd ed. Harlow, Essex: Longman.

Calhoun, Craig, Frederick Cooper, and Kevin W. Moore, eds. 2006. *Lessons of Empire: Imperial Histories and American Power*. New York: The New Press.

Cameron, Alan. 1970. *Claudian: Poetry and Propaganda at the Court of Honorius*. Oxford: Clarendon Press.

Cameron, Averil. 2006. *The Byzantines*. Oxford: Blackwell Publishers.

Campbell, Elena. 2007. "The Muslim Question in Late Imperial Russia." In Burbank, von Hagen, and Remnev 2007: 320–47.

Cannadine, David. 2001. *Ornamentalism: How the British Saw Their Empire*. Oxford: Oxford University Press.

Canny, Nicholas. 1973. "The Ideology of English Colonization: From Ireland to America." *William and Mary Quarterly* 30: 575–98.

———. 1988. *Kingdom and Colony: Ireland in the Atlantic World, 1560–1800*. Baltimore: Johns Hopkins University Press.

———. 2003. *Making Ireland British 1580–1650*. Oxford: Oxford University Press.

Canny, Nicholas, and Anthony Pagden, eds. 1987. *Colonial Identity in the Atlantic World, 1500–1800*. Princeton, NJ: Princeton University Press.

Carlyle, Thomas. [1840] 1971. "Chartism." In *Thomas Carlyle: Selected Writings*, edited by Alan Shelston, 151–232. Harmondsworth: Penguin Books.

Carr, E. H. 1956. "'Russia and Europe' as a Theme of Russian History." In *Essays Presented to Sir Lewis Namier*, edited by Richard Pares and A.J.P. Taylor, 357–93. London: Macmillan.

Carr, Raymond 2000. "Introduction." In *Spain: A History*, edited by Raymond Carr, 1–9. Oxford: Oxford University Press.

Carrère d'Encausse, Hélène. 1989. "Organizing and Colonizing the Conquered Territories." In Allworth 1989: 151–71.

———. 1992. *The Great Challenge: Nationalities and the Bolshevik State 1917–30*. Translated by Nancy Festinger. New York: Holmes and Meier.

Carter, Miranda. 2010. *The Three Emperors: Three Cousins, Three Empires and the Road to World War One*. London: Penguin Books.

Carter, Stephen. 1993. *Russian Nationalism*. London: Pinter Publishers.

Chafer, Tony, and Amanda Sackur, eds. 2002. *Promoting the Colonial Idea: Propaganda and Visions of Empire in France*. Houndmills, Basingstoke: Palgrave.

Chamberlain, Lesley. 2015. "New Eurasians." *Times Literary Supplement*, May 15, 14–15.

Chamberlain, M. E. 1999. *Decolonization: The Fall of the European Empires*. 2nd ed. Oxford: Blackwell Publishing.

Champion, Craige B., ed. 2004. *Roman Imperialism: Readings and Sources*. Malden, MA: Blackwell.

Chang, Sung-Hwan. 1974. "Russian Designs on the Far East." In Hunczak 1974: 299–321.

Chaudhuri, Nirad C. 1990. *Thy Hand, Great Anarch: India 1921–1952*. London: The Hogarth Press.

Cherniavsky, Michael. 1969. *Tsar and People: Studies in Russian Myths*. New York: Random House.

———, ed. 1970a. *The Structure of Russian History: Interpretive Essays*. New York: Random House.

———. 1970b. "The Old Believers and the New Religion." In Cherniavsky 1970a: 140–88.

———. 1975. "Russia." In *National Consciousness, History, and Political Culture in Early-Modern Europe*, ed. Orest Ranum, 118–43. Baltimore: Johns Hopkins University Press.

Chinn, Jeff, and Robert Kaiser. 1996. *Russians as the New Minority: Ethnicity and Nationalism in the Soviet Successor States*. Boulder, CO: Westview Press.

Chudoba, Bohdan. 1952. *Spain and the Empire 1519–1643*. Chicago: University of Chicago Press.

Chulos, Chris J. 2000. "Orthodox Identity at Russian Holy Places." In Chulos and Pirainen 2000: 28–50.

Chulos, Chris J., and Timo Pirainen, eds. 2000. *The Fall of an Empire, the Birth of a Nation*. Aldershot: Ashgate.

Chulos, Chris J., and Johannes Remy, eds. 2002. *Imperial and National Identities in Pre-revolutionary, Soviet, and Post-Soviet Russia*. Helsinki: Suomalaisen Kirjallisuuden Seura/ Finnish Literature Society.

Cirakman, Asli. 2001. "From Tyranny to Despotism: The Enlightenment's Unenlightened Image of the Turks." *International Journal of Middle East Studies* 33 (1): 49–68.

Clark, Bruce. 2006. *Twice a Stranger: The Mass Expulsions That Forged Modern Greece and Turkey*. Cambridge, MA: Harvard University Press.

Clarke, Peter. 2008. *The Last Thousand Days of the British Empire: Churchill, Roosevelt, and the Birth of the Pax Americana*. New York: Bloomsbury Press.

Claudian. [c. 370–404 CE] 1922. *Claudian*. Translated by Maurice Platnauer. 2 vols. Loeb Classical Library. Cambridge, MA: Harvard University Press.

Cleary, Joe. 2006. "Postcolonial Ireland." In Kenny 2006c: 251–88.

———. 2007. "Amongst Empires: A Short History of Ireland and Empire Studies in International Context." *Eire-Ireland: A Journal of Irish Studies* 42 (1/2): 11–57.

Clogg, Richard. 1982. "The Greek *Millet* in the Ottoman Empire." In Braude and Lewis 1982a: 1:185–207.

Cobban, Alfred. 1961. *A History of Modern France*. Vol. 2, *1799–1945*. Harmondsworth: Penguin Books.

Coetzee, J. M. 2002. "Emperor of Nostalgia." *New York Review of Books*, February 28, 18–21.

Cohen, Ariel. 1996. *Russian Imperialism: Development and Crisis*. Westport, CT: Praeger.

Cohen, Gary B. 2007. "Nationalist Politics and the Dynamics of State and Civil Society in the Habsburg Monarchy, 1867–1914." *Central European History* 40 (2): 241–78.

Cohn, Bernard S. 1983. "Representing Authority in Victorian India." In Hobsbawm and Ranger 1984: 165–209.

Cohn, Bernard S., and Nicholas B. Dirks. 1988. "Beyond the Fringe: The Nation State, Colonialism, and the Technologies of Power." *Journal of Historical Sociology* 1 (2): 224–29.

Cole, Douglas. 1971. "The Problem of 'Nationalism' and 'Imperialism' in British Settlement Colonies." *Journal of British Studies* 10 (2): 160–82.

Cole, Juan. 2007. *Napoleon's Egypt: Invading the Middle East*. New York: Palgrave Macmillan.

Cole, Laurence, and Daniel Unowsky, eds. 2007. *The Limits of Loyalty: Imperial Symbolism, Popular Allegiances, and State Patriotism in the Late Habsburg Monarchy*. New York: Berghahn Books.

Colley, Linda. [1992] 1994. *Britons: Forging the Nation 1707–1837*. London: Pimlico.

———. [2002] 2004. *Captives: Britain, Empire, and the World, 1600–1850*. New York: Anchor Books.

Collins, James B. 1995. *The State in Early Modern France*. Cambridge: Cambridge University Press.

Collins, Robert O., James McDonald Burns, and Erik Kristofer Ching, eds. 1994. *Historical Problems of Imperial Africa*. Princeton, NJ: Marcus Wiener Publishers.

Conklin, Alice L. 1997. *A Mission to Civilize: The Republican Idea of Empire in France and West Africa, 1895–1930*. Stanford, CA: Stanford University Press.

Conklin, Alice L., Sarah Fishman, and Robert Zaretsky. 2015. *France and Its Empire since 1870*. 2nd ed. New York: Oxford University Press.

Connor, Walker. 1984. *The National Question in Marxist-Leninist Theory and Strategy*. Princeton, NJ: Princeton University Press.

Conquest, Robert, ed. 1986. *The Last Empire: Nationality and the Soviet Future*. Stanford, CA: Hoover Institution Press.

Constantine, Stephen. 1986. "'Bringing the Empire Alive': The Empire Marketing Board and Imperial Propaganda, 1926–33." In MacKenzie 1986: 192–231.

———. 1999. "Migrants and Settlers." In Brown and Louis 1999: 163–87.

Cooke, James L. 1973. *New French Imperialism 1880–1910: The Third Republic and Colonial Expansion*. Newton Abbot: David and Charles; Hamden, CT: Archon Books.

Cooper, Frederick. 2005. "States, Empires, and Political Imagination." in *Colonialism in Question*, 153–203. Berkeley: University of California Press.

———. 2007. "Provincializing France." In Stoler, McGranahan, and Perdue 2007: 341–77.

———. 2014. *Citizenship between Empire and Nation: Remaking France and French Africa, 1945–1960*. Princeton, NJ: Princeton University Press.

Cooper, Frederick, and Ann Laura Stoler, eds. 1997. *Tensions of Empire: Colonial Cultures in a Bourgeois World*. Berkeley: University of California Press.

Cornwall, Mark. 2000. *The Undermining of Austria-Hungary: The Battle for Hearts and Minds*. Houndmills: Macmillan.

———, ed. 2002. *The Last Years of Austria-Hungary: A Multi-National Experiment in Early Twentieth-Century Europe*. Exeter: University of Exeter Press.

———. 2009. "The Habsburg Monarchy." In Baycroft and Hewitson 2009: 171–91.

Coyle, J. Kevin. 1987. "Augustine and the Apocalyptic: Thoughts on the Fall of Rome, the Book of Revelation, and the End of the World." *Florilegium* 9: 1–34.

Cracraft, James. 2004. *The Petrine Revolution in Russian Culture*. Cambridge, MA: Harvard University Press.

Cramb, J. A. [1900] 1915. *The Origins and Destiny of Imperial Britain and Nineteenth Century Europe*. New York: E. P. Dutton and Company.

Creighton, John. 2006. *Britannia: The Creation of a Roman Province*. London: Routledge.

Crews, Robert. 2003. "Empire and the Confessional State: Islam and Religious Politics in Nineteenth-Century Russia." *American Historical Review* 108 (1): 50–83.

———. 2006. *For Prophet and Tsar: Islam and Empire in Russia and Central Asia*. Cambridge, MA: Harvard University Press.

Crisp, Olga, and Linda Edmondson, eds. 1989. *Civil Rights in Imperial Russia*. Oxford: Clarendon Press.

Cromer, Earl of. 1910. *Ancient and Modern Imperialism*. New York: Longmans, Green and Co.

Crone, Patricia. 2006. "Imperial Trauma: The Case of the Arabs." *Common Knowledge* 12 (1): 107–16.

Crosby, Alfred W. 1972. *The Columbian Exchange: Biological and Cultural Consequences of 1492*. Westport, CT: Greenwood Press.

Crowder, Michael. [1964] 1994. "Indirect Rule—French and British Style." In Collins, Burns, and Ching 1994: 179–88.

Cunningham, Michele. 2001. *Mexico and the Foreign Policy of Napoleon III*. Houndmills: Palgrave.

Dale, Stephen F. 2010. *The Muslim Empires of the Ottomans, Safavids, and Mughals*. Cambridge: Cambridge University Press.

Darian-Smith, Kate, Patricia Grimshaw, and Stuart Macintyre, eds. 2007. *Britishness Abroad: Transnational Movements and Imperial Cultures*. Melbourne: Melbourne University Press.

Darling, Linda. 2000. "Contested Territory: Ottoman Holy War in Comparative Context." *Studia Islamica* 91: 133–63.

Darwin, John. 1980. "Imperialism in Decline? Tendencies in British Imperial Policy between the Wars." *Historical Journal* 23 (3): 657–79.

———. 1984. "British Decolonization since 1945: A Pattern or a Puzzle?" *Journal of Imperial and Commonwealth History* 12 (2): 187–209.

———. 1986. "The Fear of Falling: British Politics and Imperial Decline since 1900." *Transactions of the Royal Historical Society*, 5th ser., 36: 27–43.

———. 1988. *Britain and Decolonisation: The Retreat from Empire in the Post-War World*. Houndmills: Macmillan.

———. 1991. *The End of the British Empire: The Historical Debate*. Oxford: Basil Blackwell.

———. 1999. "A Third British Empire? The Dominion Idea in Imperial Politics." In Brown and Louis 1999: 64–87.

———. 2005. "Bored by the Raj." *Times Literary Supplement*, February 18, 5–6.

———. 2008. *After Tamerlane: The Rise and Fall of Global Empires, 1400–2000*. London: Penguin Books.

———. 2009. *The Empire Project: The Rise and Fall of the British World-System 1830–1970*. Cambridge: Cambridge University Press.

———. 2012. *Unfinished Empire: The Global Expansion of Britain*. London: Allen Lane.

Daughton, J. P. 2006. *An Empire Divided: Religion, Republicanism, and the Making of French Colonialism, 1880–1914*. Oxford: Oxford University Press.

Davies, R. R. 2000. *The First English Empire: Power and Identities in the British Isles 1093–1343*. Oxford: Oxford University Press.

Dawisha, Karen, and Bruce Parrott, eds. 1997. *The End of Empire? The Transformation of the USSR in Comparative Perspective*. Armonk, NY: M. E. Sharpe.

Deák, István. 1990. *Beyond Nationalism: A Social and Political History of the Habsburg Officer Corps, 1848–1918*. New York: Oxford University Press.

———. 1997. "The Habsburg Empire." In Barkey and von Hagen 1997: 129–41.

———. 2012. "Where's Charlemagne When We Need Him?" *New York Times*, July 1, SR4.

Deak, John. 2014. "The Great War and the Forgotten Realm: The Habsburg Monarchy and the First World War." *Journal of Modern History* 86 (2): 336–80.

———. 2015. *Forging a Multinational State: State Making in Imperial Austria from the Enlightenment to the First World War*. Stanford, CA: Stanford University Press.

de Gantes, Gilles. 2002. "Migration to Indochina: Proof of the Popularity of Colonial Empire?" In Chafer and Sackur 2002: 15–28.

Dench, Emma. 2005. *Romulus' Asylum: Roman Identities from the Age of Alexander to the Age of Hadrian*. Oxford: Oxford University Press.

Deringil, Selim. 1993. "The Ottoman Origins of Kemalist Nationalism." *European History Quarterly* 23 (2): 165–91.

———. 1999. *The Well-Protected Domains: Ideology and the Legitimation of Power in the Ottoman Empire 1876–1909*. London: I. B. Tauris.

Derrick, Jonathan. 2002. "The Dissenters: Anti-Colonialism in France, c. 1900–40." In Chafer and Sackur 2002: 53–68.

Deschamps, Hubert Jules. [1963] 1994. "Association and Indirect Rule." In Collins, Burns, and Ching 1994: 165–78.

Deudney, Daniel. 2001. "Greater Britain or Greater Synthesis? Seeley, Mackinder, and Wells on Britain in the Global Industrial Era." *Review of International Studies* 27: 187–208.

Díaz, Bernal. 1963. *The Conquest of New Spain*. Edited and translated by J. M. Cohen. London: Penguin Books.

Di Cosmo, Nicola. 1998. "Qing Colonial Administration in Inner Asia." *International History Review* 20 (2): 253–504.

Dilke, Sir Charles Wentworth. 1869. *Greater Britain: A Record of Travel in English-Speaking Countries during 1866 and 1867*. 3rd ed. London: Macmillan and Co.

———. 1899. *The British Empire*. London: Chatto and Windus.

Dilley, A. R. 2008. "The Economics of Empire." In Stockwell 2008a: 101–29.

Dixon, Simon. 1996. "The Russians and the Russian Question." In Smith 1996: 47–74.

———. 1998. "The Past in the Present: Contemporary Russian Nationalism in Historical Perspective." In Hosking and Service 1998: 149–77.

Donnelly, Alton. 1988. "The Mobile Steppe Frontier: The Russian Conquest and Colonization of Bashkiria and Kazakhstan to 1850." In Rywkin 1988: 189–207.

Dowling, Linda. 1985. "Roman Decadence and Victorian Historiography." *Victorian Studies* 28 (4): 579–607.

Doyle, Michael W. 1986. *Empires*. Ithaca, NY: Cornell University Press.

Duara, Prasenjit, ed. 2004. *Decolonization: Perspectives from Now and Then*. London: Routledge.

Dumont, Paul. 1982. "Jewish Communities in Turkey during the Last Decades of the Nineteenth Century in the Light of the Archives of the Alliance Israélite Universelle." In Braude and Lewis 1982a: 1:209–42.

Duncan, Peter J. S. 2000. *Russian Messianism: Third Rome, Revolution, Communism and After*. London: Routledge.

Dunlop, John B. 1983. *The Faces of Contemporary Russian Nationalism*. Princeton, NJ: Princeton University Press.

———. 1993. *The Rise of Russia and the Fall of the Soviet Union*. Princeton, NJ: Princeton University Press.

———. 1997. "Russia: In Search of an Identity?" In Bremmer and Taras 1997: 29–95.

Dunne, Tom. 1982. "*La trahison des clercs*: British Intellectuals and the First Home-Rule Crisis." *Irish Historical Studies* 23 (90): 134–73.

Duverger, Maurice, ed. 1980. *Le Concept d'empire*. Paris: Presses Universitaires de France.

Ebel, Charles. 1976. *Transalpine Gaul: The Emergence of a Roman Province*. Leiden: E. J. Brill.

Eddy, John, and Deryck Schreuder, eds. 1988. *The Rise of Colonial Nationalism: Australia, New Zealand, Canada and South Africa First Assert Their Nationalities, 1880–1914*. Sydney: Allen and Unwin.

Edwards, Catherine. 1999a. "Introduction: Shadows and Fragments." In Edwards 1999b: 1–18.

———. 1999b. *Roman Presences: Receptions of Rome in European Culture, 1789–1945*. Cambridge: Cambridge University Press.

———. 1999c. "Translating Empire? Macaulay's Rome." In Edwards 1999b: 70–87.

Edwards, Catherine, and Greg Woolf. 2003. "Cosmopolis: Rome as World City." In *Rome the Cosmopolis*, edited by Catherine Edwards and Greg Woolf, 1–20. Cambridge: Cambridge University Press.

Eisenmann, Louis. 1910. "Austria-Hungary." In *The Cambridge Modern History*, vol. 12, *The Latest Age*, edited by A. W. Ward, G. W. Prothero, and Stanley Leathes, 174–212. Cambridge: At the University Press.

Eisenstadt, S. N. [1963] 1993. *The Political Systems of Empires*. New Brunswick, NJ: Transaction Publishers.

Eley, Geoff, and Ronald Grigor Suny, eds. 1996. *Becoming National: A Reader*. New York: Oxford University Press.

Eliot, T. S. 1957. "Virgil and the Christian World." In *On Poetry and Poets*, 122–40. London: Faber and Faber.

Elkins, Caroline. 2005. *Imperial Reckoning: The Untold Story of Britain's Gulag in Kenya*. New York: Henry Holt.

Elliott, J. H. 1970. *Imperial Spain 1469–1716*. London: Penguin Books.

———. 1984. *Richelieu and Olivares*. Cambridge: Cambridge University Press.

———. 1989a. *Spain and Its World 1500–1700: Selected Essays*. New Haven, CT: Yale University Press.

———. 1989b. "Spain and Its Empire in the Sixteenth and Seventeenth Centuries." In Elliott 1989a: 7–26.

———. 1989c. "The Decline of Spain." In Elliott 1989a: 215–40.

———. 1989d. "Self-Perception and Decline in Early Seventeenth-Century Spain." In Elliott 1989a: 241–61.

———. 1989e. "Art and Decline in Early Seventeenth-Century Spain." In Elliott 1989a: 263–86.

———. 1992. "A Europe of Composite Monarchies." *Past and Present* 137: 48–71.

———. 1993. "Ottoman-Habsburg Rivalry: The European Perspective." In Inalcik and Kafadar 1993: 153–62.

———. 2006. *Empires of the Atlantic World: Britain and Spain in the Americas, 1492–1830*. New Haven, CT: Yale University Press.

Elton, G. R., ed. 1982. *The Tudor Constitution: Documents and Commentary*. 2nd ed. Cambridge: Cambridge University Press.

Emerson, Rupert. [1960] 1962. *From Empire to Nation: The Rise to Self-Assertion of Asian and African Peoples*. Boston: Beacon Press.

———. 1969. "Colonialism." *Journal of Contemporary History* 4 (1): 3–16.

Englund, Steven. 2004. *Napoleon: A Political Life*. Cambridge, MA: Harvard University Press.

Epstein, Mark A. 1982. "Leadership of the Ottoman Jews in the Fifteenth and Sixteenth Centuries." In Braude and Lewis 1982a: 101–15.

Etherington, Norman. 1982. "Reconsidering Theories of Imperialism." *History and Theory* 21 (1): 1–36.

———. 1984. *Theories of Imperialism: War, Conquest and Capital*. London: Croom Helm.

Etkind, Alexander. 2011. *Internal Colonization: Russia's Imperial Experience*. Cambridge: Polity Press.

Evans, Martin, ed. 2004. *Empire and Culture: The French Experience, 1830–1940*. Houndmills, Basingstoke: Palgrave Macmillan.

———. 2012. *Algeria: France's Undeclared War*. New York: Oxford University Press.

Evans, R.J.W. 1991. *The Making of the Habsburg Monarchy 1550–1700: An Interpretation*. 3rd impression. Oxford: Clarendon Press.

———. 1994. "Austrian Identity in Hungarian Perspective: The Nineteenth Century." In Robertson and Timms 1994: 27–36.

———. 2006. *Austria, Hungary, and the Habsburgs: Essays on Central Europe, c.1683–1867*. Oxford: Oxford University Press.

Evans, R.J.W., Michael Schaich, and Peter H. Wilson, eds. 2011. *The Holy Roman Empire 1495–1806*. Oxford: Oxford University Press.

Faber, Richard. 1966. *The Vision and the Need: Late Victorian Imperialist Aims*. London: Faber and Faber.

Fanning, Steven. 1991. "Bede, *Imperium*, and the Bretwaldas." *Speculum* 66 (1): 1–26.

Farmer, Paul. 1960. "The Second Empire in France." In *The New Cambridge Modern History*, vol. 10, *The Zenith of European Power 1830–1870*, edited by J.P.T. Bury, 442–67. Cambridge: Cambridge University Press.

Faroqhi, Suraiya. 1994. "Crisis and Change, 1590–1699." In Inalcik with Quataert 1994: 413–636.

———. 1995. "Politics and Socio-Economic Change in the Later Sixteenth Century." In Kunt and Woodhead 1995: 91–113.

———. 2006. *The Ottoman Empire and the World Around It*. London: I. B. Tauris.

Favell, Adrian. 2001. *Philosophies of Integration: Immigration and the Idea of Citizenship in France and Britain*. 2nd ed. Houndmills: Palgrave.

Febvre, Lucien. 1973. "*Civilisation*: Evolution of a Word and a Group of Ideas." In *A New Kind of History: From the Writings of Febvre*, edited by Peter Burke, 219–57. New York: Harper and Row.

Fedorowich, Kent. 2008. "The British Empire on the Move, 1760–1914." In Stockwell 2008a: 63–100.

Fedorowich, Kent, and Andrew S. Thompson. 2013a. "Mapping the Contours of the British World: Empire, Migration and Identity." In Fedorowich and Thompson 2013b: 1–41.

———, eds. 2013b. *Empire, Migration and Identity in the British World*. Manchester: Manchester University Press.

Fedyshyn, Oleh S. 1980. "The Role of Russians among the New, Unified 'Soviet People.'" In Allworth 1980b: 149–58.

Feenstra, Robert. 1992. "Law." In Jenkyns 1992b: 399–420.

Ferguson, Niall. 2004. *Empire: How Britain Made the Modern World*. London: Penguin Books.

————. 2005. *Colossus: The Rise and Fall of the American Empire*. Paperback ed. New York: Penguin Books.

Ferro, Marc. 1997. *Colonization: A Global History*. Translated by K. D. Prithipaul. London: Routledge.

Fichtner, Paula Sutter. 2003. *The Habsburg Monarchy 1490–1848: Attributes of Empire*. Houndmills: Palgrave Macmillan.

Fieldhouse, D. K. 1961. "'Imperialism': An Historiographical Revision." *Economic History Review*, 2nd ser., 14 (2): 187–209.

————. 1999. "The Metropolitan Economics of Empire." In Brown and Louis 1999: 88–113.

Figes, Orlando. 2002. *Natasha's Dance: A Cultural History of Russia*. New York: Picador.

Findley, Carter Vaughn. 2005. *The Turks in World History*. New York: Oxford University Press.

————. 2010. *Turkey, Islam, Nationalism, and Modernity: A History, 1789–2007*. New Haven, CT: Yale University Press.

Finer, S. E. 1999. *The History of Government from the Earliest Times*. 3 vols. Oxford: Oxford University Press.

Finkel, Caroline. 2007. *Osman's Dream: The History of the Ottoman Empire*. New York: Basic Books.

Finley, M. I. 1976. "Colonies—an Attempt at a Typology." *Transactions of the Royal Historical Society*, 5th ser., 26: 167–88.

————. 1978a. "Empire in the Greco-Roman World." *Greece and Rome*, 2nd ser., 25 (1): 1–15.

————. 1978b. "The Fifth-Century Athenian Empire: A Balance Sheet." In Garnsey and Whittaker 1978a: 103–26.

Flenley, Paul. 1996. "From Soviet to Russian Identity: The Origins of Contemporary Russian Nationalism." In Jenkins and Sofos 1996: 223–50.

Folz, Robert. [1953] 1969. *The Concept of Empire in Western Europe from the Fifth to the Fourteenth Century*. Translated by Sheila Ann Ogilvie. London: Edward Arnold.

Fortna, Benjamin C. 2008. "The Reign of Abdülhamid II." In Kasaba 2008: 38–61.

Foster, Russell. 2015. *Mapping European Empire: Tabulae imperii Europaei*. London: Routledge.

Fradera, Josep. 2007. "Spain: The Genealogy of Modern Colonialism." In Aldrich 2007: 44–67.

Francis, Mark, ed. 1985. *The Viennese Enlightenment*. Beckenham, Kent: Croom Helm.

Frank, Alison. 2009. "The Pleasant and the Useful: Pilgrimage and Tourism in Habsburg Mariazell." *Austrian History Yearbook* 40: 157–82.

————. 2011. "Continental and Maritime Empires in an Age of Global Commerce." *East European Politics and Societies* 25 (4): 779–84.

Franklin, Simon, and Jonathan Shepard. 1996. *The Emergence of Rus 750–1200*. London: Longman.

Freeman, Edward A. 1886. *Greater Greece and Greater Britain and George Washington, the Expander of England: Two Lectures with an Appendix*. London: Macmillan and Co.

Freeman, Phillip. 1996. "British Imperialism and the Roman Empire." In Webster and Cooper 1996: 19–34.

Freeze, Gregory L. 1986. "The *soslovie* (Estate) Paradigm in Russian Social History." *American Historical Review* 91 (1): 11–36.

Frémeaux, Jacques. 2007. "France: Empire and Mère Patrie." In Aldrich 2007: 112–75.

Gaddis, John Lewis. 2004. *Surprise, Security, and the American Experience*. Cambridge, MA: Harvard University Press.

Gallagher, John. 1982. *The Decline, Revival and Fall of the British Empire: The Ford Lectures and Other Essays*. Edited by Anil Seal. Cambridge: Cambridge University Press.

Gallagher, John, and Ronald Robinson. 1953. "The Imperialism of Free Trade." *Economic History Review*, new ser., 6 (1): 1–15.

Gallagher, John, and Anil Seal. 1981. "Britain and India between the Wars." *Modern Asian Studies* 15 (3): 387–414.

Garnsey, P.D.A., and C. R. Whittaker, eds. 1978a. *Imperialism in the Ancient World*. Cambridge: Cambridge University Press.

———. 1978b. "Introduction." In Garnsey and Whittaker 1978a: 1–6.

Geary, Patrick J. 2002. *The Myth of Nations: The Medieval Origins of Europe*. Princeton, NJ: Princeton University Press.

Gellner, Ernest. 1983. *Nations and Nationalism*. Oxford: Blackwell.

———. 1994. "The Price of Velvet: Tomas Masaryk and Vaclav Havel." In *Encounters with Nationalism*, 114–29. Oxford: Blackwell.

———. 1998a. *Nationalism*. London: Phoenix.

———. 1998b. *Language and Solitude: Wittgenstein, Malinowski and the Habsburg Dilemma*. Cambridge: Cambridge University Press.

Georgacas, Demetrius John. 1947. "The Names of Constantinople." *Transactions and Proceedings of the American Philological Association* 78: 347–67.

Geraci, Robert P. 2001. *Window on the East: National and Imperial Identities in Late Tsarist Russia*. Ithaca, NY: Cornell University Press.

———. 2009. "Minorities and Empire." In *The Blackwell Companion to Russian History*, edited by Abbott Gleason, 243–60. Oxford: Blackwell.

Geraci, Robert P., and Michael Khodarkovsky, eds. 2001. *Of Religion and Empire: Missions, Conversion, and Tolerance in Tsarist Russia*. Ithaca, NY: Cornell University Press.

Gergel, Tanya, ed. 2004. *Alexander the Great: Selected Texts from Arrian, Curtius and Plutarch*. London: Penguin Books.

Gernet, Jacques. 1980. "Comment se présente en Chine le concept d'empire?" In Duverger 1980: 397–416.

Geyer, Dietrich. 1986. "Modern Imperialism? The Tsarist and Soviet Examples." In Mommsen and Osterhammel 1986: 49–62.

Gibb, H.A.R., and Harold Bowen. 1950–57. *Islamic Society and the West: A Study of the Impact of Western Civilization on Moslem Culture in the Near East*. Vol. 1, *Islamic Society in the Eighteenth Century*, in two parts. London: Oxford University Press.

Gibbon, Edward. [1776–88] 1995. *The History of the Decline and Fall of the Roman Empire*. 3 vols. Edited by David Womersley. London: Penguin Books.

Gibbons, Herbert A. 1916. *The Foundation of the Ottoman Empire*. Oxford: Clarendon Press.

Gibney, John. 2008. "Early Modern Ireland: A British Atlantic Colony?" *History Compass* 6: 1–11.

Gilbert, Martin. 2010. *In Ishmael's House: A History of Jews in Muslim Lands*. New Haven, CT: Yale University Press.

Gildea, Robert. 1994. *The Past in French History*. New Haven, CT: Yale University Press.

———. 2009. *The Children of the Revolution: The French 1799–1914*. London: Penguin Books.

Gilroy, Paul. 2004. *After Empire: Melancholia or Convivial Culture?* Abingdon, UK: Routledge.

Girardet, Raoul. 1972. *L'Idée coloniale en France de 1871 à 1962*. Paris: La Table Ronde.

Gladstone, W. E. 1876. *Bulgarian Horrors and the Question of the East*. London: John Murray.

Go, Julian. 2008. *American Empire and the Politics of Meaning: Elite Political Cultures in the Philippines and Puerto Rico during U.S. Colonialism*. Durham, NC: Duke University Press.

———. 2011. *Patterns of Empire: The British and American Empires, 1688 to the Present*. Cambridge: Cambridge University Press.

Göçek, Fatma Müge. 1993. "The Social Construction of an Empire: The Ottoman State under Süleymân the Magnificent." In Inalcik and Kafadar 1993: 93–108.

———. 1996. *Rise of the Bourgeoisie, Demise of Empire: Ottoman Westernization and Social Change*. New York: Oxford University Press.

———. 2015. *Denial of Violence: Ottoman Past, Turkish Present and Collective Violence against the Armenians, 1789–2009*. Oxford: Oxford University Press.

Goerg, Odile. 2002. "The French Provinces and 'Greater France.'" In Chafer and Sackur 2002: 82–101.

Goff, Barbara, ed. 2005. *Classics and Colonialism*. London: Duckworth.

Goffart, Walter. 2008. "Rome's Final Conquest: The Barbarians." *History Compass* 6 (3): 855–83.

Goffman, Daniel. 1994. "Ottoman Millets in the Early Seventeenth Century." *New Perspectives on Turkey* 11: 135–58.

———. 2002. *The Ottoman Empire and Early Modern Europe*. Cambridge: Cambridge University Press.

Goffman, Daniel, and Christopher Stroop. 2004. "Empire as Composite: The Ottoman Polity and the Typology of Dominion." In *Imperialisms: Historical and Literary Investigations, 1500–1900*, edited by Balachandra Rajan and Elizabeth Sauer, 129–45. New York: Palgrave Macmillan.

Gökalp, Ziya. 1959. *Turkish Nationalism and Western Civilization*. Translated with an introduction by Niyazi Berkes. New York: Columbia University Press.

Good, David F. 1984. *The Economic Rise of the Habsburg Empire, 1750–1914*. Berkeley: University of California Press.

Gorski, Philip S. 2000. "The Mosaic Moment: An Early Modernist Critique of Modernist Theories of Nationalism." *American Journal of Sociology* 105 (5): 1428–68.

Gott, Richard. 1989. "Little Englanders." In *Patriotism: The Making and Unmaking of British National Identity*, edited by Raphael Samuel, 3 vols., 1:90–102. London: Routledge.

Goubert, Pierre. 1970. *Louis XIV and Twenty Million Frenchmen*. Translated by Anne Carter. New York: Vintage Books.

Gould, Eliga. 1999. "A Virtual Nation: Greater Britain and the Imperial Legacy of the American Revolution." *American Historical Review* 104 (2): 476–89.

Grainger, J. H. 1986. *Patriotisms: Britain, 1900–1939*. London: Routledge and Kegan Paul.

Green, E.H.H. 1999. "The Political Economy of Empire, 1880–1914." In Porter 1999: 346–68.

Greenfeld, Liah. 1992. *Nationalism: Five Roads to Modernity*. Cambridge, MA: Harvard University Press.

Greenlee, J. G. 1976. "'A Successions of Seeleys': The 'Old School' Re-examined." *Journal of Imperial and Commonwealth History* 4 (3): 266–82.

———. 1979. "Imperial Studies and the Unity of Empire." *Journal of Imperial and Commonwealth History* 7 (3): 321–35.

Griffin, Miriam. 1990. "Claudius in Tacitus." *Classical Quarterly* 40 (2): 482–501.

Gruen, Erich S. 1992. *Culture and National Identity in Republican Rome*. Ithaca, NY: Cornell University Press.

Guroff, Gregory, and Alexander Guroff. 1994. "The Paradox of Russian National Identity." In *National Identity and Ethnicity in Russia and the New States of Eurasia*, edited by Roman Szporluk, 78–100. Armonk, NY: M. E. Sharpe.

Haberer, Erich. 1995. *Jews and Revolution in Nineteenth Century Russia*. Cambridge: Cambridge University Press.

Hagerman, C.A. 2009. "In the Footsteps of the Macedonian Conqueror: Alexander the Great and British India." *International Journal of the Classical Tradition* 16 (3/4): 344–92.

———. 2013. *Britain's Imperial Muse: The Classics, Imperialism, and the Indian Empire, 1784–1914*. Houndmills: Palgrave Macmillan.

Hall, Catherine, ed. 2000. *Cultures of Empire: A Reader*. Manchester: Manchester University Press.

———. 2002. *Civilising Subjects: Metropole and Colony in the English Imagination 1830–1867*. Chicago: University of Chicago Press.

Hall, Catherine, and Sonya O. Rose, eds. 2006. *At Home with the Empire: Metropolitan Culture and the Imperial World*. Cambridge: Cambridge University Press.

Haltzel, Michael H. 1977. "National Elites and Russification in the Baltic Provinces of the Russian Empire, 1861–1914: The Case of the Baltic Germans." In Rowney and Orchard 1977: 148–63.

Hamilton, Earl J. [1938] 1954. "The Decline of Spain." In *Essays in Economic History*, edited by E. M. Carus-Wilson, 1:215–26. London: Edward Arnold.

Hanioglu, M. Sukru. 2008. *A Brief History of the Late Ottoman Empire*. Princeton, NJ: Princeton University Press.

———. 2011. *Atatürk: An Intellectual Biography*. Princeton, NJ: Princeton University Press.

Hansen, Randall. 2000. *Citizenship and Immigration in Post-war Britain*. Oxford: Oxford University Press.

Hardt, Michael, and Antonio Negri. 2001. *Empire*. Cambridge, MA: Harvard University Press.

Hargreaves, Alec G. 2007. *Multi-Ethnic France: Immigration, Politics, Culture and Society*. 2nd ed. New York: Routledge.

Harlow, Barbara, and Mia Carter, eds. 2003a. *Archives of Empire*. Vol. 1, *From the East India Company to the Suez Canal*. Durham, NC: Duke University Press.

———, eds. 2003b. *Archives of Empire*. Vol. 2, *The Scramble for Africa*. Durham, NC: Duke University Press.

Harris, Bob. 1996. "'American idols': Empire, War and the Middling Ranks in Mid-Eighteenth-Century Britain." *Past and Present* 150: 111–41.

Hart, Jonathan. 2004. "'English' and French Imperial Designs in Canada and in a Larger Context." In Rajan and Sauer 2004: 187–202.

———. 2008. *Empires and Colonies*. Cambridge: Polity Press.

Hathaway, Jane. 1996. "Problems of Periodization in Ottoman History: The Fifteenth through the Eighteenth Centuries." *Turkish Studies Association Bulletin* 20 (2): 25–31.

Hazareesingh, Sudhir. 1994. *Political Traditions in Modern France*. Oxford: Oxford University Press.

Headley, John M. 1998. "The Habsburg World Empire and the Revival of Ghibellinism." In Armitage 1998: 45–79.

Heather, Peter. 2006. *The Fall of the Roman Empire*. London: Pan Macmillan.

Hechter, Michael. [1975] 1999. *Internal Colonialism: The Celtic Fringe in British National Development*. 2nd ed. New Brunswick, NJ: Transaction Books.

Heckel, Waldemar, and Lawrence A. Tritle, eds. 2009. *Alexander the Great: A New History*. Malden, MA: Wiley-Blackwell.

Heer, Friedrich. [1968] 2002. *The Holy Roman Empire*. Translated by Janet Sondheimer. London: Phoenix Press.

Hellberg-Hirn, Elena. 1998. *Soil and Soul: The Symbolic World of Russianness*. Aldershot: Ashgate.

Hentsch, Thierry. 1992. *Imagining the Middle East*. Translated by Fred A. Reed. Montreal: Black Rose Books.

Herrin, Judith. 2008. *Byzantium: The Surprising Life of a Medieval Empire*. London: Penguin Books.

Hess, Andrew C. 1972. "The Battle of Lepanto and Its Place in Mediterranean History." *Past and Present* 57: 53–73.

———. 1977. "The Forgotten Frontier: The Ottoman North African Provinces during the Eighteenth Century." In Naff and Owen 1977: 74–87.

———. 1978. *The Forgotten Frontier: A History of the Sixteenth-Century Ibero-African Frontier*. Chicago: University of Chicago Press.

Hingley, Richard. 2000. *Roman Officers and English Gentlemen: The Imperial Origins of Roman Archaeology*. London: Routledge.

———, ed. 2001. *Images of Rome: Perceptions of Ancient Rome in Europe and the United States in the Modern Age*. Portsmouth, RI: Journal of Roman Archaeology Supplementary Series Number 44.

———. 2005. *Globalizing Roman Culture: Unity, Diversity and Empire*. London: Routledge.

———. 2008. *The Recovery of Roman Britain, 1586–1906: A Colony So Fertile*. Oxford: Oxford University Press.

Hinsley, F. H. 1963. *Power and the Pursuit of Peace: Theory and Practice in the History of Relations between States*. Cambridge: Cambridge University Press.

Hirsch, Francine. 2005. *Empire of Nations: Ethnographic Knowledge and the Making of the Soviet Union*. Ithaca, NY: Cornell University Press.

Hirst, Derek. 2012. *Dominion: England and Its Island Neighbours 1500–1707*. Oxford: Oxford University Press.

Hobsbawm, Eric. 1984. "Mass Producing Traditions: Europe, 1870–1914." In Hobsbawm and Ranger 1984: 263–307.

———. 1987. *The Age of Empire, 1875–1914*. London: Weidenfeld and Nicolson.

———. 1992. *Nations and Nationalism since 1780*. 2nd ed. Cambridge: Cambridge University Press.

———. 1994. *Age of Extremes: The Short Twentieth Century 1914–1991*. London: Abacus.

Hobsbawm, Eric, and Terence Ranger, eds. 1984. *The Invention of Tradition*. Cambridge: Cambridge University Press.

Hobson, J. A. [1902, 1938] 1988. *Imperialism: A Study*. 3rd ed. London: Unwin Hyman.

Hodeir, Catherine, and Michel Pierre. 1991. *L'Exposition colonial, 1931*. Brussels: Editions Complexe.

Hoffmann, David L., and Yanni Kotsonis, eds. 2000. *Russian Modernity: Politics, Knowledge, Practices*. Houndmills, Basingstoke: Macmillan Press.

Hofmann, Michael. 2012. "Joseph Roth: Going over the Edge." *New York Review of Books*, December 22, 79–80.

Holland, R. F. 1985. *European Decolonization 1918–1981: An Introductory Survey*. Houndmills, Basingstoke: Macmillan.

Holland, Robert. 1999. "The British Empire and the Great War, 1914–1918." In Brown and Louis 1999: 114–37.

Hopkins, A. G. 2002. "The History of Globalization—and the Globalization of History?" In *Globalization in World History*, edited by A. G. Hopkins, 11–46. London: Pimlico.

———. 2008. "Rethinking Decolonization." *Past and Present* 200: 211–47.

Hopkins, Keith. 1965. "Elite Mobility in the Roman Empire." *Past and Present* 32: 12–26.

Horak, Stephan M. 1988. "Russian Expansion and Policy in Ukraine 1648–1791." In Rywkin 1988: 103–22.

Horne, Alistair. 1965. *The Fall of Paris: The Siege and the Commune 1870–1*. London: Macmillan.

Horsman, Reginald. 1981. *Race and Manifest Destiny: The Origins of American Racial Anglo-Saxonism*. Cambridge, MA: Harvard University Press.

Hosking, Geoffrey. 1998a. *Russia: People and Empire, 1552–1917*. London: Fontana Press.

———. 1998b. "Can Russia Become a Nation-State?" *Nations and Nationalism* 4 (4): 449–62.

———. 2006. *Rulers and Victims: The Russians in the Soviet Union*. Cambridge, MA: Harvard University Press.

———. 2012. *Russia and the Russians*. 2nd ed. London: Penguin Books.

Hosking, Geoffrey, and Robert Service, eds. 1998. *Russian Nationalism Past and Present*. Houndmills: Macmillan.

Howard, Douglas A. 1988. "Ottoman Historiography and the Literature of 'Decline' of the Sixteenth and Seventeenth Centuries." *Journal of Asian History* 22: 52–77.

Howe, Stephen. 1993. *Anticolonialism in British Politics: The Left and the End of Empire, 1918–1964*. Oxford: Oxford University Press.

———. 2002a. *Empire: A Very Short Introduction*. Oxford: Oxford University Press.

———. 2002b. *Ireland and Empire: Colonial Legacies in Irish History and Culture*. Paperback ed. Oxford: Oxford University Press.

———. 2005. "When—If Ever—Did Empire End? Recent Studies of Imperialism and Decolonization." *Journal of Contemporary History* 40 (3): 585–99.

———. 2006. "Historiography." In Kenny 2006c: 220–50.

Huet, Valérie. 1999. "Napoleon: A New Augustus?" In Edwards 1999b: 53–69.

Hume, David. [1748] 1987. "Of the Original Contract." In *Essays, Moral, Political, and Literary*, edited by Eugene F. Miller. Indianapolis: Liberty Classics.

Hunczak, Taras, ed. 1974. *Russian Imperialism from Ivan the Great to the Revolution*. New Brunswick, NJ: Rutgers University Press.

Huntington, Samuel P. 1999. "The Lonely Superpower." *Foreign Affairs*, March–April, 35–49.

Hutchins, Francis G. 1967. *The Illusion of Permanence: British Imperialism in India*. Princeton, NJ: Princeton University Press.

Huttenbach, Henry R. 1988a: "Muscovy's Conquest of Muslim Kazan and Astrakhan, 1552–56." In Rywkin 1988: 45–69.

———. 1988b. "Muscovy's Penetration of Siberia: The Colonization Process 1555–1689." In Rywkin 1988: 70–102.

Hyam, Ronald. 1999. "The British Empire in the Edwardian Era." In Brown and Louis 1999: 47–63.

———. 2006. *Britain's Declining Empire: The Road to Decolonisation 1918–1968*. Cambridge: Cambridge University Press.

Imber, Colin. 1995. "Ideals and Legitimation in Early Ottoman History." In Kunt and Woodhead 1995: 138–53.

———. 2002. *The Ottoman Empire 1300–1650: The Structure of Power*. Houndmills: Palgrave Macmillan.

Inalcik, Halil. 1954. "Ottoman Methods of Conquest." *Studia Islamica* 2: 103–29.

———. 1973. "Application of the *Tanzimat* and Its Social Effects." *Archivum Ottomanicum* 5: 97–127.

———. 1977. "Centralization and Decentralization in Ottoman Administration." In Naff and Owen 1977: 27–52.

———. 1981–82. "The Question of the Emergence of the Ottoman State." *International Journal of Turkish Studies* 2 (2): 71–79.

———. 1991. "The Status of the Greek Orthodox Patriarch under the Ottomans." *Turcica* 21–23: 407–36.

———. 1993. "State, Sovereignty and Law during the Reign of Süleymân." In Inalcik and Kafadar 1993: 59–92.

———. [1973] 2000. *The Ottoman Empire: The Classical Age 1300–1600*. London: Phoenix.

———. 2006. *Turkey and Europe in History*. Istanbul: EREN Press.

Inalcik, Halil, and Cemal Kafadar, eds. 1993. *Süleymân the Second [sic] and His Time*. Istanbul: The Isis Press.

Inalcik, Halil, with Donald Quataert, eds. 1994. *An Economic and Social History of the Ottoman Empire, 1300–1914*. Cambridge: Cambridge University Press.

Ingrao, Charles. 1994. *The Habsburg Monarchy 1618–1815*. Cambridge: Cambridge University Press.

Isaac, Benjamin. 2006. *The Invention of Racism in Classical Antiquity*. Princeton, NJ: Princeton University Press.

Itzkowitz, Norman. 1962. "Eighteenth-Century Ottoman Realities." *Studia Islamica* 16: 73–94.

———. 1977. "Men and Ideas in the Eighteenth Century Ottoman Empire." In Naff and Owen 1977: 15–26.

———. 1980. *Ottoman Empire and Islamic Tradition*. Chicago: University of Chicago Press.

Jackson, Alvin. 2006. "Ireland, the Union, and the Empire, 1800–1960." In Kenny 2006c: 123–53.

Jackson, Ashley. 2006. *The British Empire and the Second World War*. London: Hambledon Continuum.

James, Lawrence. 1998. *Raj: The Making and Unmaking of British India*. New York: St. Martin's Press.

Janik, Allan, and Stephen Toulmin. 1973. *Wittgenstein's Vienna*. New York: Simon and Schuster.

Janowski, Maciej. 2004. "Justifying Political Power in 19th Century Europe: The Habsburg Monarchy and Beyond." In Miller and Rieber 2004: 69–82.

Jasanoff, Maya. 2005. *Edge of Empire: Conquest and Collecting in the East 1750–1850*. London: Fourth Estate.

Jászi, Oscar. [1929] 1961. *The Dissolution of the Habsburg Monarchy*. Chicago: University of Chicago Press.

Jeffery, Keith, ed. 1996. *'An Irish Empire'? Aspects of Ireland and the British Empire*. Manchester: Manchester University Press.

———. 1999. "The Second World War." In Brown and Louis 1999: 306–28.

Jenkins, Brian, and Spyros A. Sofos, eds. 1996. *Nation and Identity in Contemporary Europe*. London: Routledge.

Jenkyns, Richard. 1981. *The Victorians and Ancient Greece*. Oxford: Basil Blackwell.

———. 1992a. "The Legacy of Rome." In Jenkyns 1992b: 1–35.

———, ed. 1992b. *The Legacy of Rome: A New Appraisal*. Oxford: Oxford University Press.

Jennings, Eric T. 2005. "Visions and Representations of French Empire." *Journal of Modern History* 77 (3): 701–21.

Jersild, Austin Lee. 1997. "From Savagery to Citizenship: Caucasian Mountaineers and Muslims in the Russian Empire." In Brower and Lazzerini 1997: 101–14.

———. 2000. "'Russia', from the Vistula to the Terek to the Amur." *Kritika* 1 (3): 531–46.

John, Michael. 1999. "'We Do Not Even Possess Our Selves': On Identity and Ethnicity in Austria, 1880–1937." *Austrian History Yearbook* 30: 17–64.

Johnston, William M. [1972] 1983. *The Austrian Mind: An Intellectual and Social History 1848–1938*. Berkeley: University of California Press.

———. 1986. "A Nation without Qualities: Austria and Its Quest for a National Identity." In Boerner 1986: 177–86.

Jones, Colin. 1999. *The Cambridge Illustrated History of France*. Cambridge: Cambridge University Press.

———. 2003. *The Great Nation: France from Louis XV to Napoleon*. London: Penguin Books.

Jones, Ernest. 1964. *The Life and Work of Sigmund Freud*. Edited and abridged by Lionel Trilling and Steven Marcus. Harmondsworth: Penguin Books.

Jowitt, Kenneth. 1992. *New World Disorder: The Leninist Extinction*. Berkeley: University of California Press.

Judd, Denis. 2010. "Web Masters." *Times Literary Supplement*, April 2, 22.

Judson, Pieter M. 2016. *The Habsburg Empire: A New History*. Cambridge, MA: Harvard University Press.

Judt, Tony. 1998. "The Reluctant Moralist: Albert Camus and the Discomforts of Ambivalence." In *The Burden of Responsibility: Blum, Camus, Aron and the French Twentieth Century*, 87–135. Chicago: University of Chicago Press.

Kafadar, Cemal. 1993. "The Myth of the Golden Age: Ottoman Historical Consciousness in the Post-Suleymanic Era." In Inalcik and Kafadar 1993: 37–48.

———. 1995. *Between Two Worlds: The Construction of the Ottoman State*. Berkeley: University of California Press.

Kagan, Robert. 2004. *Of Paradise and Power: America and Europe in the New World Disorder*. 2nd ed. New York: Alfred A. Knopf.

Kahler, Miles. 1984. *Decolonization in Britain and France: The Domestic Consequences of International Relations*. Princeton, NJ: Princeton University Press.

Kaiser, Robert J. 1994. *The Geography of Nationalism in Russia and the USSR*. Princeton, NJ: Princeton University Press.

Kamen, Henry. 1978. "The Decline of Spain: A Historical Myth?" *Past and Present* 81: 24–50.

———. 1991. *Spain 1469–1714: A Society of Conflict*. 2nd ed. London: Longman.

———. 2003. *Empire: How Spain Became a World Power 1492–1763*. New York: HarperCollins.

———. 2005. "Depriving the Spaniards of Their Empire." *Common Knowledge* 11 (2): 240–48.

Kann, Robert A. [1950] 1970. *The Multinational Empire: Nationalism and National Reform in the Habsburg Monarchy 1848–1918*. 2 vols. New York: Octagon Books.

———. [1957] 1973. *The Habsburg Empire: A Study in Integration and Disintegration*. New York: Octagon Books.

———. 1977. "Trends toward Colonialism in the Habsburg Empire, 1878–1918: The Case of Bosnia-Hercegovina, 1878–1914." In Rowney and Orchard 1977: 164–80.

———. 1980. *A History of the Habsburg Empire 1526–1918*. Berkeley: University of California Press.

———. 1991a. *Dynasty, Politics and Culture: Selected Essays*. Edited by Stanley B. Winters. Highland Lakes, NJ: Atlantic Research and Publications.

———. 1991b. "The Dynasty and the Imperial Idea." In Kann 1991a: 45–67.

———. 1991c. "The Social Prestige of the Habsburg Officer Corps in the Habsburg Empire from the Eighteenth Century to 1918." In Kann 1991a: 221–51.

———. 1991d. "The Austro-Hungarian Compromise of 1867 in Retrospect: Causes and Effect." In Kann 1991a: 193–218.

———. [1966] 2011. "Should the Habsburg Empire Have Been Saved? An Exercise in Speculative History." *Austrian History Yearbook* 42: 203–10.

Kann, Robert A., and Zdenek V. David. 1984. *The Peoples of the Eastern Habsburg Lands, 1526–1918*. Seattle: University of Washington Press.

Kanya-Forstner, A. S. 1972. "French Expansion in Africa: The Mythical Theory." In Owen and Sutcliffe 1972: 277–94.

Kappeler, Andreas. 1992. "The Ukrainians of the Russian Empire, 1860–1914." In *The Formation of National Elites*, edited by Andreas Kappeler, in collaboration with Fikret Adanit and Alan O'Day, 105–32. Aldershot: Dartmouth; New York: New York University Press.

———. 2001. *The Russian Empire: A Multi-Ethnic History*. Translated by Alfred Clayton. Harlow, Essex: Longman.

Kappeler, Andreas, Zenon E. Kohut, Frank E. Syusyn, and Mark von Hagen, eds. 2003. *Culture, Nation, and Identity: The Ukrainian-Russian Encounter, 1600–1945*. Edmonton: Canadian Institute of Ukrainian Studies Press.

Karpat, Kemal H. 1972. "The Transformation of the Ottoman State, 1789–1908." *International Journal of Middle East Studies* 3 (3): 243–81. (Also in Karpat 2002: 27–74.)

———. 1982. "*Millets* and Nationality: The Roots of the Incongruity of Nation and State in the Post-Ottoman Era." In Braude and Lewis 1982a: 1:141–69.

———. 2002. *Studies in Ottoman Social and Political History: Selected Articles and Essays*. Leiden: Brill.

Kasaba, Resat, ed. 2008. *The Cambridge History of Turkey*. Vol. 4, *Turkey in the Modern World*. Cambridge: Cambridge University Press.

Kaspe, Sviayoslav. 2007. "Imperial Political Culture and Modernization in the Second Half of the Nineteenth Century." In Burbank, von Hagen, and Remnev 2007: 455–93.

Kates, Gary. 1989. "Jews into Frenchmen: Nationality and Representation in Revolutionary France." *Social Research* 56 (1): 213–32.

Kaufmann, Eric P., ed. 2004. *Rethinking Ethnicity: Majority Groups and Dominant Minorities.* London: Routledge.

Kautsky, John H. [1982] 1997. *The Politics of Aristocratic Empires.* New Brunswick, NJ: Transaction Books.

Kayali, Hasan. 2008. "The Struggle for Independence." In Kasaba 2008: 112–46.

Keane, John. 2003. *Global Civil Society?* Cambridge: Cambridge University Press.

Kelly, Christopher. 2009. *The End of Empire: Attila the Hun and the Fall of Rome.* New York: W. W. Norton. (Published 2008 in London by The Bodley Head as *Attila the Hun: Barbarian Terror and the Fall of the Roman Empire.*)

Kelly, J.N.D. 1975. *Jerome: His Life, Writings, and Controversies.* London: Duckworth.

Kendle, John. 1997. *Federal Britain: A History.* London: Routledge.

Kennedy, Duncan F. 1999. "A Sense of Place: Rome, History and Empire Revisited." In Edwards 1999b: 19–34.

Kennedy, Paul. 1983. "Why Did the British Empire Last So Long?" In *Strategy and Diplomacy 1870–1945: Eight Studies,* 197–218. London: Allen and Unwin.

———. [1988] 1990. *The Rise and Fall of the Great Powers: Economic Change and Military Conflict from 1500 to 2000.* London: Fontana Press.

Kenny, Kevin. 2006a. "Ireland and the British Empire: An Introduction." In Kenny 2006c: 1–25.

———. 2006b. "The Irish in the Empire." In Kenny 2006c: 90–122.

———, ed. 2006c. *Ireland and the British Empire.* Oxford: Oxford University Press.

Khalid, Adeeb. 2006. "Backwardness and the Quest for Civilization: Early Soviet Central Asia in Comparative Perspective." *Slavic Review* 65 (2): 231–51.

———. 2007. "The Soviet Union as an Imperial Formation: A View from Central Asia." In Stoler, McGranhan, and Perdue 2007: 113–39.

Khazanov, Anatoly. M. 1995. *After the USSR: Ethnicity, Nationalism, and Politics in the Commonwealth of Independent States.* Madison: University of Wisconsin Press.

———. 2003. "A State without a Nation? Russia after Empire." In *The Nation-State in Question,* edited by T. V. Paul, G . John Ikenberry, and John H. Hall, 79–105. Princeton, NJ: Princeton University Press.

Kiernan, V. G. 1974. "The Marxist Theory of Imperialism and Its Historical Formation." In *Marxism and Imperialism,* 1–68. London: Edward Arnold.

———. 1982. "Tennyson, King Arthur, and Imperialism." In *Culture, Ideology and Politics,* edited by R. Samuel and G. S. Jones, 126–48. London: Routledge and Kegan Paul.

———. [1982] 1998. *Colonial Empires and Armies 1815–1960.* Stroud, Gloucestershire: Sutton Publishing. (Previously published under the title, *European Empires from Conquest to Collapse, 1815–1960.*)

King, Desmond. 2006. "When an Empire Is Not an Empire: The US Case." *Government and Opposition* 41 (2): 163–96.

Kiser, John W. 2009. *Commander of the Faithful: The Life and Times of Abd el-Kader.* London: Monkfish Book Publishing Company.

Kitsikis, Dimitri. 1994. *L'Empire Ottoman.* 3rd ed. Paris: Presses Universitaires de France.

Kivelson, Valerie. 1997. "Merciful Father, Impersonal State: Russian Autocracy in Comparative Perspective." *Modern Asian Studies* 312 (3): 635–63.

Klier, John Doyle. 1986. *Russia Gathers Her Jews: The Origins of the "Jewish Question" in Russia, 1772–1825.* Dekalb: Northern Illinois University Press.

————. 1989. "The Concept of 'Jewish Emancipation' in a Russian Context." In Crisp and Edmondson 1989: 121–44.

————. 1995. *Imperial Russia's Jewish Question, 1855–1881*. Cambridge: Cambridge University Press.

————. 2001. "State Policies and the Conversion of Jews in Imperial Russia." In Geraci and Khodarkovsky 2001: 92–112.

Klyuchevsky, Vasilii. 1958. *Peter the Great*. Translated by Liliana Archibald. Vol. 4 of *The History of Russia*. New York: Vintage.

Knapp, Robert C. 1977. *Aspects of the Roman Experience in Iberia, 206–100 BC*. Anejos de Hispania antiqua, 9. Valladolid: Universidad.

Knight, Nathaniel. 2000. "Ethnicity, Nationality and the Masses: *Narodnost'* and Modernity in Imperial Culture." In Hoffmann and Kotsonis 2000: 41–64.

Koditschek, Theodore. 2011. *Liberalism, Imperialism, and the Historical Imagination: Nineteenth-Century Visions of a Greater Britain*. Cambridge: Cambridge University Press.

Koebner, Richard. 1961. *Empire*. Cambridge: Cambridge University Press.

Koebner, Richard, and Helmut Dan Schmidt. 1964. *Imperialism: The Story and Significance of a Political Word, 1840–1960*. Cambridge: Cambridge University Press.

Koenigsberger, Helmut. 1987. "*Dominium Regale* or *Dominium Politicum et Regale*: Monarchies and Parliaments in Early Modern History." In *Politicians and Virtuosi: Essays in Early Modern History*, 1–25. London: The Hambledon Press.

Kohn, Hans. 1961. *The Habsburg Empire 1804–1918* (Text and documents). Princeton, NJ: Van Nostrand.

————, ed. 1962. *The Mind of Modern Russia: Historical and Political Thought of Russia's Great Age*. New York: Harper Torchbooks.

————. 1965. *Nationalism: Its Meaning and History*. Rev. ed. Princeton, NJ: Van Nostrand.

————. 1971. "Soviet Communism and Nationalism." In Allworth 1971: 43–71.

Köprülü, M. Fuad. [1935] 1992. *The Origins of the Ottoman Empire*. Translated and edited by Gary Leiser. Albany: State University of New York Press.

Koshar, Rudy. 1998. *Germany's Transient Pasts: Preservation and Memory in the Twentieth Century*. Chapel Hill: University of North Carolina Press.

Kotkin, Stephen. 2001. "Modern Times: The Soviet Union and the Interwar Conjuncture." *Kritika* 2 (1): 111–64.

Kreindler, Isabelle. 1977. "A Neglected Source of Lenin's Nationality Policy." *Slavic Review* 36 (1): 86–100.

Kristof, Ladis K. D. 1967. "The State-Idea, the National Idea and the Image of the Fatherland." *Orbis* 11 (Spring): 238–55.

Kumar, Krishan. 2000. "Nation and Empire: English and British National Identity in Comparative Perspective." *Theory and Society* 29 (5): 578–608.

————. 2001. *1989: Revolutionary Ideas and Ideals*. Minneapolis: University of Minnesota Press.

————. 2003. *The Making of English National Identity*. Cambridge: Cambridge University Press.

————. 2005. "When Was the English Nation?" In *When Is the Nation? Towards an Understanding of Theories of Nationalism*, edited by Atsuko Ichijo and Gordana Uzelac, 137–56. London: Routledge.

————. 2010. "Nation-States as Empires, Empires as Nation-States: Two Principles, One Practice?" *Theory and Society* 39 (2): 119–43.

———. 2012a. "Empire, Nation, and National Identities." In Thompson 2012: 298–329.

———. 2012b. "Greece and Rome in the British Empire: Contrasting Role Models." *Journal of British Studies* 51 (1): 76–101.

———. 2015. *The Idea of Englishness: English Culture, National Identity, and Social Thought*. London: Ashgate.

Kundera, Milan. 1984. "The Tragedy of Central Europe." *New York Review of Books*, April 26, 33–38.

Kunt, I. Metin. 1982. "Transformation of *Zimmi* into *Askeri*." In Braude and Lewis 1982a: 1:55–67.

Kunt, Metin, and Christine Woodhead, eds. 1995. *Süleyman the Magnificent and His Age: The Ottoman Empire in the Early Modern World*. London: Longman.

Kupchan, Charles A. 1994. *The Vulnerability of Empire*. Ithaca, NY: Cornell University Press.

Kuzio, Taras. 2002. "The Myth of the Civic State." *Ethnic and Racial Studies* 25 (1): 20–39.

Kuzmics, Helmut, and Roland Axtmann. 2007. *Authority, State and National Character: The Civilizing Process in Austria and England, 1700–1900*. Aldershot: Ashgate.

Kwarteng, Kwasi. 2012. *Ghosts of Empire: Britain's Legacies in the Modern World*. London: Bloomsbury.

Lal, Deepak. 2004. *In Praise of Empires: Globalization and Order*. New York: Palgrave Macmillan.

Lampert, E. 1957. *Studies in Rebellion*. London: Routledge and Kegan Paul.

Landes, David S. 1961. "Some Thoughts on the Nature of Economic Imperialism." *Journal of Economic History* 21 (4): 496–512.

Lane Fox, Robin. 1986. *Alexander the Great*. London: Penguin Books.

Lapidus, Gail W., and Victor Zaslavsky, with Philip Goldman, eds. 1992. *From Union to Commonwealth: Nationalism and Separatism in the Soviet Republics*. Cambridge: Cambridge University Press.

Larson, Victoria Tietze. 1999. "Classics and the Acquisition and Validation of Power in Britain's 'Imperial Century' (1815–1914)." *International Journal of the Classical Tradition* 6 (2): 185–225.

Laruelle, Marlène. 2008. *Russian Eurasianism: An Ideology of Empire*. Translated by Mischa Gabowitsch. Baltimore: Johns Hopkins University Press.

Laurence, Ray, and Joanne Berry, eds. 1998. *Cultural Identity in the Roman Empire*. London: Routledge.

Lebovics, Herman. 1994. *True France: The Wars over Cultural Identity, 1900–1945*. Ithaca, NY: Cornell University Press.

———. 2004. *Bringing the Empire Back Home: France in the Global Age*. Durham, NC: Duke University Press.

LeDonne, John P. 1997. *The Russian Empire and the World 1700–1917: The Geopolitics of Expansion and Containment*. New York: Oxford University Press.

Lee, Mark. 2004. "The Story of Greater Britain: What Lessons Does It Teach?" *National Identities* 6 (2): 123–42.

Lenin, V. I. [1917] 1939. *Imperialism: The Highest Stage of Capitalism*. New York: International Publishers.

———. 1962. *Critical Remarks on the National Question* [1913] and *The Right of Nations to Self-Determination* [1914–16]. Moscow: Foreign Languages Publishing House.

Leatherbarrow, W. J., and D. C. Offord, eds. 1987. *A Documentary History of Russian Thought: From the Enlightenment to Marxism*. Ann Arbor, MI: Ardis.

Leonhard, Jörn, and Ulrike von Hirschhausen, eds. 2011. *Comparing Empires: Encounters and Transfers in the Long Nineteenth Century*. Göttingen: Vandenhoeck and Ruprecht.

Le Rider, Jacques. 1994. "Hugo von Hofmannsthal and the Austrian Idea of Central Europe." In Robertson and Timms 1994: 121–35.

Lester, Alan. 2002. "British Settler Discourse and the Circuits of Empire." *History Workshop Journal* 54: 25–48.

———. 2006. "Imperial Circuits and Networks: Geographies of the British Empire." *History Compass* 4 (1): 124–41.

Lewis, Bernard. 1958. "Some Reflections on the Decline of the Ottoman Empire." *Studia Islamica* 9: 117–27.

———. 1962. "Ottoman Observers of Ottoman Decline." *Islamic Studies* 1: 71–87.

———. 1968. *The Emergence of Modern Turkey*. 2nd ed. London: Oxford University Press.

———. [1982] 2001. *The Muslim Discovery of Europe*. New York: W. W. Norton and Co.

Lewis, Sir George Cornewell. [1841] 1891. *An Essay on the Government of Dependencies*. New ed. Edited by C. P. Lucas. Oxford: Clarendon Press.

Lewis, Martin Deming. 1962. "One Hundred Million Frenchmen: The 'Assimilation' Theory in French Colonial Policy." *Comparative Studies in Society and History* 4 (2): 129–53.

Lichtheim, George. 1974. *Imperialism*. Harmondsworth: Penguin Books.

Lieven, Dominic. 1989. *Russia's Rulers under the Old Regime*. New Haven, CT: Yale University Press.

———. 2001. *Empire: The Russian Empire and Its Rivals*. New Haven, CT: Yale University Press.

Lindner, Rudi Paul. 1983. *Nomads and Ottomans in Medieval Anatolia*. Bloomington: Research Institute for Inner Asian Studies, Indiana University.

Lintott, Andrew. 1981. "What Was the 'Imperium Romanum'?" *Greece and Rome*, 2nd ser., 28 (1): 53–67.

Livi-Baci, Massimo. 1992. *A Concise History of World Population*. Translated by Carlo Ipsen. Cambridge, MA: Blackwell.

Livy. [c. 25 BCE] 1998. *The Rise of Rome*: *Books One to Five*. Translated by T. J. Luce. Oxford: Oxford University Press.

Lloyd, T. O. 1996. *The British Empire 1558–1995*. 2nd ed. Oxford: Oxford University Press.

Locke, John. [1689] 2010. "A Letter concerning Toleration." In *Locke on Toleration*, edited by Richard Vernon, 3–46. Cambridge: Cambridge University Press.

Longworth, Philip. 2006. *Russia's Empires. Their Rise and Fall: From Prehistory to Putin*. London: John Murray.

Lorcin, Patricia M. E. 1995. *Imperial Identities: Stereotyping, Prejudice and Race in Colonial Algeria*. London: I. B. Tauris.

———, ed. 2006. *Algeria and France 1800–2000: Identity—Memory—Nostalgia*. Syracuse, NY: Syracuse University Press.

Losemann, Volker. 1999. "The Nazi Concept of Rome." in Edwards 1999b: 221–35.

Louis, W. Roger, ed. 1976. *Imperialism: The Robinson and Gallagher Controversy*. New York: New Viewpoints.

———. 1992. *In the Name of God, Go! Leo Amery and the British Empire in the Age of Churchill*. New York: W. W. Norton.

———, editor-in-chief. 1998–99. *The Oxford History of the British Empire*. 5 vols. Oxford: Oxford University Press.

———. 1999a. "Introduction." In Brown and Louis 1999: 1–46.

———. 1999b. "The Dissolution of the British Empire." In Brown and Louis 1999: 329–56.

Louis, Wm. Roger, and Ronald Robinson. 1994. "The Imperialism of Decolonization." *Journal of Imperial and Commonwealth History* 22 (3): 462–511.

Löwe, Heinz-Dietrich. 2000. "Poles, Jews, and Tartars: Religion, Ethnicity, and Social Structure in Tsarist Nationality Policies." *Jewish Social Studies* 6 (3): 52–96.

Lowry, Heath W. 2003. *The Nature of the Early Ottoman State*. Albany: State University of New York Press.

Lucas, Sir C. P. 1912. *Greater Rome and Greater Britain*. Oxford: Clarendon Press.

Lugard, Frederick, Lord. 1965. *The Dual Mandate in British Tropical Africa*. London: Frank Cass.

Lundestad, Geir, ed. 1994. *The Fall of Great Powers: Peace, Stability and Legitimacy*. Oxford: Oxford University Press/Scandinavian Press.

Lupher, David A. 2006. *Romans in a New World: Classical Models in Sixteenth-Century Spanish America*. Ann Arbor: University of Michigan Press.

Lustick, Ian S. 1993. *Unsettled States, Disputed Lands: Britain and Ireland, France and Algeria, Israel and the West Bank–Gaza*. Ithaca, NY: Cornell University Press.

Lynch, John 1991. *Spain 1516–1598: From Nation State to World Empire*. Oxford: Blackwell.

———. 1992. *The Hispanic World in Crisis and Change: 1598–1700*. Oxford: Blackwell.

Lynn, Martin. 1999. "British Policy, Trade, and Informal Empire in the Mid-Nineteenth Century." In Porter 1999: 101–21.

Macaulay, Thomas Babington. [1840] 1907. "Ranke's History of the Popes." In *Critical and Historical Essays by Thomas Babington Macaulay*, 2 vols., 2:38–72. London: J. M. Dent and Sons.

———. [1835] 2003. "Minute on Indian Education." In Harlow and Carter 2003a: 227–45.

MacCormack, Sabine. 2009. *On the Wings of Time: Rome, the Incas, Spain, and Peru*. Princeton, NJ: Princeton University Press.

MacDonald, Robert H. 1993. *Sons of the Empire: The Frontier and the Boy Scout Movement, 1890–1918*. Toronto: University of Toronto Press.

———. 1994. *The Language of Empire: Myths and Metaphors of Popular Imperialism, 1880–1918*. Manchester: Manchester University Press.

Machiavelli, Niccolò. [1531] 1970. *The Discourses*. Translated by Leslie J. Walker. Edited by Bernard Crick. Harmondsworth: Penguin Books.

MacKenzie, David. 1988. "The Conquest and Administration of Turkestan, 1860–85." In Rywkin 1988: 208–234.

MacKenzie, John M. 1984. *Propaganda and Empire: The Manipulation of British Public Opinion 1880–1960*. Manchester: Manchester University Press.

———, ed. 1986. *Imperialism and Popular Culture*. Manchester: Manchester University Press.

———. 1999a. "Empire and Metropolitan Culture." In Porter 1999: 270–93.

———. 1999b. "The Popular Culture of Empire in Britain." In Brown and Louis 1999: 212–31.

———. 2001. "The Persistence of Empire in Metropolitan Culture." In Ward 2001: 21–36.

———, ed. 2011. *European Empires and the People*. Manchester: Manchester University Press.

Mack Smith, Denis. 1977. *Mussolini's Roman Empire*. Harmondsworth: Penguin Books.

MacLachlan, A. 1996. "'A Patriotic Scripture': The Making and Unmaking of English National Identity." *Parergon* 14 (1): 1–30.

MacLachlan, Colin M. 1991. *Spain's Empire in the New World: Role of Ideas in Institutional and Social Change*. Berkeley: University of California Press.

Macmullen, Ramsay. 2000. *Romanization in the Time of Augustus*. New Haven, CT: Yale University Press.

Magee, Gary B., and Andrew S. Thompson. 2010. *Empire and Globalisation: Networks of People, Goods and Capital in the British World, c. 1850–1914*. Cambridge: Cambridge University Press.

Maier, Charles. 2000. "Consigning the Twentieth Century to History: Alternative Narratives for the Modern Era." *American Historical Review* 105 (3): 807–31.

———. 2006. *Among Empires: American Ascendancy and Its Predecessors*. Cambridge, MA: Harvard University Press.

Majeed, Javed. 1999. "Comparativism and References to Rome in British Imperial Attitudes to India." In Edwards 1999b: 88–109.

Mamatey, Victor S. 1995. *Rise of the Habsburg Empire 1526–1815*. Malabar, FL: Krieger Publishing Company.

Mandler, Peter. 2006. *The English National Character: The History of an Idea from Edmund Burke to Tony Blair*. New Haven, CT: Yale University Press.

Manger, Philip. 1985. "'The Radetzky March': Joseph Roth and the Habsburg Myth." In Francis 1985: 40–62.

Mann, Michael. 1984. *The Sources of Social Power*. Vol. 1, *A History of Power from the Beginning to A. D. 1760*. Cambridge: Cambridge University Press.

———. 1993. *The Sources of Social Power*. Vol. 2, *The Rise of Classes and Nation-States, 1760–1914*. Cambridge: Cambridge University Press.

———. 2003. *Incoherent Empire*. London: Verso.

Manneh, Butrus Abu. 1994. "The Islamic Roots of Gülhane." *Die Welt des Islams* 34: 173–203.

Mantena, Karuna. 2010. *Alibis of Empire: Henry Maine and the Ends of Liberal Imperialism*. Princeton, NJ: Princeton University Press.

Mantena, Rama Sundari. 2010. "Imperial Ideology and the Uses of Rome in Discourses on Britain's Indian Empire." In Bradley 2010a: 54–73.

Mantran, Robert. 1980. "L'Empire ottoman." In Duverger 1980: 231–51.

———. 1982. "Foreign Merchants and the Minorities in Istanbul during the Sixteenth and Seventeenth Centuries." In Braude and Lewis 1982a: 127–37.

Mardin, Serif. 1962. *The Genesis of Young Ottoman Thought: A Study in the Modernization of Turkish Political Ideas*. Princeton, NJ: Princeton University Press.

———. 1969. "Power, Civil Society and Culture in the Ottoman Empire." *Comparative Studies in Society and History* 11 (3): 258–81.

Marshall, D. Bruce. 1973. *The French Colonial Myth and Constitution-Making in the Fourth Republic*. New Haven, CT: Yale University Press.

Marshall, P. J. 1993. "No Fatal Impact? The Elusive History of Imperial Britain." *Times Literary Supplement*, March 12, 8–10.

———, ed. 2001. *The Cambridge Illustrated History of the British Empire*. Cambridge: Cambridge University Press.

———. 2007. *The Making and Unmaking of Empires: Britain, India, and America c. 1750–1783*. Oxford: Oxford University Press.

Martin, Ged. 1972. "Was There a British Empire?" *Historical Journal* 15 (3): 562–69.

Martin, Ged, and Benjamin E. Kline. 2001. "British Emigration and New Identities." In Marshall 2001: 254–79.

Martin, Janet. 1988. "Russian Expansion in the Far North: X to mid-XVI Century." In Rywkin 1988: 23–43.

Martin, Terry. 2001. *The Affirmative Action Empire: Nations and Nationalism in the Soviet Union, 1923–1939*. Ithaca, NY: Cornell University Press.

———. 2002. "The Soviet Union as Empire: Salvaging a Dubious Analytical Category." *Ab Imperio*, no. 2: 98–108.

Marx, Anthony. 2003. *Faith in Nation: Exclusionary Origins of Nationalism*. New York: Oxford University Press.

Marx, Karl. [1851–52] 1962. "The Eighteenth Brumaire of Louis Bonaparte." In Karl Marx and Frederick Engels, *Selected Works in Two Volumes*, 1:243–344. Moscow: Foreign Languages Publishing House.

Marx, Karl, and Frederick Engels. 1972. *Ireland and the Irish Question: A Collection of Writings*. New York: International Publishers.

Matikkala, Mira. 2011. *Empire and Imperial Ambition: Liberty, Englishness and Anti-Imperialism in Late-Victorian Britain*. London: I. B. Tauris.

Mattingly, David. 2006. *Imperial Possession: Britain in the Roman Empire, 54 BC–AD 409*. London: Allen Lane.

May, Alex. 2001. "Empire Loyalists and 'Commonwealth Men': The Round Table and the End of Empire." In Ward 2001: 37–56.

Mazower, Mark. 2005. *Salonica, City of Ghosts: Christians, Muslims and Jews 1430–1950*. London: Harper Perennial.

———. 2009. *No Enchanted Place: The End of Empire and the Ideological Origins of the United Nations*. Princeton, NJ: Princeton University Press.

———. 2015. *Governing the World: The History of an Idea*. London: Penguin Books.

McCagg, William O., Jr. 1992. "The Soviet Union and the Habsburg Empire: Problems of Comparison." In Rudolf and Good 1992: 45–63.

McDonough, Terence, ed. 2005. *Was Ireland a Colony? Economy, Politics, Ideology and Culture in Nineteenth-Century Ireland*. Galway: Irish Academic Press.

McGowan, Bruce. 1994. "The Age of the Ayans, 1699–1812." In Inalcik with Quataert 1994: 637–758.

McIntyre, W. David. 1999. "Commonwealth Legacy." In Brown and Louis 1999: 693–702.

McMahon, Deirdre. 2006. "Ireland, the Empire, and the Commonwealth." In Kenny 2006c: 182–219.

Medish, Vadim. 1980. "Special Status of the RSFSR." In Allworth 1980b: 188–99.

Mehta, Uday Singh. 1999. *Liberalism and Empire: A Study in Nineteenth-Century British Liberal Thought*. Chicago: University of Chicago Press.

Messud, Claire. 2013. "Camus and Algeria: The Moral Question." *New York Review of Books*, November 7, 56–58.

Metcalf, Thomas R. 1997. *Ideologies of the Raj*. Cambridge: Cambridge University Press.

———. 2005. "Architecture and Empire: Sir Herbert Baker and the Building of New Delhi." In *Forging the Raj: Essays on British India in the Heyday of Empire*, 140–51. New Delhi: Oxford University Press.

Miles, Gary B. 1990. "Roman and Modern Imperialism: A Reassessment." *Comparative Studies in Society and History* 32 (4): 629–59.

Miller, Alexei. 2008. *The Romanov Empire and Nationalism: Essays in the Methodology of Historical Research*. Budapest: Central European University Press.

Miller, Alexei, and Mikhail Dobilov. 2011. "'The Damned Polish Question': The Romanov Empire and the Polish Uprisings of 1830–1831 and 1863–1864." In Leonhard and von Hirschhausen 2011: 425–52.

Miller, Alexei, and Alfred J. Rieber, eds. 2004. *Imperial Rule*. Budapest: Central European University Press.

Miller, Christopher L. 1994. "Unfinished Business: Colonialism in Sub-Saharan Africa and the Ideals of the French Revolution." In *The Global Ramifications of the French Revolution*, edited by Joseph Klaits and Michael H. Haltzel, 105–26. Cambridge: Cambridge University Press.

Milner-Gulland, Robin. 1999. *The Russians*. Oxford: Blackwell Publishers.

Mommsen, Theodor. [1909] 1974. *The Provinces of the Roman Empire from Caesar to Diocletian*. 2 vols. Translated by William P. Dickson. Chicago: Ares Publishers.

Mommsen, Wolfgang J. 1978. "Power Politics, Imperialism and National Emancipation." In *Nationality and the Pursuit of National Independence*, edited by T. W. Moody, 121–40. Belfast: The Appletree Press.

———. 1982. *Theories of Imperialism*. Translated by P. S. Falla. Chicago: University of Chicago Press.

———. 1986. "The End of Empire and the Continuity of Imperialism." In Mommsen and Osterhammel 1986: 333–58.

———. 1990. "The Varieties of the Nation State in Modern History: Liberal, Imperialist, Fascist and Contemporary Notions of Nation and Nationality." In *The Rise and Decline of the Nation State*, edited by Michael Mann, 210–26. Oxford: Basil Blackwell.

Mommsen, Wolfgang J., and Jürgen Osterhammel, eds. 1986. *Imperialism and After: Continuities and Discontinuities*. London: Allen and Unwin.

Montaigne, Michel de. [1580] 1958. "On Vehicles." In *Essays*, translated by J. M. Cohen, 264–85. London: Penguin Books.

Moore, Robin J. 1999. "Imperial India, 1858–1914." In Porter 1999: 427–46.

Morefield, Jeanne. 2005. *Covenants without Swords: Idealist Liberalism and the Spirit of Empire*. Princeton, NJ: Princeton University Press.

———. 2007. "'An Education to Greece': The Round Table, Imperial Theory and the Uses of History." *History of Political Thought* 28 (2): 328–61.

Moreland, John. 2001. "The Carolingian Empire: Rome Reborn?" In Alcock et al. 2001: 392–418.

Morgan, Hiram. 1994. "An Unwelcome Heritage: Ireland's Role in British Empire-Building." *History of European Ideas* 19 (4/6): 619–25.

Morris, James. [1968] 1980a. *Pax Britannica: The Climax of an Empire*. San Diego, CA: Harcourt, Brace, Jovanovich.

———. [1978] 1980b. *Farewell the Trumpets: An Imperial Retreat*. San Diego, CA: Harcourt, Brace, Jovanovich.

Morris-Jones, W. H., and Georges Fischer, eds. 1980. *Decolonisation and After: The British and French Experience*. London: Frank Cass.

Morrison, Alexander. 2012. "Metropole, Colony, and Imperial Citizenship in the Russian Empire." *Kritika* 13 (2): 327–64.

Morrison, Kathleen D. 2001. "Sources, Approaches, Definitions." In Alcock et al. 2001: 1–9.

Morton, Frederic. 1980. *A Nervous Splendor: Vienna 1888/1889*. New York: Penguin Books.

Motyl, Alexander J. 1992. "From Imperial Decay to Imperial Collapse: The Fall of the Soviet Empire in Comparative Perspective." In Rudolph and Good 1992: 15–43.

———. 2001. *Imperial Ends: The Decay, Collapse, and Revival of Empires*. New York: Columbia University Press.

Muldoon, James. 1999. *Empire and Order: The Concept of Empire, 800–1800*. Houndmills, Basingstoke: Macmillan.

Müller, Max. [1876] 2003. "The Aryan Section." In Harlow and Carter 2003a: 239–45.

Mumford, Lewis. 1961. *The City in History: Its Origins, Its Transformations, and Its Prospects*. New York: Harcourt Brace Jovanovich.

Munck, Ronaldo. 2010. "Marxism and Nationalism in the Era of Globalization." *Capital and Class* 34 (1): 45–53.

Münkler, Herfried. 2007. *Empires: The Logic of World Domination from Ancient Rome to the United States*. Translated by Patrick Camiller. Cambridge: Polity Press.

Murdoch, Alexander. 2004. *British Emigration, 1603–1914*. Houndmills: Palgrave Macmillan.

Murphy, Agnes. [1948] 1968. *The Ideology of French Imperialism 1871–1881*. New York: Howard Fertig.

Murray, Gilbert, Francis W. Hirst, and John Laurence Hammond. 1900. *Liberalism and the Empire: Three Essays*. London: R. B. Johnson.

Musil, Robert. [1930–32] 1979. *The Man without Qualities*. Translated by Eithne Wilkins and Ernst Kaiser. 3 vols. London: Pan Books.

Muthu, Sankar. 2003. *Enlightenment against Empire*. Princeton, NJ: Princeton University Press.

———, ed. 2014. *Empire and Modern Political Thought*. Cambridge: Cambridge University Press.

Naff, Thomas. 1977a. "Introduction to Part I." In Naff and Owen 1977: 3–14.

———. 1977b. "Ottoman Diplomatic Relations with Europe in the Eighteenth Century: Patterns and Trends." In Naff and Owen 1977: 88–107.

Naff, Thomas, and Roger Owen, eds. 1977. *Studies in Eighteenth Century Islamic History*. Carbondale: Southern Illinois University Press.

Naipaul, V. S. [1967] 1985. *The Mimic Men*. New York: Vintage.

Namier, Sir Lewis. 1946. *1848: The Revolution of the Intellectuals*. London: Oxford University Press.

———. 1962. "The Downfall of the Habsburg Monarchy." In *Vanished Supremacies: Essays on European History 1812–1908*, 139–202. Harmondsworth: Penguin Books.

Nasson, Bill. 2006. *Britannia's Empire: A Short History of the British Empire*. Stroud, UK: Tempus.

Nathans, Benjamin. 2002. *Beyond the Pale: The Jewish Encounter with Late Imperial Russia*. Berkeley: University of California Press.

Nelis, Jan. 2007. "Constructing Fascist Identity: Benito Mussolini and the Myth of *Romanità*." *Classical World* 100 (4): 391–415.

Neumann, Franz. [1944] 1966. *Behemoth: The Structure and Practice of National Socialism, 1933–1944*. 2nd ed. New York: Harper.

Newman, Gerard. 1987. *The Rise of English Nationalism: A Cultural History 1740–1830*. London: Weidenfeld and Nicolson.

Newman, John Henry. [1853] 1894. "Lectures on the History of the Turks, in their relation to Europe." In *Historical Sketches*, 3 vols., 1:1–238. New York: Longmans, Green and Co.

Nicholas, Sian. 2003. "'Brushing Up Your Empire': Dominion and Colonial Propaganda on the BBC's Home Services, 1939–45." In Bridge and Fedorowich 2003: 207–30.

Nicol, Donald M. 1967. "The Byzantine View of Western Europe." *Greek, Roman and Byzantine Studies* 8 (4): 315–39.

Nimni, Ephraim J. 2000. "Introduction for the English-Reading Audience." In Bauer [1907, 1924] 2000: xv–xlv.

Nutton, V. 1978. "The Beneficial Ideology." In Garnsey and Whittaker 1978a: 209–21.

OED 1989. *Oxford English Dictionary*. 2nd ed. Oxford: Oxford University Press.

Offer, Avner. 1993. "The British Empire, 1870–1914: A Waste of Money?" *Economic History Review* 46 (2): 215–38.

———. 1999. "Costs and Benefits, Prosperity and Security, 1870–1914." In Porter 1999: 690–711.

Ohlmeyer, Jane H. 2006. "A Laboratory for Empire? Early Modern Ireland and English Imperialism." In Kenny 2006c: 26–60.

Okey, Robin. 2002. *The Habsburg Monarchy c.1765–1918*. New York: Palgrave Macmillan.

O'Leary, Brendan. 2002. "In Praise of Empires Past: Myths and Method of Kedourie's *Nationalism*." *New Left Review* 18: 106–30.

Oliver, James H. 1953. *The Ruling Power: A Study of the Roman Empire in the Second Century after Christ through the Roman Oration of Aelius Aristides*. Philadelphia: American Philosophical Society.

Olson, Robert W. 1979. "Jews in the Ottoman Empire in Light of New Documents." *Jewish Social Studies* 41 (1): 75–88.

Osterhammel, Jürgen. 1986. "Semi-Colonialism and Informal Empire in Twentieth-Century China: Towards a Framework of Analysis." In Mommsen and Osterhammel 1986: 290–314.

———. [1995] 2005. *Colonialism*. Updated and expanded ed. Translated by Shelley Frisch. Princeton, NJ: Markus Wiener Publishers.

Ousby, Ian. 2003. *The Road to Verdun: France, Nationalism and the First World War*. London: Pimlico.

Owen, Roger. 1975. "The Middle East in the Eighteenth Century—an 'Islamic' Society in Decline?" *Review of Middle East Studies* 1: 101–11.

———. 1977. "Introduction to Part II." In Naff and Owen 1977: 133–51.

———. 2005. *Lord Cromer: Victorian Imperialist, Edwardian Proconsul*. Oxford: Oxford University Press.

Owen, Roger, and Bob Sutcliffe, eds. 1972. *Studies in the Theory of Imperialism*. London: Longman.

Ozouf, Mona. 2015. *Jules Ferry: La Liberté et la tradition*. Paris: Gallimard.

Pagden, Anthony. 1987. "Identity Formation in Spanish America." In Canny and Pagden 1987: 51–93.

———. 1990. *Spanish Imperialism and the Political Imagination: Studies in European and Spanish-American Social and Political Theory 1513–1830*. New Haven, CT: Yale University Press.

———. 1994. *European Encounters with the New World: From Renaissance to Romanticism*. New Haven, CT: Yale University Press.

———. 1995. *Lords of All the World: Ideologies of Empire in Spain, Britain and France, c. 1500–c. 1800*. New Haven, CT: Yale University Press.

———. 2003. *Peoples and Empires: A Short History of European Migration, Exploration, and Conquest, from Greece to the Present*. New York: The Modern Library.

———. 2004. "Bush Is No Emperor." *Los Angeles Times*, November 14.

———. 2008. *Worlds at War: The 2,500-Year Struggle between East and West*. New York: Random House.

———. 2015. *The Burdens of Empire: 1539 to the Present*. Cambridge: Cambridge University Press.

Palen, Marc-William. 2014. "Adam Smith as Advocate of Empire, c. 1870–1932." *Historical Journal* 57 (1): 179–98.

Pares, Richard. [1937] 1954. "The Economic Factors in the History of the Empire." In *Essays in Economic History*, edited by E. M. Carus Wilson, 1:416–38. London: Edward Arnold.

Parkinson, C. Northcote. 1961. *Parkinson's Law, or the Pursuit of Progress*. London: John Murray.

Parla, Taha. 1985. *The Social and Political Thought of Ziya Gökalp*. Leiden: Brill.

Parrot, Bruce. 1997. "Analyzing the Transformation of the Soviet Union in Comparative Perspective." In Dawisha and Parrott 1997: 3–29.

Parry, J. H. 1940. *The Spanish Theory of Empire in the Sixteenth Century*. Cambridge: Cambridge University Press.

———. [1966] 1990. *The Spanish Seaborne Empire*. Berkeley: University of California Press.

Parry, J. P. 2001. "The Impact of Napoleon III on British Politics, 1851–1880." *Transactions of the Royal Historical Society*, 6th ser., 11: 147–75.

Parsons, Timothy H. 2010. *The Rule of Empires: Those Who Built Them, Those Who Endured Them, and Why They Always Fall*. Oxford: Oxford University Press.

Paul, Kathleen. 1997. *Whitewashing Britain: Race and Citizenship in the Postwar Era*. Ithaca, NY: Cornell University Press.

Paxman, Jeremy. 2012. *Empire*. London: Penguin Books.

Payne, Matt. 2001. "The Forge of the Kazakh Proletariat? The Turksib, Nativization, and Industrialization during Stalin's First Five-Year Plan." In Suny and Martin 2001: 223–52.

Pearson, Raymond. 1989. "Privileges, Rights, and Russification." In Crisp and Edmondson 1989: 85–102.

Pedersen, Susan. 2015. *The Guardians: The League of Nations and the Crisis of Empire*. Oxford: Oxford University Press.

Peirce, Leslie P. 1993. *The Imperial Harem: Women and Sovereignty in the Ottoman Empire*. Oxford: Oxford University Press.

Perdue, Peter C. 2005. *China Marches West: The Qing Conquest of Central Eurasia*. Cambridge, MA: Belknap Press of Harvard University Press.

Persell, Stuart M. 1974. "Joseph Chailley-Bert and the Importance of the *Union Coloniale Française*." *Historical Journal* 17 (1): 176–84.

Pick, Daniel. 1989. *Faces of Degeneration: A European Disorder, c.1848–c.1918*. Cambridge: Cambridge University Press.

Pipes, Richard. 1964. *The Formation of the Soviet Union: Communism and Nationalism: 1917–1923*. Rev. ed. Cambridge, MA: Harvard University Press.

———. [1974] 1995. *Russia under the Old Regime*. 2nd ed. London: Penguin Books.

Pirenne, Henri. 1939. *Mohammed and Charlemagne*. London: Allen and Unwin.

Pitts, Jennifer. 2005. *A Turn to Empire: The Rise of Imperial Liberalism in Britain and France*. Princeton, NJ: Princeton University Press.

——. 2016. "Oriental Despotism and the Ottoman Empire." Paper presented at the University of Virginia, March 18, 2016.

Plutarch. 1871. "The Fortune or Virtue of Alexander the Great." In *Plutarch's Morals*, edited by William W. Goodwin, 5 vols., 1:475–516. Boston: Little, Brown, and Company.

Pocock, J.G.A. 1977. "Between Machiavelli and Hume: Gibbon as Civic Humanist and Philosophical Historian." In Bowersock, Clive, and Graubard 1977: 103–19.

——. 1985. *Virtue, Commerce and History*. Cambridge: Cambridge University Press.

——. 2005. "Empire, State and Confederation: The War of American Independence as a Crisis in Multiple Monarchy." In *The Discovery of Islands: Essays in British History*, 134–63. Cambridge: Cambridge University Press.

Polybius. 1979. *The Rise of the Roman Empire*. Translated by Ian Scott-Kilvert. London: Penguin Books.

Porter, Andrew, ed. 1999. *The Oxford History of the British Empire*. Vol. 3, *The Nineteenth Century*. Oxford: Oxford University Press.

Porter, Bernard. 1968. *Critics of Empire: British Radical Attitudes to Colonialism in Africa, 1895–1914*. London: Macmillan.

——. 1982. "The Edwardians and Their Empire." In *Edwardian England*, edited by Donald Read, 128–44. London: Croom Helm.

——. 2004a. *The Lion's Share: A Short History of British Imperialism 1850–2004*. 4th ed. Harlow, UK: Pearson-Longman.

——. 2004b. *The Absent-Minded Imperialists: Empire, Society, and Culture in Britain*. Oxford: Oxford University Press.

——. 2006. *Empire and Superempire: Britain, America and the World*. New Haven, CT: Yale University Press.

——. 2008. "Further Thoughts on Imperial Absent-Mindedness." *Journal of Imperial and Commonwealth History* 36 (1): 101–17.

Powell, J. Enoch. 1969. *Freedom and Reality*. London: B. T. Batsford.

Price, Richard. 2008. *Making Empire: Colonial Encounters and the Creation of Imperial Rule in Nineteenth-Century Africa*. Cambridge: Cambridge University Press.

Price, S.R.F. 1984. *Rituals and Power: The Roman Imperial Cult in Asia Minor*. Cambridge: Cambridge University Press.

Prizel, Ilya. 1998. *National Identity and Foreign Policy: Nationalism and Leadership in Poland, Russia, and Ukraine*. Cambridge: Cambridge University Press.

Prochaska, David. 1990. *Making Algeria French: Colonialism in Bône, 1870–1920*. Cambridge: Cambridge University Press.

Quataert, Donald. 1994. "The Age of Reforms, 1812–1914." In Inalcik with Quataert 1994: 761–943.

——. 2000. *The Ottoman Empire 1700–1922*. Cambridge: Cambridge University Press.

Quinn, Frederick. 2002. *The French Overseas Empire*. Westport, CT: Praeger.

Raeff, Marc, ed. 1966. *Russian Intellectual History: An Anthology*. New York: Harcourt, Brace and World.

——. 1971. "Patterns of Russian Imperial Policy toward the Nationalities." In Allworth 1971: 22–42.

Rajan, Balchandra, and Elizabeth Sauer, eds. 2004. *Imperialisms: Historical and Literary Investigations, 1500–1900*. New York: Palgrave.

Raphael, Frederick. 2012. "Double Vision." *Times Literary Supplement*, February 17, 3–5.

Rasiak, Ruslan O. 1980. "'The Soviet People': Multiethnic Alternative or Ruse?" In Allworth 1980b: 159–71.

Raun, Toivo U. 1977. "National Elites and Russification in the Baltic Provinces of the Russian Empire, 1861–1914: The Case of the Estonians." In Rowney and Orchard 1977: 123–47.

Ray, Himanshu Prabha, and Daniel T. Potts, eds. 2008. *Memory as History: The Legacy of Alexander in Asia*. Delhi: Eastern Book Corporation.

Rayner, A. J. 1942. "Christian Society in the Roman Empire." *Greece and Rome* 11 (33): 113–23.

Rees, E. A. 1998. "Stalin and Russian Nationalism." In Hosking and Service 1998: 77–106.

Reid, Donald M. 1996. "Cromer and the Classics: Imperialism, Nationalism and the Greco-Roman Past in Modern Egypt." *Middle Eastern Studies* 32 (1): 1–29.

Reinkowski, Maurus. 2011. "The Imperial Idea and *Realpolitik*: Reform Policy and Nationalism in the Ottoman Empire." In Leonhard and von Hirschhausen 2011: 453–71.

Reisz, Emma. 2010. "Classics, Race, and Edwardian Anxieties about Empire." In Bradley 2010a: 210–28.

Renan, Ernest. [1882] 2001. "What Is a Nation?" In *Nations and Identities: Classic Readings*, edited by Vincent P. Pecora, 162–76. Malden, MA: Blackwell.

Riasanovsky, Nicholas V. 1959. *Nicholas I and Official Nationality in Russia, 1825–1855*. Berkeley: University of California Press.

———. 1965. *Russia and the West in the Teaching of the Slavophiles: A Study of Romantic Ideology*. Gloucester, MA: Peter Smith.

———. 2005. *Russian Identities: A Historical Survey*. Oxford: Oxford University Press.

Rich, Paul B. 1990. *Race and Empire in British Politics*. 2nd ed. Cambridge: Cambridge University Press.

Richards, Jeffrey. 2001. *Imperialism and Music: Britain 1876–1953*. Manchester: Manchester University Press.

Richardson, J. S. 1991. "*Imperium Romanum*: Empire and the Language of Power." *Journal of Roman Studies* 81 (1): 1–9.

Richter, Melvin. 1963. "Tocqueville on Algeria." *Review of Politics* 25: 362–98.

Robertson, Ritchie, and Edward Timms, eds. 1994. *The Habsburg Legacy: National Identity in Historical Legacy*. Edinburgh: Edinburgh University Press.

Robinson, Ronald, and John Gallagher, with Alice Denny. [1961] 1981. *Africa and the Victorians: The Climax of Imperialism*. 2nd ed. London: Macmillan.

Rodkiewicz, Witold. 1998. *Russian Nationality Policy in the Western Provinces of the Empire (1863–1905)*. Lublin: Scientific Society of Lublin.

Rodrigue, Aron. 1995. "Difference and Tolerance in the Ottoman Empire." *Stanford Humanities Review* 5 (1): 81–90.

Rogers, Adam, and Richard Hingley. 2010. "Edward Gibbon and Francis Haverfield: The Traditions of Imperial Decline." In Bradley 2010a: 189–209.

Rogger, Hans. 1962. "Nationalism and the State: A Russian Dilemma." *Comparative Studies in Society and History* 4 (3): 253–64.

———. 1983. *Russia in the Age of Modernisation and Revolution 1881–1917*. London: Longman.

Ross, Kristen. 1995. *Fast Cars, Clean Bodies: Decolonisation and the Reordering of French Culture*. Cambridge, MA: MIT Press.

Ross, Robert J., and Gerald J. Telkamp, eds. 1985. *Colonial Cities: Essays on Urbanism in a Colonial Context*. Dordrecht: Martinus Nijhoff Publishers.

Roth, Joseph. [1932] 1995. *The Radetzky March*. Translated by Joachim Neugroschel. New York: The Overlook Press.

———. [1938]. 2002. *The Emperor's Tomb*. Translated by John Hoare. New York: The Overlook Press.

———. 2012. *A Life in Letters*. Translated and edited by Michael Hofmann. New York: W. W. Norton and Company.

Rowley, David G. 1997. "Aleksandr Solzhenitsyn and Russian Nationalism." *Journal of Contemporary History* 32 (3): 321–37.

———. 2000. "Imperial versus National Discourse: The Case of Russia." *Nations and Nationalism* 6 (1): 23–42.

Rowney, Don Karl, and G. Edward Orchard, eds. 1977. *Russian and Slavic History*. Columbus, OH: Slavica Publishers.

Roy, Arundhati. 2004. "People vs. Empire." *In These Times*, December 14. http://www.alternet.org/story/20734. Accessed November 11, 2004.

Rozenblit, Marsha L. 2005. "On the Cult of Franz Joseph: Jews and the Habsburg Monarchy in the Nineteenth Century." Paper delivered at the conference "Religion, Identity, and Empire," Yale University, April 16–17, 2005.

Rudolph, Richard L., and David F. Good, eds. 1992. *Nationalism and Empire: The Habsburg Monarchy and the Soviet Empire*. New York: St. Martin's Press.

Rushdie, Salman. 1992. *Imaginary Homelands: Essays and Criticism 1981–1991*. London: Granta Books.

Russell, Conrad. 1995. "Composite Monarchies in Early Modern Europe: The British and Irish Example." In *Uniting the Kingdom? The Making of British History*, edited by Alexander Grant and Keith J. Stringer, 133–46. London and New York: Routledge.

Rywkin, Michael. 1980. "The Russia-Wide Soviet Federated Socialist Republic (RSFSR): Privileged or Underprivileged?" In Allworth 1980b: 179–87.

———, ed. 1988. *Russian Colonial Expansion to 1917*. London: Mansell.

Saada, Emmanuelle. 2012. *Empire's Children: Race, Filiation, and Citizenship in the French Colonies*. Translated by Arthur Goldhammer. Chicago: University of Chicago Press.

———. 2013. "Nation and Empire in the French Context." In Steinmetz 2013: 321–339.

Sabine, George H. 1960. *A History of Political Theory*. 3rd ed. London: George Harrap.

Şahin, Kaya. 2015. *Empire and Power in the Reign of Süleyman*. Cambridge: Cambridge University Press.

Said, Edward W. 1979. *Orientalism*. New York: Vintage.

Sakharov, A. N. 1998. "The Main Phases and Distinctive Features of Russian Nationalism." In Hosking and Service 1998: 7–18.

Salzman, Ariel. 1993. "An Ancien Regime Revisited: 'Privatization' and Political Economy in the Eighteenth-Century Ottoman Empire." *Politics and Society* 21 (4): 393–423.

———. 2004. *Tocqueville in the Ottoman Empire: Rival Paths to the Modern State. The Ottoman Empire and Its Heritage*. Leiden: E. J. Brill.

———. 2010. "Is There a Moral Economy of State Formation? Religious Minorities and Repertoires of Regime Integration in the Middle East and Western Europe, 600–1614." *Theory and Society* 39 (3): 299–313.

Samman, Khaldoun. 2007 *Cities of God and Nationalism: Mecca, Jerusalem, and Rome as Contested World Cities*. Boulder, CO: Paradigm Publishers.

Sandner, Günther. 2005. "Nations without Nationalism: The Austro-Marxist Discourse on Multiculturalism." *Journal of Language and Politics* 4 (2): 273–91.

Sarkisyanz, Emanuel. 1974. "Russian Imperialism Reconsidered." In Hunczak 1974: 45–81.

Sartre, Maurice. 2006. *The Middle East under Rome*. Translated from the French by Catherine Porter and Elizabeth Rawlings. Cambridge, MA: Harvard University Press.

Sauer, Walter. 2007. "Austria-Hungary: The Making of Central Europe." In Aldrich 2007: 196–219.

Saunders, David. 1982. "Historians and Concepts of Nationality in Early Nineteenth-Century Russia." *Slavonic and East European Review* 60 (1): 44–62.

———. 1992. *Russia in the Age of Reaction and Reform 1801–1881*. London: Longman.

Schiavone, Aldo. 2000. *The End of the Past: Ancient Rome and the Modern West*. Translated by Margery J. Schneider. Cambridge, MA: Harvard University Press.

Schivelbusch, Wolfgang. 2004. *The Culture of Defeat: On National Trauma, Mourning, and Recovery*. Translated by Jefferson Chase. London: Granta Books.

Schmidt, H. D. 1953. "The Idea and Slogan of 'Perfidious Albion.'" *Journal of the History of Ideas* 14 (4): 604–16.

Schorske, Carl E. 1980. *Fin-de-Siècle Vienna: Politics and Culture*. New York: Alfred A. Knopf.

———. 1991. "Freud: The Psychoarchaeology of Civilisations." In *The Cambridge Companion to Freud*, edited by J. Neu, 8–24. Cambridge: Cambridge University Press.

Schreuder, D. M. 1976. "The Cultural Factor in Victorian Imperialism: A Case Study of the British 'Civilising Mission.'" *Journal of Imperial and Commonwealth History* 4 (3): 283–317.

Schulze, Max-Stephan. 1997. "Economic Development in the Nineteenth Century Habsburg Empire." *Austrian History Yearbook* 38: 293–307.

Schumpeter, Joseph. [1919] 1974. "Imperialism." In *Imperialism and Social Classes: Two Essays*, translated by Heinz Norden. New York: New American Library.

Schwarz, Bill. 2013. *The White Man's World*. Vol. 1, *Memories of Empire*. Oxford: Oxford University Press.

Scobie, Alex. 1990. *Hitler's State Architecture: The Impact of Classical Antiquity*. University Park: Pennsylvania State University Press.

Scott, Paul. [1975] 1977. *A Division of the Spoils*. London: Granada.

Seeley, J. R. 1869. "Roman Imperialism." Three Lectures. *Macmillan's Magazine*, July (185–97), August (281–91), October (473–84).

———. [1883] 1971. *The Expansion of England*. Chicago: University of Chicago Press.

Semyonov, Alexander, Marina Mogilner, and Ilya Gerasimov. 2013. "Russian Sociology in Imperial Context." In Steinmetz 2013: 53–82.

Sergeev, Evgeny. 2013. *The Great Game, 1856–1907*. Baltimore: Johns Hopkins University Press.

Seton-Watson, Hugh. 1964. "Nationalism and Multi-national Empires." In *Nationalism and Communism: Essays 1946–1963*, 3–35. New York: Praeger.

———. 1986. "Russian Nationalism in Historical Perspective." In Conquest 1986: 14–29.

Shaw, Stanford. 1976. *History of the Ottoman Empire and Modern Turkey*. Vol. 1, *Empire of the Gazis: The Rise and Decline of the Ottoman Empire, 1280–1808*. Cambridge: Cambridge University Press.

———. 1991. *The Jews of the Ottoman Empire and the Turkish Republic*. New York: New York University Press.

Shaw, Stanford J., and Ezel Kural Shaw. 1977. *History of the Ottoman Empire and Modern Turkey.* Vol. 2, *Reform, Revolution, and Republic: The Rise of Modern Turkey, 1808–1975.* Cambridge: Cambridge University Press.

Shepard, Todd. 2008. *The Invention of Decolonization: The Algerian War and the Remaking of France.* Ithaca, NY: Cornell University Press.

Sherwin-White, A. N. 1967. *Racial Prejudice in Ancient Rome.* Cambridge: Cambridge University Press.

———. 1973. *The Roman Citizenship.* 2nd ed. Oxford: Clarendon Press.

Shipway, Martin. 2008. *Decolonization and Its Impact: A Comparative Approach to the End of Colonial Empires.* Malden, MA: Blackwell Publishing.

Shumate, Nancy. 2006. *Nation, Empire, Decline: Studies in Rhetorical Continuity from the Romans to the Modern Era.* London: Duckworth.

Simon, Gerhard. 1991. *Nationalism and Policy toward the Nationalities in the Soviet Union: From Totalitarian Dictatorship to Post-Stalinist Society.* Translated by Karen Forster and Oswald Forster. Boulder, CO: Westview Press.

Singer, Barnett. 1991. "Lyautey: An Interpretation of the Man and French Imperialism." *Journal of Contemporary History* 26 (1): 131–57.

Sinha, Mrinalini. 2014. "Whatever Happened to the Third British Empire? Empire, Nation Redux." In Thompson 2014: 168–87.

Sked, Alan. 1981. "Historians, the Nationality Question, and the Downfall of the Habsburg Empire." *Transactions of the Royal Historical Society,* 5th ser., 31: 175–93.

———. 2001. *The Decline and Fall of the Habsburg Empire 1815–1918.* 2nd ed. Harlow: Pearson Education.

Slezkine, Yuri. 1994. *Arctic Mirrors: Russia and the Small Peoples of the North.* Ithaca, NY: Cornell University Press.

———. [1994] 1996. "The USSR as a Communal Apartment, or How a Socialist State Promoted Ethnic Particularism." In Eley and Suny 1996: 203–38.

———. 1997. "Naturalists versus Nations: Eighteenth-Century Russian Scholars Confront Ethnic Diversity." In Brower and Lazzerini 1997: 27–57.

———. 2000. "Imperialism as the Highest Stage of Socialism." *Russian Review* 59 (2): 227–34.

———. 2004. *The Jewish Century.* Princeton, NJ: Princeton University Press.

Slocum, John W. 1998. "Who, and When, Were the *Inorodtsy*? The Evolution of the Category of 'Aliens' in Imperial Russia." *Russian Review* 57 (2): 173–90.

Smith, Adam. [1776] 1910. *The Wealth of Nations.* Edited by Edwin R. A. Seligman. 2 vols. London: Dent and Sons.

Smith, Anthony D. 1986. *The Ethnic Origins of Nations.* Oxford: Blackwell.

———. 1991. *National Identity.* London: Penguin Books.

———. 2003. *Chosen People: Sacred Sources of National Identity.* Oxford: Oxford University Press.

———. 2004. "Ethnic Cores and Dominant Ethnies." In Kaufmann 2004: 17–30.

Smith, Graham, ed. 1996. *The Nationalities Question in the Post-Soviet States.* 2nd ed. London: Longman.

Smith, Jeremy. 1999. *The Bolsheviks and the National Question, 1917–1923.* New York: St. Martin's Press.

Smith, Michael E. 2001. "The Aztec Empire and the Mesoamerican World System." In Alcock et al. 2001: 128–54.

Smith, Robert O. 2007. "Luther, the Turks, and Islam." *Currents in Theology and Mission* 34 (5): 351–65.

Smith, Tony. 1978. "A Comparative Study of French and British Decolonization." *Comparative Studies in Society and History* 20 (1): 70–102.

Smith, William H. C. 1991. *Napoleon III: The Pursuit of Prestige*. London: Wayland Publishers.

Snyder, Jack. 1991. *Myths of Empire*. Ithaca, NY: Cornell University Press.

Solzhenitsyn, Alexander. [1990] 1991. *Rebuilding Russia: Reflections and Tentative Proposals*. Translated by Alexis Klimoff. London: The Harvill Press.

———. [1994] 1995. *The Russian Question at the End of the Twentieth Century*. Translated by Yermolai Solzhenitsyn. London: The Harvill Press.

Spencer, Diana. 2009. "Roman Alexanders: Epistemology and Identity." In Heckel and Tritle 2009: 251–74.

Spencer, Herbert. 1902. "Imperialism and Slavery." In *Facts and Comments: Selected Works of Herbert Spencer*, 157–71. New York: D. Appleton and Company.

Spencer, Terence. 1952. "Turks and Trojans in the Renaissance." *Modern Language Review* 47 (3): 330–33.

Spiel, Hilde. 1987. *Vienna's Golden Autumn 1866–1938*. London: Weidenfeld and Nicolson.

Spruyt, Hendrik. 2005. *Ending Empire: Contested Sovereignty and Territorial Partition*. Ithaca, NY: Cornell University Press.

Stalin, Joseph. [1934] 1975. *Marxism and the National-Colonial Question: A Collection of Articles and Speeches*. San Francisco: Proletarian Publishers.

Stanbridge, K. A. 1997. "England, France and Their North American Colonies: An Analysis of Absolutist State Power in Europe and the New World." *Journal of Historical Sociology* 10 (1): 27–55.

Stapleton, Julia. 1994. *Englishness and the Study of Politics: The Social and Political Thought of Ernest Barker*. Cambridge: Cambridge University Press.

Starr, S. Frederick. 1978. "Tsarist Government: The Imperial Dimension." In Azrael 1978: 3–38.

Steinmetz, George. 2005. "Return to Empire: The New U.S. Imperialism in Comparative Historical Perspective." *Sociological Theory* 23 (4): 339–67.

———, ed. 2013. *Sociology and Empire: The Imperial Entanglements of a Discipline*. Durham, NC: Duke University Press.

Steinwedel, Charles. 2000. "To Make a Difference: the Category of Ethnicity in Late Imperial Russian Politics, 1861–1917." In Hoffmann and Kotsonis 2000: 67–86.

———. 2007. "How Bashkiria Became Part of European Russia, 1762–1881." In Burbank, von Hagen, and Remnev 2007: 94–124.

Stockwell, A. J. 2006. "British Decolonisation: The Record and the Records." *Contemporary European History* 15 (4): 573–83.

Stockwell, Sarah, ed. 2008a. *The British Empire: Themes and Perspectives*. Oxford: Blackwell Publishing.

———. 2008b. "Ends of Empire." In Stockwell 2008a: 269–93.

Stoler, Ann Laura, and Frederick Cooper. 1997. "Between Metropole and Colony: Rethinking a Research Agenda." In Cooper and Stoler 1997: 1–56.

Stoler, Ann Laura, Carole McGranahan, and Peter C. Perdue, eds. 2007. *Imperial Formations*. Santa Fe, NM: School for Advanced Research Press.

Stone, Marla. 1999. "A Flexible Rome: Fascism and the Cult of Romanità." In Edwards 1999b: 205–20.

Stone, Norman. 1966. "Army and Society in the Habsburg Monarchy, 1900–1914." *Past and Present* 33: 95–111.

Stone, Norman, Sergei Podbolotov, and Murat Yasar. 2004. "The Russians and the Turks: Imperialism and Nationalism in the Era of Empires." In Miller and Rieber 2004: 27–45.

Stourzh, Gerald. 1992. "The Multinational Empire Revisited: Reflections on Late Imperial Austria." *Austrian History Yearbook* 23: 1–22.

Strang, David. 1991. "Global Patterns of Decolonization, 1500–1987." *International Studies Quarterly* 35 (4): 429–54.

Strayer, Joseph R. 1971. "France: The Holy Land, the Chosen People, and the Most Christian King." In *Medieval Statecraft and the Perspectives of History*, 300–314. Princeton, NJ: Princeton University Press.

Stremooukhoff, Dimitri. 1970. "Moscow the Third Rome: Sources of the Doctrine." In Cherniavsky 1970a: 108–25.

Struck, Manuela. 2001. "The *Heilige Römische Reich Deutscher Nation* and Hermann the German." In Hingley 2001: 91–112.

Sugar, Peter F. [1977] 1993. *Southeastern Europe under Ottoman Rule, 1354–1804*. Seattle: University of Washington Press.

Sullivan, Robert E. 2009. *Macaulay: The Tragedy of Power*. Cambridge, MA: Harvard University Press.

Sunderland, Willard. 2005. *Taming the Wild Fields: Colonization and Empire on the Russian Steppe*. Ithaca, NY: Cornell University Press.

Suny, Ronald Grigor. 1989. *The Making of the Georgian Nation*. Bloomington: Indiana University Press.

———. 1993. *The Revenge of the Past: Nationalism, Revolution, and the Collapse of the Soviet Union*. Stanford, CA: Stanford University Press.

———. 1995. "Ambiguous Categories: States, Empires and Nations." *Post-Soviet Affairs* 11 (2): 185–96.

———. 2001. "The Empire Strikes Out: Imperial Russia, 'National' Identity, and Theories of Empire." In Suny and Martin 2001: 23–66.

———. 2015. *"They Can Live in the Desert but Nowhere Else": A History of the Armenian Genocide*. Princeton, NJ: Princeton University Press.

Suny, Ronald Grigor, and Terry Martin, eds. 2001. *A State of Nations: Empire and Nation-Making in the Age of Lenin and Stalin*. Oxford: Oxford University Press.

Swain, Joseph Ward. 1940. "The Theory of the Four Monarchies: Opposition History under the Roman Empire." *Classical Philology* 35 (1): 1–21.

Syme, Ronald. 1958. *Colonial Élites: Rome, Spain and the Americas*. London: Oxford University Press.

Szporluk, Roman. 1990. "The Imperial Legacy and the Soviet Nationalities Problem." In *The Nationalities Factor in Soviet Politics and Society*, edited by Lubomyr Hajda and Mark Beissinger, 1–23. Boulder, CO: Westview Press.

———. 1997. "The Fall of the Tsarist Empire and the USSR: The Russian Question and Imperial Overextension." In Dawisha and Parrott 1997: 65–93.

————. 1998. "Nationalism after Communism: Reflections on Russia, Ukraine, Belarus and Poland." *Nations and Nationalism* 4 (3): 301–20.

Taagepera, Rein. 1978a. "Size and Duration of Empires: Systematics of Size." *Social Science Research* 7 (2): 108–27.

————. 1978b. "Size and Duration of Empires: Growth-Decline Curves, 3000–600 BC." *Social Science Research* 7 (2): 180–96.

————. 1979. "Size and Duration of Empires: Growth-Decline Curves, 600 BC to 600 AD." *Social Science History* 3 (3/4): 115–38.

————. 1988. "An Overview of the Growth of the Russian Empire." In Rywkin 1988: 1–7.

Tacitus. 1996. *The Annals of Imperial Rome.* Translated by Michael Grant. London: Penguin Books.

Taddia, Irma. 2007. "Italy: The Last Empire." In Aldrich 2007: 254–77.

Tarn, W. W. 1948. *Alexander the Great.* 2 vols.. Cambridge: Cambridge University Press.

Taylor, A.J.P. 1954. *The Struggle for Mastery in Europe 1848–1918.* Oxford: Oxford University Press.

————. 1967. "The Failure of the Habsburg Monarchy." In *Europe: Grandeur and Decline,* 127–32. Harmondsworth: Penguin Books.

————. [1948] 1990. *The Habsburg Monarchy 1809–1918: A History of the Austrian Empire and Austria-Hungary.* London: Penguin Books.

Taylor, Miles. 1991. "Imperium et Libertas? Rethinking the Radical Critique of Imperialism during the Nineteenth Century." *Journal of Imperial and Commonwealth History* 19 (1): 1–23.

Teich, Mikulas, and Roy Porter, eds. 1993. *The National Question in Historical Context.* Cambridge: Cambridge University Press.

Teschke, Benno. 2006. "Imperial Doxa from the Berlin Republic." *New Left Review* 39 (May–June): 128–40.

Thaden, Edward C. 1990a. *Interpreting History: Collective Essays on Russia's Relations with Europe.* New York: Columbia University Press.

————. 1990b. "The Beginnings of Romantic Nationalism in Russia." In Thaden 1990a: 179–201.

————. 1990c. "Russification in Tsarist Russia." In Thaden 1990a: 211–20.

————. 1990d. ""Russian Nationality Policy, 1881–1914." In Thaden 1990a: 221–36.

Thody, Philip. 1985. "Adieu to the Colonies." *Times Higher Education Supplement,* October 5, 13.

Thomas, Carol G. 2007. *Alexander the Great and His World.* Malden, MA: Blackwell.

Thomas, Martin, Bob Moore, and L. J. Butler. 2008. *Crises of Empire: Decolonization and Europe's Imperial States, 1918–1975.* London: Hodder Education.

Thompson, Andrew S. 1997. "The Language of Imperialism and the Meanings of Empire: Imperial Discourse in British Politics, 1895–1914." *Journal of British Studies* 36 (2): 147–77.

————. 2000. *Imperial Britain: The Empire in British Politics, c. 1880–1932.* Harlow, UK: Longman.

————. 2003. "The Languages of Loyalism in Southern Africa, c. 1870–1939." *English Historical Review* 118 (477): 617–50.

————. 2005. *The Empire Strikes Back? The Impact of Imperialism on Britain from the Mid-Nineteenth Century.* Harlow, UK: Pearson-Longman.

————, ed. 2012. *Britain's Experience of Empire in the Twentieth Century.* Oxford: Oxford University Press.

————, ed. 2014. *Writing Imperial Histories.* Manchester: Manchester University Press.

Thomson, J.K.J. 1998. *Decline in History: The European Experience.* Cambridge: Polity Press.

Thornton, A. P. [1959] 1968. *The Imperial Idea and Its Enemies: A Study in British Power.* New York: Anchor Books.

Tidrick, Kathryn. 1992. *Empire and the English Character*. London: I. B. Tauris.

Timms, Edward. 1991. "National Memory and the 'Austrian Idea' from Metternich to Waldheim." *Modern Language Review* 86 (4): 898–910.

Toal, Gerard, and John O'Loughlin. 2014. "How People in South Ossetia, Abkhazia and Trans-nistria Feel about Annexation by Russia." *Washington Post*, March 20.

Tocqueville, Alexis de 2001. *Writings on Empire and Slavery*. Edited and translated by Jennifer Pitts. Baltimore: Johns Hopkins University Press.

Todd, Emmanuel. 2003. *After the Empire: The Breakdown of the American Order*. Translated by C. Jon Delogu. New York: Columbia University Press.

Tolz, Vera. 2001. *Russia*. London: Arnold.

———. 2005. "Orientalism, Nationalism, and Ethnic Diversity in Late Imperial Russia." *Historical Journal* 48 (1): 127–50.

Tombs, Robert, and Isabelle Tombs. 2007. *That Sweet Enemy: The French and the British from the Sun King to the Present*. London: Pimlico.

Torke, Hans-Joachim. 2003. "Moscow and Its West: On the 'Ruthenization' of Russian Culture in the Seventeenth Century." In Kappeler et al. 2003: 87–107.

Toynbee, Arnold. 1962–63. *A Study of History*. Paperback ed. 12 vols. London: Oxford University Press.

Treadgold, Warren T. 1997. *A History of the Byzantine State and Society*. Stanford, CA: Stanford University Press.

Trevor-Roper, Hugh. [1976] 1991. *Princes and Artists: Patronage and Ideology at Four Habsburg Courts 1517–1633*. New York: Thames and Hudson.

Turner, Frank M. 1999. "Christians and Pagans in Victorian Novels." In Edwards 1999b: 173–87.

Turner, Frederick Jackson. 1920. *The Frontier in American History*. New York: Holt.

Turoma, Sanna, and Maxim Waldstein, eds. 2013. *Empire De-Centered: New Spatial Histories of Russia and the Soviet Union*. Farnham, UK: Ashgate.

Tyrell, Ian. 1991. "American Exceptionalism in an Age of International History." *American Historical Review* 96 (4): 1031–55.

Ullmann, Walter. 1979. "'This Realm of England Is an Empire.'" *Journal of Ecclesiastical History* 30 (2): 175–203.

Unowsky, Daniel. 2001. "Reasserting Empire: Habsburg Imperial Celebrations after the Revolutions of 1848–1849." In Bucur and Wingfield 2001: 13–45.

———. 2005. *The Pomp and Politics of Patriotism: Imperial Celebrations in Habsburg Austria, 1848–1916*. West Lafayette, IN: Purdue University Press.

———. 2011. "Dynastic Symbolism and Popular Patriotism: Monarchy and Dynasty in Late Imperial Austria." In Leonhard and von Hirschhausen 2011: 237–86.

Urbanitsch, Peter. 2004. "Pluralist Myth and Nationalist Realities: The Dynastic Myth of the Habsburg Monarchy—a Futile Exercise in the Creation of Identity?" *Austrian History Yearbook* 35: 101–41.

Vance, Norman. 1997. *The Victorians and Ancient Rome*. Oxford: Blackwell.

———. 1999. "Decadence and the Subversion of Empire." In Edwards 1999b: 110–24.

———. 2000. "Imperial Rome and Britain's Language of Empire 1600–1837." *History of European Ideas* 26: 211–24.

Vasunia, Phiroze. 2005. "Greater Rome and Greater Britain." In Goff 2005: 38–64.

———. 2013. *The Classics and Colonial India*. Oxford: Oxford University Press.

Veugelers, John W. P. 2010. "Tocqueville on the Conquest and Colonization of Algeria." *Journal of Classical Sociology* 10 (4): 339–55.

Veyne, Paul. 1980. "L'Empire romain." In Duverger 1980: 121–30.

Vidal-Naquet, Pierre. 1995. *Politics Ancient and Modern*. Translated by Janet Lloyd. Cambridge: Polity Press.

Vinkovetsky, Ilya. 2011. *Russian America: An Overseas Colony of a Continental Empire, 1804–1867*. Oxford: Oxford University Press.

Visser, Romke. 1992. "Fascist Doctrine and the Cult of the *Romanità*." *Journal of Contemporary History* 27: 5–22.

Voltaire. [1763] 1912. "On Toleration, In Connection with the Death of Jean Calas." In *Toleration and Other Essays*, translated by Joseph McCabe, 1–87. New York: G. P. Putnam's Sons.

———. 1901. *Ancient and Modern History*. Vol. 30 of *The Works of Voltaire*. Edited by John Morley. Translated by William F. Fleming. 42 vols. Paris and London: E. R. Dumont.

Walbank, F. W. 1972. "Nationality as a Factor in Roman History." *Harvard Studies in Classical Philology* 76 (1): 145–68.

Walicki, Andrzej. 1975. *The Slavophile Controversy: History of a Conservative Utopia in Nineteenth-Century Russian Thought*. Oxford: Oxford University Press.

———. 1979. *A History of Russian Thought: From the Enlightenment to Marxism*. Stanford, CA: Stanford University Press.

Walzer, Michael. 1997. *On Toleration*. New Haven, CT: Yale University Press.

———. 2003. "Is There an American Empire?" *Dissent*, Fall, 3–8.

Wandruszka, Adam. 1964. *The House of Habsburg: Six Hundred Years of a European Dynasty*. Translated by Cathleen and Hans Epstein. London: Sidgwick and Jackson.

Wangermann, Ernst. 1973. *The Austrian Achievement 1700–1800*. New York: Harcourt Brace Jovanovich.

Wank, Solomon. 1997a. "The Habsburg Empire." In Barkey and von Hagen 1997: 45–57.

———. 1997b. "Some Reflections on the Habsburg Empire and Its Legacy in the Nationalities Question." *Austrian History Yearbook* 28: 131–46.

Ward, Stuart, ed. 2001. *British Culture and the End of Empire*. Manchester: Manchester University Press.

———. 2008. "Imperial Identities Abroad." In Stockwell 2008a: 219–43.

Ward-Perkins, Bryan. 2005. *The Fall of Rome and the End of Civilization*. Oxford: Oxford University Press.

Warren, Allen. 1986. "Citizens of the Empire: Baden-Powell, Scouts and Guides, and an Imperial Ideal." In MacKenzie 1986: 232–56.

Weber, Eugen. 1976. *Peasants into Frenchmen: The Modernization of Rural France, 1870–1914*. Stanford, CA: Stanford University Press.

Weber, Max. 1963. *The Sociology of Religion*. Boston: Beacon Press.

———. 1978. *Economy and Society*. Edited by Guenther Roth and Claus Wittich. 2 vols. Berkeley: University of California Press.

Webster, Jane, and Nicholas J. Cooper, eds. 1996. *Roman Imperialism: Post-Colonial Perspectives*. Leicester: Leicester School of Archaeological Studies.

Webster, Wendy. 2007. *Englishness and Empire 1939–1965*. Oxford: Oxford University Press.

Weeks, Theodore R. 1996. *Nation and State in Late Imperial Russia: Nationalism and Russification in the Western Frontier, 1863–1914*. DeKalb: University of Northern Illinois Press.

———. 2001. "Russification and the Lithuanians, 1863–1905." *Slavic Review* 60 (1): 96–114.

Weil, Patrick. 2008. *How to Be French: Nationality in the Making since 1789*. Translated by Catherine Porter. Durham, NC: Duke University Press.

Welker, Walter F. 1968. "The Ottoman Bureaucracy: Modernization and Reform." *Administrative Science Quarterly* 13 (3): 451–70.

Wells, H. G. 1937. *The Outline of History*. 8th rev. London: Cassell and Company.

Werfel, Franz. 1937. "An Essay upon the Meaning of Imperial Austria." In *Twilight of a World*, translated by H. T. Lowe-Porter, 3–39. New York: The Viking Press.

Wessel, Martin Schulze. 2011. "Religion, Politics and the Limits of Imperial Integration: Comparing the Habsburg Monarchy and the Russian Empire." In Leonhard and von Hirschhausen 2011: 337–58.

Whaley, Joachim. 1994. "Austria, 'Germany', and the Dissolution of the Holy Roman Empire." In Robertson and Timms 1994: 3–12.

———. 2012. *Germany and the Holy Roman Empire*. 2 vols. Oxford: Oxford University Press.

Wheatcroft, Andrew. 1996. *The Habsburgs: Embodying Empire*. London: Penguin Books.

White, Mary E. 1961. "Greek Colonization." *Journal of Economic History* 21 (4): 443–54.

White, Owen, and J. P. Daughton, eds. 2012. *In God's Empire: French Missionaries and the Modern World*. Oxford: Oxford University Press.

Wilder, Gary. 2005. *The French Imperial Nation-State: Negritude and Colonial Humanism between the Two World Wars*. Chicago: University of Chicago Press.

———. 2009. "Untimely Vision: Aimé Césaire, Decolonization, Utopia." *Public Culture* 21 (1): 101–40.

Wilson, Kathleen. 1998. *The Sense of the People: Politics, Culture and Imperialism in England, 1715–1785*. Cambridge: Cambridge University Press.

———. 2003. *The Island Race: Englishness, Empire and Gender in the Eighteenth Century*. London: Routledge.

———, ed. 2004. *A New Imperial History: Culture, Identity and Modernity in Britain and the Empire, 1660–1840*. Cambridge: Cambridge University Press.

Wilson, Peter H. 1999. *The Holy Roman Empire 1495–1806*. Houndmills, Basingstoke: Macmillan.

———. 2016. *Heart of Europe: A History of the Holy Roman Empire*. Cambridge, MA: Harvard University Press.

Wimbush, S. Enders. 1978. "The Great Russians and the Soviet State: The Dilemmas of Ethnic Dominance." In Azrael 1978: 349–60.

Wingfield, Nancy M. 2007. "Emperor Joseph II in the Austrian Imagination up to 1914." In Cole and Unowsky 2007: 62–85.

Winn, Peter. 1976. "British Informal Empire in Uruguay in the Nineteenth Century." *Past and Present* 73: 100–126.

Wittek, Paul. 1938. *The Rise of the Ottoman Empire*. London: The Royal Asiatic Society of Great Britain and Ireland.

Wood, Ellen Meiksins. 2005. *Empire of Capital*. Paperback ed. London: Verso.

Woodhead, Christine. 1987. "'The Present Terrour of the World'? Contemporary Views of the Ottoman Empire c1600." *History* 72: 20–37.

———. 1995. "Perspectives on Suleyman." In Kunt and Woodhead 1995: 164–90.

Wolfe, Patrick. 1997. "History and Imperialism: A Century of Theory, from Marx to Postcolonialism." *American Historical Review* 102 (2): 388–420.

Woolf, Greg. 1994. "Becoming Roman, Staying Greek: Culture, Identity and the Civilizing Process in the Roman East." *Proceedings of the Cambridge Philological Society* 40: 116–43.

———. 1998. *Becoming Roman: The Origins of Provincial Civilization in Gaul*. Cambridge: Cambridge University Press.

———. 2001. "Inventing Empire in Ancient Rome." In Alcock et al. 2001: 311–22.

———. 2012. *Rome: An Empire's Story*. Oxford: Oxford University Press.

Woolf, Stuart. 1989. "French Civilisation and Ethnicity in the Napoleonic Empire." *Past and Present* 124: 96–120.

———. 1992. "The Construction of a European World-View in the Revolutionary Napoleonic Years." *Past and Present* 137: 72–101.

Wortman, Richard S. 2006. *Scenarios of Power: Myth and Ceremony in Russian Monarchy, from Peter the Great to the Abdication of Nicholas II*. Princeton, NJ: Princeton University Press.

———. 2011. "The Tsar and the Empire: Representation of the Monarchy and Symbolic Integration in Imperial Russia." In Leonhard and von Hirschhausen 2011: 266–86.

Wright, Gwendolyn. 1991. *The Politics of Design in French Colonial Urbanism*. Chicago: University of Chicago Press.

———. 1997. "Tradition in the Service of Modernity: Architecture and Urbanism in French Colonial Policy, 1900–1930." In Cooper and Stoler 1997: 322–45.

Wyke, Maria. 1999. "Screening Ancient Rome in the New Italy." In Edwards 1999b: 188–204.

Yapp, M. E. 1987. "British Perceptions of the Russian Threat to India." *Modern Asian Studies* 21: 647–65.

———. 1992. "Europe in the Turkish Mirror." *Past and Present*, no. 137: 134–55.

Yaroshevski, Dov. 1997. "Empire and Citizenship." In Brower and Lazzerini 1997: 58–79.

Yates, Frances A. 1975. "Charles V and the Idea of Empire." in *Astraea: The Imperial Theme in the Sixteenth Century*, 1–28. London: Routledge and Kegan Paul.

Young, Robert J. C. 2001. *Postcolonialism: An Historical Introduction*. Oxford: Blackwell.

———. 2008. *The Idea of English Ethnicity*. Oxford: Blackwell Publishing.

Zeldin, Theodore. 1973. *France 1848–1945*. Vol. 1, *Ambition, Love, Politics*. Oxford: Oxford University Press.

Zielonka, Jan. 2006. *Europe as Empire: The Nature of the Enlarged European Union*. Oxford: Oxford University Press.

Zimmer, Oliver. 2003. *Nationalism in Europe, 1890–1940*. Houndmills, Basingstoke: Palgrave Macmillan.

Zimmern, Alfred. 1927. *The Third British Empire*. 2nd ed. London: Oxford University Press.

Zückert, Martin. 2011. "Imperial War in the Age of Nationalism: The Habsburg Monarchy and the First World War." In Leonhard and von Hirschhausen 2011: 500–517.

Zürcher, Erik J. 1997. *Turkey: A Modern History*. Rev. ed. London: I. B. Tauris.

———. 2010. *The Young Turk Legacy and Nation Building: From the Ottoman Empire to Atatürk's Turkey*. London: I. B. Tauris.

INDEX

Note: Page numbers in italic type indicate illustrations.

A NOTE ON THE TYPE

THIS BOOK has been composed in Arno, an Old-style serif font in the classic Venetian tradition, designed by Robert Slimbach at Adobe.